MEDIEVAL
CIVILIZATION

By the Same Author

DISSENT AND REFORM IN THE EARLY MIDDLE AGES

(University of California Press, Berkeley and Los Angeles, 1965)

On the title page

THE MEDIEVAL HIERARCHY; from the fresco "Ecclesiastical and Civil Authority," by Andrea da Firenze. In the center is the pope. To his left, seated, is the emperor and beside the emperor, also seated, are first a king and then a nobleman. In front of the king and nobleman are representatives of the other orders of medieval society including townsmen and peasants. To the pope's right, seated, is a cardinal and to the cardinal's right a bishop. Standing are representatives of the secular and regular clergy—priests, monks, canons, and nuns. The sheep represent the Christian people; the two watchdogs the spiritual and temporal guardians of the flock.

Jeffrey Burton Russell

UNIVERSITY OF CALIFORNIA, RIVERSIDE

JOHN WILEY & SONS, INC.   NEW YORK, LONDON, SYDNEY

MEDIEVAL
CIVILIZATION

For Dinny with love

Preface

THIS book is intended as an investigation of the civilization of western Europe from the third to the fifteenth centuries. It presents not only the results, but some of the important problems, of contemporary scholarship in medieval history. It follows a topical treatment of economic, social, political, and cultural history within a chronological framework. Rather than trying to achieve consistently detailed coverage of every aspect of medieval civilization, I have concentrated upon individual or collective examples of important ideas, attitudes, institutions, or events. Discussions of the sources appear in each chapter, and the sources are quoted frequently in the body of the text in order to permit the reader to feel, as well as intellectually to grasp, the nature of medieval life. Pictures and maps are integrated with the text as illustrations of the topics discussed.

Whatever the merits of this book, they are in large part owing to a number of people for whose advice I am indebted. Edwin S. Gaustad and John W. McKenna of the University of California at Riverside, Donald Howard of Johns Hopkins University, George P. Cuttino of Emory University, Jan Hajda of Portland State College, and Herbert Heaton of the University of Minnesota read and criticized certain chapters; Gene Brucker of the University of California at Berkeley read and criticized the entire manuscript. My wife, Diana, helped very much at various stages. An excellent job of editing was done by Harriet McDougal of John Wiley and Sons, and the attractiveness of the book should be attributed to the attentions of William L. Gum, Robert Goff, Nancy T. Unger, and others at Wiley. The University of California was generous with help for clerical expenses, and the interlibrary-loan staff of the library of the Riverside campus was very long-suffering. I hope that Neal Brengle is not permanently bent from the tall stacks of books he carried to and from my office.

Jeffrey B. Russell

Riverside, California
July, 1967

Contents

List of Maps

Maps by Russell H. Lenz

MEDIEVAL
CIVILIZATION

ACCORDING to the view fixed in the popular mind by outdated textbooks, teachers, and television programs, the broad sunlit uplands of classical Greece and Rome bank off precipitously into the dark, bristling valleys of the Middle Ages, only to rise again a thousand years later in the glorious range of light known as the Renaissance. Yet common sense, if nothing else, suggests that intelligence and talents do not fluctuate with the centuries and that it is impossible that everyone should suddenly have become, and then for a thousand years remained, simple, ignorant, and corrupt.

How then did the Middle Ages acquire its bad press? Medieval men themselves, with characteristic humility, believed that they were dwarves standing upon the shoulders of the giants of antiquity and, anticipating the imminent end of the world, had little conception of the social change and progress taking place in their times. Beginning in the fourteenth century a number of movements arose, each hostile to the Middle Ages though from different points of view. A pious and uncritical age could not be admired by the Renaissance humanists; an age that was Catholic could not be endorsed by the Protestants of the Reformation; and an age that was religious could not be approved by the rationalists of the eighteenth century. Nineteenth-century evolutionary pragmatism and positivism postulated a world continually elevating itself above the level of human progress represented by the Middle Ages. Imbued with the idea of progress, we assume that every century is better than the one preceding. If there was absolutism in the seventeenth century, how much worse it must have been in the thirteenth; if there was slavery in the fifteenth, it must have been more degrading in the eleventh; if there was a fanatical Inquisition in the sixteenth, it must have been more fanatical in the twelfth; and so on. The mind that has accepted this nonsense for the Middle Ages rebels against imposing it upon the Greeks and Romans, and the result is the absurd idea of an age of darkness interrupting the perennial growth of progress, which now—we assume—will continue without breaks into the future.

For a hundred years serious historians have rejected these prejudiced views and have been increasingly aware of the constructiveness and creativity of the Middle Ages. As early as 1864 a French writer observed that "no one nowadays" could still be so uninformed as to believe that the Middle Ages were dark; but nothing is harder to erase than a tenaciously held absurdity.

The Middle Ages are not a refuge for escapists but a broad and varied terrain for men vitally concerned with the human condition. The study of the Middle Ages, like ancient history, provides scope of time and space for the broad questions of history that cannot be considered in more parochial studies. Here we may ask, what is civilization? Why do civilizations arise and why do they fall? What are the varieties of political, philosophical, and artistic expressions that occur to men at different ages and times, and what accounts for changes in cultural fashions? How do civilizations rebuild after enormous shocks? Further, events of the distant past are more broadly, though less directly, influential upon the present than those of modern history. Had John Kennedy not been assassinated, many things would now be different; had the Moslems conquered Gaul in the eighth century, everything would be different. Many of the assumptions established by Plato and Saint Augustine have been so deeply engraved in so many minds throughout the history of western civilization as to have incomparably greater importance for an understanding of what we now think than any but the most powerful of modern beliefs.

Our understanding of earlier history is often more balanced because we can look at it in a longer perspective. Think of how our interpretation of World War I has changed since 1919 and how it will continue to change as its ultimate consequences come slowly to light; we have yet to see it from the variety of points of view that make true historical perspective. In this sense we can make more accurate judgments on the Peloponnesian War or the Crusades. Modern history, while often of more immediate practical use than earlier history, is correspondingly less fruitful of philosophical comprehension.

Another value of medieval history is that a sophisticated

understanding of our own assumptions and customs is enhanced by comparison with others. And this sophisticated understanding enables us to glimpse the most important, and most difficult, truth that history has to teach: that those things that we consider self-evident today are not self-evident tomorrow; that what we confidently "know now" will in a few years likely turn out to be a silly absurdity.

ONE of the characteristics of the Middle Ages was that it was an age of acceptance, not so much in the sense of assent to a body of doctrine but in that of acceptance of, and commitment to, the whole way of life in which one was placed. In the Middle Ages, *libertas* meant the occupation of one's proper place in the world order. "Men need an order within which they can locate themselves, an order providing coherence, continuity, and justice."[1] Men seek this requisite order in the cosmos, in society, and in themselves. One of the characteristics of contemporary western life is its loss of the sense of acceptance, its loss of the sense, though not of the need, of order. We cannot manufacture an artificial commitment, and we do not wish, even if we could, to return to that of the Middle Ages. But by becoming aware of a society that did have faith, we can place our own lack of it in perspective.

Another, related, characteristic of medieval society is that it was the last in the heritage of western civilization to have a *sacred* view of the world: rather than perceiving the world as consisting of objects to be exploited, medieval men more often thought of it as containing beings with which they should adopt a proper relationship. At its crudest, this attitude is one of simple animism or magic; at its most refined it is a manifestation of that sense of the "Other" or the "Thou" that modern theologians like Rudolf Otto, Martin Buber, and Mircea Eliade have indicated is the truly religious sense. "We have here the original sense of the word 'religious', not referring to a particular religion, but to an attitude of respect, or beyond that, of worship, or more still, a feeling of giddiness on the edge of the abyss. . . . This attitude may refer either to a god . . . or to the festal reality of the world—a godly world or a world full of gods—or even to the Nihil in a completely godless world."[2] This understanding of the sacred was expressed in an agricultural society by a closeness to nature that is represented in the festivals and the art of the Middle Ages. This relationship of man to nature may seem meaningful not only to the modern theologian but also to the ecologist or conservationist in a world where nature is everywhere wantonly exploited and deformed.

The sacred view held by the Middle Ages was not in *opposition* to the profane. On the contrary, medieval society did not admit the existence of the profane. Secular society as we understand it, as well as the things of nature, was itself sacralized and sanctified. Thus medieval religion expressed the *life* of the whole community, rather than being the personal possession of the pious.

Medieval society was also characterized by a general adherence to the ideal, if not to the practice, of a united Christendom; by a general acceptance of Christian principles; by a strong trust in human reason and a close connection of philosophy and religion in the form of theology; by adherence to the ideal of a divine and absolute law on the one hand and to tradition and custom on the other, both principles limiting the power and scope of the state and inhibiting the growth of nationalism. The problems of the Middle Ages were very different from our own. Where we face the enormously complex problems of an enormously complex technical society, all demanding the mobilization of vast resources on a natural scale, such problems were utterly absent from the simpler world of the Middle Ages.

The idolatries, as well as the problems, of the medieval world were different from ours. Every age is idolatrous in enlisting the support of God for its own convictions. The idolatry of medieval Christianity brought about the Crusades and the persecution of the Jews; the idolatry of the modern nation and the flag have brought about the world wars and the concentration camps. The undemocratic Middle Ages were at least spared democratic total wars.

Perhaps the most fundamental difference between medieval and contemporary times is that the Middle Ages were the rude and vigorous beginnings of a civilization of which we are approaching the refined maturity or, as some fear, the degenerate end. For better or worse, they were creating the materials with which we are still building. There are not only differences, but also important connections, between us.

Our technology is founded upon theirs, and experimental science originated in the fourteenth and fifteenth centuries. Modern universities are direct descendants, not of Greek or Roman schools, but of the universities established in western Europe beginning in the thirteenth century. The institutions and doctrines of the Christian religion, of most of the Protestant denominations as well as of the Catholic Church, were established and developed during this period. The modern theater's origins are to be found, not upon the proscenia of Epidaurus and Athens, but in front of the west portals of churches in the market places of medieval Bourges and Trier. The western European languages that we speak achieved their identity in the Middle Ages. Not only our speech, but our manners, bear the traces of our medieval forefathers: when we listen to the latest love songs or hold the door open for a lady, we are acting in accordance with a respect for the importance of woman that was established by the courts of love of the eleventh and twelfth centuries. We open a book, instead of unrolling it: the form of the bound book with pages, the *codex,* was popularized in the Middle Ages. When we look at the book, the lowercase letters we see were formed in the monastic *scriptoria* of the Carolingian period. The national state itself developed from the thirteenth or fourteenth century onwards, and the forms and divisions familiar to modern governmental administration were already established in the advanced systems of England, France, and Sicily by the twelfth and thirteenth. The legal system and legal principles of the United States and most of the Commonwealth of Nations derive from medieval English law; one of our most cherished institutions, the jury, is of purely medieval ancestry. In political theory, the ideas of natural rights, of the limited power of the state, and of the social contract have their roots in medieval conceptions of the natural law on the one hand and feudalism on the other. Modern banking, currency, and exchange originated during the eleventh and twelfth centuries when pilgrimages and crusades encouraged commerce with distant lands.

BUT what were the Middle Ages? How is the period defined? The term "Middle Ages" is itself only somewhat less invidious than "Dark Ages." It was coined by the humanists of the fourteenth century to designate the years that by divine oversight had been allowed to intrude between imperial Rome and Italian Renaissance; and the division of history into ancient, medieval, and modern was established by an obscure seventeenth-century German historian. We have already noted the attitudes that determined such a view of history. Since all periodization in history is artificial, the arrangement is no worse than any other, except that by pasting a label upon a period of a thousand years it has led people unthinkingly to assume that those thousand years were monotonous and without change. In fact, the Middle Ages were sluggish only in comparison with the rapid changes of the nineteenth and twentieth centuries, but dynamic compared with most periods in the history of most civilizations.

The Middle Ages lasted roughly a thousand years. But which thousand? Until a few decades ago the date 476 A.D. for the "fall of Rome" and the date 1453 A.D. for the fall of Constantinople were taken as the reasonable limits of things medieval. The date 476 no longer seems very important, and most historians will carry the study back to about 300 in order to include the edicts of toleration for Christianity or even, as did Gibbon himself, back into the political and economic troubles of the Roman world in the third century. The fall of Constantinople no longer seems quite as important for the history of civilization in the West as it used to, and historians have moved the date for ending the Middle Ages either forward to the Protestant Reformation or back to the important watershed of events around 1300. The beginning of the fourteenth century is certainly an epoch fatal to medieval ideas, but the next two centuries comprised a transition zone that can be labeled either the "waning of the Middle Ages" or the "Renaissance" depending upon whether one looks forward or backward. The years 1492–1500, when Europeans first discovered that there was a New World that they could call upon to redress the imbalance of the Old, are as logical a time as any for taking leave of the Middle Ages and entering modern times.

There are two further drawbacks to the term "Middle Ages." The first is that it is reasonable to understand the Middle Ages not as the "middle," but as the beginning, of our civilization. There is an analogy between the third to eighth centuries A.D., a period of barbarian invasions, cultural crudity, and heroes, and the thirteenth to seventh centuries B.C., when, in another age of heroes, cultural crudity, and barbarian invasions, Greek civilization was replacing the Minoan-Mycenean. The second drawback is that the term "medieval" has been used absurdly to apply to areas that had no relationship to western civilization. One hears of medieval Japan, medieval China, and even medieval America in reference to the indigenous Indian population! The term can be applied with some meaning to the Byzantine and Slavic East, but it is best to keep its meaning as clear as possible by limiting it to western Europe from Scandinavia to Spain and Ireland to Italy.

ONE more thing is needed to understand the importance of the study of the Middle Ages in the twentieth century, and that is to grasp how they have been, and are being, studied by scholars. There were roughly two strands in the study of medieval history before the nineteenth century, one the philosophical, the other the erudite. The philosophical school, including Bayle, Montesquieu, and Voltaire, included religion, commerce, and the arts in their discussion as well as military and political events; and they directed their discussion towards a defense of the Enlightenment and consequently a condemnation of the religious Middle Ages. The erudite tradition was expressed in the first great critical editions of medieval source materials that were issued by the seventeenth-century Benedictines of Saint Maur—the Maurists —and their students, men like Mabillon and Muratori; and by the Jesuit Bollandists who began in 1643 to produce the critical and erudite collection of saints' lives that is known as the *Acta Sanctorum* and that is still in progress. The strength of erudition was its careful scholarship and its attention to facts; its weakness was its pedantic detachment from living philosophical problems. The strength of the philosophers was in the breadth of their vision; their weakness was their sometimes cavalier attitude towards facts.

Edward Gibbon aimed at correcting the weaknesses of each school by using the strengths of the other. It has been said that the study of medieval history began on the day in October 1764 when Gibbon, musing amidst the ruins of imperial Rome, determined to write his *Decline and Fall*, which eventually became a European history on the grand scale down to the fall of

Constantinople. Gibbon's work is a perennial cause of wonder and admiration for the lucidity and wit of his style, the vigor of his philosophy, and the patience with which he examined the sources at a time when they had not yet been assembled in handy collections. It is a source of encouragement as well as of awe for students of the Middle Ages that their first modern interpreter is generally reputed the greatest historian ever to have written in the English language.

The early nineteenth century witnessed two developments of unequal importance in the historiography of the Middle Ages. The first was the revival by the Romantics of interest in the colorful aspects of the Middle Ages. Sir Walter Scott and his contemporaries added fancies about knights-errant and deeds of derring-do for ladies fair to the more somber images of gloomy monks that already occupied the popular mind. The more important development was the great expansion of serious scholarship. To the ecclesiastical motivations of those who prepared enormous source collections like Migne's *Patrologia Graeca* and *Patrologia Latina* were added the national aspirations of the German historians who from 1819 were engaged on the *Monumenta Germaniae Historica,* an effort to gather, criticize, and publish all of the sources relating to the Middle Ages, particularly in Germany, and those of the British historians, who were doing the same thing in their *Rerum Britannicarum Medii Aevi Scriptores,* familiarly known as the Rolls Series.

In the latter part of the last century these endeavors had made possible two gigantic strides forward in the study of medieval history, strides that were to place it in the forefront of historical activity. The first was a renewed interest in medieval philosophy, theology, art, and literature. The epics, romances, Gothic architecture, and scholastic philosophy of the time were recognized as the products of high cultural achievement and worthy of both scholarly study and popular appreciation. The second was a renewed understanding of the debt our laws and political institutions owe to the Middle Ages. Frederick William Maitland, the only medieval historian writing in English whose wit and wisdom as well as style and philosophy compare with Gibbon's, made it clear that we should never understand the common law, the workings of our government, or the principles we apply to law and government without first understanding their antecedents in the Middle Ages.

From the 1880s to World War I the Middle Ages dominated European interest in history. Even now, when the horrors of twentieth-century society preempt the attention of analysts, the study of medieval history continues to be strong in Europe. European scholars have been immensely patient and careful in applying themselves to the study of the sources. American medievalists have often preferred painting large canvasses in broad strokes to laboring over details. Europeans are more familiar with the older auxiliary disciplines of history like paleography, philology, and diplomatic (the study of documents); Americans are more familiar with the newer aids lent history by psychology, sociology, and the other social sciences.

Medieval scholarship in the United States, at first merely imitative of the work done in Europe, has now become in many respects more original and vital. Serious interest in the Middle Ages began in late nineteenth-century America with Henry Adams at Harvard, the first professor of medieval history in America. It was a non-professional scholar, Henry Charles Lea, who first established an international reputation for American medieval studies. The care and thoroughness of his research matched that of the best European scholars, and his books on the inquisition and other subjects have become classics. So thoroughly did he ransack European collections that Benjamin Disraeli remarked that Mr. Lea, were he not checked, would soon have spirited all the libraries of Europe off to Pennsylvania.

The advance of American scholarship in general after the First World War was reflected in medieval studies. Charles Homer Haskins made Harvard an internationally known center of medieval studies, and in the 'twenties the Medieval Academy of America was founded and began to publish its journal *Speculum*. By the 1930s and 1940s more American scholars had the opportunity to study in Europe, and American resources were greatly enhanced by the immigration of fine European scholars like Gerhart Ladner. But since World War II American medievalists have not only begun to equal their European counterparts in the ability to master the techniques and details of conventional scholarship but have been in the forefront of new approaches. American medievalists are drawing from the techniques and insights of the social sciences and from the comparative study of culture, religion, folklore, and institutions, and their leadership in these respects gives them at present the opportunity to lead medieval scholarship in new and creative paths.

The comparison of medieval institutions and ideas with other medieval, non-medieval, and even non-western institutions and ideas, and the re-examination of the great philosophical questions of history are the kinds of problems with which medievalists will be concerned. What is the nature of the transformation of the Roman world into the medieval? Were the early medieval centuries more creative than destructive? To what degree did the ideal of a Christian society render medieval culture cohesive? What were the motors of social change? Was the direction of medieval political history towards greater control by the central authority or towards greater power on the part of representative institutions? Can a church wedded to secular power preserve its integrity? Can holiness, as well as wealth or status, be a fundamental human motivation? Have societies found roads to truth other than the scientific? These are only a few of the questions that excite the philosophical, as well as the historical, curiosity; and scholars have now the means of investigating them more fully than ever before.

NOTES

[1] Edward Shils, "Charisma, Order, and Status," *American Sociological Review,* xxx (1965), 203.
[2] C. Kerenyi, *The Religion of the Greeks and Romans* (New York, 1962), p. 14.

PART ONE

*The Transformation
of the
Roman World
and the Foundations
of the Middle Ages*

Chapter One

THE CRISIS OF THE THIRD CENTURY

THE history of the Middle Ages, since it does not constitute a homogeneous and unchanging whole, is divisible into four periods, the first and last of which are essentially periods of transition. There was no moment when ancient man, awakening in the morning, stretched his arms and suddenly found himself in the Middle Ages. Rather, between a time that bore the unmistakable traits and characteristics of what we call classical civilization and a time that clearly was what we call medieval, stretched a period of five centuries. This first period of transition lasted from about 200 A.D. until about 700 A.D. It was followed by the early Middle Ages (ca. 700–ca. 1050), the central Middle Ages (from about 1050 to 1300), and finally the second period of transition, from medieval to modern society, which ended about 1500.

Gibbon knew that the end of the empire in the West was the beginning of the Middle Ages, and he knew that the story of that end did not begin with the traditional date of 476 but rather with the close of the Age of the Antonines almost three centuries earlier. Following the death of the last worthy Antonine emperor, Marcus Aurelius, in 180, came an enigmatic century of crisis, when the decline and fall of the Roman Empire began.

The terms "decline" and "fall" are of only limited usefulness. They inevitably bring to mind an absolute ruin of civilization with the corollary that the ages that followed must have been dark. This conception is exaggerated to the point of being false. The period of transition was not a decline of civilization in the absolute sense, but a decline of certain values and institutions typical of classical civilization, coupled with the corresponding slow growth of elements that would form the future medieval civilization. This was a process of transformation, not of eradication.

Why did the transformation of the old civilization occur? Since no institutions or attitudes are permanent, it might be thought that the question needs no asking. Yet other societies, like the Egyptian or the Chinese, continued for millennia without such a major transformation. Furthermore, the political, economic, and military dislocation of the empire that took place in the West hardly occurred in the richer, more densely populated, and more zealously protected East, where the continuity of the Roman state, although with many changes, was maintained down till 1453, almost a thousand years after the conventional date of the end of the empire in the West. The transformation that occurred in the West does require explanation.

This transformation, of which Christianity was the chief motor, changed pagan, classical Roman civilization into medieval, Christian civilization. It was thus both creative and destructive. It created a new civilization by effecting a synthesis of diverse cultures over a period of time. First Judaism and Hellenism were united in Christianity, and then Christianity was itself wed to Roman culture and institutions. Later, Teutonic and Celtic elements were added. The process of synthesis was generally complete by the end of the eighth century. What was destroyed were those ideas, attitudes, and institutions that we consider typical of classical civilization. The city of Rome itself did not decline or fall: Rome was, after all, still the center of European civilization in the thirteenth century. What declined and fell was that Rome which we somewhat arbitrarily define as classical: the Rome of the first two centuries B.C. and the first two centuries A.D.

By the first century A.D. the Romans had built a state extraordinary not only in its wealth, extent, and luxury, but in its tolerance of cultural diversity and its responsiveness—at least till the time of the Caesars—to the will of the people. The old Roman virtues praised by Cato and Cicero—seriousness, hard work, and patriotism—maintained, as they had built, the stability and order of the empire. What the Romans lacked in cultural creativity and imagination they adopted from the Greeks,

The Roman Forum.

so that Greek ideas were incorporated in Roman religion and philosophy, and much of Roman literature and art is derivative from Greece. The citizens of the city of Rome, at the center of this empire, enjoyed transacting business and politics in the forum, relaxing at the baths, and entertaining at their homes. They were protected from undue worry and harassment not only by the size of the empire and the strength of its armies, and by the wealth that these brought the city, but by efficient institutions of administration and justice. They were sheltered from undue struggles of conscience or intellect by their strong adherence to tradition and by their unquestioning acceptance of the idea that religion was and ought to be public rather than individual and inseparable from other public matters. They considered both religion and government indivisible manifestations of politics, which they, like the Greeks, defined as the life of the city. Roman society was not uniformly happy, but it was well-ordered, and its order and prosperity seemed to culminate at the end of the first century under the rule of the Antonines.

The Golden Age of the Antonines (96–180) was the period in the history of the world, according to Gibbon, "during which the condition of the human race was most happy and prosperous."[1] He observed that "in the second century of the

Christian era, the Empire of Rome comprehended the fairest part of the earth, and the most civilised portion of mankind."[2] Further,

> . . . it is not alone by the rapidity, or extent of conquest, that we should estimate the greatness of Rome . . . the firm edifice of Roman power was raised and preserved by the wisdom of ages. The obedient provinces of Trajan and the Antonines . . . were united by laws and adorned by arts. They might occasionally suffer from the partial abuse of delegated authority; but the general principle of government was wise, simple, and beneficent.[3]

Rome was not a European empire. Its power made the Mediterranean a unifying center of, rather than a division between, the three continents of Europe, Africa, and Asia. From Mesopotamia to Scotland and from north Africa to the Danube, the *pax romana* protected territories now shared by no less than thirty-six sovereign states. Of this vast domain, supporting a population of at least eighty millions, the provinces boasted busy cities, centers of art, literature, and philosophy as well as of commerce and industry; fields and orchards fruitful in cattle, grapes, olives, grain, and other products of the soil; and public works massive in their size and majestic in their execution. The Antonine Emperor Hadrian encouraged all the human arts, settled desert areas, reclaimed wasteland, and constructed monuments to the public benefit and to his own glory in every province of the empire. With the loyalty of the Senate and the support of their subjects, the Antonine emperors ruled over a state that could boast both inner tranquility and security from external dangers. Protected by mighty fleets and sustained by numerous and valorous armies, Rome created a prosperous economy that brought her into contact with China and India, a legal system still the basis of procedure in many countries, and, through gradual extension of citizenship and the mutual benefits of prosperity, a sense of community and responsibility on the part of her subjects. The virtues of the Roman community were in some measure those of the Greek polis writ large: the virtues of happy and prosperous citizens freely united in a community of interest.

YET in the third century, defects in this hitherto successful system began to be evident.

Gibbon thought he knew the moment when the decline began: the succession to the throne in 180 of Commodus, the unworthy son of Marcus Aurelius. Though it is false to consider the vices of the emperors a cause of decline—there had been too many corrupt rulers earlier, among them Nero—it is true that the brilliance of the Age of the Antonines dimmed and grew tarnished in the succeeding century. Though it is improper to speak of this period of transition solely as a decline and fall since it included positive attainments, it is clear that some things did decline, notably those institutions and attitudes that had maintained the empire, and bolstered the morale, of the Roman people: the army, the system of justice, the imperial administration, and the imperial office itself.

The causes of this decline have long been, and will continue to be, disputed, for the third century has left us few historical sources. Aside from coins, inscriptions, and other artifacts, we are left only the fragmentary works of inferior historians like Dio Cassius, Herodian, the biographers of the *Historia Augusta,* and some even less reliable chroniclers of the fourth and fifth centuries. For the reign of Diocletian (284–305) we have also the *Notitia dignitatum,* a list of civil and military officers of high degree, and the works of the Christian writers Eusebius and Lactantius. The bias of all the third-century historians interferes with our understanding, for the Christians freely expressed their natural antipathies to persecuting emperors; and the senators, like Dio, their dislike of rulers who infringed upon the privileges of their order. It is easier, therefore, to raise questions about the third century than to answer them.

Nevertheless, many answers have been suggested. Gibbon emphasized the corruption of institutions (particularly the army) the effete influence of Christianity, the "immoderate greatness" of the empire, and the onslaught of the barbarians; Christian historians used to view the disaster as a punishment of pagan sins. Recently Professor Piganiol has insisted that the barbarian attacks were solely responsible for the ruin. Historians have over the centuries emphasized one or another of these themes; some also have argued economic causes—the outward drain of gold, the exhaustion of the soil, the decline of population owing to malnutrition, plagues, and infertility, or the intrusion of pirates into the sea lanes and highways. Yet others have urged social causes, sometimes in direct opposition: the increase of the power and influence of the lower classes corrupted the standards of the elite; the decrease in the power and influence of the people alienated them from the government.

One problem with the concept of Roman "decline and fall" is that it has been applied to all kinds of cultural phenomena where it is in fact irrelevant, rather than restricted to the political and military institutions typical of classical Rome. The problem has thereby been expanded to wholly unmanageable proportions. Another is that it is difficult to say exactly when the process even of political decline and fall was completed— Gibbon, after all, extended his history to 1453. Still another problem is that differing conditions in different parts of the empire make all generalizations dubious. Finally, it is true here as elsewhere that in the extremely intricate and large web of human events, threads of cause and effect too often intersect and knot in a random fashion, and chance (or fate if you prefer) plays a very large part. It is impossible to select any one cause or series of causes for the phenomenon of decline. What follows here is therefore a description of how, more than an analysis of why, the decline took place. The great question of the ultimate reasons for the fall of the West's grandest empire will continue to be debated.

It is possible that the most significant feature of the decline was the strain put upon Roman institutions and liberties by the construction and maintenance of the empire, just as Periclean Athens was obliged to suffer the destruction of its democratic institutions in its efforts to construct a Greek empire. The concentration of energy upon the defense of distant frontiers and upon the attempt to preserve existing institutions inhibited the flexibility and creativity necessary to preserve old values under new circumstances.

One of the most telling weaknesses of the empire was its lack of responsibility, and responsiveness, to the will of the people. Aurelius Victor remarked concerning Augustus, "in the 722d year of the city there began at Rome the habit of obedience to one man." The history of the Republic had been marked by the slow growth of popular participation in government, a growth that was ended in the first century B.C. by the intrigues and quarrels of the demagogues. The victory of the most successful military demagogue, Julius Caesar, was approved both by the undiscriminating populace and by the cowed Senate. It was legitimized in the rule of his adopted son Augustus, who took the titles of *princeps* and *imperator* while retaining republican institutions as a window-dressing for his tyranny. The tyranny grew, after the death of Augustus, more capricious and more isolated from the people. By the third century its wasting effects were plain to see: the emperor and the army ruled as it pleased them with or without the consent, and for or against the interests, of the citizens. Centralization and autocracy alienated the people without protecting them. "Both in theory and in the practice of the constitution the emperor's powers were absolute. He controlled foreign policy, making peace and war at will: he could raise what taxes he willed and spend the money at his pleasure: he personally appointed to all offices, civil and military: he had the power of life and death over all his subjects. He was moreover the sole fount of law and could make new rules or abrogate old at pleasure . . . ."[4] The delicate balance of powers that Polybius had attributed to the Roman constitution in the second century B.C.—even then somewhat unrealistically—had vanished; there was now no limitation to the emperor's power save whatever brute force rebels might raise; and where Augustus had been *princeps*, "first citizen," Diocletian (284–305) became *dominus*, or "lord."

The occupant of the throne, however absolute his power, had no means of assuring the succession of his heir. The gravest constitutional deficiency of the Roman monarchy was that succession was fixed neither by heredity, by election, nor by the wishes of the outgoing ruler himself. In theory the monarchy was elective and in the hands of the Senate, but the emperors themselves had done so much to emasculate that body that by the third century it could do no more than submit docilely to the ruler imposed upon it by the army. Succession passed to the strongest—to the man who could command the loyalty of the army and especially of the powerful Praetorian Guard, the chief military force in the city itself and that which could best seize the centers of power during an interregnum. The acclamation of the army became the most regular means of election to the throne, and the army became the chief power in the state. Dependent upon the military for tenure in office, the emperor was obliged to do everything to please the troops. "Take care of the army," a dying ruler advised his successor, "and let everything else go." Obliged to fight at the head of his troops in the field, since he dared not delegate command to any general who might achieve enough popularity with the soldiers to rise against him, the emperor had to expose himself to the dangers of war and leave the civil rule of the empire to those who remained behind. This situation rendered continuity of policy and consistency in executing it extremely difficult.

The military control of the state eventually brought about the ruin of both the state and the army. Not only was the emperor committed to constant wars, which ended in overextending the strength and resources of the empire; not only were the soldiers irresponsible in their political intrigues, their demands for money, and their propensity for looting their own cities when their pay was in arrears; they obliged the emperors to cling to outmoded military strategies. As it had done to the Spartans, militarism caused the Romans to develop a closed and defensive mentality: the army existed for the protection of the sacred institutions of Rome, but the most sacred institution of Rome had become the army.

When the prince became a prisoner of the army's favor, other institutions declined. The proudest and most ancient of all, the Senate, was completely humiliated. Defeated in its struggle against the demagogues in the first century B.C., browbeaten by a Tiberius and insulted by a Caligula, it was treated with friendly if condescending respect by the Antonines. But after the death of Marcus Aurelius, Commodus showed it open hostility, relying instead upon the army and upon hosts of secret police and informers. The emperor Carus did not bother to inform the Senate of his elevation by the troops in 282; and even reforming emperors like Septimius Severus and Diocletian had, in order to be effective, to ignore the Senate in favor of less phantasmal sources of power. As it was with the Senate, so it was with the lesser institutions of the state. All that was preserved, and all that preserved its power, did so by subservience to the emperor, himself the slave of the army.

The rot of military cynicism and corruption came to penetrate the entire society. The Antonines had made the civil service salaried and professional. But since the favor of the

Arch of Septimius Severus in the Roman Forum.

emperor and army was the only control or limitation imposed upon the civil service, it grew in the third century into an enormous, greedy, and sycophantic bureaucracy, sucking up the taxes of the citizens and offering in return no service beyond the flattery of its superiors. The Roman law itself, justly celebrated as the greatest achievement of Roman civilization, became venal and corrupt. Untrained short-term judges presided for their own profit over courts with conflicting jurisdictions and cases that inevitably required high fees and long journeys on the part of the litigants, and even longer delays in getting judgments.

The cynical abuse of power on the part of those who had it, and the decay of decent and responsible institutions, gradually sapped the political virtues of the Roman people. Too many were excluded from the benefits and decisions of government to retain the old sense of loyalty and devotion to the polis. Local

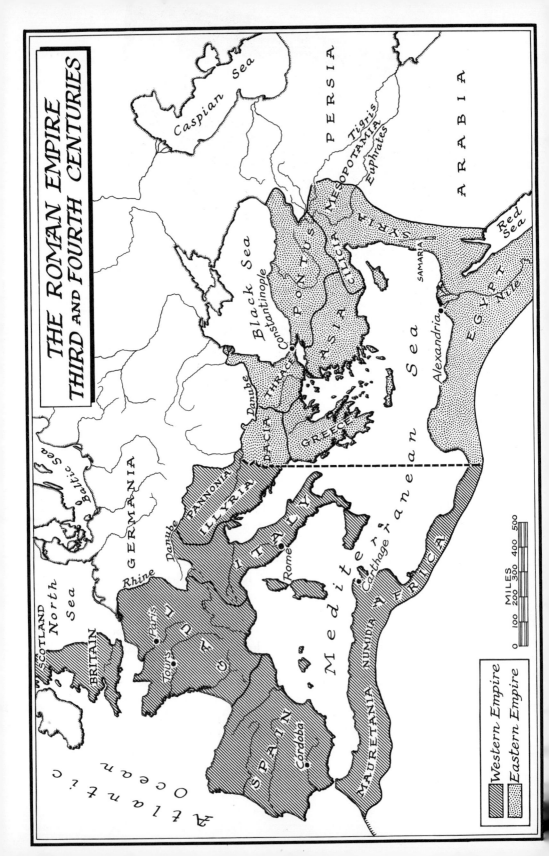

THE ROMAN EMPIRE
THIRD AND FOURTH CENTURIES

Caspian Sea

PERSIA

ARABIA

Black Sea

Tigris
MESOPOTAMIA
Euphrates

Red Sea

PONTUS

ASIA

CILICIA

SYRIA

Constantinople

THRACE

DACIA

SAMARIA

Danube

GREECE

Alexandria

EGYPT

Nile

Mediterranean Sea

PANNONIA

ILLYRIA

ITALY

Danube

Rome

Carthage

AFRICA

Rhine

GERMANIA

Baltic Sea

North Sea

SCOTLAND

BRITAIN

G A U L

Paris

Tours

NUMIDIA

MAURETANIA

SPAIN

Cordoba

Atlantic Ocean

MILES

0 100 200 300 400 500

Western Empire

Eastern Empire

loyalties had perhaps always been greater than loyalty to Rome itself, but now in the third century cities unashamedly took advantage of civil strife to wage war against their neighbors. As venality grew in the capital, it flourished in the provinces. Even the great public works erected in the cities were often extravagances whose purpose was to flatter the pride of the city or the vanity of the emperor rather than to stimulate the economy. The citizens of Rome itself, whose models had once been Cincinnatus or Cato, increasingly sought means of avoiding military service, leaving the army to the greedy, the wanton, and eventually, in the fourth century, to the barbarian. In 212, Caracalla extended citizenship throughout the empire, more to increase the number of those liable to military service than to secure the loyalty of the populace. It was not only the size of the empire, but the fact that the idea of a mutually beneficial community had been lost, that was at fault.

ADDED to the internal weaknesses of the empire, the increased pressure of external enemies in the third century proved intolerable. About 250 the Franks burst across the barrier of the Rhine to pillage Gaul and Spain; at about the same time the Alamanni and Marcomanni crossed the upper Danube into Pannonia and Italy. From 249 the Goths were beleaguering the Balkans and Asia Minor. Pirates infested the sea lanes and robbers the roads. In the East, the ineffective Arsacid dynasty of the Persians yielded in 227 to the vigorous Sassanids, who pursued an aggressive policy against Rome and whose King Shapur I conquered Syria and in 260 took the emperor Valerian prisoner. Like the Persians, the Teutonic barbarians became an increasing threat, and in the fourth century the incursions of the Huns into Teutonic lands drove their terrified occupants willy-nilly against the Romans, whom they found a much less formidable foe. One reason was that these fourth-century Germans were more formidable than the Germans of the first had been; they had improved their technology and had learned to forge much better weapons.

It was not for lack of will that the Romans faltered. The third-century army may have numbered about 300,000 men; Diocletian may have increased it to as many as 450,000, and it may have gone as high as 600,000 in the fourth century. Thus, in the period of decline, the army's size was actually increasing; moreover, the attentions of men like Septimius Severus and Diocletian were largely devoted to making it more efficient. But even an army of 600,000 was not sufficient against active enemies on all fronts in an age when rapid transportation on the modern scale was impossible. Good as the Roman roads were, they could not provide mobility enough. None of the Teutonic peoples could count more than twenty or thirty thousand warriors, but when even these small numbers were suddenly hurled at one point of the frontier, irruption proved impossible to prevent, especially when the army was so often distracted from its task of defense by intrigue and rebellion.

THE political weaknesses of the Roman state contributed to the increasing weakness of the Roman economy, which in turn inhibited political and military recovery. This economic weakness was to bring about a depression that lasted with minor fluctuation from the third century into the eighth, and was the central fact of European economic history throughout the period of transition.

Under the Antonines the *pax romana* created a large united area of trade in which to find resources, as when Italy came to depend upon the grain supply of Egypt. To the natural wealth and fertility of their empire, the Romans had been accustomed for centuries to add the tribute of frightened neighbors, the booty of conquered peoples, and the taxes of subdued provinces.

In the third century these advantages ceased. The borders of Rome had stopped expanding, and sources of booty and tribute dried up; after defeats by the Persians the Romans were sometimes even obliged to pay indemnities themselves. The greed of the bureaucracy and the army, the extravagance of the emperors, and the need of the starving unemployed increased taxes beyond the point of stifling initiative to that of bringing many merchants and small farmers to ruin. The government's need for money grew as the ability of the people to pay lessened, and its increasingly strict economic measures only weakened the economy further. Debasement of the coinage led to inflation and further debasement. The *curiales,* influential citizens in the cities entrusted with administrative duties and the collection of taxes, were asked to pay into the treasury more tax money than they could collect from the impoverished towns. The result was the ruin of the class. The freezing of trades and crafts, the binding of children to the vocation of their fathers, stifled initiative. Price ceilings established in attempts to curb inflation were simply ignored. Meanwhile, gold was being sent east to pay the Persians indemnities and to pay for the luxuries required by the effete ruling classes.

The two most fundamental motors of economic downfall, however, were the decline of agriculture and of population. Ecologists observe that few lands in this overpopulated world today have been so thoroughly ravaged by man as the territory once occupied by the Roman Empire on the shores of the Mediterranean. We are accustomed to thinking of Greece, Syria, North Africa, and southern Italy as barren countries, but there was a time when the now brown and eroded hills supported thick forests and fruitful orchards. Uncomprehending and heedless of the future, men exploited and stripped these lands until their fertility was destroyed. The speed of this disastrous process is surpassed only by that of our own destruction of the fertility and wild life of North America.

What ecological folly did not accomplish, tax programs did. Small farmers were ruined and forced to sell out to their more prosperous neighbors. These proceeded to build huge landed estates known as *latifundia,* which they devoted in small part to serious agriculture and in large part to hunting preserves and pleasure gardens. The romance of the land was always in the Roman mind, as the romance of the frontier is in the American, and long after the sturdy yeoman farmer had ceased to be the political backbone of Rome, the Romans continued to sing his praises. The pastoral and farm poems of Vergil and Horace were written by men who had little more to do with real farming than the New York owner of a summer place in Wyoming has to do with ranching. For the wealthy, the land became a place of recreation, not of production; this is a luxury the Americans can afford but the Romans could not. As A. H. M. Jones has said, "The basic economic weakness of the empire was that too few producers supported too many idle mouths."[5] The decline of agricultural production was only temporarily offset by the agricultural settlements of the Antonines. Abandonment of land, which had already begun in the third century, by the fifth accounted for ten to fifteen percent of the formerly arable land in some sectors, and as much as fifty percent in North Africa. The most important result of driving the farmers off the farms was the creation of a large, unemployed, and unskilled urban mob, who ate up large supplies of food in the dole, produced nothing for the economy, and added another element of political unrest to the state.

The other basic economic problem was the decline in population. The third century brought recurring epidemics of malaria and other diseases, and bubonic plague, ravaging vast areas from 251 to 266, killed two-thirds of the population in some localities. Such universal disease would not be seen again until the fourteenth century. The death rate in a society without high medical or hygienic standards is always high, and these third-century developments made it all the more necessary to match the high death rate from disease and war with a correspondingly high rate of birth. Yet as nearly as we can determine, the birth rate was actually declining. This was partly owing to famines, disease, wars, and sexual irregularities, but mostly to the heavy taxes that did not permit people of modest means to keep their families alive. Infanticide, as well as abortion and contraceptives, was employed, and many children who were not deliberately destroyed succumbed to malnutrition.

Under these conditions of corruption, poverty, disease, and famine, it was difficult to find enough men for the army or to collect the revenues necessary for the effective functioning of the state, and a growing number of citizens, deprived of their land or of productive jobs, became alienated from, or indifferent to, its welfare.

A DECLINE in morality has always been cited, from the time of Tacitus, as a cause for the general decline of the Roman state. But it is difficult to measure the morality of any given time. The twentieth century, for example, may have looser sexual customs than the nineteenth, but its humane concern for the public welfare is generally much greater. Further, it may be that the moral vigor of a period is better measured by the presence of effective movements for reform than by the actual standards prevailing at the moment. The growing success of Christianity with its strict moral code is a positive indication of the strengthening of moral concern, even in the third century. There was, therefore, no absolute decline of morals, and it cannot be made one of the causes of the general "decline and fall."

Nonetheless, what did occur was a gradual sapping of devotion to the public welfare. As the state ceased to be a polis, a community of interest for its citizens, its virtues were replaced by what the Greeks called *idiocy*—the pursuit of personal gain.

The greed and pleasure-seeking of the emperors and the armies were reflected in the habits of the upper classes, whose mores were described with scorn by Tacitus, with cynicism by Martial, and with satirical disdain by Juvenal. *Moritur et ridet,* the Christians said of Rome: "it dies laughing." The old Roman virtues extolled by Cato and Vergil—seriousness, hard work, patriotism, honor—had already begun to disappear at the time the latter was writing. The orgies of Messalina, the murdering brutality of Sejanus, the *vomitoria* of Trimalchio, and the baths characterized the leaders of society in the first century of the principate; for the lower classes there were the spectacles in the Colosseum. It is difficult to consider the Middle Ages a "decline" from the Roman Empire when one contemplates the spectacles. Men hacking or clubbing one another to death, criminals and Christians disemboweled and eaten alive by wild animals, the squealing of beasts; these were the sights that pleased the eye, and the sounds that delighted the ear, of the Roman populace. Whatever the faults of the early Christians, they must have redeemed many of them by their condemnation and eventual elimination of these pastimes.

At the beginning of the third century, the emperor Commodus demonstrated how the refined vices of the upper classes could be united with the crude evils of the lower. This representative of classical culture, when he was not amusing himself in his harem of 300 girls and 300 young boys, used to dress himself in the garb, and pride himself in the titles, of Hercules. Going to the Colosseum, he would personally slaughter, with javelin, arrow, or club, crowds of animals, slaves, and criminals herded before the royal box. All of this was done to the delight, or to the sycophantic applause, of the spectators, and when, at the age of thirty-two, Commodus was removed from this world, the deed was done not by moralists or reformers but by one of his whores with the aid of a wrestler friend.

THOSE too decent, or too poor, to pass their time in vice faced a terrible spiritual crisis. The old Roman religion had become a hollow shell, and the official deification of emperors like Commodus cannot have enhanced its appeal. Stoicism, the philosophy that had strengthened the fiber of duty and devotion of the Roman people from Cicero to Marcus Aurelius, was losing its influence. The old institutions were no longer proper objects of faith, and the alternatives were on the one hand cynicism, idiocy, and despair, and on the other new ideologies. Romans who did not yield to the former alternative turned to mystical philosophies like neoplatonism, to the mystery cults, to the salvation cults of the East, and to Christianity.

THE same failure of the old traditions was visible in the realm of the intellectual and the artistic. Civilizations are great according to the degree they permit man to be a rational as well as social animal, that is, according to the creativity and diversity that they produce. Historians have often spoken of the cultural decline of Rome; in fact this is very difficult to measure. It is true that the "Golden Age" of Roman literature was the first century B.C., and the first two centuries A.D., and both the quantity and the elegance of literature seems to have fallen off from the third century. Nonetheless, whole new genres were developed: the liturgical and theological literature of the new religions, and the romantic and satirical novels. In law the later empire was as creative as any period in Roman history, including that of Cicero. In painting, sculpture, and mosaics there was no evident decline, but rather a shift in taste away from classical realism and individualization to a style fixed, symbolic, two-dimensional, and hieratic.

It is possible to argue that since Roman culture as a whole was less creative than Greek, the entire Roman period represents the decline of Hellenic civilization. But this does not help to explain the "decline and fall" of Rome. What does happen in the history of any culture is simply this: there comes a time when the possibilities of a particular tradition have been exhausted and its continuation brings only stale repetition and imitation. At this point cultures may continue to make use of the form whose spirit is dead, or they may turn to new and vital modes of thought and expression. The philosophy of the Christian fathers, ill-formed in comparison with that of Plato, was a living philosophy in the third century and eventually grew into the mature work of Augustine. Later Latin poetry, inferior as a whole in style to that of Horace or Catullus, produced at its best lyric works that were natural and pure. There was no decline of culture in the absolute sense. Those things typical of classical Greco-Roman civilization were slowly fading, and those things that would come to be typical of the new, medieval civilization were slowly growing.

Not all energetic and vital men had given up Roman institutions for dead in the third century. Quite to the contrary, this paradoxical age witnessed the rule of a number of competent emperors, like Septimius Severus, Claudius Gothicus, Gallienus, Aurelian, and Probus. The virtues of these emperors, however, were limited: the "good" emperors were those who could control the army; the "bad" ones those who could not. The lack of fixed succession, which produced military revolts, civil wars, twenty-six emperors in fifty years, and as many as nineteen pretenders to the throne at one time, combined with the occasional degenerate emperors like Heliogabalus and Caracalla, meant that it was impossible to implement long-term reforms or to assure continuity in policies.

Yet the century ended with an emperor great enough to hold the decline in check. This was Diocletian (284–305), to the Christians an "inventor of crime and contriver of wickedness, (who) ruined everything and did not spare God himself."[6] It was usually the better emperors who prosecuted the Christians, for it was they who had vigor enough to resist the threat that Christianity posed to traditional Rome.

An Illyrian of low birth, Diocletian was a man of great military, and greater administrative, abilities. Recognizing the limitations of his time, he pursued a cautious policy. He worked to establish the autocracy on a sound administrative and military basis, and to this purpose shared the empire with other Illyrians as crude and as able as he. The first of these was Maximian, whom he made "caesar" in 285 and "augustus" in

286. Maximian and Diocletian ruled jointly, Maximian in the West and Diocletian in the more powerful half of the empire, the East. In 293, Diocletian decided upon a fourfold division of the empire. In the East, the augustus Diocletian was to be assisted by Gaius Galerius as caesar, while in the West the augustus Maximian was to be supported by the caesar Constantius Chlorus, the father of Constantine the Great. In addition, Diocletian split the provinces that Severus had established into even smaller units, thus increasing the degree of control that the rulers could exercise over them.

This fourfold rule was militarily a good idea, as it allowed four rulers to be in the field at one time against enemies both foreign and domestic. Ultimately, however, the system was harmful, for in sharing, rather than delegating, authority, Diocletian opened the gate to future conflicts. As long as he was alive and well, his associates masked their personal ambitions and greed, but when he was forced by ill health to abdicate in 305 and obliged Maximian to abdicate with him, a new period of civil unrest ensued and continued until 312, when Constantine was able to consolidate his own power. While the good effects of the division faded, the evil effects remained, and the basic separation between the eastern and the western Roman Empire was a hundred years later restored for good.

Diocletian's other reforms had similar short-term benefits and long-term disadvantages. In order to enhance his prestige, Diocletian adopted the scepter and diadem and affected the pomp and ceremonial of oriental courts. Henceforward one desiring audience of the emperor approached him as his *dominus* (lord) and was obliged to offer him *adoratio*, kneeling and kissing the hem of his garment. This notion of imperial authority was translated by Constantine and his successors into a Christian context and became the origin of the medieval conception of the emperor as the vicegerent of Christ on earth.

Diocletian completely reorganized the army, offering greater inducements to recruits, using the draft, and dividing the army into frontier defenders and mobile reserve troops—an invaluable strategic innovation that helped preserve the empire for another hundred years. He abolished most indirect taxes and used a sophisticated form of direct tax that was levied both upon individuals and upon their property, a lucrative measure

Palace of Diocletian at Split.

that ultimately hastened the destruction of the small farmers; by
322 they had become unfree *coloni,* bound by law to the soil. He
reformed the currency, and in 301 established a price ceiling
in words that might apply to times other than his own:

> Is anyone so dull and unfeeling as not to know, not to have seen,
> that the high prices in our markets, on which the daily life of our
> cities depends, are not checked by abundance or bumper crops? . . .
> Men with enough wealth to satisfy whole nations try to capture smaller
> fortunes and strive after ruinous percentages; concern for humanity
> in general persuades us to set a limit to the avarice of such men.
> Now we must detail the facts whose urgency has finally overcome our
> tolerance.[7]

The edict, rather than having salutary effects, created a scarcity
of goods, since people simply withheld them from the market
rather than sell them at low prices.

Thus the emperor's policies had the ultimate effect of weakening the economy, driving numbers of farmers into the state of serfdom, dividing the empire, and, by increasing the autocracy, widening the chasm between the government and the citizens. They made necessary repairs in some parts of the engine, but that engine had been too long abused. Gibbon's gloomy epigram remains true: "Such was the unhappy condition of the Roman emperors that, whatever their conduct, their fate was commonly the same."[8] No matter what policies they undertook, they met defeat and ruin. As Horace had already put it in the first century:

> What does this wretched day forbode?
> The age of our parents, worse than that of our grandparents,
> Has borne us who are still more worthless—and we in turn
> Shall give rise to a yet more vicious generation.[9]

THE true way out was not to refurbish the old but to create anew. Victory would ultimately come, not to Diocletian, but to the creators of the new world. In the second century had already appeared a figure that typifies the new direction society would take. This man, a Samarian Greek named Justin, converted to Christianity ca. 130 after investigating the ancient religions and philosophies. Before his martyrdom ca. 165, he wrote three notable works bringing together Greek and Christian thought— two *Apologies* and a *Dialogue with Trypho*. Justin Martyr's importance is that unlike the early Judaeo-Christians, who shunned this world, he accepted it. He linked Christianity with pagan philosophy and made it a living part of Roman culture, expressing the life force of the community in a way that paganism had ceased to do.

The *Apologies* and the *Dialogue* are part of a tradition of Christian literature that began in the second century and culminated in Augustine's *City of God:* essentially they were justifications of Christianity against the charges of corruption brought by pagan writers. Justin argued not only that Christianity was true, but that Christians made the best citizens of the state and that they were in fact the best representatives of Roman culture! In the course of this argument, Justin, who had been strongly influenced by Stoicism, worked out a doctrine of the Christian word of God (*Logos*) that was similar to the

Stoic idea of *logoi spermatikoi,* "seminal words or ideas." According to Justin, God had revealed himself not only to the Jews but to the Greek philosophers: Christ, the *Logos,* has shown "every race of man that which is always and in all places just, so that every type of man knows that adultery, fornication, murder, and so on, are evil." This is a doctrine of natural law enforced by the idea of the immanence of Christ in the world. Indeed, he argued, Euripides, Xenophon, Plato, and all the other ancients, pagan or barbarian, who lived by reason were truly Christians.

Justin challenged the Roman philosophers on their own ground, that of reason: "If you think our statements in accord with reason and truth, respect them; if they seem silly, despise them." There were plenty who would continue to despise, but what Justin had done was both further to Hellenize Christianity and to make it more acceptable to Roman intellectuals: he built a bridge between Christian revelation and Greco-Roman thought.

THE "decline and fall" of Rome was not the decline of all civilization but only of that particular civilization that we somewhat arbitrarily classify as *the* Roman: that of Rome at the height of its political, military, and economic powers. Different aspects of this Roman civilization declined at different rates, and some not at all. Insofar as decline actually did occur, it appears to have been the third century in which it reached the point beyond which it could no longer be checked. But as new, healthy forces of religion, culture, and even politics were beginning to arise at the same time, it is better not to speak of a decline but of a transformation.

The modern eye has understandably been more impressed by the spectacle of the toppling towers of the old civilization than by the almost imperceptible beginnings of the new. It has followed the tragedy of men like Septimius Severus and Diocletian, trying vainly to shore up the ruins of their society, more readily than it has the courage and creativity of those more obscure but more original men who dared to make the leap to a new faith and a new hope and made the rebuilding of civilization possible. In this we have been deceived into taking shadow for the substance and the substance for the shadow.

There was a twilight in the evening of the Roman world, but
that same twilight was the first light of the new dawn.

NOTES

[1] *Decline and Fall of the Roman Empire* (New York, 1932). I, ch. 3, 70. This is
the Modern Library edition, to which all citations from Gibbon in my
text are made.

[2] Gibbon, I, ch. I, I.

[3] Gibbon, I, ch. 2, 25.

[4] A. H. M. Jones, *The Later Roman Empire 284-602*. 2 vols. (Norman, Okla.:
Univ. of Oklahoma Press, 1964), I, 321.

[5] A. H. M. Jones, II, 1045.

[6] Lactantius, *On the Deaths of the Persecutors,* 7, trans. Moses Hadas in
Hadas, *A History of Rome.* Copyright © 1956 by Moses Hadas. Reprinted
by permission of Doubleday & Company, Inc. (New York, 1956), p. 180.

[7] *Edictum Diocletiani de Pretiis Venalibus,* trans. Hadas in *History,* pp. 179–180.

[8] Gibbon, I, ch. 12, 274.

[9] *Odes,* III, 6.

Chapter Two

CHRISTIANITY

THE old religions, morality, and philosophies of the Romans were by the first century A.D. ceasing to command assent or to express the life of the community. Those who despaired of reviving them turned to new expressions offering greater personal satisfaction and pointing the way to a transcendent truth beyond this material world. Of these expressions Christianity was originally only one; but it came to be the most important force in the transformation of the Roman world into the medieval.

Christianity's rivals for the allegiance of the Romans were numerous and varied. Neoplatonism, a mystical doctrine elaborated by Plotinus (d. 270), taught that an individual might, through successive stages of purification, achieve union with the One. The old agricultural mysteries of pre-classical times were also revived, often united with fertility cults imported from the Middle East. These mystery cults ["mystery": secret rites] had been introduced at Rome as early as the third century B.C., and in the first centuries of the empire spread widely. Their central myths explained the seasons: a god dies and descends to the underworld, and the land becomes bare and brown; the god is brought back to life, and the land begins to turn green again. The object of the cults was to achieve immortality for the believer by uniting him with the rising god through ceremonial acts. These dying-and-rising gods were numerous: the Egyptian Osiris, the Greek Dionysius, the Syrian Attis, and the lovers of the Egyptian Isis and of the Anatolian Great Mother. Yet another religion of the empire, one vastly popular with soldiers, was Mithraism, a variation of Persian Zoroastrianism in which Mithra, identified with the sun, is the bearer of light and salvation to

37

Christ as the Sun God: an illustration of religious syncretism in the later Roman Empire.

his followers, who rise through a series of mystic steps to achieve union with him.

CHRISTIANITY began to gain strength at the same time as these mysteries. The origins of Christianity have been and continue to be the subject of hot debate among scholars, although historical sophistication and new archeological discoveries have permitted substantial progress in the last half-century. Beyond their intrinsic interest, these origins are important for an understanding of the passage from Roman to medieval; Christianity, the most fundamental expression of medieval life, was rooted in the classical Mediterranean world.

Was Christianity another mystery cult? Like the mystery cults, it worshiped a dying-and-rising god, had ceremonies of initiation and communion, and emphasized the search for individual salvation. Christianity has an even closer parallel to Mithraism: Mithra was born of a virgin on the night of the winter solstice, calculated as occurring on December 25. But Mithra's birthday was deliberately chosen by the Church Fathers to mark the birth of Christ in order to prevent the faithful from hedging their bets by attending the feasts of both gods. Other differences from the cults were even more pronounced. The gods of the mystery cults lived in some mysterious non-time; Christianity took pains from the beginning to emphasize the historicity of its founder, who, as the Nicene Creed explicitly puts it, "suffered under Pontus Pilate," an historical and verifiable procurator of Judaea. Finally, the Christian sacraments have more in common with Judaism than with the cults. Unlike the mysteries, Christianity by no means rejected the world entirely: far from sapping the strength of the empire, Christians were often its most active and vital subjects.

If Christianity was not one of the cults, what were its true origins? As so often in ancient history, the answer is obscured by inadequate source materials. Of non-Christian writers, only a few trouble to mention the rise of what seemed a small and merely troublesome sect. Much of what is ascribed to the Jewish writer Josephus may be a later interpolation; of the Romans, Tacitus, Pliny, and Suetonius mention the Christians, but do not deign to discuss their origins. Fortunately we have the New Testament, a fuller collection of sources than we possess for most problems of ancient history.

The New Testament has always been difficult to understand. In the first place, the details are sparse, and the materials are not arranged with historical exposition in mind, but for various theological purposes that are difficult for the modern literal and historical mind to follow. In the second place, the texts emanate from only one group of early Christians, the Hellenizers who were struggling to overcome the Judaeo-Christians' prejudice against the Gentiles.

The preliminary problem recognized by modern Biblical scholars is to analyze the New Testament in its present form and, by understanding its component parts and how they were put together, to come closer to an understanding of the intention of its authors. Modern scholars generally agree upon the dates when the books of the New Testament were written, the earliest being the Pauline epistles (ca. 50–64 A.D.); the Gospels of Mark, Matthew, and Luke appearing (probably in that order) about 65–70; and the Gospel of John probably about 90. Most scholars also consider that the Gospels are themselves compositions of earlier, diverse, oral or written traditions, in which can be recognized miracle stories, conversations, proverbs, apocalyptic sayings, and sayings concerning the law. Since the pre-literary forms of these component parts have been lost, and since each of the evangelists had his own point of view and method in arranging the materials, it is difficult to be certain that everything they attributed to Christ was actually his.

"WHO say you that I am?" Jesus asked his followers, and Peter answered, with the approval of his master: "The Christ, the Son of the Living God." But according to the third chapter of Mark, Jesus' own relatives worried about his sanity, and the Scribes for their part were sure that his inspiration was diabolical rather than divine. The orthodox Jews called him an illegitimate blasphemer, and the pagan Romans mocked at his death as the crucifixion of an ass. Since the beginning of Christianity Christians have held opinions of Jesus almost as diverse as these, and few would have been recognized in the Middle Ages or by most modern Christians.

In the eighteenth century the Deists attacked Christianity as irrational. Some German Christians replied by trying to construct a version of Christianity that would fit eighteenth-century notions of rationality. They concluded that Jesus thought himself an earthly Messiah and that his apostles, horrified at his failure and death, invented the whole story of his divinity and resurrection in order to justify him and themselves. Others rationalized the miracle stories, claiming for example that though Jesus did not really walk on water, atmospheric conditions made it appear to his disciples that he had. The rationalists' attempt at reconciling reason and religion was clumsy; in the early nineteenth century David Friedrich Strauss developed a more sophisticated theory according to which the apostles transformed

The Good Shepherd; Roman statue of Jesus, fourth century.

the earthly Jesus into the divine Christ, not through self-justification or gullibility, but through the creation of a myth which, Strauss believed, was poetically valid though historically false.

After Strauss's death his ideas were developed in three directions. The first development led to the creation of many wild myth-theories, in which Jesus was simply a version of the fertility gods Tammuz and Adonis, or the Vedic god Agni. Signs of this sort of interpretation may be found today in the work of Robert Graves, but not in the work of any serious historian. The second train of thought led to the school of liberal theology, which proclaimed Jesus the most advanced, but still wholly human, teacher of morality. This school still has its followers in Britain and America but has generally been rejected as contrary to the evidence of Biblical criticism. The third led to the modern "eschatological" [eschatology: the study of the "last things"—death, the end of the world], which perceives in Jesus a mystical prophet who believed that the end of the world was imminent and that his mission was to call men to face their God wholly and fully in the immediate hour.

All these interpretations have tailored the idea of Jesus to fit the prevailing intellectual fashion of the time: the eschatological interpretation, for example, is very congenial to existentialism. Albert Schweitzer, reviewing the literature in his famous *Quest of the Historical Jesus*, abandoned hope of history's fully confronting the object of its search.

But this is an abandonment, not of the historical quest, but of the nineteenth century's approach to the historical quest. The modern quest of the historical Jesus does not ask the same questions or expect the same answers as did nineteenth-century historians. Modern historians do not claim, as their grandfathers did, to be able to find the "objective reality" about any person or event. The historically sophisticated mind attempts to *encounter* historical personalities, including that of Jesus, by understanding how they *appeared* to others and to themselves. This kind of question can be asked and answered about Jesus with as much success as about many other historical personalities.

The Biblical and historical criticism of the last sixty years have gone far in the direction of an answer. If historians cannot say who Jesus was, they can say who he was not, for criticism has demolished some of the theories that it once raised. The essential questions now debated are: To what degree is the New Testament historical and to what degree mythological (always understanding that myth, as well as history, has truth and meaning)? Did Christ reject or accept the material world? Did he really claim to be divine? What did he mean by "the Kingdom of God"—the new aeon that would come with the end of the world; a construction based upon church or sacraments; or a transformation of the hearts of believers?

These are the approaches taken by modern historians. The medieval mind, on the other hand, was by and large not only historically unsophisticated but almost unhistorical. It allowed its view of Christ to be formed, not by critical investigation, but by tradition—a tradition that emphasized the formality and remoteness of the divine Christ in proportion as the institutions of society became more formalized. Medieval kings drew upon the divinity of Christ as a sign of their own powers; but the idea of Christ the King was in turn partly derived from medieval kingship.

WHATEVER the nature of Christ, it is unquestionable that his teaching and to an even greater degree the teaching of his followers is in large part a synthesis of certain Jewish and certain Greco-Roman attitudes and ideas. It was the first great step in the synthesis of western culture which would be further advanced by the addition later of Teutonic and Celtic elements.

JESUS was himself closer to orthodox Judaism than to any other tradition. He held firmly to the Judaic monotheism; he kept its feasts and read its Scriptures, he attended the synagogue, and he taught the Mosaic law that he said he had come to fulfill, not to destroy. He accepted the linking of religion with morality that had been one of the great contributions of the Jewish religious genius, and many of his sayings resemble those of the great rabbis of the first century B.C., particularly Hillel. The Messiahship of Jesus as claimed by his followers was explicitly borrowed from both of the two orthodox Jewish Messianic traditions: the conquering king who would lead the Jews against their earthly enemies, and the suffering servant who would take upon himself the sins of the people. In their sacraments the Christians followed the Jewish notion of a ritual as an external act signifying the gift of the individual to God.

Most of Jesus' principles, except for his apparent belief in his own divinity, differed from orthodox Judaism only in their emphasis. The suffering servant tradition had long conceived of the Messiah as otherworldly rather than political. Later Jewish thought was increasingly concerned with resurrection and the last judgment, with faith as superior to the letter of the law, and with the eventual conversion of the Gentiles. Jesus went beyond Jewish orthodoxy on these points, but he did not depart from it radically. Jesus was a Jew in life and belief as well as in birth.

ANOTHER Jewish element in early Christianity was Essenism. This Jewish sect, which flourished from ca. 175 B.C. until the fall of Jerusalem in 70 A.D., was little known or understood until 1947. In that year a Bedouin shepherd looking for a lost

The Isaiah scroll from the Essene Dead Sea community.

sheep in a cave came across an old vase containing some ancient scrolls written by the Essene community of Qumran. These scrolls, and others discovered in a series of dramatic finds, contain Biblical and other early holy works as well as some hitherto entirely unknown writings of the Essenes themselves, including their *Rule* and the *War of the Sons of Light with the Sons of Darkness.*

Though scholars no longer think it possible to identify Jesus with the mysterious Essene "Teacher of Righteousness," Essenism made a profound impression upon early Christianity, particularly upon the Gospels of Matthew and John, the *Apocalypse,* and the writings of Paul. Before 1950 scholars had begun to regard John as very much under Hellenistic influence, but it is now believed that the influence is Essenic. John may represent attitudes toward Jesus that, far from being late and metamorphosed, are early and direct. John and Paul both use the contrasting images and metaphors (e.g., light vs. darkness) that are typical of the Essenes.

The similarities between Essenism and Christianity appear not only in phraseology, but in the conception that each community was itself the true fulfillment of the Law. Both the Christian and the Essenic communities represented the "traditional piety and the national hope of the Jewish people,"[1] both were highly concerned with traditional ethics, and both came into conflict with the religious authority of the orthodox. But the most important influence of Essenism upon Christianity was in eschatological thought. Both the Essenes and their Christian contemporaries expected the imminent end of the world. There is an ancient tension within Christianity, and one that seems to have been present within Christ himself, between acceptance and rejection of this world. Jesus seems to have drawn world-accepting attitudes from traditional Judaism and world-rejecting ones from the Essenes, who were themselves influenced by Persian and Canaanite dualism.

An Essenic distrust of this world, associated in Paul and later Christian thinkers with Platonic dualism, became, with Stoicism, the source of the Christian asceticism and puritanism that continued through the Middle Ages and persists today.

Christianity is no mere derivation from Essenism. The Essenes differed from the Christians in many important ways. They believed that only Jews could be saved; they were militantly hostile to those outside their sect; they emphasized the letter of the Law over its spirit; they placed strong hope in the Messiah as conquering king, and they emphasized their exclusive—almost professional—priestliness. The Essenes fled from the world; the Christians distrusted it but went out to meet it.

CHRISTIANITY developed in Jewish Palestine, but Palestine was also part of the Roman Empire, and was still under the strong influence of Greek civilization, which had dominated the area in the Hellenistic period (ca. 300–50 B.C.). Alexandria in Egypt was the center and symbol of this Greek commercial and cultural domination. Hence Christianity partook, not only of Jewish, but also of Greek, elements. The Greeks, unlike most early civilizations, believed that all phenomena were the result of a rational principle acting upon nature; that philosophy—the use of reason—enables us to understand nature. Christianity deepened its meaning and perception by incorporating both Greek rationality and the more common miraculous-magical view of the world.

Christianity incorporated Judaic concern with morality, but its Greek antecedents made it concerned with objective truth, with *dogma*, a Greek word meaning affirmation of an abstract proposition. There is little of the Hellene about Jesus himself; Christian theology—the application of Greek philosophical method to the study of God—began when his followers tried to explain the circumstances of his life and death. As Gibbon said, "Christian theology begins . . . with the self-adjustment of the church of Jerusalem to the death of Jesus and with its correlation of that death to the Old Testament."[2] That Christianity "became the religion *about* Jesus, rather than the religion *of* Jesus," is only partly true, but the cliché indicates Christianity's intellectuality, which made it able to preserve Greek rationality in and after the Middle Ages.

Not only the method, but also the concepts, of Greek thought had their influence upon the new religion. Salvation through escape from time (heaven) and salvation through the fulfillment of time on earth (the Second Coming) are both present in Christianity; the former is Platonic and the latter Jewish. From this ambivalence arose the medieval uncertainty as to whether to look for the Golden Age in a mythical past or in the historical future.

Christianity wed the Essenes' distrust of the world with the dualism of Plato, who held the spirit better and more real than the flesh. The offspring of this union was an identification of the spirit as good and the flesh as corrupt, and a lasting mistrust of this world that reinforced asceticism and puritanism. It also made possible the development of western mysticism, the search for ultimate reality in another world.

Christianity united the morality of Judaism with that of Stoicism and the law of Moses with the natural law of Cicero, a happy combination of revealed and natural morality that became the basis of medieval ideas of justice. The Stoic influence was so strong that some of the Christian fathers occasionally sound more like Cicero or Aristotle than like Jesus; thus Saint Clement of Alexandria: "Everything that is contrary to right reason is sin . . . . Virtue itself is a state of the soul rendered harmonious by reason in respect to the whole life . . . . Christian conduct is the operation of the rational soul in accordance with a correct judgment and aspiration after the truth." Only belatedly does Clement add that "Virtue is a will in conformity to God and Christ."[3]

AFTER Jesus himself, Saint Paul is indisputably the man who had the most effect upon nascent Christianity. Born at Tarsus in Cilicia in Asia Minor, a center of learning as well as of commerce, Paul came from a wealthy Jewish family and, like others of his class, had both a Jewish name, Saul, and a Greek name, Paulos, for use in contacts outside the Jewish community. He received a strict Jewish upbringing and was remarkable for his piety, which led him, like other devout Jews, to consider the beliefs of the Christians blasphemies. After being a leader of the Jewish repression of the Christians, he was suddenly and, according to his account, miraculously, converted. Though he henceforth became the leading apostle of the Christians and a champion of the Gentiles, the spirit of Judaism never left him. Where Greek discourse was direct, rational, and logically consequent, Jewish thought was allusive, poetic, and repetitive, and that Paul continued to express himself in the Jewish idiom is evident both in his writings and in his failure to make any impression upon the philosophers at Athens.

According to the recent calculations of one of our modern gods—a computer—Saint Paul was the author of only four of the epistles ascribed to him. Human scholars have been more generous than the machine, but the question is less than crucial, for the other "Pauline" epistles, whether or not actually composed by the apostle, bear the clear impression of his thought. His writings, his conversation with Christians in all parts of the Mediterranean as far west as Italy, his leadership in the missionary effort from his first journey in 45 to his death (which probably occurred in Rome in 67), and his influence upon the Christian community in Palestine, all entitle him to be called the most cosmopolitan leader of the early Church. It was he who made the Church truly universal in character by creating a synthesis between Judaism and Hellenism.

Judaism and Hellenism were at first antagonistic elements within Christianity. Though the teachings of Jesus himself had made it clear that the Gentiles were not to be excluded from the Kingdom, some of his followers maintained that Gentile converts ought to be obliged to remain on the fringes of the community, and others insisted that they follow all the traditional Jewish practices, including circumcision. This group, the Judaeo-Christians, seems to have included the majority of the apostles;

North
Sea

Baltic Sea

Atlantic Ocean

IRELAND

BRITAIN

London
Canterbury

SAXONS

Reims
Battle of Châlons (451)
Châlons-sur-Marne
ALAMANNI
BOHEMIA
MORAVIA

GAUL

Lyon
Marseille
PYRENEES

ITALY

PANNONIA

ILLYRICUM

MOE

SPAIN

CORSICA
Rome
SARDINIA

Thessalonika?

Mediterranean

Athens

Hippo (Bona)
Tagaste
Carthage
SICILY

MAURETANIA
NUMIDIA

SOUTH OF THIS LINE LOST

AFRICA

MILES
0   100   200   300   400   500

Christianized Territory Ca.400
Additional Christianized Territory Ca.500
"   "   "   Ca.500-800

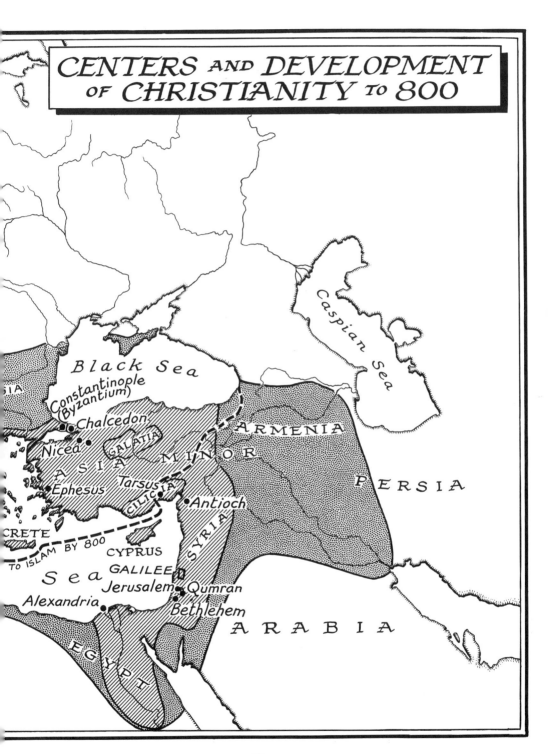

CENTERS AND DEVELOPMENT OF CHRISTIANITY TO 800

Black Sea

Caspian Sea

Constantinople (Byzantium)

Chalcedon

ARMENIA

Nicea

GALATIA

ASIA MINOR

PERSIA

Ephesus

Tarsus

CILICIA

Antioch

SYRIA

CRETE

CYPRUS

TO ISLAM BY 800

Sea

GALILEE

Jerusalem

Qumran

Alexandria

Bethlehem

ARABIA

EGYPT

Saint Peter was indecisive; it was Saint Paul who took the lead in favor of the Gentiles at the Council of Jérusalem in 49. The Jewish revolt of 66–70 and the sack of Jerusalem by the Romans in 70 dealt a final blow to the Judaeo-Christians. It was thenceforth Paul's theology, still Jewish yet increasingly Hellenized, that prevailed. Owing to Paul, Christianity was fully established as a universalist, world religion instead of an exclusive sect or a mere minor variant of Judaism. Upon his theological principles of faith and grace the foundations of Christian theology were laid.

THE apostles, particularly Paul, began very early to evangelize outside Palestine, and in the first century Christianity spread in the Jewish and Greek communities within the cities of the East. Later, and with more difficulty, it penetrated the Latin communities of the West. A religion whose backgrounds were Jewish and whose Scriptures were Greek had smaller attraction in the less cosmopolitan West, though the Christian community at Rome was established by Peter and Paul, both of whom there became martyrs. In the second century, Christianity spread into Asia Minor, Spain, Italy, and southern Gaul, and then into Africa, Egypt, and Britain. The third century saw the penetration of Christianity into areas beyond the borders of the empire, such as Persia and India. By 300, perhaps a quarter of the population in the eastern part of the Roman Empire was Christian, and perhaps ten percent in the West.

The missions enjoyed their most notable early successes among two groups: the slaves, women, and other downtrodden people of the cities; and the cosmopolitan commercial middle classes. Toward the end of the third century, converts were found increasingly among the aristocracy, a tendency that was encouraged when Constantine inaugurated his era of toleration. Christianity had least success on the one hand with the always conservative peasants (in fact, *pagani*, "pagans," actually meant "hicks"), and on the other with the intellectuals, who despised Christian ideas as vulgar and the Greek of the Christian Scriptures as crude. Justin Martyr with his calm, philosophical adoption of the religion of the Galilean was an exception among the cultured; it was left to Augustine to set the new religion firmly upon its intellectual feet.

OPPOSITION to Christianity led to sporadic persecutions. The intellectuals' contempt for Christianity was combined with a crude and unreasoning popular hatred that ascribed to Christians as many vices as Christians later attributed to Jews and heretics. There was an African proverb: "There's a drought; the Christians have caused it." The followers of Christ were accused of atheism and worshiping a donkey; and the believers in the Sermon on the Mount, of sexual orgies, incest, ceremonial infanticide, and cannibalism. So great was the common hatred of Christians that during a period of over two hundred years they were exposed to frequent and bloody persecutions by mobs, magistrates, and emperors. Whether Nero actually roasted Christians alive is doubtful, but the persecutions by Domitian and the Antonines are well attested, and those by the emperors Diocletian and Galerius notorious. Many Christians throughout the empire were forced to choose between their life and their God. Many yielded to a natural fear; many more were borne up by a supernatural courage: as the aged Saint Polycarp said as he made his decision to die rather than to renounce Christ, "I have served my lord eighty-six years, and he has done me no wrong. Shall I blaspheme the king who has saved me?"

Of the religious policy of the pagan Romans, Gibbon observed:

> The policy of the emperors and the senate, as far as it concerned religion, was happily seconded by the reflections of the enlightened, and by the habits of the superstitious, part of their subjects. The various modes of worship, which prevailed in the Roman world, were all considered by the people, as equally true; by the philosopher, as equally false; and by the magistrate, as equally useful. And thus toleration produced not only mutual indulgence, but even religious concord.[4]

How was it that this tolerant paganism could tolerate for two and a half centuries a bloody intolerance of the Christians? The essential reason lay beyond simple distaste or hatred. In all ancient societies, religion was considered, not the right of the individual conscience, but the domain of the state; there was no distinction between religion and politics; and a citizen of the state took part automatically in the public cult. To this rule the Roman Empire was no more an exception than medieval

"The Crucified Donkey," a graffito by a pagan of the second century.

Catholicism. Political loyalty and public piety demanded that all citizens participate, no matter how perfunctorily, in the official worship of the gods. Of all the religions in the empire, only the Christian, the Jewish, and the Manichaean did not permit their members to offer worship to the emperor; and the Romans persecuted all three, the Christians the most only because they were the most numerous and therefore the most dangerous.

The Christians made a distinction that Roman paganism could not tolerate—a distinction between the community of the faithful and the community at large. In their natural desire for domestic tranquility, the emperors again and again held out the olive branch to the Christians on the condition that those stubborn people sacrifice publicly and thereby avoid the scandal that their reticence was causing. The Emperor Aurelian, magnanimity itself, offered to include Christ along with Mithra and Apollo as one of the manifestations of the Sun-God, but his generosity was scornfully repulsed.

The Christians contemned the perfunctory externalism of paganism as much as the pagans detested the insistence of the Christians that they had the only true God. The best emperors prosecuted the Christians; the best Christians resisted the emperors.

OTHER Christians sprang up in their place, for the blood of the martyrs was the seed of the Church. Christianity, which had arisen as a religion prophesying from outside against the expiring life of pagan Rome, ended by becoming the new life force of medieval Europe. The Church grew not only in numbers but in confidence, as is revealed in the slow building of doctrine and traditions by those writers and teachers we call the Fathers of the Church. The Fathers continued the work of Saint Paul in building a theology by reflecting upon and building upon the career and teachings of Jesus.

The great majority of the early Fathers spoke and wrote Greek; they lived and taught in the cosmopolitan centers of the eastern part of the empire. As Greeks and intellectuals, they had, like Justin Martyr, a respect for Greek philosophy; they also had a corresponding contempt for the corruption and decadence of Greco-Roman society. Their sometimes exaggerated hostility to paganism was aimed at more than the corruption of paganism itself: paganism was the hostile and firmly entrenched Establishment against which they had to struggle. Just so, in the eighteenth century, the Rationalists of the Enlightenment were irrationally severe in their censures of the historical Church—by then the Church was the Establishment they had to fight. As with the rationalists, the early Christians' loathing of the faults of pagan society blinded them to its virtues, and with their background of dualism from both Greeks and Essenes, the more extreme of the Fathers taught a morality that was uncharitable and a philosophy that was antiphilosophical. Tertullian (ca. 145–220), whose fanaticism eventually led him into heresy, advised as his prescription for the repentant adulterer: "Lead (him) into the church and prostrate him there in haircloth and ashes, an example of disgrace and horror, before the widows and the elders. Let him beg the compassion of all, licking their feet and embracing their knees." And in regard to the philosophical basis of Christianity, he asked scornfully, "What do Athens and Jerusalem, the academy and the church, have in common?" He concluded that Christianity "is certain because it is absurd."

The great Fathers—Ignatius of Antioch, Justin, Irenaeus, Clement of Alexandria, Origen, and Cyprian—raised the great fundamental questions of Christian belief: questions on the Trinity, the nature of Christ, the salvation of the individual,

An early Christian praying in the "orans" position, standard until the tenth or eleventh century (from the Catacomb of Priscilla).

and the purpose of the sacraments in relation to the coming end of the world. These were issues that would be further, and fiercely, debated by bishops and emperors.

THE Alexandrian Fathers did most to create the symbolizing mentality that came to characterize medieval thought. Saint Clement of Alexandria (ca. 150–210) carried on the philosophic tradition of Justin Martyr and, with Origen, his successor in the schools of the great commercial and cultural metropolis, established principles of interpreting the Scriptures that helped form the thought of Augustine, and, through him, that of western civilization. Clement had a respectful and grateful attitude toward the pagan philosophers: "Philosophy," he said, "was necessary to the Greeks for righteousness, until the coming of the Lord. And now it assists toward true religion as a kind of preparatory training for those who arrive at faith by way of demonstration. . . . Philosophy was a 'schoolmaster' to bring the Greek mind to Christ, as the Law brought the Jews."[5] For Clement, the Greek poets as well as philosophers had intimations of immortality, and so Hellenized was his notion of faith that he slighted the Pauline sense of that virtue as personal commitment and interpreted it rather as intellectual assent to a doctrine or as an Aristotelian act of willing obedience to that doctrine.

Clement and Origen derived from the Jewish Alexandrian Philo and from the traditional Greek exegesis of Homer a notion of allegory that is their greatest contribution to philosophy and literature. Believing in the divine inspiration of the Scriptures, they accepted the Bible in its entirety and held that every letter and word had eternal significance. But they found that the simple, "corporeal" meaning was in some instances contrary to reason. As a result they imitated the Romans in rationalizing their mythology (e.g., "Jupiter embracing Juno" is really "the sun embracing the air") and interpreted the Scriptures on various levels. Augustine later established four standard levels of interpretation. Take as an example the exodus of the Jews from Egypt under Moses. This text could be read: (1) historically (corporeally): the children of Israel left Egypt to return to the Promised Land; (2) tropologically (morally): the soul leaves the fleshpots and returns to purity; (3) allegorically: the Jews left the kingdom of this world for the Kingdom of God; (4) anagogically (eschatologically): the Holy Family will themselves come out of Egypt to return to Judaea. The method permitted the reconciliation of revelation and reason and has always, except among fundamentalists, been in use in the Christian Church. Moreover, it encouraged the symbolic tradition of both religious and profane literature that is still very much with us today. So strong was the tradition in the Middle Ages that the reader of all medieval literature must keep in mind that the medieval writer always kept it in his.

The wedding of Judaeo-Christian revelation with Greco-Roman rationality produced in the Fathers a powerful and original form of thought: theological philosophy. This thought would dominate much of medieval intellectual activity.

EARLY Christianity, complex and often unsure of itself as it sought its identity, is the first of the great syntheses that stand at the origin of our own western civilization, the synthesis between Hebrew and eastern thought on the one hand and Greek and western on the other. It was left to the next centuries, not only to consolidate and institutionalize the Church, but to combine Judaeo-Greek Christianity with Latin culture and then with the Teutonic and Celtic elements brought by the barbarians from the North.

NOTES

[1] Lucetta Mowry, *The Dead Sea Scrolls and the Early Church* (Chicago, 1962), p. 59.

[2] Arthur Darby Nock, *St. Paul* (New York, 1938), p. 45.

[3] *Paedagogus,* I, xiii, in *The Ante-Nicene Fathers* (New York, 1890), II, 235.

[4] Gibbon, *Decline and Fall,* I, ch. 2, 25.

[5] Clement, *Stromateis,* I, p.28, trans. H. Bettenson in Bettenson, ed. *Documents of the Christian Church,* 2d ed. (London, Oxford University Press, 1963), pp. 8–9.

Chapter Three

THE PEACE OF THE CHURCH
AND THE END OF THE EMPIRE
(305-590)

THE idea of the universal Christian Church replaced the idea of the universal pagan empire and brought about the creation of "Christian society," the fundamental medieval political ideal. As a side effect it also caused the separation of the eastern and western halves of the empire, for the East did not submit to the authority of papal, as it had to that of imperial, Rome.

THE sources for the political history of the Roman world from Constantine to Justinian are not plentiful. In the fourth century the pagan Ammianus Marcellinus wrote his *Histories* in an effort to supplement and extend the work of Tacitus. Ammianus' hero was Julian the Apostate. That of his Christian counterpart, Eusebius, was Constantine. Eusebius wrote at the beginning of the century an *Ecclesiastical History* and a *Life of Constantine,* but these works were less investigations into the deeds of men than respectful accounts of the workings of God. Besides these two great writers there were the Christian Orosius; Procopius, the author of the highly biased *Secret History* of the reign of Justinian; and a number of minor historians like Zosimus and Aurelius Victor. None was remarkable for his impartiality, and none of their works is thorough. Other sources, however, particularly of cultural history, exist in greater bulk: letters and personal writings, notably those of Julian, Ambrose, Jerome, Augustine, and Symmachus; theological tracts and conciliar documents; literature (like the poems of Ausonius); and legal codes.

CONSTANTINE the Great, the figure who more than any other helped transform classical into Christian society, was born about 280 to Constantius Chlorus, later caesar and augustus, and apparently a devotee of the popular military deity, the Unconquered Sun. Constantine's mother was the Christian Helena, later canonized for discovering the wood of the True Cross. Helena had little opportunity to instill her religion into the mind of her son, who was sent off to the court of Diocletian to learn obedience and flattery. After the abdication of the old emperor, Galerius gained the throne and, fearful of Constantius's power, designed to keep his son hostage. Constantine contrived to escape and to rejoin his father in Britain. Constantius, by then one of the augusti, was preparing to advance his fortune even farther when death overtook him in 306; immediately the legions proclaimed his son emperor, and the reign of Constantine began.

The person, as well as the mind, of Constantine had been enriched by nature with her choicest endowments. His stature was lofty, his countenance majestic, his deportment graceful; his strength and activity were displayed in every manly exercise, and, from his earliest youth to a very advanced season in life, he preserved the vigour of his constitution by a strict adherence to the domestic virtues of chastity and temperance.[1]

So fit a young man could hardly fail in his efforts to compose the empire under his sole rule, though first he had to overcome the opposition of a number of competitors. It was in the course of his wars with one of these, Maxentius, that the gaze of the young ruler was turned away from the "Unconquered Sun" of his father to the "Only-Begotten Son" of God. Eusebius tells us that Constantine later affirmed with a solemn oath that, upon preparing to cross the Alps into Italy, he had seen a fiery cross in the sky with the legend "Conquer by this." Lactantius sets the occurrence more directly before the Battle of the Milvian Bridge in 312 and more modestly confines it to a dream, in which Constantine learned that if he emblazoned the symbol ☧ [for ΧΡΙΣΤΟΣ:CHRISTOS] upon his standard and upon the shields and helms of his warriors he would win the battle. Constantine did win. Whether his success was owing to divine or only to human resources, he attributed it to the former and from that moment condescended to benevolence towards Christianity. Constantine now established his colleague Licinius as emperor in the East, and himself in the West, but the ambitions of the great ruler could not be satisfied in so narrow a territory, and after years of desultory warfare he finally succeeded, in 324, in depriving his rival of both his throne and his life.

As sole emperor (324–337), Constantine devoted himself to the double purpose of fulfilling Diocletian's administrative policies, and of establishing the welfare of the Christian Church. Constantine had learned to be distrustful of the institution of the augusti, and, unlike Diocletian, did not, after his victory over Licinius, raise other rivals to this dignity; instead he relied upon caesars, whose interests he succeeded in binding closely to his own. Diocletian had chosen the East, rather than the West, as the seat of the imperial power, and Constantine ratified this preference when he chose Byzantium as the site for a new capital.

Adorning this New Rome with all the splendors of the Old, he lavished his wealth upon palaces, churches, statues, walls, a hippodrome, a market place, roads, and harbors. Establishing there a senate, spectacles, statuary, and all that he might borrow of the Old Rome, he modestly named this great new center of the world Constantinopolis. The greater security of the spot, the greater population and military strength of the East, and its far greater commercial wealth, were all considerations that commended themselves to his practical mind.

Constantine followed his pagan predecessor in his efforts to stabilize the currency, to centralize and reform the bureaucracy, and to make the army both more mobile and more responsive to the imperial will. "Masters of infantry" and "masters of cavalry" were established in supreme command of the armies, with orders to report directly to the emperor; and a "master of offices" was introduced as a kind of chief of staff for civil affairs. Constantine also collected a *comitatus,* a group of men personally responsible and indebted to himself, and entrusted to them the protection of his person and his treasury. This *comitatus* was an institution very similar to the *household* of the medieval kings.

Constantine's religious program was as vigorous and as cautious as his military and civil policies. Although he believed

Head of Constantine the Great on the Capitoline Hill in Rome.

that the victory of the Milvian Bridge had been secured for him by the Christian deity, he made no immediate conversion. Medals were struck in honor of other gods till 318; the Unconquered Sun was not denied this privilege until after 323; and it was not until 324 that the emperor forbade the worship of statues of himself. Yet Constantine made it his immediate policy to free the Christians from the disadvantages they had suffered under the edicts of Diocletian and Galerius. In 311, the dying persecutor Galerius himself, tormented, to the just satisfaction of the Christian writers, by worms, rescinded his repressive laws. The Christians, who had earlier been told *Non licet esse vos:* "It is forbidden to be you," were now the beneficiaries of an order that proclaimed: "Let there be Christians again." Constantine and Licinius prudently anticipated the worms and immediately upon their victory issued a series of laws of toleration. The traditional "Edict of Milan" (313) probably never existed, but as a whole the liberal legislation of the decade 311–320 removed the Christians' handicaps and even gave them an advantage. Full toleration of all religions was granted, Church property was restored, grants of money were given to the Christian clergy, bequests to the Church were legalized, the authority of bishops' courts was recognized, and the clergy was exempted from taxation, military service, and other public duties. The "Peace of the Church" had been achieved.

Whether Constantine was really a Christian is not of crucial importance. It seems that he was not baptized until he was on his deathbed, and certainly he was moved by considerations of state as well as of conscience. But the cynicism attributed to him by Gibbon and Burckhardt does not seem likely. The Christians were not yet powerful enough to make care for their welfare a prime requirement of statesmanship, and there is no reason why Constantine should not have been in his own way a worshiper of the Christian God. In any event, his acquiescence in the new religion helped preserve the empire. Had he attempted, like Diocletian before him or Julian after him, to reestablish the old pagan virtues, he would certainly have failed, and the failure might have brought about a far more complete ruin of civilization than did occur. Rather, he threw in his lot with a party which, if not yet the majority, was the most vital force in the state.

Constantine arranged that his death should be no ordinary thing: people are said to have remarked, while the imperial corpse lay upon a golden couch adorned in all its regalia and deferred to by the courtiers as if it were alive, that "Constantine alone, by the peculiar indulgence of Heaven, had reigned after his death."[2]

SUBSEQUENT events proved how vulnerable were the defenses that Diocletian and Constantine had built round the declining institutions of Rome. Autocracy continued to grow, while the effective power of the state weakened. Disputes over succession broke out at the death of Constantine and recurred at frequent intervals over the succeeding years.

The religious quarrels between Christianity and paganism were resolved only by the gradual repression of the latter. The efforts of the emperor Julian the Apostate (361–363) to restore

Julian the Apostate.

paganism were unavailing, not only because of the brevity of
his reign but because his subjects considered his revival of old
cults only amusing. In 382 the Christian emperor Gratian removed the venerable altar of victory from the *curia* (the meeting
place of the Senate in Rome) and deprived pagan priests of
public support. There followed in 384 a debate between Saint
Ambrose and the pagan prefect Symmachus, who had peti-
tioned for the restoration of the altar. The Christian won the
debate, and the pagan's petition was denied. Edicts of the
emperor Theodosius I in 391–394 against both public and
private practice of paganism finished the process of establishing
Christianity as the official religion of Rome.

Whatever tranquility was gained in this fashion was lost
in the growing hostility of Christians to one another and the
entry of imperial authority into religious politics. Economic
decline and social demoralization were unchecked. All the
emperors, irrespective of their religious persuasion, were faced by

increasingly intolerable pressures from the Persians to the East and from the Teutonic barbarians to the North. When the division of the empire between East and West became complete after the death of Theodosius I (379-395), neither half could count upon effective support from the other against their common external enemies. Of the two halves, the eastern was better able to preserve its territorial integrity because it was the wealthier, the more heavily populated, and, for those reasons, the more carefully guarded by imperial armies.

The territory effectively ruled by the western emperor began to shrink rapidly from the beginning of the fifth century, and its weaknesses were exacerbated: with increasing need for money and soldiers, there was a decreasing amount of area upon which to levy taxes and from which to recruit troops. From the time of Constantine the citizen-armies were gradually replaced with barbarian troops, even the highest office, that of "master of the army" being filled by the Vandal Stilicho under Theodosius. When from the middle of the fourth century the Romans had to rely increasingly upon the *federates*, barbarian allies who had their own rulers and armies and no particular loyalty to the emperor, the military reforms in the direction of mobility and the creation of the personal *comitatus* of the emperor were not enough to overbalance the defects of the system.

The crisis became acute in the second half of the fourth century, when the Huns, entering Europe, drove the terrified Goths before them across the Danube. After a long series of unsuccessful negotiations that ended in the defeat and death of the emperor Valens (378), Theodosius finally settled them within the boundaries of the empire as *federates* of Rome. Only eleven years after Theodosius' death the Rhine frontier was permanently breached and Frankish and Burgundian settlements established to the west of the river (406-407). Only four years later Rome itself was sacked by a foreign army for the first time since the Celts had taken it 800 years earlier.

The capture of Rome by Alaric I and his Visigoths in 410 was the event that made the most impression upon contemporaries: it was then that it seemed to them Rome fell. "When the brightest light on the whole earth was extinguished, when the Roman Empire was deprived of its head, when, to speak more correctly, the whole world perished in one city, then 'I was dumb with silence"' was Saint Jerome's cry when he heard the news.[3] Nevertheless, the invasion of the Huns had been even more disruptive, for Attila did more than attack the empire itself; his attacks on the Teutons drove those peoples in turn against the empire.

After the Hunnic invasions, the western empire was at the mercy of the Teutonic warriors without and the mercenaries within. Mercenaries ruled behind one imperial figurehead after another. When the Teutonic chieftain Odovacar was refused one-third of all the land of Italy, he deposed the last Roman emperor in the West, Romulus Augustulus, in 476. Though the Roman Julius Nepos attempted to reestablish the purple shortly thereafter, the western empire had effectively ceased to exist. For all their energy and devotion, Constantine, Theodosius, and their descendants could never overcome the inherent limitations of Diocletian's policies, which could only retard, but not reverse, the course of history.

THE religious policies of Constantine and his successors had a happier consequence: if the empire faltered, the Church flourished. Though the Church was inherently conservative ("Let nothing be introduced save that which has been handed down by tradition," as an early pope said), change occurred with enough rapidity, and differences of custom and opinion with enough bitterness, that Christianity might early have been divided into a number of sects, had not Fathers, councils, and emperors affirmed its unity and organized its structure.

BOTH monasticism and heresy, though impeding unity and organization, yet provoked their establishment through opposition.

After the free-wheeling, wandering "prophets" of the early Church had disappeared, the urge toward an individual encounter with God seemed best fulfilled by a withdrawal from the community into a desert place. Such withdrawal found Scriptural antecedents in the retreat of Christ into the wilderness, and it appealed to the ascetic, world-rejecting elements that Christianity had derived from the Essenes. It seemed to the monks [*monachus:* "one who dwells alone"] that the way to Christ lay in solitude, not through organized society.

Saint Anthony, whose spiritual life was written in detail by

Saint Athanasius, was one of the first monks. He retired as a hermit [*erêmos:* "solitude, desert"] to the desert about 285, and so many others followed his example that he soon found himself surrounded by a crowd of emulators whom he was obliged to teach how best to become solitaries themselves. The numbers of monks at last became so great that by about 310 it was found most convenient to group the monastic cells under a common administration and a common rule. It was Saint Pachomius who first adopted this form of *coenobitical monasticism* (an apparent contradiction in terms meaning "living apart in a community"), and soon community monasticism became standard.

The huge migration to the desert that occurred, particularly in Egypt and Syria, in the third and fourth centuries is, like the Crusades, one of the most dramatic and to modern eyes incomprehensible phenomena of history. Why should thousands of men and women, many of them of wealthy families and with good personal prospects, have given up everything and withdrawn completely from the world? It has been suggested that the monastic exodus can be explained in terms of despair with the declining fortunes of Rome, but there is no evidence that any such general despair existed; further, other great periods of monastic expansion (like the twelfth century) occurred at a time of economic and social advance.

Rather, monasticism represents an assent to Christ's demand to take up the cross and follow him, and is the best possible fulfillment of that part of his teaching that called for rejection of the world. Monasticism enabled men to withdraw from the distractions of this world and to concentrate entirely upon the other. It was the fulfillment of *peregrinatio,* the Christian idea that we are only travelers passing through a world less real than the world of God, and had best keep our eyes upon our true goal. The purpose of monasticism was to seek God on behalf of all men, and the monks believed that prayer to this purpose was the most important part of their task. The mind that judges the monks selfish men seeking their own salvation fails to do justice to the fact that, if one believes in prayer at all—and the monks certainly did—it is neither selfish nor useless to spend one's time praying for the welfare of one's fellows. Monasticism again and again brought to the Church a prophetic spirit that judged the organization by the standards of a higher reality. Benedict in the sixth century, Bernard in the twelfth, and Francis in the thirteenth revived the flagging and jaded spirits of a Church grown too worldly. As a monk wrote of the fourth-century monastic communities of Egypt:

Nowhere have I seen love so in flower, nowhere so quick compassion, or hospitality so eager . . . . One by one they abide in their cells, a mighty silence and a great quiet among them; only on the Saturday and the Sunday do they come together to church, and there they see each other face to face as folk restored in heaven.[4]

HERESY was the other path of individual expression, and, though Tertullian announced that "a controversy over the Scriptures only upsets either the stomach or the brain," many questions left unsettled by the Church Fathers continued to be debated. Moreover, there was a large body of common opinion in the Church that had not yet been judged correct or incorrect. As debates arose, some of this opinion was accepted as doctrine and some rejected as heresy. In each debate the opinions of the winning party were established as orthodoxy; the losing party were castigated as heretics. Thus the body of orthodox doctrine grew larger, and the number of heretical sects multiplied.

The greatest of the early heresies was so rooted in non-Christian soil as to be as much another religion as a sect of Christianity. Gnosticism, described by one historian as "the acute secularizing or Hellenizing of Christianity" and by another as "the verbal Christianizing of paganism," originated among Jews who had expected the Messiah to appear when Jerusalem was destroyed by the Romans in 70 A.D. A mingling of Jewish, Essenic, Zoroastrian, Christian, and Neoplatonic ideas, Gnosticism taught a markedly dualistic doctrine of continual cosmic warfare between the powers of light and spirit and those of darkness and flesh. Gnostics believed that the souls of men are little sparks of light and life that have become imprisoned in the dark, devil-created flesh; their escape can be effected only by the attainment of *gnosis* (esoteric knowledge). Those Gnostics who were particularly Christian in orientation taught that Christ was a messenger of the divine whose function was to bring men to salvation by teaching them *gnosis*. Those who had been saved were infused with the divine spirit and could by definition do no wrong; as this happy state was interpreted in two opposite ways, some Gnostics became libertines and others puritans. The influence of Gnosticism upon the main body of Christianity was always small, but its grotesque exaggerations of Christ's world-rejecting attitudes have endured through the ages as a kind of mirror distorting the features of the Church. From the first to the twentieth century many heresies, the most famous of which is the Catharist or Albigensian, have borne the gnostic stamp. Perhaps the most important gnostic sect, really a separate religion, was Manichaeism, the creation of the Babylonian prophet Mani (d. 275 A.D.), who combined gnostic with Jewish, Christian, Buddhist, and Zoroastrian ideas. Mani taught an absolute dualism featuring a cosmic war between independent powers of good and evil.

OTHER questions produced other heresies and other orthodoxies.

The Fathers had not agreed upon the relationship between the Persons of the Trinity. At the first ecumenical council at Nicea in 325, Athanasius, an Alexandrian cleric, secured the condemnation of another Alexandrian, Arius, who argued the subordination of the Son and the Holy Spirit to the Father. The judgment of Nicea that the Three Persons were equal was confirmed by the second ecumenical council (at Constantinople) in 381 and enshrined in the Nicene Creed—the foundation of Catholicism. But Arianism long persisted among the Romans and was spread by missionaries to the Teutonic tribes, so that it remained a divisive force for centuries.

The question of Christ's nature produced further heresies. The Nestorians, who argued that Christ was two discrete personalities (two persons and two natures), were condemned at the third ecumenical council (Ephesus, 431), and the Monophysites, who taught the opposite belief that he was wholly divine, were condemned at the fourth (Chalcedon, 451). The Church elected the middle ground (Christ is one person, but with two natures) between the two extremes, but the divisive disputes dragged on to the detriment of both the Church and the empire.

THE most important question underlying all these debates was: Who had the authority to determine and to proclaim what was orthodoxy and what not? The pragmatic need of the early Church to evolve some structure of authority and organization was great. It was this pragmatic need that transformed a transcendent creed of salvation into an effective organization in this world. It may be that in organizing itself the Church courted failure as a religion, removing or weakening the sense of direct personal encounter with God. It may also be that at times the organized Church approached idolatry in the sense of setting itself up in the place of God as absolute arbiter. Yet the organization was absolutely necessary. Without it, Christianity would soon have splintered into fragments. Divisions, both doctrinal and moral, would have increased unchecked; local and personal rivalries would have triumphed over love and common sense.

Saint Paul had already called the Church the mystical body of Christ. With borrowings from the Roman theory of corporations, it became a legally constituted body with recognizable characteristics. As early as the time of Saint Ignatius (ca. 60–ca. 107) the notion of an "invisible" Church of believers had become a "visible" Church, with a visible organization and recognized authorities.

Already in the first century of the Church the clergy had become distinct from the laity by virtue of their presiding over the administration of the sacraments. By the second century, the office of bishop was separated from, and elevated above, that of priest, one bishop having charge of the Christian community in each major city. The doctrine of Apostolic Succession taught that the authority of the bishop derived through consecration in direct succession from the apostles; in practice it derived from the necessity of having an arbiter of disputes in every community. The bishops themselves proved prone to disagree, and so the bishops of the larger and more renowned sees, Rome, Alexandria, Antioch, Jerusalem, and, after 330, Constantinople, came naturally to exert a certain authority over their lesser colleagues.

The extent and limitations of these "patriarchal sees," as they were called, were unclear. It was generally assumed by most of the early Fathers that the bishops together formed a kind of college or corporation empowered to formulate decisions in unity of opinion and will, and from this idea derived the authority of the ecumenical councils. The difficulty and expense of convoking bishops from all over the empire, and then of securing their agreement, proved shortcomings of the conciliar idea. Hence arose a natural tendency to monarchy, either of the pope or of the emperor.

The papacy, like the other institutions of the Church, developed only gradually in the course of the centuries. The supremacy of the pope over the other bishops was justified in theory on the ground that Peter had been the first bishop of Rome, and had been granted pre-eminent powers by Christ, who in the "Petrine texts" of the New Testament is reported as saying: "Thou art Peter, and upon this rock I will build my church." It was bolstered in practice by the natural prestige of Rome, by the fact that from the beginning of the fourth century the competing authority of the emperor had been removed to Constantinople, by Rome's position as the sole major patriarchate in the West, by the administrative skill of the chancery in Rome, and by the rapidly increasing wealth and property that the Roman bishops were amassing through the welcome generosity of gifts and legacies. With pragmatism anticipating that of King Henry IV of France, the pagan leader Agorius Praetextatus exclaimed: "Make me bishop of Rome and I'll be a Christian tomorrow."[5]

The slow growth of papal influence began no later than ca. 95, when the church of Rome intervened to settle a dispute at Corinth, and as the Protestant historian Harnack observed, "from the close of the first century the Roman church was in a position of practical primacy over Christendom." It is not, of course, to be supposed that this primacy entailed anything like the power of later popes. In its first few centuries, the papacy only gradually obtained, and probably without conscious plan or intent, the admission first of its primacy in honor, then of its right to intervene in other sees, then of its right to limited administration over the Church as a whole, and finally of its right to pronounce unilaterally upon matters of doctrine. It was not until 451 at the Council of Chalcedon that a pope (Leo I) played a deciding role in a doctrinal dispute. Yet less than a century later, Pope Hormisdas (514–523) first intimated the final degree of papal claims, infallibility, when he said: "The Catholic religion has always been immaculately preserved in the apostolic see." By the reign of Gregory I (590–604) the pope had considerable influence over the whole western Church.

Bishop: ca. 110
Archbishop (*Metropolitan*): ca. 300
Pope: ca. 303; also used by some other bishops at the time
Patriarch: ca. 450
Servant of the Servants of God: established by Gregory I
Apostolic See: 6th century
Vicar of Peter: until 1200
Vicar of Christ: after ca. 1200
Pontifex Maximus: 1464—the title the emperors had
       taken as high pagan priests!

THE foremost rival of the pope for supreme authority in the Church was the emperor, and the foremost problem of the Church was its adjustment to the pagan, and then to the Christian, empire.

On the one hand, the empire was both transformed and preserved by the Church. Though the emperor ceased to be deified, he became the vicegerent of Christ. "Invested as he is," said Eusebius in his eulogy of Constantine, "with a semblance of heavenly sovereignty, he directs his gaze above, and frames his earthly government according to the pattern of that Divine original. . . . Our emperor is one, appointed by, and representative of, the one Almighty Sovereign. . . ."[6] One God, one Christ, one Emperor. In effect, Eusebius was baptizing the oriental absolutism that had flourished from the time of Diocletian. The notion of the emperor's supernatural powers had been successfully transplanted from pagan to Christian soil and, flourishing in its new bed, was one of the justifications of medieval emperors for claiming ecclesiastical authority.

Not only the ruler but the customs of Rome as well were made to conform to the new order. Roman statutes were recast to combine the Judaeo-Christian moral law with the old Roman natural law. The cruel spectacles of the Colosseum were banned, infanticide outlawed, and divorce restricted. The salutary effect of the new morality and the new laws upon the family enabled that institution to revive, flourish, and become, along with the Church, one of the elements of stability essential to the creation of the new civilization. The most pertinent effect of Christianity upon the empire was to strengthen those institutions that were needed to hold society together while the transformation of the world was being completed.

Oɴ the other hand, the effect of the triumphal "Peace of the Church" upon Christianity itself was not an unmitigated blessing. Once a community of devoted confessors and martyrs, after Constantine's edicts of toleration the Church was inundated by sycophants and office seekers who, now that they saw an advantage in Christianity, hastened to applaud the faith, and procure the favors, of the Christian emperors. The Church that had proclaimed the ideal of *peregrinatio,* and longed only for the coming of that other world that was the Kingdom of God, now began to acquire enormous properties and huge stores of wealth. The successors of the apostles began to adorn themselves in luxurious robes and ornaments, and even monasticism, whose origins lay in a protest against increasing worldliness, had by the sixth century in large part been formalized and made an important part of the ecclesiastical system.

Most of all, the Church that had protested the bloody repression of Christianity by paganism now hastened to repress not only pagans but heretics with such ferocity that Ammianus observed that the wild beasts did not treat each other so savagely. Theodosius established not only Christianity, but the Catholic version of Christianity, as the only acceptable religion. Those who differed "We adjudge demented and insane . . . they shall be smitten first by divine vengeance and secondly by the retribution of our own initiative. . . . They shall also pay the penalty of high treason with their life and blood."[7] Rome was to prosecute deviation from its new public cult with as much severity as it had deviation from the old.

The favor of the emperors had gained the Church great wealth and influence; that very wealth and influence made it necessary for the emperors to intervene in ecclesiastical affairs. Confronted with this challenge, the Church had only two choices: it could yield up its wealth and influence, or it could fight to retain them and independence too. The former course of action never seemed to occur, let alone to recommend itself, to any but the most radical reformers; the latter course engendered the constant struggles between pope and emperor that mark the history of the Middle Ages.

IN the fourth and fifth centuries, these issues were already current. Popes and emperors were already disputing ultimate authority. There were three major positions possible in this dispute: that the emperor received his authority from God and delegated matters spiritual to the pope and bishops; that the pope received his authority directly from God and delegated matters material to the emperor; that both received parallel authority from God in their own spheres.

The imperial position was at first dominant. Eusebius had considered Constantine the peer of the apostles, and the emperor Constantius had declared in 355: "Whatever I will must have the force of ecclesiastical law." The episcopal and papal forces, however, were preparing their defenses. When Valentinian I ordered Saint Ambrose to turn over the churches of Milan to the Arians, the bishop replied: "Do not deceive yourself, sir, with the fancy that you have any imperial right over divine things!" Ambrose even had the courage in 390 to excommunicate Theodosius, Catholic emperor though he was, for his part in the massacre of the citizens of Thessalonike as reprisal for the assassination of his master of the army.

Ambrose was claiming only the independence of the spiritual from the temporal, but by the reign of Leo I (440–461), the papacy was already hinting at its superiority. Leo held that the Roman church not only held authority from God but also *principatus*, dominion over the entire world. This idea was further developed by Pope Gelasius I (492–496): "There are, most august emperor, two powers by which this world is ruled: the sacred authority (*auctoritas*) of the popes and the royal power (*potestas*). The responsibility of the priestly power is much greater than that of the secular, since it is responsible to God for kings themselves."[8] To what practical extent Gelasius intended this authority to prevail is not clear, and the text was used later to justify both the position of papal regulation of the secular and the idea that the emperor and the pope both had commissions for their respective spheres directly from God. In any event, the imperial theory prevailed over the papal in most quarters until the eleventh century.

THE changes wrought in the Roman world by Christianity and barbarism were profound; but they were the occasion of the transformation, not of the ruin, of civilization. In the minds of Romans and barbarians alike, the idea of the Roman Empire outlived the deposition of Augustulus in 476. Indeed, eventually revived by Charlemagne and Otto I, it was to persist until Napoleon finally abolished the Holy Roman Empire in 1806. The empire in the East continued almost without hiatus until 1453; and the popes have carried on the universal claims of the eternal city into the twentieth century. In the fourth century the old ideals and institutions had passed away, but at least one commentator could see in this no grounds for pessimism: "Now the earth is in concord . . . ," said Prudentius, "now Christ, a world receives thee which peace and Rome hold together in a bond of union."9

ONE last epilogue to the story of the Roman Empire in the West was written by the East. The Emperor Justinian I (527–565) believed that he had been sent to establish both Catholic Christianity and the ideal of a united empire throughout the Mediterranean. In an effort as audacious and imaginative as it was futile and disastrous, he bent all the resources of the empire to a reconquest of the lands lost to the barbarians. Building huge fleets and employing huge armies under the able command of generals like Belisarius and Narses, he succeeded in bringing Africa, Italy, and part of Spain under the rule of Constantinople, as well as in inaugurating a massive building program in the capital itself. Unfortunately these efforts could only be made at the cost of draining the treasury and making even more severe demands upon the weakened economy than before; nor did the able emperor's thrift and skill in reorganization save the government enough money to make up for its losses. His conquests were ephemeral; their ultimate effect was the further weakening of the eastern, without the resurrection of the western, part of the empire.

Of much more permanent value was Justinian's creation of the *Corpus Juris Civilis,* a collection of imperial legislation and decrees, together with the commentaries of lawyers and the addition of such new laws as the emperor thought proper. This *Corpus,* which superseded the Theodosian Code published by the lawyers of Theodosius II in 438, became the foundation for the later study and development of Roman law in the Middle Ages.

THE Christianizing of the empire and the Romanizing of Christianity were great steps in the synthetic process that produced our civilization. Greco-Judaic Christianity was now wed to Latin culture, and Christianity now served as the bridge that united the Romans with the barbarians. With the coming addition of Teutonic, Celtic, and Slavic elements, the synthesis of our civilization would be completed.

NOTES

[1] Gibbon, *Decline and Fall,* 1, ch. 18, 561.
[2] Gibbon, 1, ch. 18, 577–578.
[3] A. H. M. Jones, *The Later Roman Empire 284–602* (Norman, Okla.: Univ. of Oklahoma Press, 1964), II, 1025.
[4] Quoted by Helen Waddell, *The Desert Fathers,* 2d ed. (Ann Arbor, University of Michigan Press, 1957), pp. 53–54.
[5] A. H. M. Jones, 1, 151.
[6] Eusebius, *Life of Constantine,* in Philip Schaff and Henry Wace, *A Select Library of the Nicene and Post-Nicene Fathers* (New York, 1890), 584, 591.
[7] *Theodosian Code,* 1, 2; 1, 4, ed. Clyde Pharr (Princeton, 1952).
[8] Letter of Gelasius to Emperor Anastasius I. There is a translation in James A. Corbett, *The Papacy* (Princeton, 1956), p. 98.
[9] Quoted by Moses Hadas, *A History of Rome* (New York, 1956), p. 277.

Chapter Four

SAINT AUGUSTINE

Dᴜʀɪɴɢ the fourth century, when the empire still stood but the barbarians were already pressing on its borders, three great teachers united classical with Christian, and humanist with philosophical, thought, advancing the process of synthesis and forming the western mind as a whole and western religion in particular for centuries to come. These three, Jerome, Ambrose, and Augustine, together with the later Gregory the Great, are known as the Fathers of the western Church. The Latin as well as the eastern Fathers of the fourth century showed an openness to the world and its culture greater than that of the earlier, more suspicious, Christian philosophers. They were most of them from sophisticated and influential families, for Christianity had become fashionable among the elite, and it was they, the natural leaders of the whole community, who were the natural leaders of Christian communities.

The personal wealth, privilege, and sophistication of the Fathers taught them about the corruption, disaffection, and lassitude of the ruling classes; they had themselves been tempted by the sweet life; and they interpreted correctly the meaning of the barbarians' distant battle-cry. Rather than yielding to the temptations of soothing delights or easy despair, they took up arms and struggled, in the midst of a world going wrong, for the perfection of man. The very vigor of their resistance often engendered in them extreme attitudes, particularly in regard to sex, that repel the modern sensibility and even suggest aberration. Yet the twentieth-century historian, standing again, as did they, on the edge of a great gulf, can have some sympathy for the violence of their reactions. They had little hope for the stabilization of society. Recognizing that something was disastrously wrong with the kingdoms of this world, they longed for the Kingdom of God.

SAINT JEROME was the most cosmopolitan of the Fathers. By 419, when he died at a monastery at Bethlehem, he had lived in most parts of the empire, from the palaces of Rome and Constantinople to the hermits' cells of the Syrian desert. He was a scholar, the author of many letters, and translator of the Old and New Testaments from the original tongues into Latin. His translation, known as the Vulgate, became the standard Bible of the Middle Ages. Jerome was also both a passionate and a solitary man, and his hatred of the world came to encompass scholarship itself. Seeking solitude—"To me a town is a prison, solitude paradise"[1]—he sought refuge in books, but even these betrayed him: in a famous dream he saw himself rejected at the gates of paradise for being more a Ciceronian than a Christian. After a period of revulsion he returned to classical writers; when reproached by Christians even more puritanical than he, he argued that one must meet the pagans on their own grounds and that by retaining what was compatible in them with Christianity one could build up a valuable body of Christian literature.

The personal attachments Jerome formed were few but exceedingly strong, and he easily felt himself disappointed and betrayed by friends. His bitter pen put him in the center of numerous disputes, and at one point he allowed himself to look forward to seeing, in paradise, the suffering of his enemies in hell. His hatred of women and sex owed something to a legitimate revulsion against the immorality of contemporary society, and something to Stoicism, but more to the exaggerated dualism that declared all flesh the work of the Devil. Rejecting all sex as evil, Jerome was willing to tolerate marriage only on the grounds that it produced more virgins, and he publicly doubted that married couples should presume to take holy communion. He warns mothers to dress their little girls plainly and modestly and to keep them out of company, especially that of little boys. The matron Blaesilla is praised for mourning her loss of virginity more than the loss of her husband, and Origen, who mastered his lusts by the expedient of emasculating himself, is offered as an exemplary model. It is impossible now to read Jerome without mental reference to Freud. Such exaggerated fears of sex never became dominant in Christianity, but they have persisted as an unhealthy undercurrent through the Middle Ages and down to the present.

Jerome, for all his cosmopolitan background and travels, and for all his learning, retained, in comparison to Ambrose and Augustine, much of the harshness, intolerance, and gnostic puritanism of the earlier Fathers. There is something in Jerome of Tertullian. Yet Jerome's was a mastery rather than a rejection of classical culture. That mastery is even more evident in the careers of Ambrose and Augustine.

SAINT AMBROSE (ca. 339–397) had a less lurid and more conventional mind. The son of the prefect of Gaul, he was raised in a palace in Trier and from his birth was marked for high office. His proclivities showed themselves early. He was nicknamed "the bishop" even as a child, and in 374, though not yet in holy orders, he was chosen bishop of Milan by the general acclamation of the people. In contrast to most of the early Fathers, including Jerome, Ambrose added great political skill and tact to intelligence and piety. Well versed in the classics, he took a deep interest in education. With a skill like that of Saint Bernard, the later ascetic politician, Ambrose used his wealth, prestige, and connections to raise Milan to the temporary position of the most powerful see in the empire. It was he who debated with the pagan orator Symmachus, faced down the Emperor Valentinian, wrested the Italian Church from the Arians, and shamed the great Emperor Theodosius into doing penance for his sins. It was Ambrose who encouraged the conversion to the Church of its most influential thinker since Saint Paul.

THE importance of this new convert, Saint Augustine, can hardly be overstated. One recent writer has said that Augustine towers like a colossus over all of western thought. Not only was the Christian philosophy of the early Middle Ages almost wholly Augustinian, not only did the scholastics of the later Middle Ages and the Protestants of the Reformation base their systems upon his principles, but twentieth-century theologians, both Catholic and Protestant, are turning again to his wisdom. Even modern secular thought, issuing in its origins from Christianity, owes much to principles and attitudes that are in origin Augustinian.

AUGUSTINE'S personality is better known to us than that of any other Christian thinker before the Renaissance. Partly for this reason and partly because of his enormous energy and concern for the world in which he lived, he seems the most human of the Fathers. He was born in 354 at Tagaste in Numidia to a pagan father and an ambitious Christian mother. The province of Africa, centered around Carthage, was at that time immensely well endowed materially and intellectually. More even than Italy or Gaul, it was the center of the Latin Christian culture to which Augustine would now give the impress of a first-rate mind.

In 370, when Augustine was only sixteen, he was sent off to school at Carthage. His experience in leaving home resembled that of many young men both before and after, though his sensitivity to it was unusual. "To Carthage then I came," he wrote in the third book of his *Confessions,* "where there sang all around me in my ears a cauldron of unholy loves." He acquired a mistress at seventeen and at eighteen an illegitimate son, whose name, Adeodatus ("Gift of God"), showed how little his father was then ashamed of him, whatever his later sentiments.

> to Carthage then I came
>
> Burning burning burning burning
> O Lord Thou pluckest me out
> O Lord Thou pluckest
> burning[2]

Augustine burned not only for women but for wisdom. His mother, Saint Monica, had not been able to secure the loyalty of her son to Christ, and in the great city he interspersed feverish bouts of pleasure with equally feverish bouts of study, reading Cicero, the philosophers, and the poets as well as the Scriptures. Finishing his education, he settled down at Carthage with his mistress and child to earn his living as a teacher of rhetoric, the most popular subject of study and therefore the most lucrative to profess. Still seeking wisdom, he adopted Manichaeism about the time his son was born, and adhered to it for ten years, a period quite long enough to leave permanent traces of dualism in his thought and to infect him to a milder degree with the same unhealthy distrust of the flesh that obsessed Jerome. Augustine at last came to question his religion, but remained confident that its greatest teachers could assuage his doubts, until Faustus, the greatest philosopher of the Manichaeans, came to Carthage in 383. Faustus was unable to answer the eager young man's questions satisfactorily. Augustine, discouraged but still determined, took his family the same year to Italy where he could continue his search for truth while teaching rhetoric. After a time in Rome he moved to Milan where he fell under the influence of Ambrose. With the bishop he studied the Christian religion more thoroughly than he had been able to explore it with his mother. For a while he was strongly inclined toward Neoplatonism, but one day in 386 his conversion to Christianity came suddenly. He was seated alone in his garden musing when he heard in the distance the voice of a child at play chanting words which sounded like *tolle lege,* "take up and read." Augustine hastened to the house, where he threw open the Bible at random. It opened to Romans XIII, 13: "Let us walk honestly, as in the day; not in rioting and drunkenness, not in lust and wantonness, not in strife and envying. But put ye on the Lord Jesus Christ, and make not provision for the flesh, to fulfil the lusts thereof." Suddenly the seeking, the worry, and the tensions dissolved: the long personal crisis was over. The next year Augustine was baptized a Christian.

That year also brought the death of his mother, and in 388 he decided to return to Africa. It was at this point that enthusiasm overstepped humanity, and obedient to the letter rather than the spirit of the Gospels, he decided to send away a mistress who, after seventeen years, might have expected to continue to enjoy the privileges of a wife. Only a year later, the fruit of their union, Adeodatus, died, at just the age his father had been when the "Gift of God" was born.

Back in Africa, Augustine settled down at Tagaste. With a few friends he pursued a life of seclusion that borrowed something from that of Socrates and his group and something from Christian monasticism, and became the model of the semi-monastic "Augustinian Rule" of the Middle Ages. He was ordained a priest in 391 and in 395 became bishop of the large city of Hippo (modern Bône). His youthful optimism was gradually yielding, under the influence of the times, his readings of Saint Paul, and possibly his separation from his family, to a pessimism that brought him to dwell more and more upon the other world and the Pauline theories of sin and grace. As bishop, he had to struggle with the laxity of his own congregation, with the numerous heretical puritans known as the Donatists, and with a paganism that was still strong among both the educated and the uneducated. The capture of Rome by the Visigoths in 410 made as great an impression upon the old bishop as upon most of his contemporaries, and when in 429 the Vandals invaded Africa the ruin of the empire seemed too much for him to bear. He died in 430, while the Vandals besieged his city, with his eyes upon the penitential psalms.

Augustine always had an extremely nervous and driving personality, which made him subject to attacks of physical weakness and probably induced his occasional harshness. His restless pen produced 113 books, at least 218 letters, and more than 500 sermons. His most famous works are the *City of God,* on which he labored for fourteen years (412–426), and the *Confessions.* The latter bear only a superficial resemblance to later personal outpourings like the egotistic horrors of Rousseau, which are reminiscent of Saint Jerome at his most violent. The word "confess" meant originally to bear witness, and Augustine meant to praise God rather than himself: the first lines of the book are: "Great art Thou O Lord, and greatly to be praised." The *Confessions* contain passages of profound psychological introspection and passages of brilliant philosophy, as in the great Book Eleven where the nature of God and of time are described with a vision that seems prophetic of Einstein.

UNLIKE Aquinas or Aristotle, Augustine never organized his thought into a logical system. His style of theology has been described as "psychological and analogical" as opposed to the geometrically rigorous "essential analysis" theology of Aquinas or the "existential" theology of today. Augustine used insights, images, metaphors, allusions, and breathtaking inspirational leaps, rather than dry logical analysis. The richness of his thought is like that of great literature: it cannot be grasped in paraphrase. Yet, because medieval Christian thought and assumptions are so largely Augustinian, it is useful here briefly to indicate their purport, without hope of conveying anything like their depth and complexity.

Unlike his former Manichaean coreligionists, who believed

Saint Augustine, the earliest extant portrait (from a mural).

that matter was the creation of the devil, Augustine holds that God created all things and that nothing he created is bad. The world proceeds from the mind of God like a work of art from the mind of its creator. The human body is an artifact of God, not a prison created by the devil for the purpose of holding us captive. Evil arises not from matter itself but from the misuse of matter. Matter and body may offer temptations, but the evil lies in yielding.

Since the world is not essentially evil, philosophy, the examination of the world for truth and wisdom, is possible. Augustine was perfectly aware of the epistemological skepticism that has existed from Plato's time to ours: the disbelief in the powers of the human mind to arrive at objective reality. He had been such a skeptic himself. But he had gone on to a belief in "a truth which thou canst not call thine, or mine, or any man's, but which is present to all. . . ."[3] Our minds are capable of creating not only an internally *coherent* system but one that *corresponds* to objective reality. We can discover truth and to this truth add wisdom, which is lack of excess: "For there was never truth without true measure, nor true measure without truth. . . ." Augustine's abandonment of dualism and acceptance of the world permitted and encouraged western thought to pursue philosophical, scientific, and historical problems within the context of time and this world, rather than seeing everything, as the Eastern Church tended to do, in terms of eternity. Such was the enormous prestige of Augustine's thought that it is difficult to imagine the western world's having developed its scientific and humanistic interests to nearly so great a degree had the bishop of Hippo instead taught total contempt for the world.

Augustine was a Christian and a Platonist, and, real and good though the phenomenal world might be to him, there was another world better and more real: the Kingdom of God, the world of grace, the world of spirit and ideas. To Augustine, the ultimate purpose of examining the material world is not to understand it for its own sake, but to use our knowledge of it to understand the other world. God is the ultimate end of every intellectual quest—a sentiment echoed in our own time by Teilhard de Chardin, who said that research was very like adoration. Yet this end can never be wholly attained. Our minds cannot reach out and grasp God; they can only be attentive, ready, and open to receive *his* grasp.

Augustine's conception of God is, like Aquinas' later, pure being, an idea based upon the Old Testament text I AM WHO AM and upon Greek speculation about the absolute. The existence of God so far from being open to doubt is the only thing of which we can be sure, for if anything is, God is, and all that is derives its being from God. God is, and God is good; God is absolute being and absolute goodness. Evil, therefore, is a negative quantity. Nothing in itself, it is the absence of perfection, and absolute evil is absolute non-being. The universe is rather like a Swiss cheese; its only imperfections are the holes, which are merely "cheeselessness"; and even these imperfections must exist in order for the whole to be perfect. Augustine thus hinted at an idea which was to be picked up and made explicit by the scholastics and later philosophers, that of the Great Chain of Being on which all beings, from God at the top to nothingness on the bottom, can be arranged on an ontological scale.

Time, like space, is a measure and both were created with the universe. Time and space are real qualities with which we must deal, but they exist only within the created universe. God exists outside of time and space. To God, all times and spaces are one; he sees, as it were, everything in the universe at one moment and in one point. Thus there never was "a time" before the universe existed, though for us inside it it has a beginning and an end.

Man is the only creature with self-consciousness and the ability of rational choice. (Augustine was unaware of the possible existence of intelligent races on other planets; if he had been, his argument would simply have been extended.) God created the universe for one purpose: to extend moral goodness. Moral goodness cannot exist apart from the free choice of good or evil, and only rational creatures possess such an ability to choose. Hence God created the world for rational creatures.

What is the proper end of man? Augustine encompasses the Aristotelian idea that man should fulfill his essence, his rationality, but he holds that this fulfillment can take place only when man has found God, the ultimate reason and the ultimate good. Man's task on earth, therefore, is to seek God. The first requisite of the search is not intelligence, but humility and love—the humble and grateful opening up of the mind to God, and the setting aside of any material considerations that distract us from this openness. The next requisite is faith. Augustine used the word "faith" inconsistently both in the Hebraic sense of personal commitment and in the Greek sense of assent to intellectual propositions. A man must have both commitment and willingness to believe; these then can lead his intellect to understanding.

We achieve this understanding partly through the use of reason and logic but even more through what we would call psychological and artistic perception, and mysticism (here Augustine's thought is opposed to Aquinas'). First we examine the world around us, seeking in it analogies of God. The symmetry of a tree, the majesty of a mountain, the complexity of an animal, the reason of a man, all of these are analogies of qualities of God. Created things derive these qualities from God; in them is expressed imperfectly what in God is expressed perfectly. The truth, beauty, and goodness of God are infinitely beyond any-thing we call by those names on earth; but only by understanding the limited, earthly analogies can we get a glimpse of those divine perfections: "I saw Thy invisible things understood by the things which are made." Introspection follows observation: having looked at God in the world without, we turn to look at God within. The human mind and spirit are the closest analogies to God that we know; the order, proportion, and harmony that we see in nature are received and understood by the order, proportion, and harmony of our souls.

The final step toward God is mystical union. The basic prin-ciple of mystical theology is that God, by virtue of his transcen-dent qualities, can never really be comprehended. Augustine anticipates it: "If thou hast been able to comprehend Him as thou thinkest, by so thinking thou hast deceived thyself. This then is not God, if thou hast comprehended it; but if this be God, thou hast not comprehended it . . . ."[5] Insofar as man can attain God, it is God who grasps man, not man who grasps God.

This idea of the immeasurable greatness of God in compar-ison to man lies at the bottom of Augustine's doctrines of sin, grace, and free will. Evil, as has been said, is non-being. Sin therefore consists of the essentially negative act of turning away from God, preferring our own limited will to his perfect will: "The will . . . commits sin when it turns away from immutable and common goods, toward its own private good. . . ."[6] Or, again: "All sins are contained in this one category, that one turns away from things divine and truly enduring, and turns towards those which are mutable and uncertain."[7]

God created man for the purpose of extending the moral goodness in the world. Because moral goodness consists of a free choice of God, God had to make man free—truly free—to choose between God and self. In Adam, man chose self. Augustine con-siders all mankind to have taken part in the sin of Adam and Eve, a cosmic event which (though he does not put it this way himself) may be conceived of as having occurred in eternity rather than in time. This original sin is therefore shared by all men, who suffer from its consequences. The worst consequence of original sin is that it has destroyed man's freedom. Adam was perfectly free to choose between good and evil, but men are now cut off from God and chained to sin.

God and man made a contract that man would continue to be happy in return for his obedience to the will of God; man broke the contract; hence God in justice can abandon man. Abandonment is the true meaning of hell: hell is separation from God, and man, by choosing to follow his own desires, creates hell for himself. Yet God is not only just, but merciful. In fact, so great is his mercy that he himself became man. Christ, the Son of God, was the New Adam opening again for all men the road to paradise that the Old Adam had closed. Christ died to break the bonds of sin that attached man to evil. Man's sin is his own choice; his salvation is God's.

The individual man has, therefore, but one hope of salvation from the hell that man has built: he must cast himself upon the mercy of God. Augustine entered into a long dispute with a theologian from Britain named Pelagius, who maintained that man could, by diligence, prayers, fasting, and study, achieve his own salvation. On the contrary, said Augustine, whatever bad there is in man is his own; whatever good is God's. There is nothing in the world that one can do to save oneself but to accept Christ wholly and completely, to have faith, in the Pauline sense of total commitment, in the Savior.

But, if man is bound to sin by his choice in Adam, is he even free to choose to have faith? This question was never resolved by the Church, and Augustine was not wholly clear in his own answer, which tended, however, to be no. As it is God who saves mankind in general, it is God who saves the individual man in particular. To some, and not to others, God gives his grace, which brings about faith on their part and achieves their salvation. To others God does not send this grace. God's mercy is extended to some men; the others are left, in God's justice, to perish in the hell they made for themselves. This is no limitation of God's justice, for the damned are damned of their own free will, but it does seem to be a limitation of God's mercy, of man's freedom, and of the doctrine that Christ died for all men—principles that Augustine always affirmed. His position was not logically consistent; perhaps it was not intended to be; and in any case it may be contended that religion, like art, need not be wholly logical.

Augustine thus raised, but did not settle, the great question of predestination. He asked himself: "How can the following two propositions, that (1) God has foreknowledge of all future events and that (2) we do not sin by necessity but by free will, be made consistent with each other? 'If God foreknows that man will sin,' you say, 'it is necessary that man sin.' "[8] In other words, if God foreknows all and is all powerful, how can he not be responsible for man's choice to sin? Augustine denied that he was. To begin with, the question must be taken out of time, since God exists out of time, and this is difficult to do since we do not have any verb-forms to express timelessness. But, using the present tense to indicate timeless action, it can be said that God, rather than foreknowing or foreordaining, simply knows and ordains. He wills the salvation of all but, in order to allow freedom to choose, permits the choice of evil. He knows that B has faith and is saved and that C does not and is left to his own damnation. He wills to give B the grace of faith; for some reason he withholds that grace from C. He brings B into heaven; he leaves C to hell. Against these doctrines many theologians have urged that God leaves greater freedom to both B and C. "We conclude that a man is not justified by the precepts of a holy life, but by faith in Jesus Christ. That is to say, not by the law of works, but by that of faith; not by the letter, but by the spirit; not by the merits of deeds, but by gratuitous grace."[9] On the other hand, Calvin went beyond Augustine to the logical extremes and held that God actively willed the damnation of C as well as the salvation of B. In any case, it was the Augustinian ideas, with all their complexity, profundity, and inconsistency, that dominated medieval thought on these subjects.

AUGUSTINE was too concerned with the justice of God to concern himself greatly with the ethics of society. After his conversion, he adopted the sexual puritanism common to many of the early Fathers, but good sense prevented him from going as far: when the young matron Ecdicia gave away all her money and put on widow's garments while her husband still lived, Augustine warned her that she was driving her husband to adultery and that his sin was on her head.

Towards social institutions repugnant to the modern conscience, slavery for example, Augustine was complacent, merely urging slaveholders to treat their slaves with mercy. It must be added that none of the most enlightened figures of antiquity,

Christian or pagan, perceived the inherent injustice of this institution which had always existed in every society. This is one demonstration of the historical axiom that the deepest assumptions of a society, those that are never questioned because "everybody knows are true," are precisely those—like nationalism, or materialism, today—that are the most vulnerable to rational analysis. One of the unquestioned assumptions of both ancient and medieval society was that men, far from being created equal, were created each in his proper place. As water naturally seeks its own level, so man is happiest, and possesses true "liberty," in his natural and proper station in life, whether it be as a slave or as an emperor. This hierarchical view of society was scarcely questioned before the eighteenth century.

SAINT AUGUSTINE applied himself to historical problems in the *City of God*, begun in 412, two years after the taking of Rome by the Visigoths. His work was intended to answer the complaints of the pagans, who held Christianity responsible for the ruin of the empire, and to remove the doubts of the Christians, who had previously been taught that Christianized Rome was a Providential creation. Against the pagans, Augustine urged that the weakness of Rome lay in declining and decadent paganism, rather than in vital and patriotic Christianity. Then he turned to the murmuring Christians and pointed out that they need not grieve overmuch for Rome, for it is not the City of God. The City of God is not to be found in any earthly state, but in the Kingdom of God that is not of this world. The City of God, which comprises "all who from the beginning of the world have been righteous (and who) have Christ for their head," is, in fact, constantly at war with the "city of man" or the "city of this world," which comprises "those who live according to man (rather than) according to God." The City of God is identified with the mystical body of Christ and with the Church; the city of man with those who are not saved. This analysis was scrupulously applied by Augustine's disciple Orosius to a detailed and tedious historical review of all past empires, and the idea appears in the writings of many medieval historians.

Augustine has frequently been credited with originating the modern idea of history. Most of the classical writers had little idea of any direction in history. Augustine conceived of it as a straight line from creation through the Incarnation to the end of the world. God had created time, so that it was necessarily good; he had allowed time to elapse between the Fall of man and the Incarnation of Christ, and since he does nothing without purpose, that time must have had meaning. Drawing from the earlier Fathers, Augustine argued that God had delayed the Incarnation in order to prepare man for the advent of Christ; and preparation implies progress of a sort. Since God now allows more time to elapse between the Incarnation and the Second Coming, progress must still be continuing. The idea of Augustine and the other Fathers that it was possible to have a *reformatio in melius,* a movement of progress in time, encouraged the perennial efforts of western man to reform first ecclesiastical, and then secular, society. Some critics have argued that Augustine's thought is anti-historical in his conception of history as the unfolding of the purpose of a superior being rather than of the efforts of men, but his unilinear idea of time and progress created a sense of the meaning of history and of hope in the future.

Augustine's greatness lies in his universality; the immensity, diversity, and complexity of his thought have made him intelligible to men of diverse ages. His was the most important part in the union of classical and Platonic philosophy with Christian and Pauline thought. He completed the intellectual synthesis from which the thought of the Middle Ages proceeded.

NOTES

[1] Letter 125.
[2] T. S. Eliot, *The Waste Land,* III, lines 307–311. Reprinted by permission of Harcourt, Brace & World, Inc. New York.
[3] *De Libero Arbitrio,* II, xii, quoted in *An Augustine Synthesis,* ed. Erich Przywara (New York, 1958), pp. 14–15.
[4] *De Beata Vita,* IV, 33, 34, quoted by Przywara, p. 35.
[5] *Sermo* III, vi, quoted by Przywara, p. 81.
[6] *De Libero Arbitrio,* II, xix, in *On the Free Choice of the Will,* trans. and ed. Anna Benjamin and L. H. Hackstaff (New York, 1964), p. 82.
[7] *De Libero Arbitrio,* I, xvi, quoted by Przywara, p. 124.
[8] Benjamin and Hackstaff, p. 90.
[9] *De Spir. et Lett.,* XIII, xxii, quoted by Przywara, p. 316.

Chapter Five

AN AGE OF DARKNESS OR OF CREATIVITY?
(400–700)

THE epithet "Dark," long removed from the Middle Ages as a whole, is still occasionally bestowed upon the period from the fifth to the eighth centuries. This age of invasions, continued economic decline, and scant intellectual activity, so the argument goes, was the nadir of western civilization. But it is not a good argument. Although the light of these centuries is dim, it is as much the dimness of approaching dawn as of fading evening.

The era was not only a time of troubles, but an age of heroes analogous to that which ended the Aegean civilization and opened the Hellenic. The new barbarians are Teutons instead of Dorians, and the new heroes Beowulf and Charlemagne instead of Hector and Agamemnon, but there is a similitude reinforced by the likenesses between early Greek and Germanic kingship, laws, religion, and customs. With our classical-Renaissance frame of mind we look upon the earlier time of troubles as *creative* of things Hellenic, not *destructive* of things Minoan, but this same frame of mind makes us read the more recent time of troubles in the opposite fashion: as *destructive* of things Roman rather than as *creative* of things medieval or "western." The more judicious historian will describe the era from the fifth to the eighth century A.D. as creative of a new civilization as well as destructive of the old.

There were several "Middle Ages," and this first and earliest was the most original and creative. The failures of Rome—in economics, society and politics, technology, and religion—opened men's minds to new possibilities and in this period the seeds of innumerable later assumptions and beliefs were sown. Moreover, as William C. Bark has observed, the very shattering of peaceful and complacent conformity by the invasions released the forces of creative energy, as did the addition of Celtic and Teutonic elements to the Roman-Christian synthesis.

This encounter of Latin-Christian civilization with the barbarians resulted in a double process of assimilation and synthesis. In assimilation, one culture conquers and absorbs the other. In many areas and in many aspects of culture Latin culture absorbed barbarian; in some the barbarian absorbed the Latin. In other respects a true synthesis between the two was attained, in which each acted to transform the attitudes and institutions of the other. Accompanying this process was a shift northward from the Mediterranean of the centers of culture. The result of the division of the Mediterranean world into three parts, western, Byzantine, and Islamic, this shift meant that the northern "fringe" areas of Greco-Roman civilization would become the heartland of the new western civilization. This, some historians suggest, is the most important distinction between the classical and medieval worlds.

These developments began in the fifth through seventh centuries, when the elements of synthesis were assembled, and were completed in the eighth, which is therefore considered the end of the period of transformation of the Roman world. These changes meant that the tone of life would be very different in the eighth century from what it had been in the fifth.

This new tone of life is not best described as a barbarization of the Roman Empire. If the word "barbarian" is taken in its root sense of "outsiders," then the invaders were of course barbarians, since they came from outside the empire. But the word is accompanied by the implication that when the Teutonic peoples irrupted into the empire they were wholly ignorant of civilized life, customs, and religion. This is false. The Teutons had long been in contact with Roman civilization, and they had learned a great deal about culture, technology, and even religion. The Teutons of the fifth century were not the simple savages that Tacitus described four centuries earlier.

BEFORE their entry into the empire the Teutons had had considerable exposure to Christianity. The Goths, while dwelling in what is now the Ukraine, were the first of the Teutonic peoples to receive missionaries. Though a very few converts had previously been made among them by traders, returning mercenaries, and Christian slaves, there had been no concerted effort to bring them into the fold. About 341, however, the patriarch of Constantinople, Eusebius of Nicomedia, sent a priest named Wulfila to minister to the needs of the Christians who were dwelling among the Goths. Eusebius was one of the leaders of the Arian party, which at that time was dominant in the empire; as a result, Wulfila's Christianity was of the Arian, rather than of the Catholic, variety. Wulfila soon decided that the Goths as well as their Roman slaves should hear the Gospel, and he translated the Bible into Gothic, for the first time establishing a Teutonic dialect as a written language. Wulfila was obliged to flee the heavy hand of an unsympathetic ruler, but the groundwork for conversion had been laid: the Visigoths (the "wise" or "western" Goths) were converted in the 380s and 390s, the Ostrogoths (the "brilliant" or "eastern" Goths) about 460.

The establishment of Christianity among the other Teutonic and Celtic barbarians began somewhat after the time of Wulfila, but before their conquest of the empire, the Vandals, Burgundians, and Lombards became Arians. One result of these conversions was to create in many of the kingdoms a tension between Arian Germans and Catholic Romans that would retard the achievement of peaceful synthesis. Of all the peoples who invaded the empire only two converted directly to Catholicism, in both cases after the invasion: the Franks and the Anglo-Saxons. As a result, the papacy on the one hand and the Franks and the English on the other became natural allies and eventually the dominant forces in western Europe. In any event, those who wish to attribute the weakness of Rome to Christianity should bear in mind that most of the conquerors of Rome were themselves Christians.

The conversion of the Teutons illustrates that this age of transition affected not only the Roman, but the Teutonic, world. Some German historians have gone so far as to mourn the decay of old Germanic ideas and attitudes as much as other historians have mourned the passage of those of classical Rome. Certainly the quality of German life changed as the invaders settled down

The Visigothic King Receswinth.

among the towns and fields, with access to the churches and schools of the empire, while their presence in turn changed the quality of life in the empire: the two cultures acted upon one another in the process of synthesis.

Unquestionably the life of the Roman population changed greatly between the fifth and eighth centuries. The repeated invasions encouraged political insecurity and economic weakness. The unity of the old empire was preserved in theory, but in fact power passed into the hands of local chieftains or administrators. The economic depression that had begun in the third century was deepened, and there was a general depopulation of the towns and even, in many areas, of the countryside, where formerly cultivated fields reverted to waste. Everywhere, particularly in northern Europe, the towns lost their commercial, cultural, and political importance, so that the centers of life were in the countryside: either castle or monastery. The availability and use of luxury goods were curtailed, and leisure was devoted less to the spectacles, baths, and conversations of the town and more to the diversions of the outdoors, like hunting and games. Communications were often disrupted or discouraged by the lack of commerce, and opportunities for exchanging philosophical and other ideas declined. Regional idiosyncracies developed almost unchecked, and a host of vernacular dialects began to replace Latin. Even the unity of the Church was qualified by the regional divergencies in liturgy, practice, organization, and even doctrine that political and commercial fragmentation encouraged. Seventh-century Europe badly wanted a center: in the eighth century this center was provided in the Franco-papal alliance.

THE records of the period are so sparse as to constitute a lesson in humility for the historian. As the French historian Lucien Musset puts it, the scholar's fate is much like that of Penelope at her loom: he must undo every night what he has woven during the day. Our understanding of the period, both in its general form and in its particulars, is very tentative.

In addition to the information provided by artifacts, inscriptions, myths, legends, and epics, there are some writers of the period who show a purpose and a fidelity to detail that make them generally trustworthy sources. Gregory of Tours' *History of the Franks* is our main source of information about those people in the sixth century. The history of the Lombards into the eighth century was composed by Paul the Deacon, a scholar of Charlemagne's time. A history of the Goths was written by Cassiodorus, but is now available only in the inferior version of Jordanes (ca. 550); and the history of the Goths, Suevi, and Vandals into the seventh century survives only in the chronicle of the unreliable Isidore of Seville. The Anglo-Saxon conquest is recounted by the British monk Gildas, by the *Anglo-Saxon Chronicle,* and by Saint Bede's *Ecclesiastical History of the English Nation.* These histories are supplemented by law codes, saints' lives, and letters—especially those of Cassiodorus, Sidonius Appollinaris (in fifth-century Gaul), and Pope Gregory the Great.

THE invasions of the third and following centuries were but the latest in a long series of migrations from the East into the West that began deep in the prehistoric past and continued with the Celts in the sixth century B.C., through the Teutons, Huns, Magyars, Mongols, and Turks, down to the eighteenth century. In this long history the relative stability of the Roman world between the Celtic and the Gothic captures of the city was an exception.

By the fourth century A.D., there were four important groups at the periphery of, or outside, the empire: the Celts, the Teutons, the Slavs, and the Ural-Altaic peoples. All but the last were Indo-Europeans like the Latins themselves, with whom the Celts and Teutons had had relatively close relations in prehistoric times. The pristine Celts and Teutons lived in central Europe (probably in southern Germany) in such close proximity that the Roman writer Strabo was unable to tell them apart.

In numbers, linguistic and cultural independence, and geographical extension, the Celts had every claim to equality with the other Indo-European peoples. Known as *Galatai* as well as *Keltoi*, they moved outward from their central European homeland ca. 500 B.C., until they occupied areas from Galatia in Asia Minor to Galicia in Poland, to Gaul, to Britain [Gallia: Wales], and to Iberia. About 390 B.C. they took Rome, and from that time until about 150–100 B.C. dominated much of the continent. Thereafter their star declined, and they were gradually conquered, killed, or expelled from their great territories by the Latin Romans from the south and the Teutons from the north, so that after Caesar's conquest of Gaul they retained independent control only of Britain and Ireland. After the English (Anglo-Saxon) invaders of the fifth and sixth centuries had overcome the resistance of British chieftains like Arthur, the "King Arthur" of later legend, the Celts were thrust back wholly into the "Celtic Fringe" of Ireland, Wales, Cornwall, the Scottish Highlands, and across the Channel into Armorica, which henceforward bore their name: Brittany. So meager did their political and military influence become that Gibbon did not consider it worth his while to speak of the Celts once. The only Celtic state that remained through the Middle Ages was the Kingdom of Scotland, and even that was largely English in population, government, and speech.

The contemporaries of the medieval Celts had little better opinion of them than did Gibbon. Said one twelfth-century writer (Gerald of Wales) about the Irish: "Secluded from civilized nations, they learn nothing, and practice nothing, but the barbarism in which they are born and bred, and which sticks to them

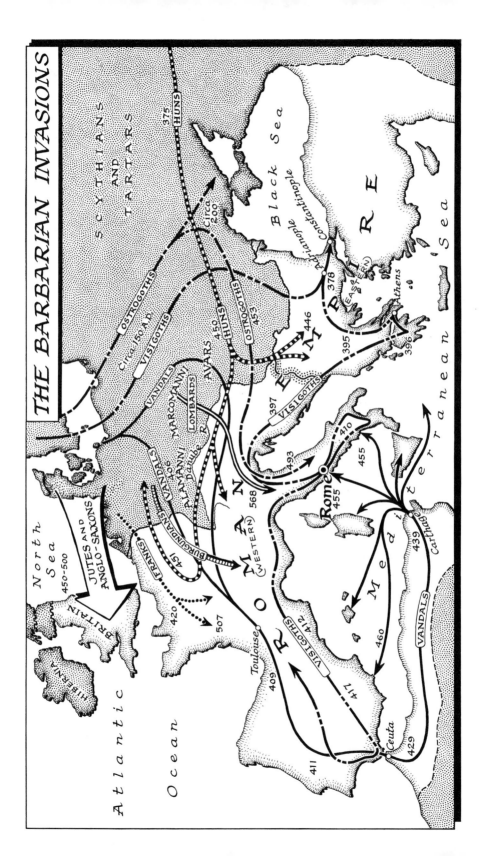

THE BARBARIAN INVASIONS

like a second nature. Whatever natural gifts they possess are excellent; in whatever requires industry they are worthless." The modern historian is more favorably impressed. The Celts had a great influence upon the prehistoric Teutons; and in historical times, their art and their literature have flowed into the deepest wells of our imagination. The voyage stories, the lyric poetry, and the legends of the Irish enjoy a just renown, and the Arthurian cycle known to the Middle Ages as the "Matter of Britain," including the famous stories of the Grail and the Fisher King, is visible in the work of Wagner, Eliot, and Hemingway as well as in that of the medieval Chrétien de Troyes.

Toynbee exaggerates when he speaks of an abortive but distinct "Far Western Civilization" among the Celts of Ireland, Scotland, and Wales. The Celts never achieved their own civilization, but they did make several unique contributions to the Western synthesis. The most profound influence exercised by the Celts in Europe was that of the Irish missionaries. Ireland had been converted from paganism in the mid-fifth century, at least partly through the efforts of Saint Patrick (d. 461). Patrick had probably been a student in the strict monasteries of southern Gaul; in any case, the Irish adopted an unusually strict form of Christianity, emphasizing fasting, chastity, mortification, and the eremitical and monastic life. So powerful were the monasteries that until the conquest of Ireland by the English in the twelfth century, abbots, rather than bishops, directed the Irish Church.

The Irish, who had always been fond of wandering and voyaging, quickly found in the Christian principle of *peregrinatio* a reason in Christ to do so. The Christian notion that man is a pilgrim in this life was translated by the Irish into specific action, and for centuries they poured out of their island in great numbers to evangelize the world. Saint Colum Cille (Colum the Hermit) aided in the conversion of Scotland in the sixth century, and his successors were preaching to the heathen Anglo-Saxons years before Gregory the Great sent Saint Augustine of Canterbury to win them to the Catholic faith. Saint Columbanus and many others went to the continent, where they preached to the pagan Teutons, founded monasteries, and established schools. In the sixth and seventh centuries, when learning was in eclipse among the crude and unlettered Franks and Lom-

Page from a Irish gospel book. In the corners are the stylized figures of the four evangelists. The stylization is typical of early Irish art.

bards, the Irish monasteries preserved and imparted a knowledge of the pagan and Christian classics; and Irish artists and writers produced some of the most beautiful works of art of the early Middle Ages.

In the seventh and eighth centuries the Irish Church suffered two grave setbacks. At the Synod of Whitby in 663 or 664 King Oswy of Northumbria declared after a public debate that he would follow Roman, not Irish, Catholicism, and Irish influence throughout England declined. On the continent, the Irish monasticism that had been spread by Saint Columbanus and his followers was gradually replaced by the Benedictine Rule. But Irish practices like private (as opposed to public) confession

Irish art: A page from the eighth-century Book of Kells showing the sacred monogram XPI [*CHRI(sto)*].

and penance had been established throughout the Church, and the assimilation of the Irish into the Roman Church did not make them less fervent in their pursuit of *peregrinatio*. Throughout the Middle Ages Irish bishops, abbots, priests, and monks were found in France, Germany, Italy, and as far east as Kiev.

THE Slavs had no direct effect upon the Roman world, but they are, with the Latins and Teutons, one of the three major linguistic groups of Europe. Their name, which meant "glory" in their own language, came to mean "slave" in the Latin and Teutonic tongues, so ruthlessly were they exploited by their neighbors. The Slavs, originally dwelling in the great European plains, moved westward to occupy the regions vacated by the Germans in *their* westward drift, and by the seventh century they had settled in the area east of the Elbe that is now Poland. In the East, they penetrated the whole Balkans to such an extent that few nations in that area, including modern Greece, are not strongly Slavic in blood. Upon conversion to Christianity, the southern Slavs moved into the orbit of Constantinople and Eastern Orthodoxy, while the northern Slavs, with the single great exception of the Russians, moved into the orbit of Rome and adopted the Latin alphabet and religion.

THE Teutons [*Theut–Theod–deutsch*: "people"] occupied the area (called by the Romans *Germania*) from the Rhine eastward past the Danube and Vistula. These peoples, whose anthropological and even linguistic unity was tenuous, consisted of two main groups, the southern tribes, with whom the Romans had long been familiar as the *Germani*, including the Suevi (Swabians), Alamanni ("All-men," a confederation of Swabians), and Thuringians; and the eastern and northern tribes, the Vandals, Goths, Burgundians, Franks, and Anglo-Saxons. It was these northern and eastern tribes that began to raid the empire in the third century. Changes in climate, pressures of population, desire for booty, and especially the need for more productive agricultural lands had long made the Teutonic peoples restive. In the fourth century improved weapons made them for the first time a match for the heavily armed Romans, and their natural desire to seize the riches of the empire was reinforced, in the next century, by their even greater craving to escape the Huns at their rear.

THE Mongoloid Ural-Altaic peoples occupied the vast Eurasian plains of what is now the Soviet Union, from which, unhindered by any natural barriers, they again and again swept into Europe, from the fifth-century invasions of the Huns through those of the Avars, Magyars, Mongols, and Turks.

Theoderic's tomb in Ravenna.

It was the assault of the Huns upon the Teutonic peoples that in the fifth century hurled the latter westward against the empire. The Huns, possibly to be identified with the Hiong-Nu who had for centuries been harrying the Chinese, inspired terror in Roman and Teuton alike:

> (They) surpass every measure of savagery. From earliest infancy their cheeks are deeply furrowed with steel, so that the deep scars retard the growth of hair when it comes to sprout . . . . They all have compact and sturdy limbs and thick necks and are so monstrously ugly and misshapen that you might suppose they were two-legged animals . . . . They need no fire or prepared food but live on wild roots and the flesh of any kind of animal, eaten half raw; they warm it a little by putting it between their thighs and the backs of their horses.[1]

Until the fifth century these terrifying nomads had been separated by tribal rivalries, but by ca. 425 they formed a state in the Balkans to which Attila, "the Scourge of God," succeeded as king in 434. Attila was a savage, but he had had some experience of the Romans in Ravenna, where in his youth he was sent as a hostage. Attila early decided to plunder the Romans, as well as to enslave the Teutons. When the emperors refused further tribute and botched their attempt to have him murdered, and the princess Honoria secretly offered herself in marriage to the already two-hundred-times wed barbarian chieftain, Attila seized the occasion to invade the empire. Electing to take possession of the western empire first, and counting upon the neutrality of the Teutons, Attila invaded Gaul. But the Visigoths and Franks already had enough established interests in that region to rally behind the remnant of the Roman forces under the Roman general Aëtius, who ironically had been a child hostage at the Hunnish court while Attila was hostage to the Romans, to administer a decisive defeat to Attila in 451 at the Battle of the Catalaunian Fields near Troyes. Attila withdrew but returned to invade Italy, from which he was expelled only by the payment of an increased tribute and by an attack of the eastern emperor at his rear. His preparations of war against the East were extinguished by his death, which, it was said, was owing to overenthusiastic celebration of his nuptials with a captive Teutonic princess.

THE first people whom the Huns encountered in their march westward into Europe were the Goths, who, with the Vandals, Burgundians, and Suevi, were propelled westward as part of the first general wave of invasion. The Goths may, as patriotic Swedes claim, have originated in Scandinavia (as indeed, the names Götaland and Gotland suggest); by the third century they occupied the Ukraine, forming two major groups, the Visigoths and Ostrogoths. The Visigoths were attacked in the Ukraine by the Huns about 375 and were driven westward to settle first in the Balkans, and then within the western empire. Under King Alaric I the Visigoths invaded Italy, took Rome (410), passed on to Gaul still looking for richer farmlands, and finally, under Alaric's successor, established a kingdom in Spain. The Ostrogoths were conquered and enslaved by the Huns, but after the defeat of Attila at the Battle of the Catalaunian Fields they revolted. Under Theoderic [*Theude-rik*: "king of the people"], they invaded Italy, at that time ruled by the Odovacar who had deposed Romulus Augustulus in 476. After the murder of Odovacar and the massacre of his troops, Gothic rule was established in Italy

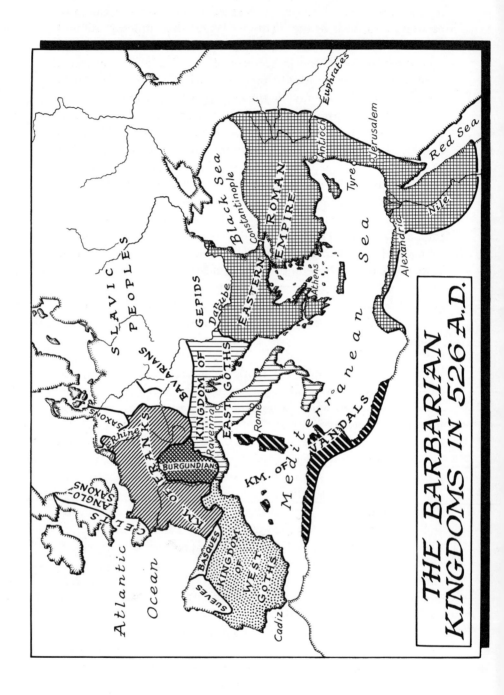

THE BARBARIAN
KINGDOMS IN 526 A.D.

(493). Only sixty years later the armies of Justinian brought it to an end.

While the Visigoths were approaching Rome, the Vandals broke across the Rhine (406–407) and ravaged Gaul, Italy, and Spain, where their temporary rule gave their name to the province of [V]Andalusia. Under their able ruler Geiseric they finally conquered north Africa, taking Carthage in 439 and making it their capital until their overthrow by the armies of Justinian in 533–548. The Burgundians, crossing the Rhine early in the fifth century, established a kingdom on the upper Rhône.

The second wave of invasions began in the fifth century and continued into the sixth. The Anglo-Saxons and Franks had raided the empire earlier, but the withdrawal of Roman troops southward to deal with the Goths left Britain, and to a lesser extent Gaul, open to full-scale invasion. From the beginning of the fifth century desultory raids were replaced by conquest and settlement.

The English, or Anglo-Saxons, who originally dwelt along the coast of the North Sea from the present Netherlands to Denmark, began the serious conquest of Britain shortly after 410 and had completed most of their work by 600. The English were the only Teutonic people who chose to exterminate, rather than to rule or assimilate, the population of the province they conquered. (It is a curious historical coincidence that in the later conquest of the New World the English also outshone all other European peoples in their annihilation of the American Indians.) The adherence of the English to Roman Catholicism in 663 foreshadowed their future political union, though there was no united kingdom of England until the reign of Alfred the Great (871–899).

THE most successful of the invading Teutonic peoples were the Franks ["proud people"]. This group of diverse tribes was formed some time in the third century. There was little political unity among the Frankish tribes; each was ruled by its own chieftain, and each pursued its own course of migration and settlement. Some tribes remained to the east of the Rhine in what came to be called Franconia; others crossed the Rhine and settled in the empire, where they entered into an alliance with the Romans. Then around 410 other Franks crossed the river, refused an alliance, and penetrated deep into Belgium, where they made Tournai the capital of an independent kingdom. Even then they cooperated with the Romans against more savage invaders, and the semilegendary ruler Merovech, who gave his name to the Merovingian dynasty, supposedly came to the aid of Aëtius at the Battle of the Catalaunian Fields. The wealth and power of the early Merovingian kings, who eventually ruled all the Franks, was first discovered when the tomb of Childeric, Merovech's son, was unearthed at Tournai in 1653: it was filled with magnificent ornaments, gold, and jewels.

In 482 Childeric's son Clovis or Chlodovech [Chlodovech–Hludovicus–Lodovicus: Ludwig, Louis, or Lewis], succeeded as *cuning* ["kin leader": king] of the Franks. Clovis' career is obscure owing to the lack of sources other than Gregory of Tours, but it is evident that it was he who chiefly was responsible for the elevation of the Franks from relative obscurity to the rank of one of the great powers of Europe. A shrewd politician as well as a skillful warrior, Clovis not only extended his borders by the sword but secured the loyalty of his new subjects by a lenient and civilized policy. He rapidly subjugated the Alamanni, the kingdom of the Roman general Syagrius, the Burgundians, the Thuringians, and the Kingdom of Tongres. In 511 at the Battle of Vouillé he almost doubled his realm by defeating the Visigoths and annexing most of the southern portion of Gaul. When he died later that year, his dominions stretched from the Pyrenees across the Rhine and deep into the forests of central Germany.

Clovis' masterful policy was to use ruthlessness or conciliation in accordance with the demands of the moment. He repressed, by assassination and savage punishments, any sign of disloyalty among his Teutonic subjects, and he showed himself as a mild and gentle ruler to the Gallo-Roman population, which in many places outnumbered the Teutons. It was probably largely as a political gesture that Clovis converted to Catholicism. According to the story of Gregory of Tours, patently modeled upon Eusebius' life of Constantine, Clovis was on the eve of his battle with the Alamanni at Zülpich persuaded by his Catholic wife to pray to Christ rather than to pagan deities, and consequent to his victory he embraced the true faith. It is now suspected that Clovis was not converted until well after the battle, but the effects were the same whenever the conversion took place: the Franks were obliged to follow their leader into the new religion, and its precepts eventually transformed their customs. Moreover, Clovis gained possession of a valuable political tool. As a Catholic, he could not only rely more securely upon the loyalty of the Gallo-Roman population in his own domains but also upon the support of the Catholic subjects of other Teutonic rulers. The success that Clovis had against the powerful Visigoths was one of the fruits of this policy, for the Catholic population of southern Gaul, led by their bishops, welcomed Clovis as a liberator from their Arian masters. Returning from the campaign of 511, Clovis was crowned at Tours with the title of "consul or augustus," and with his reign the history of Frankland, as distinguished from the history of Roman Gaul, begins.

Clovis' successors completed the conquest of Gaul and much of Germany, but unfortunately for the Franks, Clovis' united kingdom did not outlast him. Under Frankish law, the father's kingdom was, like his private property, divided among his sons, and except for an occasional short period of a few years it is more correct to speak of Merovingian kingdoms than of one kingdom.

The Franks transformed, and were transformed by, the Gallo-Roman civilization they conquered. When they entered the empire they consisted of small and unimportant tribes numbering only a few thousands each. Their petty chieftains, and then their kings, relied for support upon the Frankish infantryman, the backbone of the community. Land that was conquered from the Romans or other Teutonic people was apportioned to these warriors and their voices ruled the assemblies of state. They now undertook to govern one of the richest and most civilized provinces of the empire, with its cities, its schools, and its sophisticated population. As the years passed, their rule was confirmed, and their culture, blending with that of the Romano-Gallic population, became part of the new synthesis. The skill of the Franks united with the wealth and culture of Gaul to render it possible for Frankland to become, in the eighth and ninth centuries, the center of the emerging western civilization.

A FINAL wave of invasion struck the empire in the sixth and seventh centuries, not long after Justinian had put an end to Ostrogothic rule in Italy (553) and restored that country temporarily to the effective rule of Constantinople. This time the invaders were the Lombards ["long-beards"(?) or "long battle-ax" (*barda*)], who had remained on the upper Rhine while the other Teutons pressed westward. Before the end of the sixth century, however, the Lombards were impelled against Italy by the thrust of the Ural-Altaic Avars at their rear, and began their invasions. The Lombards were divided into independent tribes and continued to display disunity almost as long as their kingdom endured, but they were gradually able to restrict Roman control to a few important cities. At last, about 700, they formed a united kingdom with its capital at Pavia, in what is now called Lombardy.

The sixth- and seventh-century wars in Italy, first of the Romans against the Ostrogoths and then of the Lombards against the Romans, ravaged and weakened that country much more disastrously than the overthrow of the western empire by Odovacar or of Odovacar by Theoderic in the fifth century. The cause of western unity was in the long run strengthened by the ruin of Italy, for it meant that there would be no effective competitor with the Franks for the domination of the West, and that the papacy, in order to secure its independence from both the Lombards and Constantinople, would be obliged to enter into a close alliance with the Frankish crown.

THE penetration of Teutonic (Germanic) customs into western culture was as deep as the Teutons' penetration into the territories of the empire. They brought both elements generally barbaric and elements peculiarly Germanic. As barbarians, they provided the heroes—Attila, Siegfried, Beowulf—for the new epic age; as barbarians they did the necessary job of tearing down the old so that the new might be constructed in its place. It has also been suggested that they purified Europe of Roman decadence; but if they were innocent of some of the effete vices of the Romans (and these they quickly learned), the murders, rapes, feuds, robberies, poisonings, and other brutalities of the Merovingians and their contemporaries do not suggest a new Golden Age. Nor do contemporary accounts support the surmise that the Frankish conquest of Gaul was a polite occupation that made no essential break with the Roman past. "The whole of Gaul burned like a vast funeral pyre," contemporaries observed; "I have seen the ground heaped with dead, bodies of both sexes,

Meeting place of the Icelandic Parliament at Thingvellir.

naked and torn, exposed to the birds and the dogs. The stench of corpses infected the living." The barbarians imparted to society new vigor, but not new virtue.

As Teutons, the invaders established their language in a small portion of the empire (Britain and northeastern Gaul), though in the greater portion they adopted the local dialects of Latin that would shortly become the nascent Romance languages. Most of the literature of the early Middle Ages is in Latin. Even literature in the Germanic tongues was already heavily Christianized and Romanized. In the arts, in technology, and in religion, the Germans drew from the Latins rather than the opposite.

The Teutons made their greatest contributions, as befitted a conquering and ruling people, in law and political theory. Germanic conceptions of personal loyalty and responsibility, and Germanic notions of land tenure, were wedded to similar Roman notions to produce feudalism and manorialism. Germanic legal procedures and institutions, many of which, like the jury, remain essential to our own system of law, dominated the courts of northern Europe. The German idea that the people, rather than the ruler, was the source of law, gave rise later to ideas of popular election and the right of resistance that ultimately helped create the concept of social contract.

SCOTLAND

IRELAND

NORTHUMBRIA

WALES

CORNWALL

Anglo-Saxons

Salisbury

GÖTALAND

BORNHOLM

Elbe

FRISIA

GERMANIA

Tournai   Cologne

Zülpich

ARMORICA
(BRITTANY)

Tongres   AUSTRASIA

NEUSTRIA   Laon

Paris   Châlons   Metz   Rhine

Vouillé   Loire   Troyes

Danube

KM. OF THE SUEVES

Toulouse

PYRENEES

KM. OF

THE VISIGOTHS

ANDALUSIA

PILLARS OF HERCULES

KM. OF THE BURGUNDIANS

Pavia

KM. OF THE LOMBARDS

Ravenna

Rome

PAPAL
STATES

K M .   O F   T H E   F R A N K S

G A U L

Mediterranean

KINGDOM OF THE VANDALS

Justinian's Empire (527-565).

Boundaries of Barbarian Kingdoms — 700 A.D.

EUROPE 527-700

GOTLAND

Vistula

S l a v s

Kiev

UKRAINE

Dneister

r s

Ural-Altaic peoples

Huns, Avars, Magyars

Danube

BALKANS

Adrianople ×

Black   Sea

Constantinople

Nicomedia

a n   S e a

MILES
0   100   200   300   400

THE question whether the disruption caused by the barbarian movements of the fifth century constitutes a break, or merely the beginning of a transition, in the history of civilization has for decades been focused upon the "Pirenne thesis."

Henri Pirenne was a great Belgian historian who deserves to be remembered for more than one "thesis," but the argument he developed in his book *Mohammed and Charlemagne* achieved special fame. The "Pirenne thesis" declared that (1) there was no serious discontinuity in the fifth century; (2) there was a fundamental preservation of *Romanitas* (the sense of being Roman) through the seventh century; (3) in the seventh and eighth centuries the massive Moslem intrusion into the Mediterranean brought about the real discontinuity between ancient and medieval; and (4) revival began in the late tenth and eleventh centuries.

Pirenne defended, and subsequent historians have modified, his thesis with reference to economics, politics, and culture. To begin with, the question of continuity and discontinuity must always be limited to the western part of the empire, for economic, political, and cultural continuity in the East is undeniable.

In economic matters, Pirenne was correct that there was no discontinuity in the fifth century. The general economic depression that had begun about 250 continued, but it did not grow worse. Coinage, commerce with the East, and trade between Gaul, England, and Frisia were relatively vigorous, though continued low population levels made any full revival of commerce or urban life impossible. On the other hand, Pirenne seems to have been misled in believing that the Islamic invasions caused a discontinuity in the eighth century. Some historians claim that the Moslems actually stimulated trade. Many now agree that the general revival of population and the economy began, not in the tenth, but in the ninth, or even eighth, century.

Seen in perspective, the fifth, sixth, and seventh centuries represent economically a continuation of the great depression of 250–750, to which the barbarian invasions contributed: the Vandal pirates of the fifth and sixth centuries and the long wars in Italy in the sixth created conditions unfavorable to economic prosperity. The introduction of the Christian notion that wealth was to be mistrusted, and of the Germanic contempt for occupations unrelated to warfare, may also have had deleterious effects, though the contempt for trade persisted through the genteel times of Jane Austen and Trollope without impeding modern economic growth. A more harmful attitude was that which induced kings, bishops, and abbots, as well as other men, to hoard up huge stores of specie in the form of jewelry, ecclesiastical ornamentation, or coins and other treasure buried for safekeeping, causing a shortage of money that made the economy of the West to some degree an economy of barter. Economic continuity was in most respects the rule, though it was a continuity of decline until the eighth century.

CONTINUITY was also evident in political theory, though not in political practice. The authority of the emperor at Constantinople was recognized in theory throughout the West until the eighth century. Stilicho the Vandal and Alaric the Goth held the titles of Roman "masters of the army"; Theoderic I and Clovis were consuls; Athaulf the Visigoth fancied himself the "restorer of the Roman world"; and the murderous Theoderic primly averred that his task was to keep the barbarians out of the empire! The Teutonic rulers often used Roman administrative personnel and codified their laws on Roman models. The Church adopted Roman administrative divisions, while the pope carried on the traditions of the "eternal city" and the one "universal empire." Rome and other cities preserved the physical aspects that had characterized them in classical times, including pagan temples and monuments. The Senate, as well as praetorian prefects, notaries, and the other ancient offices of the empire were retained at Rome at least until the eighth century. Neither Roman nor Teuton had any idea of nationhood, and neither could conceive of any state other than the Roman. When Charlemagne took the imperial crown in 800, his action was viewed by contemporaries, not as the resurrection of an empire that had been dead over three hundred years, but as the confirmation of an imperial continuity that had never ceased.

While in theory the kingdoms upheld the notion of the continuing *res publica*, in practice they were developing separately. Though the idea of *Romanitas* persisted, the barbarism and anarchy of Merovingian Gaul indicates that it had but little effect. While the titles of emperor, senator, and consul remained, they were increasingly empty of power; those of king, bishop, and count came gradually to preempt their realities. The center of European power was slowly shifting away from the Mediterranean towards the former peripheries of civilization in Gaul, Britain, and the Rhine. Politically, the fifth to seventh centuries are a period of transition within continuity.

CONTINUITY in culture was assured by the triumph of the Roman Catholic religion and of the Latin language and its Romance derivations. Those who find discontinuity have found it in the ending of classical, pagan culture, but this had been superseded within the empire even before the barbarian attacks. Late Roman culture was Christian Roman culture, and if this definition is accepted, the continuity is clear in both the idiom and the ideology of most of the literature and all of the philosophical, legal, and theological thought of these centuries.

Yet the transition period would have been culturally sterile indeed if all that it had done was to continue the decaying literary and artistic forms of the Romans. The worst productions of the period are the writings of men like Ennodius, who attempted unsuccessfully to imitate the forms and language of a classical Latin that was already dead and had never really been alive. The *sermo classicus* of Horace or Cicero had even in the first century been no more a living language than the poetry of Pope was the living language of the eighteenth century. The people of the first century used the *sermo cotidianus* (everyday speech) derived from the old vulgar Latin, whose traces can be found in Terence and Plautus. This popular speech divided into dialects and eventually into the vernacular Romance languages. The most successful writers of the early Middle Ages, like Gregory of Tours, used the common idiom.

The philosophers of the time carried on the Roman and Christian traditions. Boëthius, a philosopher and administrator at the court of Theoderic, composed a profound treatise on the *Consolation of Philosophy*. He made popular the study of the "seven liberal arts," an idea borrowed from a fifth-century writer named Martianus Capella. The seven arts, studied throughout the Middle Ages, later became the core of the university curriculum. Cassiodorus, a senator and administrator under Theoderic, upheld the value of both Christian and pagan thought in his *Institutes*.

Founding a monastic community which devoted much time to the copying of manuscripts, Cassiodorus did much to establish the learned tradition in western monasticism and thus to preserve works of antiquity which otherwise would certainly have been lost. A sixth-century Syrian writer, for centuries confused with the Dionysius converted by Saint Paul on the Areopagus and therefore impressively known as Pseudo-Dionysius the Areopagite, wrote mystical treatises that had a profound influence throughout the Middle Ages upon Christian mystical thought. The Celtic and Teutonic peoples were evolving their own artistic and literary forms, epics and legends like those of Beowulf or Arthur that had vigor and life if not polish.

These centuries were not in any sense a Golden Age of philosophy or literature, for the old forms were dead or dying, and the new forms had not yet matured. The crude ideas expressed in the seventh century by that epoch's only notable writer, Isidore of Seville, are testaments: "*Nox* (night)," he wrote seriously, "is derived from *nocere*, to injure, because it injures the eyes. And it has the light of the moon and the stars in order that it may not be without beauty and that it may comfort all who work by night . . ."[2]

But this does not mean that the age was not creative. The Golden Age of Greece in the fifth century B.C. was possible only because preceding centuries had slowly introduced new and living ideas that could later be perfected; the same is true of the Augustan Age in Rome and of all Golden Ages, and the generalization holds in the present instance. The great flowering of medieval culture in the twelfth and thirteenth centuries had its ultimate origins in the sixth and seventh.

THE barbarian invasions produced, not a deep discontinuity, but a gradual transition from things identifiably Roman to things identifiably medieval. They produced decline from the point of view of things Roman, but creativity from the point of view of the new and emerging civilization. In this period all the elements of synthesis that would make modern Europe were assembled. The synthesis would be achieved in the course of the next century, the eighth; but before turning to this century of synthesis in the West, the historian must first observe the rise of two other great Mediterranean civilizations, Islam and

Byzantium. For in the eighth century the Mediterranean, formerly *mare nostrum* and the center of civilization, was divided into three parts.

NOTES

[1] Ammianus Marcellinus, 31.2.1, trans. Moses Hadas, *A History of Rome,* Copyright © 1956 by Moses Hadas. Reprinted by permission of Doubleday & Company, Inc. (New York, 1956), pp. 203–204.
[2] Quoted by Colman Barry, *Readings in Church History* (Westminster, Md., 1960), p. 262.

Chapter Six

THE MEDITERRANEAN WORLD
IN THREE PARTS

In the eighth century, the century of synthesis in the West, the Mediterranean ceased to be the center of a unified civilization. That sea became the border between three separate cultures—the West, Byzantium, and Islam. On the one hand Byzantine power was eliminated in the West and in the Middle East, and the eastern empire became increasingly Greek in character; and on the other hand Islam expanded rapidly. The divisive forces already at work were confirmed in the eighth century by a series of deeply important changes: the succession in 717 of the Isaurian dynasty in Byzantium and in 750 of the 'Abbasid dynasty in Islam confirmed the particular qualities of each empire; in the West, the establishment of the Carolingian dynasty was accompanied by the formation of a papacy oriented towards the Franks rather than towards Constantinople.

The culture of the West did not emerge in a vacuum; though communications in the Mediterranean had deteriorated, they had by no means ceased; and the West was aware of the existence, and constantly exposed to the pressures, of the two other communities with which it shared that corner of the world. Westerners felt this exposure the more because life in both Byzantium and Islam was, until the twelfth or thirteenth century, more comfortable and enlightened. Byzantium and Islam enjoyed a greater continuity with the older Roman and Persian civilizations, which conferred upon them an initial advantage. The West received a series of greater shocks; its focus was removed to the periphery of the old world; and it had to build its civilization anew upon a much less complete foundation. But this "misfortune" made upon its creative energies more demands than were placed on Byzantium and Islam, and after the initial period of inferiority, the West came to outshine its rivals in resourcefulness, creativity, and variety.

This is not to say that western civilization is necessarily "better" than Byzantine or Islamic. A society that can, like the Byzantine, preserve itself for a millennium without many radical upheavals enjoys a stability that may reflect the contentment, rather than the dullness, of its members; it may be our own western values that lead us to make the opposite judgment—that the civilization that raises the more questions and offers the greater variety of answers to human problems is the higher.

THE sources for Byzantine history to the eleventh century are numerous, and many have still not been translated from the Greek. The histories and chronicles of Theophanes, Nicephorus, John Zonaras, Symeon Logothetes, John Scylitzes, and particularly Michael Psellos are superior to most of their counterparts in the West; and these are supplemented by lives of saints and emperors, and by the decisions of councils. The *Book of the Popes* and Bishop Liutprand of Cremona's account of his visit to Constantinople in the tenth century reveal something of the relations between the West and Constantinople. The sources for the history of Islam are, even aside from the language problem, relatively limited compared to those for Byzantium. There is the Qur'ān (Koran) itself, and early collections of traditions (Hadīth) about the Prophet. Then there are the Arab annals and chronicles, and the great history of the fourteenth-century Ibn Khaldûn, as well as scientific writings. For both Byzantium and Islam, these sources are supplemented by legal codes and administrative decrees, literary and artistic monuments, philosophical and theological writings, and coins, seals, and other artifacts.

GIBBON's belief that the history of the Byzantine Empire was uniform and tedious expressed a prejudice that has only recently been dispelled. Far from being stagnant, the East was undergoing a gradual transition, in language, culture, religion, and politics, from "Roman" to "Byzantine." Essentially this transformation was the reassertion of the Greek and Hellenistic backgrounds of the eastern empire, a process that established a Byzantine civilization independent of the West and of the Roman Empire that had given birth to both of them.

Reckoning from the foundation of Constantinople, the continuation of the Roman Empire in the East endured for more than eleven hundred years, six times as long as the independent United States to date. Its sources of internal weakness were relatively few. The extravagance of the Byzantine rulers (if it really existed) probably did not substantially weaken their empire; but there was an economic weakness in the increasing tendency to invest in land rather than in industry and commerce, and the landed feudal magnates, as well as the military and civil aristocracy, caused difficulties. The most deeply felt, and the most frequent, source of internal discord was religious disputes. But with all of these the empire might forever have coped successfully. Its one great weakness was its wealth, which, like that of China, made it a constant lure for invaders from without. No society has been so savagely assaulted by so many foreign enemies over so long a time: Huns, Teutons, Persians, Slavs, Avars, Magyars, Arabs, Bulgars, Lombards, the papacy and its Frankish allies, the Khazars, Patzinaks, Seljuks, Normans, crusaders, Italians, and Ottomans, all hurled themselves at the empire, inhibiting both constructive domestic policy and even consistent attention to any one area of foreign policy. That Byzantium so long endured is a testament to its considerable resources. Besides its material wealth, large population, commercial vigor, and well-trained armies, the empire enjoyed widespread cultural and religious influence. Constantinople became for the Slavs as well as for the Greeks what Rome was for the West.

Not the least of Byzantium's assets was its succession of able rulers, a succession made possible by the salutary innovation of hereditary monarchy. We are so used to looking at hereditary monarchy with the jaundiced eyes of eighteenth-century revolutionaries that we easily overlook its great virtues. The principle of hereditary succession restricts civil wars and succession disputes, and limits both the excessive power of the army and the excessive exercise of venality. Though the Byzantines changed dynasties, occasionally with violence, on eight major occasions, "Byzantine intrigue" was seldom as disruptive and never as frequent as that which contributed so heavily to the downfall of the old Roman Empire.

Justinian and his followers; mosaic from San Vitale Basilica, Ravenna.

In politics, the transformation of the East occurred between the reign of Justinian (527–565) in the sixth century and that of Leo III (717–741) in the eighth. Justinian had still been a Roman, he had thought of himself as ruler both of East and of West, and his great law code and decrees were published in Latin. Certain aspects of the late empire were continued and even exaggerated as the East developed, such as centralized government, heavy taxes, and state regulation of industry and religion. The emperor became increasingly orientalized and autocratic. Augustus had modestly claimed the title of first citizen; his successors on the Bosphorus demanded that their subjects prostrate themselves upon entering into the sacred presence of the emperor. Yet even the most awesome emperors were limited by the army, by the patriarch of Constantinople, by the lawyers, by the mob, and even occasionally by the Senate.

The gradual transformation of Roman into Byzantine began, ironically, with Justinian's attempt to restore the boundaries of the old empire. The treasure he expended in the conquest and maintenance of his vast domains seriously weakened the state and rendered it difficult of defense by his successors. It was the first ruler of a new dynasty, Heraclius (610–641), who achieved a brief revival of waning fortunes. The ancient enemy of the Romans in the East, the Persians, had succeeded in conquering Egypt and Syria, the wealthiest provinces of the empire. Heraclius marshaled an efficient army and, proclaiming a crusade for the recovery of Jerusalem, not only expelled his enemies from the occupied provinces but brought the Sassanid dynasty of Persia to a disastrous end. The prospects of the empire, having eliminated its most dangerous rival, seemed bright; but the year in which Heraclius undertook his crusade against the Persians was the year in which Mohammed fled Mecca for Medina and founded the Moslem state (622). Within decades Heraclius, victor over the Persians, was vanquished by the Arabs, and the provinces regained at the cost of so much blood were lost again at the expense of more. George Ostrogorsky, one of the greatest Byzantine scholars of this century, believed that the reign of Heraclius marked the beginning of the Byzantine as opposed to the eastern Roman Empire. To set such a precise date is probably as futile as choosing a particular moment at which the empire in the West ceased to exist, but by the accession of the Isaurian dynasty in 717 the process of transformation in the East was nearly complete.

In 717 the Arabs were advancing on Constantinople, and the weak emperor Theodosius III panicked and refused to take the measures necessary to defend the city. One of his generals, Leo the Isaurian, an able and vigorous commander from Asia Minor, took matters into his own hands. He crossed the straits and entered the city; Theodosius, less angry than grateful to escape responsibility, abdicated, and the Isaurian was crowned Emperor Leo III by the Patriarch in the Cathedral of Hagia Sophia.

Leo's military vigor and administrative skill restored the confidence that had been seriously diluted by the demoralizing rapidity of the Arab conquests. The Greek army and navy were aided by the secret "Greek fire," a preparation something like napalm, which, sprayed upon the Arab vessels, caused them to burst into flames. Leo was further assisted by the rigors of a hard winter and a plague the following summer, after which the Arabs departed. His successors were able to reoccupy Asia Minor, and it was not until 1453 that the Moslems again threatened the city. The state had been preserved.

But it had also been transformed. The loss to the Arabs of the Semitic eastern provinces, of North Africa, and of Spain, and the decreasing influence of the empire in Italy and the West, confirmed and enhanced the Greek characteristics of the remaining territory. Leo issued a law code (called the *Ecloga*) which contained a summary of Justinian's code in addition to the decrees of later emperors, but all translated into Greek; Greek now became the official administrative and legal language of the land. By introducing Judaeo-Christian humanitarian modifications to the law, Leo's code achieved in the East what would be achieved in the West only during the legal renaissance of the twelfth and thirteenth centuries: the wedding of the Roman conception of rational, natural law with the Christian idea of divinely revealed law.

Leo's religious policy did as much as anything else to set the Greek East apart from the Latin West, for it was he who introduced a policy of Iconoclasm by issuing his decree against images in 725 or 726. His motives have often been debated and remain obscure. The Moslem Caliph Jezid of Baghdad had outlawed images in his own domains in 723; this fact and Leo's birth in Isauria (or in another of the provinces bordering upon Islam) make it probable that he was influenced by Moslem principles, though he could easily have drawn as well upon a tradition of puritanical Iconoclasm in some of the earlier Christian sects. These Christian Iconoclasts observed that the veneration of pictures and statues of Christ, the Virgin, and the saints was often carried to superstitious extremes and tended to obstruct a direct relationship with God; and they remembered the Biblical injunctions against idols. They further asserted that a good life was a better image of God than any picture. Their doctrines are rational and easily comprehended; what was not rational was the vindictive fanaticism with which they argued them. Defenders of images argued that while superstition doubtless did exist, the ordinary veneration of images

Byzantine icon of Christ. As divinity was supposed to be truly present in icons, their style changed little through the centuries.

was not blasphemous, for the images served only as reminders of the spiritual. The majority of the people in the East never embraced Iconoclasm; several patriarchs protested the imperial policy; and the monks, led by the powerful abbey of Studion in Constantinople, opposed it vigorously. Leo's successor Constantine V, fondly nicknamed *Copronymous* ("Excrement") by unsympathetic Byzantine historians, pursued a policy of repression against the iconodules (defenders or images), while the mob, always pleased to kill in the name of Christ, tore a monk to pieces alive for his refusal to conform to the will of the ruling party. Iconoclasm had some muted echoes in the West, but was firmly opposed by the popes. In fact, the popes used the Iconoclast heresy of the emperors as a weapon to secure their religious and political independence of Constantinople, which was one of the most serious consequences of the Isaurians' policy. The widening split between the pope at Rome and the emperor at Constantinople on this and other issues encouraged the development of separate and discrete eastern and western civilizations.

In spite of their folly in pursuing a divisive religious policy, the military and administrative successes of the Iconoclast emperors preserved and revived the strength of the empire and averted another real crisis until the eleventh century. The Amorian and Macedonian dynasties, which succeeded the Isaurian, continued successfully to repulse external enemies, though the militarization and feudalization promoted by the constant threat of war, and the concomitant shortage of money in the imperial treasury, prepared future internal dissensions. The death of the able emperor Basil II in 1025 touched off feudal and military upheavals, and about 1050 the Seljuk Turks arrived in force in the Near East to take advantage of these discords. The decisive victory of the Turks over the Byzantines at Manzikert in 1071 caused the East to call upon the West for military help and inaugurated a wholly new era of East-West relations, that of the Crusades.

THE history of Byzantine culture, like that of the state, reveals a gradual transformation from Roman to Greek. Greek had always been the common spoken language in the East, even during the height of Roman rule, and after the reign of Justinian it came gradually to replace Latin as the language not only of government but of culture as well. The chairs of Latin at the academy in Constantinople were gradually replaced by chairs of Greek, and philosophical, theological, and literary writing was done in Greek. After Justinian closed the ancient secular Academy at Athens in 529, education was placed more and more in the hands of the monks. It was imbued with the eastern monastic hues of Christianity, though it never became the exclusive privilege of the clergy as it did in the West: the tolerance of the Greeks went so far as to permit the education of little girls.

The wealth and commercial activity of the Greeks encouraged the continuation of an urban environment happy both in material luxuries and in cultural productivity, so that in the twelfth century Constantinople ranked with Baghdad and Córdoba as one of the three great centers of culture west of China. The Byzantine world produced a wholly distinctive style of art and architecture, of which the Cathedral of Hagia Sophia in Constantinople and the mosaics of the Church of San Vitale in Ravenna are the most renowned monuments. Like the Roman Christian art from which it developed, Byzantine art is governed by sacred purposes. Sculpture was eschewed as too reminiscent of idols. Painting was almost wholly devoted to the making of icons. The style of the icons changed little, because they were treated as holy objects through which the Divine Spirit passed to believers. It is difficult not to feel, upon entering a richly decorated Byzantine church, some of the awe and majesty that its builders meant to convey. As Yeats expressed it:

> O sages standing in God's holy fire
> As in the gold mosaic of a wall,
> Come from the holy fire, perne in a gyre,
> And be the singing masters of my soul.[1]

Most literature, history, and theology was written in imitation of the old Attic Greek, just as a large part of medieval literature in the West attempted to imitate classical Latin; but there were also good stories, lyrics, and saints' lives written in the living, spoken *koinê* (common tongue).

Westerners have always been inclined to see in Byzantium a certain lack of innovation, a certain stylistic rigidity both in art and in thought. It is true that the Byzantine East never achieved the great cultural variety of the West, but it must be remembered that its history does not extend past the fifteenth century, that very period when the West was enjoying its most brilliant Renaissance. The medieval West before that period enjoyed little, if any, greater cultural variety than the East; if there was any difference at all, the explanation is in the influence in the West of Celtic and Teutonic influences and of the Augustinian view that there is value in observing and investigating the material world, as opposed to the more mystical and other-worldly tendencies of eastern Christianity.

The Eastern Church was characterized by a tendency not

*Divine authority bestowed upon Byzantine rulers: Christ crowning the
Emperor Romanus and his wife Eudocia.*

only to mysticism, but to intricate theological debates. The
virtue, or the vice, of theorizing was even in the ancient world
more common in the speculative East than in the practical
West. Theological disputes did much to weaken Byzantine society, though from the eleventh century they declined, perhaps
from sheer exhaustion, while in the same period religious dissent was rising to a new high in the West. Caesaropapism—
the idea that the emperor has supreme religious authority—is
usually attributed to the Eastern Church. But the ecclesiastical
power of the emperor was limited by the patriarch and other
bishops, by councils, by the monks, and for centuries even by
the pope. And though the kings in the West usually enjoyed
less control over their churches it was seldom for want of trying.

As Byzantine culture and policy became more Greek, it diverged more and more from that of the West. The Teutonic kings had continued to nurture the illusion of the united Roman Empire for centuries after there had ceased to be an emperor at Rome, so that Constantinople was considered the capital both East and West. Justinian had attempted to turn this illusion into a reality; ironically, his ultimate failure, and the unpopularity of the new taxes that Constantinople imposed upon Italy, helped to bring ruin not only to the reality but to the illusion itself. The gradual recession of Byzantine power from Italy in the seventh century produced only the sentiment of joy among the Lombards and among the Roman nobles and the Roman popes, whose pride had been too often injured and whose purses too often invaded not to wish for political independence from Byzantium.

The increasing political disaffection of the West was encouraged by religious differences. The popes had long resented the claims of the patriarchs of Constantinople to equality in rank and dignity, and the two prelates disputed the jurisdiction over several Balkan and Slavic ecclesiastical districts. The popes resented even more the interventions of the emperor. In the first place, they believed that he had no business intruding in ecclesiastical matters. In the second, they observed that his ideas were often "heretical." The successors of Constantine had supported Arianism; later emperors had defended monophysitism and monothelitism. The eighth century brought the innovation of Iconoclasm in the East, which was unacceptable to the West, and the spread of the *Filioque* clause in the West, which was unacceptable to the East.* In addition, numerous diverging practices set the churches apart: the use of Greek in the East and of Latin in the West, the marriage of the eastern clergy and the celibacy of the western, and the Greek habit of closing the doors of the sanctuary during mass. A Christian of the fourth century might have felt at home both in Rome and in Constantinople, but by the ninth or tenth he was likely to feel that the religion of one was foreign to the other.

* The original Nicene Creed, approved at the First Council of Constantinople, affirmed that the Holy Spirit proceeded from the Father; from the sixth century the western Church came gradually to include the doctrine of "double procession" and to affirm that the Holy Spirit proceeds from the Father *and the Son (Filioque).*

When the eighth-century popes procured the disengagement of Italy from the political and spiritual power of Byzantium and turned instead to the Franks, and when Frankish King Pepin turned over the lands he had conquered from the Lombards to the pope rather than to the emperor, political relations cooled still further. The coronation of Charlemagne as emperor in 800 was merely the most dramatic event in the long story: it symbolized the final separation of the West from the eastern empire. Economic and cultural contacts declined, particularly after the Islamic invasions, and in the ninth century the conflict between the popes and the Patriarch Photius frayed ecclesiastical relations even further.

The Great Schism between the churches in 1054 had thus long been in preparation. The degeneracy of the tenth-century papacy aroused contempt in the East, and the efforts of the vigorous popes of the eleventh century to reassert their influence elicited only hostile resistance. In 1043 the proud and opinionated Michael Kerullarios obtained the patriarchate; eager to repudiate the papacy, he incited the mobs of Constantinople to desecrate the Latin churches. Pope Leo IX (1048–1054) attempted to establish better relations with Constantinople, but though he found the emperor willing, the patriarch was recalcitrant. Leo accordingly sent to Constantinople an embassy of legates headed by Humbert of Silva Candida, who was as proud and opinionated as the patriarch. The emperor received the papal legates amicably, but their relations with the patriarch consisted of mutual insults, and at last they went into the Cathedral of Hagia Sophia and laid upon the high altar a bull which excommunicated the patriarch and somewhat tactlessly listed the errors and deviations of the Greek Church. The emperor attempted to calm all parties, but Kerullarios published the contents of the bull to the angry populace, and the legates departed without condescending to discuss matters further. When they returned to Rome, Leo IX was dead, but his successors took the obstinacy of the patriarch quite seriously, as did the patriarch the rudeness of the Romans. The result was a schism that has separated the Roman Catholic and the Eastern Orthodox Churches to this day, though in 1965 Paul VI somewhat belatedly lifted the excommunication of Kerullarios.

The separation of Rome and Constantinople had effects

throughout Europe. If the western countries became Roman Catholic, most of the emerging eastern nations were attracted religiously and culturally to Constantinople. The northern Slavs were converted to the Roman Church, often by German missionaries. The Moravians were converted in the ninth century by Saints Cyril and Methodius, who provided them with a Slavic alphabet (the Cyrillic). Cyril and his brother had originally been sent by Constantinople. Upon their return from the North, however, they were met at Venice by representatives of the pope and enticed to Rome; and the pope obtained the submission of the Moravian church to the western, rather than to the eastern, patriarchate. The southern Slavs, notably the Serbs, Vlachs (Rumanians), and Slavicized Bulgarians, adopted eastern Christianity. The greatest addition to eastern Christendom was Russia, which was converted to Christianity by King Vladimir (ca. 980–1015). The Russian rulers kept relations with Rome open for a while, but they had their seat at Kiev, a wealthy city with close trading relations with Constantinople, and were inevitably drawn into the eastern sphere. The incorporation of Russia into the Eastern Orthodox civilization contributed to the perennial isolation of that country from the West.

THOUGH Islam owed much to Greco-Roman civilization, it was not, like Byzantium or the West, a successor state of the Roman Empire. It was dominated by the Arabs, a people who had for the most part lived beyond the borders and the influence of the empire, and who until the seventh century were wanting in political cohesiveness. The term "Arab" is difficult to define: generally speaking, the Arabs of today are Moslem in religion, Semitic by race, and linguistically united in the use of the Arabic tongue; they retain, as present policies indicate, the memory of the united Arab empire that stretched from Morocco to Iraq. Before the seventh century, the Arabs were limited to the Arabian Peninsula. They were nomadic in habit and animistic in religion, their chief cultic center being the huge black stone at Mecca called the Ka'ba. Each tribe was governed by a sheikh chosen by the elders in accordance with the customs (*Sunna*) of his people. Yet the Arabs had known wealth and sophistication even before Mohammed. The ancient Kingdom of Saba (the Biblical Sheba whose queen visited

Atlantic Ocean

Whitby
York
ANGLO-SAXON KINGDOMS
Canterbury
FRISIA
Elbe
RUSSIA
Kiev
Liège
AUSTRASIA
Aachen
St. Denis
Herstal
Paris
Terry
NEUSTRIA
Tours
BURGUNDY
GAUL
AQUITAINE
MORAVIA
Covadonga
PYRENEES
Aniane
Arles
Venice
Vlachs
Danube
SPAIN
Nursia
Serbs
BULGARIA
Black
Constantinople
Córdoba
Rome
Monte Cassino
Seville
Granada
Naples
GIBRALTAR
Mediterranean
ASIA
ANATOLIA
ISAURIA
Carthage
AFRICA
Athens
Sea
Alexandria
ISLAM
Cairo
EGYPT
Nile

MILES
0   200   400   600   800   1000

Byzantine Empire ca. 700
Western Christendom ca. 700
Islam ca. 700

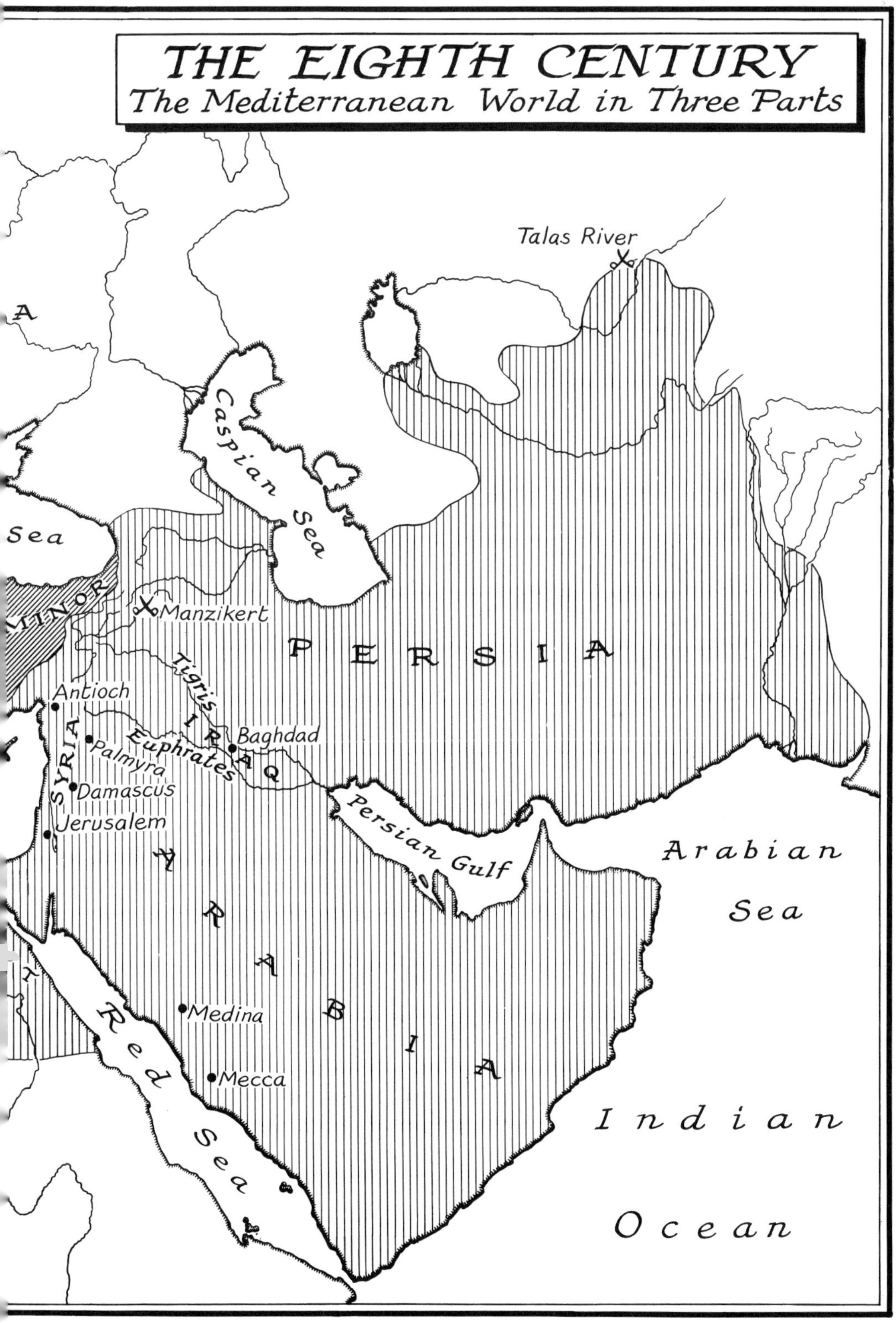

THE EIGHTH CENTURY
The Mediterranean World in Three Parts

Talas River

Caspian Sea

A

Sea

MINOR

Manzikert

PERSIA

Antioch

Tigris

IRAQ

Baghdad

Euphrates

SYRIA

Palmyra

Damascus

Jerusalem

Persian Gulf

Arabian

Sea

ARABIA

Red Sea

Medina

Mecca

Indian

Ocean

Solomon in all his glory), in the southwestern corner of the peninsula, had enjoyed enormous wealth centuries before Christ. In the north, the Arab state of Palmyra flourished under Roman domination. The northern Arab tribes had cultural as well as commercial relations with Romans, Jews, and Christians, and by the time of Mohammed some had been converted to Christianity.

One of the most commercially active tribes were the Quraish of Mecca, among whom Mohammed was born about 570. Mecca was a cosmopolitan trading community, like Tarsus where Saint Paul was born, and young Mohammed had the opportunity to hear many ideas and teachings other than those of his own people. About 610 Mohammed had a call to preach. The Archangel Gabriel, he said, revealed to him the contents of a book whose prototype was in the seventh heaven; and Mohammed in turn revealed the contents of this sacred text, the Qur'ān, in a series of inspired verses. Modern religious scholarship in the West, freed from centuries of ignorant prejudice against Islam, recognizes the sincerity of Mohammed and his place in the succession of inspired prophets. Like the ancient poets, like Ezekiel, and like Paul, Mohammed was filled with a spirit that impelled him to speak.

The revelation of the Qur'ān was not agreeable to the leaders of the Quraish, who were devoted to the established paganism, and in 622 Mohammed was obliged to flee Mecca to the more receptive city of Medina. From the year of this journey, known as the Hijra, the Moslem calendar is dated. It is difficult for the westerner to appreciate in translation the beauty and profundity of the Qur'ān; even in the original versions the chapters were disarranged and disconnected by the mistakes of early Arab scribes. These misunderstandings, added to simple ignorance and prejudice, caused medieval Christians to consider Mohammed a Christian heretic, an ignorant pagan, or even an evil sorcerer.

In reality the religion of Islam is more simple and direct, if less sophisticated, than Christianity. More Semitic and less Hellenized than that religion, it is more ethical and less theological. The center of its teaching is an uncompromising monotheism that shunned the Christian Trinity. This monotheism was derived in part from Mohammed's familiarity with Judaeo-Christian writings; in part it was a refinement of the monotheism that was latent in Arab, as it is in most, animism. In Mohammed's revelation, the one God, Allah, is the creator of the universe and of man. Allah has complete control over the world of his creation and leaves no room whatever for human freedom. Allah ordains the belief and disbelief of individuals in ways and for reasons inscrutable to man. Mohammed accordingly taught submission (*Islam*) to the will of Allah; the Moslem ("one who submits") must yield to Allah and to Mohammed's revelation of Allah: "Whoso believe, and do things that are right, and believe in what hath been sent down to MUHAMMAD—for it is the truth from their Lord—their sins will He cancel, and dispose their hearts aright"[2].

This submission to Allah is expressed by fulfillment of the moral precepts revealed by the Prophet. The ethic of the Qur'ān is social and rational, demanding benevolence, social responsibility, and cooperation for the love of Allah. It was an ethic of moderation, rather than of extreme asceticism, more permissive than Christianity in sexual matters, and stricter in others, such as fasting and abstention from alcohol. The Five Pillars of Faith as established by Moslem theologians are (1) prayer five times a day and public prayer at the mosque on Fridays, (2) a verbal profession of faith, (3) almsgiving, (4) pilgrimage, particularly to the great stone Ka'ba at Mecca, which Mohammed declared to have been erected by Abraham, (5) the yearly fast of Ramadan, lasting a month; and some theologians added a sixth principle, that of *jihâd*, or holy war. Islam respected the warrior in particular and the male in general, its greatest moral weakness being the very inferior position allotted to women in both this world and the next. In this life the woman is to submit to her husband as her husband submits to Allah, and as many as four wives were allowed Moslems who could afford them. In the next life, the wife of a believer followed him to paradise, but the joys of the Moslem heaven must have appealed to men more than to any normal woman, for they include (Sura 37) not only banquets, gardens, and limpid drinks, but the "large-eyed ones with modest refraining glances, fair like the sheltered egg." It was said that women regained their comely, virginal forms in heaven, the better to please their masculine partners.

The determinism of Islam had perhaps more effect upon the lives of Moslems than any other of their principles. Determinism may enervate or stimulate. There is an apocryphal story of a Turkish admiral who, upon the approach of the Venetian fleet, refused to prepare for action on the grounds that Allah would bring the foreordained victory or defeat whether or not the Turkish ships gave battle. A more common response was the superhuman vigor displayed by the Moslem warrior endowed with the absolute confidence that Allah was fighting on his side.

It was this vigor that brought Mohammed his success. His religion was simple; it expressed the courage, dignity, and generosity of his people; and by declaring him the successor of Moses and Jesus, it gave him a place in an already established higher religious tradition. Mohammed was able before his death in 632 to achieve the conquest of Mecca and the Arabian Peninsula.

THE success of Islam after the Prophet's death was even more phenomenal. By 640 the Moslems had conquered Syria and by 642 they had subdued Egypt. Upon the fall of Alexandria its conqueror wrote the Caliph Omar: "I have captured a city from the description of which I shall refrain. Suffice it to say that I have seized therein 4000 villas with 4000 baths, 40,000 poll-tax paying Jews and four hundred places of entertainment for the royalty."[3] If the Byzantine crown thus lost one of its most precious jewels, its ancient rival of Persia was completely cast down, that whole country being annexed to Islam by 652. Between 670 and 677 the Moslems were at the gates of Constantinople. There they met their first significant repulse, but if they were denied entrance to Europe in the East, they were more successful in the West. By 698 Carthage and the Province of Africa had fallen, and in 711 the Arab chieftain Tarik crossed the straits that henceforth were to bear his name [Gibraltar: Gebel-al-Tarik, "the Rock of Tarik"]. By 713 the Visigothic Kingdom of Spain was conquered, and in 733 the Moslems confronted the Frankish chieftain Charles Martel at the Battle of Tours (Poitiers) in central Gaul. Charles turned them

Mohammed declares Ali his successor.

back, as did Leo the Isaurian in their second attempt upon Constantinople in 717–718. By the mid-eighth century the tide of conquest began slightly to turn, and for centuries thereafter, with only minor fluctuations, the border between Christianity and Islam was stabilized in Asia Minor in the East and just south of the Pyrenees in the West. Meanwhile the Battle of the Talas River in 751 secured Central Asia for Islam and opened the way for its penetration of India and eventually Southeast Asia.

No academic theories suffice to explain this tornado sweep of a people who had heretofore been almost entirely without influence, but some suggestions are permitted. A perennial infiltration by the Arabic tribes into fertile lands had begun long before Islam. In part the expansion of Islam was a continuation of this pattern, and in part it was owing to the skill and courage of the Arab warriors. The Arabs quickly learned the administrative and cultural secrets of the ancient Persian civilization, and, once Islam absorbed Persia, it succeeded to the territory and wealth of the venerable and powerful Sassanid monarchy that Heraclius had destroyed in the 620s. Arabic, previously an obscure Semitic tongue, was made a vehicle of beauty and culture by the Qur'ān; and it now became as great a unifying element in Islam as Latin had once been in the Roman Empire.

In addition to these assets, the Moslems had in the seventh and eighth centuries the additional and decisive advantage of the "fullness of time." Their rivals were exhausted and divided at just the moment that they themselves could marshal their greatest vigor: Byzantium and Persia had worn each other out through constant warfare. Much of the Semitic population of Syria and Egypt was sympathetic to the Semitic Arabs. Many Egyptians and Syrians were Monophysite or Nestorian Christians and felt the weight of official Byzantine religious intolerance as well as that of repressive taxes, so that the Arabs, with their leniency toward non-Moslems, appeared less as conquerors than as liberators.

It was this leniency, this adaptability, on the part of the Arabs which was the greatest force in permitting them to gain and retain their vast provinces. Like the successful Romans before them, they permitted the continuation of local customs, reformed taxation and administration, and permitted Christians and Jews, for the consideration of a not insupportable surtax, to retain their religion and their professions as well. Rather than being faced with an intolerable choice between apostasy and persecution, a choice that would certainly have provoked resistance and revolt, the citizens of Roman Syria and Africa were permitted to compromise with Islam without compromising their consciences. They gradually came to accept the language, the customs, and at last even the religion, of the Arabs, and it requires an effort of imagination today to remember that Tunisia, Egypt, and Syria were once the centers of Greco-Roman Christianity or that Egyptian Alexandria' and Tunisian Carthage were the homes of Saints Clement and Augustine. Yet, tolerant as Islam initially was, it is undeniable that fervent devotion to the religion of the Prophet was an important element in its success. Mohammed replaced the narrow tribal loyalties of the pagan Arabs by the broad religious bonds of the *Umma,* a conception of legal, political, and institutional unity embracing all Islam, and this permitted the maintenance of unity in an empire larger than that governed by Trajan or Hadrian. The caliphs, the successors of Mohammed, combined the functions of the Christian pope with those of the Christian emperor and functioned as the supreme secular and religious authority in Islam.

In 660 the Umayyad dynasty obtained the caliphate, which they ruled, from Damascus, until 750. The Umayyads, while constructing an efficient state, discriminated not only against the Dhimmis (the Jewish and Christian subjects of Islam) but even against the Mawalī, Moslems who were not Arab by nationality. The Mawalī, many of whom were wealthy merchants and artisans, and, especially in Persia, men of great learning and culture, dominated the wealthy cities, which resented the rule of the pastoral Arabs. In 750, the 'Abbasids rallied the Mawalī and discontented elements among the Arabs, replaced the Umayyads, and moved the capital from Damascus to Baghdad in the old Persian area of Mesopotamia. The 'Abbasid dynasty was to transform and consolidate Islam. The remnant of the Umayyads, fleeing to Spain, established their power there at Córdoba, which became an artistic and cultural center comparable only to Baghdad itself. Constantine's feat of building himself a new capital was surpassed by that of the Caliph al-Mansur, who in 762 ordered Baghdad or, as it was called, Dar-al-Salaam, the Abode of Peace, raised from the sand and dust at a point where the Tigris and Euphrates drew close together. In the land of ancient Babylon and Nineveh now arose a new great city, built by a hundred thousand workmen. At its center was a great square around a huge domed mosque; its four great gates stood at the four cardinal points of the compass; and its roads and caravan routes linked Europe and Africa with Persia, India, and China.

Adopting Persian administrative patterns and Persian absolutism (the caliph became the "Deputy of God"), the 'Abbasids insured the permanence of Arab rule by completing the transition from a purely Arabic empire to a cosmopolitan Moslem one. As the Greeks under Alexander the Great conquered by ceasing to be wholly Greek, the Arabs ruled by ceasing to be wholly Arab. Baghdad's libraries, bookstores, and academies became the clearing houses of Greek, Babylonian, Indian, and Persian learning. Books from all these tongues were translated into the Arabic, and the scholars of Baghdad, armed with all the wisdom of the ancients, created a culture which, if largely derivative, was nonetheless brilliant. The architecture of 'Abbasid Baghdad was reportedly magnificent, but it was destroyed in the Mongol invasion of the thirteenth century; the most impressive relics of the great age of Islam are in Spain: the mosque (now the cathedral) at Córdoba, the Alhambra at Granada, and the Alcazar at Seville. A century of translation (750–850) of Greek scientific materials was followed by centuries of activity in which Arab astronomers, mathematicians, and physicians surpassed the achievements of the ancients. By the eleventh century, when ibn-Sina (Avicenna) wrote his *Book of Healing,* the Moslems knew so much of drugs, hygiene, and hospitals, that they were frankly incredulous of the crude practices of European physicians. The Arabic adaptation of Indian numerals and invention of the zero made modern arithmetic and mathematics possible. Al-Khuwārizmi and Umar al-Khaiyam (better known in the West for his poetic works) developed algebra. The Arabic geographer al-Idrīsi produced a world atlas of seventy detailed maps. The Arabic influence upon our culture and economy is barely suggested by the many loan-words taken from their language, among them alcohol, algebra, alkali, alchemy, almanac, admiral, chemistry, zero, cotton, sugar, lemon, cheque, and traffic.

The wealth and trade of the 'Abbasid empire were enormous, and it was 'Abbasid traders who invented banking and credit, skills that could be borrowed by the West at the time of the Crusades.

The brilliance of Moslem culture seems to have ebbed by the thirteenth century. Its superiority had derived in great part from its absorption of the learning of the ancients; now this learning was available elsewhere, while few new works were

Interior of the Mosque at Córdoba.

translated into Arabic. Islamic culture became stagnant and has generally remained so till the present, while from the twelfth century the Christian West made great advances. In part the decline was the result of the deteriorating political and religious unity of Islam. The first political schism in Islam—the foundation of the Umayyad state in Spain—was followed by the rise of the Fatimids in Egypt in the early tenth century, the establishment of petty principalities in Central Asia and in Spain, and then the assaults of the Seljuk Turks and the Mongols, Ural-Altaic invasions that caused even more damage to Islam than to Christendom. Religious divisions, which had begun even in the seventh century, were encouraged by political divisions and increased in the ninth and tenth. The material, as well as the cultural, preeminence of Islam began to pass as early as the time of the Crusades.

RELATIONS between Islam and Christendom were always conditioned by the initial sweep of the Moslem sword. Neither Byzantium nor the West soon forgot the loss of the African and Asian provinces that contained the wealthiest cities and the oldest cultural centers of the old empire, three out of the five patriarchal sees (Alexandria, Antioch, and Jerusalem), and the very land where Christ had taught and died. The Christian resentment of this loss and desire to make it good by reconquest were persistent. The Moslems were not initially hostile to either Christians or Jews as long as they did not offer military resistance, for they regarded them as Hanif (monotheists) and "People of the Book." The Qur'ān declares in Sura 2: "To Moses gave we 'the Book,' and we raised up apostles after him; and to Jesus, son of Mary, gave we clear proofs (of his mission), and strengthened him by the divine spirit." Moslem tradition holds that Jesus, upon his second coming, will call the faithful to prayer from the minaret of the mosque at Damascus. Though Christianity and Judaism largely disappeared in North Africa, they both persisted in Spain, where the Jewish community was particularly vigorous and the Christian Church survived, though in isolation, until the *Reconquista*. The Battle of Covadonga in 718, only five years after the Moslem conquest, was the first step of the process of the reconquest that ended with the final expulsion of the Moors by Ferdinand and Isabella in 1492 and that set a precedent for the Crusades of the eleventh and later centuries.

Conditioned by resentment, Christian attitudes towards the Moslems were always much more hostile. Their attacks upon Mohammed as a false prophet were supplemented by exaggerations of the sexual liberties permitted by the Qur'ān; Dante's *Divine Comedy*, that great *summa* of medieval attitudes, placed Mohammed in hell, his body split to the waist to represent his role as the author of schisms. Until the nineteenth century Islam always was more of a threat to both eastern and western Europe than the other way round: the Moslems pounded at the gates of Constantinople, penetrated Gaul, and ravaged the coasts of Italy, but even during the Crusades the Christians never menaced Baghdad, and their assaults upon Egypt were impotent and futile. Fear was thus added to the resentment of the Christians, and it is fair to say that not until the present century was there a beginning of better understanding on the part of Christians; but now the Moslems, themselves recently the victims of European colonialism, are less responsive to the establishment of amity.

Direct relations between Moslem and western powers before the Crusades were very rare. Harun-al-Raschid of Baghdad sent an embassy to Charlemagne (and the gift of an elephant), in the hope of cementing an alliance against Umayyad Spain, but relations ended almost as soon as they had begun. From the time of the Crusades, contacts, though seldom friendly, were established in southern Italy as well as the Levant; the Normans in Sicily learned much from Arab administrative methods; and in the twelfth and thirteenth centuries Moslem writers like Avicenna and Averroes had an immense influence upon Christian theology. Until that time the West was only threatened, never instructed, by its Islamic neighbor.

In the eighth and following centuries, then, the Mediterranean world was divided into three parts. Though each was to affect the others, each was isolated enough to develop its own identity. This was true of Byzantium under the Isaurians, of Islam under the 'Abbasids, and of the West under the combined aegis of the popes and the Frankish monarchy.

NOTES

[1] W. B. Yeats, *Sailing to Byzantium*, 1928, 1956, Macmillan, New York. (Reprinted with permission of the publisher.)
[2] Qur'ān, Sura 47.
[3] Quoted by A. A. Vasiliev, *History of the Byzantine Empire 324–1453*, 3d ed. (Madison, 1961), pp. 211–212.

Chapter Seven

THE FORMATION OF THE
EUROPEAN SYNTHESIS

THE elements of the new civilization, Judaeo-Christian, Greco-Roman, Celtic, and Teutonic, were assembled in the fifth and sixth centuries. The process of synthesis was completed in the eighth; the result was the formation of a new, western civilization distinct from both its Greco-Roman antecedents and its Eastern Orthodox contemporary.

At the beginning of the eighth century western political power was still fragmented. The Franks and Anglo-Saxons were disunited, the Visigoths independent in Spain, Italy torn and divided among Byzantium, the Lombards, and the papacy; much of Germany was not as yet even converted to Christianity. Split by heresies, beset by the ignorance and superstitious practices of the only partially converted heathen, divided by differences of custom, the Church lacked a strong and universally recognized authority. The papacy had yet to achieve its independence of Byzantium, and it had yet to unify the Church and provide a center of loyalties. The ideal of a united Christian society was preserved, but throughout most of the West only the vaguest lip service was rendered to the emperor at Constantinople, and there was no independent imperial authority in the West. Localities had become politically and economically isolated. Everywhere laws, customs, traditions, and tongues were divergent. Where Byzantium had its center in Constantinople and Islam its center in Baghdad, western Europe at the beginning of the eighth century still had no recognized center or recognizable identity.

By the end of the eighth century a center for the new

civilization had been established, though less by the extension of unity from the centers of civilization and power than by a general centripetal tendency on the part of peripheral elements. The centers to which authority and power were drawn were the papacy, which was the heir of Saint Peter's apostolic powers and of the ancient capital of the Roman Empire, and the Frankish monarchy, which enjoyed, once its unity was established, the resources of military and governmental skill and of wealth. In the meanwhile, the competitors of the popes and the Franks were being slowly eliminated. By the eighth century most of the Arians in the West had been converted to Catholicism and the Irish Church persuaded to adopt the practices of Rome. The decline of Byzantine power in the West in the seventh and eighth centuries, while disrupting the unity of the Mediterranean world, permitted the West to find an identity of its own by forming and developing its own institutions. The conquests of the Ostrogoths and Vandals by the Byzantines, the Visigoths by the Arabs, and the Burgundians and Lombards by the Franks reduced the number of competing peoples, and the repulse of Islam by the Franks meant there would be no new, indigestible element to swallow. In the eighth century, the remaining western pagans were converted, the authority of the papacy grew, and a common culture was formed. Largely through the efforts of Anglo-Saxon missionaries, the papacy and the Frankish monarchy were brought into an alliance which became the axis upon which Western unity could be posited. The culmination of the process occurred exactly one week before the end of the century, on Christmas Day 800, when the Christian pope placed the imperial diadem of the Roman Empire upon the brow of the Teutonic ruler of the Franks, Lombards, and Burgundians.

THE sources remain sparse. The *Book of the Popes* begins to be reliable in the eighth century; and there are the monastic rules and lives of the saints, like Gregory the Great's *Life of Saint Benedict* and Jonas' *Life of Saint Columban*. There is an increasing number of chronicles, and two varieties of local histories, the monastic annals and the *Gesta* ("Deeds"), like Paul the Deacon's *Deeds of the Bishops of Metz,* begin. There are literary and philosophical writings; there are many useful letters, particularly those of Gregory the Great and Saint Boniface. There are the usual ecclesiastical documents and one unusual forgery, the "Donation of Constantine." Secular documents include law codes, diplomas (charters consisting of grants by kings to churches or individuals), and capitularies (ordinances or "legislation").

THE results of synthesis varied among the peoples of the West. The Ostrogothic kings had attempted to build a society in which Roman and Teutonic pursued parallel but independent courses. The Visigoths resisted any synthesis for a long while and then, just as they were on the verge of achieving a viable one, were conquered by the Moslems. Of the Teutonic kingdoms, that of the Franks achieved the best synthesis, particularly in Gaul, where the entity known as France was emerging from the fusion of Frankish and Gallo-Roman elements. The Church began to combine its divergent elements, largely through the efforts of monks, missionaries, and the papacy.

IN Rome the Ostrogoths, under King Theoderic, adopted a policy called *civilitas,* which aimed neither at the destruction of Roman culture nor at synthesis but consisted of an effort to encourage, without uniting, the best virtues of both Roman and Goth. The fiction that the Roman Empire was still intact and that they were a part of it was maintained. Culture and commerce were left in the hands of the Romans, for even the king of the Goths was illiterate and had laboriously to trace his approval of documents through a golden stencil. As a consul of the Roman Empire, Theoderic "kept the barbarians out of Italy," used Romans like Cassiodorus and Boëthius in his administration, and allowed only Romans to hold the ancient dignities of senator, praetor, and the other old public offices. "Our care," said Theoderic to the Senate of Rome, "is for the whole Republic, in which, by the favour of God, we are striving to bring back all things to their former state; but especially for the City of Rome." Theoderic supported the games, rebuilt fallen monuments, repaired the city walls, and established the rule of Roman law for his Roman subjects.

Theoderic ruled over the Gothic portion of his subjects with the old, unwritten Teutonic law and left the army in their hands. When Roman and Goth came into conflict, the conflict

A coin of Theoderic the Great.

was usually resolved in favor of the latter. When both Goths and Romans were involved in legal disputes, a Gothic count passed final judgment. The religion of the Goths was Arian, and though it was Theoderic's professed policy to give the Catholics equal protection, his spirit was never ecumenical. His intolerance increased with age and at last brought him into an open conflict with the Catholic hierarchy, during which he flung Pope John I (523–526) into a Gothic cell to die. Theoderic was consul of the Romans and king of the Goths, but the functions were never united. The two nations prospered under his rule in an often peaceful but always separate existence. The result was that the Roman subjects of the Goths greeted Justinian's armies as their countrymen, and the Gothic kingdom was extinguished (553). The policy of *civilitas,* useful in its hour, left no permanent Gothic impression upon Italy.

THE Ostrogoths had less than a century of rule; their Visigothic cousins enjoyed nearly three. In Visigothic Spain a policy of cooperation similar to that of *civilitas* gradually yielded to synthesis. King Athaulf (d. 414) toyed with the idea of supplementing *Romania* by *Gothia,* then gave it up on the grounds that the Goths were too unruly and decided instead to "restore the Roman name." Initially, the hostility between invaders and invaded, between Arians and Roman Catholics, was supplemented by a deliberate policy of the Visigothic kings to maintain a distance between the two peoples. In 506 Alaric II issued the *Breviarium,* derived from Roman law but with modifications appropriate to the Spanish situation; but this law Alaric applied only to his Roman, not to his Gothic, subjects.

In the seventh century synthesis and assimilation began to occur. The dialect of Latin that would develop into Spanish became the common language; Catholicism had replaced Arianism as the official religion of the Goths when King Recared (586–601) was converted; intermarriage between the two peoples was permitted; and King Receswinth issued a *Liber Judiciorum* which codified Gothic law under Roman influence. A viable, synthetic culture at least the equal of that of the Franks might have been achieved in Visigothic Spain. But the persistence of internal dissensions, first between Arians and Catholics, then between pro-clerical and anti-clerical parties, made the kingdom an easy prey for the conquering Arab armies of 711–713. Nevertheless, even their inchoate synthesis ensured the persistence of Visigothic influence in the Spanish Church and in Spanish laws and government long after the fall of the Visigothic state. Historians still debate how much the institutions of the emerging Spanish kingdoms of the later Middle Ages owed to Visigothic precedents.

It was in the Kingdom of the Franks that the widest and most perfect synthesis was achieved. This was in part owing to the geographical extent of the Frankish state, which at its broadest bordered upon the Baltic as well as upon the Mediterranean and the Adriatic. It was also owing to the labors of the Irish and Anglo-Saxon missionaries.

The Merovingian kingdoms after the time of Clovis did not on the surface show encouraging signs of order, let alone synthesis. Shattering civil wars and blood feuds produced an anarchy which neither a divided and often impotent monarchy nor a yet undeveloped feudal system could repress. The Frankish practice of dividing the kingdom among all the sons of the dying monarch was the occasion of much disruption. The broad territories ruled by the Frankish kings were occupied by diverse peoples often hostile to one another: the Burgundians, the Aquitanians of southwestern Gaul, the Austrasian (Eastern) Franks in what is now Germany, and the Neustrian (New territory) Franks in what is now northern France. Economic and political dislocation and isolation were producing even smaller divisions.

A story told to a Frankish King (Theoderic) by Bishop Leudegasius of Mainz illustrates the isolation of men in such an atomized society: "There is a countryman's tale," said the bishop, "that tells how a wolf went up into the hills with her cubs, and when they had started to hunt she called them round her and said: 'As far as your eyes can see, and in whatever direction, you have no friends, except a few of your own kind.'"[1] Even allowing for the exaggeration of the chroniclers, the era was brutal. At a battle in which two Merovingian kings met for a brotherly passage of arms, "the carnage on both sides was such that in the fighting line there was no room for the slain to fall down. They stood upright in their ranks, corpse supporting corpse, as if they still lived . . . . The whole countryside was strewn with their bodies."[2]

Yet in the midst of this futile anarchy preparations for creative synthesis were being made. Roman law prevailed in southern Gaul, while in the latter years of Clovis (481–511) the Teutonic Salic law was already being codified by Roman lawyers in the Latin language, and the law, if fundamentally Germanic, showed modifications by Gallo-Roman legal practices. For example, primitive Teutonic law was purely customary and traditional: things were done because they had always been done. Under the influence of Roman legal theory, Teutonic law began to show signs of jurisprudence (the philosophy and theory of law) in an examination and adjustment of the laws in conformity to the principles of natural law and Christian law. In the course of the sixth century, legal distinctions between the Franks and Gallo-Romans disappeared, and, rather than separate codes governing each, one law ran for all.

Assimilation, rather than synthesis, was the rule in language. The Teutonic tongue prevailed in areas beyond the limits of the old empire or within those limits wherever Frankish settlement was particularly thick. Southward and westward the Gallo-Roman tongue, by the end of the sixth century beginning to evolve into French, prevailed. The line between the two areas was fixed in the eighth century almost where it is today. In government and Church, however, Latin was adopted as the official language on both sides of the line. By the eighth century, then, most of the distinctions between Gallo-Roman and Frank were removed.

In the meanwhile, the Merovingian monarchy was declining. With the exception of a very few able kings like Dagobert I (629–639), the Merovingians became *rois fainéants,* drawn from one part of their domains to another in their sacred ox-carts, their heads crowned with the long and flowing locks that were the badge of their rank and their virility. The increasing weakness of these long-haired kings was matched by the increasing effectiveness of their chief advisers, the Carolingian *maiores domus.* These "chief officers of the household," having established their control over the king's private affairs, extended it to the treasury and the public lands, and eventually all the affairs of state, thereby becoming more chief ministers than simple "mayors of the palace," a term that conveys little to the modern ear.

The change from Merovingian to Carolingian dynasty in shifting Frankish attention northward was not as important as used to be thought. Though the Carolingians moved their capital from Neustrian Paris to Austrasian Aachen, they retained an interest both in Paris and in the Mediterranean, while most of the weaknesses of the Merovingian state—its divisions, decentralization, feuds, and lack of trained leaders—persisted into Carolingian times. The Carolingians were more powerful and effective than their predecessors, but that they failed to make the institutional changes necessary to render their gains permanent is witnessed by the rapid decline of their own house in the ninth century.

In the beginning, however, the Carolingians showed vigor and skill. They arose in Austrasia from a union of the son of the powerful bishop of Metz with the daughter of Pepin of Landen (Pepin I), the chief minister of the Merovingian King Dagobert. From the death of Dagobert, Pepin and his family effectively controlled Austrasia. The fruit of the union of the family of Pepin with that of the bishop was a son called Pepin II or Pepin of Herstal, from his estate in Austrasia.

Pepin II extended the power of the Carolingians by defeating the chief minister of Neustria at the Battle of Tertry in 687. This great step toward the unification of the Franks led to the even greater successes of Pepin's illegitimate but illustrious son, Charles Martel (the Hammer). Charles succeeded his father as chief minister of Neustria and Austrasia and added to these dominions Burgundy and Aquitaine, repelling the Saracens at

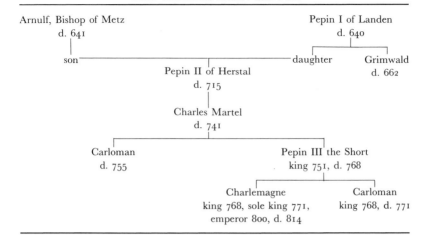

Arnulf, Bishop of Metz
d. 641

Pepin I of Landen
d. 640

son

daughter

Grimwald
d. 662

Pepin II of Herstal
d. 715

Charles Martel
d. 741

Carloman
d. 755

Pepin III the Short
king 751, d. 768

Charlemagne
king 768, sole king 771,
emperor 800, d. 814

Carloman
king 768, d. 771

the Battle of Tours in 733 and later attacking their strongholds on what is now the Riviera. It is at least possible that the Saracens would have been able to complete their conquest of western Europe had they not been opposed by the Carolingian power.

At about this time the Moslems introduced the stirrup into the West and reintroduced effective cavalry. Some historians argue that by so doing the Arabs helped to cause a technological and social revolution. The Franks and the Teutons had previously preferred to fight as infantrymen. The horses of the Germans were small, and without stirrups it was difficult to retain one's balance in the midst of a battle. Now the fleeter and larger Arabian stock was introduced to make the western horse more effective, and the stirrup (which seems to have come to the Moslems from the Far East) made it possible to keep one's seat better as well as to use the lance. With lance thrust forward, the body lined up with that of the horse, and the feet braced in the stirrups, the cavalryman became a formidable soldier and was now preferred by the kings to infantry. But only men of a certain wealth could afford the horse and weapons required, as well as the heavier armor now needed for protection. Hence the old host of Frankish freemen serving as infantry was gradually supplemented and then largely replaced by an elite force of cavalry, whose position was further enhanced by the gratitude and rewards of the kings. Society was now divided between the man who could afford a horse (a knight, in French *chevalier:* "horseman" and in German *Ritter:* "rider") and the man who could not. The former became the feudal nobleman of the new Europe and the latter the commoner.

Charles Martel's military campaigns obliged him to promote the growth of this aristocracy by rewarding his knights in some way. Money to pay a professional army was lacking, and the free and warlike Franks would in any event have sneered at the idea of salaried troops. Charles had to rely upon free warriors, and to pay them with grants of land. The result was his confiscation of some of the vast properties of the Church, which under ecclesiastical administration supplied no money for the minister's coffers and no men for his armies.

The confiscation of Church property was a military necessity and did not prevent Charles Martel from endowing monasteries, supporting missionaries, and in other ways comporting himself as a Christian ruler so long as it was to his advantage. His sons, Pepin III and Carloman, had an even closer relationship with the Church. Charles Martel died in 741, and in accordance with the Frankish custom that bound the chief ministers as well as the kings and private landholders, his domains were divided between his two sons. They ruled with unusual fraternal cooperation for nine years, after which Carloman quite voluntarily abdicated and withdrew into a monastery, leaving Pepin chief minister for the whole kingdom. Pepin's vigorous policies in driving the Saracens from Provence and mounting a successful invasion of Lombard Italy were matched by his equally vigorous support of the Church, which gained him, in 750, ecclesiastical approval of his assumption of the title of king. Having secured Pope Zachary's approval, he was crowned by the Frankish bishops at Soissons in 751. The event was accompanied by the tonsuring of the last Merovingian king, who was sent—in his case unwillingly —to retirement in a monastery.

The Carolingians had long been kings in fact; the Merovingians could offer no effective opposition; yet the coronation was noteworthy. Though the idea that the ruling family were descendants of the gods had been discouraged by the reception of Christianity, the Merovingians were still considered to have a supernatural right to rule that was symbolized by their long hair. Pepin therefore took pains to gain Divine favor, or its appearance, not only by obtaining the approval of the pope and the bishops, but by causing himself to be anointed at Saint Denis in 754 by Pope Stephen III, as Solomon had been anointed king over Israel by Zadok the Priest and Nathan the Prophet. This anointing, an innovation in Europe deliberately derived from the Biblical ceremony, gave the Carolingian house the supernatural aura it required and set the precedent for the imperial coronation of Charlemagne in 800.

The synthesis of cultures that had begun in Merovingian Gaul was consummated under the Carolingians by their close association with the papacy and the Church. The Carolingians always retained a firm control over the Church in their own realm, but it remained Latin in its language and increasingly Roman in its liturgy. Dominated by Benedictine monasticism, nurtured by the missionaries, fostered by the papacy, the Frankish Church was attentive, if not uniformly obedient, to the papal will. The Frankish wedding of Gallo-Roman with Teutonic culture performed at the altar of the Roman Church at last provided western civilization with a focus.

THE Church itself was given a badly needed focus by the monasteries, the missionaries, and the papacy.

In the sixth and seventh centuries in the West monasticism enjoyed an enormous growth, during which the number of houses and monks increased by as much as six times. This phenomenal growth was owing partly to the skill and devotion of monasticism's founders, and partly to its function as one of the few institutions in the transition period that offered peace to the people and the advantages of good organization to the rulers. The monks gave alms to the poor, cared for widows and orphans, and provided medical care when these services were otherwise unavailable. As the old Roman schools disappeared, monastic schools became virtually the only ones in Europe; and while the papacy relied upon the monks to spread the teachings of the Church, the monarchs relied upon them to train administrators.

But monasticism could not fulfill its potential as a center of synthesis as long as it was itself divided. Several different varieties of monasticism appeared in the West in the fifth and sixth centuries. Rules were established by Cassian, Caesarius of

Arles, and Cassiodorus. The strict, ascetic Rule of the Irish Saint Columbanus prevailed, through the labors of Irish missionaries, in vast numbers of monastic houses all over Europe.

The Rule that enjoyed the most permanent success was that of Saint Benedict of Nursia (ca. 480–543). A wealthy young man, Benedict abandoned family and fortune to become a hermit. The fame of his sanctity attracted many followers, and at last the saint went with a few disciples to form a community on the hill of Monte Cassino, on the road between Rome and Naples.

For this community he wrote a Rule whose purpose was to avert the opposite dangers of laxity and exaggerated asceticism. Some of the more educated monks were priests; but in the beginning the lay brothers, who were not in holy orders, were in the majority. The monks as a whole were known as *regular* clergy (because they followed a rule, *regula*) as opposed to the nonmonastic clergy, which was called *secular* (because its task lay in working in the world). The Rule enjoined the three traditional monastic observations. The first, chastity, was directed against the lusts that most often divert younger men from attention to God; the second, poverty, was aimed at curbing the desires for material security that beset older men; and the third, obedience, was directed at the root of all sin, which is pride, the assertion of the self against God. The abbot [*abbas,* from Aramaic *abba:* "father"] had, as the symbol of the authority of God, almost complete power over his monks. He was expected to rule with justice and moderation, but compliance even to unreasonable orders on his part was enjoined as part of the mortification of pride. "Let no one in the monastery," says the Rule, "follow his own inclinations, and let no one boldly presume to dispute with his abbot, whether within or without the monastery." Those who found the monastic life too rigorous were permitted to abandon it, but as long as they professed it they were obliged to follow the Rule.

To aid the spirit in its struggle to be free of worldly cares, the monks' food was simple and spare, their clothing uniform and rough, their beds simple and usually set together, as was the medieval style, in a dormitory. "And these beds are frequently to be searched by the abbot for private property. And, if anything is found belonging to anyone which he did not receive from the abbot, he shall be subjected to the most extreme discipline." Yet the purpose of these rigors was a positive wish to free the spirit, not a fanatical desire to punish the body, and Benedict insisted that "all things be done with moderation . . . on account of the fainthearted . . . . Indeed we read that wine is not suitable for monks at all. But because, in our day, it is not possible to persuade the monks of this, let us agree at least to the fact that we should not drink to excess, but sparingly."[3]

The purpose of the monastic community was the worship of God. Accordingly, Benedict ordered his community so that prayer was its first duty. Private prayer and devotions were continuous; indeed every human action, performed devoutly, rendered praise to the Lord. The center of monastic life, however, was the *Office,* the assembling of the community in the chapel every three hours for the recitation and singing of prayers and hymns.

Second in importance to prayer itself Saint Benedict considered, was manual labor, to which the monks devoted six hours a day. The purpose of manual labor, aside from the principle that "to work is to pray," was to teach the monks humility, to give them exercise, and to provide for the economic needs of the self-sufficient monastery: the monks grew and prepared their own food, made their own clothes, constructed their own buildings and furniture, and in every other way provided for themselves. A third activity was study. Those monks who were literate copied books in the *scriptorium,* taught the young, and read sacred and secular works.

The Rule of Benedict was strict enough, but also moderate and flexible enough, to become the most effective vehicle of the monastic ideal. By the eighth century, the Benedictines had, under the influence of Cassiodorus and the Irish, allowed a greater place to study, which henceforth became a distinguishing characteristic of their order. The declining particularism of the Irish in that century brought about a gradual absorption of their houses by the Benedictines, whose growth was encouraged by the popes and the Frankish monarchy as a force for unity and stability. Charlemagne and his son Louis I encouraged the monk Benedict of Aniane to extend the rule of his namesake to all the houses of the Frankish kingdom, and in 817 the Diet of Aachen officially imposed the Benedictine Rule upon every monastery in the kingdom. From that time until the end of the

Matins: 12 Midnight
Lauds: 3 A.M. (sometimes combined with Matins
   to allow the monks uninterrupted sleep)
Prime: 6 A.M.
Terce: 9 A.M.
Sext: 12 Noon
None: 3 P.M.
Vespers: 6 P.M.
Compline: 9 P.M.

eleventh century it was the only monastic Rule in general use in Western Europe. The Benedictines were one of the most potent forces in binding Europe together in cultural and religious unity.

THE second such potent force was the missionary spirit. The great age of the missions began with Gregory the Great (pope 590–604), but his successors took little active rôle in the missionary endeavor. Most of the missionaries were not really sent out by anyone. Individuals inspired by the ideal of *peregrinatio,* they undertook their missions on their own. Their most spectacular efforts occurred in the seventh and eighth centuries, but even in the eighth century their attention was already diverted from "external" to "internal" missionary work, concentrating upon problems of reform and standardization in the areas already nominally Christian, and endeavoring to eradicate the pagan practices and assumptions that underlay the superficial veneer of Christianity.

The methods of the missionaries were varied. They preached, taught, and even engaged in debates with pagans. Bishop Daniel of Winchester advises the missionary Saint Boniface to ask questions that penetrated the illogicalities of the pagan religion: "How did the gods bring under their sway a universe that existed before them? Whence or by whom was the first god or goddess begotten?"[4] And so on. These were questions that a sophisticated pagan like Julian the Apostate might have taken in his stride, but there were few sophisticates in the forests of Thuringia or the marshes of Frisia. The moral example of the Christian missionaries was also effective. But if moral and intellectual suasion failed to convert to the Prince of Peace, the missionaries did not hesitate to threaten the pagans with the forces of the king of the Franks. Charlemagne enjoyed considerable success with the Saxons by telling them that if they did not permit him to convert them he would kill them.

The purpose of the Carolingians and the popes in supporting the missions was not wholly pious. The Franks realized that the pagans on their northern and eastern frontiers would be easier to subdue and pacify when they were incorporated into the Christian Church. The papacy did not find it amiss that the organizational work of the missionaries was binding the northern churches in closer allegiance to Rome. The missionaries themselves, however, set out without ulterior motive, often in groups of thirteen in imitation of Christ and his twelve, for the pure purpose of spreading the Good News of the coming of the Savior.

The first great missionary endeavors in the medieval West were undertaken by the Irish; the Gauls and Germans also labored in the harvest; but it was the Anglo-Saxons who were most successful. So ubiquitous did the English become that when a Saxon visited a Frankish monastery to see his compatriot Alcuin, the monks exclaimed: "This Briton or Irishman (sic) has come to see the other Briton (sic) who lies within. O God, deliver this monastery from these Britons (sic), who all come to this man like bees returning in every direction to their queen."[5]

The Anglo-Saxons had originally all but eliminated Romano-British culture, but now they became one of the greatest forces for synthesis. Teutonic in race and speech, they absorbed elements of Celtic culture, not so much from the Celts whom they had conquered as from the Irish missionaries who in turn conquered them by the Book. The English Kingdom of Northumbria became a center of Celtic learning. Then, from 597, when Saint Augustine of Canterbury arrived to convert Kent, England was also under strong Roman influence. The English missionaries to the continent were therefore the bearers of a synthetic Teutonic-Celtic-Latin culture. From Canterbury they learned devotion to the Roman see; from the Irish they learned asceticism and the ideal of *peregrinatio*. They were the chief builders of external missionary work, the conversion of the heathen, but also of internal missionary work, the uniting of northern Christendom under the authority of the papacy.

The first of the English to preach to the pagans on the continent did so almost by mistake. This was the politically powerful and controversial Saint Wilfrid of York, who in 678 undertook one of his several journeys to Rome to seek papal support against opponents at home. Wilfrid was unable to take the direct route to Rome through Neustria owing to the fact that the Neustrian chief minister was one of his numerous enemies, and he landed in Frisia (the present Netherlands) instead. Shocked at the ignorance of the natives, he remained during the winter and preached to them, without much success.

But Wilfrid had a young pupil, Willibrord (born ca. 658), who had learned the missionary spirit in Ireland. Hearing from his mentor about the need of the Frisians, he carefully planned a mission and crossed the Channel in 690. He knew that the success of any mission to the continent depended upon the support of the chief minister of the Franks and of the pope, and he successfully applied to both. Willibrord worked vigorously and with some success among the Frisians and even made one missionary journey to Denmark. His holiness was renowned. "Many of the brothers have testified that they have frequently seen a wonderful light over the bed on which he gave back his blessed soul to his Creator, and perceived there a ravishing fragrance and most sweet odour." [6]

WILLIBRORD'S successor in missionary labors was Winfrith, whose barbarous name the pope, unable to pronounce, changed to Boniface. Winfrith (ca. 680–755), who may have been born in Devon, early felt the call of the Spirit. His biographer, a better hagiographer than a child psychologist, improbably relates that when the little fellow "reached the age of five he conceived a desire to enter the service of God and began to think deeply on the advantages of the monastic life. Even at this early age he had subdued the flesh to the spirit and meditated on the things that are eternal rather than on those that are temporal." [7] Wholly devoted to his task, Boniface grew into a man bluntly intolerant of opposition, and certainly a less determined man could not have accomplished the half of his Herculean labors.

In 716 Boniface, like his predecessors, began his efforts in Frisia, and preached with as little effect as they had done. Still following in Willibrord's footsteps, he then went in 717 to visit Charles Martel, whose support he obtained, and in 718 he was in Rome with Pope Gregory II. Gregory sent him to preach in the wild forests of Thuringia, and in 722 the pope consecrated him bishop and gave him license to preach at large among the Germans. In 732 Gregory III made him archbishop of Mainz with an effective primacy over Germany. From 735 he worked to reorganize the Bavarian church, meanwhile promoting good relations with the chief ministers. He may have helped crown Pepin king in 751, although this is now questioned: in any event, he ended his career where he had begun it, preaching to the Frisians, who always appeared less eager to adopt the Cross than to grant the grace of martyrdom to its adherents. At Dokkum in the Frisian wilderness, where one could still have journeyed directly eastward all the way to the Pacific without encountering a Christian church, Boniface and his friends were in 755 attacked and murdered at dawn by a band of pagans who coveted the large chests the saint had with him, imagining them to contain silver and gold.

Boniface's mission was one of the most important undertakings for the formation of Europe. He converted much of Germany. His "internal" mission resulted in the founding of monasteries and schools that became the centers of spiritual revival, reform, and intellectual activity. A great movement for the reform of the Church now began, promoting moral reform in the monasteries, among the secular clergy, and among the laity, and encouraging the intellectual revival that would be further advanced by Charlemagne. Later monastic reforms, the papal reform and revolution of the eleventh century, and the cultural advance of the twelfth century were all rooted in the movement begun by Boniface and his companions. He almost singlehandedly reorganized the Frankish Church, creating dioceses and arch dioceses which he staffed with the able and numerous men who had followed him from England. These new churches he established as outposts of loyalty to the Roman see, and, with the concurrence of the Carolingians, he brought the whole Church north of the Alps into closer unity with the papacy. In 722 he took an oath of allegiance which he never violated and which illustrates his deep loyalty to the ideal of ecclesiastical unity under Roman leadership: "I will not agree to anything opposed to the unity of Universal Church, no matter who should try to induce me, but I will maintain complete loyalty to you (Gregory II) and to the welfare of your Church."

In retrospect the unity of medieval Europe under the papacy seems natural, but it was by no means inevitable. The theological notion of a single Christian society combined with the still living memory of the one Roman Empire called for some kind of institutional unity. But that the papacy came to provide the framework for such unity was the result of devoted labor on the part of the monks and the missionaries, and also on the part of a number of very able popes.

The growth of papal power consisted both in gaining firmer control over the Church in particular and in extending its influence over society as a whole. It is unlikely that the popes at this time entertained long-range plans to either effect or that Gregory I ever dreamed of the wide powers that his successors in the twelfth century would enjoy.

The primary efforts of the papacy from the sixth to the ninth century were directed at securing firmer control over ecclesiastical administration throughout the Church as a whole. Such authority demanded moral stature, independence from undue influence by laymen, especially the emperors and the Roman nobility, intellectual prestige, political acumen, and wealth. The popes made an effort to advance their standing in these respects, and, by leading the fight against heresy, pronouncing on matters of doctrine, and acting to standardize the liturgy, they enhanced both their administrative and their doctrinal authority.

Rome was helped to become the chief see of the Catholic Church by the failure of its competitors. Of the five original patriarchal sees three fell to the Moslems in the course of the sixth century—Antioch, Jerusalem, and Alexandria. The prestige of the fourth—the patriarchate of Constantinople—was always dimmed by the preeminence of the imperial authority, while the fading political and military influence of Byzantium in the West meant that the emperor was himself less and less an effective competitor. The popes' diligent concern with the problems of every area, illustrated by their voluminous correspondence, and the support lent by the missionaries and monasteries, encouraged appeals to Rome and permitted increasing papal intervention in disputes. In Italy, the papacy played the Byzantine and Lombard powers against one another so that neither could secure control over the entire peninsula or over the papacy itself. By steadily increasing their own wealth and territory, the popes became themselves the *de facto* rulers over much of central Italy, a position that enabled them to assert their spiritual independence from the emperor and other lay powers. Papal theorists in the meanwhile gradually developed arguments for the supremacy of the papacy in the Church and the superiority of the papacy over the empire. These processes were immeasurably aided by the careers of brilliant and effective popes like Gregory I (590–604) and Gregory II (715–731); and they were accelerated by the alliance between the papacy and the Franks established under Stephen III (752–757).

GREGORY I was born about 540 to an influential and noble Roman family, and at first he pursued a career as a civil magistrate, becoming prefect of the city in 573. When his father died in 575 Gregory turned over the family estates to the monasteries and himself became a monk at Rome. His light was not to remain hidden in a cloister: his abilities were well known, and after seven years of retirement from the world he was made a deacon, then sent on papal diplomatic missions, notably one to Constantinople, and finally, in 590, elected pope.

Pope Gregory the Great, as he was later called, enhanced the authority of Rome over the clergy, exerting his influence directly upon the Italian bishops and over the prelates of northern and western Europe as well. The extent of his efforts is measured in his voluminous, vigorous correspondence. He made his power felt, though not as much as he would have liked, even in the eastern churches. Carrying the talents he had learned as a civil administrator into his ecclesiastical career, he wrote a *Book of Pastoral Care* detailing the duties of a bishop; he was also the author of a powerful, if unsubtle, commentary on Job that became a standard textbook in medieval schools; and he created a synthesis in the liturgy by combining Gallic, Italian, Visigothic, and other practices into a standard Roman rite. In spite of bad communications and the sea of Arian heresy that surrounded him, Gregory was able to establish close relations with the newly converted Visigothic King Recared. He vigorously combated the Donatist heretics in Africa, and he maintained a working relationship with the emperor at Constantinople.

The emperor's power in Italy was declining. The successful attacks of the Lombards upon the Byzantine possessions in Italy had nearly isolated Rome, and Gregory found himself in effect the governor of the city. It was Gregory, as an imperial officer representing Constantinople, who paid the soldiers and civil servants and collected the taxes, he who fed the poor, and he who conducted the defense of the walls.

This imperial office was one of the sources of the temporal power of the papacy. The other was the patrimony, land given or willed to the see of Saint Peter by pious donors or acquired through purchase. Gregory managed the patrimony extremely well, improving its administration and drawing upon its resources for the temporal needs of the city.

The ineffectiveness of imperial rule in Italy, combined with the increasing responsibilities of the papal office, obliged Gregory to look northward and westward for stronger reeds on which to lean. It was he who sent Saint Augustine of Canterbury to the English, and their conversion gave the papacy leverage in the West that it could at the right moment use to obtain complete independence.

That time had not yet come in the seventh century. The emperors were too weak to impose their will upon the papacy with uniform success, but not yet weak enough not to make the attempt on every occasion. Constans II (641–668), having failed to induce Pope Martin I (649–655) to adopt an imperially sponsored heresy, had the pontiff arrested and carried off to the Crimea to die in exile. The heresies and heavy-handedness of the emperors instilled into the popes an increasing eagerness to break away.

THE revolution that had begun under Gregory the Great was completed in the eighth century. Under the leadership of Gregory II and his successors, the papacy exchanged its ties with the East for ties with the West.

Gregory II, like his great namesake a scion of noble birth who became an able ecclesiastical administrator, served his predecessors as subdeacon, treasurer, deacon, and finally as "librarian," at this time the pope's chief adviser. He was the natural choice for pope in 715, and in that office he seems deliberately to have emulated both the piety and the vigor of his illustrious namesake. Gregory II at first cooperated loyally with the emperor. The popes had continued to develop their two temporal functions, first as rulers of the "patrimony," and second as Byzantine administrators, the "dukes of Rome," responsible to Constantinople for the collection of taxes, the repair and defense of the city, and the administration of public policy in the area around the city. Gregory II in his capacity as duke of Rome was the emperor's chief representative in Italy outside of Ravenna (where the emperor Leo III established a sort of viceroy known as the exarch).

Some time about 729 the working relationship between Gregory II and the fiery Emperor Leo III deteriorated. The emperor had long since lacked the ability to defend Rome against its enemies; rather, he called to Rome to send the exarch troops for the campaigns against the Lombards. Though the emperor was no longer able to protect his Italian possessions he continued to tax them, and though money flowed out of Rome to help balance the imperial budget, no money flowed back for the relief of Rome's citizens. Further, the exarch was continually interfering in Roman politics. A final grievance was that the emperor was attempting to impose Iconoclasm upon the Church.

Gregory II judged that the papacy need no longer tolerate these annoyances. In customs and in sentiment, in language and liturgical practices, the western and eastern churches were gradually separating. The increasing resentment of imperial taxation on the part of the Italian people gave the pope a weapon against imperial authority, and the presence of the Lombards made it possible to play the exarch and the Lombard king off against each other. Most important, the work begun by Gregory the Great gave the papacy increasing support in the North. The cult of Saint Peter had grown enormously throughout the West in the seventh century, when people made pilgrimages to Rome from as far away as Ireland and England, and now in the eighth the English missionaries were uniting the Frankish churches in devotion to the Apostolic See. From at least the ninth century, the English Church had become so loyal as to send the pope a voluntary yearly contribution known as Peter's Pence.

With these sources of support, Gregory II determined to

defy the emperor, and from 729 he refused both to accept the imperial decrees on Iconoclasm and to continue to collect taxes for the imperial treasury. When Leo remonstrated with him, he replied with a scathing letter:

> Listen to us, emperor: change your present course . . . matters of faith are not the business of the emperor, but of the pope . . . . The emperor has no right to interfere in the affairs of the Church . . . . You persecute and annoy us like a violent tyrant, while we, harmless and defenseless, having no armies on earth, call upon Christ, who commands all the armies of creation, all the hosts of angels, to send down a demon upon you . . . .

The exarch of Ravenna replied by fostering an unsuccessful plot to murder Gregory, who died in peace and in power in 731. He was succeeded by another independent pope, Gregory III (731–741).

The Lombards were as hostile to the papacy as the emperors were, and the popes dared not enter into an alliance with them. Caught between Scylla and Charybdis, they turned their eyes northward for help. There was only one other major Christian power: the Franks. Gregory III appealed to Charles Martel for support against the Lombards, but Charles refused; he had an alliance with that people. Thus matters stood until 750, the year in which Pepin III obtained Pope Zachary's approval of his deposition of the Merovingians. The next year Ravenna fell to the Lombards. Henceforth Byzantine power in Italy was negligible, leaving the Lombards with power throughout the peninsula and able to carry out their designs upon papal territories.

Under the force of this threat, Zachary's successor, Stephen III (752–757), prepared to beseech the new king of the Franks for aid. It was probably at this moment that a scheme to establish and augment the pope's temporal power recommended itself to the mind of someone at the papal court. From the fifth century a wholly unfounded legend had been current at Rome. According to this "Legend of Saint Sylvester," Constantine the Great, dying of leprosy, had been told by his pagan counselors that he could be cured only by bathing in the blood of innocent children. Constantine ordered the babes assembled, but, less cruel than Herod, he was unable to give the fatal order. Rewarding his restraint, Pope Sylvester cured the emperor by bathing him in holy water. In gratitude, Constantine bestowed gifts of great price upon the pope. This story was implicitly believed at the Rome of Stephen III, the only difficulty being that there was no document recording the gifts. Someone in the papal court determined to remedy this defect. The result was the "Donation of Constantine," the most famous forgery in history.* It was itself accepted as genuine and conditioned much medieval political theory and practice until it was at last debunked by Lorenzo Valla in the fifteenth century. Specifically, the Donation asserts that the empire exists for the purpose of protecting the Church, that the emperor offered Sylvester the imperial diadem, though the pope graciously refused it, and that Constantine not only bestowed upon the pope authority over all sees and the right to judge all matters of doctrine, but also gave him direct rule over all of western Europe. These ideas were not forgotten by later popes like Gregory VII and Innocent III.

When Stephen III began his journey northward in 753, the Donation seems already to have been known among the Franks. When on January 6, 754, he met King Pepin at Ponthion, Pepin's young son, later to be known as Charlemagne, watched his father dismount and perform the office of groom for Stephen exactly as the Donation described Constantine's having done for Sylvester. The next year at Easter the pope gave Pepin the title of "Roman patrician," which had previously been held by the Byzantine exarch, and Pepin in return offered the "Donation of Pepin," promising to the pope large territories in Italy then held by the Lombards. The alliance was sealed at Saint Denis in June of 754, when the pope himself confirmed the coronation of Pepin by anointing him with holy oil, setting another precedent for the imperial coronation of Charlemagne. This shift in papal allegiance from East to West is indicated by the documents issued by the papal chancery, which at the beginning of the century were dated by the regnal year of the eastern emperor, then by that of the pope, and finally by that of the Frankish king.

*The chronology given here for the forgery is the most likely, but some historians contend that it originated later in the century. The events of 754 do not prove absolutely the existence of the document but only of some of its ideology.

Saint Peter bestowing power upon Pope Leo III and Charlemagne.

In 754 or 755 Pepin invaded Italy, defeated the Lombards, and took Ravenna. Emissaries from Constantinople approached him and asked for the return of the city to their emperor, but Pepin was too good a student of the forged Donation; instead, he "returned" the city to the pope, who had never possessed it.

The independence and the extent of the papal states was thus confirmed and augmented, the Lombard and Byzantine power was emasculated, and the formation of the papal states inhibited for eleven hundred years the growth of a united Italy that could deprive the papacy of political sovereignty. But all was not rosy. The pope had lost most of his own influence at Constantinople, while in the West he had to face a newly powerful Roman nobility and to endure the embrace of the Franks, which, though friendly, proved overpowering. But though the papacy was not to reign supreme in Europe until nearly four hundred more years had passed, the foundation of its power had been laid. The coronation of Charlemagne in 800 symbolized the great synthesis which, aided by monks and missionaries, the popes and the Carolingians had created.

Any century is a century of decision, but the eighth was more decisive than most, completing as it did the processes of synthesis and assimilation that were forming the new society. Between 700 and 800 the Islamic conquest of Spain was achieved, but further Moslem expansion in both East and West was halted; the 'Abbasid caliphate was established at Baghdad. The Isaurian dynasty revived the vigor of the eastern Roman Empire and inaugurated policies that made it more Greek and alienated it from the West. The independence of the papacy from Byzantium was effected and the Lombards removed as an independent force. The papacy's temporal power was enormously enhanced, and through the efforts of the Anglo-Saxon missionaries and the Benedictine monks the western Church was brought into close relationship with the Roman see. The conversion of the Germans was greatly advanced. The Carolingian monarchy was founded and the Franco-papal alliance established that would provide a focus for a united western society. The leaders of that society, the eighth century indicated, would be the pope and the emperor—not of Byzantium—but of the Franks. The monks and missionaries began a movement of moral and intellectual reform that gradually gathered strength until it culminated in the eleventh and twelfth centuries. A distinctive western culture began to be formed among the English and the Franks.

Thanks to the general desire for unity, thanks especially to the two great figures of the century, Boniface and Charlemagne, the fabric of society rent in the third century was rewoven by the eighth. The pattern, however, was new, and in it one can for the first time discern the configuration of our own civilization. The transformation of the Roman world was complete.

[1] *The Fourth Book of the Chronicle of Fredegar with Its Continuations,* ed. J. M. Wallace-Hadrill (London, Thomas Nelson and Sons, Ltd., 1960), p. 31.

[2] Wallace-Hadrill, pp. 30–31.

[3] All quotations from the *Rule,* in *Documents of the Christian Church,* trans. and ed. Henry Bettenson. 2d ed. (London, Oxford University Press, 1963), pp. 161–179.

[4] In *Anglo-Saxon Missionaries in Germany,* trans. and ed. C. H. Talbot (Copyright Sheed and Ward Inc., New York, 1954), p. 76.

[5] Quoted by Wilhelm Levison, *England and the Continent in the Eighth Century* (Oxford, 1946), p. 169.

[6] Alcuin's *Life of Willibrord,* in Talbot, p. 19.

[7] Willibald's *Life,* in Talbot, p. 25.

PART TWO

The Formation
of a
New Civilization

Chapter Eight

FROM CHARLEMAGNE TO CHAOS

The establishment of the new European culture and synthesis was consummated by the brilliant rule of Charlemagne (768–814). The "first Europe" had been established, and men might have hoped that events would have progressed to make possible, for the first time in centuries, the realization of stability and order in government, the Church, the economy, and culture. The transformation of the "Kingdom of the Franks" into the "Christian Empire" is symbolic of the high hopes of the time. But soon after the death of the great king, order was shattered by a terrible period of chaos, internal collapse, and a renewal of the barbarian invasions. Many of the creative advances of the eighth century were suspended. It was as if civilization, having pulled itself at great cost and labor up onto a safe ledge, was swept suddenly down again for a hundred years. It was not until the latter part of the tenth century that the quest for order and security could be resumed in earnest.

Nonetheless, many of the institutions and ideas that were to characterize the Middle Ages at their height received their initial stamp under the Carolingian Empire.

Among the sources for the period are a number of biographies, of which the *Life of Charlemagne* by his contemporary Einhard is the best known; a later *Deeds of Charles* by the monk Notker is less reliable. There is Asser's *Life of Alfred* (the Great), Nithard's *Sons of Louis the Pious,* and an anonymous *Life of Louis* himself. Monastic annals, chronicles, and histories, which first appeared in the seventh and eighth centuries, multiplied in number and length in the ninth and tenth. Besides the usual ecclesiastical and governmental monuments, of which the capitularies are the most important, we have a treatise by Archbishop Hincmar of Reims (*De Ordine Palatii*) on the nature of kingship and the conduct of royal government. The letters of Einhard, Alcuin, and Lupus of Ferrières further illuminate the personalities of their contemporaries.

FROM the accession of Charlemagne, the Carolingian state passed through two phases. The first, continuing through the early reign of Louis the Pious, was constructive and creative; the second was marked by internal dissension and a fresh wave of invasions from without.

Charlemagne and his brother Carloman shared the inheritance of their father, Pepin, upon his death in 768. There was little love lost between them, and the death of Carloman in 771 had the virtue of sparing the kingdom an overt struggle for power. The vitality of the man who now became sole ruler presaged his future success. Strong and determined, merry at table, swift on a horse, Charlemagne was quick to understand and quick to decide. Like Alexander the Great, Augustus, and all really great rulers, he respected both intellectuals and the intellectual life. Though he had difficulty writing, he spoke not only his native language (East Frankish, which was developing into Old German), but Latin and even a little Greek. The impetus his wide interests gave to theology, poetry, architecture, and history created the climate of cultural activity that is sometimes known as the "Carolingian Renaissance." His private morals were less unimpeachable. Besides many mistresses, he acquired five wives, the last of whom was only thirteen years old. So varied were his merits, demerits, and activities, that he became one of the great legendary figures of the Middle Ages. We find him in the *Song of Roland,* immensely old and wise; and in 1165 the emperor Frederick Barbarossa took the step, never approved by the pope, of canonizing him. Modern generals and statesmen, including Napoleon and Charles de Gaulle, have invoked the spirit of this man, who is justly honored as the creator of the first united western European state.

THIS creation was, like Napoleon's, largely military. Having subdued rebellion and discontent at home, Charlemagne moved to assure the security and tranquility of his frontiers by foreign wars. In 773, eager to enhance his family's alliance with the papacy, he answered Pope Hadrian I's appeal for help against the continuing Lombard menace. By the following year, far surpassing the exploits of his father in Italy, Charlemagne had taken the capital of the Lombards and himself assumed their iron crown. The Lombard kingdom was henceforth a dependency of the Frankish throne. Charlemagne further imitated his father by confirming to the popes a "Donation of Charlemagne," but Frankish power in Italy was sufficient to assure papal obedience to the royal benefactor.

The Frankish power, centered as it was on the Rhine, could contemplate independent and hostile powers in Germany with even less equanimity than it could such threats in Italy. Accordingly, Charlemagne completed with the sword the pacification and Christianization of the Germans that Boniface had commenced with the Book. The duchy of Bavaria, which had maintained its autonomy, was now incorporated into Carolingian Germany, and after thirty-two years of campaigning (772–804) Charlemagne defeated the savage and stubbornly independent Saxons. No German people now remained free of Frankish control. Having secured Germany, Charlemagne was now obliged to protect it against the incursions of the northern Slavs and the Ural-Altaic Avars, who had been raiding and looting for decades. He achieved the submission of the Slavs to his nominal rule and destroyed the Avar power by sending his son Pepin at the head of an army that seized the Ring, the great Avar fortress system in what is now Hungary. The treasure that the Franks brought away from the Ring helped finance further wars and may have caused a slight improvement in the economy.

In order to protect southern Gaul from Moslem raids, the great king undertook his most renowned campaign, though one of the least fruitful. This was his expedition against the Umayyad caliphs of Spain, which ended in frustration, retreat, and the famous attack by the Basques upon the Frankish rearguard under Count Roland at the Pass of Roncesvalles (778). Years later, Charlemagne conducted a more successful Spanish campaign in which the Franks secured the "Spanish March" north of the Ebro.

Though Charles' motivation in these constant military activities was defensive, they resulted in spectacular conquests, securing to the Frankish kingdom a vast territory that became the heartland of western civilization: its borders are very close to those of the twentieth-century Common Market.

IN these wars of expansion, there was, beyond simple defense or conquest, one other motive: the desire to restore or to re-create the old universal state. Both the ideal of Roman imperial unity and the Christian ideal of a united Christendom as the external expression of the mystical Body of Christ called for a unified Christian society. The extension of Frankish rule (*regnum Francorum*) was considered to involve a transformation as well—a transformation into the *imperium Christianum,* symbolized by the imperial coronation of Charlemagne on Christmas Day 800.

In the background of the coronation was the politics of Rome. Since the subjection of the Lombards by Charlemagne gave the papal states autonomy, the power and pretensions of the Roman nobility had been growing. As in the Renaissance, the noble families were split into feuding political factions; quarreling among themselves, they agreed upon their common desire to control the popes. Pope Hadrian I had been a representative of one of the most powerful families; his successor, Leo III, a stubborn man of obscure birth, antagonized the family of the former pope. The hostile nobles waylaid Leo in the streets of Rome, beat him savagely, and then justified their actions by accusing him of perjury and adultery. In answer to an appeal from the pope, Charlemagne came to Italy, and, having investigated the matter and received an oath of innocence from Leo, adjudged him innocent. On Christmas Day,

> . . . when the king, at mass before the tomb of the blessed apostle Peter, arose from prayer, Pope Leo placed upon his head a crown and the whole Roman people acclaimed him: Life and victory to Charles, Augustus, crowned by God, the great and peaceful Emperor of the Romans! And after the laudation he was adored by the pope in the manner of ancient princes . . . .[1]

These were the events; but there is little agreement among historians today as to their purport. To begin with, we are not sure whether Charlemagne wished to be crowned emperor or

Charlemagne.

whether the whole thing was a stratagem of the pope's. The notion that Charlemagne was surprised and indignant at his sudden elevation derives from the usually reliable Einhard, whom the majority of historians are still inclined to believe, holding that the king would not have wished gratuitously to offend the eastern emperor by disputing his title. Others argue that it is inconceivable that the frightened, weak, and politically exposed pope, who owed everything to Charlemagne, would have dared to risk his wrath by crowning him without his permission. They find it hard to imagine the scene in the cathedral as Einhard describes it: Charlemagne too engrossed in prayer not to notice the purpose of the pope as he approached him or too timid, once the people had acclaimed him, to decline the honor.

The question of what this new "empire" was has recently been explored more deeply by Peter Munz in an original and convincing argument. Munz says that the "empire" had no objective meaning, but only different constructions placed upon it by different people. There is no one answer to the question. But there are reasonable guesses as to what people meant when they talked about the empire.

Pope Leo was obviously and undeniably one of the planners of the coronation, whether or not it surprised the king. His motives are easy to discern. By flattering Charles, he hoped forever to secure his support against his Roman enemies. By crowning Charles emperor, he was protecting himself from the claims of Constantinople that it had imperial rights over Rome. As for Charles, his acquiescence in the cathedral is not the only evidence that he wanted the empire. He began using the title of emperor at once and officially passed it on to his son. After a war with the eastern empire he finally extracted its recognition, in a treaty, of his imperial dignity. None of these events make it credible that he did not want the title; no one could have obliged him to use it against his will. What, then, might Charles have had in mind by becoming "emperor"? The revival of learning had acquainted him with several venerable ideas. The study of Saint Augustine's idea of natural law made him wish to be no longer a Germanic king ruling by conquest, but a Christian emperor ruling according to justice and with divine approbation. The unction with holy oil, which he and his father had received in imitation of the kings over Israel, so impressed him that he liked his courtiers to address him as David. The imperial coronation was thus a confirmation of the sacred nature of his kingship. It is also quite credible that Charles or his political theorists wished to use the imperial title to enhance the prestige of the ruler and thus to enhance his authority over his diverse subjects. The term *imperium Francorum* had been used before 800, and the idea that Aachen was an imperial seat was early enshrined in an anonymous poem envisioning Charles, "the head of the world, the delight and the glory of his people, the venerable chief of Europe, hero, Augustus," supervising the construction of his capital at Aachen: "the second Rome . . . . Here he disposes the forum, there the sacred senate . . . ."[2]

Of all Charles' advisers, it was Alcuin who had for years been the most enthusiastic cultivator of the imperial idea. His conception of the empire was grander than that of the Aachen advisers. The revival of learning and the Donation of Constantine had led to a rediscovery of that ruler and his Christian Empire, and Alcuin seems to have envisioned a restoration of an orthodox *imperium Christianum* in place of the heretical eastern empire. The new emperor, the true successor of Constantine, was to be the superior of all men, including the pope, in spiritual, as well as temporal, authority. This idea of Alcuin's ultimately prevailed and throughout the Middle Ages dominated the thought of the defenders of the imperial against the papal.

The coronation, whatever its motives, had wide effects. It strengthened the papal-Frankish alliance and united the West more securely than ever. It excluded forever the influence of Constantinople from the West, and it established Frankish control over Italy, including the papal states. The idea of an indivisible *empire,* had it been able to eliminate the idea of the divisible *kingdom,* might have been a stabilizing and unifying force capable of holding the Carolingian state together. The weaknesses of that state became apparent soon after the death of Charlemagne.

FORTUNATELY for the unity of the kingdom, all of Charlemagne's sons save one died before their father. The empire, and the kingdom, passed entire into the hands of the survivor, Louis, later called "the Pious." Louis' reign was not without its virtues. He encouraged the cultural revival begun by his father, and he carried out a number of sensible and humane administrative reforms. He favored the Jewish community, possibly because of the respect for Judaism produced by the Carolingians' study of the Old Testament, and helped it to develop its influence. But his nickname betrays the difference between his personality and that of his father. Slow, deliberate, grave and modest in speech and in dress, the husband of only two wives (the first died), he lacked his father's exuberance. His reign was marred by his weak but irritable personality, which suffered from periods of excessive timidity followed by periods of extravagant revenge. It was also marred by increasing evidence of the inherent weaknesses of the Carolingian monarchy, which had been minimized by the skill of Charlemagne.

Charlemagne had obtained a huge domain, but the resources of his successors were inadequate to maintain it. The economy was weak, and too much power lay in the hands of local lords and ecclesiastics; there was no adequate system of administration binding the empire together; communications were too limited for either civil or military efficiency; many areas of the empire, notably Saxony, had scarcely emerged from barbarism; and even in the more civilized portions of the realm, there was enormous cultural diversity and disunion in an empire that comprised Franks, Burgundians, Lombards, and Romans, among others.

The most serious weakness of the Frankish monarchy under Louis the Pious was the same as that of the Merovingians: the quarrel of the sons over the father's legacy. Louis and his first wife had three sons, Lothar, Pepin, and Louis, and the emperor attempted to arrange a succession that would answer to Frankish customs and still avoid the inherent dangers to unity. In 817 he arranged that each of his three sons should receive a kingdom but that Lothar, the eldest, should inherit the title of emperor. The other two sons were to owe him a certain undefined amount of leadership. This settlement provoked a rebellion on the part of the emperor's nephew Bernard and sowed the seeds of future dissatisfaction on the part of the younger sons. In 823 Louis arranged that his son Lothar should be crowned by the pope, thus assuring his succession to the imperial title. It was Louis' hope, and the hope of his ecclesiastical advisers, who, in the tradition of Alcuin, believed in an *imperium Christianum,* that the future of the empire would thus be assured. But in the meanwhile a new complication had arisen. Louis' first wife had died, and he had remarried. His second wife, Judith, an extremely ambitious woman, gave birth in 823 to a son, Charles. For this baby the new queen "brought her power to bear upon the rule of all the realm; she stirred up waves and seas; she drove the winds; she turned the hearts of men to all that she willed . . . . "[3] By the time Charles was six, Judith had persuaded her husband to make a new division

Lothar I.

of the kingdom in the little fellow's favor, and the result was
a new rebellion, this one led by the three older sons. In 833
Louis suffered an ignominious humiliation at the hands of his
sons at the place called the Field of Lies, where the king's
troops and supporters crept over singly or in small groups to
join the rebels. Louis was forced to confess his sins against the
realm and to promise to amend his life; but the overweening

THE CAROLINGIANS FROM CHARLEMAGNE

Kings capitalized, emperors capitalized and **boldface**

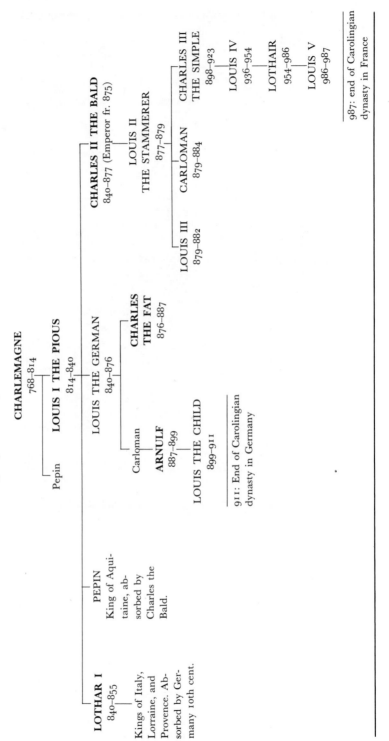

pride of the eldest son, Lothar, so alienated the other two that they went back to their father's side. These disputes continued until 840, when the old king died.

Fortunately his son Pepin had preceded him to the grave, so that only three sons—Lothar, Louis, and Judith's son Charles —now divided the kingdom among them. At first there was an attempt to keep the kingdom together under Lothar with his two brothers as sub-kings, but they quickly defeated him in battle (841) and made an alliance against him at a meeting at Strasbourg in 842. In 843 their alliance forced Lothar to agree to the Partition of Verdun, which left him the title of emperor but allowed him only the middle third of the realm. The King-dom of the West Franks, largely Romance-speaking, was given to the youngest son, to whom age brought the name "Charles the Bald." The Kingdom of the East Franks, Germanic in lan-guage, was the portion of Louis, hence called "the German." Thus were the outlines of the future nations of France and Germany drawn for the first time, though the intentions at the time were scarcely nationalistic; the idea was simply to arrive at a roughly equal division between the three rulers.

But the divisions had not ceased with Verdun. The death of Lothar I in 855 was followed by a division of his middle kingdom into three, one portion going to each of his sons. One got Provence, another Italy, and the third, Lothar II, the ter-ritory along the Rhine and westwards, which now took its name (Lotharingia, or Lorraine) from the name of its ruler. Upon Lothar II's death, Lorraine was divided between France and Germany (870), exactly 1,000 years before the first of the three major wars of contemporary times fought between the same nations over the same territory. Italy was abandoned to a num-ber of princelings disputing the imperial title; it was finally absorbed by Germany in the tenth century and did not regain nationhood until 1861.

In Germany, Carolingian power was increasingly attenuated and almost vanished after the reign of the lethargic Charles the Fat, who proved incapable of defending against the bar-barian assaults. Upon the premature death of the Carolingian Louis the Child in 911, the German dukes chose one of their own number as king.

In France, there was a similar deterioration of the cen-

Charles the Bald and his court.

tral government. A successful revolt in Burgundy made that area a separate kingdom, and the duchy of Aquitaine in the south and that of Francia in the north (whence modern France), obtained near independence from the king. The Carolingians, having learned from the mistakes of the Merovingians, never appointed chief ministers who might supplant them; but they could not prevent the rise of these feudal lords. The duchy of France, with its center at Paris, was ruled by the able Robertian—Capetian family, which so limited the Carolinginans' strength that at last King Louis IV (936–954) retained no more than one castle in his own name. The failure of Charles the Fat to defend against the Vikings during the siege of Paris in 885–887 had led to his deposition and to the succession, in the West Frankish Kingdom, of Odo the Capetian. The crown

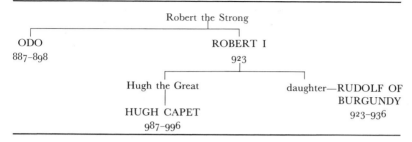

passed back and forth between the Carolingian and Capetian families until at last in 987 Hugh Capet put an end to the Carolingian dynasty.

THE events attending the break-up of Charlemagne's empire shaped the map of Europe for a millennium. United Europe existed henceforth only in the world of ideas; and France, Germany, and Italy were all to go their own particular ways. But the rise of the nations was yet to come. The process of deterioration went even farther, and those French, German, and Italian kingdoms themselves lacked effective central governments. It was left to feudalism, building upwards from small, local bases, to reconstruct a stable society. The immediate effect of Carolingian chaos was the interruption for a hundred years of the movement for reform, education, and stability that had commenced in the eighth century. The work was resumed in the tenth century, but only after a painful interlude.

THE hundred years of pain was produced, not only by the internal collapse of the empire, but also by the calamity of the barbarian invasions, which now resumed with ferocity and violence. The Vikings and Hungarians visited upon the people of western Europe a savagery and ferocity unexceeded by the Goths. These external pressures upon a weakened state hastened, but did not cause, the disruption of the empire, which would in any event have collapsed owing to internal weaknesses. It has been suggested that the internal decline actually brought about the attacks by rendering the empire an easy prey. This

North
Sea

MERSEN
AACHEN

WEST
FRANKISH
KM.

Verdun

EAST

FRANKISH

KM.

Rhine

ITALY 870

Pavia

Venice

Rome

TREATY OF VERDUN 843
Kingdom of Charles
Kingdom of Lothar
Kingdom of Louis

TREATY OF MERSEN 870
——— Boundary of East
and West Frankish Kingdoms.
Lothar's Kingdom divided
between Charles and Louis

FAEROE IS.

NORTHMEN PENETRATED
AS FAR AS ICELAND,
GREENLAND, AND VINLAND

NORWEGIA

SCOTLAND

IRELAND

DANISH OCCUPIED

ENGLAND

Wedmore

SAXON

Mersen
Aachen
AUSTRASIA

Reims

FRANCIA

Verdun

BRITTANY

NEUSTRIA

LORRAINE

Rhine

Ferrières

BA

AQUITAINE

BURGUNDY

St. Bernard P

Pavia

KM. OF
ASTURIAS

Roncesvalles

SPANISH MARCH

PROVENCE

Rom

Ebro

UMAYYAD

CALIPHATE

CORSICA

BALEARIC IS.

SARDINIA

Mediterranean

MILES

0   100   200   300   400   500

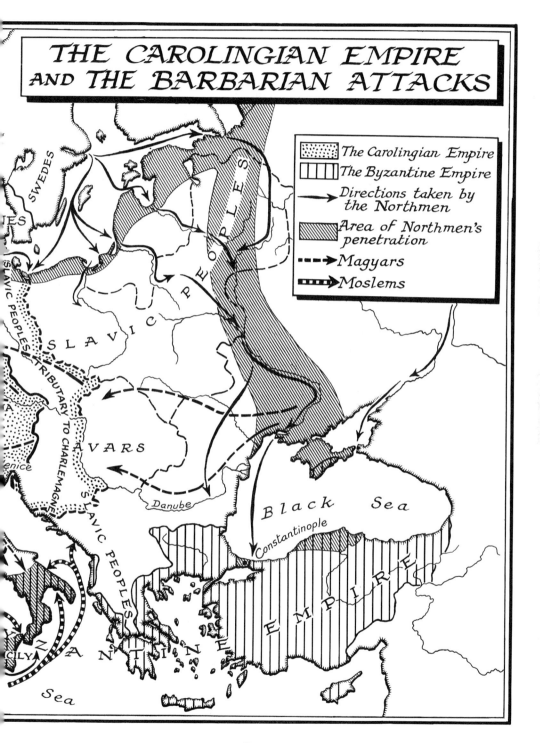

THE CAROLINGIAN EMPIRE
AND THE BARBARIAN ATTACKS

The Carolingian Empire

The Byzantine Empire

Directions taken by the Northmen

Area of Northmen's penetration

Magyars

Moslems

SWEDES

SLAVIC PEOPLES

SLAVIC PEOPLES TRIBUTARY TO CHARLEMAGNE

AVARS

Venice

SLAVIC PEOPLES

Danube

Black Sea

Constantinople

BYZANTINE EMPIRE

SICILY

Sea

is only partly true. The Merovingian state had been weaker than the Carolingian state ever was, yet the Merovingians had been spared the barbarian scourge. Moreover, barbarian raids had been slowly increasing even at the height of Charlemagne's power. Climatic and other considerations urged the barbarians to move, and their assaults were encouraged, but not caused, by the inability of Europe to resist.

The attacks came from three directions. From the South the Moslems, prevented from conquering Europe, mounted incessant raids against the European population. The Saracens (as the men of the Middle Ages called them) established themselves in Sicily and Sardinia, as well as in bases all along the Mediterranean shore of the continent. So deep into Europe did they press, and so presumptuous were they, that in 972 they dared kidnap Abbot Maieul of Cluny, one of the most important men in Europe, as he was crossing the Saint Bernard Pass between Italy and Switzerland!

From the East, the Ural-Altaic peoples menaced again. First were the Avars, who by the seventh century had enslaved many of the Slavs and by the eighth were raiding Frankish territories. The Franks met this challenge successfully, bringing the Avars under the yoke by ca. 805. By 894, however, a new Ural-Altaic foe, the Magyars or Hungarians, appeared along the Middle Danube, established a base in what thereafter became Hungary, and began raiding and looting as far west as the Rhine and even Belgium.

From the North, the most terrible foe of all appeared in the Vikings, a name of uncertain origin which by the ninth century meant terror to every town and village of Europe. Moved by love of war and booty, driven by overpopulation, utilizing new maritime techniques, and encouraged by the weakness of their wealthy adversaries, the Vikings, or Northmen, began by the end of the eighth century an era of vigorous expansion.

Each of the three Scandinavian peoples chose a different direction. The Swedes chose "the eastern passage," moving down through Russia to trade with Constantinople. Though warlike and daring, the Swedes were usually less dangerous and more tractable than their Danish and Norwegian cousins.

The Danes chose the "middle passage," raiding England and northern Gaul, thrusting up the Seine to besiege Paris from

Prow of Viking ship (ninth century) found in excavations at Oseberg, near Oslo, in 1903.

885 to 887, and circling Spain and appearing in the Mediterranean to raid Italy in 859. The Danish raids were soon replaced by permanent settlements, particularly in Gaul and in England. They wintered on the continent for the first time in 826, and thereafter more frequently, until they became so thick and powerful on the northern coast that King Charles the Simple was forced in 911 to grant their leader, Rollo, a territory which was to become the duchy of Normandy (*Northmannia*).

In England, the Danes began their raids in 786 and wintered for the first time in 850–851. Their success in overwhelming the eastern part of the island eliminated all the English kingdoms save one, the Kingdom of Wessex. The success of Wessex in resisting their assaults permitted its king to extend his rule to all of

Model of a Viking camp, c. 1000.

England. The present sovereign of Great Britain is a direct descendant of King Alfred the Great (871–899), whose energy in building the English navy, constructing defensive fortifications, and organizing resistance against the Danes laid the foundations of the English state. At first Alfred was obliged to partition the island with the Northmen and to agree to the payment of an annual tribute (the Danegeld). That the payments were really made is witnessed by the great numbers of Anglo-Saxon coins found by archeologists in Denmark and southern Sweden (then ruled by the Danes). By 878, however, Alfred's successful resistance obliged the Danes to agree to the Treaty of Wedmore, which checked their further advance, provided for their conversion to Christianity, and prepared their assimilation into a united English kingdom. Alfred's successors, who had to deal with further attacks not only by the Danes but also by the Norwegians, were successful in reducing Danish territory bit by bit and completing the formation of a united England. That their task was a fierce one is indicated by an old chronicle's report of the Battle of Bruanburh in which King Ethelstan fought the Norwegians (in Tennyson's interpretation):

> Also the brethren,
> King and Atheling,
> Each in his glory,
> Went to his own West-Saxonland,
> Glad of the war.

Many a carcase they left to be carrion,
Many a livid one, many a sallow-skin—
Left for the white-tailed eagle to tear it, and
Left for the horny-nibbed raven to rend it, and
Gave to the garbaging war-hawk to gorge it, and
That gray beast, the wolf of the weald.

The victories of Alfred's successors were only temporarily negated by the folly of Ethelred II the Redeless ["Without Counsel"], who failed to save his throne from the Northmen. The Norwegian chief Olaf Tryggvason and the Danish chief Sweyn Forkbeard disputed the island between them; at last the Danish party triumphed, and though Sweyn had died, his son Canute obtained in 1016 a kingdom that united England and Denmark and subsequently Norway as well. The Danish rule was again short-lived, for when Canute's young son Harthacanute died of drink in 1042, the English Edward the Confessor managed to gain the throne. England had on the whole responded well to the Danish challenge, for by 1042 it had achieved what few other European peoples had at that time: a united, efficient government, an insular sense of identity, and a vigorous culture. After the Conquest of 1066 united England with Normandy, it commanded great influence throughout Europe and more than once caused the thrones of France and Germany to totter. The advantages England enjoyed over the continental countries arose precisely from this early achievement of unity.

The exploits of the Norwegians, though less influential than those of the Danes, were even more dramatic. By the eighth century they had taken the Faeroe Islands and had begun to raid Ireland, Scotland, and England. By the ninth century they were in Iceland (whose boreal shores may first have been touched by the Irish a century earlier), by 984 in Greenland, and about 1000 in America, which they called Vinland.

Until recently there was no absolute proof of the Norse discovery of America, though the literary evidence was good, there even being an account of a bishop sent to the new continent in 1121. But the famous Minnesota "rune stone" turned out to be a fake, and there were historians skeptical of the whole affair. In the 1960s, however, additional evidence has appeared. In 1963 excavations in Newfoundland unearthed the remains of a settlement that was unquestionably Norse. Even more dra-

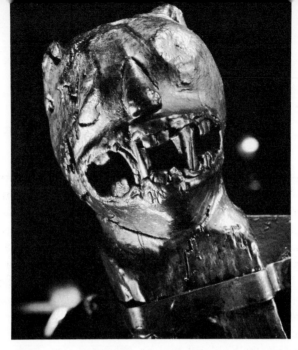

The Viking Terror: Corner post of a sleigh discovered in archeological excavations at Gokstad near Oslo.

matically, in 1965 Yale University published the "Vinland Map," drawn in a Swiss monastery at least fifty years before Columbus and showing portions of the North American continent labeled "Vinland." The Yale map's authenticity has been questioned, but so far unconvincingly. The Norse discovery does not of course detract from Columbus' merits, for it was his discovery, not theirs, that was followed by thorough exploration and settlement. And the laurels for the original discovery of America belong neither to Italians nor to Norwegians, but to the ancestors of the Amerinds who about 10,000 B.C. crossed the Bering Straits from Asia.

The European settlements of the Vikings, particularly of the Danes, were large enough to oblige us to count them another important element in the western synthesis. In general, their culture and religion were similar to those of the other Teutonic tribes, and their sagas, eddas, and other writings, compelling in themselves, give us an insight we would otherwise lack into the pagan Teutonic mind. The contributions of the Normans in France and Italy have already been mentioned; but to a large extent they were assimilated into the religion, culture, and languages of the people they conquered. Norse influence in Normandy is today visible only in a few place names (Harfleur–Harfloth: "Har Bay") and in the physical traits of the Norman people. The conversion of the Scandinavians (except those who settled in England and France) came late, in the eleventh and twelfth centuries, and they formed an integral part of Latin Christendom for only four centuries before they broke away in the Protestant Reformation.

With the Saracens as far north as Switzerland, the Magyars as far west as Belgium, and the Vikings as far south as Italy, there was no town, village, castle, or farm in western Europe safe from the threat of destruction. Any day might dawn to the sound of the barbarian horn at the gate; in 950, as again after 1950, every home in western civilization was liable to annihilation virtually without warning.

The political collapse of Carolingian Europe reflected the absolute terror and demoralization that everywhere prevailed. A few anecdotes will illustrate. The Annals of Saint Vaast for 882 state:

> The Northmen . . . horribly devastated the kingdom of Carloman . . . . The Northmen ceased not from rapine and drove all the inhabitants who were left beyond the Somme . . . (884): The Northmen ceased not to take Christian people captive and to kill them, and to destroy churches and houses and burn villages. Through all the streets lay bodies of the clergy, of laymen, nobles, and others, of women, children, and suckling babes. There was no road nor place where the dead did not lie.[4]

In 1012 the archbishop of Canterbury was pelted to death with the bones of animals eaten at a banquet of his Viking conquerors. In 954 a girl of noble family was captured near Worms by the Magyars, who sold her into slavery in the marketplace of that very city. An Icelander was teased by his comrades for being the "children's man" because he was the only one who did not indulge in the sport of impaling babies upon his spear. Marc Bloch cited the wanderings of the monks of Saint Philibert as illustration of the total insecurity in which people lived. The monks first founded their house at Noirmoutier, an island at the mouth of the Loire, but in 819 were obliged to build a temporary refuge on the mainland. In 836, the refuge became their temporary home, while they built a new place of retreat farther up the river. They moved upstream again in 858 and again in 862; in 872–873 they fled far inland, and finally found security only in 875, in a fort on the banks of the Saône near modern Switzerland.

EUROPE possessed resilience enough to outlast its century of terror and to resume its development, but in the process its unity and order had been shattered. It was necessary to rebuild with the smallest fragments; hence the construction of the new order rested upon the small units of the manor and the fief. Yet the memory of Carolingian unity, and the trace of Carolingian institutions, persisted. These institutions bear mention, not only because of their future influence, but also because they were the tools with which the short period of Carolingian order was constructed.

Charlemagne made whatever efforts were consonant with his limited powers to deal with the economic weaknesses of his realm. He increased the silver content of the coinage and established as the common coin the silver penny or *denier,* which became almost the only denomination struck in the West for four centuries. In an attempt to limit inflation, Charles issued edicts against usury and attempted to stabilize prices. He moved to concentrate economic power in royal hands by forbidding anyone other than the king to mint money. In other capitularies, he strove to stimulate commerce, industry, and markets. He worked to administer his personal property in an efficient manner, ordering in the *Capitulare de villis* a thorough census of his lands. The reports of his census-takers abound in astounding detail. The census of one royal estate lists, among many other objects, "Utensils: 2 brass kettles, 2 drinking cups, 2 brass cauldrons, 1 iron one, 1 frying-pan."[5]

The revenues of the royal fisc—domains held directly by the king—were the major source of the government's income, which also included revenues from mints, mines, and forests, judicial fines, presents voluntary and otherwise, tribute and booty from conquered peoples, and the *heerban,* collected from those who did not appear for military duty. An attempt to impose a direct head-tax failed when it was discovered that fathers were killing their children in preference to paying. But if royal income was irregular, royal expenses were small, and it is probable that the pettiness of the operations of the government was what permitted the limited revenues, rather than the limited revenues forcing the government to restrict its activities.

Royal government was indeed very restricted, and nothing is more absurd than the common notion that Charlemagne was an absolute monarch. Medieval monarchy was not even strictly hereditary. Two principles were recognized in Germanic kingship, "kin-right" and election. In the primitive Germanic tribes the man was chosen chief who showed the greatest strength and the most qualities of leadership. If he were related in blood to the former chief, this gave him an additional, but by no means a decisive, advantage. As the Frankish and English monarchies developed, the hereditary principle was reinforced by the notion that the kings were descendants of a god; and from his transcendent "ancestor" the king derived semi-priestly, even magical, powers. The kings of Wessex, for example, derived their line from Woden, and one finds today, in the literature of the eccentric "Anglo-Israelite" sect, genealogical tables tracing Queen Elizabeth II's ancestry to Solomon and David on the one side and Woden on the other. Yet the idea of election never wholly passed, and with it was cherished the old Germanic idea of the "right of resistance." A tribal chief who proved cowardly and incompetent might be replaced by his followers; and it was assumed (and overtly admitted at the Council of Coulaines in 843) that the Frankish or English people had a right to depose a wicked or incompetent ruler.

The adoption of Christianity brought with it the idea that the king was the servant of God. This notion operated in two different ways. On the one hand, as the anointing of Pepin and the coronation of Charlemagne suggest, it reinforced the pagan idea of divine kingship and encouraged the idea that the king's divine commission to rule permitted him to claim semi-priestly powers and ultimately authority over the Church. On the other hand, it encouraged the idea that the king was limited by Christian principles, and that, if he violated them, he would be a tyrant worthy of deposition. All these ideas were worked out more clearly in later medieval political theory, but they were present in embryo in the Carolingian period and acted as restraints upon monarchical power.

Royal power was limited in practice by the meagerness of the king's resources and restricted even in theory. The idea that the king, or the government, should deal with all the economic and social problems of society was foreign to the Middle Ages. The king's job was to lead the army, defend the realm and the faith, and administer justice under the law. He could subsist on a small income because his only expenditures were in the maintenance of his household and the construction of a very few public buildings. Education, roads, health, even the army, put few monetary demands upon the royal treasury.

Charlemagne, in spite of his building program at Aachen, had no permanent residence or capital; the officers of government were obliged to follow him and his successors on their journeys. The government was almost totally informal. It consisted of a household, a vague sort of "cabinet," and the Great Council. The household officers were essentially servants of the king whose offices, originally personal and menial, had been elevated to the level of public functions. For example, the seneschal, who originally waited on table, became a military officer, while the chamberlain, who attended to the king's bedchamber and therefore to the strongbox kept at the foot of the royal bed, naturally became the treasurer. When the king moved from place to place, his household brought with them his treasury and the other necessities of government.

The "cabinet" was entirely undefined, and simply consisted of those prelates or magnates who at the moment possessed the king's confidence and respect.

The Great Council, an extension of the old tribal council, originally consisted of a yearly gathering of all freemen of the Frankish nation. Owing to the increase in the size and population of the realm, attendance at the Great Council was limited even in Merovingian times to the lay and ecclesiastical magnates of the land. The council advised the king and consented to his plans. It served as the high court of justice for the realm, as a place of assembly for the year's military campaign, as a consultative assembly, and as a religious synod, though in the last case the clergy most often met separately from the laity.

The Carolingian council met yearly in June or July (it had originally met in May and continued with medieval consistency to be called the Mayfield), because by that time the spring thaws were over and the ground was good for military expeditions. These expeditions were supposed to last three months out of every year, and in the beginning every Frankish freeman was obliged to serve. The difficulties of this system for agriculture and ordinary business were recognized, and the old national *heer*—the gathering of the tribe for war—was gradually replaced by a feudal army, the obligation to serve being limited to those who possessed a certain amount of land.

The great council issued capitularies (so called because they were divided into chapters, *capitula*), which were ordinances for the governance of the realm. These were issued by the king with the *"consensus"* of the assembly, and in purport and content were administrative rather than legislative. Bound by legal traditionalism, the Franks, like other medieval peoples, believed that law was not made but discovered. The law existed in the traditional customs of the tribe, which were eternal and unchanging, and which, now that the Franks were Christians, were supposed to reflect natural and divine law. Hence law could not be changed and legislation in the modern sense was thought to be impossible. The capitularies were considered administrative orders proceeding from the king's "ban" (*bannum*), his power to command or prohibit under pain of punishment, and they covered a wide range of problems from defense and economics to ecclesiastical organization and discipline and even personal morality. Other orders proceeding from the royal ban were memoranda on various points and responses to the queries of government officials.

Among these officials were men responsible for the administration of the king's will throughout his wide domains. Charlemagne used three very different means to secure loyalty to his person. First, in 802, he exacted a personal oath of loyalty to the emperor from every freeman. Second, he employed the power of local magnates to keep order. These magnates were originally public officers who later acquired feudal status, and their powers varied according to their original functions. The count was the civil administrator of an area which came to be called a county. The viscount assisted the count. The duke [Latin *dux:* "military commander"] or, in Germany, the *Herzog* [O. H. G. *herizogo:* "helper of the king"] was responsible for the military defense of several counties. The margrave [German *mark graf:* "count of the march"] protected exposed frontiers. Bishops were used when necessary in either a civil or a military capacity. In Charlemagne's time, all these were still public officers rather than feudal barons, and to keep these officers under his supervision, Charlemagne instituted the *missi dominici,* who traveled about in pairs (one bishop and one baron) to make sure that the king's will was obeyed. They reported directly to the king, and they had authority to supervise any territory but that belonging to themselves. The capitulary on the *missi* observes: "Where anything which is not right and just has been enacted in the law, (the king) has ordered them to inquire into this most diligently and to inform him of it; he desires, God willing, to reform it."[6]

Finally, Charlemagne, recognizing that he could not fully control his realm even with this sensible system, was obliged to rely more and more upon ties of a feudal nature. Capitulary 64 states: "Let each man so control his dependents that they shall the better obey and accept the imperial orders and decrees." Charlemagne hoped, by asserting firm control at the top of the feudal hierarchy, to use feudalism as a tool of central control. The weakness of his successors rendered this infeasible, but the technique of manipulating feudalism was to be used with more success by the French kings in the twelfth century. Feudalism became the system according to which Europe was organized from the tenth century to the end of the Middle Ages.

NOTES

[1] *Annales Regni Francorum ad ann. 801,* trans. Helen Wieruszowski in Stewart C. Easton and Helen Wieruszowski, *The Era of Charlemagne,* copyright 1961, D. Van Nostrand Company, Inc., Princeton, New Jersey, p. 127.
[2] In F. J. E. Raby, *The Oxford Book of Medieval Latin Verse* (Oxford, 1959) pp. 89–90.
[3] Quoted from Paschasius Radbert by Eleanor Shipley Duckett, *Carolingian Portraits* (Ann Arbor, 1962), pp. 33–34.
[4] J. H. Robinson, *Readings in European History* (New York, 1904), I, 163–164.
[5] *University of Pennsylvania, Translations and Reprints,* III, 2, pp. 2–4, quoted by Easton and Wieruszowski, p. 135.
[6] J. H. Robinson, I, 139.

Chapter Nine

FEUDALISM

During the decentralized Middle Ages most men had only a vague idea of the theory of the united Christian commonwealth, and an even vaguer notion of the national state, but the most vivid impression of the relationship between a man and his immediate lord. For this reason it is as important to an understanding of the Middle Ages to know about feudalism as to know about Christianity or kings.

{ The word "feudalism" is an artificial one unknown in the Middle Ages and invented in the seventeeth century. }

One group of contemporary historians, viewing feudalism as a complex of loosely connected political, military, and legal institutions, define it as *a system in which a free man binds himself personally to a lord, offering him loyalty and military service in return for protection and the use of a property (usually land)*. The vassal then begins to exercise public functions—administrative and judicial—as a property right. Feudalism so defined contrasts with manorialism (see Chapter Ten below), in which the contract is between an unfree man (the serf) and a free man (the lord) and involves agricultural, not military, duties.

Other historians, taking the broad view, insist that feudalism can be understood only as part of a whole social, political, and economic system dominating medieval life. This opinion has the merit of emphasizing the economic basis of feudalism but has otherwise been exaggerated. Marxists explain the whole structure of medieval society in terms of aristocratic control of the manor—the agricultural means of production. Comparative historians find the "feudal system" in Japan, ancient Egypt, Russia, and India; some writers, using "feudal" as a synonym for "medieval," speak vaguely of feudal art, architecture, literature, or theology. A final, preposterous, misuse of the word is as a synonym of "reactionary." Feudalism was certainly reactionary in the eighteenth century, when writers began to use the term pejoratively, but in the ninth and tenth it was new, vigorous, and progressive. The broad view was brilliantly expounded by the great French historian Marc Bloch, but as a whole it is best to use terms in their most precise sense. One advantage of the restricted definition given above in italics is that it permits us to perceive the difference between feudalism and manorialism. Another is that it has the virtue of limiting generalizations about enormously complex and varied institutions.

PRACTICALLY every history, poem, story, picture, or document conceived by the medieval mind says something, directly or indirectly, about feudalism. The assumptions people made without thinking about them, always the most important though the least easily defined aspects of a culture's thought, were feudal assumptions. Certain documents, of course, are the most helpful. These include (1) *formularies* (forms used by scribes in setting down feudal contracts), (2) *charters* (written records of feudal grants), (3) *laws* or *administrative edicts* dealing with feudalism (the Carolingian capitularies, for example, or the later *établissements* of Saint Louis), and (4) *theoretical writings* pertaining to feudalism, like those of Fulbert of Chartres or John of Salisbury.

THE first question to ask about feudalism is how it began; the second is how it came gradually to dominate. To the first, there are three subsidiary questions: whence, when, and why?

In the nineteenth century, inspired by patriotic vigor, French historians ascribed Roman origins to feudal institutions; the Germans insisted they were Teutonic. The dispassionate historian today will probably admit the preponderance of the Germanic in the feudal system and Roman preponderance in the manorial. The Germans were the warriors of early medieval society, and feudalism was a military system.

The question of *when* feudalism appeared is still a live one. Some define sixth- and seventh-century institutions as feudal or proto-feudal; others reserve such terms until the tenth. The debate over England is whether Anglo-Saxon institutions were feudal or whether feudalism was introduced only at the time of the Norman Conquest. There are two ways to answer these questions. The first is an arbitrary one. The term "feudalism" derives from *feodum* ("fief" or "fee") which in turn derives from the German *Vieh:* "cattle," expanded to mean any chattel or property. Since the granting of a fief—almost always land, but occasionally money or goods—in return for military service did not become common until the eighth century, it is possible to argue that feudalism began only in the eighth century. The second way, though less satisfyingly clean-cut, has the virtue of being more historical than etymological: feudalism did not suddenly spring up full-grown, but underwent gradual development. The earliest elements of feudalism date back to ancient Rome and Germania; by 1100 the system was complete but already obsolescent; and its remnants remained at least until 1789.

With these ideas in mind, the question of *why* feudalism appeared can be answered more intelligibly. Between the third and seventh century a centralized state had been replaced by a highly decentralized society. One modern historian puts the next question succinctly: was feudalism "the cause or consequence of decentralization"?[1] The initial decentralization following the barbarian invasions of the fourth and fifth centuries made it difficult for government to function, and the Merovingians allowed local authorities to build up their power. Charlemagne was obliged to encourage the growth of local power, hoping to use it, but his successors, engaged in dynastic disputes, let their control of the local leaders lapse. With the ninth- and tenth-century invasions, the central governments, already weakened, practically ceased to exist, and people everywhere turned desperately to whatever source of security they could find. Their situation was much like what ours might be if there were any survivors after an atomic war. They turned to their families, but since families were not large or powerful enough, they naturally placed their trust in the local magnates. These leaders, enjoying virtual independence, now did not hesitate to defend it against all the claims of central authority. Feudalism was originally called into existence by decentralization, but once it was established, self-interest impelled the feudal magnates to perpetuate it.

Since feudalism was established by local leaders in small communities, its practices and forms varied greatly from region to region, as F. L. Ganshof and others have shown. The generalizations that follow are, therefore, subject to almost infinite exceptions in time and place.

ONCE introduced, feudalism passed through five stages of development, which are in part reflected in the elements of the ceremony that occurred when a man entered into the feudal relation with his lord, much as geological changes can be seen in the strata of a cross section of earth.

The count asked each one if he wished to become wholly his man, and the latter replied, "I so wish," and with his hands clasped and enclosed by those of the count, they (the lord and his man) were bound together by a kiss. Secondly, he who had done homage pledged his faith to the count's spokesman in these words: "I promise on my faith that I will henceforth be faithful to Count William and that I will maintain my homage toward him completely against everyone, in good faith and without guile." And in the third place he swore an oath to this effect on the relics of the saints. Then the count, with a wand which he held in his hand, gave investiture to all those who by this compact had promised loyalty and done homage and likewise had taken an oath.[2]

There are three essential elements in this typical ceremony: (1) homage (cf. *homme*), in which a person becomes the "man" of his lord by giving him his hands to hold (indicating that the lord has the use of them from now on) and by making a simple declaration of loyalty; (2) a religious oath; (3) investiture or seisin, wherein the lord bestows upon the man some symbol (often a clod of earth or stalk of wheat) of the fief he now receives. These elements, and two others not included in the ceremony—heredity and chivalry—represent five stages in the growth of feudalism.

THE first element was the personal bond between lord and man. With the breakdown of central authority, men "commended themselves" to one who could protect them and lead them in battle. In effect there was a contract between the lord [A.S. *hlaford:* "loaf-keeper," a person in authority over a household; cf. German *Herr* and French *seigneur* from Latin *senior*] and his

A feudal lord receiving his knights.

vassal [from the Celtic *gwas:* "boy" or "servant"; cf. *Knight,*
from A.S. *cnihta:* "boy"]. This was a purely practical military
contract, and if either party was unable or unwilling to continue to fulfill his obligations under the contract, the other
party was considered quit of his. As early as 847 such a personal contract was prescribed for everyone in the Frankish kingdom: "We will moreover," says the capitulary of Mersen of that
year, "that each free man in our kingdom shall choose a lord,
from us or our faithful, such a one as he wishes." [3] Under this
system, had it worked ideally, the kings could have controlled
society through a pyramidal feudal hierarchy: the king calls
upon his vassals, who call upon *their* vassals, who call upon
theirs, until every free man in the kingdom has been reached.
But another element—land—was added to feudalism that made
it infinitely more complicated.

THE second element of feudalism was the land that came to
be added to the personal relationship. When society had attained some degree of tranquility, the vassal began to feel that
the protection given him was no longer important enough to
justify the cost of rendering military service. This feeling increased from the eighth century, when cavalry for a while became the most important element in warfare, and the cost of
service increased enormously. The eighth-century introduction
of the stirrup and the larger and more powerful war horse

(*destrier*) made the mounted warrior, leaning forward along his horse's body with his lance set forward, a formidable engine of assault. Unfortunately, other knights had lances too, and the warrior was obliged in defense to use heavier and more complete armor. Horse, lance, armor, and shield all cost a great deal of money, and the rulers had to reimburse their warriors by grants of land. Sometimes the knights obtained their land, not by gift, but by force, taking advantage of the weakness of central authority to seize territory. Land seemed desirable because it conferred status upon its possessor, and—more basically —because the knights received attached to the land a servile population which harvested its products and yielded a monetary income sufficient to feed, clothe, shelter, and arm the knight and his household.

The amount of service a man owed his lord depended upon the amount of land that he held from him. Hence military service came to be allotted, not only to the tenant, but to his holding: each bit of property owed the lord so many knights' services. The value of property considered worth one knight's service varied. In twelfth-century England, for example, land worth £20 a year was often considered one "knight's fee (fief)" owing one knight's service. If Lord A granted land worth £200 per annum to Lord B, Lord B would owe Lord A ten knights' services and, when summoned, would be obliged to appear himself with nine other knights. Lord B might keep these nine knights around him in his own castle. In this event he would hold the whole fief personally as his demesne, which would be worked by peasants. Or he might grant out land worth £60 to Lord C, who would then owe him three knights' services, and land worth £120 to Lord D, who would owe him six. Lord D could then grant land worth £40 to Sir E, and so on. This process was known as subinfeudation, and it was usually much more complicated than the foregoing illustration suggests. A vassal holding less than one knight's fee would, by tradition, have to go in with someone else to provide the one knight's service. A capitulary of 808 states: "Every free man who has four *mansi* (*mansus:* a measurement of land) of his own property, or as a benefice from any one, shall equip himself and go to the army, either with his lord, if the lord goes, or with his count. He who has three *mansi* . . . shall be joined to a man who has one *mansus* . . . and shall aid him so that he may serve for both."[4] The *établissements* of Saint Louis over four hundred years later ordered that "the baron and all vassals of the king are bound to appear before him when he shall summon them, and to serve him at their own expense . . . with as many knights as each one owes . . . ."

∠The effects of this union of land and personal contract were diverse. First, feudal land law became immensely complicated. To cite only one of the simpler complications: a man might hold land from several different lords, owing each one several knights' services. But to whose host was he to go himself? Or what if one of his lords should go to war against another? To solve this problem one was designated as the liege lord [from *lego*: "to bind"] to whom the vassal was bound above all others. A second complication was that a man might, in modern slang, "wear many hats." In 1175, for example, one man was at the same time king of England, duke of Normandy, count of Anjou, and duke of Aquitaine. As king of England he owed no one service, but as duke of Normandy he was a vassal of the king of France and was obliged to render service to that monarch even when the latter went to war with the king of England. Of course the English king in question did not stand about smiting himself with his own sword: practical politics intervened, and he simply did not appear to render his services to France. A third, and eventually crippling, complication of the system was brought about by subinfeudation. As long as there were only a limited number of vassals the king could hope to control the feudal system; but with the decline of the Carolingian Empire vassals indulged more and more frequently in giving out parts of their own fiefs to subvassals, and eventually ways were found to circumvent the system and to avoid sending the king the military service owed him. Hence the addition of the element of land to the system encouraged further decentralization and anarchy.

It also had another, quite different, but equally important effect: welding wealth and status to military power, it helped to create a new class structure, for no poor man could hope to afford a knight's equipment.

∠THE third element of feudalism proceeds from the introduction of land: feudalism was transformed from a mutual contract

Investing a knight with arms.

for utilitarian military purposes to a class structure. This transformation was completed by the triumph of the hereditary principle. The original terms for land held by the vassal were *precarium*, something you got by *preces,* humble request, and held only under good conduct (whence "precarious") and *beneficium,* which had a similar connotation. But the hereditary nature of fiefs, already visible by the ninth century, was established in the eleventh. This meant, first of all, that the original use and purpose of feudalism had disappeared: a child or an incompetent who succeeded to a fief could hardly render his lord the military service required of him under the original system. The hereditary principle was useful in securing peaceable succession to a throne, but from the moment when feudalism created an hereditary aristocracy, it began to be obsolescent as a military system. Medieval society was seriously injured by the freezing of class lines, the restriction of social mobility, and the consequent denigration of ability in favor of birth, limitations that persisted until quite recently in Britain and other European countries.

The most powerful of these hereditary aristocrats were generally the dukes, though in England there were none until the fourteenth century. After the dukes there were the counts (in England, earls), the viscounts, the marquesses, and the barons. "Baron" [late Latin *baro*: "man"] was also used as a general term to describe tenants of a higher rank than that of simple knight.

The French jurist Beaumanoir defined a "baron" as a noble who holds a court, indicating the importance of the judicial functions of the nobility. In France and Germany these nobles attained enormous power; in England they were always limited by the royal efforts to use less powerful, and more loyal, officers like the sheriffs in place of the feudal nobility.

THE fourth element in feudalism is the religious, represented by the vassal's oath of fealty taken upon the Bible or the relics of a saint. The Church, faced with the pervasiveness of feudal values, attempted to baptize them. The oath of fealty made it not only illegal but also sinful to break the feudal contract. Feudal warriors were taught, though the lesson seldom took, to regard themselves not as mere knights but as knights of Christ whose job was, as John of Salisbury put it, to "defend the Church, assail unorthodoxy, venerate the priesthood, protect the poor . . . ."

CHIVALRY, the fifth element, was introduced towards the end of the eleventh century. Chivalry and courtly love made of the knight a romantic figure, lonely, mysterious, ready to die for God or for his lady love. Chivalry illustrates the growing obsolescence of feudalism as a military institution but also its ability to express varied and changing manifestations of the life of the community.

THESE were the theoretical principles of feudalism; what was it in ordinary practice? The fief was not owned, but simply possessed, by the tenant. In the beginning, when the Frankish people conquered Gaul, all the land was designated the land of the people (in England, "Folk Land") and each man was considered to have a portion. In some areas, a few people continued to own their land free of service (this kind of holding was called an "allod"), but for the most part "Folk Land" was gradually turned into "King's Land." By the twelfth century in England it had become a legal principle that the king owned all the land, and in that kingdom underground resources or discovered hoards are still deemed the property of the crown. By the thirteenth century the principle (*nulle terre sans seigneur*) that almost all land had some kind of service attached to it became common.

The king, owning the land, gave some to the Church, retained

Dover Castle, Kent, England.

Donnington Castle, Berkshire, England; fourteenth century.

Castel del Monte, Apulia; thirteenth century.

Castle of the Counts of Flanders, Ghent; twelfth century.

some as his royal demesne (as forest, hunting preserve, or most usually, agricultural land farmed by his own serfs), and gave the rest out to feudal vassals. These vassals and (if they subinfeudated) their own vassals did not own the land; they had the usufruct of it, and they had that only so long as they tendered the services due for it. The principle, not a foolish one, was that one has right to his property only so long as he fulfills his obligations to society and does not use it to the public detriment.

How did the land thus held by the vassal (called the benefice, fief, or fee) fit into the feudal pattern?

What the vassal received from his lord under the feudal contract was (1) the fief itself; (2) protection—the lord was obliged to defend the vassal's life and property by warfare or by taking his case to court, and to refrain from harming his vassal; and (3) often a grant of "immunity." These grants of immunity derived from the fact that in the Carolingian period the holders of public offices (called "honors") were granted fiefs and that the offices, like the land itself, came to be part of a feudal grant. Hence the lord could grant, in addition to the fief, the right to collect one's own taxes, to run one's own system of justice, to take tolls, even to coin money. These were called "immunities" because the vassal holding them was *immune* in the sense of enjoying the rights that the king ordinarily would have in these respects. Immunities varied from fief to fief: "The king has justice over all the lands which he has in his domain. He can make manors out of these lands and give them (to a vassal) with complete or shared rights of justice. He can also give manors but keep the justice of himself."[5]

In return for these benefits, the vassal owed his lord four types of service: *auxilium, consilium,* aids, and incidents. *Auxilium* (military service) included yearly duty in the feudal host (usually forty days in peacetime, occasionally as much as two or even three months in wartime) and escort duty or garrison duty ("castle-guard"). These duties could be avoided by the offering of a valid excuse and the payment of *scutage* [from *scutum*: "shield"] or fine, and in fact the later medieval kings often preferred to collect fines and pay their own professional soldiers, for a feudal campaign might well come to a sudden halt upon the expiration of the agreed term of service. *Auxilium* was, like the vassal's other duties, owed to his direct lord, and only in England was the rule early and firmly established that a man could not be summoned by his lord to serve against the king.

∠ In addition to *auxilium*, the vassal owed *consilium* ("advice"). He had to come when called to help his lord make decisions or to serve in his court of justice. The vassal was also obliged to furnish *aids*, payments of money to help ransom his lord if he were captured or to pay for the knighting of the lord's eldest son or the marriage of his eldest daughter, affairs which required a considerable outlay for trappings and entertainment. The vassal was subject to certain *incidents:* when he received his fief, he paid the lord a "relief"; if the vassal were a minor, he or she became the lord's ward, and the lord not infrequently continued to manage his ward's estate to his own advantage. If the vassal died without visible heirs, the estate went back into the lord's hands in the process of "escheat." If the vassal broke the feudal contract, his land was "forfeit." Finally, the lord had the inconvenient *droit de gîte* requiring his vassal to provide him and a sometimes numerous retinue food and lodging for weeks on end. The most shameless prototypes of the Man Who Came to Dinner, the medieval monarchs often used the *droit de gîte* as a regular means of relieving the pressures on the royal treasury.

∠THE feudal contract was binding on both parties, though it could be dissolved by mutual agreement. If the vassal broke his part of the contract, he forfeited his fief; if the lord violated his, the vassal was theoretically released from his side of the bargain and had the right of going to the lord's court and throwing the symbol of investiture back in his face (a process given the resounding title "exfestucation"), though the exercise of this right may have depended upon how many burly friends the vassal had brought with him. Violation of the feudal contract might be adduced as justification for the deposition of a monarch, but again military might did more than legal theory to determine the outcome of such a proceeding.

IN the borderlands of medieval legal practice, there were other free tenures that were not strictly feudal. Bishops, abbots, and other churchmen usually held at least some of their lands in feudal tenure and were obliged to render military service, which, for the most part, choosing to keep their vestments clean of blood, they did through substitutes. But God and the saints might hold land, through the churches consecrated to them, in the non-feudal tenures either of "divine service" or of *"frankalmoign"* ("free alms"). A lord might upon his death leave a certain property to the Church of Saint X upon the condition that Saint X's priests say *y* number of masses a year for the repose of his soul ("divine service"), or he might leave them the land, still to ensure the welfare of his soul, but without requiring any specific spiritual services (*"frankalmoign"*).

THE most curious tenure was serjeanty, neither strictly free nor strictly servile. Serjeanty illustrates the curious fact that in the Middle Ages neither the extent of one's holdings nor the form of one's tenure was a sure guide to status, for a large estate did not necessarily make one a baron or even a knight, and on the other hand a free man might in some cases hold in servile tenure. The term "serjeant" (from which, of course, comes our modern "sergeant") derives from the Latin *servire,* "to serve." Serjeants were men who themselves or whose fathers had been stable boys, waiters, gardeners, or the like. The king, well pleased with their services, had given them gifts of land, and if a serjeant were loyal or clever enough he could obtain wide possessions. The serjeants were obliged to do some service for the land, but they had become too wealthy and powerful to be expected to continue cooking in the kitchen; on the other hand, their servile origins prevented them from becoming knights. A few eventually held their land by some kind of military service, but most continued to hold by the performance, once a year, of some act symbolic of their original functions. Thus in the reign of Henry I of England (1100–1135), one John Belet performed all the functions of a butler, but by 1256 his descendant held the family land simply by coming once a year to court and handing the Earl Warenne a cup to pass to the king. Another serjeant held by putting the king's chessmen in their box once a year. One Rolland of Hemingstone was obliged to come to the royal court once a year to make a hop, to whistle, and to break wind.

ANOTHER kind of tenure was that in England called socage: the socager was a free man holding his land by the payment of rent and so falling into the category of neither serf nor noble.

FEUDALISM may have retarded the growth of political unity on a national level. It concentrated power in the hands of a small aristocracy of warriors who retained their privileges long after their military utility had declined. These feudal lords were insufficiently subject to the supervision of a central government. The authority of the lords is expressed in the French lawyer Beaumanoir's phrase: "each baron is sovereign in his barony." For practical purposes this was often true in France before the twelfth century and in Germany after the thirteenth. Such lords had most of the rights and privileges we associate with the sovereign state today. Europe was broken into tiny feudal fragments over which the kings were not sovereigns, but only suzerains (feudal overlords).

Yet political development after Charlemagne's unsuccessful effort at establishing a universal empire depended upon the utilization of feudalism. Feudalism permitted local centers of political stability to be formed, and the new monarchies used these centers as building blocks in the establishment of a larger polity. It was, therefore, in countries like England and France, where feudalism was initially strong, that the central power finally emerged most powerful; in countries like Germany and Italy, where it was initially weak, an impressive central authority failed to emerge. The political history of later medieval Europe is in large part the history of the central power's trying to convert suzerainty into sovereignty, the feudal system into a centralized state.

Economically, feudalism, by encouraging the growth first of a small class of warriors and then, through the development of scutage, of a paid, professional army, for centuries freed the bulk of the population from the obligations of military service for more productive labors.

If feudalism encouraged anarchy and promoted local feuds and wars, it also inhibited the kind of total war associated with the ancients and with the twentieth century. Feudal wars were fought spasmodically, by small forces, and for limited objectives; and the behavior of the knights, while frequently brutal (as that of warriors often is), was modified by the institutions of chivalry, a code based in part upon Christian ethics and in part upon the ethics of personal loyalty. The Church made the only efforts before the modern Geneva Convention to limit war, attempting to outlaw "unjust wars" and to impose the "Peace of God" (ca. 990) prohibiting assaults upon noncombatants, and the "Truce of God" (ca. 1030), prohibiting fighting on Friday, Saturday, Sunday, certain feast days, and at certain seasons. Personal loyalty, honor, obedience to one's lord, generosity, frankness, and openness were the qualities of *prowess,* the code of the *preux chevalier,* or perfect knight, and this code had its advantages. Its remnants inhibited, if they did not always prevent, the indiscriminate destruction of hospitals, schools, and civilian homes, until our own times again approved the idea that nothing should be permitted to limit the national interest.

THERE are many *preux chevaliers* in literature—perhaps Roland, Gawain, and Galahad are the most famous—but there were *preux chevaliers* in real life as well, and of these William Marshal, Sidney Painter's "knight-errant, baron, and Regent of England" is one of the most justly celebrated. His career illustrates what a knight was supposed to be as opposed to the more numerous examples of what he was supposed not to be.[6]

William Marshal was exposed to feudal warfare at the early age of five, when in 1152 King Stephen of England, engaged in a civil war to protect his throne from the claims of the Countess Matilda, attacked the castle of William's father, one of her supporters. The father held off Stephen's attack by promising not to reinforce the castle while negotiations for capitulation were under way, and in surety offered his son as hostage. Little William was accordingly delivered over to the king, whereupon his devoted sire immediately violated the truce by sending in a strong garrison, leaving the child "in an extremely precarious position."[7] Stephen sent a message threatening to hang the boy, to which the father, caring more for castles than for children, contemptuously replied that it did not matter, "for he had the anvils and hammers with which to forge still better sons."[8] Upon receipt of this reply Stephen would have carried out his threat, had not the boy's youth caused him to repent. So weak was this king that he not only called off the hanging but squelched the suggestion of one of his more ingenious advisers that he should order the little fellow hurled over the battlements of the beleaguered castle by a siege engine.

The family's support of the Angevins against King Stephen

was rewarded by Countess Matilda's son, King Henry II, and William Marshal received both the honors of the king and the attentions of the queen, the notorious Eleanor of Aquitaine. (There is an amusing ballad about the queen and "the earl marshall"—William's title only much later—but it probably does William an injustice. It would be difficult to do one to Eleanor.) The king appointed him the tutor of the young Prince Henry, an office that had nothing to do with books and pens but a great deal to do with horses and weapons. Fighting was the métier of the feudal class, but the true knight-errant was supposed to fight for glory as well as out of necessity. William taught the young prince to ride, to use the sword and the lance, and to cultivate the newer and gentler virtues that priests and ladies were coming to expect of their knightly companions— generosity, courtesy, and a tongue as mild as the sword was sharp.

William's courage and courtesy were so well thought of that he was able to indulge his love of warfare in the various and sundry feudal and dynastic disputes of the time without incurring the permanent displeasure of any of the kings in whose reigns he lived. Perhaps his youthful experience with King Stephen had taught him the value of tact in dealing with Henry II, Richard the Lion-Hearted, and John; in any case, he was able to fight against them on occasion without permanently relinquishing their friendship. For more than half his life he was landless but renowned, a respected and beloved figure at courts and tournaments, a true knight-errant. Then, by marriage with a landed heiress, and by inheriting his own family properties and the office of master marshal of the king's court at his brother's death in 1194, he became one of the most powerful barons of the realm.

As a soldier and as a loyal knight William was without peer. He combined with knightly valor the two very unknightly virtues of intelligence and obedience. Richard the Lion-Hearted (1189–1199) was amazed during a campaign in France in 1194 to find that William could be relied upon to obey as well as to kill. A battle was fought in which the enemy was put to rout, and Richard and his knights wished to pursue them for the purposes of ransom and booty, so the king asked William Marshal to hold his own knights back from the pursuit in order to act as a rear guard. It was extraordinary enough that William should forego the pleasure of the chase but even more extraordinary that he should be able to restrain his followers from the looting, and Richard no more forgot this incident than he forgot that at fifty-three the marshal could still lead his men in a scramble up a siege ladder onto the battlements of a castle and there cut down a defending knight with one blow of his sword.

William's relations with King John (1199–1216) were strained for a long while, but his support of the king during the dark time when most of Europe was against him restored him to even that monarch's favor; with Stephen Langton, William Marshal was a leader of the moderates during the struggle that culminated in Magna Carta (1215). The year after, when King John died, William became regent for the young King Henry III. In this capacity, in spite of advancing age, he defeated the French, reorganized the administration, approved a new charter of liberties, and died peacefully in office with his renown unimpaired.

What was as extraordinary, he died with his wife and children round him shedding unaffected tears and more concerned with their dying father than with their future estates. On his deathbed he is said to have exclaimed to his friend John d'Erley, "I am going to tell you an extraordinary thing. I do not know why it is, but it has been three years or more since I have had as great a desire to sing as I have had for the last three days." John told him to go ahead, but he demurred, saying, "It would not do me any good, and everyone would believe me to be crazy."[9] At last, asking his family and friends to gather closely round his bed, he said, "I am dying. I commend you to God. I can no longer be with you. I cannot defend myself from death."[10]

FEUDALISM could no more defend itself from death than could the great feudal knight, but for half a millennium, feudalism, with the manor upon which its economy rested, was the basic fact of life in western Europe, where people's almost sole contact with power and government was through their lord and *seigneur*.

[1] R. S. Hoyt, *Feudal Institutions: Cause or Consequence of Decentralization* (New York, 1961).

[2] Galbert of Bruges, *The Murder of Charles the Good,* trans. and ed. James Bruce Ross (New York, Columbia University Press, 1960), pp. 206–207.

[3] Norton Downs, *Basic Documents in Medieval History* (Princeton, 1959), p. 46.

[4] *Translations and Reprints from the Original Sources of European History,* Univ. of Pennsylvania (Philadelphia, 1899), p. 9.

[5] Cited and trans. by Joseph R. Strayer, *Feudalism* (New York, 1965), p. 131, from the *Leges Henrici Primi.*

[6] This short account follows the late Sidney Painter's excellent biography, *William Marshal* (Baltimore, Johns Hopkins Press, 1933).

[7] Painter, p. 14.

[8] Painter, p. 14.

[9] Painter, p. 286.

[10] Painter, p. 288.

Chapter Ten

THE AGRICULTURAL ECONOMY
AND COMMUNITY

"Some pray, some fight, and others work," said Adalbero of Laon, a tenth-century bishop, describing the threefold division of medieval society into clergy, knights, and peasants. The last comprised upwards of ninety percent of the early medieval population, and it does not require a Marxist point of view to recognize that a group itself so large in number, and so necessary for the livelihood of other classes, was an essential, if anonymous, part of medieval society. That society was agricultural; it rested upon the shoulders of the peasants.

The peasant was first and foremost a member of a family; beyond the family he felt himself a part of the village community. The village was small, neighborly [neighbor–"nigh boor": "near farmer"], and its members acted as a group.

The agricultural community of the Middle Ages may be viewed as a village, a *vill*, or a manor. Considered as a village, it consisted of peasants who had come together for mutual advantage, communal living and cooperation being natural in the fertile and temperate countries of western Europe. In the village lived peasants in varying degrees of freedom. Earlier historians, in their eagerness to distinguish the legal status of the free from the unfree, came to the conclusion that less than a quarter of the population of a village was likely to be "free," while the rest were serfs. But these distinctions were wholly irrelevant in terms of life of the village community. The "free" and the "unfree" lived in similar conditions, did the same kind of work, often held about a similar amount of land, and fraternized without inhibition.

Knights attacking peasants.

It is fair to say that if the manorial system and its attendant legal distinctions had not existed, the village community would have taken much the same form. It was the natural way of life.

The differences in the sizes of the holdings of the peasants were seldom great. In much of western Europe the land was communal and "open-field." Each peasant had a small "door-yard" around his hut and sometimes an "assart" as well, a bit of land he had personally claimed from the waste. Aside from these small properties, however, his land was disposed about the manor in unfenced and unhedged strips distinguished from those of the other peasants only by a double furrow. This arrangement was designed to prevent any one person from getting particularly good or bad soil, and to facilitate the ploughing, which was done with draft animals and heavy ploughs which the individual peasant could not afford and which he had to share with his neighbors. They ploughed, weeded, sowed, and harvested together, but the system was one of cooperation rather than of communism, for after the work had been done each man received the produce of his own holdings. Besides the ploughed fields there was a common pasture on which the animals of all the peasants might graze. This open-field, common-pasture system persisted in some isolated areas into modern times.

THE agricultural community was also a *vill,* a unit of local government, responsible to the king and his officers for the maintenance of order and the reporting of crimes. The local court, called the "hundred court" in England, was a public court attended by the free peasants, though later in the Middle Ages it often, by falling into the hands of the nobility, became a private court. Then, in order to procure justice for the common people, the Tudor kings were obliged to create special prerogative courts, like the Star Chamber, where secret proceedings protected plaintiffs from the vengeance of their lords.

THE agricultural community may also be viewed as a manor. In France, Germany, or England there was no "free village" exempt from seignorial exactions: each village was connected with a manor. It seems natural that the manor and the village should be coextensive, and this was often the case in the early Middle Ages, but by the twelfth century land tenures had become more complicated. Sometimes a manor would comprise more than one village; more often, a village would be divided between two or more manors. A manor was part of the lord's fief: for it he owed feudal obligations to his own suzerain; but from it he himself received servile, rather than military, benefits.

THE seignorial, or manorial system [Latin *manere:* "to dwell"] is different from the feudal system; the feudal vassal was a free man having certain contractual rights in regard to his lord, while the serf or villein [*villanus:* "inhabitant of a *vill*"] was an unfree tenant holding from a lord by rendering servile labor. This taint of servitude remained with him for life and passed to his descendants unto the last generation (*in perpetuum*). The two systems were distinct, and the manorial could and did exist in some areas, like Sardinia, where the feudal did not. But the feudal could not exist without the manorial, for the manor was the economic foundation of the castle. Said one medieval writer, "It is seemly that the men should plow and dig and work hard that the earth may yield the fruits from which the knight and his horse shall live."[1] Almost every lord, whether king, bishop, or baron, was at the same time a manorial lord and lived by the sweat of his peasants' brows.

Knights greeting a peasant.

Ploughmen.

Peasants plowing, sowing, and planting; detail from the Bayeux Tapestry
(eleventh century).

YET many historians still continue, after the discoveries of the last hundred years and the excellent work of Bloch, Verriest, Duby, and others, to give short shrift to the nine-tenths of the medieval population engaged directly in agriculture. Medieval writers themselves were as reticent on the subject as Jane Austen about the personalities of her heroines' servants, but tracts on estate management like Walter of Henley's *Treatise on Husbandry,* manorial archives, archeology, and the new techniques of aerial photography have been of great help, as have been public laws and surveys like William the Conqueror's *Domesday Book.* Many studies have recently been done of particular manors and local conditions, and these are gradually producing a picture that is clearer, if more complex, than before. The manorial system in its pure form existed only in France, England, and Germany and, even in the countries where it was strongest, varied considerably from locality to locality and from century to century. As with feudalism, most generalizations about the medieval village are subject to many exceptions that vary according to time and place.

The chronological development of agricultural institutions is particularly important. Nineteenth-century historians debated whether the manor originated in the Roman *villa* or in the depression of an originally free Germanic population. The primitive Germans formed villages collectively, but in what degree of "freedom" or "servitude" it is impossible to determine. Whatever the status of individual German peasants, the origins of the manor are more clearly to be found in the late Roman *villa,* a large landed estate worked by slaves and *coloni.*

The manor developed from the *villa* according to the exigencies of the feudal system, coupled with the abandonment of slavery and the depression of the free man (if not of the imaginary "free village").

Beginning in the seventh century slavery gradually disappeared from most of Europe. The reasons for this decline are obscure, but we may guess at a few. The first was that, since slave populations did not adequately reproduce themselves, new slaves had constantly to be imported, and the recession of Roman military power caused the cessation of new supplies of slaves. In France, where the supply was wholly lacking, slavery disappeared completely in the course of the ninth century. In Spain and Portugal, which continued to be able to draw on Moslem imports of slaves, and to enslave captured Moslems themselves, the institution continued into modern times. The second reason was religious. The ancient polis, while permitting the enslavement of those outside its politico-religious limits, protected its own citizens from slavery. Christianity extended the notion of the polis to Christian society as a whole and, while long permitting the enslavement of infidels, forbade the enslavement of other Christians. The third reason is that masters found that men permitted at least a few liberties and incentives were better workers. The *servus,* in the sixth century a "slave," had in most parts of western Europe by the ninth century become a "serf." By the twelfth century the word *villanus* increasingly replaced the word *servus.* Religion and economic advantage happily united to remove an institution that had, in Babylon, Athens, and Rome alike, been accepted and practiced by all the ancients.

The elevation of the slave was unhappily countered by the depression of the free man. While the agricultural economy of most of Europe had probably always rested to a large extent upon unfree labor, there were large numbers of ordinary freemen among both the indigenous populations and the invading Teutons. But in the period of barbarian attacks that lasted until the mid-tenth century many of these men lost their freedom. Some were simply seized by lords taking advantage of troubled times when the king's law could be disregarded; some who gradually had come to do more and more servile labor found their *de facto* status as serfs changed by legal definition into *de jure* status; some inherited their servility, for if one's father were a serf, one was automatically a serf oneself. When the invasions were over, the economic advance did not help the small holder, for increased population put too heavy a burden on his land and forced at least some of his heirs into servitude.

Most commonly the free man became a serf of his own will, though of economic necessity, by the process of "commendation." As the free man of some wealth and standing commended himself to a lord as a feudal vassal, the poor free man without means commended himself as a serf to a manorial lord, offering servile labor in order to obtain the security, protection, and land that he needed.

At least in the beginning, serfdom was a constructive rela-

A medieval cart found at Oseberg.

tionship between serf and lord advantageous to both parties. As a modern American president said, "a necessitous man is not a free man": a man who is crushed by utter lack of material security, even though he is technically "free," is practically speaking deprived of spiritual as well as physical freedom. It is difficult in today's affluent society, where even the extremely poor have their most fundamental needs taken care of, to imagine the total lack of security that threatened the man of the early Middle Ages. A wholly "free" man was free to come and go as he pleased and to do as he liked without any obligations, but there was nowhere for such a man to go and nothing he might do. Until late in the eleventh century there were no towns where he could seek employment. If he wanted to farm, there would be no opportunity to earn money to buy land or a plow. He could not "squat" on uncleared land, because even land not in use was in possession of one lord or another. The roads were unsafe and there were no police, and if he traveled he would very likely be beaten or murdered. He might take to crime and live for a while as a robber, but when caught he would be speedily hanged. At best he might spend his life as a beggar, living out on the steps of a church eating whatever scraps were thrown him and dressed in whatever rags people were charitable enough to give him. When he fell sick, no one would tend him. In short, there was no way whatever such a "free" man could find food, clothing, and shelter for himself or his family. Freedom without obligations was freedom to starve. In order to possess minimal material security, then, a man had to enter into a relationship of dependence. He had to enter a monastery or else to commend himself to a lord.

The distinction between "free" and "unfree" has been exaggerated by legal historians. The Middle Ages did not conceive of "liberty" as a positive quality in itself, except to indicate the proper place that every man must occupy in society. When "liberties" were mentioned, they meant not positive rights but exemptions from certain duties. Hence there was no clear-cut distinction between free and unfree.

Further, it was believed that serfdom was a natural manifestation of the subjection of all men as the servants of God. To symbolize this, the wealthy Saint Gérard of Brogne went every other year to Rome in the costume of a serf, and the popes adopted the title *servus servorum Dei* ("slave of the slaves of God"). Medieval thinkers admitted that bondage was not natural; it had not existed in Eden and was one of the consequences of the Fall of Man. But in our present fallen state, we are all *servi* in one way or another, and the condition of the serfs was felt to be no scandal.

THE purpose of the manor was of course agricultural production, and numerous improvements were made in agricultural techniques. Almost all the peasants were engaged in a variety of activities pertaining directly to the cultivation of the soil and the raising of stock, chiefly cattle, sheep, and pigs. Some had specialized skills and filled the other needs of the lord and the community as masons, carpenters, smiths, or millers. Some had other occasional duties, like haywards (who took care of the hedges [*haia*]), woodwards, or ditch- and canal-diggers.

Medieval farm technology was creative and progressive. The ancients had tilled the shallow soil with light scratch plows, but more extensive use of iron in the period from the sixth through the ninth centuries made possible the invention and use of the heavy wheeled plow, rendering cultivation of deeper soils much more efficient. The animals used to draw the plow were also the beneficiaries of invention. The horseshoe, the horse-collar, and a greatly improved harness were introduced in the eighth or ninth century to encourage the replacement of the ox by the horse and to make the horse a more effective machine.

About the eighth century too came a great improvement of

PLAN of the MANOR

- The lord's demesne, in open fields
- The glebe (strips in open fields held by the parish church)
- The peasants' strips in open fields

WASTE

WOODLAND

FALLOW

COMMON PASTURE

Road

Road

SPRING PLANTING

WOODLAND

AUTUMN PLANTING

PARSONAGE

CHURCH

MANOR

WASTE

Pond

Stream

Mill

VILLAGE

MEADOW

Road

CLOSES

MARSH

THE THREE-FIELD ROTATION SYSTEM

	Year *1*	Year *2*	Year *3*
Field 1	WINTER: wheat	SPRING: peas, beans, oats	Fallow
Field 2	SPRING: peas, beans, oats	Fallow	WINTER
Field 3	Fallow	WINTER: wheat	SPRING

cultivation methods. Both the Romans and the primitive Germans had used a two-field rotation system: wheat would be planted in one field while the other was left fallow, the process being reversed the next year, so that in any one year only half the land was under cultivation. The old system remained in wide use, but in unusually fertile areas the new three-field rotation was adopted with enthusiasm, and production was greatly increased. In the new system, both winter and spring crops were sowed, and a period of fallow was also used, as in the accompanying chart.[2]

The increase in population from the tenth century led to great clearings of marshes and forests within the heartland of Europe and to expansion into the East from Germany, creating a great agricultural boom and preparing the eventual transformation of the manorial system into the modern system of agricultural free labor.

THE center of the manor was the lord's manor house, surrounded by his close; nearby were the church and the rectory surrounded by its own small garden. In 1265 one Robert le Moyne received a manor house that contained

> . . . a sufficient and handsome hall well-ceiled with oak. On the western side is a suitable bed, on the ground, a stone chimney, a wardrobe and a certain other small chamber; at the eastern end is a pantry and a buttery. Between the hall and the chapel is a sideroom. There is a decent chapel covered with tiles. . . In the hall are four tables on trestles. There (is) likewise a good kitchen well covered with tiles . . . .[3]

The lord would sometimes live in this manor house himself, though he would more often prefer to reside at the household of a greater lord, and in any event he would often be away fulfilling his feudal obligations. In the lord's absence, his place was taken by the seneschal ("oldest servant"), an honorary title usually borne by the steward, who was usually a man of some rank and often a close relative of the lord himself. As steward, this man was in charge of all the lord's estates. Under the steward was a bailiff (hence Bailey), a free man most often in charge of only one of the estates. The steward and the bailiff were in charge of keeping order and ensuring that the proper services would be performed. Under them was the reeve [French *prévôt*] a peasant acceptable to both lord and serfs who served as a kind of foreman and an indispensable link between the rulers and the ruled.

Besides his close, the lord also held the forest and strips of land throughout the manor. All these properties, which he held directly, were known as his "demesne." The priest, or rather the manor church, also held such strips of land interspersed among the peasants' holdings: these were known as the "glebe."

In addition to his demesne, the lord was likely to have a mill, a wine-press, and other appurtenances that figured large in the peasants' lives. He also held a manorial court, quite independent of the royal and public courts, that met in the hall or, when the weather was fine, on the village green. The manorial court had jurisdiction over disputes between peasants and over the lord's tolls, market rights, and other privileges. The courts varied in power; many lords had gained from the king jurisdiction over petty criminal matters, and a few had usurped jurisdiction over all crimes, though the kings hotly contested such pretensions whenever they were able. These courts not only permitted the lord to keep order in his own manor with a minimum of royal interference but also yielded him a good income in fines. A serf could not sue the lord in his own court, and after the early Middle Ages he was hardly ever permitted to go to law against him in the king's courts, so that he had little recourse against a lord who was truly vicious. But since the lord did not act secretly or unilaterally, but rather in a court attended by the peasants of the manor, the unfairness of the system was alleviated.

AMONG the peasants themselves were numerous degrees of servitude. The reeve was a serf with a considerable amount of re-

Model of a third-century peasant's house. This is fairly typical of peasant dwellings throughout the early Middle Ages.

sponsibility and power, and there were others, like the butler, in charge of the lord's table, or the constable, in charge of his stable, who stood above their fellows and occasionally rose to the peculiar status of serjeanty. Lowest among the serfs were those who were attached wholly to the lord's land and held none of their own; in England these were known as cottars. Between the highest and the lowest was a wide range of ill-defined grades of servitude, carrying different burdens.

The serf, unlike the ancient slave, had certain rights. The lord might not harm him and owed him protection against his enemies. This right of protection was in fact often violated. Feudal wars harmed the serf more than anyone else, for knights shut themselves up inside castles or forts while their besieging enemies systematically ravaged their land—that is to say, their peasants' land. The serf had a right to his land. He had little remedy if the lord chose to drive him off his land, but all custom was against such an action. In any case, the lord was usually much more concerned with keeping peasants working on the land than with driving them away. The serf had an absolute right to his wife and family. Unlike the ancient slave or the Negro slave in America, the serf was considered a human being rather than a piece of property, and he could not be sold away from his family or they from him.

THE AGRICULTURAL ECONOMY AND COMMUNITY

He had a right not to work on holidays, a right guaranteed him by the Church, and in theory he might relax every year on as many as fifty holy days in addition to fifty-two Sundays. In practice this right was curtailed by the lords as much as they dared, so that fifteen holidays a year is probably a high average estimate; and more than one lord, bishop as well as baron, found it in his conscience to permit his serfs no rest on the day the Lord took his. In general, however, the number of free days was not inconsiderable, and the peasants took advantage of them to feast and carouse and otherwise find surcease from their daily toil.

The duties of serfs exceeded their rights, and although the services varied according to time, place, and the amount of land held, few serfs got off easily. The serf rendered a certain percentage of the produce of his own land to the lord and another ten percent—the tithe—to the church. In addition, he was obliged to work from one to three days every week on the lord's demesne (week-work), manuring, dung-carting, weeding, ditch-digging, fruit-gathering, flock-shearing, hedge- or fence-making, hay-cutting, threshing, winnowing, and caring for stock. At the busy seasons of the year, he was obliged to do extra work called (obviously from the lord's point of view) "boon-work": ploughing, sowing, and harvesting. In such seasons the lord's crops came first, and boon-work was one of the most bitterly resented—and shirked—jobs on the manor. The record shows that in one incident a lord "wickedly slew William Bright with a dung fork, because he found him idling in his service."[4] Other "occasional services" included tree-felling or *corvées* when the king demanded the repair of a highway or a bridge.

One of the most annoying impositions on the serf was the rendering of little gifts established by custom. The phrase "three times make a custom" was zealously used by stewards and bailiffs against the serf. The bailiff might wander by one Easter and "ask" for a gift of a dozen eggs, a request which the serf would scarcely dare to refuse, and if the eggs were given three Easters in a row the serf and his posterity to the end of the world would be legally accountable for the yearly dozen. Moreover, the serf was obliged to use the lord's mill, his bake-oven, his brewery, his wine-press, his stud animals, all in return for a payment as high as the lord wished to make it. Then there was the "tallage," a payment of money to the lord at irregular intervals and for unspecified purposes.

Some servile duties resembled feudal aids. When a serf died, his heirs would have to pay the lord a "heriot," which in effect consisted of the lord's selecting for himself whatever possession of the dead man seemed of most value. Occasionally there was a payment exacted upon the accession of a new lord, the so-called *joyeux avènement,* which could be less than joyful for the serfs. The serf, like the feudal vassal, might have to play host to the lord or his representative for a period of time, though this was a custom used sparingly and apparently only on the continent; the lord's vassals usually had better accommodations to offer.

Frequently, especially in France, the serf paid an annual head-tax to the lord. One duty so different from anything owed by a free man that it was often used in court as a test of servitude was the payment of "merchet" [French *formariage:* "marriage outside"]. Merchet had to be paid in order for the serf to obtain the lord's permission for his daughter to marry, and the payment was especially high if the girl was marrying off the manor, because in that case the lord lost her services and those of her children. The famous *droit de seigneur* or *jus primae noctis* satirized by Beaumarchais and Mozart in the *Marriage of Figaro,* the lord's purported right to enjoy brides on their wedding nights, is, sadly, only the prurient result of an eighteenth-century scholar's misreading of the documents.

THE peasant's inability to leave the land without permission was a prohibition that mattered little in the early Middle Ages, when he had little desire to be "free," for "freedom" could mean only destitution unless he was otherwise provided for, and in a society where there was virtually no industry or trade there was little for him to do but work the land. In the later Middle Ages, however, the restriction became irksome. The manorial, like the feudal, system gradually became more rigid and more arbitrary as it departed from its original purpose. The mutually beneficial aspect of serfdom, originally recognized in the king's courts as a kind of contract, disappeared. Gradually the serf's rights were abridged and then abrogated, while his burdens were increased. The relatively respected serf of the eleventh century became the oppressed, despised, and intensely hostile serf who from the fourteenth to the sixteenth century rose up again and again against his hated masters in England, France, and Germany. These risings in part resulted (paradoxically) from increasing opportunities owing to the growth of towns and other economic and social changes. These had eliminated the original need for the manor, and the efforts of the nobility to retain a system that was now of use only to themselves heightened class hostilities. Under such conditions the desire for freedom grew.

Throughout the Middle Ages freedom could be obtained by entering holy orders, and in the Church the child of a serf might even rise to a position of influence. Legislation sometimes limited this possibility by insisting upon the lord's consent to a serf's going into the Church, but it remained an open possibility, a safety valve for the ambitions of a particularly able young serf. Another means of winning freedom was to do some deed of enormous bravery that would gain the serf knighthood in the field: needless to say this was not a frequent event.

Flight was another possibility. After four days' successful flight, the serf could, if recaptured, go to the king's court with a writ that put the burden of proof of servitude upon the lord. If the serf could reach a free town and there remain a year and a day, he had won his freedom and could not be retaken. Finally, he might win from the lord a charter of manumission. "Let all know," says a charter of 1278, "that we have manumitted and liberated from all yoke of servitude William, the son of Richard of Wythington, whom previously we have held as our bondman, with his whole progeny and all his chattels, so that neither we nor our successors shall be able to require or exact any right or claim in the said William . . . ."[5] Manumission might come as a reward for some unusual service done the lord, as a deed of charity pleasing in the eyes of God, or in return for a money payment.

LIKE feudalism, the manor began to be obsolescent at the very time it was becoming firmly established. The rise of the towns from the eleventh century weakened the manor by providing a place of refuge for runaway serfs and opportunities for their employment. The rising population, especially that of the towns, served as consumers of the excess in agricultural products made possible by technological improvements and deforestation. This encouraged the growth of a money economy, which in turn encouraged the commutation of manorial services into money payments. The old servile duties gradually vanished, and the lords came to rely either upon leasing land to free tenants or upon hiring free agricultural labor for money. The fact that the commuted payments were fixed in amount combined with the gradual inflation occurring from the eleventh to fourteenth century to give the peasants more and more surplus cash with which to buy freedom and other benefits.

The reduction in population by the famines and plagues of the fourteenth century meant that those peasants who still owed servile duties were obliged to work harder than in the past, since there were fewer hands to help. These peasants rose in rebellions, like the French *Jacqueries,* against increased oppression. Other rebellions were raised by free peasants whose rising expectations led them to demand social and political reforms that would lessen the differences separating the classes. These rebellions often took the form of, or were allied with, apocalyptic religious movements against wealth and power and for Christian egalitarianism.

Though relics of the manorial system persisted on the continent as late as 1848, and though its last vestiges were not removed from English law until 1926, it had undergone constant change and transmutation within the Middle Ages themselves.

NOTES

[1] Ramon Lull, quoted by Joseph Dahmus, *A History of Medieval Civilization* (New York, 1964), p. 334.
[2] Chart adapted from Lynn White, jr., *Medieval Technology and Social Change* (New York, Oxford University Press, 1962), p. 71.
[3] University of Pennsylvania *Translations and Reprints* (Philadelphia, 1902) III, #5, pp. 30–31.
[4] Henry S. Bennett, *Life on the English Manor* (Cambridge, Eng., 1937), p. 113.
[5] J. H. Robinson, *Readings in European History* (Boston, 1904), I, 405–406.

Chapter Eleven

THE CHURCH: RUIN AND RENOVATION

From the time of Constantine onwards the Church grew ever more rich and powerful, and "this was worse than a persecution."[1] The Church, whose message is of the other world, had embraced this world. A religion must express the life of the community or, like the old Olympian religion, be abandoned. Yet if a transcendent religion identifies too fully with society it loses its character as an instrument of Divine judgment, and society, rather than standing under the judgment of God, establishes its own values as God. The medieval Church was ambivalent, holding to its eschatology and otherworldliness and at the same time throwing itself so enthusiastically into feudal society that it often thought of the Lord of hosts as a feudal lord.

From the time of Constantine to the eighth century, the Church had shared in the general dislocation. Most of its energies were expended in converting the heathen, reconciling the heretics, and establishing enough of an organization to allow it to survive. Insofar as it enjoyed unity, it did so at the suffrance of the emperor in Constantinople.

In the eighth century, at least in the West, some of these problems were resolved. Major doctrinal disputes no longer arose, and schisms were less common; the skill of Gregory II and his successors had advanced the independence of the western Church from the eastern emperor. Yet poor education and discipline remained among both clergy and laity. Superstition and the remnants of paganism lurked everywhere, particularly in those areas only recently converted to Christianity. The weakness of Church organization permitted laymen to exercise undue influence in the Church on every level, from the papacy to the smallest parish.

Nonetheless, the mission of Saint Boniface and his contemporaries had added a great leaven of reform to the Church, and from his time it showed indelible signs of vigor. Though decadence persisted and in some ways deepened, Boniface's mission began a rising countercurrent of reform. All ages are corrupt; their vigor is to be measured in the amount of resistance they offer to corruption, and by this standard the Church of the eighth century was very much alive. Schools were created, monasteries reformed, morals improved, and a great popular swell of religious devotion arose such as had not been seen for centuries. The spiritual revolution of the eleventh century was being prepared in the great reform movements of the preceding centuries.

The crudity and disorder of the early Middle Ages were of course not abolished by the efforts of the eighth-century reformers. The collapse of the Carolingian Empire pulled the Church down with it, and the renewal of the invasions revived anarchy in Church as well as state. The educational and moral advance begun in the eighth century was suspended in the later ninth and early tenth.

To the old crudities were now added new problems created by the very growth of the Church in wealth, independence, and power. The freedom that the papacy had won from the eastern empire in the eighth century only bound it more closely to the western. When the Carolingians were strong, they maintained the papacy in health, but also in subservience; and when they were weak, they left the papacy a prey to the quarrels and dissensions of the Roman nobility, whose desire to control the Church grew with its power and wealth. The desire of bishops and popes for freedom from political dependence caused them to create ecclesiastical states whose care and government chained them to political activity and which became ever more tempting prizes for political rapine. Church property, ten percent of European soil in the eighth century, swelled to thirty percent by the ninth and then only gradually declined. In the meanwhile, the division between clergy and laity widened as the organization of the Church became more complicated and bureaucratized, and gradually the Church was transformed from the mystical unity of Christ's people into an ecclesiastical hierarchy.

These problems arising from the Church's participation in

temporal power and wealth persisted through the Middle Ages, but they constantly provoked protests and movements of reform.

For the reform spirit set in motion by Saint Boniface continued, based upon the educational, moral, and organizational reforms of Boniface, Charlemagne, and the eighth-century papacy. While there was no one movement of reform extending to the eleventh century, persistent manifestations appeared among the clergy, in the monasteries and in the papacy, and, in the form of popular piety or popular heresy, among the laity as well.

These movements for the reform of the Church were supported and encouraged by the gradual pacification of society. External missionary activity continued in the ninth and tenth centuries, bringing the Scandinavians, Slavs, and Magyars inside the pale of Christian society, and the internal missionary labors at which Boniface had excelled were continued, directed at the education and edification of already nominal Christians.

In the mid-tenth century, when the barbarian invasions began to be checked again and political order restored, it became possible to attack the anarchy within the Church and to restore it to order. With the help of the kings who from that time began to restore tranquility to their domains, the Church could enforce discipline and enhance education. As the economy became stronger and the towns grew in size, more money and more leisure were available for education, and there was more opportunity to exchange ideas. The consequent elevation of intellectual and cultural standards encouraged the revival of theology and the establishment of a higher moral and intellectual climate throughout the Church.

The culmination of these movements of reform was the reform papacy of the eleventh century. By 1050, society was stabilized, anarchy reduced, and political theory advanced to the point that the great issue of who was the appropriate ruler of Christian society and leader of reform could be debated and, after a fashion, resolved. In the eleventh-century papacy the reform spirit was combined with a political program that transformed all of society.

THE sources for Church history between Boniface and Hildebrand include the lives of the popes in the *Liber Pontificalis,* those of the saints in the *Acta Sanctorum,* and those of bishops and abbots in many *Gesta* or *Deeds*. There are letters, notably those of Gerbert of Aurillac and Rather of Verona. There are popular stories and legends. There are the decrees of councils and local synods, and treatises and tracts—especially those of the reformers, whose impassioned rhetoric the historian should beware of taking too seriously.

THE reformers of the ninth and tenth centuries had ample material on which to work. The first problem was that the organization of the medieval Church was increasingly hierarchical. The unity of Christian society was accepted by all parties, the question being limited to whether emperor or pope was the first representative of God on earth. The other body that had traditional claim to headship of the Church, the ecumenical council, was not called between 870 and 1123, and by that time the papacy had firmly established its control of Christendom. Below the high authority of pope or emperor, yet higher than the bishops, stood the metropolitans or archbishops, each ruling over a province consisting of several dioceses, their power varying over the centuries and from place to place. The diocese was ruled by the bishop, whose clergy originally lived round him at the cathedral but by the ninth century increasingly lived out among the people, each in his separate parish. The monasteries, initially subject to episcopal authority, gradually attained "immunity" or independence.

In the years between Charlemagne and the reform papacy of the eleventh century, this hierarchy was in the power of laymen. The kings and the emperor insisted upon their right to control the churches. They could hardly do otherwise. The enormous wealth of the Church had in some way to be tapped by rulers who were always in want of money. Kings did not hesitate to tax and exact feudal dues from their ecclesiastical tenants or to leave bishoprics or abbacies vacant in order to collect their revenues; sometimes the king would occupy the position of abbot himself, like Hugh Capet, who made himself the lay abbot of the wealthy monastery of Saint-Denis. The bishops could be used against the agents of feudal atomization by the kings, who therefore strove to obtain the right to appoint them. Quite naturally, such royal appointments were made on the grounds of political loyalty and administrative ability rather than sanctity or devotion.

The kings argued that God had made them the protectors of the Church. In this they followed the tradition of Constantine. They also supposed that the anointing received at their coronation gave them semi-sacerdotal powers: Through anointing the king became the channel of God's will. Said Charlemagne to the pope: "My task is to defend the Church of Christ. . . . Yours, most holy father, is to aid us with your prayers." The king protects and governs; the pope and the clergy aid him with their prayers. This did not mean that the rulers were indifferent to Church reform. Many of them, notably Henry II and Henry III of Germany or Ethelstan and William I of England, took their duty of guiding and protecting the Church quite seriously. But any good and able king living in this rough age had perforce to put spirituality fairly well down his list of priorities. For the king, the welfare of the Church was dependent upon that of the state.

The effects of this arrangement were, as they almost always are when Church and state are united, deleterious to the Church. The worldly success that the Church obtains by such union invariably drains it of its spirituality. The medieval Church, rather than resisting its secularization, participated with enthusiasm in its own betrayal. Churchmen argued that they were acquiring wealth and power in order to win independence and influence for the Church, but in accordance with the dictates of human frailty, they soon began to think of the wealth and power first and the spiritual goals only afterwards.

The bishops, many of them political appointees, were seldom men of spiritual stature. The best of them, men like Bruno of Cologne or Hincmar of Reims, kept their eyes more zealously upon the throne than upon the Cross. The worst of them set new records of hypocrisy. Simony (the buying and selling of offices), nepotism, and luxurious dress were the least of their offenses. Bishops like Odo of Bayeux participated in feudal combat with the zest of secular warriors, though one bishop is reported to have exclaimed piously "God forgive me" each time he bashed a man's head in with his mace. Archbishop Manasses of Reims exclaimed that the archbishopric would be a great thing if one were not obliged to sing mass for it. Bishop Megingaud of Eichstätt always preferred a short mass to a short meal and used to have a hot plate of fish put in front of the cathedral choir in order to induce them to finish the office quickly. Before a journey to Rome he requested from his cathedral chapter a dispensation for a quantity of blasphemies for use among the difficulties of the road and then, before he had proceeded very far on his way, was obliged to send back for more.

THE diocese of Liège is an example of the worldly connection between bishops and kings. It was not unusual among dioceses in being caught up in a quantity of intricate relationships. It was largely French-speaking, but its political overlords were the German duke of Lower Lorraine and the German king. Its ecclesiastical overlord was the German archbishop of Cologne, while the neighboring German-speaking diocese of Cambrai owed ecclesiastical suit to the French archbishop of Reims. In and around Liège were a number of feudal counts whose power was early suppressed (though in other great cities the count long persisted as an additional complication). From the twelfth century the burgers of the city attained increasing independence and self-government. The great monastery of Stavelot-Malmédy had virtual independence; and the archdeacon and the cathedral chapter also wielded power on their own. In the midst of these confused jurisdictions, the bishop himself had two distinct rôles. He was the *spiritual* ruler of the diocese of Liège. He was also the *temporal* ruler of expanding feudal holdings, which later became the "Principality of Liège," conferring upon the bishop a title —"Prince-Bishop"—which in apostolic terms may appear self-contradictory.

The effect was to make the bishop of Liège a political figure of some importance. Originally the bishops of the Church had been elected by acclamation of the clergy and people of the diocese; later the cathedral chapters had claimed the right to elect; and in the tenth and eleventh centuries the king, who needed the bishop as an administrator, directly appointed half of the bishops of Liège. By comparison, the number of royally appointed bishops in France was gradually increasing, and the king of England chose virtually all of the bishops in his realm. The question of who had the right to name the bishop would produce the fiercest debate in the eleventh-century war between the pope and the secular rulers.

Both wishing to suppress the power of the feudal lords, the bishop of Liège entered into a natural alliance with the king. The bishop became the king's main support against the local feudality; in return, the king aided the bishop in adding the territories of these lords to that of the principality of Liège. The king granted the bishop rights of mint, legal jurisdiction, and other immunities as well as land and the powers previously enjoyed by the count.

Bishop Otbert (1091–1119) was only one example of the effect this relationship had upon the episcopal dignity. King Henry IV of Germany sold him the diocese of Liège for 300 marks. Otbert got the sum back by selling lesser offices to the highest bidders, so that simony permeated the entire diocese. Otbert loyally supported Henry IV and the antipopes against the reform papacy. Liège became the most imperialist of cities, backing Henry IV in his struggles to the death against his rebellious son and then becoming equally loyal to the son when he in turn attacked the papacy. Otbert's epitaph was: "His loyalty to Caesar never faltered in adversity." Ironically Liège, the bastion of empire, was also one of the chief intellectual centers of the reform movement.

This venal, corrupt episcopacy would be blamed by the papalist reformers upon the evil of the kings. Few of the reformers realized that as long as the Church refused to abandon the political power and economic wealth that made it tempting it could not be purified of worldliness.

THE worldliness of the great prelates penetrated down to the parish clergy. In a period when lay participation in the Church is deemed praiseworthy, it is hard to recollect that the Church of the early Middle Ages suffered from too much of a certain kind of such participation. As the kings dominated dioceses, so petty feudal lords dominated the parish churches as "lay proprietors." Sometimes this was not wholly unjust, for the lord might have founded the church to begin with, but the result was the spread of venality and simony. Either the lord would obtain the right to the parish revenues and then use a fraction of them to hire a priest, or he would grant the living as a benefice in return for a cash payment or percentage. In either case the appointment was made for money, and by a layman. In England, the proprietary church is still common. In 1961, Brigadier Anstruther-Gough-Calthorpe was still selecting the pastor of Acle, Norfolk; Mrs. Power-Clutterbuck had that right at Ozleworth, Wotton-under-Edge; and the Misses Nind chose the clergyman at Parracombe, Devon.

The picture of the clergy that resulted in the Middle Ages from this arrangement is not an attractive one. A poem of the eleventh century observed:

> The clerks (clerics) in their hatred
> Quarrel with each other;
> They all teach evil
> And sow scandal . . . .
> Nothing on earth was more vile
> Than the acts of clerks
> Or the morals of clerks . . . .[2]

The sale of the sacraments, the keeping of women, illiteracy, drunkenness, lewdness, brawling, these were the common faults of the clergy. Nor were they exempt from even cruder vices. A provost of Saint Déodat had children by his own daughter. One priest wore especially large sleeves so that he might, by tilting the offertory plate, surreptitiously fill them with the congregation's contributions. One synod even warns against the unseemliness of priests' bathing in the holy water. Another was thus described: "The priest of Wanestanville (violated) a certain one of his parishioners whose husband on this account went beyond the sea, and he kept her for eight years, and she is pregnant; also he plays at dice and drinks too much, he frequents taverns, he does not stay in his church, he goes hawking in the country as he wishes . . . ."[3] As the parish priest was that representative of the Church which the ordinary person was most likely to encounter, it is no wonder that the reform movement, including its heretical manifestations, became popular.

THE corruption was most evident at the very pinnacle of the hierarchy, the papacy itself. A short period of papal brilliance often occurred during times when the empire was weakened but when the resulting anarchy had not yet overtaken Church as well as state. Under Charlemagne the popes were controlled by the king; but following the decline of Frankish power there was a brief period of papal independence. The great Pope Nicholas I (858–867) forced emperors to bend the knee to his decrees and published theories of papal power that would be used to advantage by the later papalists. But after the death of Nicholas' second successor, the papacy, deprived of imperial support as well as of imperial interference, fell into the hands of the contentious Roman nobility. The treatment of Pope Formosus shows what they were capable of.

Formosus (891–896) was a moral and upright, if ambitious, man, who during his pontificate had offended one faction of the Italian nobility, the House of Spoleto. Nine months after Formosus' death, the Spoletans seized Rome and determined to wreak vengeance upon their enemy. With the concurrence of the vicious Pope Stephen VI, they had the now putrefied papal corpse exhumed, dressed in pontifical robes, and set upon a throne. Behind the body was placed a deacon who was ordered to answer for the thing, which was now placed on trial, deposed, stripped of its robes, and thrown into the Tiber.

Another Roman family, the House of Theophylact, boasted as one of its chief ornaments the Princess Marozia, mistress of one pope, mother of another, and herself murdered by the angry Roman mob. The Renaissance popes sinned, but they did so with some taste and style; their predecessors of the tenth and early eleventh centuries were merely brutal. Marozia's grandson, John XII, was deposed by Otto I for living in open adultery with the matrons of the city. "His rapes of virgins and widows had deterred the female pilgrims from visiting the tomb of Saint Peter, lest, in the devout act, they should be violated by his successor."[4]

It is astonishing under the circumstances, not that there should have been protests and heresies in the tenth and eleventh centuries but that there should not have been a Protestant revolt. After all, both the theoretical and the actual power of the papacy was much less than it would be in the sixteenth century, and there was widespread sentiment against Rome. Said Archbishop Arnoul of Reims in 991: Rome had always been honored because of the memory of Saint Peter but one must not forget the canons. If the pope was a good and intelligent man, his decrees were worthy of attention; otherwise they were not. Ignorance, fear, and cupidity now ruled at Rome, and under these circumstances neither the pope's opinion nor his silence was to be considered. "O wretched Rome . . . ," he concluded, "who held aloft the clear light of the Fathers to our ancestors, but has shadowed our own time with monstrous crimes that will be notorious in that of our children."[5]

The reason there was no rebellion against the papacy in the eleventh century is partly sociological and partly practical. Society was not compartmentalized enough to allow radical movements to grow up in any one area of thought without being checked from other quarters. Any revolt within the medieval framework had to be "norm-oriented" rather than "value-oriented," that is, it had to be concerned with reforming existing institutions rather than creating new ones. Thus even the great Gregorian "papal revolution" of the eleventh century took place within the existing framework of society. The second reason has to do with that revolution itself. There have been three great times of ferment in Church history: one in the eleventh century, the second in the sixteenth, and the third in the twentieth. The papacy failed to reckon with the second until it was too late, and it remains to be seen whether it is dealing adequately with the third. But the papacy of the latter eleventh century gained stature by putting itself squarely at the head of the reform movement. Even during its period of decadence, the papacy's power was increasing. The papacy achieved a balance of power in Italy and prevented any one authority from dominating the whole peninsula and threatening the papal states; the temporal power of the popes was growing; the establishment of feudalism bolstered hierarchical notions; the papacy was asked to mediate disputes; and Roman liturgy and customs were widely adopted.

ONE final source of disaffection in the Church and of the deterioration of Christianity was the state of the liturgy. The mass, which had been the center of Christian communal worship, the feast of Christians around the altar, had become almost meaningless to most of the congregation. Churches grew in size, choirs were set between the altar and the people, and the altar was turned away from the congregation to face the eastern wall. The language of the liturgy, which in the fourth-century West had been changed from Greek to Latin in order to make it intelligible, now remained in Latin after that language had in turn become incomprehensible to all but a few. Most priests mumbled, and many mispronounced, the Latin. The raised bread which had been consecrated and symbolized the people's participation in the mass was replaced by unleavened wafers which had no relation to the bread eaten in daily life. The offertory processions of the people were discontinued, and singing and responses in church grew less and less frequent. Cut off from an understanding of the central sacrament of their religion, they began to develop private devotions and externals like genuflection, holy water, and later the rosary, and they developed paraliturgies in the form of religious drama. The gap between priest and laymen increased. These defects, unremedied until our own time, were deleterious to Christianity and to the unity of Christian society.

AMIDST all this decadence and decline the Church proved its perennial ability to reform itself. The labors of the Irish and Anglo-Saxon missionaries, aided by the popes and the Frankish kings, especially Charlemagne, had laid the foundations for moral reform and intellectual advance as early as the eighth century. This impetus towards reform continued, here weaker, there stronger, but unbroken, until it culminated in the reform papacy of 1048. The impetus to reform, at first moving from the peripheries of the Church inwards, and then taken up and propagated by its centers, affected clergy and laity alike.

The reform movements had many aspects good and bad: moral reform, educational improvement, doctrinal development, popular piety, heresy, crusades, and pogroms; and they eventually led to a political revolution under the leadership of the papacy. The frequent and numerous efforts of synods, kings, monks, and preachers both orthodox and heretical, to improve the state of the Church are evidence of the pervasive spirit of reform.

Each age of reform nonetheless had its own characteristics. In the later eighth and early ninth centuries reforms were prompted chiefly by the Frankish kings. In the later ninth century the weakness of the Frankish monarchy enabled the papacy of Nicholas I briefly to prevail. From the end of the ninth century, the growing power of the English and German kings made them leaders of reform. Fostering education, founding schools and monasteries, calling synods for the reform of clergy and laity, they took seriously their function as protectors of the Church.) Thus Alfred the Great (871–899) was a promoter of reform in England, and Otto I of Germany (936–973) was so impressed with his responsibilities that he went beyond Charlemagne's role in the judgment of Pope Leo III and deposed Pope John XII. The tradition of royal reform continued on into the eleventh century: kings like Edgar the Peaceful of England (959–975) and Henry II and Henry III of Germany being most responsible in their religious duties.

But from the early tenth century the monasteries became important centers of reform. Royally and episcopally fostered monastic reform had become common from the time of Saint Boniface, witness the establishment of the Rule of Saint Benedict of Nursia for all monasteries in the Frankish empire, formally approved through the efforts of Saint Benedict of Aniane at the courts of Charlemagne and Louis the Pious. But in the tenth century movements of monastic reform that were largely independent both technically and intellectually arose in three areas, Lorraine, Burgundy, and Italy. From these centers they gradually spread to all of western Europe.

The monastic reforms were aimed primarily at moral and intellectual improvement. The monasteries had, like the parishes, become debased and corrupted, the Rule being ignored more than it was respected, and monks keeping concubines. When Abbott Abbo of Fleury attempted to enforce the rule of chastity, his monks conspired to murder him. Much of the energy of the reformers was absorbed in reestablishing the observance of the Rule.

Among the monastic reformers there was also a common desire to free the monasteries from the control of bishops and laity in order to secure their proper place in society and to free them from untoward and harmful influences.

But in regard to the relation of the monasteries with the world there were two schools of thought. Monasticism had enjoyed great success in the affairs of the world; having a virtual monopoly of education, monasteries produced the great scholars and administrators that graced the courts of Europe, and possessed enormous influence and wealth. Monasticism had become "the expression of the corporate religious ideals and needs of a whole community."[6] The purpose of the conservative, or moderate, reformers was to elevate morals and education and to return to the strictness of the Rule while retaining wealth and influence and holding back from dedicating themselves to the reform of society. Essentially they desired a return to the position of the earlier Benedictine monasteries: they wished to be respected and influential in the world but to avoid the responsibilities of participation in the community around them.

Cluny was the most famous expression of this school of thought. Founded in 909, Cluny's strict observance of the Rule attracted both a flood of novices and the enthusiastic support of the wealthy. By the year 1000, the abbot was one of the greatest figures in Europe and presided over a large and tightly organized system of houses crowned by an abbey so rich and powerful that it could without inconvenience entertain a king with all his courtiers. Yet the influence of Cluny upon society as a whole has been exaggerated. She used her great political influence for the limited purposes of her monasteries. Until 1100 she had little influence in northern Europe, except in England, where Saint Dunstan and his colleagues, inspired by the example of one of Cluny's daughter houses, reformed English Benedictine monasticism. Uninterested in the problems of society, Cluny had very little to do with the revolutionary program of the reform papacy and never questioned the predominance of the emperor. The self-centered worldliness of Cluny was apparent a hundred years after its founding, and the abbey underwent a severe financial crisis in the twelfth century owing to the high living of its residents, which inspired the contempt of the puritanical Cistercian Saint Bernard. The precious ornaments, the great marble pillars, the great corona of lights—all this, Bernard observed, could clothe the Church in glory from without but not the souls of the monks in Christ's glory within.

The second school of monastic thought as regards the world, the ascetic tradition that in the twelfth century produced Saint Bernard, was represented earlier by hermit ascetics. In the eleventh century its most outspoken representative was Peter Damian. Its purpose was to penetrate beyond the superficial problem of monastic morality to its roots: to return to, and then to preach in the world at large, a completely other-

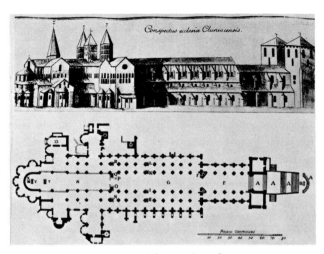

The monastery of Cluny, eleventh century.

worldly attitude, an attitude of simplicity, solitude, and attention to God, an attitude that spurned political influence as it spurned the temptations of the flesh. Here is the paradox: Cluny, worldly herself, cared little for the fate of the world around her; the ascetics, renouncing the world, sought to bring its people to an understanding of the Kingdom of God. It is the ascetics who connect the monastic and the papalist reformers. While spurning the papalist argument that the Church had to obtain power in order to renovate the world in the image of Christ, the ascetics approved and abetted that renovation in their own way. Few men were as active in the world they contemned than Peter Damian or Bernard of Clairvaux.

Peter Damian was born in 1007 into a poor family of Ravenna and was soon orphaned. One of his brothers recognizing his talents and procuring his education, Peter became a successful scholar and teacher at Parma, where he began to make a fair amount of money. In 1035 he renounced this worldly success and joined a semi-eremitical monastic community at Fonte Avellana, whose prior he became in 1043. Continuing his writings, he attacked the lack of true Christianity in the Church, particularly in his *Book of Gomorrah,* an excoriation of the morals of the secular clergy. Peter had contempt for the Church's rôle in politics, even when it was directed toward a desirable end.

He characterized the fiery Hildebrand, later Gregory VII, as "a holy Satan," and asserted that "whoever thinks that he can at the same time be a monk and diligently serve at the papal court is mistaken. A man who leaves the cloister to concern himself with the welfare of the world is making a bad bargain." So he spoke, but in 1058 he became cardinal bishop of Ostia and one of the most vigorous and persuasive preachers to the world of the life that is not of the world. Peter was skilled in canon law and rhetoric and was an effective politician. Like the other wealthy and successful men who flocked to the cloister (among them the great Berno of Cluny, Gerard of Brogne, Bernard, Dunstan, Oswald, and Francis) Peter had proved that he was able to function in the world. Monks were not misfits or outcasts, difficult as this may be for the modern secular mind to grasp.

Peter Damian, though a great politician in the world of men, always loved the ascetic life best. To mortify the flesh he prayed, doused himself with cold water, used the whip (for other than masochistic reasons, it is today necessary to add), and fasted, taking a few vegetables three days a week and nothing but bread and water the other four. Exhorting his brethren to contempt of the world, he said: "Let (the monk) confine himself within the walls of his cloister, let him love spiritual quiet, let him have a horror of running about in the world . . . ." To those who faltered, he exclaimed: "Come now, brother, what is this body which you clothe with such diligent care and nourish gently as if it were royal offspring? Is it not a mass of putrefaction, is it not worms, dust, and ashes? . . . Let the holy mind not fear therefore to share the cross of Christ in scourging . . . ."[7]

The effect of the monastic reforms was limited. For the most part they stood apart from the great political debates of Christian society. Monastic morals, once reformed, tended quickly to relax again in accordance with the historical rule that the inflation of morals occurs as readily as that of currency: the bad drives out the good, and gradual devaluation from a high standard occurs until revolutionary measures are again needed. Thus the painstaking victories of the tenth century had to be won again in the twelfth. Moreover, the monks were gradually losing the dominant place they had occupied in society since the time of Saint Benedict and Gregory the Great. They lost this place partly owing to their deliberate turn to asceticism and partly because of the increasing complexity of a society in which bishops were pushing their cathedral schools far beyond the limits of monastic education and kings were finding other and better sources for monetary and military support. Ironically, as monasticism became less socially useful and lost much of its influence, there was more room in the monasteries for the spiritual life. It is no accident that almost all of the great medieval mystics appeared after the power of the monasteries began to wane in the eleventh century.

ONE other aspect of reform must be mentioned, the popular. Enthusiasm for reform stirred not only the clergy but the laity, whose enthusiastic participation in the pilgrimages, popular devotions, and Crusades of the eleventh and twelfth century is testament to its effect. Another form that popular enthusiasm took, a quite natural one in view of the decreasing rôle of the laity in the Church, was religious dissent. Dissent, usefully defined in a broad sense, included not only strict heresy but magic, skepticism, or anything that opposed or ignored the generally accepted traditions of the Church.

The amount and the vigor of medieval dissent may have increased in the eleventh and twelfth centuries, but it began, with the reform movement itself, in the eighth. It differed from the ancient heresy that preceded it in that, with a few anachronistic exceptions, it centered less around intellectual questions of doctrine than around morality, and it differed from the dissent of the later Middle Ages in its lack of clear social implications and in its freedom from outside, eastern influences. The dissent of the early Middle Ages was indigenous and for the most part moral.

An exception was the implicit dissent in the use of magic and superstition that persisted largely as a continuation, under the veneer of Christianity, of ancient Germanic paganism. These pagan ideas held on in folklore (e.g., the maypole) and in the superstitious reverence paid to relics, as well as in the overt use of forbidden magical rites.

But for the most part the religious dissenters of the period from the eighth through the early twelfth centuries were Reformists. Typically they arose something like this: outraged at the ignorance and immorality of the local clergy, a layman would begin to protest openly. If sufficiently motivated and gifted he would then begin to preach to his friends and neighbors, without any license from the bishop so to do. This would earn him the enmity of the clergy and in his opposition to them he would pass from attacking their morals to questioning the whole institution of the clergy and the hierarchy. The sacraments would then become mere symbols, something that any devout layman could confer. At last he would argue that his justification came from the Holy Spirit, the inner light that dwelt within him. One unfortunate man insisted that the Spirit had taken the form of a swarm of bees lodged in his abdomen.

The authorities were for centuries quite tolerant of all this. Far from arranging *autos-da-fé,* the hierarchy usually contented itself with severe admonitions addressed to these wanderers from the faith (it may well be asked, of course, whether in this era of ecclesiastical degradation the hierarchy was not wandering as much as the dissenters). From the eleventh century, however, the state, having extended its power and wishing no civil disturbance, began to interest itself in the matter. The first heretics executed in western Europe since the sixth century met their fiery doom at Orléans on the Feast of the Holy Innocents 1022, and from then on repression of dissent grew steadily more severe.

THE history of the Church from the eighth to the eleventh century is that of the growing vigor of the reform movement against a background of desperate need. The movement would culminate in the eleventh century and come to a conclusion in the triumph of the papacy in the twelfth.

NOTES

[1] Hans Küng.
[2] *Gesta Pontificum Cameracensium,* ed. Charles de Smet (Paris, 1880) p. 4.
[3] Odo of Rigaud, trans. James Bruce Ross, in Ross and McLaughlin, *The Portable Medieval Reader* (New York, 1949), pp. 78–79.
[4] Gibbon, III, 46.
[5] Trans. Jeffrey B. Russell, in Russell, *Dissent and Reform in the Early Middle Ages* (Berkeley and Los Angeles, 1965), pp. 147–148.
[6] R. W. Southern, *The Making of the Middle Ages* (New York, 1953), p. 161.
[7] Trans. James Bruce Ross in Ross and McLaughlin, *Medieval Reader,* pp. 49–55.

Chapter Twelve

EARLY MEDIEVAL THOUGHT AND CULTURE

The sources for cultural history in the period 750–1050 are in some ways more direct than those for political or economic history. Rather than documents telling about the events, the historian has here the "events" themselves: poems, carvings, letters, and artifacts. Yet even here the gap between the thought and the expression of the thought remains. A man can never wholly enter into the state of mind of another being, particularly if his way of looking at things has long vanished. The sight of such a simple thing as a chair or a bird, let alone the consideration of art or religion, brought to the medieval mind countless associations and impressions wholly foreign to us.

The end of the eighth century has often been characterized by modern historians as the beginning of something called the "Carolingian Renaissance." Tired of hearing of the wonders of the "Renaissance" of the fifteenth century, they invented first a "Renaissance of the Twelfth Century," then a "Carolingian Renaissance," and more. Like the term "revolution," "renaissance" has been inflated until it scarcely means anything. In accordance with the root of the word, a true renaissance must be a rebirth of something that has died. No known renaissance (not even the most famous one) really fits this definition: certainly the Carolingian does not. Far from being dead in the centuries before Charlemagne, culture was rapidly creating new, if inchoate, ideas, while those aspects of the Roman past that really had died returned under Charlemagne only as ectoplasm. The Carolingian Renaissance, like all renaissances, was not a rebirth but a quickening of the pace of intellectual and artistic activity. One distinction to keep in mind is that the classical revival of the Carolingian period was more limited to a smaller elite than that of the fifteenth-century Renaissance.

SOME of Charlemagne's contemporaries were aware that something was happening, but they were as mistaken as to its nature as the modern enthusiasts for renaissances. They called what was going on a *renovatio* and believed that they were really reviving the Golden Age of the past; in fact, they believed they were combining Israel, Greece, and Rome into one glorious new Golden Age centered at Charlemagne's court at Aachen. Charlemagne affected the name of David, his friend Alcuin was Horace, Angilbert was Homer, Theodulf was Pindar; in fact, everybody who was anybody was somebody else.

In reality, the revival, such as it was, was limited almost wholly to the Romans. Few eighth-century scholars besides Saint Bede had more than a smattering of Hebrew and, except for Bede and John Scotus Eriugena, even fewer knew Greek, for one could pick up some of the language of Jeremiah from the local rabbi but had to travel to Constantinople to learn that of Theocritus. Of the Roman authors, Horace, Virgil, Ovid, and Cicero were the best known and the most revered.

The Carolingians' attempts at imitation failed to bring back the glory that was Greece and the grandeur that was Rome. Though they were not able to reproduce a dead culture, in trying to do so they produced, willy-nilly, something new. Enamored of the arches and groves of ancient Greece and Rome, it never occurred to the Carolingians to long for a return to the camps and forests of the ancient Celts and Teutons. But those influences were there, and so, much more strongly, was that of Christianity. The interesting thing about early medieval culture is its morphology, its involuntary modification of classical forms according to its own non-classical background and assumptions. The continuity of classical forms was better preserved in the East, where they tended to become stereotyped. The West, having been shattered by external and internal upheavals, was more creative because it was forced to rebuild and to establish a new synthesis.

THE Carolingian Renaissance was a period of rapid cultural advance, but it did not spring from nothing. It was the heir of

The reading desk of St. Radegund, a Frankish princess of the sixth century.

the labors of the Irish, Anglo-Saxon, and Italian scholars of the preceding centuries and of their descendants who assembled at Charlemagne's court. The particular brilliance of the time depended upon the very fact of the assemblage, for scholars shine best when they meet and exchange ideas with others.

The low cultural level of the seventh century was gradually raised by the increasingly efficient systematic education begun by the Irish and transmitted by the Anglo-Saxons to Frankland. Cultural advance is most often the result of social need. The society of the eighth century was more settled than that of the sixth and seventh, and it demanded the establishment of social order. Hence intellectual advances were encouraged and promoted by the rulers, and Charlemagne took up the intellectual work of Saint Boniface as well as the religious. The reform movement of the eighth century touched learning as well as morals.

It was Charlemagne's will and the wealth he acquired from conquest and tribute that made it possible to found schools and libraries and to attract foreign scholars. He encouraged systematic education in Latin with the double purpose of teaching clergymen to understand the Bible and the Fathers and of preparing them to act as efficient ecclesiastical and civil administrators. Further, he and the other great lay and ecclesiastical lords who also patronized the arts found that the world could now again afford the luxuries of learning. This learning was essentially Christian, but reverence for the pagan classics had never disappeared. A by-product, but an important one, of the educational reform was a growth of knowledge and appreciation of the classics that was to flower in the twelfth century. Already in the ninth century Lupus of Ferrières strove consciously in his letters to achieve the purity of diction of classical writers; and scribes even copied the plays of Terence complete with labeled pictures of prostitutes and pimps.

The center of educational reform was the palace school, consisting of the scholars collected at the court and their pupils. Peter of Pisa, a grammarian whom Charlemagne had brought up with him from Italy, was the first head of this school, but in 782 Alcuin, an English scholar whom Charles had met at Parma, replaced Peter. Alcuin brought with him the pattern of education established at the school of York. Alcuin is a perfect example of how the older English tradition of learning was exported to the continent. The popes had sent Theodore and Hadrian to Canterbury in the seventh century, and they had taught Bennet Biscop, who taught Bede, who taught Egbert of York, who taught Alcuin, who now returned to the continent.

What Charlemagne and Alcuin were trying to accomplish was less what we could call a liberal education than what we would call social engineering: they were using education as a means to build the kind of unified, orderly Christian society they wanted. The Bible, the Fathers, and the pagan authors were all sifted for information and attitudes *useful* to this purpose. Culture has almost always been promoted on pragmatic grounds.

In his efforts to spread the salutary benefits of education throughout his domains, Charlemagne urged that each monastery and diocese, and even the parishes where possible, should have schools for the training of clergy and laity. His efforts were only partially successful, especially as regards the laity. The idea that in the Middle Ages only the clergy could read and write is a gross exaggeration, but it remains true that such accomplishments among the laity were exceptional. Charlemagne encouraged the formation of libraries, particularly around the monastic *scriptoria* or writing-rooms—no mean achievement at a time when books

were handmade and in exceedingly short supply. Lupus of Ferrières felt constrained to refuse to lend a book to Archbishop
Hincmar of Reims by messenger lest the valuable item be stolen
along the way. "It is too large to hide in one's cloak," he explained, "and its beauty would excite the cupidity of thieves . . . .
Therefore I am inclined to let you have it when it can be transferred with complete security, that is to say the next time we
meet in person."[1] One manuscript bore the warning: "Whoe'er
this book to make his own doth plot, / the fires of Hell and
brimstone be his lot."[2]

In Carolingian Italy there were fewer centers of learning
and fewer spectacular advances because town life had survived
more than in the North and literacy was generally more widespread. The learning of the South was in the ninth century
(as in the nineteenth) much less systematic, but sometimes richer,
than that of the north.

AT the palace school, Alcuin followed Boëthius and Cassiodorus
as well as his masters at York in organizing a curriculum based
upon the seven arts. The seven arts were of course taught in
Latin and throughout the Middle Ages formed the core of undergraduate education. Alcuin was the first to divide the seven into
the trivium (grammar, dialectic, and rhetoric) and the quadrivium (arithmetic, geometry, astronomy, and music), an arrangement they were to retain into the Renaissance. The study of
the seven arts was of enormous importance for the development
of medieval thought. Grammar, the intense study of the Latin
language and Latin authors, was the font of renewed interest in
the classics and of the development of a superior Latin style.
The fruits of the study of grammar ripened in the classical
humanism of the twelfth century. The study of rhetoric helped
to lay the foundation for the revival of legal studies and, once
it had broken free from its earlier limitations, for original poetry;
that of dialectic, which taught rational thinking, was the basis
for the growth of rational scholasticism in the twelfth and thirteenth centuries. The quadrivium provided the background for
the development of scientific studies.

ALCUIN was not only the originator, but the chief propagator,
of the seven arts in Charlemagne's dominions. He taught rhetoric

*Allegory: Grammar, one of the seven liberal arts, personified
as a teacher with her pupils.*

and dialectic and wrote poetry and theology. Towards the end
of his life, when he was at the monastery of Tours, he helped
perfect the "Caroline minuscule," the script upon which modern
lowercase letters are based.

THROUGH the efforts of Charlemagne and his helpers, the level
of intellectual attainment gradually rose, and the "Carolingian
Renaissance" did not end with Charlemagne. In the later ninth
and early tenth centuries, society, reeling from the new barbarian
blows, was unready to make any new cultural demands, and the
intellectual life of this period was a continuation and development of eighth-century ideas. Theodulf of Orléans, poet, builder,
and theologian; Einhard, Charlemagne's biographer; and others
continued their activities after the death of the great emperor.
The court of Charles the Bald at Paris, that of Alfred in England,
and the monasteries of Germany built upon what Charlemagne
and Alcuin had begun. Rather than a series of independent
renaissances, there was a continuity of cultural development.

UNDER Charles the Bald flourished the poets Sedulius Scotus
and Walafrid Strabo and the great philosopher John Scotus
Eriugena ("the Irishman"). As Alcuin continued the *peregrinatio*
of the Anglo-Saxons to the continent, Eriugena continued that
of the Irish. Born shortly after 800, he came to the continent in
the 840s and was named head of the palace school under Charles
the Bald. Charles, who had been taught by Walafrid Strabo,

was no dullard, and the king and the Irish scholar enjoyed repartee. On one occasion the king got the worse of the encounter. Seated across the table from the Irishman, he pointedly demanded: "What separates a Scot from a sot?" to which Eriugena quickly replied, "Only the table, your grace."

THE later tenth century inaugurated a "pre-scholastic age" in which increasing peace, tranquility, and affluence permitted and encouraged the development of the classical heritage in the full sense of appreciation of the classics for themselves rather than as mere treasuries from which to draw useful knowledge. At the same time, society now demanded a further advance of learning. The emerging urban communes took an interest in the city states of the classical world; the increasingly complex needs of government required an understanding of classical law and encouraged an appreciation of classical administration; the urban upper classes desired to enrich their leisure hours with classical literature. This pre-scholastic age was an age of borrowing and compilation from the ancients; it was to be followed by an age of rapid assimilation and growth, the scholastic age of the twelfth and thirteenth centuries.

Toward the end of the tenth century the West Frankish Kingdom produced some notable schools and scholars, notably at Chartres, which in the eleventh and twelfth centuries produced such great names as Fulbert, Bernard, John of Salisbury, and Yvo the lawyer. The most notable scholar of the end of the tenth century was Gerbert of Aurillac, who became Pope Sylvester II under the patronage of Emperor Otto III. A bishop and a skillful politician, Gerbert found the time to pursue an unusual interest in mathematics and astronomy that earned him the reputation among the people of being a magician. In a letter of 989 to a monk of Trier, he observed: "Since we are not unmindful of your kindness we have begun to make the (astronomical) sphere—a most difficult piece of work—which is now being polished in the lathe and skillfully covered with horsehide . . . ."[3] Gerbert's greatest contribution was his revival of the study of logic based upon the works of Boëthius. Now that people again had the facilities and the leisure to reflect upon the nature of the world, they longed for a tool with which to understand it. Dry though the medieval uses of pure logic may seem today, they summoned an eager glint to the eyes of men brought up in the even drier and more useless traditions of rhetoric. Gerbert was still too conservative to do more than develop the principles of logic, but in the twelfth and thirteenth centuries these principles were applied with exciting results to philosophy, theology, and science.

In Germany and Italy, the Ottonian rulers patronized scholars like Gerbert and Liudprand of Cremona, who wrote perceptive and amusing accounts of visits to Constantinople in which he described Emperor Nicephorus Phocas as "a monstrosity of a man, a dwarf, fat-headed and with tiny mole's eyes; disfigured by a short, broad, thick beard half going grey; disgraced by a neck scarcely an inch long; pig-like by reason of the big close bristles on his head . . . as the poet (Juvenal) says, 'You would not like to meet him in the dark.'"[4] More important than the Ottonian court was the monastery of Fulda, where men like Raban Maur, Walafrid Strabo, and Lupus of Ferrières, trained first among the western Franks, came to make the ancient monastery founded by Saint Boniface the center of learning in central Europe.

In England, the tradition of learning reached its height in the eighth century with Bede, Egbert, and Alcuin. Then, at the end of the ninth, it was revived by King Alfred the Great, who had natural proclivities for learning and had been impressed by the intellectual activities of the court of Charles the Bald. Alfred encouraged the vernacular. "We . . . should turn into the tongue which we can all understand," said the king, "certain books which are most necessary for men to know . . . (so) that all the youth which now is in England of freemen who have wealth enough to be able to apply themselves to it, be set to learning . . . ."[5] Alfred himself set a good example by personally rendering Gregory the Great's *Book of Pastoral Care* and other works into English.

This early medieval culture may be grasped through its implicit assumptions, and through its conscious expressions.

The fundamental assumption was the sacred nature of the world. The world of the supernatural was always vividly present to the mind of the sophisticated, as to that of the illiterate. The material world was a mask of appearances hiding the more real world of ideas, the world of God. Such a sacred view of the world, wholly Christian as it is, is uncongenial to the mind of the modern positivist and materialist, but the undogmatic spirit recognizes that the idealist view of the world is philosophically at least as plausible as the materialist. There are superstitions of science as well as superstitions of religion: "supernatural" is not a synonym of "superstitious."

The sacred view implied a distrust of the material world summed up in the phrases "contempt of the world" or "vanity of vanities." The world was transitory and full of vanities, and the man who put his trust in it would surely be deceived.

> I have seen Henry, the king's son, habited in robes of silk interwoven with gold, surrounded by troops of attendants and guards, and brilliant with almost celestial splendour. . . . This prince, so pampered. . . , from his proud eminence fixed his thoughts on his future kingdom; but God said, "Not so. . . ." And it came to pass that the head which should have worn a crown of gold, was rudely dashed against the rocks; instead of wearing embroidered robes, the prince floated naked in the waves; and instead of ascending a lofty throne, he found his grave in the bellies of fishes at the bottom of the sea.[6]

So the twelfth-century historian Henry of Huntingdon expressed this most common of medieval attitudes in his analysis of the death of Prince Henry, son of Henry I of England, in the wreck of his pleasure boat, the White Ship. It is one which might also have occurred to Americans as they watched, only the day after the President's assassination in November 1963, the sad spectacle of his rocking chair and other belongings rushed hurriedly across the street from the White House to storage.

The most vivid expression of distrust of the world is the pervasive sense of impending doom. The old idea that everyone expected the world to come to an end in the year 1000 is exaggerated, but the belief in the Second Coming and the Last Judgment was real, and no man knew when the Messiah would come. Any day could bring the end of the world.

Another corollary was the exegetical searching for, and the artistic production of, various levels of meaning. In literature, art, history, and science alike, men were less interested in the development, structure, function, or physical attributes of an object than in its place in the real, spiritual, world. A fruit is not only a fruit but a symbol of temptation; a pelican is less a bird than a symbol of Christ; a nightingale may be a wandering poet.

Yet another corollary is that medieval men had criteria for greatness and success different from ours. Modern sociologists speak of the fundamental drives to wealth and status, but the devoted medieval Christian spurned wealth and fame; he sought holiness. The idea of greatness in the Middle Ages was wholly unlike the Renaissance and modern conceptions. Artists and poets seldom signed their productions, or, if they did, it was only with an apology or a plea for the prayers of their audience. The lack of Cellinis in the Middle Ages indicates not that they lacked great men, but that their idea of greatness was based, not upon vainglory and boasting, but upon the two principles of *peregrinatio* and *ordo.* The mystic, the monk, and the missionary were great because they recognized that life in the world is only *peregrinatio,* a brief journey to our true native land in God. Preachers and prelates were great because they worked for *ordo* in this world, a unified Christian world order penetrating all of society and constructed according to the will of God. Those who sought God's world, and those who tried to make this world according to his will: these were the great, and often nameless, men of the Middle Ages. To medieval man, the individual seeking fame, prestige, or an "image" was quite literally a damned fool, just as to Hellenic man he was quite literally an "idiot." Experience may yet prove that their view of the world was healthier than ours.

In the earlier Middle Ages, monastic conceptions of Christianity were especially important. The monastic theology of the time was quite distinct from later scholasticism. Rather than the "essential analysis" of pure reason employed by Aquinas, it used a psychological, intuitive, partly mystical approach deriving from Plato and Augustine. The monks searched the world, the universe, and man for intimations of the Divine. This is why most medieval historians were monks: they perceived the workings of the Divine will in individuals rather than in syllogisms.

Medieval creativity had other sources as well. An actively investigative attitude toward the world, employed in the Middle Ages for mystical purposes as in modern times for the aims of science, is characteristic of the West. It is in part the product of the tradition that the world, created by God, is good and worthy

A medieval vision of hell.

of study. It may also be in some part the product of Christian sexual morality. The sexual tension preached by puritanical Christianity led, when people paid attention to it, to repression, to sublimation, and hence to creativity.

Another aspect of puritanism was less productive. Inheriting the Roman ideal of *gravitas,* medieval churchmen sometimes connected mirth with sin and praised saints whom "no one had ever heard angry, upset, grieving, or laughing" (Saint Martin). Fortunately these precepts were often disobeyed, and the comic element—everything from wit to broad caricature—appears in epics, student songs, lyrics, and occasionally even in the saints' lives themselves. Medieval songs and dances are also testaments to the fact that the puritans did not usually get their way.

The excessive dependence of the Middle Ages upon the past is part of that Golden Age complex which besets most civilizations, though medieval men carried it to an unusual degree. They believed that they were "little men in the twilight of the world" or "dwarves sitting on the shoulders of giants" (the ancients). Both the primitive Church and Augustan Rome loomed out of the mist of the past as towers of civilization from which society had fallen, no matter if the Augustan Romans saw themselves as degenerates from the time of Cato, who in turn bewailed the lost *Saturnia regna.* Had the medieval mind looked only backwards to Eden, medieval thought would have been primitivistic; it would have had no idea of progress. But the fact that the incarnation came after the fall, and the resurrection after the crucifixion, was productive of hope. Nonetheless, exaggerated respect for the past caused several medieval eccentricities, among them the curious practice of reverse plagiarism. A modern plagiarist takes the writings of a famous man and passes them off as his own; with greater modesty, a medieval writer was likely to gain an audience for his own writings by attaching to them the name of a great pope or Father. Their worship of the past checked originality, just as our own worship of everything new promotes superficiality. The use of the word "primitive" is instructive. To us it means crude and barbaric; but through the time of Samuel Johnson its connotation was favorable: the Good Old Days.

ALL these cultural traits, which obscure the true individualism of medieval society, gave rise to the once-common generalization that it was a society wholly corporate in nature.* Aside from the fact that nothing could have been less individualistic than the ancient polis to which such critics compare the society of the Middle Ages, the generalization itself is false. It is true that Church, manor, gild, and university were considered corporations. It is

---

*We use the word "corporation" today to denote a business organization with a legal personality. The word derives from the Latin *corpus* ("body") and in Roman and medieval usage referred to any organization considered to have an essence, or real existence, of its own. Thus the Christian people as a whole was considered a corporation—the mystical body of Christ.

also true that the concept of a *societas christiana* as the mystical body of Christ is quite literally a corporate theory. But these were theories. In practice there was weak government, varying laws, feudal atomization, heresy and dissent, wandering scholars, and drifting peasants. If anything, the Middle Ages were more individualistic than both ancient and modern civilization.

Individual isolation was alleviated for the peasant by the village community and for the knight or noble by the feudal attitudes of loyalty, honor, and comradeship in battle. But to a very large extent the individual was at the mercy of nature and his fellows. His life expectancy was short, and he was exposed to cold, wet, drought, and disease more than is today conceivable in this country. In times of famine there was no provident Joseph, let alone a Department of Agriculture or a Welfare Commission, to care for him; in sickness the physician was as likely to do him harm as good; and there were no police to call upon for protection from murderers or thieves. Medieval man had to face the distinct possibility of death and judgment at any moment. Perhaps largely because of this, he was obliged to do what the modern existentialists ask of us today, to face reality in every given moment, avoid rationalization, and take responsibility for our actions. This is the way that Fulcun Geroy behaves in H. F. M. Prescott's superb historical novel, *Son of Dust*. Fulcun's passion for the wife of another man brings ruin to his family, misery to himself, and war to his peasants, but he never whines about how badly God or the world or the Church or society are treating him. He cannot renounce his love, but he has no doubt that he must take full responsibility for it.

These were the implicit assumptions of the eighth through tenth centuries.

THEY found explicit expression. In theology and philosophy there were controversies over the eucharist, Iconoclasm, and predestination, but none at a particularly high level. The only great philosopher was John Scotus Eriugena, who was in the psychological and mystical tradition of the early Middle Ages. Though John, with a hint of gnosticism, said that "no one could be saved except through philosophy," he did not have in mind the systematic philosophy of Aristotle but something more akin to Plato and more especially to the neoplatonists. Perhaps the strongest influence upon Eriugena was that of the fifth-century Syrian monk known as Pseudo-Dionysius, himself a mystic influenced by the neoplatonists. John's view of God as something wholly beyond the power of human reason to describe, let alone to grasp, derives from Pseudo-Dionysius. For John, God "is not Being but more than Being . . . . God is not one of those things that are, but is more than those things that are." God is not "good" but something far more than good. At one point he even said that God is "Nothing:" nothing in the sense in which we mean anything. This "negative theology" was most beautifully expressed by Pseudo-Dionysius in his *Mystical Theology:*

We maintain that It (God) is not soul, or mind, or endowed with the faculty of imagination, conjecture, reason, or understanding; nor can It be described by the reason or perceived by the understanding since It is not number, or order, or greatness, or littleness, or equality, or inequality, and since It is not immovable nor in motion, or at rest, and has no power, and is not power or light, and does not live, and is not life; nor is It personal essence, or eternity, or time; nor can It be grasped by the understanding since It is not knowledge or truth; nor is It any other thing such as we or any other being can have knowledge of; nor does It belong to the category of non-existence or to that of existence; nor do existent beings know It as it actually is, nor does It know them as they actually are . . . nor is It darkness, nor is It light, or error, or truth; nor can any affirmation or negation apply to It . . . .

God is not, not because he fails to attain being, but because he is infinitely above it. It is difficult to imagine within the western Christian tradition an analysis more in variance with that of Aristotle and Thomas Aquinas.

In his great work *On the Division of Nature,* John speaks of an emanation from and a return to God, in a tradition that stretches from Empedocles through the neoplatonists down to Teilhard de Chardin in our own day. In John's view, there are four stages in cosmic time: the first is God the source of all, uncreated and creating; the second is the world of primal causes or Platonic ideas, created and creating; the third is the phenomenal world, created and uncreating; and the last is the return to God uncreated and uncreating. The microcosmic individual comes from and returns to God in much the same way as the cosmos itself. On account of this doctrine John was accused after his death of pantheism, quite inaccurately. For the pantheist,

The inferiority of the temporal to the spiritual: King Ethelstan bows as he presents Bede's Life of St. Cuthbert *to the saint himself.*

God is wholly immanent: all things are God, there is no distinction between things and God, and God is nothing other than all things. Eriugena was an emanationist: all things are God, but there is room for distinction, and God is more, much more than that which he has created. He escaped formal condemnation as a heretic until four hundred years after his death, but his mystical profundity and use of allegory were far above the comprehension of his contemporaries, who respected him intellectually but distrusted him theologically.

I<small>F</small> John was the only really interesting philosopher of the time, there were a number of exciting developments in language and literature.

This period was the critical moment in the development of the modern European languages. English and the Scandinavian tongues had developed by the seventh and eighth centuries. The

O.F.: Pro deo amur et pro christian poblo et nostro commun salvament d'ist di in avant, quant Deus savir et podir me dunat . . . .

O.H.G.: In Goddes minna ind in thes christianes folches ind unser bedhero gehaltnissi, fon thesemo dage frammordes, so fram so mir God geuuizci indi mahd furgibit . . . .

Trans.: For the love of God, the Christian people, and the welfare of both of us, from this day on, so far as God gives me the ability and the power . . . .

first monuments we have in either Old French (O.F.) or Old High German (O.H.G.) are the Oaths of Strasbourg taken by Charles the Bald and Louis the German against their brother Lothar in 842. There was some vernacular literature even in this early period, when Latin was considered the proper written language and people disputed whether God in heaven spoke Latin or Hebrew. The English *Beowulf* and the German *Hildebrandslied* are among the best examples in the vernacular.

Since Latin was believed by most to be the proper medium for literature, most of the relics of the period are in that tongue. Much is imitative of the ancients and consequently poor, but much too is fresh and original, like the Swan sequence of the ninth century:

I shall sing, my children, of a voyage of the wingèd swan who crossed the seas. O how bitterly did she weep to depart the shores with their flowers and to turn her head to the empty deep! And she said: Unhappy bird, alas, what shall I do? When daylight has faded I shall not be able to keep aloft here in the spray. Buffeted by the waves, swept here and there by the winds, I fly an exile. I see schools of fish but dare not go down to take the food I need. Sunrise and sunset I fly, and at night I see the shining stars in every region of the sky. Orion I see, half veiled by the scudding clouds. While thus silently she mused, ruddy dawn came, and, catching its fire on her wings, she began to recover her strength. Rejoicing now . . . singing sweetly, she flew to the pleasant shores.[7]

THE FORMATION OF A NEW CIVILIZATION

The Oaths of Strasbourg.

There are conventions here, and the poem is an allegory of *pere-grinatio,* but it has a sensitive feel to it all the same.

Some of the Latin hymns of the time are attractive, like the one to the Virgin beginning

Ave, maris stella,
Dei mater alma,
atque semper virgo,
Felix caeli porta.[8]

Hail, Star of the Sea,
Fostering Mother of God,
Ever-virgin,
Blessèd gate of heaven.

Some poets had their eyes on less ethereal maidens:

Come, sweet friend, and be with me,
Darling of my heart, my treasure!
Come now into my chamber—see,
It is fresh-decked and fit for pleasure.

I have put cushions in the seats,
And hung bright cloths about the room,
Set fragrant herbs to mix their sweets
With flowers fresh-plucked and all in bloom.[9]

THE drama began as an extension of the liturgy and was developed further by the nun Roswitha of Gandersheim in a number of plays which no one has thought to revive for Broadway. Here is part of the dialogue from her *Paphnutius:*

PAPHNUTIUS: What greater injury can we conceive than this—that while the greater world is obedient, and subject to his rule, the lesser world resists his guidance?
DISCIPLES: What do you mean by the lesser world?
PAPH.: Man.
DISC.: Man?
PAPH.: Yes.
DISC.: What man?
PAPH.: Every man.
DISC.: How can this be?[10]

IN medieval historical writing there were two traditions, the high philosophical, and the low didactic. The high philosophical tradition derived from Saint Augustine's theory of history. The Greeks and Romans had written history that lacked a sense of development and sought to draw eternal lessons from unchanging human nature. The ancients mined the past for *exempla,* examples of the greedy tyrant, the enlightened king, the foolish commander. The Christian Fathers, especially Saint Augustine, for the first time formulated a real theory of history in averring that since God created time it must have meaning and since there is a beginning and an end to time there must be within it a process which is meaningful. They believed that history is guided by Providence in the direction of progress, progress from man's state after the Fall to his reunion with God. As the Jews were slowly prepared for the first coming of Christ, the history of the world after the Incarnation is the slow preparation for the Second Coming. This idea that the historical process is real, meaningful, and progressive is one of the greatest contributions of early Christian thought to western civilization. Further, the ancient historian was, with only one notable exception (Herodotus), concerned with the history of his own polis; Augustinian history was universal and encompassed the entire world. Within this context high history interpreted the world according to the sacred view. Miracle stories in this high history, far from being crude superstition, are part of the manifestation of Divine Providence to man.

In practice, medieval historians usually reverted to the *exempla* history of the ancients, modifying it to fit the principles of Christianity. Martyrologies and hagiographies, the commonest forms of writing about the past, used conventional images and *exempla* in order to show in individual lives how trust in the world is rewarded and how good men win their way to heaven.

From the seventh century, annals and chronicles appeared as another common form of recording the past. At first the annals consisted of very brief insertions into the calendars used for computing the date of Easter: "1024. In this year died Bishop Robert." Longer and more detailed annals are called chronicles. The annals lacked all historical analysis or development of theme. The chronicles often were not much more sophisticated, but the better chroniclers did have plan and direction.

There was only one great historian in the early Middle Ages: Saint Bede, the equal of Augustine in historical perception and the peer of the ancients in care and accuracy. Born in 672 near the monastery of Jarrow on the coast of Northumbria, he was brought up on that lonely shore and "passed all the days of my life in that monastery; I devoted myself to meditating on

Holy Scripture, observing the discipline, and daily singing the office. My whole life I was always pleased to learn from others, and to write and teach myself." Bede led a perfectly uneventful, ideal scholar's life.

Like many men of imagination, this cloistered scholar who never traveled more than a few miles from home had a marvelous understanding of the world and of the ways of men. Bede was an adept at mathematics and astronomy, writing books on natural science and making original and startlingly accurate observations upon the variation of tides according to latitude and the configuration of the shore, but his great contribution was to history. He wrote saints' lives, a short universal chronicle, and a treatise on chronology in which he popularized that division of time into A.D. and B.C. that we now take for granted.

His greatest work, and one of the greatest works of the Middle Ages, was *The Ecclesiastical History of the English Nation.* It is difficult to say what is most impressive about this extraordinary book. In an age when most chroniclers took few pains in examining the sources of their information, Bede subjected all of his sources, written and oral, to rigorous criticism, and in his eagerness to learn borrowed books from distant libraries and even commissioned acquaintances going abroad to copy material for him in the papal archives and other continental repositories. Not since Herodotus had an historian shown such vigor in collecting his evidence. Bede believed in miracles and wrote about them, which is not surprising, for he was a Christian, but his principles of criticism were utterly sound for his day: he demanded as accurate evidence for a purported miracle as for any other purported event. The purpose and plan of the book, clear, highly structured, and unobtrusively executed, is a model. Never forgetful of historical and literary unity, Bede shapes his central theme, the gradual conversion of the English and their unification in the Catholic faith, with skill and with effective use of illustration. His style is lively and quick, and his powers of characterization and dialogue surpassed anything since Suetonius. In an age when chronicles and annals were centered upon the events at one monastery or city or court, Bede wrote a history of a whole nation, a feat even more remarkable in view of the fact that that nation had never been united, and would not be for a century and a half after his time. In almost every instance

Carolingian architecture: The Abbey of Corvey (ninth century) in old Saxony.

in which modern historians have been able to check his facts
Bede has proved accurate. The final, and not the least, tribute
one can pay him is to observe that he is one of the few medieval
writers of prose that can still delight as well as instruct.

EARLY medieval art was permeated by the same assumptions as
literature. Charlemagne encouraged the arts in order to imitate
the grandeur of the ancients and also, recognizing their didactic
possibilities, as a practical measure of education. The Carolingians, though Theodulf of Orléans was a sedulous student of
Vitruvius, seldom attempted, and never achieved, anything on
the scale of the Romans. Few architectural monuments of the
time remain, and those that do, like the cathedral or the restored palace at Aachen, disappoint the eye accustomed to the
later grandeurs of the Gothic. Carolingian art concentrated upon

Saint Luke, from the Gospel Book of Archbishop Ebbo of Reims. The Roman influence can be seen, but with the peculiar Carolingian rendering of the clothing. An exaggerated imitation of Roman sculpture results.

the so-called cloister-crafts, book illumination, metalwork, carved ivories. One of the most interesting of early medieval creations is the Bayeux Tapestry, made in 1077–1082 for the bishop of Bayeux. Drawn by clerics (though embroidered by women), it portrays the Norman Conquest as the story of the divine retribution dealt the noble Harold for violating his oath to Duke William.

The Carolingian period, characterized as it was by tendencies toward synthesis, produced a general western European style of art. The models used were primarily Roman, because

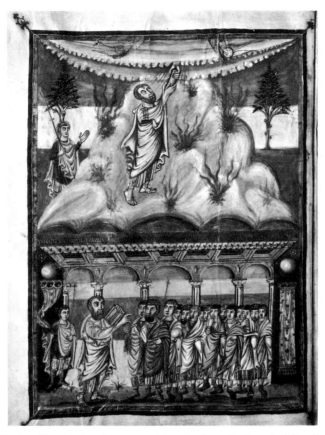

Carolingian illumination: Moses receiving the Law (top) and giving it to the Israelites (below); from the Grandval Bible.

the Carolingians revered things classical and because they found the representational art of the Romans much more congenial to their didactic purpose than the abstract art of the Celts and Teutons. The artist, like the poet and the historian, wanted his work to *mean* something: he employed symbols and allegories, and he shunned pure aesthetics. The creativity of the art of the period, as of the literature, lies in the modification of Roman models by other traditions or ideas.

In accordance with their didactic purpose and their belief in the mystical reality of things, artists modified the classical precepts of representational art in several fascinating respects. In looking at medieval pictures for the first time, one is struck by several apparent crudities. In the first place, the artists seem to have been quite naive in their conception of the past: Joshua's soldiers at Jericho wear eleventh-century armor, and Joseph and Mary wander on their mule through countryside that looks a great deal more like France than like Egypt. But this is not naïveté. It is an attempt to bring home the timelessness, the eternity of God's actions in regard to man. For the medieval artist as for the modern existentialist, all things are the present moment. Artists who today paint Jesus wearing overalls and riding a motorcycle have the same idea in mind.

Another apparent crudity is the disproportionate size and ceremonial stiffness of the figures. Again, rather than the result of clumsiness, this is a deliberate attempt to portray things *the way they really are* in the spiritual sense: the king in the picture is larger than his courtiers because he is greater than they. The figures of the great and the holy are removed from the petty perspectives of this world of appearances into the dimension of the sacred. The same is true of the stiffness of the figures. The impassive Christ of the Romanesque crucifix, and the emperor fixed in majestic posture and clothed in all his robes of state, are representational, not of the physical, but of the mystical, reality. The art of the Middle Ages was more flexible than that of the Renaissance, which insisted upon physical reality.

There is another way in which medieval art may possibly have been more sophisticated then Renaissance art. Even apart from the size of great men, the perspective of medieval pictures troubles one: things seem out of joint. It is likely that this, like other apparent "mistakes," was deliberate. Renaissance painters saw everything from one perspective, photographically, "realistically," but medieval painters looked at a scene from several different perspectives at once. A medieval picture looked at with this in mind becomes very exciting indeed. It is as if the artist is everywhere at once: the castle is tiny as if seen from afar; the men on its battlements huge as if encountered face to face; this lake is seen from that distance and that tree from this. Medieval pictures, like Christian thought, have many dimensions.

It would be folly to ascribe to medieval art supreme virtues which it lacked: many of the pictures are crude, and it is clear that in most respects technique was much inferior to what it later became. But it is also true, unless we restrict our vision

*Gold Hen and Chickens, one of Queen Theudelinda's possessions
(early seventh century).*

with Renaissance blinders, that the art of the early Middle Ages
is as often wonderful as it is strange, and it may bear a closer
relation than the art of the Renaissance to much of what is
being done today.

IF early medieval history and art were creative, the same can
scarcely be said for early medieval science. The early Middle
Ages had lost much of what was valuable in ancient scientific
thought, particularly Aristotle's works on natural science. The
knowledge they retained, such as the medicine of Galen and the
geography of Ptolemy, they preserved uncritically. Nowhere were
they as uncreative or as slavishly attached to the "authorities"
of the past as in science. Experimentation seemed unnecessary
to the exaggerated humility of the day: if Galen didn't know it,
how could they? The word of a Father of the Church was more
readily challenged than the diagnosis of an ancient physician.
This is in part because of the preoccupations of medieval men
with the other world, but even from their own point of view
they missed an opportunity: the advance of science has disclosed
wonders from which the religious spirit can derive a notion of
the Divine more awesome than anything conceived of in the
tight little cosmology of the tenth century. It must be added
that while western science slept, the Arabs were avidly learning

from the science of the Greeks and the mathematics of the Babylonians and the Indians.

Nevertheless, the Middle Ages were quite productive of practical technology. Medieval men were interested on the one hand in God and on the other in making a living. As Lynn White observes, Christianity, by replacing animism, modified the sacred view of the world and made it possible to exploit nature. Before the eighth century calendars depicted the seasons by their natural elements (sun for summer, wind for fall); thereafter they tended to indicate them by their human activities, such as sowing or reaping. It may be that modern technology begins in these eighth and ninth centuries. The advances made in agricultural technology in the eighth century were matched by equally impressive advances in mechanical technology from the end of the eleventh. Ideas were introduced from the East, even from as far away as India, Tibet, and China, as eagerly as inventions were pursued at home. The windmill and the tidal mill were invented; sophisticated uses of water power occurred from the ninth century; motor techniques were perfected; and, in the later Middle Ages, the crank, the turbine, gunpowder, the suction pump, the coach with suspended body, and the mechanical clock appeared.

THE fifth to the seventh centuries form a period when the elements of European culture were being gathered. In the eighth they were synthesized. From the ninth to the eleventh the synthesis was completed, attitudes and forms of expression took shape, and the forces of creativity gathered strength for the introduction of new ideas in the twelfth and thirteenth.

NOTES

[1] Lupus, letter #108, in *Loup de Ferrières*, ed. Léon Levillain (Paris, 1935), I, 146.

[2] Max L. W. Laistner, *Thought and Letters in Western Europe* A.D. *500–900*, 2d ed. (London, 1957), p. 237.

[3] Letter #156, in Harriet Pratt Lattin, *The Letters of Gerbert with His Papal Privileges as Sylvester II* (New York, 1961), p. 184.

[4] Frederick A. Wright, *The Works of Liudprand of Cremona* (London, Routledge and Kegan Paul, Ltd., 1930), p. 236.

[5] Cited by W. O. Hassall, *Medieval England* (Oxford, 1957), p. 22.

[6] Trans. Thomas Forester, in *The Chronicle of Henry of Huntingdon* (London, 1909), pp. 301–319.

[7] *Oxford Book of Medieval Latin Verse* (Oxford, 1959), #68.

[8] *Oxford Book,* #71.

[9] Trans. Howard Mumford Jones, in Charles W. Jones, *Medieval Literature in Translation* (New York, 1950), p. 259.

[10] Trans. Christobel Marshall in C. W. Jones, p. 211.

Chapter Thirteen

THE RECONSTRUCTION OF
POLITICAL SOCIETY

I<small>N</small> the tenth and eleventh centuries the new configurations of political power that would eventually become the states of modern western Europe emerged from the dissolved Carolingian Empire.

At the end of the ninth century a dispassionate observer of the state of Europe might have concluded that it would take centuries to repair the damages wrought by the barbarian invasions and internal strife. Yet, before the following century was half over, significant steps had been made toward the reestablishment of order and a resumption of the process of building that had begun so auspiciously in the eighth century. The barbarian invasions were checked, partly through the military efforts of able rulers like Alfred the Great and Otto the Great, partly through the expedient of settling and assimilating the invaders, as in Normandy. Almost every section of the population was eager for the restoration of stability. The needs of the Church, of commerce, of peasants and townsmen who for decades had been subject to constant fear, were added to the natural desire of rulers to rule.

The initial regrouping and reorganization was often most effective on the local level. The failure of the later Carolingian kings to protect their subjects against the barbarians induced people to rally round their local strong-man, usually a military leader or important civilian administrator. The result was the growth of the feudal relationships discussed in Chapter Nine and the accrual of considerable power and independence to these local leaders. More than ever, real power lay in the hands of these feudal magnates, and no king could hope to rule effectively without either destroying or controlling them.

This is one of the problems that make the period exciting: it was by no means preordained that the fission of political authority characterizing the later Carolingian period would cease before tiny principalities like Anjou or Brittany emerged as sovereign states. Nor was it predetermined, on the other hand, that the supranational ideal of the unified Christian society should fail to be realized. The jelling of authority at the level of the nation is no more logical or necessary than at that of the principality or the polis, and probably less logical than at that of universal dominion. The history of Germany, which did not attain nationhood until 1871, is witness to the existence, if not the practicality, of the alternatives.

Why should central governments headed by kings have been able to supplant or at least substantially to modify the independence of the feudal magnates? One reason was that the ideal of order represented in the concepts of the universal Roman Empire and the universal Christian society persisted. Another was the sense, encouraged by the practice of anointing as well as Roman and German traditions of kingship, that the ruler had a dignity exceeding, not only in quantity but in quality, that of any lesser lord. Even the most powerful feudal lords took care to link their authority with that of a Carolingian king or one of his successors. Most of all, society needed the extension of law and order over a territory larger than that of the fief. The Church required order for the improvement of morals and the conduct of education, let alone the safety of its ministers. Commerce required the safety of traveling merchants and their goods; the people longed for a security that could never be fully attained while their lords were permitted to wage war against one another at their will. Far from being a symbol of oppression, the distant king in London or in Paris often appeared as a defender of the people against anarchy and the rapacity of the barons. Finally, it was true in Middle Ages, as it is today, that there is a natural growth of government, a natural extension of power outward until checked by internal imbalance or external competition. As government grew, it required more administrators and a larger army; these in turn required more revenues; and the need for larger revenues in turn demanded an extension of territory or at least of taxation. The little extra dignity and authority that the kings possessed over that of their subjects made them the natural centers of this natural extension of authority.

Why should the centers of authority have taken the shape of the nations known as England, France, Germany, and Italy? England enjoyed natural frontiers and a people generally united in language and culture, though even there it took the shock of the Danish invasions to make Alfred the Great and his successors able to organize a really united monarchy. On the continent, the boundaries of the kingdoms inherited by the sons of Louis the Pious were at first very arbitrary, but slowly changed as the divisions of language, culture, and laws that predated Charlemagne's conquest reasserted themselves. Italy was set apart from the North by all these divisions and by natural boundaries as well. The lack of natural frontiers between France and Germany and the consequent artificiality of their common border made it one of the perennial causes of dispute in European history.

All these countries inherited certain similarities from their common background in the eighth-century synthesis and the Carolingian Empire: a kingship both elective and hereditary, a feudal structure, and a powerful Church.

But there were significant differences among them as well, differences that encouraged them to develop differently. England achieved effective political unity much earlier (ca. 900) than either France or Germany, and it enjoyed both a well-organized Church and a strong monarchy, whose effectiveness was reinforced after 1066 by the efficient and centralized administration of the Normans. At the same time, England had a powerful nobility and strong feudal institutions, which were also reinforced by the importation of French feudalism after 1066. The result was that neither the centripetal monarchy nor the centrifugal feudal elements could defeat the other, and there developed a continual tension in English politics that eventually established a beneficent balance of power and created the eighteenth-century constitution that Montesquieu and Jefferson so admired.

In France, the originally weak monarchy was heir to all the difficulties of the later Carolingians and suffered from the long disputes between Carolingian and Capetian, during which the great lords established their virtual independence. But, partly through luck and partly through skill, the Capetian kings were able to strengthen and eventually transform the feudal bonds that tied the lords to them into means of effective centralized control.

The German Carolingians' power deteriorated like that of the French, but in Germany the Saxon dynasty gained the throne with much less trouble than the Capetians had. From early in the tenth century a succession of able rulers established a strong monarchy with the help of the Church. But the size of the kingdom, its lack of a political center and of natural frontiers, combined with imperial schemes beyond the Alps, were initial disadvantages that it was hard to overcome. When in addition the German rulers chose the policy of assaulting, rather than building upon, feudal institutions, and when at the end of the eleventh century they began to quarrel seriously with the Church, their troubles only increased. In the end, the monarchy lost its power to the nobility, and the establishment of the German nation was deferred until the nineteenth century.

In Italy, the quarrels of Normans, Germans, papacy, and towns rendered the attainment of order, let alone a national state, extremely difficult, and Italy, like Germany, never achieved unity in the Middle Ages.

From the beginning of the eleventh century, the sources increase greatly in number if not in reliability. There are multitudes of minor chronicles, annals, lives of saints, deeds of bishops, and collections of charters and decrees. Archives, which in general contain large quantities of materials from the twelfth century, offer a few from the eleventh, many of which have never been edited. There are many published sources including the writings of Richer, Regino of Prüm, Liudprand of Cremona, Widukind of Corvey, Flodoard of Reims, Thietmar of Merseburg, Radulf Glaber, Florence of Worcester, Orderic Vitalis, Landolfo of Milan, and William of Malmesbury.

GERMANY. When Louis III the Child died in 911, the East Frankish line of Carolingians came to an end. Lorraine briefly attached itself to France, which was still ruled by the Carolingians, but the rest of the German dukes chose as king one of their own

Coronation chair of the Carolingian kings at Aachen.

number, Conrad of Franconia, who was accepted without significant opposition. After eight years Conrad died, having named as his heir the duke of Saxony, Henry I the Fowler. The Saxon dynasty persisted from 919 until 1024, when it was replaced by the "Salian" dynasty originating in Franconia (where the "Salic" Franks were falsely supposed to have arisen.)

The Saxon and Salian kings were able and devoted men who meant to rule well and to consolidate their power, and they had initial advantages over and beyond their ability. They eliminated the Carolingian custom of dividing the kingdom among the sons, while retaining at least part of the Carolingian administrative apparatus. They had on hand a well-organized Church; the prestige of kingship, to which they later added that of empire; and opportunities for expansion eastwards.

With these advantages they might well have built a viable state had their corresponding disadvantages not proved immense and unmanageable. The very geographical location that gave

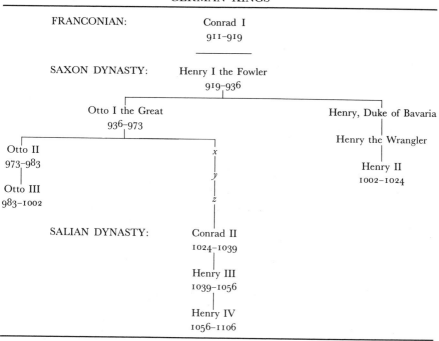

FRANCONIAN: Conrad I
911–919

SAXON DYNASTY: Henry I the Fowler
919–936

Otto I the Great   Henry, Duke of Bavaria
936–973

Otto II   Henry the Wrangler
973–983

Otto III   Henry II
983–1002   1002–1024

x
y
z

SALIAN DYNASTY: Conrad II
1024–1039

Henry III
1039–1056

Henry IV
1056–1106

Germany the opportunity of expansion also left it open to attack. The disadvantage of its exposure on both eastern and western flanks has both frequently and recently been demonstrated. Further, the German kings lacked crown lands, a weakness increased by changes of dynasty. They lacked a natural capital such as France possessed in Paris or England in London; the only large cities in Germany were on the Rhine in Lorraine, a territory disputed with the French and never well integrated into the German kingdom. Too much power lay in the hands of the bishops, who could not always be counted on, especially as the papacy increased its influence, and in the hands of the even less loyal local barons. Finally, whether from necessity or folly, the German kings dangerously overextended their power by political and military ventures beyond their frontiers.

Like all the Teutonic monarchies, the German combined election with heredity. Heredity was the rule as long as a dynasty was strong, but when it failed, or no heir was forthcoming, dislocation was bound to occur. The tension at the time of the

THE RECONSTRUCTION OF POLITICAL SOCIETY

277

election of Conrad II, the first Salian emperor, is conveyed by his biographer:

> While all the magnates, and, so to say, the valor and the vitals of the kingdom, had convened . . . , they pitched camps on this side and in the region about the Rhine . . . . An affair of supreme importance was in question; there was hesitation in view of the possibility of an indecisive election. Hung between hope and fear . . . , members of the same households long explored alternate desires among themselves.[1]

Once the king was elected, his deposition was permitted, in ill-defined circumstances, by several political theories: the old Germanic right of resistance against an inept or unjust tribal leader, the feudal theory of breach of contract, and the ecclesiastical theory of the unjust ruler. Secure kings did not have to worry about such theories; but from the end of the eleventh century the kings of Germany were seldom secure.

Their insecurity arose from fragmentation and localization. Although enough of the Carolingian administrative structure was retained to hold the dukes to some kind of allegiance to the king, many of the German nobles considered their holdings allods (lands for which they were responsible to no one). The king's lack of a strong centralized feudal hierarchy made it difficult for him to use feudalism to evolve a national system.

This difficulty was exacerbated by the dukes' propensity, after having chosen one of their own number to replace the last Carolingian king, to regard the ruler as their peer rather than as their superior and to accord the crown only nominal reverence. Given only a slight change in circumstances, the great duchies might have themselves become little monarchies. Called the *Stamm* ("tribe" or "race") duchies, because they used inaccurately to be regarded as the extension of the ancient Germanic tribal divisions, they in fact derived from their function as administrative units of the Carolingian Empire.

The methods employed by the kings to combat the power of the dukes proved even more dangerous than the dukes themselves. The king had always first to secure control of his own duchy and Franconia, whose central location made it indispensable. Next he had to hobble the other dukes as much as possible by erecting royal castles and extending the royal domain, by using *ministeriales* (the German equivalent of serjeants, who, owing the king everything, were in some things loyal) and by making alliances with the bishops, the towns, and the lesser nobility.

Such a policy might have been successful, even with the civil strife that it constantly engendered, had feudalism existed to a degree that permitted a close relationship between the king and the lesser nobility. The power of the latter was growing rapidly. The result of the anti-ducal policies of the kings was to earn the permanent hostility of those who, like the duke of Bavaria, retained their power, and to replace the others with lesser nobles who in the long run proved even harder to control. In their efforts to secure centralization the policy of the kings led directly to further atomization. Only in the alliance with the Church and the towns did they have any lasting success, and the ambitions of the papacy were to rob them of the support of one of these two pillars as well.

ANOTHER means of expanding royal power was the assumption of the imperial title. Historians have long, and sometimes angrily, debated whether the empire was beneficial or destructive to German political unity, and whether it was a tool of military expansion, an expression of the Christian ideal of unified society, or a revival of the Roman imperial ideal. Many recent historians, notably Geoffrey Barraclough, consider the theory and ideal of the empire less important than its practical use to the German kings.

The empire was revived by the second Saxon king, Otto I, a young and vigorous monarch who succeeded his father Henry I in 936. Otto's reign is an example of how much the most successful German rulers were able to accomplish. If the chronicler does not exaggerate too much, Otto was an impressive ruler in more ways than one: he was

. . . in all his doings the most resolute of men, always amiable, so long as the kingly dignity (was) not weakened; liberal in gifts, sparing of sleep . . . . To his friends he denied nothing; he was loyal beyond the endurance of a man . . . . He could read and understand whole books. He could talk, besides, in French and Slavonic. He was an assiduous huntsman . . . ; he rode a horse with kingly bearing. His

Crown of Otto I.

fine and royal figure fitted this part—he had a good head of grey hair, and blazing eyes, whose glance shot out like lightning . . . .[2]

Early in his reign Otto extended his power westward. To secure Lorraine he appointed his youngest brother Bruno archbishop of Cologne and effective vicegerent for the western duchy. Bruno's personal power was immense. He divided and ruled the duchy effectively and made of it a bulwark of royal strength. He carried the influence of Germany even farther westwards, so establishing his influence among the last French Carolingians that France might possibly have been reunited with the empire had not the Capetian dynasty arisen and expressed different ambitions.

Otto's activities in Italy were even more spectacular than his brother's in France. But invasion of the South was dictated less by dreams of empire than by the requirements of a purely German policy. Italy was a power vacuum. No effective authority ruled its northern part, which was in effect divided into nearly independent cities, bishoprics, and fiefs. The papacy, dominated by noble factions and intrigues, had fallen into disrepute. The policy of the king of centrally located and exposed

Germany had to be to secure and pacify all areas of possible disruption upon its periphery. This was the basis of Bruno's policy in France, and it was the basis of Otto's in Italy. In Italy the stakes were, if anything, far higher. Otto feared that the Swabian and Bavarian dukes would take control of Italy and even extend their power to Burgundy and Lorraine, thereby recreating that middle kingdom that had been the lot of Lothar I at the partition of Verdun and isolating the northern German duchies on the fringes of Europe. To eliminate this possibility Otto conquered Italy and assumed its crown himself (962).

For Italy the conquest was a blessing, for Otto and his successors gave it a degree of unity and supported the papacy against the turbulent Roman nobility. For the Saxon kings the effect was less salutary. They had conquered Italy in order to give their policy in Germany greater leverage, but they now found that they had to expend an immense amount of energy in Italy dealing with Byzantines, Saracens, Lombards, and Normans in southern Italy as well as with the disjointed politics of the papacy and the cities in the north.

The fantastic complication of Italian politics in the eleventh century may be illustrated in the difficulties that Conrad II had with Milan. Milan had long been ruled by a duke who owed feudal allegiance to the king. Ariberto, Archbishop of Milan since 1018, successfully usurped the duke's powers with the help of the capitanei, the noble upper class which resented the duke's authority. The valvassores, or petty nobles, who hated the capitanei, now rallied to the duke. Since the king had to support his vassal, the duke, there was now an alliance between king, duke, and valvassores against archbishop and capitanei. Conrad summoned Ariberto to explain his actions; Ariberto failed to appear, and the king then ordered his arrest, an order that no one was able to execute. Ariberto declared that he no longer considered Conrad king and offered the crown of Italy to Otto, the king of Burgundy. In their hatred for the archbishop, the valvassores had meanwhile become connected with the semi-heretical movement of the Patarenes. The pope now entered the picture, but on the side of the heretics. Desirous of keeping good relations with the king, he excommunicated the archbishop. The alliance was now one of King Conrad, the pope, the duke, the valvassores, and the heretics, against the archbishop, King Otto of Burgundy, and the capitanei. By this time, everyone was somewhat confused as to whom he was supposed to hate, and the Milanese patched up their quarrels and united against the king. Conrad died without having resolved the issue. His son Henry III achieved a temporary peace with the city, but another internal war broke out shortly between the valvassores and the merchants, followed by a war in which the valvassores and the merchants united against the capitanei and the archbishop. In the course of this last war, the archbishop was forced out of town, and a commune was established. Ariberto finally died in 1045. Henry III and the nobles chose a successor, Guido, who was opposed by the merchants as a tool of the aristocracy and by the papacy as a corrupt simoniac. Open civil war followed, and the perennial troubles of the city finally merged into the larger quarrel between empire and papacy under Hildebrand and Henry IV. German power in Italy rested upon treacherous quicksand.

OTTO the Great clearly wanted the imperial crown when he assumed it in 962—it was he who suggested the coronation to Pope John XII—but it is probable that he was less interested in reviving the Age of Augustus than in obtaining additional prestige to impress his new Italian subjects as well as the dukes at home. As emperor, he became something more than one *Stamm* duke ruling at the suffrance of the others. The imperial coronation also legitimized the Saxon line and lent it a semi-sacred quality that further enhanced its prestige. In the eleventh century it became a useful tool in opposing the claims of the papacy.

The imperial idea was of further use in the eastern lands and in Burgundy. Burgundy became the third kingdom in the empire, along with Germany and Italy, in 1033, when Conrad II inherited it peacefully.

In the ninth and tenth centuries the powers to the east of Germany were gradually consolidating. Previously in a nomadic, unlettered, and primitive state, the eastern peoples settled down, adopted Christianity, learned letters, and formed political states. One was the Magyar kingdom of Hungary. The others were the Slavic states of Bohemia, Moravia, and Poland. Between Poland and Germany—that is, between the Elbe and the Oder—were other groups of Slavs, the Wends and Abodrites, completely wild and uncivilized.

No threat was exerted against these peoples from the East by a Russia that was still inchoate and uncivilized, but from the ninth century the Germans began their *Drang nach Osten*—their effort to incorporate the Slavic territories. As the Americans used the ideology of "manifest destiny" to justify their relentless thrust to the Pacific, so the Germans evolved ideologies to justify their ruthless pressure to the East: Germany became, in the minds of Germans throughout history, the bulwark of Christendom, the bulwark of western civilization, and, most recently, the bulwark against Bolshevism. The gradual extension of German power eastward began with Charlemagne, culminated in 1942 at Stalingrad, and suffered a total reversal in 1945. In one demonic wager, the German people lost in six years of war what their ancestors had gained in a millennium. The present border between Germany and Poland is almost precisely where it was one thousand years ago.

Under the Saxon and Salian rulers the *Drang nach Osten* took two main thrusts, the first being to exterminate the Slavs and colonize and annex their lands, and the second being to extend to them the beneficent influence of the German nation.

The policy of colonization was aimed particularly at those Slavs who were least civilized and most contiguous to German territory. Charlemagne had extended his lordship vaguely as far as the Oder, and King Henry I began a deliberate advance in that direction. The most permanent inroads into Slavic territories were accomplished by barons whose lands lay upon the frontier and who undertook to extend them as a matter of private enterprise independent of royal policy: such a family were the Billungs, who colonized the regions bordering the North Sea. The Church also took part in the process of "conversion" (which can be understood, like the modern "liberation," in a number of ways). Most striking was the influx of ordinary settlers, largely from the overpopulated Low Countries, who made their way eastward into the wilds in much the same way as American settlers later moved West. As one American medievalist observed, the following passage from a medieval chronicle might have been written about the Pilgrim Fathers:

For they had left the sweet soil of their native country and entered into an alien land, in which their future was to be, where for many years they were destined to endure hardships without hope of return homeward . . . . They came from a fertile homeland, peaceful and quiet, and penetrated a country of horror and vast solitude and baneful war.[3]

They even made up ballads that sound a little "Looking-Glass" to Americans: "Oh, we'll ride out east . . . ."[4] Against these settlers the Slavs, like the American Indians, rose in revolt that was occasionally successful but never permanently effective, and by the middle of the eleventh century the boundary of German settlement had reached the middle Oder. To the South, the Bavarian dukes pursued their own policy of expansion into what came to be called *Ostmark* and then *Österreich* ["Eastern Kingdom": Austria].

The process of extermination and annexation was checked by the relatively stable states of Bohemia, Moravia, Hungary, and Poland that now arose in the East. Their conversion to Christianity made it impossible for the Germans to treat them quite as brutally as they did their pagan cousins to the West. Bavarian missionaries had penetrated into Bohemia and Moravia in the ninth century. In the tenth, northern bishoprics like Magdeburg and Meissen were set up with jurisdiction eastwards. Germany accepted the independence of the eastern countries, the understanding being that they would form part of western civilization by adopting Catholicism and accepting German influence. Here the Church was more successful than the state, and Poland, Hungary, and Czechoslovakia today remain Catholic.

Otto III seems to have entertained the notion of including the eastern countries in a kind of loose federation under the empire, and to that purpose went so far as to take a goodwill tour of Bohemia and Poland. His early death, however, brought to the throne a man with different tastes. Henry II was a *Kleindeutscher* who preferred the immediate advantages of the German kingdom to the long-range advantages of an imperial confederation. Substituting aggression for persuasion, Henry drove the great Duke Boleslaw Chrobry (992–1018) of Poland into assuming the royal crown and renouncing his allegiance to the emperor. At about the same time the independent Hungarian throne was established. The Germans had more success in forcing Bohemia into the German orbit, but the hostility which might have been avoided by the policies of Otto III was left to grow and fester

Otto III surrounded by his ecclesiastical and temporal advisors.

on the eastern frontiers. The present hostility to Germany in
eastern Europe has roots deep in medieval history.

The German rulers seem to have taken their imperial pretensions increasingly seriously. Otto I had dispatched Liudprand
of Cremona to Constantinople in the hope of achieving some
kind of recognition for his empire, but Liudprand's report could
not have been pleasing to his master:

> On the fourth of June . . . we arrived at Constantinople and
> waited with our horses in heavy rain outside the Carian gate until
> five o'clock in the afternoon. At five o'clock (the eastern emperor)
> ordered us to be admitted on foot, for he did not think us worthy to
> use the horses with which your clemency had provided us, and we were
> escorted to . . . (a) hateful, waterless, draughty stone house.

There they were insulted by their official guide, given unpleasant
food and drink, and watched closely by Byzantine soldiers. The

marshal of the court finally received Liudprand: "We tired our-selves with a fierce argument over your imperial title. He called you not emperor, which is Basileus in his tongue, but insultingly Rex, which is king in yours."[5]

At length Otto I procured a Byzantine princess as wife for his son Otto II, and this lady, Theophano, became the mother of Otto III. The young king, under the influence of his mother, adopted certain Byzantine rituals at court, placed the motto *Renovatio imperii Romanorum* on his seals, and secured the election of Gerbert Aurillac as pope, who took the name of Sylvester II in imitation of the papal contemporary of Constantine the Great. Otto's successor, Henry II, bore at his coronation the orb of the world and wore the "world-mantle," a garment embroidered with the shapes of the planets and stars. Later emperors spun dreams that grew as their actual powers waned: Frederick I (1152–1190) added the title of "Holy" to his "Roman Empire," and his son Henry VI sought meaningless recognition of imperial overlordship from the crowned heads of Europe and the whole Mediterranean region. In the end, Voltaire's epigram, which was close to being the epitaph of the empire, was accurate: it was neither Holy, nor Roman, nor an Empire. Few nations outside Germany took the title very seriously even in the tenth and eleventh centuries, when the kings of England and those of Leon and Castile occasionally affected the title of emperor themselves.

Imperial notions were a result, rather than a cause, of the overextension of German power. In turn, the overextension was the result of a desperate desire to establish some kind of effective royal control within Germany and to secure her fatally exposed frontiers against external threats or anarchy. It was not the ideal of a unified Christian Empire under German leadership that ruined Germany, but its failure to develop a workable political system. In 1056, at the death of Henry III, the ruin was still impending. Germany still stood the proudest power in Christendom. But the barons and the popes were soon to push hard upon the structure, which proved to be all too topheavy. The future hegemony of Europe would pass from the empire to the popes and to the kings of France and England.

FRANCE. France began with certain initial advantages: a geo-graphical position protected by seas and mountains and open only in the northeast, relative cultural unity, a strong and settled Church, and wealth and population second to no country in Europe. There were also disadvantages, differences of linguistic, legal, and institutional customs between northern and southern France, and an initial weakness relative to Germany and England. The transition from Carolingian to Capetian in France was more difficult than that from Carolingian to Saxon in Germany, and the result was a greater breakdown of the Carolingian administrative system and the undermining of the public authority of the king.

The French kingship, like the English and the German was partly elective and partly hereditary, but the dynastic disputes that lasted from 888 to 987 made its elective aspect more evident than in the other two kingdoms and put the royal power at a further disadvantage. Archbishop Adalbero of Reims could thus debate in open assembly the succession to the throne in 987:

> We are not ignorant of the fact that Charles of Lorraine, the uncle of Louis V, has his partisans who maintain that he ought to succeed by hereditary right to the throne. But if one examines this question, one sees that the throne is not hereditary at all. One ought to place at the head of the kingdom only a man who is distinguished not only by nobility of race but also by his spiritual and intellectual qualities, a man whom honor recommends and statesmanship supports.

It was an argument for the election of Hugh Capet, but it could very easily have been turned against the Capetians in the future. No Frenchman knew in 987, as no Englishman knew at the accession of the Tudors in 1485, that the dynastic wars were over. Hugh Capet's situation was as precarious as that of Henry the Fowler: he had been a duke himself, the duke of Francia, and as such the dukes of Normandy and Aquitaine were naturally lacking in deference towards him. There was no national administration, no national army, no national system of revenues, and but a small royal domain to back up the royal power. All the king held directly was a bit of land around Paris called the Ile de France, and even that was a *congeries* of small baronies rather than a unified domain.

But France had hidden resources that would eventually make her the strongest of the three great realms of the West. The king built up his administration and gradually, by standard-

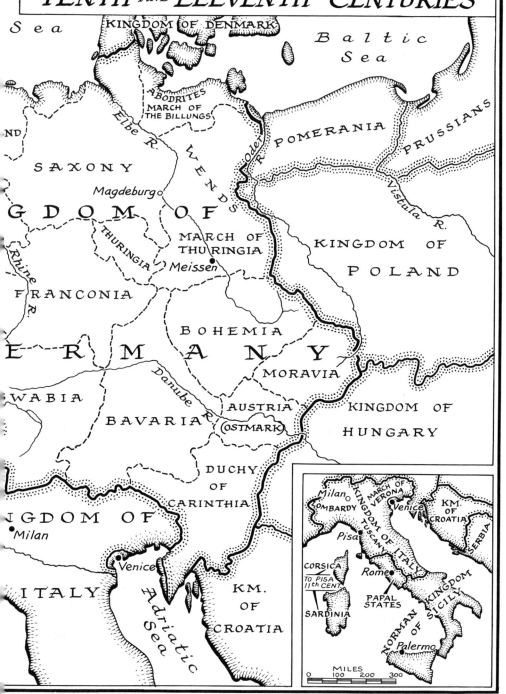

THE NEW KINGDOMS
TENTH AND ELEVENTH CENTURIES

Sea

KINGDOM OF DENMARK

*Baltic
Sea*

ABODRITES
MARCH OF
THE BILLUNGS

ND

POMERANIA

PRUSSIANS

Elbe R.

W E N D S

Oder R.

Vistula R.

S A X O N Y

Magdeburg

G D O M   O F

THURINGIA

MARCH OF
THURINGIA

Meissen

KINGDOM   OF

P O L A N D

Rhine R.

F RANCONIA

E R M A N Y

B O H E M I A

MORAVIA

W A B I A

Danube R.

AUSTRIA
(OSTMARK)

KINGDOM OF

H U N G A R Y

B A V A R I A

DUCHY
OF
CARINTHIA

I GDOM   OF

Milan

I T A L Y

Venice

*Adriatic
Sea*

KM.
OF
CROATIA

Milan O
LOMBARDY

MARCH OF
VERONA

Venice

KM.
OF
CROATIA

KINGDOM OF ITALY

TUSCANY

SERBIA

Pisa

CORSICA

TO PISA
11th CENT.

Rome

SARDINIA

PAPAL
STATES

NORMAN KINGDOM

OF SICILY

Palermo

MILES
0   100   200   300

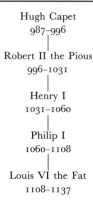

Hugh Capet
987–996

Robert II the Pious
996–1031

Henry I
1031–1060

Philip I
1060–1108

Louis VI the Fat
1108–1137

izing and generalizing feudal obligations, transformed his feudal suzerainty into royal sovereignty. From feudal overlord he became an effective monarch. This was not a far-seeing and deliberate process: Hugh Capet, like Louis VI after him, looked ahead not to Louis XIV or Napoleon but only to the next problem in the pressing task of building a viable government. But the Capetians used good sense, and they had a great deal of luck.

To begin with, they, like the Germans, abolished the Carolingian policy of dividing the kingdom, and they took care to crown their young sons and give them partial responsibility for affairs of state as early as possible, in order to assure the succession. In addition, no Capetian king for well over three centuries failed to produce a male heir, something of a record among the world's dynasties and a biological phenomenon that firmly established hereditary over elective principles.

Feudalism, more strongly ensconced in France than anywhere else, there proved constructive precisely because of its strength. The French nobles, even during the weakest periods of the monarchy, recognized their obligations: both Henry I and Louis VI were able to raise something like national armies in time of emergency. The existence of feudal bonds was exploited by the kings, who gradually drew up the chain of feudal command link by link till they had it all in their hands. The kings did not attempt to destroy the greater nobles, but slowly exerted their control over them even as the nobles extended theirs over their own vassals. The French kings worked with, not against, feudalism.

Like the German kings, the Capetians relied upon the bishops, appropriating to themselves ecclesiastical appointments not only within the Ile de France, but throughout the kingdom. Also like the Germans, they chose their administrators from among humble men who could derive no advantage from attacking their king, and they gradually let lapse the great offices of state occupied by nobles. At first the kings relied upon the advice of the great lay and ecclesiastical lords, but even such early Capetians as Henry I and Philip I turned to lesser persons whose titles—usually that of count—were owing to royal patronage and favor.

The heart of the extension of royal power was the increase of the royal domain, land held directly by the king. At first this consisted only of the Ile de France, but the kings added to it by every conceivable means: marriage, purchase, conquest, and the use of all the feudal possibilities of escheat (the reversion of lands to the king in the absence of a legitimate heir) and wardship (the lord's right to administer the estates of vassals who were not of age). Gradually too the system of royal justice was extended throughout the land, and royal officers were sent out to supervise local government. In all this the king had in mind the limitation of the power of the nobles and the increase of his own.

THE French kings of the tenth and eleventh centuries were petty, weak, and almost destitute; and some of their powerful vassals were building territories every bit as extensive and impressive as the Ile de France. The county of Anjou is an example. In the early tenth century the counts established their power in the Loire Valley, and there Count Fulk the Black (987–1040) built castles, founded abbeys, and fought successful battles. Gradually the Angevins extended their power, reducing the lesser nobility, appropriating their lands or bringing them into obedience. What they could not obtain by marriage or by purchase, they seized by exploiting the opportunities offered by "a minority, the chance offered by the enemy's engagement elsewhere, or a lucky battle."[6] The most important city in the region, Tours, was taken in 1044. By then Anjou was confronted by powerful neighbors: Blois,

Normandy, Brittany, and Poitou, all of which had gradually built up their own power in a similar fashion. This was an international system in miniature, and the counts of Anjou built up a government and a legal system requisite to such a position. They encouraged education for its own sake as well as for the purpose of training administrators, and one of the counts, Fulk Rechin, is one of the few lay lords of the Middle Ages who wrote a book. Another count, replying to a king who was mocking him for his scholarly habits, rejoined: "Know, sir, that an illiterate king is only a crowned ass." In 1128, Count Geoffrey Plantagenet of Anjou married the Princess Matilda, heiress to the English throne, and their son, King Henry II, ruled one of the largest and most efficient domains in Europe.

The same process that created the county of Anjou created the other counties and duchies, and affairs might have jelled at this level, creating sovereign principalities. But the king of France emerged eventually as king in fact as well as in name. How?

First of all, he held Paris, the ancient center of power of the Merovingian kings. Second, he was the king and at the top of the feudal chain, and the very consolidations of power made by the counts of Anjou and the dukes of Normandy were to his advantage when he finally was able to incorporate their territories in his own. Finally, and most important, he was the consecrated king, the *christus Domini*. Angevins, Normans, and Champenois alike had a notion of France as an entity, *France la douce* of the *Song of Roland,* and the king, in a sense, was France. The mystique of the French monarchy was fully developed only by the time of Joan of Arc, but even earlier the king could invoke the aid of Saint Denis, the patron of France, and the memory of Charlemagne. It was the king with whom the Byzantine emperor, the pope, or the prince of Kiev treated when they wished to speak to the head of the country, and it was only he who could summon all the hosts of France in a national emergency. The king of France was little more than *primus inter pares* but that little more made possible the formation of the French nation.

THE NORMANS AND ENGLAND. The Normans, rulers after 911 of one of the largest French duchies, were the most dramatically successful people of the tenth and eleventh centuries. In Scandinavia itself, the homeland of the Normans, the period of expansion that had begun in the ninth century was followed by an age of conversion and then, in the twelfth and thirteenth centuries, increasing political stability and economic prosperity. But the transplanted Northmen went on to dominate large sections of Europe.

The English historian William of Malmesbury saw something special in the virtues of the Normans. They "live in large edifices with economy; envy their equals; wish to excel their superiors . . . ." They were a proud and ambitious race, skillful alike in war and in government. Their phenomenal success was owing in part to their natural love of adventure and war, which enabled them to extend their power by conquest. But this was supplemented by their ability to rule. In the duchy of Normandy they succeeded in reducing the smaller vassals to a state of dependence; they organized an excellent army in which Bretons, Flemings, and others were added to the Norman core; and they early produced a systematic and efficient central administration. The duchy was naturally a fertile land, and efficiency made of it one of the most prosperous areas of France.

The Normans who settled with their leader Rollo in northern Francia and there founded the duchy of Normandy were incorporated into the French political system and culture without losing any of their mental vigor. Norman pilgrims arriving in southern Italy on their way to the Holy Land in the eleventh century found that territory troubled by Saracens and stopped to protect the inhabitants. More Normans followed, pressed by overpopulation in Normandy and lured by the love of conquest. Among these was Robert Guiscard of the house of Hauteville, who transformed protection into domination and domination into rule. By 1070 Guiscard's successors were fully in control of the former Byzantine, Saracen, and Lombard possessions in southern Italy and had made a treaty of friendship with the papal states. From southern Italy they moved on to take Sicily. King Roger II (1101–1154), making his capital at Palermo, combined all the skills of Arab, Greek, Latin, and Norman to make it a center of culture and the seat of the best-administered country in Europe. The Norman Kingdom of Sicily achieved something like a modern centralized government centuries before the rest of Europe. Roger II went on to occupy parts of North Africa and even projected the conquest of the Byzantine Empire.

No less spectacular was the Norman conquest of England. In that process the accession of King Edward the Confessor in 1042 is almost as important a date as 1066 itself, for Edward took immediate steps to remove England from the Danish-Norwegian orbit, to limit the power of the Danish nobility, and to encourage his country's connection with France and Normandy. Edward had been in exile at the court of Normandy while the Danish Canute and his sons were on the throne, and when he returned home he brought with him Norman advisers, bishops, and knights. In effect a three-way struggle ensued between the Danish, Norman, and old English elements; at last Edward's partiality for the Normans drove the English to choose the Danes as the influence they disliked the less. The appointment by Edward of the Norman Robert of Jumièges as archbishop of Canterbury in 1051 led to a general rising against the Normans the next year, the replacement of Robert with an Englishman, Stigand, and the general diminution of Norman influence. The Danish party now obtained the support of many Englishmen, and although Edward retained the throne the seeds of future war had been sown.

When Edward the Confessor died without issue in 1066 there were four claimants to the throne. The first, a boy of sixteen, was set aside because of his youth. The second was Harold, earl of Wessex, the leader of the Danish party, and a mature man of forty. Harold was on the spot when the old king died, and, claiming that Edward had on his deathbed chosen him to succeed, he secured the consent of those members of the English nobility he could assemble at short notice and had himself proclaimed king within six hours. But there were two other claimants who did not yield gracefully to these hasty proceedings. One was Harold Hardrada, the king of Norway. The other was William, the duke of Normandy. William was a distant cousin of King Edward's with little claim to the throne by blood. But he was understandably skeptical of the Confessor's "deathbed bequest" and preferred to remember that it was he himself to whom Edward had earlier promised the crown. William bolstered his claim by referring to the peculiar events of 1064: the future King Harold had come to Normandy, stayed some time in apparent amity with the duke, and finally taken a sacred oath to support his claims to the English throne. The dire consequences of the breach of this oath constitute the message of the Bayeux Tapestry. William could also rely, of course, upon the Norman party in England, but he also had the support of the pope, who disapproved of the uncanonical fashion in which Robert of Jumièges had been removed from office and who regarded Stigand as an usurper.

THE man who now assembled the power of Normandy for the conquest of England was the illegitimate son of Duke Robert and a tanner's daughter. Robert died in 1035, leaving his duchy to his seven- or eight-year-old son. The circumstances of William's conception earned him a nickname which succeeding generations have respectfully changed to "the Conqueror:" to his contemporaries he was simply "the Bastard." Tall, ruddy, quick, and ambitious, William was an effective duke, subduing the lesser nobles, building a stronger administration, forging a close relationship with the Church, and defeating the count of Anjou in war. By 1066 Normandy was probably the strongest, and certainly the best run of the French principalities.

William's enemy Harold was no less able a man, but the events of 1066 proved too much for him. Like any new king, Harold had to pacify dissent at home, but before he could get this job fairly under way, the invasion of the Norwegians under Harold Hardrada was announced. He was forced to assemble his army and hurry quickly to Yorkshire. He defeated the Norwegians in a bloody battle at Stamford Bridge, but the reward of his victory was the report that William of Normandy had already invaded the southern coast. Rushing his exhausted army on foot from Yorkshire to Kent, he faced the Normans less than three weeks after he had fought the Norwegians. Some years ago an intrepid group of Englishmen attempted to hike the distance between Stamford Bridge and Hastings in the time that Harold's troops had been obliged to do it. A few of them made it, aching, footsore, and, though none of them had been obliged to cope with unfriendly Norwegians, uneager to participate in even a simulated Battle of Hastings. It is no wonder, then, that Hastings ended in the victory of William and the death of Harold the oath-breaker.

The effects of the Norman Conquest upon England have long been debated. In popular tradition English history begins in 1066, just as in royal tradition the kings are numbered from that date. But the historian will recognize that "the essential continuity of English life"[7] was preserved. English agriculture and the English army, law, and local government were gradually changed, but without a break from the pre-Norman epoch.

The Anglo-Norman realm was advantaged by the blending of English with Norman centralization and efficiency. William established a very close working relationship with the Church, replacing Saxon with Norman bishops and using them as royal administrators. The Norman kings used feudalism but placed themselves securely atop it. William built castles throughout England to pacify that country as he had pacified Normandy— the most famous of these monuments forms part of the present Tower of London. He deprived most of the English nobility of their fiefs and broke up the old earldoms, bringing in Norman nobles instead, though some of the English were permitted to retain their land. He assured the loyalty of the Norman knights to both his Norman and English interests by granting them land on both sides of the Channel, and he secured himself from revolt by scattering their holdings as much as possible. In 1086 the greatest landholders were obliged to come to Salisbury plain to swear that they would never do war against the king and that they would support him even against their own immediate lords. William ordered the compilation of the *Domesday Book* to take stock of his new kingdom and to secure for himself all the taxes to which he was entitled: "Then the king sent his men all over England into every shire to ascertain how many hundreds of hides of land there were in each shire, and how much land and livestock the king himself owned in the country, and what annual dues were lawfully his from each shire . . . ."[8]

The conquest blended French with English law and French with English feudal customs. It also created a cultural and class distinction. The French language and culture became the language of good society, the result being that England enjoyed the benefits of closer contacts with continental culture while suffering a two-hundred-year eclipse of her once flourishing vernacular literature. It was not until the reign of Edward III (1327–1377) that an English king was even fluent in the English language. Yet the hatred between Englishman and Norman has been grossly exaggerated by Sir Walter Scott and Hollywood producers on the evidence of a chronicle now known to be a later forgery. A twelfth-century writer more accurately observed that "With the English and Normans dwelling together and alternately marrying and giving in marriage, the races have become so fused that it can scarcely be discerned at the present day—I speak of freemen alone—who is English and who is Norman by race."[9] Perhaps the most important effect of the conquest was an external one: the long-lasting involvement of England in the little system of French principalities and eventually in the larger questions of Europe.

William the Conqueror ended his reign with as much vigor as he had begun it, fighting the Danes, the Flemish, the French, and the Angevins. He died raising his eyes to heaven and commending his soul to the protection of the Virgin. The events that followed immediately upon his last breath revealed to the medieval mind the vanities of worldly power; to ours, the distance between those times and the settled condition of modern states. The attendants of the king, seeing him dead,

> . . . the wealthiest of them mounted their horses and departed in haste to secure their property. But the inferior attendants . . . laid hands on the arms, the plate, the robes, the linen, and all the royal furniture, and, leaving the corpse almost naked on the floor of the house, they hastened away.[10]

Alas, how deceitful and untrustworthy is this world's prosperity. He who had been a powerful king and lord of many a land, had then of all the land only a seven-foot measure; and he who was once clad in gold and gems, lay then covered with earth.[11]

The work of the tenth- and eleventh-century kings may seem less vain to the modern historian. At the end of the eleventh century, feudalism and localism persisted, and disorder was common. But the kings had made great strides in the establishment of a stable political order on an extensive scale, and their successors in the following centuries would build to advantage upon their work.

NOTES

[1] Wipo, *Deeds of Conrad II*, in *Imperial Lives and Letters of the Eleventh Century*, ed. Theodore E. Mommsen and Karl F. Morrison, (New York, Columbia University Press, 1962), p. 61.

[2] Widukind, *Rerum Gestarum Saxonicarum Libri Tres,* II, xxxvi, trans. Christopher Brooke, in Brooke, *Europe in the Central Middle Ages 987–1125* (New York, Holt, Rinehart, and Winston, 1964), p. 162.

[3] Peter von Dusburg, quoted by James Westfall Thompson, *Feudal Germany* (New York, 1928), II, 527–528.

[4] Thompson, II, 552.

[5] *The Works of Liutprand of Cremona,* trans. F. A. Wright (London, Routledge and Sons, 1930), pp. 235–238.

[6] R. W. Southern, *The Making of the Middle Ages* (New York, 1953), p. 88. I follow Southern's admirable sketch of Angevin history throughout this account.

[7] David C. Douglas, *William the Conqueror* (Berkeley–Los Angeles, 1964), p. 367.

[8] *The Anglo-Saxon Chronicle E,* 1085, ed. Dorothy Whitelock (London, 1961), p. 216.

[9] Richard fitz Nigel, *Dialogue of the Exchequer,* cited in W. H. Hassall, *Medieval England* (New York, 1965), p. 43.

[10] Orderic Vitalis, trans. Thomas Forester (London, 1854).

[11] *The Anglo-Saxon Chronicle E,* 1087, ed. Dorothy Whitelock (London, 1961), p. 163.

PART THREE

*The Central
Middle Ages
1050–1300*

Chapter Fourteen

THE CENTRAL MIDDLE AGES AND
THEIR ECONOMY

The mid-eleventh century is a watershed between the earlier and the central Middle Ages. The institutions and ideas created by the early Middle Ages were now mature. About 1050 began the formidable conflict between the papacy and the kings that has been called the "investiture controversy"; in fact, this controversy was part of a much larger series of changes that some historians designate "the papal revolution." The conception and organization of the Church was changed in the course of this revolution from a relatively loose polity in which the pope had certain limited authority beyond that of other bishops to a highly centralized papal monarchy. The power of this new and mature papacy came naturally into conflict with the growing power of the kings, who had efficiently been strengthening and broadening their own jurisdiction. About the same time, monasticism underwent a severe crisis. In the simple and uncomplicated, if anarchic, society of the early Middle Ages the monasteries were one of the chief bulwarks of order, and they played a central role in education, culture, and even politics. Now in a society that was at once more settled and more complicated, the monasteries lost this special role. Education shifted to the bishops' schools in the towns, where a broader and more liberal course of studies was available. There scholars gathered eagerly and exchanged new ideas. Theology and philosophy were no longer expressed solely in the discursive and allusive style made typical by Saint Augustine, but increasingly in the rigorously logical style, influenced by Aristotle, that is known as scholasticism. In the early Middle Ages, almost all literary and historical writing, all painting was done by monks and their pupils; now, with spreading literacy, secular clerks, students, and even laymen painted and wrote. Often they chose secular subjects.

This change in the tone of life was rendered possible by the restoration in the eleventh century of that order and stability in society for which previous ages had yearned. Feudal divisions remained, governments were still far from assuring perfect tranquility, let alone happiness, to their subjects, and life was still rude for most people. But these limitations apply to most ages. A late twelfth-century chronicler boasted that in his day it was possible for a woman to walk alone from one end of England to the other without fear of being harmed. The claim may have been exaggerated, but we would not even think of making it today, and in any event it illustrates the enormous improvement effected since the age of invasions in the early tenth century. Efficient and powerful governments had learned to keep off outside invaders and, by an effective system of administration and laws, to restrict internal disorder. For the first time since the Age of the Antonines, population grew rapidly; old cities regained their former size, and new ones were erected. Commerce and industry emerged from the long depression that had begun in the third century, and in their new vigor they encouraged rapid change in society, Church, and politics. New classes arose in society and gave it new forms.

This flowering of European civilization had been prepared by the hard work and painful struggles of the preceding centuries. The synthesis of Christian and Roman with Celtic and Teutonic that was completed in the eighth and maintained in the ninth and tenth centuries made the new brilliance possible, and the creativity of the earlier Middle Ages should not be forgotten. But now creativity seemed more vital, more confident, and a European civilization emerged with its own character and with a brilliance comparable to that of Rome or any other.

In the background of this rapid change in the tone of life was a rapid change in the nature of the economy.

THE historian's understanding of the medieval economy has of late become at once more complex and more perplexed. His awareness of economic expansions and contractions, rising and falling population figures, the relation of western Europe to the outside world, commerce and industry, social classes, organization and policy, has been transformed by new information and by new methods derived from the social sciences. The historian will search in vain for the final word on most disputes and will be obliged to refer for the latest theories to the increasing periodical literature.[1] His realization is growing that the medieval economy was itself changing, and that it was dynamic rather than static. Broad generalizations have yielded to cautious recognition that conditions varied from year to year and from one valley or town to the next.

The sources are sparse at the beginning of the period because men were not conscious of economic developments in the same way that they were conscious of political, religious, or even intellectual events. Their observations on the economy were imprecise, scattered, prejudiced, and uncritical. From the twelfth century this became less true as the volume and variety of sources increased. Technological treatises on mining and other industries, documents relating to the wool trade and other commerce, journals of merchants, notarial letters, contracts, and wills, gild ordinances, town charters and municipal regulations, bankers' accounts, bills of exchange, coins, canon and civil laws and theological treatises, royal edicts, legislation, trade treaties, the *Hanserecessen* (records of the meetings of the Hanseatic League), perceptive chronicles like that of Giovanni Villani of Florence: the list is almost as inexhaustible as the documents it categorizes are still unexhausted by research.

OUTLINE OF ECONOMIC CHANGE. The establishment of a political and cultural synthesis in the early Middle Ages was accompanied by an economic revival from the great depression that had begun in the third century. Our grandfathers ascribed the end of the great depression to the effects of the Crusades; our fathers observed that the tenth century seemed more the turning point than the eleventh; and the present generation perceives signs of revival in the ninth, or even the latter eighth, century. The point is important, not only in itself, but because of its implications for the *reason* the decline came to an end. Some historians and demographers maintain that population growth precedes and causes growth in economic activity, and these argue that the economy expanded owing to the stabilization of society after the barbarian raids of the ninth and early tenth centuries. Others insist that the rise in population was preceded by a revival of commerce stimulated by Byzantine and Arab trade and gold. Far from accepting Pirenne's idea that the Arab invasions broke up Mediterranean trade and dealt the final blow to a tottering economy, these historians insist that the presence of the Arabs was largely beneficial.

There is no general agreement on this question, but there is an increasing disposition to admit a great and positive effect exerted by the eastern economy upon that of the West and to place that effect well before the Crusades. The commercial superiority of the West over the East, accepted today as the natural state of affairs, began only six or seven centuries ago. Maurice Lombard recently postulated a set of stages in this process: (1) third and fourth centuries: decline of cities in the Roman West, continued growth in the Roman East; (2) fifth to seventh centuries: continued decline in the West, growth of towns in Persia, decline and then revival in the Roman East; (3) seventh to eleventh centuries: growth in Byzantine world, rapid growth of the Moslem world, and subsequent revival in the West. In this view, the West is not an entity in itself, developing without reference to the world outside, but rather strongly influenced by the economic advances of the other civilizations of the Mediterranean.

WHETHER or not population growth preceded the revival of commerce, the two, once started, were mutually stimulating. The period from the ninth century to the fourteenth was one of rapidly growing prosperity. Population seems to have increased from about 800, certainly from the tenth century, and it is even possible that popular monastic and heretical movements, pilgrimages, and Crusades resulted from population pressures on the land as well as from increased wealth and mobility. Population increased spectacularly from the eleventh century to the fourteenth. That of England, for example, increased from something like 1,000,000 in 1086 to about 3,700,000 about 1340. That of the city of Pisa increased from about 11,000 in 1164 to about 38,000 in 1293. Fourteenth-century towns were extremely large in comparison with their counterparts of three centuries earlier, though still very small in comparison with ours. The population of London may have been about 40,000, that of Bruges about 35,000, that of Paris 80,000, and that of the great Italian centers like Venice and Milan about 100,000. The average town was well under 10,000. The population of Italy at the beginning of the fourteenth century was about 10 million and that of France, the most populous and prosperous country of Europe, a surprising 22 million, or half the population presently dwelling within what were then French borders.

THE growth of population in Europe from the tenth through the thirteenth centuries resulted in migration into the towns, for that is where the opportunities for employment were. At first the average medieval town was little more than a village, still very much a part of the agricultural economy: there were open fields within its walls as well as in the broad verdure of forest, field, and pasture without. As the towns gradually developed their commercial and industrial functions, some of them became centers of trade and communication and of culture as well, markets for the exchange of ideas as well as of goods, for a high civilization is as unlikely as a high economy without the existence of large towns. Some of the towns always remained small, serving primarily as markets for the surrounding peasantry who could walk to market and back in the course of a day. Their condition is natural; it is the great towns that need explanation.

Even during the great depression of the third to the eighth centuries, most of the Roman towns of the West continued to exist, though with drastically reduced populations. When urban economy again emerged, these old Roman towns became natural centers of population, particularly since many had become the seats of episcopal power. Hence Reims, Trier, Lyon, Milan, London, and other old cities again became the centers of a lively commerce. Artisans and others came to service the settled population of clergymen and other inhabitants, and thereby became part of the population themselves, attracting yet other service people and merchants. Around the old episcopal city sprang up new quarters for this new population. In such cities the history can still be traced in the names of the quarters or streets. In Liège, for example, there is a street still called the Rue Neuvice ("Newquarter Street"), because it was built for

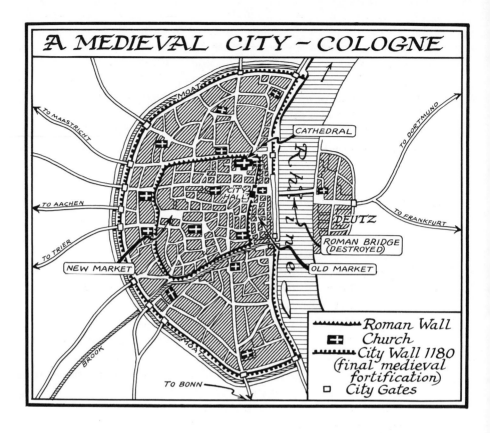

A MEDIEVAL CITY – COLOGNE

Legend:
- Roman Wall
- Church
- City Wall 1180 (final medieval fortification)
- City Gates

Map labels: TO MAASTRICHT, TO AACHEN, TO TRIER, NEW MARKET, BROOK, TO BONN, MOAT, CATHEDRAL, TO DORTMUND, Rhine River, DEUTZ, TO FRANKFURT, ROMAN BRIDGE (DESTROYED), OLD MARKET, CITY HALL

the medieval artisans just beyond the edge of the old episcopal city; and in London there is Newgate.

Other towns arose around fortifications. In unsettled times, feudal lords and even monasteries frequently built walls and other fortifications (cf. Newcastle). Again, the population enclosed in these forts would attract service people, who would dwell outside the walls in what was called the *portus* until the *portus* became so important that new walls were built to include it as well. The word *town* itself originally meant "enclosure" [English *ton*: Northampton, Heaton ("high ton"), Taunton; Dutch *toen*: "enclosed garden"] and so did the Scandinavian suffix *-by* and the German *Burg* or English *bury* [A.S.: *burh*], though in Romance-speaking countries a *bourg* seems usually to have been unfortified. Hence the names Wis*by,* Ham*burg,* and Canter*bury* all imply original fortifications.

Other towns were created by royal policy, though if there

were no natural commercial or defensive advantage, the policy was unsuccessful. The attention lavished on Aachen by the Carolingians, for example, could not make it a great city, but from the twelfth century the kings had more lasting success with *bastides* and *villes neuves,* like the Lorris of Louis VI, that had both economic and political advantages.

It was the towns that lay on natural lines of commerce between other centers or as importing or exporting centers for larger areas that had the best chance of growth: ports like Venice, Genoa, and Bruges; towns at the mouths of rivers like Plymouth, Portsmouth, and Bordeaux; towns at bridges (Cambridge, Osnabrück) or fords (Frankfurt, Oxford); towns at river junctions (Namur, Paris, Mainz) or at stopping places on rivers (Châlons-sur-Marne, Tours) or on land routes (Brussels or the towns of Champagne).

The impressiveness and elegance of these towns grew with their size. To the simple huts of the early towns were added structures of stone or brick, and shops and places of business for artisans and merchants. Each craft usually occupied a certain street or section of town, a fact attested by the Quai des tanneurs, Threadneedlestreet, and Silberstrasse of today. Some of the more successful merchants, like the famous Jacques Coeur (d. 1456) were able to build impressive dwellings and to furnish them with expense and taste. Wealthy towns constructed great cathedrals as monuments to their glory as well as to God's, and then, to show that the authority of the city yielded nothing to that of the bishop, constructed Town Halls (*Rathaus, Stadhuis, Hôtels de Ville*) on a similar scale. In 1288, Milan was described in glowing terms:

> In regard to housing . . . the truth is there before the eyes of those who see. The streets in this city are quite wide, the palaces quite beautiful, the houses packed in, not scattered but continuous, stately, adorned in a stately manner. . . . Outside the wall of the moat there are so many suburban houses that they alone would be enough to constitute a city. . . . The main gates of the city are also very strong, and they reach the number of six. The secondary gates . . . are ten. . . . The steeples, built in the manner of towers, are about 120 in the city.[2]

Yet in his pride at the glories of medieval Italy the Western historian should not forget that at that moment at the oppo-

Market hall.

site end of the world there stood, among other great Chinese cities, the city of Kinsai (Hangchow), with a circumference of a hundred miles. Each of the twelve quarters which lay within the gates was greater than the whole of Venice. Its main street was two hundred feet wide, and ran from end to end of the city, broken every four miles by a great square.[3] Kinsai boasted twelve thousand stone bridges and beautiful parks with lakes and wooded islands.

THE glory and wealth of China would attract a few European merchants in the fourteenth century, but of necessity Europeans were primarily concerned with shorter routes and everyday products.

The rural response to the growing economy and the increasing need for food and raw materials was to supplement subsistence farming with the production of marketable staples and the establishment of rural handicrafts. Local industries were at first almost wholly agricultural and produced for local markets held perhaps weekly. Then those men who had skills turned to specialization and became Smiths, Weavers, Taylors, or Wheelwrights. At first they simply worked on materials brought to

Glassmakers.

them; as their trade grew they could set up permanent little shops and market their own goods in "retail handicraft." In the central Middle Ages these skills were very numerous and very specialized. In the cities there were butchers, bakers, candlestick-makers, greengrocers, needlemakers, potters, glassblowers, and brewers; in the country, millers, blacksmiths, and others rendered services. Among metalworkers there were goldsmiths, coppersmiths, ironmongers, and many others; among woodworkers there were carpenters, cabinet-makers, and others; among leather workers there were tanners, saddle-makers, shoemakers, and so on. The specialization in production was enormous; the difference from today is that retail was almost as specialized as production and, as one still finds to some extent in Europe,

Blacksmiths.

shopping meant a visit to a great many windows and stalls rather than to two or three great emporia.

THE growth in complexity and strength of the medieval economy required the development of regulatory policies. But in the first place there was little economic consciousness, and in the second place the fragmentation of medieval society meant that what public economic policy existed was divided among kings, lords, bishops, and towns. All these authorities evolved rudimentary policies aimed at securing tax revenues, defending the consumer against fraud, regulating commercial disputes, and protecting artisans.

Among the economic policy-making bodies of the Middle Ages the gilds were of great importance. Appearing first in Italy, the original gilds were merchant-gilds, organized for the purpose of providing mutual protection and assistance on journeys. Having banded together, the merchants realized the advantages of association and began to exercise considerable political as well as economic power. The independence of the cities from undue feudal influence was owing for the most part to the power of the merchant gilds.

From the twelfth century, as the specialization of crafts advanced, the gilds themselves became more specialized. The artisans—the ironmongers, bakers, carpenters, and the rest—grew tired of the monopoly on power exercised by the merchant gild and organized specialized gilds of their own. These gilds were associations of craftsmen in the same trade for mutual benefit. Originally having a religious, as well as an economic purpose, the gilds had patron saints, and provided for the medical care of their members, and for the care of widows and orphans in the event of death. Economically, the craft gilds regulated wages and prices, protected members from competition and established effective monopolies, and set down standards of quality. They also laid down strict rules of apprenticeship and mastership. A boy was at first apprenticed by his father to a master in the craft. After working for a number of years as an apprentice, during which time he was given only room and board, he became a journeyman (working by the day for a day's wages; French *journée:* "day"). Since the journeyman was usually hired only for a week at a time he was in fear of unemployment until such time as he had acquired money enough, and established a sufficient reputation, to open a business himself. In order to qualify as a master and have full membership in the gild, the craftsman had to produce a work of sufficient quality to meet the standards of the gild. This work was called a masterpiece, a piece entitling him to the dignity of master.

In some crafts, especially those big enough, like cloth-making, to rank as real industries, there were workers (called *salariati* in Italy) who were always in the position of wage earners. Their discontent at low wages and the threat of unemployment quickly became chronic. In 1245 at Douai and in 1274 at Ghent, these early representatives of the urban proletariat actually called strikes, which were quickly and harshly repressed as a form of insurrection.

The generally benevolent and constructive policies of the gilds not only aided the economy but served the purpose of establishing community of spirit and action among their members. They thus provided a valuable social function in a still-atomized society, and they were one of the chief political vehicles for the towns' independence from feudal authority.

THE development of interregional trade was somewhat impeded by political and ecclesiastical considerations. Feudal atomization produced a series of tolls and market taxes very burdensome to commerce, and feudal anarchy encouraged robbers and piracy. Particularism impeded the establishment of the calm social conditions that would have aided commerce. Further, most medieval commerce was a gamble. Goods were generally not sold before they were delivered, and the merchant had to undertake every trip with the expectation, but without the assurance, of being able to sell his goods at an advantageous price. Moreover, faced with the possibilities of shipwreck or piracy, the merchant was unsure of getting his goods to market at all. It is not without reason that the merchants of the Middle Ages were called "merchant venturers."

The state of the roads has often been mentioned as an impediment to medieval commerce, but this seems unjustified. In many instances Roman roads were kept under repair, and when they were neglected it was because medieval lines of commerce and communication were not identical to Roman, and the old routes were being replaced by new. Thus old roads were kept up where useful, and new roads and bridges built and maintained. Paving was frequent at the approaches to towns and the rule within towns, and artificially drained and leveled roads were common. Inns were set up to serve the traveler. Most medieval roads were dirt, rather than paved, because unlike the Roman roads, which were built for military foot traffic, they were constructed for mercantile uses. The medieval invention of the padded horsecollar made cartage efficient for the first time, and pack and cart animals required soft surfaces, especially since expensive iron shoes were rare.

Rivers were sometimes preferred to roads, but sometimes they were even slower: in 1319 two student groups left Cambridge on the same day to see the king; the group travelling by road arrived four days ahead of the group going by stream. The average time between Rome and Canterbury was seven weeks, from Italy to Champagne three weeks. Eighteen miles was a good day's journey, but "pony expresses" might make as much as 100 miles a day. The speed and convenience of travel was never much improved until the invention of steam, and Jane Austen's gentry found a journey of ten miles as uncomfortable and difficult as did Chaucer's pilgrims.

The impediments offered by the Church have likewise been exaggerated. It is true that the Church protested investment as "putting a mortgage on time" and profit as getting advantage where the Christian should give freely to those who need.* But in practice churchmen themselves engaged vigorously in buying and selling (even of their offices and the sacraments), and wealthy bishops did not hesitate to invest money in mortgages or to engage in other forms of moneylending. Bishop Otbert of Liège helped finance Godfrey of Bouillon on the First Crusade by squeezing money out of Liégeois churches and lending it to Godfrey in return for a mortgage on the castle of Bouillon. Even in theory, protestations of the value of Christian communism became more and more muted in the face of the commercial realities of the twelfth and thirteenth centuries. By the time of Aquinas the Church was delighted to recognize the legitimacy of trade and private property, though it always insisted upon honesty in exchange. The theory of the "just price" held that the price should depend, not upon supply and demand, but "justice," notwithstanding the difficulty of determining such "justice" in any particular case. Albertus Magnus insisted that if, for example, a builder constructed a house for a shoemaker, the shoemaker should pay him with a stock of footwear equal in value to the house! Ignorant of the importance of lending and credit to the economy, early medieval theologians, drawing upon both Aristotle and the Bible, attacked all usury as sinful; but later, Franciscan monks felt it within the bounds of their charity to lend at profitable interest.

COMMERCE, not greatly affected by these impediments and stimulated by Byzantine and Moslem activity, grew rapidly in the west from the tenth century. There were always two clearly defined zones of commerce, the southern and the northern, between which goods were exchanged at certain central points like Champagne. Routes themselves were not fixed but varied according to convenience. In the South, trade centered on the Mediterranean, where goods were exchanged between western countries and with the East. The West exported cloth, timber, arms, slaves, and precious metals—the last being often half the total eastbound galleys' cargo in value—in exchange for the much-desired spices, fruit, medicine, and cotton. The slave

*The proverb was *mutuum date nihil inde sperantes.*

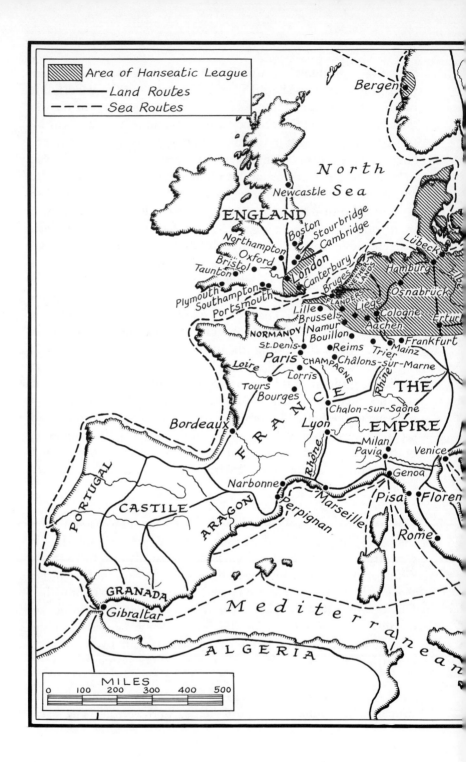

THE MEDIEVAL
ECONOMY

tockholm

Reval   Novgorod

Wisby

EDEN   Baltic Sea   Riga

alsund

MUSCOVY

Don

POLAND   Kiev

Dnieper

Vienna

HUNGARY   Danube

SERBIA   Danube

BULGARIA   Black   Sea

Constantinople

TURKEY

Aegean Sea

Sea

315

Builders.

trade had been forbidden many times, but without much effect, as a Venetian decree of 960 indicates: "In former times . . . there was the captivity of slaves by us, on account of which sin many tribulations came upon us. (The practice was outlawed, but) on account of the offensiveness of the ill-disposed . . . that decree appears to have been corrupted and broken. . . . Whence . . . we decree and confirm lastingly that no one . . . ought to purchase slaves for sale."[4] During the Renaissance the slave trade increased to proportions greater than at any time since the decline of Rome: the Portuguese brought slaves from Africa, the Spaniards and French bought Negroes from the Algerians, and the Venetians and Genoese imported Serbs, Bulgarians, and Circassians from the Turkish slave markets on the Black Sea. Innocent VIII accepted one hundred Negro slaves as a gift from Ferdinand of Aragon in 1488, and more than a few Italian churches were erected on the proceeds of the slave trade. Medieval darkness yielded to this modern enlightenment that persisted until the end of the American Civil War in 1865.

The Italian domination of the Mediterranean trade is of immense importance. Not only did it insure that Italy became the wealthiest part of Europe, and thereby made possible the Italian

Renaissance, but it also insured that the West would dominate East–West trade. The economic power of Italy seems to have increased from the sixth century in connection with the Byzantine reconquest and then expanded owing to the stimulus of both Byzantine and Moslem trade. The most important Italian cities were those that retained connections with the Byzantine Empire, particularly Venice; Pisa was the only important commercial city in the Lombard domains. For a while Marseille competed with the Italian ports, but by the eleventh century the Italian cities, especially Venice, Genoa, and Pisa, clearly dominated the trade with the Levant. The Venetians acquired a *fondaco* (a colony of merchants with warehouse privileges) in Constantinople, and, owing to the usefulness, of their shipping services, gained political leverage in the crusading states. After the conquest of Constantinople in 1204, which the Venetians financed, they acquired considerable territorial possessions in the Aegean and eastern Mediterranean.

The northern trade was less concerned with the luxuries of the East, though the Swedes established a route to Constantinople through Kiev. The Rhône was a channel for French exports, and the Rhine for German. Cologne became a great transshipment point on the route from the German hinterland through Belgium to Bruges and London. By the thirteenth century the Germans were second as traders only to the Italians, and the North Sea–Baltic Sea trading area second only to the Mediterranean in importance.

This northern trading area became the center of the Hanseatic League, one of the most important economic and political creations of the later Middle Ages. The league had two precedents. The first was in the town confederations in Germany, which the feebleness of imperial power made natural and where mercantile treaties between towns began early in the thirteenth century. The second is in the institution of the *Hanse,* originally any association of merchants formed to promote and protect trade with foreign parts. The city governments, whose power depended upon their mercantile power, gradually entered into agreements and treaties for the protection of the Hanse. These agreements were gradually expanded and developed between about 1250 and 1300 into a general league. Lübeck came to be the central city of the league, where

Riga: A Hanseatic town whose architecture reflects German influence in the Baltic.

the diets or general meetings took place. At its height the league's influence dominated Baltic and North Sea trade from Novgorod to London and comprised from 70 to 80 towns. By 1367 the league was taking united military action, defeating Denmark and imposing the Treaty of Stralsund (1370). The zenith of the league's power was reached about 1450; afterwards cities drifted out owing to mutual jealousy, and the Germans lost much of their Baltic trade to the Swedes, Dutch, and English. Nonetheless the effect of the league was to spread German culture as well as trade throughout the area. Reval, Riga,

Reval (modern Tallin in Estonia): One of the easternmost Hanseatic towns.

and other Baltic cities gained a large German population that remained until the Soviet purges of 1940–1945.

THE most important contact between the northern and southern trading areas was, until the fourteenth century, at the fairs of Champagne. Italian carriers dominated the Champagne trade, and even today Italian truckers commonly are seen on the land route that passes through Champagne on the way to the Low Countries. The fair often lasted six or eight weeks. The center of interregional commerce, it was distinguished from the local market in that it was seasonal rather than weekly or biweekly, attracted a much wider range of merchants and goods, and had certain juridical rights including special courts to settle commercial disputes on the spot. The oldest recorded fair is that of Saint Denis near Paris, founded about 635; other famous fairs were those of Pisa, Venice, Genoa, and Pavia in Italy, of Stourbridge and Boston (the fair of Saint Ives) in England, of Cologne and Erfurt in Germany, of Chalon-sur-Saône and Lyon in France, and of Bruges and Lille in Flanders. The most important were the fairs of Champagne, where merchants from the North met merchants from the South, and Germans, Flemings, and Englishmen rubbed elbows with Spaniards and Italians. Six fairs were held each year and were scheduled in such a way that there were few months or even weeks when none were in progress. The fair was organized around a religious holiday (*feria*); after the appropriate religious ceremonies, there would be eight days of installation followed by ten days allotted to the sale of woolens, in turn followed by the sale of hides and the sale of goods "avoirdupois," goods sold by weight and measure. The Champagne fairs dominated North–South commerce until the fourteenth century, when their ascendancy was brought to an end by Genoese, Pisan, and Florentine fleets sailing through the Strait of Gibraltar and establishing a direct sea route between the Mediterranean and Bruges.

Thereafter the fairs of Flanders excelled those of Champagne. The Flemish, Dutch, and English now began their slow rise to commercial ascendancy, the Company of the Staple bringing great wealth to England by the export of wool and the Merchant Adventurers, once English industry manufactured its own cloth, continuing their work by the export of woolens. From this trade Edward I and his successors derived an increasing proportion of the money they required for their increasingly complex government.

THE merchant of the twelfth or thirteenth century was as yet no Buddenbrook or even a Jacques Coeur. Sometimes he came from a wealthy landed family and began with some capital; sometimes he had a career that would have endeared him to the heart of Horatio Alger. Saint Godric of Finchale (twelfth century), a man of humble birth,

> . . . aspiring to the merchant's trade . . . began to follow the chapman's way of life, first learning how to gain in small bargains and things of insignificant price; and thence, while yet a youth, his mind advanced little by little to buy and sell and gain from things of greater expense. . . . Hence, within a brief space of time, the youth who had trudged for many weary hours from village to village, from farm to farm, did so profit by his increase of age and wisdom as to travel with associates of his own age through towns and boroughs, fortresses and cities, to fairs and to all the various booths of the market-place. . . . Then he purchased the half of a merchantship . . .[5]

After acquiring great wealth and fame, Godric eventually renounced the world and ended his life in a monastery.

Medieval shops. The proprietors ply their trades on the first floor and live on the second.

Dick Whittington, the son of a country gentleman, came to London to make money. He seems to have started with more capital than the cat that legend insists was his sole possession, and he early made money by importing luxury cloth for the future Henry IV. Three times Lord Mayor of London, Dick Whittington erected public hospitals, a college, and was in charge of rebuilding the nave of Westminster Abbey.

That the merchant was becoming increasingly useful, if not powerful, in society is illustrated by the career of Jacques Coeur. Beginning with a modest capital, he rose to power under Charles VII and ended with a great fleet of merchant ships trading to the Levant in silks, armor, furs, spices, and feathers for beds. He owned warehouses at Tours, Marseille, Paris, Perpignan, and Narbonne. For thirteen years he was in charge of purchasing for the royal household and frequently floated loans for royal projects, including the successful reconquest of Normandy from the English in 1450. His great house at Bourges is one of the most impressive and elegant medieval dwellings still in exist-

The house of Jacques Coeur in Bourges. A wealthy merchant of the later Middle Ages could live as grandly as the nobility and with more comfort.

ence. His very wealth brought about his downfall, for his debtors accused him of the murder of Charles VII's mistress Agnes Sorel, and he saved his life only by paying an enormous indemnity to the king.

COMMERCE cannot be carried on to any wide extent without a system of banking and credit. As long as a merchant had to carry cash with him in coin, the risks of travel remained prohibitive. Here again the East taught the West, for the Moslems developed a system of credit which was learned by the Europeans in the twelfth and thirteenth centuries. Before the twelfth century the European banker was simply a man who sat at his bench (*bancum*) and exchanged money from one currency into another, but after 1100 his affairs expanded considerably. By 1200 it was already common for an Italian merchant to have a bank account and to make payment by transfer of credit. Lending, in the early Middle Ages largely in the hands of the Church, became part of an established business practice including, for example, advances on the expected profits of a voyage. In northern Europe loans were largely in the hands of the Jews, Templars, and "Lombards," a term applied to almost all Italians, and by the end of the thirteenth century the English and French

The Money Changer and His Customer (*by Marinus van Reymerswael*).

governments were able to function only through credit, thus establishing governmental deficit spending.

Meanwhile various means of exchange that did not involve currency were contrived. At the Champagne fairs clearing-houses canceled out obligations of men who were both buying and selling. By 1200 banks of deposit were common, credit being transferred at the personal word of the depositor; but the bank check came into general use only in the sixteenth century. Merchants trading overseas used bills of exchange. By the end of the thirteenth century credit was so well developed that "an unbroken series of credit sales stretched from the English woolgrower to the Polish purchaser of Flemish cloth."[6]

Not only credit, but currency itself, became more versatile in response to the needs of commerce. During the long de-

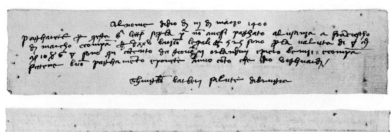

Bill of exchange.

pression of 300–800 currency was scarce and almost exclusively
limited to the silver penny, which was literally cut into halves
and quarters to make halfpennies and farthings. Until the eighth
century the penny was small and base; from that time it became a larger disk and was made of silver. For over three centuries the English penny retained its silver content, whence the
term sterling [from O.E. *stere:* "strong, fixed"], though in the
later Middle Ages it was again debased gradually, owing to the
inevitable process of depreciation and inflation that affects all
currencies. In the thirteenth century a larger coin was struck in
Italy, the *grosso* ["big"], which was adopted in England as the
groat and was worth fourpence. At about the same time a fine
and large gold coinage was introduced in Europe for the first
time since the decline of the Roman economy, the gold being
obtained from the Gold Coast, the Urals, and the Near East.
The Florentine *florin,* first struck in 1252, the Venetian *ducat,* and
the Genoese *genovino* were imitated all over the West, including
England, which in the fourteenth century minted the *noble.*

Money of account, as opposed to minted money, was needed
from the twelfth century for the purposes of banking and credit.
A method that had its origins in the seventh or eighth century
was now popularized—division into pounds, shillings, and pence
(*livres, sous,* and *deniers*), twelve pence to the shilling and twenty
shillings to the pound—though the shilling and the pound were
never minted until after the end of the Middle Ages.

Obverse (left) and reverse of silver penny of Edward I.

Obverse (left) and reverse of silver groat of Edward I.

Obverse (left) and reverse of gold noble of Edward III.

As John of Salisbury observed, society stood upon its feet, by which he meant the peasants and laborers who provided their superiors with services. In the manorial system of the early Middle Ages most of them had been serfs, but in the expanding economy of the later Middle Ages serfdom became less practical. Agricultural laborers were increasingly paid in wages, particularly from the fourteenth century, when depopulation added to the burdens placed upon the serf but enabled free laborers to demand higher pay, a discrepancy that provoked serfs to seek their freedom more vigorously than before either by flight or by revolt.

THE economic expansion of the Middle Ages came to an end in the fourteenth century, but the eleventh through thirteenth constitute a period of exceptional vigor and vitality, not only in commerce and in industry, but in every aspect of life and society.

NOTES

[1] Particularly in the *Journal of Economic History* and the *Economic History Review*.
[2] Quoted by John H. Mundy and Peter Riesenberg, *The Medieval Town* (New York, D. Van Nostrand Company, Inc., 1958), pp. 100–101.
[3] Eileen Power, *Medieval People* (Garden City, 1956), p. 45.
[4] Howard Adelson, *Medieval Commerce* (Princeton, 1962), pp. 147–148.
[5] *The Life of Saint Godric,* trans. G. G. Coulton, *Social Life in Britain from the Conquest to the Reformation* (Cambridge University Press, 1918, reprinted 1938), pp. 415–418.
[6] Herbert Heaton, *Economic History of Europe,* 2d ed. (New York, 1948), pp. 178–179.

Chapter Fifteen

PAPAL REFORM AND REVOLUTION

Between 1046 and 1125, Christian society was transformed by a great conflict. The sources for this struggle include, besides numerous chronicles and annals, a number of important *Lives* and letters, notably those of Henry IV, Gregory VII, Peter Damian, Yvo of Chartres, and Saint Anselm. The numerous polemical works produced by the theoreticians of papacy, empire, and the kingdoms are collected in the volumes of the *Monumenta Germaniae Historica* known as the *Libelli de Lite:* "Controversial Tracts."

The conflict was waged on several levels. At one level it was a controversy over investitures. Just as a lay vassal received from his lord investiture with a clod of earth or other symbol of his fief, the bishop received such a symbol from the ruler from whom he held his temporal possessions. But it had become the custom for the king to bestow, not only the symbols of temporal power, but the crozier and the episcopal ring, symbols of spiritual power. The papal reformers demanded that this practice cease and that only spiritual officers be allowed to invest the bishop. "For how does it pertain," asked Cardinal Humbert of Silva Candida, "to lay persons to distribute ecclesiastical sacraments and episcopal or pastoral grace, that is to say crozier staffs and rings. . . . The crozier staffs . . . symbolize . . . pastoral care. . . . Again, the ring is a symbol of heavenly mysteries. . . ."[1] Papalist theoreticians made much of the investiture issue, but it was really only the symbol of other and more fundamental divisions.

In the first place, it was the symbol of widespread lay interference in Church affairs, which the reformers considered intolerable. To them, *ordo* (the proper arrangement of society) and *libertas* (the proper place of each person and institution with its privileges and duties within the *ordo*) demanded that the pope be established as the head under God of Christian society and that the emperor should be subservient to the pope. The conflict thus became a struggle between the pope and the emperor for supremacy in Christian society.

Yet the struggle was more even than this, for it invaded all segments of society. Some modern historians have called it a "struggle between Church and state," but this is not accurate enough, for the emperor considered himself an ecclesiastical authority and had on his side many bishops; and the pope considered himself a temporal authority and had on his side many nobles and knights. The conflict was nothing less than a great civil war in Christian society: a reformation and a revolution combined.

THE conflict was a reformation in that it consisted in the assumption by the papacy of leadership of the reform movements that had begun with the mission of Saint Boniface three centuries earlier. From the eighth century to the eleventh, reform had been directed by the kings and by the monasteries. The old idea that the papal reformation was the continuation of monastic reform was overstated, but it has been discarded too readily by some recent historians. It was no accident that the centers of papalist theory were in Lorraine and northern Italy, precisely those regions where the monastic reform movement was strongest. The monks, however, had tended to argue that reform demanded withdrawal from the world. The papal reformers argued instead —and this was a radical leap—that in order to accomplish reform the influence of lay rulers should be removed from the Church and that this should be done by bringing society firmly under papal control. Papal policy demanded that action should replace monastic meditation and that the concern for individual moral renovation should be transcended by the concern for *ordo* in society. The mission of the papacy was to reform the whole world, to bring the proper *ordo* to all of Christian society not only by ending the domination of the Church by the laity, but by instituting the domination of empire and kingdoms by the clergy. Thus to the program of moral reform was added a political program that was revolutionary.

This revolutionary program was based upon the theory of papal supremacy rooted in the Biblical texts implying the primacy of Peter and occasionally elaborated by outspoken theorists like Gregory the Great and Nicholas I. The program was enhanced by the great advances made in the eleventh century in the study of canon law, which permitted papalists to search the decrees of the past for justification of their present position and to organize their theories into a coherent and effective program of revolution.

The revolution began in 1046 after a last spectacularly successful intervention of the imperial power in the papacy, the deposition of three popes and the appointment of another by Emperor Henry III at the synods of Sutri and Rome. In 1048, after the sudden deaths of this appointee and his successor, the emperor named as pope the bishop of Toul, Bruno, who took the throne name of Leo IX (1048–1054). Leo was from Lorraine, a center of monastic reform, social and intellectual change, and papalist theory. When he went to Rome to assume the papal crown, he took with him a brains trust of capable Lorrainers, including Humbert, later cardinal-bishop of Silva Candida; Frederick of Lorraine, the future pope Stephen IX and the brother of the powerful duke of Lorraine; and Hildebrand, an Italian by birth who had spent some time in Lorraine with the exiled Gregory VI (one of the popes deposed by Henry III) and who now returned to Italy with Leo. Henry appointed Leo with the assumption that he would achieve reform while remaining acquiescent to imperial supervision. Leo gratified the king's wishes in the first regard but not in the second. The revolution was on.

THE papalists had two related but distinct revolutionary programs. The first was the transformation of the Church from a loosely knit organization with considerable local autonomy into an efficient and centralized papal monarchy. The second was the domination of all of Christian society, including temporal matters and temporal rulers, by the pope. The ultimate purpose of these programs was moral reform, but inevitably power once achieved sought more power and eventually became an end in itself. The result was a revolution, the metamorphosis of an ill-defined Christian society under the nominal rule of the emperor into a closely organized Christendom under the effective rule of the papacy. Some historians call it one of the great revolutions in western history, and in many respects its course resembled those of more modern upheavals. But, much less cataclysmic than the French or Russian Revolutions, it is more fairly compared with the American. Even at the height of his powers the pope was not omnipotent, for he was always bound by the tradition of the Church. The papal revolution was what a modern sociologist has called "norm-oriented" rather than "value-oriented;" its purpose was not to tear down the old structure of society but simply to substitute one institution for another at its summit.

THE first part of the program promoted by the revolutionary popes was the establishment of internal order in the Church. Disorganization and corruption had rendered local ecclesiastical authority prone to weakness, simony, and lay interference. The papacy moved to establish a strong sense of hierarchy and to place itself firmly at its apex. As "the Church" was equated with the Mystical Body of Christ, so now "the Roman Church" was equated with "the Church" and the pope and the cardinals with "the Roman Church."

From 1048 onwards, particularly under Gregory VII, the centralizing efforts of the papacy were unrelenting. Papal power was brought to bear directly at all levels of the Church and to reduce wherever possible the powers of primates, archbishops, and bishops in favor of that of the pope. The popes endeavored first to remove lay influence from episcopal elections and later to name the bishops themselves. They enormously increased their correspondence in order to keep closer tabs on their subordinates; Gregory VII's frequent missives prompted the archbishop of Hamburg-Bremen to remark that the pope treated the bishops like tenant-farmers. The popes sent out legates to represent papal authority and to control the bishops throughout Europe. They granted charters of immunity to monasteries, freeing them from episcopal control and placing them directly under that of Rome. They called synods and councils under their supervision and transformed ecumenical councils into tools of papal policy. Ecumenical councils had not been called since the

POPES

These three popes were deposed by Henry III:
Benedict IX (1032–1046)
Sylvester III (1045–1046)
Gregory VI (1045–1046)

These were the first two German popes appointed by Henry III:
Clement II (1046–1047)
Damasus II (1048)

These are the important popes of the period of revolution:
Leo IX (1048–1054)
Stephen IX (1057–1058)
Nicholas II (1059–1061)
Alexander II (1061–1073)
Gregory VII (1073–1085)
Clement III (1084–1100) Antipope
Urban II (1088–1099)
Paschal II (1099–1118)
Calixtus II (1119–1124)

EMPERORS

Henry III (1039–1056)
Henry IV (1056–1106)
Henry V (1106–1125)
Lothar II (1125–1137)

ninth century, partly because imperial control of the Church made it unnecessary from the imperial point of view, and partly because from the papal point of view the popes and the cardinals were sufficiently representative of universal Church. By 1095 when Urban II summoned the great councils of Piacenza and Clermont, the papacy was insecure enough to want to enlist such public support, and secure enough not to fear imperial domination of the assemblies. The ecumenical councils of the Middle Ages differed from their predecessors in being firmly under the control of the pope rather than of the emperor.*

*The councils of Piacenza and Clermont are not classified as ecumenical. The first ecumenical council of the Middle Ages met at the Lateran palace in Rome in 1123.

Most controversial was the papacy's use of the Roman curia to rule the entire Church. The curia consisted of administrators and advisers, the most important of whom were called cardinals.* The cardinals eventually became the prime object of the hatred of the anti-papalists. Sang the poet Walter of Châtillon in the twelfth century: "In this new state of affairs the cardinals ("carnals," he calls them elsewhere) sell the birthright of the Crucified: the appearance is Peter, but the reality is Nero; the appearance is the lamb, but the reality the wolf."[2]

To the extension of jurisdiction the papalists soon added the claim to pronounce in matters of doctrine. The informal Papal Memo (*Dictatus Papae*) of 1075 says: "the Church of Rome has never erred, will never err, can never err. . . ." To the clergy of Milan Urban II wrote: "You know how dangerous it is to be in disagreement with the Roman Church, and how it is necessary for salvation to obey this Church in humility and peace."

The result of these centralizing tendencies was that by the mid-twelfth century the Church had a well-organized, hierarchical system headed by a papal monarchy. The pope ruled the Church and was responsible to none save God. The curia, dominated by the college of cardinals, shared in the authority attributed to the Holy See and served as the papal administration. Ecumenical councils became extensions of papal power. Papal legates and papal correspondence kept the archbishops and bishops in close obedience to Rome. Just as the distinction between clergy and laity had grown in previous centuries, now the distinction between the pope and the other bishops widened. It was forgotten that the pope was originally merely first among equals; from bishop of Rome he became vicegerent of God. With reforms, the bishops increased their authority within their own dioceses, so that the local clergy and laity were brought more firmly into line. The monasteries, which might have stood outside the system, had long since looked to Rome for protection and now had to yield to papal authority. It became possible as never before for the pope to draw upon the resources of the entire Church from top to bottom: the Crusades and

*The word has a curious history. It derives from the Latin *cardo,* "hinge," and was applied to bishops, priests, and deacons who were "hinged" to two churches, their own and the papal.

Gregory VII and a monk.

the pontificate of Innocent III, as well as the subordination of the lay rulers, would show how successful this program was. At the same time, the very success of papal centralization, the very tightness of the organization, discouraged originality and spiritual independence and drove many creative spirits from the Church as heretics.

The desirability of this transformation from decentralized polity to monarchy in the Church has always been the subject of debate, not only by Protestants, but by the ecumenical Council of Constance in the fifteenth century, and, with renewed vigor, by the ecumenical Second Vatican Council of 1962–1965. Whatever its long-range effects, the transformation had the initial import of aiding moral reform as well as of enhancing papal prestige.

It also led directly to the next step of the papal program: the securing of independence, and then of superiority, in regard to the temporal powers.

There are numerous possible approaches to the problem of Church and state. Most medieval approaches assumed the integrated unity of Christian society. The imperialists claimed that the ruler of this society under God was the emperor; the papalists that it was the pope. A few suggested parallel authority within the context of unity. The kings' position was somewhat anomalous. They argued that although Christian society was united, each king should have control over the Church in his own dominions.

From the time of Constantine the imperial and royal theories had generally prevailed, so that in this respect the eleventh-century imperialists were conservatives desiring to preserve the old order, and the papalists were radicals. The papalist argument itself underwent modification. It began with the moderate assertion that the popes and emperors had independent and parallel powers, so that neither had the right to dominate the other. When the papal position grew stronger, the argument shifted to a claim that papal power was superior to imperial or royal power.

The papalist claims go back to the Bible, but they were not advanced with any consistency until the eleventh century, although in the tenth some theorists already began to insist that the evils besetting the Church had their sole source in the influence of the laity. In the tenth century Rather of Liège insisted upon the superiority of the clergy to the laity. He held that bishops were to be judged by no one but God; and that their dignity was such that kings and princes should bow before them, for in honoring the clergy they honored Christ himself. Bishop Wazo of Liège, Rather's less extreme compatriot of the eleventh century, was no less insistent that the laity should withdraw from spiritual matters. Wazo's was basically a position of parallelism. "To (the emperor) we owe fidelity; to the pope, obedience. To (the king) we must answer for worldly things; to the pope for everything having to do with God's service." The arguments of Rather and Wazo were for spiritual freedom, not yet for papal supremacy, but they laid the foundations upon which the papalists would build.

The greatest of the papalist theoreticians was Humbert, the haughty and outspoken cardinal of Silva Candida. On the death of Henry III he was able to take advantage of the temporary weakness of the empire to publish his fiery tract *Against the Simoniacs.* For Humbert, any lay interference in the Church was sinful and even heretical. No matter that Emperor Henry III was a friend of reform: his place was in hell. The Roman Church was at the head of the world because it represented the mystical Body of Christ. Those who were obedient to Rome were members of the Body; those not in communion with Rome were cut off from the Body. As for the King, his job was merely to protect the Church. Humbert put his ideas into a series of metaphors: the pope is the soul, the king is the body; the pope is the sun, the king is the moon reflecting the glory of the greater luminary; the pope is the head of the Church and the king its arm.

These theories began to be put into practice by the popes after 1048. Leo IX (1048–1054) deposed simoniac bishops, called councils without the consent of the emperor, and took an extended tour of northern Europe to build support for the papacy. Nicholas II (1059–1061) made an alliance with the Normans of Southern Italy to counterbalance imperial power in the North. He presided over the Lateran Synod, which excluded the laity from the election of popes and solemnly—and for the first time formally—forbade lay investiture.

Under Gregory VII (1073–1085), revolutionary theory and practice were carried further. In part to establish a course of action, and in part to justify that which had already been established, the papacy ordered the compiling of the texts of canon law, the first great collection being the *Sentences* attributed to Humbert. Under the influence of these collections, Gregory VII in 1075 renewed the decrees against lay investiture and drew up the famous "Papal Memo" (*Dictatus Papae*), a summary of the titles of those canons which vindicated the papalist cause. According to this Memo

> . . . the Roman Pontiff alone is rightly to be called universal; he alone can depose and reinstate bishops; he alone may use the imperial insignia; the Pope is the only one whose feet are to be kissed by all princes; he may depose Emperors; he may transfer bishops; he may himself be judged by no one; the Roman Church has never erred; he should not be considered as Catholic who is not in conformity with the Roman Church; the Pope may absolve subjects of unjust men from their fealty.[3]

Such were the modest principles upon which Gregory VII based an equally modest political program: to extend semi-feudal papal suzerainty over Aragon, Naples, Kiev, Poland, Hungary, and Croatia. The king of Leon and Castile was notified in 1077 that "the Kingdom of Spain belongs to Saint Peter and the Holy Roman Church." If kings did not wish to cooperate, there was

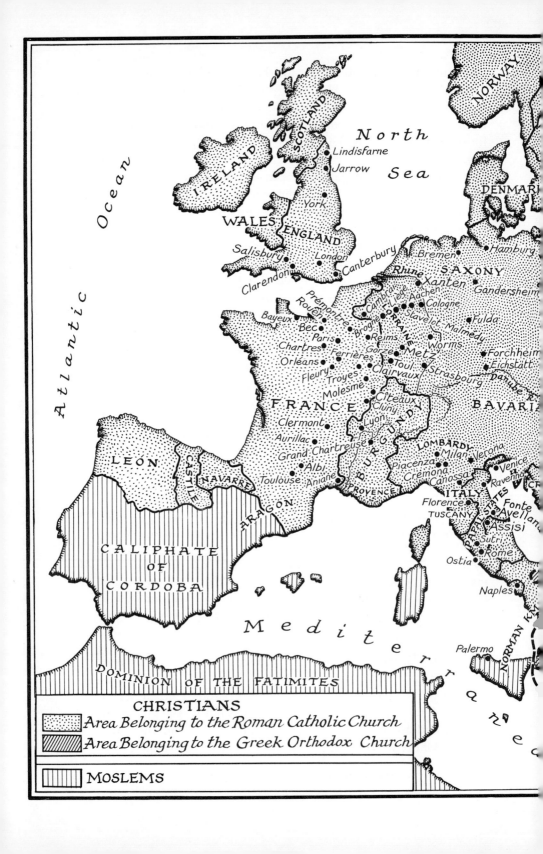

NORWAY

North

Sea

DENMARK

IRELAND

SCOTLAND

Lindisfarne

Jarrow

York

WALES

ENGLAND

Hamburg

Bremen

SAXONY

Salisbury

London

Canterbury

Rhine

Xanten

Gandersheim

Clarendon

Aachen

Cambrai

Cologne

Prémontré

Aachen

Rouen

Brogne

Stavelot-Malmedy

Fulda

Bayeux

LORRAINE

Bec

Reims

Worms

Paris

Gorze

Metz

Forchheim

Chartres

Ferrières

Eichstätt

Orléans

Toul

Strasbourg

Fleury

Clairvaux

Danube

Troyes

FRANCE

Molesme

Cîteaux

BAVARIA

Cluny

Clermont

Lyon

BURGUNDY

Aurillac

LEON

Grand Chartreuse

LOMBARDY

Milan *Verona*

CASTILE

Albi

Piacenza

NAVARRE

Toulouse

Aniane

Cremona

Cañosa

Venice

ARAGON

PROVENCE

Ravenna

ITALY

Florence

Fonte

TUSCANY

Avellana

PAPAL STATES

Assisi

CALIPHATE

Sutri

OF

Ostia

Rome

CORDOBA

Naples

Atlantic

Ocean

Mediterra

Palermo

NORMAN K

DOMINION OF THE FATIMITES

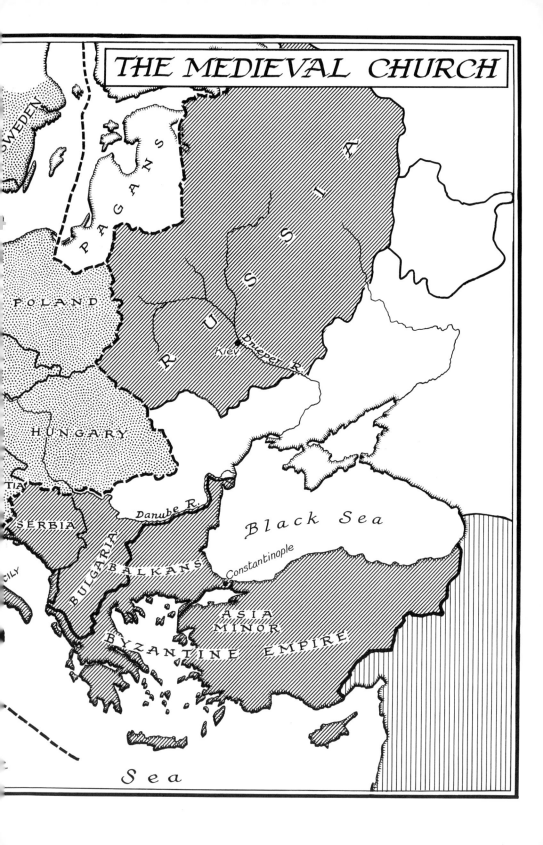

THE MEDIEVAL CHURCH

SWEDEN

PAGANS

POLAND

RUSSIA

HUNGARY

Kiev

Dnieper R.

TIA

SERBIA

Danube R.

Black Sea

BULGARIA

BALKANS

Constantinople

CILY

ASIA MINOR

BYZANTINE EMPIRE

Sea

at hand a formidable arsenal of weapons against them: the interdict, under which a whole country could be deprived of the sacraments for as long as the pope chose, thus depriving people not only of the comforts of the eucharist but of the luxuries of marriage and burial; excommunication, which theoretically excused the king's subjects from even speaking to him; formal deposition; and the ban, which combined the virtues of excommunication and deposition in one handy instrument.

The historian must remember the principles upon which this apparently excessive program was based. Gregory VII and his supporters believed that it was in the proper tradition of the Church. More than that, they believed that *ordo* would never be achieved were the papacy not to rule firmly. Most of all, the program appeared to be a requirement of logic: Christ had ordained that the world should be governed in accordance with justice. But who is to decide what is justice? If the individual, anarchy is the result. If the state, the result can be tyranny. There must be an authority on earth capable of defining justice and of securing it for society: and the papacy was the only logical candidate. It is no accident that the concept that appears most frequently in Hildebrand's letters is exactly that: *justitia.* This was the essence of the papalist theory of the eleventh century.

In the meanwhile the theoretical position of the imperialists was eroding. Logically, if Christian society were to be united, there is no reason why the emperor should not have been its ruler rather than the pope. The emperors had tradition and the memory of the Christian Roman Empire of Constantine behind them. Not only Constantine, but Theodosius, Charlemagne, Otto I, and even Henry II of Germany had showed how Christian emperors should rule. But imperial theory always had weaknesses: it enjoyed much less Biblical justification than the papacy, which could rely upon Christ's commission to Peter; and canons of the Church, now being laboriously collected and collated by the papal lawyers, were much more favorable to the papal than to the imperial cause. The real strength of the emperors had been their practical power; as that power eroded in the political deterioration of Germany and Italy, and as the power of the reform papacy grew, that strength disappeared. It was no longer possible to argue that the emperor was obviously the ruler, because he was obviously the most efficient protector, of the Church. The German emperors through weakness lost their right to rule the Church of the twelfth century.

The polemical literature of the eleventh and twelfth centuries betrays this imperial weakness. The writings and publications of Humbert and Hildebrand engendered an enormous body of controversial literature, a true battle of the books. While the papalist position was ably defended by men like the eleventh-century Bishop Bonizo of Sutri or the twelfth-century scholar John of Salisbury, equally able eleventh-century writers like Peter Crassus and Sigebert of Gembloux defended the empire. But the imperialists' arguments faltered. Thus Peter Crassus, the leading defender of Emperor Henry IV, was unsure whether he should assert imperial superiority to, or merely equality with, the papacy. He was uncertain whether he ought to defend the powers of the emperor in particular, or of the kings in general. The failure of the imperialists is visible in the degeneration of their arguments into name-calling: Gregory VII was accused of being a sorcerer, a lecher, a heretic, the paramour of Countess Matilda of Tuscany. The fertile brain of Bishop Benzo of Alba concocted marvelous variations on names, like Merdiprand and Folleprand for Hildebrand, or Asinander for Alexander II.

In effect, the imperialists retreated from the field and left opposition to the papacy in the hands of royalists, who defended the right of each king to rule over the Church in his own country. The most able royalist theoretician was an anonymous Anglo-Norman writer, from either York or Rouen, who argued that the papalists were usurping power in violation of tradition and that the kings, both traditionally and pragmatically, should rule their churches.

Both the papalist and imperialist writers left ideas that would bear ripe fruit in the later Middle Ages. The papalist writer John of Salisbury identified "the Church" with "the people" and argued that if a king were unjust the people need not obey him, though the papacy must decide in any given instance whether the ruler in question was a "just king" or an "unjust king." Later on this kind of thinking was applied to the papacy itself and bolstered conciliarism (the limitation of the papal power by the ecumenical councils), as well as the development of full-fledged populism and a theory of social contract. The imperialist arguments also helped to engender conciliarism; where they argued the independence and equality of empire and papacy they also encouraged pluralism (the division of the spiritual and the temporal realms). Royalist theoreticians greatly encouraged the later rise of nationalism.

SUCH were the theories of the papal revolution. The chief battleground upon which it was fought out was the empire, partly because the emperor was the only lay ruler claiming universal jurisdiction. It is sometimes forgotten that the battle was fought in both the eastern and the western empires, for the mission of Humbert and Frederick of Lorraine to Constantinople in 1054 was designed to bring Byzantium into the papal conception of society. But that mission was a complete and immediate failure. Hence the western empire was the battleground, the more naturally so because papal Rome was located within its imperial borders.

Henry III, who had achieved the last great imperial victory at Sutri, died in 1056, leaving the throne to a child, Henry IV, under the regency of his mother Agnes. Pious, young, and trusting, Agnes relied upon spiritual counselors whose advice was not always politically, or even spiritually, reliable. During the troubled regency the power of the papacy rose, so that a formidable adversary had been prepared for the young king when he assumed personal rule in 1066. Henry was an exceptionally able and determined ruler, and if, in facing his enormous problems, he yielded too often to emotion and violence, it is not surprising. His task, the task of any of the German kings, was too great for mortal man. With his biographer we may say "Just as all this could not be written by me without tears, so it cannot be read by you without tears."[4]

The vigorous emperor tried to extend his domain and the authority of his office, but his hold on power was always shaky; the backing of the bishops was absolutely necessary, and he could not afford to tolerate the papalism that affected nearly half of the German episcopate.

The determined Henry found in Hildebrand an equally determined enemy. The early career of Hildebrand, according to dubious legend a poor carpenter's son,* is obscure. He was

*Dubious because there had been another poor carpenter's son in Galilee.

probably very briefly a monk; he was of service to Gregory VI, and in 1046 he accompanied that deposed pontiff across the Alps into exile. He returned to Rome with Leo IX in 1048, and rose quickly in the ranks of the hierarchy: subdeacon, cardinal, legate, and in 1059 archdeacon, the second most important office in the diocese of Rome. As archdeacon he wielded a power that was recognized if not always admired: Peter Damian declaimed that "if you wish to live at Rome you must clearly declare that you obey the lord pope less than the pope's lord." Hildebrand's enthusiasm came to be equally noted, his German supporters calling him Hellbrand (Bright Fire) and his enemies Höllebrand (Hellfire). It is said that his favorite passage from the Bible was "Woe to him who holds his sword back from blood."

In 1073 he was uncanonically elected by the spontaneous acclamation of the people and took the name of Gregory VII (1073-1085). He described the scene himself: "Suddenly during the funeral procession of our lord the pope, in the church of the Savior, a great noise and tumult arose, and the people seized hold of me like madmen without giving me time to speak or to take advice. It was by force that they raised me to this apostolic government. . . ." His plan as pope was simple: "I am placed here," he wrote in 1073, "to announce to all the nations justice and truth." His purpose was to reform the Church, reclaim Spain from the Moslems, and achieve the submission to Rome of the Eastern Church. He became hostile to the western empire only when he found that it would stand in his way rather than aiding him along it. To an undeniable purity and thirst for justice he added an enthusiasm that was often rash and a high conception of the majesty of his office. His program was questionable—it was certainly questioned—but his greatness lay in his willingness to sacrifice himself as well as others for the ideas of *ordo* and *justitia* that he believed constituted the right tradition of the Church. Not pride, but earnestness, moved him. Driven into exile by his enemies, he met his end saying, "I have loved justice and hated iniquity; for this I die in exile."

In the first years of Gregory's reign he got along tolerably well with Henry IV, writing in 1073 that "it is surely fitting for (us) . . . not to disagree with one another, but rather to cleave to each other, inseparably joined with the bond of Christ."[5] But the elements of discord were already assembled. Gregory was dissatisfied with the progress of reform in Germany and was determined to use his influence over the bishops to advance it. Henry was equally determined to assert control over the Church.

Dissension in Germany procured allies for the pope. In 1073 occurred a revolt of the dukes of Saxony and Bavaria aided by the Saxon peasants, who resented royal taxation. Gregory did not then move against the emperor, because he still hoped for an accommodation, and the unlikely alliance dissolved when the peasants fell out with the nobles and the Bavarians with the Saxons. Yet the possibility remained that papacy, princes, and monks could make common cause against the king. One example is the program of monastic reforms centered at the monastery of Hirsau, which sought to free the monasteries from royal control by securing papal privileges and relying upon princely protectors. All was ready for the explosion of 1075.

This explosion had two immediate causes. The first was the publication by Gregory VII of his decree against lay investitures and the appearance of his Papal Memo; the second was a schism in the church of Milan, where the emperor appointed one archbishop and the pope another. Milan, the ancient sore spot in Italy for the emperor, now became the *casus belli* for the conflict that destroyed the empire.

At 1076, in Worms, Henry IV brought together a majority of his Bishops. He knew of the pope's intransigeance in Milan and of the extravagance of papal claims. He also knew of the unusual manner in which Hildebrand had been elevated to the papacy. His bishops accordingly wrote to Gregory that, owing to his perjury, infamy, and oppression, they would no longer recognize him as pope, and Henry wrote an even more violent missive concluding, "I, Henry, King by the grace of God, together with all our bishops, say to you: Descend! Descend!"[6] Though the deposition of popes was nothing new—Henry's father had laid out three with one blow—it appears that the king wished to bring Gregory into line rather than actually to depose him, for at this time he appointed no other pope to take his place.

Gregory's reply was to summon a synod at Rome later the

same year, where he excommunicated Henry and released his subjects from obedience. Gregory, like Henry, meant to impress his adversary rather than to depose him. But leaders have never learned that events once set into motion have a way of taking their own course.

Henry's first reaction was violent, but on second thought he let reason get the better of pride. Fearing an alliance of the papacy with the princes, he went across the Alps to meet the pope in Canossa, where he was staying at a castle owned by his ally, Countess Matilda of Tuscany. It was January 1077, the dead of winter. "On three successive days, standing before the castle gate, laying aside all royal insignia, barefooted and in coarse attire, he ceased not to beseech the apostolic help and comfort. . . ."[7] It is clear that Henry meant this spectacular act of contrition as a clever political gambit, but it is not clear whether he got sufficient goods for the price. He did secure the lifting of his excommunication and prevent the princely-papal alliance from forming immediately. He wrung a short-term advantage from Gregory's moralism—had Gregory been a more cynical politician he would have sent Henry packing with more anathemas than ever. But in the meanwhile Henry had etched indelibly into the mind of Europe the picture of the empire prostrate before the papacy.

The nobles viewed the papal moderation at Canossa with complete indifference and proceded at Forchheim to declare Henry deposed and Rudolf of Rheinfelden their king. Gregory, always moral, withheld recognition from Rudolf until it could be seen whether Henry really meant to do penance and amend his life.

Impelled by his desperate need to keep control of the bishops, Henry now violated his oath and began again intervening in episcopal elections. Gregory proceeded in 1080 formally to depose Henry and to recognize Rudolf, declaring that "Henry is justly cast down from the royal dignity for his insolence, his disobedience, and his deceit." Though Gregory groped for far-fetched precedents like Pope Zachary's approval of Pepin III's *coup d'état* over the Merovingians, the event was really revolutionary. Emperors had deposed popes, but no pope had ever dared to depose an emperor. Henry's response was predictable: he called his own synod, deposed Gregory, and set up his own antipope, "Clement III." The true nature of the struggle as a civil war in society now becomes evident: on the one side there was an emperor, a pope, certain clergy, and certain nobles; on the other side there was a pope, an emperor, certain clergy, and certain nobles. Society was split down the middle.

The civil war went against the pope. After a long struggle Henry took Rome and installed the antipope on the throne of Peter, while Peter's successor was driven off to die in exile. In Germany, Henry completed his victory by deposing the bishops who had continued, despite the political disadvantages, to support Gregory.

Gregory's successors avenged him. Urban II (1088–1099) built up the papal power by every means, negotiating alliances with the nobles and using the Council of Clermont in 1095 to gain enormous prestige by putting himself at the head of the Crusading movement. A formidable coalition had been constructed when Countess Matilda of Tuscany, who had always supported the papacy, married the heir to the Bavarian duchy. Saxony continued disaffected, and the towns of northern Italy were rebellious. A papal-Tuscan-Lombard-Bavarian-Saxon axis, while never formal or lasting, was a configuration with which Henry now had to deal. The adherents to this axis were called Welfs after Duke Welf V of Bavaria; the imperialists were later called the Weiblingen, after one of the castles of the Hohenstaufen.* The final blow was the revolt of Henry's sons, who harried him from place to place till at last he died at Liège, the only town in the empire that remained faithful to the end. Shortly before his death he wrote to King Philip of France vainly imploring his aid:

> O most illustrious prince and most faithful of our friends, in whom, after God, we place our hope! . . . To you I have thought it necessary to lament my calamities and all my woes and to mourn them. And I should even have fallen to your knees, were that possible without prejudice to the majesty of the Empire. . . . (My enemies) turned the mind of my son against me, I say the mind of my most beloved Absalom. . . . (Henry describes how he pleaded for absolution with the emissaries of the pope, who coldly turned him down, though) prostrate on the ground, I began with the greatest contrition

*The Italians, unable to pronounce *w*, translated this into the struggle between "Guelf" and Ghibelline" made famous by Dante.

of spirit to pray in the name of God. . . . (His son was also insensitive to his need. The old king had agreed to see his Absalom, but friends warned him that if he kept the appointment) either I should be taken off into perpetual captivity or I should be beheaded on the spot. Wholly despairing of our life at this news, we fled at once; and in flight I came to Cologne. Tarrying there for some days, I came afterward to Liège. In these places I always found men who were faithful and constant in good faith toward the kingly office.[8]

IF Pope Paschal II (1099–1118) expected better of the son than of the father, he was disappointed. Once the old king had been vanquished, the new king Henry V turned against his former ally, for every German ruler needed to control the bishops. The methods of Henry V were even more direct than those of Henry IV: inviting Paschal to a conference, Henry threw the pope into a dungeon and starved him until he signed a document legitimizing imperial control over the Church. The document was soon denounced, of course; but finally Henry and Paschal's successor, Calixtus II (1119–1124), reached a compromise on the question of investiture.

Such compromises had already been worked out in France (at Troyes) and England (at London) in 1107 under the influence of moderates like Yvo of Chartres and Hugh of Fleury, and the German compromise of Worms in 1122 was essentially the same: the king would invest the bishops with the symbols of their temporal authority; the pope or other bishops would invest them with the *spiritualia.* This was a moderate victory for the papacy, but it was a limited one, for the kings retained the right to influence the appointments of the bishops, a far more important point than who handed whom what symbols.

Up through 1122 the emperor had been able almost to hold his own against the revolution, but in 1125 Henry V died without a direct heir, and the crown passed to Lothar II, a scion of the papalist Saxon-Tuscan-Bavarian alliance. Further, the end of the Salian line inaugurated a renewal of fierce internal discords in Germany. Together, the popes and the princes brought the empire down. It was seldom again able to challenge the papal vicegerency of Christian society.

THE popes had to deal with royal, as well as imperial, opposition. In France, the controversy followed the same lines as in the empire, but with much less bitterness and open hostility, though Gregory VII tactfully found King Philip I (1060–1108) "the cause and fountainhead of (all crimes) under the inspiration of the Devil." Unlike the kings of Germany, those of France were growing stronger, and after the compromise of Troyes in 1107 they slowly increased their control over their bishops. It was in France, rather than Germany, that in the fourteenth century the papacy met its Appomattox.

In England, no controversy arose until the reign of William II (1087–1100). Both the English monarchy and the Norman duchy had close connections with the Church in terms of administration and reform, and William the Conqueror (1066–1087) worked in close cooperation and harmony with Lanfranc, his archbishop of Canterbury. The English Church was loyal to Rome, contributed Peter's Pence, and revered the papacy; but at the same time it was the king who dominated the choice of bishops and in general ruled the Church. Of all the monarchs of his time, William I was the least objectionable to Gregory VII, who observed that though William had not been scrupulous in all things with reference to the Apostolic See his virtues required that he be treated with patience.

It was otherwise with William II, a greedy and perverted monarch who inherited his father's will to control the Church while lacking his desire to reform it. Lanfranc died in 1089, and William II, wishing to enjoy its revenues and uncertain who its new occupant might be, kept the see of Canterbury vacant for four years. At last he agreed to the appointment of Anselm of Bec, a complaisance which he soon rued. Anselm came from Normandy and had been in touch, as Lanfranc had not, with the new currents of papalism. He and the king fell out almost immediately, the upshot being that the archbishop went back to the continent in exile. An ecclesiastical council met at Rockingham to determine whether the king or the pope had fuller power over the English Church; "soon, however, they found the wholesome and familiar counsel on which they were wont to rely; that is to say, they gave (the king) a large sum of money and were restored to (his) favor."[9]

William's brother Henry I (1100–1135) was more conciliatory and invited Anselm to return, but in the meanwhile Anselm's own position had become more extreme, and a new dispute arose that was only partly solved by the Compromise of London in 1107. Henry I continued to dominate the Church, although with more tact and justice than his brother. A period of weakness and civil war under Stephen (1135–1154) allowed the Church to regain some of the lost ground, but in 1154 Henry II succeeded, a brilliant king determined to restore the control enjoyed by his grandsire over both civil and ecclesiastical matters.

The policies of the second Henry led to the second great controversy in English Church history and the most famous dispute of the Middle Ages: Henry's quarrel with Thomas Becket. Few medieval personalities are as well known as Becket's, and few are as little understood. The son of a fairly well-to-do Norman tradesman of London, he was educated in England and Paris. Presently he came to the attention of the archbishop of Canterbury, Theobald, who offered him a position as clerk at his court. Young Thomas was always more interested in law and politics than in theology, and he took a sometimes active part in the civil wars of Stephen's time. Theobald made him archdeacon, a high post in any diocese, and Thomas served him well. When Henry had at last won his throne and was in search of a chancellor, Theobald could think of no better candidate than his able archdeacon. Thus the young clerk became the chancellor of the young king; together they governed well, hunted well, and wenched well. To Henry, Thomas seemed not only the ablest

Effigy of Henry II.

and the loyalest, but also the most amusing, companion in England. And so he was until in 1162 old Archbishop Theobald died, and Henry without delay called his friend to the see of Canterbury.

It was a logical move: a king could want no better archbishop than a clergyman with secular interests who had for years been his adviser and his drinking companion. Thomas had warned Henry what he would feel obliged to do as archbishop, but the king was unprepared for the extent to which the warning would be fulfilled.

Politically speaking, the quarrel was a resumption of that between Henry's grandfather Henry I and Anselm: the king wished to control the Church; the archbishop wished to preserve the rights of the papacy and of the English Church against unwonted intrusion. The political dispute became a bitter personal quarrel such as is only possible when two men who have been close friends fall out. The immediate occasion of the split was the king's efforts to try in his courts clergymen who had already been tried and convicted in Church courts, in order to impose harsher penalties on them. Thomas, determined to retain the independence of Church courts, refused to permit this on the grounds that it was double jeopardy. Henry issued the "Constitutions of Clarendon," which outlined the restoration of the "good old system" of the Conqueror in regard to the Church. The king, not the pope, was to have full power over the English Church and the king was to recognize the pope's authority in only a general and nominal way. To these Constitutions, most of the English bishops consented; Thomas agreed but then recanted and fled to the continent. As with Anselm, exile made Becket only the more extreme. In 1166 he wrote Henry that "Kings receive their power from the Church, not the latter hers from them but from Christ. . . . You have not the power to give orders to bishops . . . nor to drag clerks before secular tribunals. . . . (Do right). Otherwise you may know for certain that you will experience the divine severity and vengeance."[10]

Though Thomas defended papalism more vehemently than did the pope himself, he finally persuaded the latter to pronounce the majority of the Constitutions of Clarendon uncanonical and to excommunicate Henry's leading episcopal supporters. Armed with this papal support, Thomas returned to

The murder of Thomas Becket. The archbishop, kneeling, is struck down by the four knights, while one of his cathedral canons watches in horror.

carry the struggle onto English soil. It was in 1171 that Henry angrily made his famous wish that someone would rid him of the traitor, and that four knights hastened to make his wish come true. Their murder of the archbishop in Canterbury Cathedral is one of the most famous scenes of medieval history. "Are you then come to slay me?," cried the archbishop. "I have committed my cause to the great Judge of all mankind; wherefore I am not moved by threats, nor are your swords more ready to strike than is my soul for martyrdom." In the end, "bespattered with blood and brains, as though in an attitude of prayer, his body lay prone on the pavement, while his soul rested in Abraham's bosom."[11]

The outrage of all Europe at this deed was such that Henry was forced to do public penance the next year at Avranches in France and to yield to the pope precisely those points upon which Thomas had insisted. The result in England was a stand-off: king's power, bishops' power, pope's power, and barons' power were still balanced. The resulting tension brought about yet more conflicts but in the long run proved beneficial.

Historians, theologians, kings, and playwrights have for centuries debated whether Thomas was a saint, a traitor, a fanatic, a megalomaniac, or an astute politician. The Becket created by T. S. Eliot in his *Murder in the Cathedral* yields nobly and faithfully to the will of God after having resisted all temptations, including those of spiritual pride and good works. The temptation of good works was the lure most often taken by the medieval Church, but Becket rejects it:

> Temporal power, to build a good world,
> To keep order, as the world knows order.
> Those who put their faith in worldly order
> Not controlled by the order of God,
> In confident ignorance, but arrest disorder,
> Make it fast, breed fatal disease,
> Degrade what they exalt. . . .[12]

Canonized in 1173, he was for centuries the most popular saint in England; to his shrine at Canterbury came men from every shire's end of England to seek "the holy blissful martyr"; and the Pilgrim's Way upon which Chaucer's characters journeyed to the shrine still winds beautifully through the Kentish countryside.

WHAT was the result of the whole gigantic conflict that raged across Europe and left in its path the death of martyrs and the destruction of empires? The Church increased its independence from the laity and improved its morality and education. At the same time, it was centralized and transformed into a monarchy. The power of the papacy over both Church and temporal affairs grew awesome: it dominated Europe for two centuries from the

Henry II doing penance at Avranches, 1172.

time of Gregory VII to that of Boniface VIII. The revolution
that placed the papacy at the head of Christian society left
tradition in many regards unchanged. Though the popes pointed
out to the imperial traditionalists that Christ had said, "I am
the way, the truth, and the life," not "I am custom," they
themselves sought return to a Golden Age. Said Gregory VII:
"We returned to the teaching of the holy fathers, declaring no
novelties nor any inventions of our own, but holding that the
primary and only rule of discipline and the well-trodden way of
the saints should again be sought and followed."

THE papal revolution was a success in terms of its limited objectives, for it achieved the domination of society and the humiliation of its opponents. It contributed in theology, political
theory, and law to the intellectual outpouring of the twelfth
century. But its triumph was not immaculate. In the wake of

its glory it left a schism with the Eastern Church that has endured nine hundred years, a politically disrupted Germany, and a rising crop of princes and kings who, when their power at last permitted, brought the papacy as low as it had brought the empire.

The success of the papacy in establishing an ecclesiastical monarchy increased the rigidity of the Church, though it did protect it from the national control that has characterized both the Protestant and Eastern Orthodox Churches of Europe. The pope's position as arbiter of justice for all society did not long go unquestioned. Nations, councils, and individual consciences all eventually arose to judge the pope and find him wanting.

The triumph of the papacy seemed to many even in the Middle Ages not wholly consistent with the Kingdom of God. As Saint Bernard observed,

> What slavery can be more degrading and more unworthy of the Sovereign Pontiff than to be kept thus busily employed, I do not say every day, but every hour of the day, in furthering the sordid designs of greed and ambition? What leisure hast thou left for prayer? What time remains over to thee for instructing the people, for edifying the Church, for meditating upon the law? True, thy palace is made to resound daily with noisy discussions relating to law, but it is not the law of the Lord, but the law of Justinian.[13]

> (Religions may say) *yes* to society both by affirming it as a part of the divine order of creation and by striving to reconstruct and unify it in its own spirit. But it cannot stop at this point. It must go on to say *no* as well. While society is to be affirmed as part of the divine order of creation, no *particular* social order or social institution can be so affirmed.[14]

NOTES

[1] Humbert of Silva Candida, *The Three Books against the Simoniacs*, trans. Brian Tierney, *The Crisis of Church and State 1050–1300*. © 1964, Reprinted by permission of Prentice-Hall, Inc. (Englewood Cliffs), p. 40.

[2] *Oxford Book of Medieval Latin Verse* (Oxford, 1959), p. 285.

[3] Trans. S. Z. Ehler and J. B. Morrall, *Church and State throughout the Centuries* (London, 1954), pp. 43–44.

[4] *Life of Henry IV* in Theodore E. Mommsen and Karl F. Morrison, *Imperial Lives and Letters of the Eleventh Century* (New York, Columbia University Press, 1962).

[5] Mommsen and Morrison, p. 141.

[6] Mommsen and Morrison, p. 151.

[7] Letter of Gregory VII to the German princes in Ephraim Emerton, *The Correspondence of Pope Gregory VII. Selected Letters from the Registrum* (New York, 1932), pp. 111–112.

[8] Mommsen and Morrison, pp. 191–195.

[9] David C. Douglas and G. W. Greenaway, *English Historical Documents* (London, Eyre and Spottiswoode, 1953), p. 666.

[10] Douglas and Greenaway, pp. 743–744.

[11] Edward Grim, in Douglas and Greenaway, pp. 763, 768.

[12] T. S. Eliot, *Murder in the Cathedral*, in *The Complete Poems and Plays*, New York, Harcourt Brace and Co., 1952, p. 187.

[13] Bernard, *On Consideration*, trans. Tierney, *Crisis of Church and State*, p. 92.

[14] Will Herberg, *Judaism and Modern Man* (New York, Farrar, Straus, and Giroux, Inc., 1951), p. 139.

Chapter Sixteen

NEW EXPRESSIONS OF SPIRITUALITY

THE reform spirit of the early Middle Ages persisted into the central and even the later Middle Ages, for the need, and the ability, of the Church to reform itself was perennial. Much of that spirit had been diverted by the papal revolution into a political program. With the success of that revolution, the Church became more efficient and better organized, as well as more moral. But there was a Christian spirit that could not find satisfaction in efficiency and organization. This spirit, stemming from the ancient ascetic and prophetic traditions of Christianity, was less interested in the papal program of establishing a Christian order in society than in the question of how the individual in society could best escape the demands of this world in order better to live in God's. It was a manifestation of the world-rejecting elements in Christianity; it was also the result of a recognition that, as the power of the papacy and the hierarchy increased, new worldliness was coming into the Church. The papalists had argued that once lay influence were removed, the Church would return to its pristine purity, but they did not reckon upon the effects of power. As long as churchmen held great temporal power, for whatever expressed purposes, that temporal power would tend to corrupt or at least to distract. Hence the new spirituality sought new channels of development outside the ordinary organization of the Church. The Church proved flexible enough to absorb some, but not all, of these new expressions.

Thus the religion of the central and later Middle Ages was on the one hand more tightly organized and more hierarchical than before, but on the other hand productive of greater personal piety, humanity, and devotion to the Bible—heralds of

Reformation spirituality. Much of the reason for these changes was the increasing complexity, stability, and cultural productivity of the central Middle Ages, which altered the challenge that was offered the Christian life. The crudity and ignorance, and the intervention of the laity, that had characterized the early medieval Church had in some measure been vanquished. Now the problem was not how to create a purer and more stable Church, but how best to live a Christian life within the Church. Greater literacy and wiser understanding of the Bible and the Fathers encouraged the search for purity; the advance of philosophical understanding encouraged the asking of more questions; the revival of cities posed new social problems. The greater complexity of central medieval society produced a greater variety of religious experience.

The result of these new demands was to produce new varieties of monasticism, of popular piety, and of popular heresy. Through this diversity of religious expression, there is a certain continuity, consisting of the combination of the reform spirit with a particular emphasis upon the search for a purer and more intense personal religion.

THE sources are numerous and full, making the historian's task at once difficult and rewarding. In the last half-century especially, so much critical work has been done on the sources relating to monasticism and heresy that new interpretations have become possible. For monasticism there are the Rules of the new orders, the papal registers and archives, conciliar decrees, and a quantity of treatises and *Lives*. The lives of Saint Francis by Thomas of Celano and of Saint Anselm by Eadmer, the pious *Little Flowers of Saint Francis,* the correspondence of Saint Bernard and of Abbot Peter the Venerable of Cluny, the chronicles of Orderic Vitalis and William of Malmesbury, are only examples. There are many archives, which have barely begun to be exploited. For the history of heresy the situation is similar. Most of the information we have about the heretics comes from the pens of their enemies, but some Valdesian (Waldensian) and Catharist tracts have been discovered. To the long-known writings of Bernard Gui, Ermengaud of Béziers, Eckbert of Schönau, Peter the Venerable, and Saint Bernard against the heretics can be added much material discovered in the last two decades.

THE development of medieval monasticism, though continuous, passed through a number of stages. The first was a movement of monastic asceticism in the early eleventh century of which Saint Peter Damian was one of the leaders. The second began towards the end of that century following a crisis in Benedictine monasticism. The third, beginning at the end of the eleventh century and culminating in the thirteenth, was characterized by a rise of popular lay piety and of religious movements oriented towards the laity.

The crisis of monasticism in the later eleventh century sprang in part from the triumph of politics in the Church under the successful papacy; and in part it arose from the failure of the earlier reforms to resist the inevitable tendency to decay. The most important reason for the crisis, however, was the change in the rôle that monasteries as a whole were able to play in Christian society. The Benedictine monasteries had been centers of order and culture. Now the rise of the papacy, the bishops, the kings, and the towns rendered this function obsolete. Education was now centered in the bishops' schools rather than in the monasteries. Even such artistic work as manuscript illumination, hitherto the sole province of the monks, passed in the thirteenth century into secular workshops as well, such as that of Master Honoré in Paris. Towns, kings, and bishops now assured a degree of order in society that made the monasteries' role as oases of culture obsolete. The new orders replaced the spirit of power with the spirit of prophecy. Like the ancient prophets of Israel or those of the early Church, they stood apart from, yet concerned with, both secular and ecclesiastical society and bore witness to the Kingdom of God. They expressed the cry of the alien, transcendent God to a society perhaps too well organized under papal theocracy. The historian will not be surprised to see monk and Reformist heretic taking similar stances: both rejected the status quo and demanded that society be subjected to the judgment of God.

THE most influential of the new orders was the Cistercian. The "white monks," contrasted by the color of their habits with the Benedictine "black monks," were founded at the end of the eleventh century, during the period when the papacy was beginning to win its battle with the empire. "In his (Urban II's) time began the Cistercian order, which is now both believed and asserted to be the surest road to heaven," said William of Malmesbury,[1] and such indeed was their reputation.

About 1075 a group of monks settled at Molesme in northern Burgundy under the leadership of one Robert, who had been a Benedictine abbot. There they established an ideal Benedictine monastery; but its success, like that of Cluny, proved its downfall. It was not long before pious laymen began to patronize Molesme, and soon it found itself becoming wealthy. With those of his followers who could withstand the insidious attractions of ease, Robert fled in 1097 or 1098 to Cîteaux to try again. Quarrels with Molesme, sickness, and hard winters would have reduced the little community of Cîteaux almost to extinction but for the exertions of two extraordinary men.

The first was Saint Stephen Harding, third abbot of Cîteaux. Stephen drew up the *Charter of Love,* a Rule for the house that amounted to an adoption of the spirit of Saint Benedict's Rule without any concession whatever to comfort or condition. The Cistercians emphasized manual labor instead of scholarship and constant private prayer rather than an elaborate liturgy. They chose the most desolate spots for their houses, which they constructed themselves. They received no tithes, no gifts, and no lay patronage. They kept no servants and, proclaiming that "to work is to pray," took upon themselves farming, baking, weaving, carpentry, and all the other tasks of life. They kept no ornaments in their churches and no treasures: for them a simple carven crucifix was better than one ornately encrusted with precious stones. The Cistercians kept no personal possessions whatsoever.

The Cistercians slept together wholly clothed on straw sacks in a great dormitory. They were allowed seven hours sleep in winter and six in summer. Like the Benedictines, they gathered for the communal prayers of the Office, though in a simple fashion. The rest of the day was occupied with manual labor, meditation, reading and copying, the chapter where faults were confessed, and daily mass. There was one meal a day in summer and two in winter. They ate vegetables, a little fish and cheese, and bread and water. Even in the most unhospitable climates a fire was allowed only once a year at Christmas. It is no wonder that one medieval chronicler breaks off his account with the

A monastery dormitory (Cleeve Abbey in Somerset)

remark that his hands are too stiff with cold to hold his pen any longer. Always, before and after dinner and through the day, most of the monks' time was taken up with manual chores round the house.

This strict Rule had a phenomenal success. Hundreds of Cistercian houses occupied by thousands of monks had been established by the end of the twelfth century, it being remarked that "Everything is becoming Cistercian." Clearly the strictness and asceticism of Cîteaux appealed to a society whose sacred view of the world was intact and which wanted to fix its attention upon the world of God.

The second great Cistercian was Saint Bernard, whose arrival in the hard winter of 1112 with thirty other novices gave Cîteaux a new lease on life. Bernard, like so many of the monastic leaders, came from a wealthy family. Perceiving the discrepancy between his way of life and the Gospel, he determined to be a monk. Few preachers have had as compelling a charisma as Bernard. The story is that he persuaded three of his brothers, including one who was married, to accompany him to the monastery, while the fourth and youngest, left to inherit all the family fortune, bitterly complained: "What, earth for me and heaven for you! It is not a fair bargain." It may be an exaggeration that mothers hid their sons and wives their husbands when Bernard came by fishing for the souls of men, but his influence throughout Europe was vast.

In no one individual is the function of the monk as prophet so visible as in Bernard. He was the Jeremiah of the twelfth century. To mortify himself he could drink oil instead of water and when friends came to visit stop his ears with wax. He is said to have traveled all day along the shores of the Lake of Geneva amidst mountains, streams, and flowers without noticing his surroundings at all. He reproved his fellows for laughing and advised the use of self-discipline (i.e., the whip). It comes as something of a relief to learn that he was once rebuked by Stephen Harding for neglecting his evening prayers.

At twenty-five, Bernard found the life at Cîteaux too luxurious and went off with a few disciples to the Vale of Wormwood, where he founded the monastery of Clairvaux. Before his death he had personally established twenty-five Cistercian houses. With his noble connections, his influence extended far beyond the order. He persuaded the king of France to accept Pope Innocent II during a schism. He preached the Second Crusade. He smote Abelard with terrible wrath. He toured southern France preaching and debating heretics. He acted as the conscience of Europe. To Suger, the great and powerful abbot of Saint-Denis, Bernard wrote: "Two unheard-of and detestable improprieties have arisen in the Church lately. If you will pardon my saying so, one of these is the impropriety of your way of life." To another of Louis VI's most powerful ministers he did not hesitate to say: "Who would not be indignant that (such a) man should against the Gospel serve God as a deacon and Mammon as a minister of state. . . ."[2]

Saint Bernard would not have been a comfortable table companion, yet the intensity of the man was the result, not of lust for power or of cruelty, but of a burning love that left him no peace and permitted him to leave none to others. "O Love," wrote the saint, "headlong, vehement, burning, impetuous, that

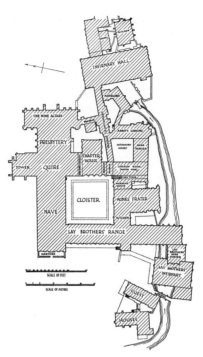

Plan of an abbey: Fountains, near York.

canst think of nothing beyond thyself, detesting all else, despising all else, satisfied with thyself! Thou dost confound ranks, carest for no usage, knowest no measure. In thyself dost thou triumph over apparent opportuneness, reason, shame, council, and judgment, and leadest them on to captivity."

The Cistercian order enjoyed enormous success owing to the fame of men like Bernard and to their reputation for holiness and zeal in a generation of great popular enthusiasm and zeal. Yet by the end of the twelfth century the Cistercians were already lax and ineffective, and Cistercian preachers in the south of France were losing converts to the heretics by reason of their openly disreputable lives. It was in part the Cistercians' very success that proved their undoing. Their wealth and influence tended to a corruption that affected them even more rapidly than it had the Cluniacs. They became as well known for their efficient management of agricultural lands, which they cleared and tilled to great advantage, as for their spiritual life. Nor was the adoption of the Cistercian Rule by some of the new military orders a good omen for an order dedicated to the cause of the Prince of Peace. The order has since undergone several reformations, and today the Cistercian Trappists represent in their many houses in Europe and America a close approximation of the original strictness of the order.

Some orders, notably the Carthusian, were far stricter than that of Cîteaux. This order was founded about 1084–1088 at the isolated site of the Grande Chartreuse near Grenoble by Saint Bruno of Cologne. The tradition was that of Saint Peter Damian carried to the extreme. Practicing extreme asceticism, the Carthusians dwelt in separate cells and meditated individually. They saw their fellows only once a week, on Sunday, when they met for mass and for a period of brief conversation wholly upon spiritual matters. The rigors of the order excluded all but the most devoted, and it is with justice that the Carthusians claim that their order "was never reformed, because it was never deformed."

But the great day of the cloistered monasteries was drawing to a close. Society was more settled than it had been, and the quiet and repose of the cloister seemed less unusual, and therefore less desirable, than it once had. Towns and cities were growing rapidly, offering their own attractions to the capable, and a new challenge to the Church. The inadequacies of the parish system in the cities combined with the growing worldliness of city life meant that a rapidly growing segment of the population was quite unaffected by monasticism and increasingly indifferent to religion in its conventional forms.

Some clergymen recognized the need to bring the new spirituality into the world and struck upon a device that would permit them to work in the world but at the same time to live under a strong spiritual rule. The idea went back to Saint Augustine, who as bishop of Hippo had gathered his clergy round him under a semimonastic rule. During the conversion of northern Europe it was usual for clerks to live together with their bishops in "cathedral chapters," where they bore the name of "canons." Gradually the parish system replaced that by which the whole diocesan clergy lived at the cathedral, and those who remained at the cathedral often became lax. In the eighth century Chrodegang of Metz and other bishops imposed order upon their chapters by placing them under a modified version of the Benedictine rule, and it also became common for parish churches to be "collegiate," that is, to be staffed by a collection (*collegium*) of clergy living under some sort of rule.

But these arrangements were not standardized and were open to abuse. From the early twelfth century the new spirituality encouraged efforts to bring under a strict rule all clergy who were living together. To fill this need *orders* of canons were established. The Premonstratensians, or "white canons," founded by Saint Norbert of Xanten (d. 1134), had a Rule resembling the Cistercian; the Augustinian or Austin canons used the Rule of Saint Augustine. The canons fasted, practiced poverty, and in general followed as much of the monastic rule as was consonant with their duties of teaching and preaching in the world.

At the beginning of the thirteenth century the older orders of canons had generally become lax, and their place was taken by the friars (*frères*). The friars lived under an ascetic rule while fulfilling the role of prophets and inspiring religious devotion in all of society. The friars preferred the active life, and they functioned to special advantage in the cities and towns. There, where the more conventional kinds of religious teaching were often ineffective, the friars preached in the parishes and in the squares and taught in the schools, eventually coming for a time to dominate many of the universities.

The Franciscan friars take their name from Saint Francis of Assisi (1182–1226). Francis was brought up to a life of luxury, parties, and polite culture. He came to love the splendors of the world and as a young squire dreamt of a life of military glory and renown. It is this perhaps that makes Francis so attractive: his exuberant love for the world in a worldly sense made his love of the world in a spiritual sense so much the stronger. As a youth Francis composed love poetry in the style of the Provençal troubadours, and poetry remained with him after his conversion:

Praised be my Lord God with all His creatures, and especially our brother the sun, who brings us the day and who brings us the light; fair is he and shines with very great splendor; O Lord, he sig-

Saint Francis preaching to the birds; fresco by Giotto in the Upper Church of Saint Francis, Assisi.

nifies to us Thee! Praised be my Lord for our sister the moon, and for the stars, the which He has set clear and lovely in heaven.[3]

Few men have expressed the sacred view of the world in word and life as eloquently as Saint Francis. Everything in the world was a living comrade. Many sources report Francis' sermon to the birds, but none so well as Thomas of Celano, his biographer:

Francis the most blessed servant of God left his companions in the way and ran eagerly to the birds. When he was come close to them and saw that they were awaiting him, he gave them his accustomed greeting. But, not a little surprised that the birds did not fly away (as they are wont to do) he was filled with exceeding joy and humbly begged them to hear the word of God (saying:) "My brother birds, much ought ye to praise your Creator, and ever to love Him. . . ." And then he went to and fro amidst them, touching their heads and bodies with his tunic. . . .

(Francis) used to pick . . . up (worms) in the way and put them in a safe place, that they might not be crushed by the feet of passers-by. What shall I say of other lower creatures, when in winter he would cause honey or the best wine to be provided for bees, that they might not perish from cold?[4]

Francis' father, who wished him to be a knight or at least to follow him in his trade, was displeased with his son's spiritual interests, and by the expenditure of his goods: Francis distributed them gratuitously among the poor. In a terrible scene at the bishop's court, Pietro Bernardone renounced his son and demanded the return of all his goods, whereupon Francis disrobed and would have left the court naked had the bishop not given him a coat. Later he took a ragged cloak and a rope belt from a scarecrow (whence the habit of the order) and tramped round the countryside with a few followers begging from the rich, giving what he could to the poor, and preaching. In 1210 Francis obtained from Pope Innocent III the right to organize a Rule devoted to apostolic poverty, and he called his associates in "holy poverty" the *fratres minores* or "little brothers." In 1223, against Francis' opposition, Honorius III provided the order with an elaborate organization. Towards the end of his life Francis' relationship with the Lord grew ever closer as that of his order grew weaker; he received the stigmata, and in his last hour he awaited his "Brother Death" in glad submission.

It was inevitable that the order founded by the apostle of poverty should have retreated from his principles. The Franciscans grew wealthy and powerful in government and in the universities. Though Francis had left a will asking that no one should change his rules binding the order to poverty, Pope Gregory IX declared only four years after his death that the will was not binding. The Spiritual Franciscans or *Fraticelli,* that segment of the order that insisted upon keeping the founder's Rule, was for a long time subject to persecution and not

Innocent III approves the Franciscan rule; fresco by Giotto in the Upper Church of Saint Francis, Assisi.

surprisingly became associated with several heretical movements.

THE second great order of friars was founded by Saint Dominic (1170–1223), a serious and studious Castilian who had come to the south of France to preach against the Albigensians and had been horrified by the laxity of the Cistercians and other Catholic preachers. The Dominican Rule, while resembling Francis' in many respects, emphasized poverty less than it did the friars' vocation to preach and teach. Hence the Dominicans' official title was the Order of Preachers. "The bow is bent by study,

Saint Dominic; fresco by Fra Angelico.

the arrow loosed by preaching," they said, and the Dominicans were among the leaders of the intellectual life of the central Middle Ages: Thomas Aquinas was a Dominican, and Dominicans were on the faculties of most of the European universities. Only in one respect was their vocation for preaching unfortunate: their vigorous pursuit of heretics led them to participate in the Inquisition. Like the other orders, the Dominicans quickly deviated from their original strictness and suffered many scandals even before the end of the thirteenth century.

PIETY was manifested not only by the monks but by the laity as well. Nobles constructed chapels and patronized monasteries, peasants gave tithes with surprisingly little complaint, and merchants paid God whatever they thought he required on account. The rush of piety touched all classes.

Many common religious attitudes were identical with those of the earlier Middle Ages. The practice of magic continued. It was believed that the presence of spirits good and bad was immediate. God intervened in lawsuits, saints wrought miracles in bewildering profusion, and demons lurked in wait for the unwary. If anything, the cult of relics increased. Every church needed, and every individual desired, some portion of the physical remains of a holy person. It was not surprising, though it was resented, that Saint Hugh, while visiting a church that possessed a relic of Saint Mary Magdalene, was covetous enough to bite off a piece of her bone with his teeth. It was commonly believed that the saints in some way inhabited churches dedicated to them. It was also common for more veneration to be paid the images of saints than was in strict accordance with the canons.

With the eleventh and twelfth centuries subtle changes in religious attitudes occurred, some of them apparently contradictory. The decline of the mass as the center of Christian worship and the increasing distance between clergy and laity explain the increase of external pieties like the use of the rosary. It also encouraged the growth of individuality in religion, encouraging both private devotions and heresy. Vernacular books of devotion and "books of hours" added to this tendency.

Just at the time the papacy was engaged in building a *societas christiana* religious consciences were turned less toward the community and more toward the individual. Yet this was the age of great cathedral building, a phenomenon that can be ascribed partly to increasing wealth, partly to the pride and ambition of architects, and partly to the expression of a common faith or at least a common spirit of community in the cities. And it was also the age when feudal institutions were blended with religious in the chivalric code that made of every knight a "knight of Christ" with a semi-religious function. The Crusades carried this conception of knighthood to its height.

On the one hand, the ideas of death and last judgment seemed to play a greater rôle than before, these fears of the very last day becoming grotesquely exaggerated in the fourteenth and fifteenth centuries.

On the other hand, there was a searching for greater humanity in religion. The images of Christ the king, Christ the creator, yield to Christ the suffering man, Christ the son of Mary. The attitude of the Savior on crucifixes changes from one of superhuman impassivity to one of real suffering. The age wished to restore to Christ his human nature. To some extent this was no longer possible: he was after all God and too thoroughly hierocratized. Personal piety toward Christ was growing but would not reach its height until the Reformation. And so the twelfth and thirteenth centuries found partial consolation in a growing veneration for saints, especially for certain favorites like Saint James of Compostella and Saint Thomas of Canterbury, and of course the Virgin Mary.

Around the Virgin a great cult developed. Her miracles were innumerable; churches sprang up in her name all over Europe, and most of the great new cathedrals were dedicated to Our Lady. Veneration of the Virgin ranged from the crudest superstition through pleasant sentimentalism, as in the story of the Juggler who wins the favor of Our Lady by performing his act before her image, through theological sophistication, to the delicate and superb expressions of Notre Dame de la Belle Verrière at Chartres and of the great hymn *Stabat Mater*. The cult of Mary the advocate of sinners is a phenomenon by no means limited to the Middle Ages, let alone to the twelfth and thirteenth centuries, but it was then that it achieved its most beautiful utterance.

One of the most consequential of the manifestations of piety was the pilgrimage. Pilgrimages had been made to Rome as early as the sixth century, but about the year 1000 they multiplied enormously. Where formerly a few had gone, now thousands set out, and not only for Rome, but for Canterbury, Compostella, and even Jerusalem itself. As Chaucer wrote in the fourteenth century:

> Thanne longen folk to goon on pilgrimages
> And palmeres for to seken straunge strondes,
> To ferne holwes kowthe in sondry londes. . . .

The pilgrimages opened roads to the Near East, bringing about a resumption of commercial and intellectual intercourse, but also provoking the Crusades and increasing intolerance of Jews

Duccio's Mother and Child, *at Siena. The cult of the Virgin places her at the center of a throng of adoring saints. It is she who sustains and supports her divine child.*

and heretics at home. In themselves, however, there is no better indication of the fervent spirit of the time than this willingness on the part of rich and poor to undertake a journey from, say, Cologne to Jerusalem and back, a journey that took an enormous amount of time and offered severe discomfort and frequent danger.

Popular enthusiasm expressed itself in a variety of ways. It is natural that some of these would prove unacceptable to the authorities and be branded as heresy.

The first important tradition of heresy in the later Middle Ages is a direct descendant of the Reformism typical of the earlier period. Reformist heresy, which grew from the eighth century along with movements of orthodox reform, demanded a return to the spirit of individual prophecy and rejected the efforts of the organized Church to build a Christian order. Like the monastic revival, this heresy was an expression of concern for the renovation of the individual in the face of a reform movement gone political. The largest of these Reformist groups was that founded by Valdes,[5] who began as a simple reformer seeking Christian perfection in the strictest observation of the most austere counsels of the gospels. Valdes was a well-to-do citizen of Lyon who, moved by the miseries of a famine, began by helping the poor and ended by giving all of his money away. There is little that differentiates his origins or motives from those of Saint Francis, and it was luck more than anything else that made of one a revered saint and of the other a heretic.

Valdes put the Scriptures into the vernacular and, together with some friends, began to preach the gospel. The bishop forbade them to preach on the grounds they had not the proper training. Valdes took his case to the third Lateran Council in 1179. He might have had some success there, as Francis was to have at Rome thirty years later when Innocent III approved his Rule, had it not been for Walter Map, an English prelate well known at home for his sharp tongue, who could not resist the opportunity of showing off his wit to the assembly by ridiculing the theologically unastute Valdes. Valdes returned to Lyon with the laughter of the bishops ringing in his ears. He returned to his preaching and went on to commit the monstrous atrocity of allowing women to preach as well. The bishop of Lyon hastened to expel Valdes and his followers from the diocese. The Valdesians now took to wandering and begging in the name of Christ and the "Poor People of Lyon." In the meanwhile Valdes remained theologically orthodox, and when he was condemned by Pope Lucius III in 1184 it was only in disciplinary terms. But even this mild reproof was enough to end Valdes' restraint. He now turned to attacking the organized Church, arguing that the clergy and sacraments were unnecessary and insisting that personal devotion to Christ was sufficient to salvation. The Valdesian (Waldensian) Church has persisted without a break into the present.

Reformism had many permutations. It became connected with Joachim of Flora's millennarianism, a belief that this world would shortly end and be replaced by a thousand-year reign of the Holy Spirit. It became connected with the pantheism of Amalric of Bena, who taught that all things are God. Eventually it underwent some strange sea-changes. The Brethren of the Free Spirit added Amalrician pantheism to the doctrine of internal illumination by the Holy Spirit and turned it into a kind of antinomianism, adjuring that "Whatever the eye sees and covets, let the hand grasp it." If, after all, the Holy Spirit is acting for me, they argued, I can do no wrong. Mixed with magic and occultism, such ideas eventually ended up with the

*Preaching in the countryside; this open-air evangelism was practised
by both the friars and the heretics.*

Luciferans, who held the convenient doctrine that whatever
they did when they went below ground into cellars or caves was
legitimate. The Luciferans also invented the most unusual line
ever handed the ladies: they claimed that a woman could restore her virginity by sleeping with one of their sect.

The second important element of later medieval heresy
was Catharism, an eastern dualist belief imported into the West
in the 1140s by Bulgarian missionaries. Rooted in ancient gnosticism, related to Manichaeism, and transferred through Asia
Minor into the Balkans and eventually into the West, Catharism
taught that there are two opposing forces in the world, one good
and one evil. Whether or not the power of evil was independent
of the good God or was one of his fallen angels was debated,
but in either event it was the evil spirit, rather than the good
God, who created the world. The world, having entrapped spirit
in matter, was evil. Man was in a difficult position: his soul
was spiritual and therefore good; he must seek to liberate it
from the flesh as effectively as he could. By living the proper
life (that is, by becoming a Catharist), one could escape the
flesh; otherwise the spirit might be doomed to reincarnation.
From this doctrine the Catharists derived a fanatical puritanism,
which seems to have been practised at least by the leaders, if
not by all the believers, of the cult.

The heresy spread rapidly through Europe and gained

enormous strength in northern Italy and southern France, where it was called Albigensianism, affecting all levels of society from the count of Toulouse to the peasants. That Catharism caught on so quickly can only be explained by the fact that Europe had been prepared for it by the puritanical aspects of reform in general and of Reformist heresy in particular. The doctrines of the Reformist heretics were marked by an exaggeration of elements latent in orthodox Christianity, and their puritanism blended easily with that of the Catharists. It is clear, for example, that at Cologne in the 1140s and 1150s an existing Reformist sect was gradually infiltrated and eventually taken over by Catharists.

Religious disaffection found other expressions, some even more extreme than the Catharist, others much less serious. Secularism was increasing, the clergy was held up to not wholly good-natured mockery in many popular stories and satires, and the doctrines of courtly love made one's lady, rather than God, the object of one's ultimate concern. Witchcraft began to be both widely practiced and widely prosecuted from at least the fourteenth century.

Most serious in its implications for society was the increasing connection between religious and social unrest. From the twelfth century onwards, heretical doctrines were used as weapons with which citizens attacked episcopal control over cities and with which the lower urban classes attacked the upper. The praise bestowed upon poverty by the heretical Reformists made their doctrines attractive to the poor, and the heretical movements of the late Middle Ages—the Lollards in England, for example—are largely peasants' and laborers' movements. Marxist historians have belabored the point, but they have a good case when they argue that much of the religious discontent of the later Middle Ages was really economic discontent expressed in religious terms because people were used to thinking of salvation's coming from another world.

The medieval heretics, particularly the Valdesians, have been called precursors of the Reformation, but this is only partly so. Catharism persisted into the fourteenth century, but it had been badly broken in the thirteenth by the Albigensian Crusade; and the Valdesians were driven into their Alpine fastnesses. It is even difficult to show a direct connection between the fifteenth-century Lollards and the English Reformation. The Protestants of the Reformation were like the Valdesians and the Reformists of the early Middle Ages, not because Luther and Calvin learned from Valdes, but because in similar situations they made similar responses and used the same weapons: the Bible, the ideal of primitive Christianity, and a zeal for reform. Even if doctrines did not linger, disaffection must have, for one curious fact is that a map showing the centers of Calvinism in Reformation France looks very much like one showing the centers of twelfth-century Catharism.

All of these spiritual activities and debates show that medieval society and its sacred view of the world were still healthy. The increased complexity of society engendered increasing varieties of religious experience and of cultural expression.

NOTES

[1] *Chronicle,* trans. J. A. Giles (London, 1847), Bk. iv, ch. 1, 347.
[2] *The Letters of Saint Bernard of Clairvaux,* ed. and trans. Bruno Scott James (London, Burns and Oates, 1953), pp. 110–118.
[3] "The Song of the Creatures," trans. Matthew Arnold.
[4] Thomas of Celano in Bryce Lyon, *The High Middle Ages* (Glencoe, The Free Press, A Division of the Macmillan Company, 1964), pp. 155, 159.
[5] Erroneously called "Peter Waldo."

Chapter Seventeen

THE GREAT CULTURAL ADVANCE

THE eleventh and twelfth centuries were centuries of great achievement and change, not only in society and in the Church, but also in philosophy, law, education, and the arts. Daring cultural originality in counterpoint to tradition made this period as much a watershed in the history of European culture as the later and more famous "Renaissance."

For forty years it has been common to speak of a "renaissance of the twelfth century," and some scholars have pushed this "renaissance" as far back as the eighth. There is now a tendency for the sake of convenience to reserve the term for the period to which it was originally applied. "Renaissance" is not a good historical term, since it implies death and rebirth and great cataclysmic changes. There are few abysses or chasms in history; there are merely times when cultural change takes place more quickly and vigorously than at others. In the Middle Ages, the eighth and ninth centuries were such a time; so were the eleventh and twelfth. The quickness of cultural change in the fourteenth and fifteenth centuries was such that we designate them "The Renaissance," the transition from medieval to modern civilization.

The acceleration of cultural advance in the eleventh and twelfth centuries is bound to changes in society as a whole. The increasing complexity of economy, social structure, and politics evoked new questions and rendered old answers inadequate. A new understanding of law, government, and society was required. Philosophical and theological doctrines had to be restated in language that was meaningful to the new era. Literacy was increasing, and the growth of the cities facilitated patronage of the arts and education. The deep change in both the practice and theory of Christian society brought about by the papal revolution required, and the new monasticism and the influence of popular enthusiasm and piety invited, correspondingly deep changes in modes of thought. The great cultural advance of the eleventh and twelfth centuries was both fulfillment and transformation of the past. It was a product of the great movement of reform that, beginning in the eighth century, encouraged political, moral, and intellectual change. It was also a motor of change itself.

The basic motor of the intellectual movement was the urge to use and to assimilate the classics, and then to turn them into the vehicle of a new synthesis. In the eighth century the study of the classics had been revived for the pragmatic purposes of building a more moral society and a more efficient government. In the tenth and early eleventh centuries a humanistic interest in the classics for their own sake flourished. In the latter eleventh century began a period of assimilation that culminated in the work of the great scholastics of the thirteenth. This process of assimilation was characterized by an effort to synthesize Christian tradition with the classics and particularly with the newly discovered works of Aristotle and others that were now imported from the Arabs and translated into Latin. Beginning in the twelfth century the fascination with grammar and classical scholarship in and of itself began to fade, to be replaced with the growing concern with dialectic (the study of logic) in the form of scholasticism, which came to dominate theology, philosophy, and science. Men were no longer content to quote classical tags. They achieved a new self-confidence, using their own reason vigorously to weld a synthesis of the old with the new.

Yet this new self-confidence was limited. It pressed and extended, but did not burst, the boundaries of tradition. The traditions of the Church still seemed the only hope and guarantee of social and intellectual order. Like most social revolts of the time, most intellectual efforts were norm-oriented, not value-oriented: they sought means of expression making the old values meaningful, not tools with which to build new ones. The fourteenth and fifteenth centuries, although no more vigorous than the twelfth, were more radical. It is for this reason that their claim to be the ushers of a new age is well justified. The spirit of scholasticism, on the other hand, was a spirit of *organization,* drawing all elements together for a final synthesis. Thomas Aquinas and Dante were the crowns of their age, the highest monuments atop a tradition hundreds of years old. But the tradition would be changed when men glimpsed the possibilities of other social and intellectual orders.

THE clearest indication of cultural change in the eleventh century was the shift from monastic to scholastic education. In the early Middle Ages education had been totally dominated by the monastic schools, which had preserved the writings and traditions of the ancients and taught the traditional, allusive, rambling, intuitive monastic theology. Now the monasteries ceased, because of the growing power and affluence of kings, towns, and bishops, to be the centers of society and its intellectual life. Too bound by tradition, they proved incapable for the most part of developing into the kind of school that could serve as the vehicle for the coming scholastic synthesis. That school would be episcopal, rather than monastic.

Episcopal schools had been founded from the time of Charlemagne, but from the end of the tenth century they began to grow in numbers and importance, led by the school of Chartres under Bishop Fulbert and that of Reims under Archbishop Gerbert. The episcopal schools profited both from the increasing importance of the bishops and from their location in the growing towns. By the mid-eleventh century they overshadowed the monastic schools. The cathedral schools, around which the new medieval universities were built, were the centers of the new philosophy known as scholasticism.

THE most startling changes of the eleventh and twelfth centuries were in philosophy, the result both of new materials and of new methods.

These new materials, consisting of lost Greek works and their commentaries, came for the most part from the Arabic. After the Moslems had conquered their great empire, they rapidly settled down to assimilating the cultures they had subdued, and from the eighth century their translators began putting Greek and Indian works into Arabic. The Greek culture they emulated was that of Alexandria rather than that of Athens: they sought mathematical, scientific, and philosophical treatises rather than literature. Having learned from the Greeks the value of reason, the Arab scholars attempted to apply it to Islamic revelation. Some of these scholars, the *mutakallimun*, accepted the primacy of Hellenistic reason; others, the *mutazilites*, were skeptical of Hellenism yet rationalized and allegorized the Qur'ān; both were opposed by the *sufis*, who rejected reason altogether and preached a mysticism based upon the principle that God was the only reality and that the world of the senses was meaningless.

These debates of Arab scholasticism began in the tenth century and lasted through the twelfth. Among the greatest Arab rationalists were al-Fārabi (d. 950), a physician and musician as well as a philosopher, whose commentaries upon Aristotle and Plato later had wide currency in the West; Ibn-Sīnā (Avicenna; d. 1037), a physician and proponent of the emanational metaphysics of neoplatonism; and Ibn-Rushd (Averroes; d. 1198). Averroes, who lived in the flourishing Moslem city of Córdoba, produced such profound and influential commentaries on Aristotle that he became known in the West as "The Commentator" par excellence, in the same way that Aristotle was called "The Philosopher." Averroes' doctrines, like emanationism or the eternity of the world, proved less acceptable and, together with the Aristotelian texts they accompained, were often banned by the Christian authorities.

The problems of Arab scholasticism were reflected by the Jewish scholastics in Spain, who could read Arabic. Solomon ibn-Gabirol and Moses Maimonides, influenced like the Arabs by Greek rationalism, attempted to reconcile Jewish revelation with reason.

The importance of the Jewish and Arab scholastics for the West is that they showed Christian philosophers that the use of reason was the way to reconcile discordant traditions. Once the materials were available in a language they could use, the Christians could create their own synthesis.

IT is one of the peculiarities of cultural history that the knowledge of Greek had been so lost in the West that Greek thought had to be reintroduced through the medium of translations from the Arabic. The process began in the twelfth century, chiefly in Spain and Sicily, where translators like Dominic Gundisalvi,

Adelard of Bath, Gerard of Cremona, and Herman the German gathered from all over Europe, impelled by the interests of humanism and science to obtain more of the classical materials they admired. Later, in the thirteenth century, when debates over the Arab commentaries grew heated, translations were undertaken directly from the Greek.

The bulk of these translations were made between 1125 and 1180, many others being added in the thirteenth century. Their effect was enormous. In science, the works of Archimedes, Euclid, Galen, and Ptolemy at last became fully known. In philosophy, the effect of the rediscovery of Aristotle's lost works was even more profound. In the early Middle Ages, only the treatises *On Interpretation* and *Categories* were known, as well as the *Introduction* to Aristotle by Porphyry and summaries of some of the advanced works made by Boëthius. These materials formed what was called the "old logic." Now in the twelfth century the rest of Aristotle's logic, "the new logic," and his scientific treatises, were added.

A Church accustomed to settling disputes by reference to ancient authority strained at swallowing the new knowledge: in 1215 the papal legate banned the study of Aristotle's metaphysics and science, contaminated as they were by Arab commentaries, from the University of Paris. The struggle between tradition and new knowledge was never resolved, for the incorporation of new ideas created a new tradition, which in turn resisted newer ideas.

New methods, as well as new materials, made the great intellectual advance possible. Partly under the influence of the new knowledge, partly because changes in society demanded a change in style, scholars deserted the allusive thought that had been typical of Augustine and took up the method of direct and logical exposition. This kind of thought had always been known, but as long as tradition was relatively undisturbed, its virtues were unapparent. Now that conflicts within tradition came to light, a method was needed to resolve them. The medieval desire for order could not tolerate intellectual pluralism or permit intellectually disparate ideas to remain discordant. It needed to restore harmony through the use of reason. The new method appears in the eleventh century in the works of Berengar of Tours and Saint Anselm, and it was perfected from the time of Abelard in the twelfth. The scholastic method, in the mature form used by Aquinas, proceeded by raising questions in logical order. Each question was stated, the objections set forth, and the authorities quoted. Reason was then brought in to resolve the question, and refutation of the objections followed. Then the next question in logical order was raised.

We are today so accustomed to the belief that experience is a better guide than pure reason that we find the enthusiasm with which the new method was propagated difficult to understand. But the self-confident use of reason untrammeled by tradition was a heady new drink in the eleventh and twelfth centuries. It produced scholastic theology and philosophy.

SCHOLASTICISM broadly defined is the theology and philosophy taught in the schools from the eleventh into the fourteenth century. There was the mystical scholasticism of Bernard and Bonaventure; there was the empirical scholasticism of the Franciscans, particularly Grosseteste and Bacon; and there was the rational scholasticism of Abelard and Aquinas. There was no essential difference between scholastic philosophy and scholastic theology, the purpose of both being to find out about the world and man the better to understand God. The rational scholastics, like their Jewish and Arab colleagues, sought by means of reason to reconcile Christian revelation with the new knowledge and to resolve conflicting positions within the Christian tradition.

THE preliminary problems of rational scholasticism were to reconcile faith with intellect, Plato with Aristotle, and traditional authority with new ideas by means of reason. Berengar of Tours and Abelard experienced difficulties with the authorities because of their insistence that a correctly guided reason should be allowed to lead where it willed even when it conflicted with tradition. Supporters of traditional authority like Peter Damian reacted to such ideas with horror, and Manegold of Lautenbach went so far as to say that a knowledge of philosophy was useless to the theologian. Even a moderate twelfth-century writer like John of Salisbury was mistrustful of the pure logic of the new philosophers: "They take refuge in subterfuge; they change front; they torture words; with tricks of magic they transform themselves until you marvel. . . ."[1] And to Saint Bernard the evil of the claims of reason lay not only in their frivolity but in their presumption. Saint Bernard believed in the virtues of humility, and to him Abelard, who "sees nothing through a glass darkly but stares at everything face to face" was a spiritually proud man. Yet Bernard himself was no dull conservative, for he made a great system of the Christian mysticism that had in the West previously existed only inchoate in the thought of Augustine and Anselm. Bernard and the School of Saint Victor were to the development of systematic mysticism what Anselm and Abelard were to that of logical scholasticism.

ABOVE the underlying problem of tradition and reason, the scholastics had to face the difficulties of dealing with new materials, methods, and vocabularies. They had to define Aristotelian terms and to resolve the problem of universals.

The problem of universals was fundamental. In the early Middle Ages Platonic idealism had always been taken for granted; there were ideas in God's mind of all things: of soul, honor, grace, tree, and chair. Now in the twelfth century idealism was challenged, and this was a radical and original departure. Defenders of the Platonic position were called "realists," because they affirmed the reality of universals, or ideas; its opponents were called "nominalists," because they maintained that the universals were only "names." The most extreme went so far as to insist that universals were only *flatus vocis,* hot air, as we should say; the moderates took a position like Abelard's conceptualism and held that the ideas were real in the human mind.

Once such preliminary problems had been aired, the scholastics could turn their attention to the high questions regarding God and man.

THE first of the great scholastics was Saint Anselm (1033–1109), abbot of Bec and then the archbishop of Canterbury who defied William II and Henry I. Anselm asserted that faith should precede understanding, but that understanding could in turn deepen faith through reason. In his *Proslogion* Anselm introduced the famous "ontological proof" of the existence of God, which is strictly speaking neither ontological nor a proof. It is not an *a posteriori* proof from the nature of the world, such as Aquinas would offer and such as Anselm himself offered in his *Monologium,* but a wholly *a priori* argument derived from within the mind. The argument runs: I can conceive of the greatest of all possible beings. But that being must exist objectively and not only within my mind, for if it existed only in my mind it would not be the greatest of all possible beings. Further, since being adds and non-being detracts, the greatest of all possible beings cannot even be conceived not to exist. Hence the greatest of all possible beings exists necessarily. The argument is both absurd and compelling. It was rejected, as soon as it appeared, by the monk Gaunilo, on the insufficient grounds that he could conceive of a perfect island. Gaunilo forgot that while perfection in islands does not entail existence, perfection in being does. Anselm's argument has been rejected by philosophers like Aquinas, Locke, and Kant, who insist, following Aristotle, that knowledge must come from without, but accepted by Bonaventure, Descartes, and Leibniz, who follow Plato in accepting knowledge from within. It has its defenders and its opponents today.

ABELARD (1079–1142), one of the most revolutionary figures of the age, was born in Brittany. He early left home to go and study with Roscelin, the leading nominalist philosopher, from whom he imbibed a skepticism in regard to the reality of Platonic ideas and a deep commitment to reason. From Roscelin he went to William of Champeaux, the leading realist, who was then lecturing in Paris. The young Abelard, whose brilliant mind had been stocked with Roscelin's best arguments against realism, contradicted William publicly and roundly defeated him in debate. The angry teacher drove his pupil out of Paris to Melun, only to find most of his other pupils deserting him to hear the upstart. In triumph Abelard returned to Paris where he taught at the School of Sainte-Geneviève; then he went to study with the old scholar Anselm of Laon, whom he ridiculed as a fusty old fool whose intellectual fires gave forth more smoke than light. Finally he returned again to Paris, having laid the foundations of his fame with his brilliance and having dug the pit of his ruin with his arrogance.

Resuming his studies at Paris, he became acquainted with a beautiful and intelligent young girl named Eloise, whom he determined to seduce. He accordingly offered to tutor the girl at her home in return for board and lodging from her uncle and guardian Fulbert. Abelard found Eloise a ready scholar and soon contrived to divert her attentions from philosophy to himself. Looking back upon the affair later, he felt some compunction for Eloise, more regrets for his own ruined career, and a considerable residue of pride at his way with women. For, he said, "so distinguished was my name, and I possessed the advantages of youth and comeliness, that no matter what woman I might favour with my love, I dreaded rejection of none. . . ." Eloise became pregnant, and Abelard went to make his complaints to Fulbert, reminding him that "from the beginning of the human race, women had cast down even the noblest men to utter ruin." Knowing that marriage would hinder his career in the Church, Abelard did not wish to enter into an open alliance with the girl, but he generously offered to marry her in secret. Fulbert agreed, but finding the arrangement an insufficient guard against the gossip of his neighbors, divulged the secret in order to preserve his own reputation. Eloise, always eager to protect Abelard, lied publicly and said that they had never married. Fulbert beat her and treated her so badly that Abelard had her placed in a convent. Believing, or affecting to believe, that Abelard meant to be rid of the girl forever, Fulbert now conceived of a more effective remedy for his dishonor, and with a band of his relations burst into Abelard's room one night and castrated him.[2]

Abelard now withdrew into the monastery of Saint Denis, where he infuriated the monks by proving that their patron saint, Denis (Dionysius), was not the same Dionysius whom Saint Paul had converted in Athens. In the meanwhile the Council of Soissons in 1121 condemned his teaching on the Trinity. He retreated to a hermitage, which his students helped him build, and eventually turned it over to Eloise as a convent. The letters of Eloise to Abelard all during the latter part of their life testify to her lasting love and devotion to him; his letters are kind but more distant and increasingly occupied with his own troubles, of which he had plenty. Returning to his native Brittany, he became abbot of the monastery of Saint Gildas, where the monks attempted to do away with him by poisoning the communion chalice. At last he came back to Paris, where he devoted himself to writing theology.

His vain and imperious personality meanwhile earned him even more enemies, and his theology was attacked by a number

Abelard and Eloise; from a carved capital in the Salle des Gardes
of the Conciergerie, Paris (fourteenth century).

of writers, particularly William of Saint Thierry and Saint Bernard. Letters condemning him as a heretic were circulated, and at last he was summoned before the Council of Sens in 1140. "Read, if you please," wrote Saint Bernard, "that book of Peter Abelard which he calls a book of Theology. . . . (Read his other books) and see how they too run riot with a whole crop of sacrileges and errors."[3] Bernard campaigned against Abelard in his best oratorical style, and the council ended by condemning certain propositions of Abelard's as heretical. Most of the propositions were scarcely unorthodox even in the view of the theology of the day, and it was clear that it was Abelard's personality and his devotion to reason, rather than any particular doctrine, which were under attack. In an access of humility, Abelard wrote to Eloise after the condemnation, "I will never be a philosopher if this is to speak against Saint Paul; I would not be an Aristotle, if this were to separate me from Christ." The next year he died at Cluny, the most brilliant, if not the most tactful, man of his generation.

It was Abelard's revolt from subservience to tradition and

his insistence upon the right of the philosopher to use his own reason that put him in the advance guard of scholasticism. In his *Sic et Non* (*Yes and No*), the book that caused the greatest stir, he showed that tradition and authority were insufficient in themselves by making a long list of questions (Is God omnipotent; do we sin without willing it; is God a substance; is faith based upon reason, etc.) and then quoting authorities on both sides of the question. Abelard left the contradictions unresolved in *Sic et Non,* though he pursued them farther elsewhere. His pupil Peter Lombard (1100–1160) used reason to arrive at the answers in his *Book of Sentences,* which became a textbook of theology in use for centuries. This would be the method of Thomas Aquinas as well; by then scholasticism had itself become a tradition.

Everywhere the need of the Middle Ages to bring order out of chaos appeared. Fortunately for them, in comparison with us, they had not only the need, but the ability, to do so. The scholastic method was popularized not only by Peter Lombard in theology, but by Gratian in canon law ["canon": a measure or rule, hence the law of the Church]. In his book (ca. 1140) *Concordia discordantium canonum,* otherwise known as the *Decretum,* Gratian stated authoritative propositions found in the canons. If a canon was not contradicted by any other, it was allowed to stand. If there were opposing statements, he attempted to reconcile them through logic, or to show that one or both had only limited application, or that one was an exception to the rule.

The development of canon law was strongly influenced by a similar growth of Roman law. Roman law had been in use through much of southern Europe throughout the Middle Ages. Its theory was taught at Ravenna continuously from Byzantine times. Yet until the eleventh century most of Europe was ignorant of both the theory and practice of Roman law, and even in the South lawyers' knowledge was derived from inferior compilations of the original codes. From the latter eleventh century, the application of new scholastic method and original thought to old texts like the *Digest* of Justinian, revived by the legal scholar Pepo at Bologna, brought a renewed study of Roman legal theory. Montpellier, Ravenna, Lombardy, and especially Bologna were the centers of this study. At Bologna, Irnerius and other "glossators," who used the scholastic method in studying Roman law, opposing differing authorities and then using logic to resolve the opposition. In northern France Placentinus, and in England Vacarius, introduced the ideas of the glossators. In the thirteenth and fourteenth centuries the "commentators," who commented on the glosses, replaced the glossators. The most famous of the commentators was Bartolus (1314–1357) whose intricacies of argument made him the prototype of the lawyer Bartolo in *The Marriage of Figaro*.

The influence of the study of Roman law was immense. Canon law was codified in the twelfth century along the lines of Roman law; and only canon and Roman law were taught at the universities until the nineteenth century, even in England, where Roman law had little relation to practice. Roman law reinforced its domination of southern Europe and slowly transformed northern France and Germany. The "Reception of Roman Law" by Germany occurred in 1495, and Roman law won its final triumph in France with the Revolution and the *Code Napoléon*.

Roman law had an important influence upon political theory in the central Middle Ages. Even when the particulars of Roman law were rejected, customary law was transposed into its terms. Hence in the northern French *coutumes de Beauvaisis* by Beaumanoir (1283), or the German *Sachsenspiegel* of the 1220s, or the *Treatise on the Laws and Customs of England* ascribed to Glanvill in the twelfth century, or Bracton's *Laws of England* in the next, Roman principles of systematic exposition were applied to the customary law.

NOT all of the brilliance of the twelfth century was expressed in incipient scholasticism. The humanistic traditions of the tenth century were continued into the eleventh and twelfth. But here too the increasing diversity of society and its increasing willingness to deal with secular matters wrought change. Humanism now began to show not only interest in the classics, but also an increased interest in the world for its own sake. This new interest would have an effect both upon the growth of scientific interest in the thirteenth century and in the development of Renaissance humanism later.

The Latin and Greek classics, particularly the former, had

been studied in the monasteries, but primarily for the purpose of illustrating Christian moral principles. From the tenth century they were increasingly studied for their own sake, and with such avidity that one less enthusiastic scholar (Walter Map) complained that everyone was so entranced with the ancients that no one had any time for the moderns: "The dead live, and the living are buried."

Together with revived interest in the classics went reaffirmation of the value of the liberal arts as the basis of education. Hugh of Saint Victor (1096–1141) and John of Salisbury (ca. 1120–1180) in particular taught the value of studying the "seven arts." John of Salisbury, a great and original thinker in his own right but suspicious of the growing enthusiasm for one of the "arts," dialectic, wrote the *Metalogicon* as a defense of the old grammar and logic. This was an interest in only *part* of what we would call a liberal education. Two educational theories have always been with us: one that the purpose of education is to discover truth and broaden the mind; the other that its purpose is to inculcate morality and conformity to societal values. Hugh and John stood firmly on the side of morality and looked with distrust upon the dialecticians' quest for answers to all metaphysical questions. Thus Hugh and John stand in a long tradition stretching from Plato through the Christian Fathers and the "social engineering" of Charlemagne. Even in the Renaissance, morality remained the chief concern of education, and it continues to be in very many circles today. The notion of education as freeing the mind, strongly advanced in some quarters in the eighteenth century, has not won full acceptance today, even in libertarian countries. The Middle Ages, with their sense of social order and unity, could not give it much scope, as the persecution of Abelard indicates.

Humanism was growing in its secular, as well as in its classical, sense. As conventional piety dominated the literate less, they turned both to new expressions of spirituality and to secularism. Hence they often expressed sentiments that were sometimes anticlerical—witness the satires on the corruption of the clergy—sometimes broadly sacrilegious, as when hymns to the Virgin were subtly altered into hymns in praise of wine, and sometimes simply more concerned with worldly than with spiritual matters, as in the student songs and the poetry of courtly love. It was not that fewer men were religious but that irreligiosity had for the first time in centuries become a "clever" and, to some, acceptable attitude. The new spirit is best expressed in the famous exclamation of the hero of *Aucassin and Nicolette:*

> Into Paradise go none but . . . aged priests, and those old cripples, and the maimed, who all day long and all night cough before the altars . . . . Such as these enter in Paradise, and with them have I nought to do. But in Hell will I go. For to Hell go the fair clerks and the fair knights who are slain in the tourney . . . . And there go the fair and courteous ladies, who have friends, two or three, together with their wedded lords . . . . [4]

In the course of the twelfth century the development of the cathedral schools culminated in the formation of what we call universities. The universities appeared because the monastic schools were in decline; their program of education was narrow, and they could provide neither the intellectual excitement nor the training in law, medicine, or scholasticism that students now demanded. It was in the schools of the flourishing medieval cities that modern universities originated. Certain cities boasted a particularly great number of schools, or particulary well-known schools, and to these scholars were naturally drawn. At first the scholars simply took up residence in rooms and gathered to talk with one another. Then students came to the rooms of a particularly gifted scholar to sit at his feet and hear him talk; finally the talks became formal lectures which the students paid to attend. A whole informal curriculum came into existence.

The bishops tried to bring this novel and growing system under their control. The greatest schools, attracting students from far away, became known as *studia generalia,* general places of study. The bishop usually extended his authority over the *studium generale* by appointing his archdeacon chancellor of the *studium,* thus bringing it into the ecclesiastical system.

In the meanwhile, the masters and students organized themselves into *universities.* The term university has nothing to do with "universal knowledge" but derives from the medieval word for a community or gild: *universitas.* There were "universities" of butchers, bakers, and now of masters and scholars, the *universitates magistrorum discipulorumque.* In the North the gilds were controlled by the masters; in southern Europe by the students. By the creation of universities, the scholars obtained greater control over their own affairs. Standardization was introduced when in the thirteenth century it was understood that no school could bear the name *studium generale* without a formal privilege, usually from the pope. The title *studium generale* gave its masters the right to teach anywhere in Christian Europe. The Church's control of the *studia* was natural, as all students were considered clerics, and the chief purpose of the schools was still the training of clergy. But tension between the chancellor and episcopal authority on the one hand and the gild on the other increased. For a long while the two organizations existed side by side, degrees having to be approved, for example, by both the gild and the chancellor. In the late thirteenth century, the chancellors lost most of their power, and the gilds triumphed, the record of their victory being preserved in the fact that today we have universities and not *studia generalia*.

In the thirteenth century Paris, Oxford, and other universities had to defend themselves against the encroachment of the Dominicans and Franciscans. The friars were among the most successful teachers at the universities, but their emphasis upon evangelization and their close organization seemed for a while about to turn the universities into teaching arms of the mendicants.

The gradual fashion in which the universities developed makes it impossible to determine which one is the oldest. There was a school of rhetoric at Bologna from about 1000, and later in the century there was a school of civil law and one of canon law as well as an episcopal school. Round these schools great scholars like Irnerius and Gratian gathered; Bologna got a charter as a *studium universale* in 1158, and by the end of the century there were four gilds, each representing a different "nation": the Lombards, the Tuscans, the Romans, and the Ultramontanes. The schools of Paris and of Salerno date back to the tenth and eleventh century as well, and there was a gild at Paris from 1170, but it was not until 1200 that Paris received its charter. Oxford became a center of scholarship only in 1167 after Louis VII drove the English students out of Paris, though Oxford had had schools before, and it was not till 1252–54 that it received its statutes. Cambridge was founded in 1209 by a similar migra-

tion of scholars from Oxford. Montpellier, Padua, Naples, Orléans, Salamanca, and Toulouse also rank among the earliest
of the universities.

Though there were sometimes riots between unruly students
and equally disorderly apprentices from town, there was no anti-
intellectual sentiment in medieval society at large. This is because
the medieval universities, like the monastic and cathedral schools
before them, were dedicated to serving the interests of society.
The universities produced literate graduates who could become
competent priests or administrators; their postgraduate schools
produced practising physicians, lawyers, and theologians, or men
who would teach others to practise. Thus the physical, legal,
and spiritual needs of that particular society were served. Before
the Renaissance, it was only unusual men like Socrates or Abelard
who questioned whether the interests of their societies were in
fact good, and such men were invariably treated roughly. It
was only with the Renaissance, which introduced the idea of
truth for the sake of truth, that intellectuals and schools were
encouraged to stand outside the assumptions of society and question them. It has never been more clear than in the violent age
in which we now live that the intellectual questioning of societal
assumptions is necessary; but it will never be popular, and the
modern intellectual is torn between his duty to question and his
desire to please. In the Middle Ages, intellectuals were not by
and large faced with this dilemma, and consequently their place
in the community was the more readily accepted.

The universities generally taught the seven arts, which
formed the core of undergraduate instruction, and they also provided graduate training in the more advanced disciplines—theology, law, and medicine. Some, like universities today, were
distinguished for one subject in particular. Thus Paris and Oxford were known for theology, Bologna for law, and Salerno
and Montpellier for medicine. Some of the younger universities,
obliged to compete with their more famous predecessors, did
not shrink from sending out circulars of advertisement. The
University of Toulouse, for example, let it be known that

> . . . the professors at Toulouse have cleared away for you the
> weeds of the rude populace and thorns of sharp sterility. . . . For here
> theologians inform their disciples . . . , logicians train the tyros in the
> arts of Aristotle . . . , decretists extol Justinian, and physicians teach

Galen. Those who wish to scrutinize the bosom of nature to the inmost can hear here the books of Aristotle which were forbidden at Paris. What then will you lack? Scholastic liberty? By no means . . . . Or do you fear the malice of the raging mob or the tyranny of an injurious prince? Fear not, for the liberality of the count of Toulouse affords us sufficient security. . . .[5]

Paris was the most famous of the medieval universities. It sprang from the three cathedral schools of Saint Victor, Sainte-Geneviève, and Notre Dame. Relations between town and gown, which had too often deteriorated into riot, in 1200 led Philip Augustus to issue Paris its charter. The statutes, or regulations, of the university were established by the papal legate Robert of Courcon in 1215 and again by Pope Gregory IX in 1231. Gregory's statutes demanded that the students and scholars be afforded adequate protection against the townsmen but provided that students who rioted would be punished with imprisonment in the bishop's jail. The chancellor was forbidden to keep the students in his own prison. "Moreover," the pope continued, "we prohibit more expressly the students from carrying weapons in the city, and the university from protecting those who disturb the peace and study. And those who call themselves students but do not frequent the schools, or acknowledge any master, are in no way to enjoy the liberties of the students."[6]

The university was organized into the undergraduate school of arts and the graduate faculties. At Paris the school of arts was divided into four nations, each of which had a proctor, while the schools of theology, canon law, and medicine each had a dean, the three deans and four proctors being responsible to the rector. The rector was himself a scholar: professional administrators and the enormous administrative bureaucracy characteristic of modern American universities were wholly lacking.

The medieval universities were small by modern standards: three or four thousand students was the norm. The age of the students varied from place to place, but each university attempted to regulate it to some extent. At Paris, a boy might begin his studies for the baccalaureate as early as the age of twelve, but he might not lecture on theology until he was a man of at least thirty-five.

A sound knowledge of Latin was prerequisite to all university work. The first four years were typically passed in working for the B.A., during which time all students studied the liberal arts, the trivium and quadrivium of Boëthius and Alcuin remaining the basis of undergraduate education. This was followed by a further two-year course for the M.A. involving further study, teaching assistantship, and the defense of a thesis. At the minimum age of 21 the student might receive his *licentia docendi* or teaching credential from the chancellor, and he was then initiated with great pomp and ceremony into the masters' gild. Trumpeters preceded him down the street, people cheered, and the procession ended with a huge and obligatory banquet—paid for by himself.

With the *licentia*, the student might now choose to teach the arts at Paris or elsewhere, to leave the university altogether, or to go on and study medicine, law, or theology. Law was perhaps the most popular of the graduate studies. At Paris theology was the usual choice of the approximately twenty percent of the students who went on past the M.A. Six years of study of the Bible and Peter Lombard's *Sentences* earned the student his D.D. (Doctor of Divinity); if he were a medical student he would get the M.D. instead; if a law student the LL.D. or the more advanced J.U.D., doctor of both civil and canon laws.* A final three years of study of the Bible and the Fathers culminated at Paris in the degree of S.T.D., Doctor of Sacred Theology, which entitled the scholar to teach theology in the same way that the M.A. entitled him to teach the arts.

Professors at medieval universities were all technically clerics, and celibacy was the rule, though there were frequent exceptions on the part of those who were not priests but only deacons or in one of the other minor orders of the Church. The professors had originally assembled for the purposes of scholarship and mutual enlightenment, but they received students with pleasure, for students paid—or were supposed to: one professor at Bologna discontinued his extra lectures because, as he said, "All desire to know but none to pay the price." The university had no central registrar or cashier, and the students left their fees with the professor at the door. What they paid for was a lecture, literally a reading, in the sense that the French word *lecture* retains today. Books were expensive, for they had

*The term doctor [from *docere:* "to teach"] means teacher.

Medieval lecturers reading the texts to their students.

to be copied painstakingly by hand upon expensive parchment, itself difficult to prepare—it often took more than a year to copy a Bible. Most students could not afford to own more than one or two books: as a result they could not own the textbooks, and the professor taught by reading the text out loud and making comments as he went along. Later the comments of some of the best lecturers were incorporated into new editions of the text.

Since parchment was too expensive to permit note-taking, the medieval student cultivated a memory that was much better trained and more retentive than that of his modern counterpart, who can rely upon all the helpful crutches of pen, paper, and books. The student day began early, at four or five A.M., and included not only the lectures, but disputes and recitations designed to reinforce the lessons.

The students came to town and settled in whatever rooms they could find. From the thirteenth century, colleges—originally the equivalent of American dormitories—were founded where they might live cheaply and with some regulation by older students and clergy. The most famous college at Paris was the Sorbonne, founded in 1256 or 1257. At Oxford and Cambridge the colleges became the most important part of the university and remain so today. The university college [from the Latin *collegium*: assemblage] resembled the colleges of canons in more ways than one: they were places where clerics (i.e., students) lived together under a Rule. The religious origins of the university colleges are evident in the chapels of those at Oxford and Cambridge: not only is the chapel the center (architecturally at least) of the college, but it is arranged like a monastic chapel with opposing choir stalls for the singing of the Office.

Even the best accomodations lacked light, heat, and space. Students who did not live in college went out to dine in taverns, and there they did more than eat. In Paris, the drinking, wenching, and singing of the students in the *Quartier Latin* (the students were supposed to speak in Latin even in their hours of relaxation) caused the bishop more than one bad moment: he was particularly unhappy when on one occasion the students were found playing dice on the high altar of Notre Dame. The students' possessions were usually meager, consisting of bedding, a few changes of clothes, a lute, some sports equipment, and possibly a book or two. Chaucer's clerk of Oxenford was an unusually studious man, "for hym was levere have at his beddes heed / Twenty bookes clad in blak or reed / Of Aristotle and his philosophie / Than robes riche, fithele, or gay sautrie." All was not fun and games even for the less serious students, and of many of them it might be said, as it was of the clerk of Oxenford: "Gladly wolde he lerne, and gladly teche."

The richest students could rent or buy houses and in the fifteenth century had liveried servants; the poorest were reduced to begging until benevolent personages provided the colleges with scholarships. Most, then as now, were of moderate means and depended upon their families for support; there were no part-time jobs. Charles Homer Haskins translated a number of form letters designed by notaries to be written by students and their parents about money. One goes:

B. TO HIS VENERABLE MASTER A., GREETING. This is to inform you that I am studying at Oxford with the greatest diligence, but the matter of money stands greatly in the way of my promotion, as it is now two months since I spent the last of what you sent me. The city is expensive and makes many demands; I have to rent lodgings, buy necessaries, and provide for many other things which I cannot now specify. . . .[8]

One angry father was not impressed by his son's solicitations:

TO HIS SON G. RESIDING AT ORLÉANS P. OF BESANÇON SENDS GREETINGS WITH PATERNAL ZEAL. It is written, "He also that is slothful in his work is brother to him who is a great waster." I have recently discovered that you live dissolutely and slothfully, preferring license to restraint and play to work and strumming a guitar while the others are at their studies, whence it happens that you have read but one volume of law while your more industrious companions have read several . . . .[9]

Most of the students were away from home, and most of the undergraduates were under eighteen, a situation which produced not only the frivolity and rioting that the authorities so dreaded but also a situation where intellectual ferment was encouraged. Gathered together in a large community away from parental or direct clerical control, the students were responsive to new ideas and to intellectual change; it was their support that gave a teacher like Abelard fame and reputation. Much of the ferment and change in theology, philosophy, and the arts and sciences can be attributed to the "peer-group" mentality of the twelfth-and thirteenth-century students.

NOTES

[1] John of Salisbury, *Frivolities of Courtiers and Footprints of Philosophers,* trans. Joseph B. Pike (Minneapolis, 1938) p. 244.

[2] Quotations from Abelard's *Historia Calamitatum,* trans. H. A. Bellows and Thomas A. Boyd (St. Paul, 1920).

[3] *The Letters of St. Bernard of Clairvaux,* trans. Bruno Scott James (Chicago, 1957), pp. 315–317.

[4] Eugene Mason, *Aucassin and Nicolette* (New York, E. P. Dutton and Co., 1958), pp. 6–7.

[5] Lynn Thorndike, *University Records and Life in the Middle Ages* (New York, Columbia University Press, 1944), pp. 34–35.

[6] D. C. Munro, *Translations and Reprints* (Philadelphia, 1899) ii, No. 3, p. 9.

[7] Charles Homer Haskins, *The Rise of the Universities* (Copyright 1957, Cornell University. Used by permission of Cornell University Press), p. 44.

[8] Haskins, 77.

[9] Haskins, 79.

Chapter Eighteen

THE PAPACY AND ITS OPPONENTS

THE papacy emerged from its period of revolution as the most powerful force in Christendom and remained so for over two hundred years. During this time, on the assumption that the Roman Church was the only vehicle of salvation and indeed, as the mystical Body of Christ, the only true society, the popes used every means at their disposal to advance the claims of that society against sinner, heretic, Jew, and Moslem. The result was reform, inquisition, pogrom, and crusade.

AT the beginning of the twelfth century the sources of medieval history become so numerous that it is impossible to do more than cite a few of the most famous. For the Crusades the best-known contemporary works are the *Gesta Dei per Francos,* William of Tyre's *History of Deeds Done Beyond the Sea,* Villehardouin's chronicle of the Fourth Crusade, and, on the side of the Greeks and Arabs, Anna Comnena's *Alexiad,* the comments of Niketas Choniates on the taking of Constantinople by the Crusaders, and the works of the Arab commentator Usāmah. For papalism and canon law, the writings of the canonists themselves—Burchard of Worms, Gratian, Ivo, Hostiensis, Huguccio, and others —are, together with the papal registers, the best sources. On the inquisition, the best-known work is Bernard Gui's *Manual of the Inquisitor;* the numerous fragmentary sources on the Christians' treatment of the Jews have been summarized by Bernhard Blumenkranz.[1] The travel accounts by John of Piano-Carpini, William of Rubruck, and John of Monte Corvino provide much of our knowledge of the Mongols.

THE papacy continued its program of reforming society, a program that reached its climax in the Fourth Lateran Council of 1215. There the idea that a truly Christian society could be obtained through organization attained its most impressive expression. The council demanded order throughout the Church, ordering each archbishop to hold a provincial council every year in order to make sure that the bishops were doing their duties properly. There were to be provincial councils of monks every three years in order to make sure that each monastic community was following its Rule. In order to prevent any disorderly multiplication of distinctions among the monasteries, it was ordained that henceforth no new Rule was to be accepted. Ignorance and heresy were to be repressed by the establishment of a strong educational system. The bishops were ordered to visit the churches of their dioceses, to preach and teach, and to make sure that every cathedral had its school, where the sons of the wealthy could be taught for pay and where the worthy sons of the poor would receive a free education. Innocent III and his successors encouraged the universities, which Innocent IV called "rivers of science that water and fertilize the soil of universal Church." The laity was enjoined to respect the property of the clergy, to pay due reverence to the Church and its courts, and to observe the rules of Christian marriage. The clergy was adjured to abstain from drunkenness, brawling, and licentiousness, and careful and exact procedures were established for the trial of disorderly clerks.

The difficulty of enforcing these rules, even in a well-organized and disciplined Church under the leadership of a powerful papacy, is illustrated by the long and drawn-out nature of the struggle against nicolaitism (the practice of marriage or concubinage by the clergy). In 1126, for example, John of Cremona, sent by the pope to fight nicolaitism in England, preached a vehement sermon against concupiscent priests, shuddering at the idea that the same hands that touched the Body of Christ should also touch the body of a wanton. That very evening, through the watchfulness of those whose sensibilities he had offended, the cardinal was surprised in his own bedchamber with a courtesan. At Reims, a young girl was prosecuted for heresy on the grounds that she refused to sleep with a handsome young priest;

and in 1299 the bishop of Orléans was murdered by an irate father.

The success of the struggle against nicolaitism and against immorality and disorder in general depended upon the papal exercise of power. Papal power was exerted by calling frequent ecumenical councils under firm papal leadership, by the appointment and control of bishops, by the use of legates and the friars, by leadership in the Crusades, and by the use of canon law, this last being the most important. The history of papal power in the twelfth and thirteenth centuries is inextricably combined with that of canon law, for it was not so much upon the individual popes but upon the tradition expressed by lawyers and political theorists that the nature of the office depended. Canon law was both the result of, and an instrument of, the establishment of an ordered and reformed Christian society. Alexander III, Innocent III, Gregory IX, and Innocent IV, the most forceful popes of the period, were themselves lawyers. Canon law aided in the creation of a great, legal-governmental system centered in Rome. Essentially it was the pratical side of social theology, the attempt to create a Christian *ordo*. It transformed Christianity into government, the Church into a corporation.

Canon law had existed from the beginning of the Church in the pronouncements of bishops, councils, and the Fathers, but it was ill-defined until collections of these pronouncements were made in the seventh and eighth centuries. The first thorough, well-organized collection was made by Burchard of Worms in the eleventh century, and then in the twelfth two great lawyers, Yvo of Chartres and Gratian, began analyzing and commenting on the texts. This revolutionary change in canon law derived from both practical and intellectual demands. The new power and organization of the Church called for a well-organized constitution; and the intellectual revival of the eleventh and twelfth centuries encouraged a more reasoned and methodical structure of law. Thus Gratian's collection, the *Decretum* (ca. 1140), or the *Concordance of Discordant Canons,* showed the influence both of Roman law and of the scholastic method of theology. His work became the basis of canon law thereafter. Following Gratian was a school of commentators on his work, called the "Decretists"; then the popes added new pronouncements, called decretals, of their own; and a modernized version of the *Decretum* was published in 1234. This in turn was commented on by the "Decretalists," and further collections were made, culminating in that of 1503, which remained the basis of Church law until 1917.

The development of canon law, in its organization, its clarity, and its borrowing from authoritarian Roman law, encouraged papalist theory and practice. Twelfth-century papalism was still basically that of Gregory VII, but it gradually changed as several unresolved questions arose, the most important being whether the pope's "plentitude of power" gave him the right to rule the temporal sphere directly or merely to influence it morally. Papalism, encouraged by canon law, advanced beyond the already extended lines defended by Gregory VII. The pope came to be thought of as the source of temporal power to whom temporal rulers were responsible. As so often in human events, theory and practice encouraged one another: papal power, and theories enhancing papal power, advanced together. The title of the pope changed subtly in the thirteenth century from "vicar of Peter" to "vicar of Christ," and he was now said to be the "high priest representing God on earth."

The first great dispute of the latter twelfth century brought about by the advance in papalism arose in 1157 when Rolando Bandinelli, later Alexander III, met the Emperor Frederick Barbarossa at Besançon and handed him a letter in which Pope Hadrian IV asserted that he had bestowed *beneficia* upon him. This term could be understood simply as "services" but it might also be read in its technical feudal sense of "benefices," in which case the implication might be that the emperor held his crown from the pope as a fief. This was the interpretation the emperor put upon it, and Bandinelli was fortunate to leave Besançon alive. The misunderstanding at Besançon might appear absurd, but the fact is that the popes were gradually extending their "suzerainty" to many of the kingdoms of Europe and the Mediterranean and that it was by no means clear whether in so doing they meant this in a feudal or in a merely indirect fashion. No one was sure about the limits of papal power. Without planning to do so, the popes and their lawyers were moving in the direction of an autocratic theocracy.

Innocent III (1198–1215) enjoys the reputation of being the most powerful of the medieval popes, a reputation merited only when placed in the proper context, for neither his personality nor his politics were very original. He was the heir and representative of a great tradition. Most modern historians doubt that he meant to make himself "prince of the world," but the policies he inherited led in that direction. He intervened, often directly, in the politics of England, France, and Germany, making King John do homage, placing France under interdict when Philip Augustus sought to have his bride put away in a convent, and alternating his support of candidates in the German civil wars. Throughout, Innocent seems to have been operating under Gregory VII's principle that the pope had the duty of preserving the integrity of the Christian *ordo* by judging the world's morals as God's representative. He therefore had not merely the right, but the duty, to right wrongs done by monarchs. This, rather than a desire to create a theocracy, was Innocent's motivation. In the decretal *Novit* he declared: "For we do not intend to judge concerning a fief, judgment on which belongs to (the king)—except when some special privilege or contrary custom detracts from the common law—but to decide concerning a sin, of which the judgment undoubtedly belongs to us. . . ."[2] Innocent III's reputation rests upon a development of existing tradition, upon the unusual energy that permitted him to apply that tradition with more vigor than many of his predecessors, and upon the intemperateness of personality that often led him into actions that he later regretted.

Gregory IX (1227–1241) and Innocent IV (1243–1254), canon lawyers themselves, did more than Innocent III to advance papalist theory. In one encyclical Gregory asserted that as vicar of God the pope had the power of judging temporal matters directly, and Innocent IV argued that it was the pope's task to enforce natural law throughout society. It was this principle that encouraged the inquisition and the persecution of the Jews. The extreme libertarianism of the Middle Ages was limited towards their end by an effort on the part of the popes to establish on a theocratic basis something like the totalitarian states of the ancient and the modern world. As ancient and modern totalitarianism makes a god of the state, so thirteenth-century papalist theory almost made a god of the papacy.

But papalism never went unchallenged. The theoretical polemics of the opponents, as well as the supporters, of the papal revolution were remembered in the thirteenth century. Many canon lawyers and other theorists even then argued that in the famous Petrine texts of the Bible it was Christ and not Peter who was "the Rock," that the Church might be infallible but not the pope, and that a vicious or insane pope might be judged by the whole Church in spite of the papalist dictum that "the supreme judge must be judged by no one." Hence emerged the conciliar theories that were to attempt to limit papal power in the fifteenth century. Oddly, the only time when papalism was completely triumphant within the Catholic Church was not in the Middle Ages at all, but from the reign of Pius IX (1846–1878) through that of Pius XII (d. 1958).

NONETHELESS the powerful papalism of the thirteenth century, having transformed the Church from a community of worshipers into a legally governed society or corporation, found it difficult to sympathize with elements of popular religion or to tolerate dissent. The repression of heretics and Jews and the Crusades must be seen in this context.

The reaction of the Church to heresy was almost universally patient and mild into the twelfth century, after which it grew rapidly more severe. In the earlier Middle Ages, the mobs were the chief instruments of persecution; but now the authorities increasingly intervened. What explains the change? First of all, the heretics became both more radical and more influential. As medievel society became more complex, religious heresy blended with social and economic protest. Discontent, no longer compartmentalized, reinforced itself, recruited more adherents, and changed its "norm-oriented" efforts to tinker with society to "value-oriented" efforts to transform or even to abolish it. Second, the increasing authoritarianism of the papacy caused it to approve harsher measures. Third, the broader heresy of the central and later Middle Ages increasingly provoked the secular authorities, who feared the political consequences of religious unrest. The first formal execution of heretics since the fourth century occurred by order of King Robert the Pious at Orléans in 1022. The Church proved only too ready to accept the services of the state and to hand convicted heretics over "to the secular arm"— "for due attention," a conscience-saving phrase that usually meant the stake.

But the Church, if leaving punishment to the rulers, was unwilling to forgo the detection and conviction of heretics. In 1184 the Council of Verona had called for each bishop to act as an inquisitor in his own diocese; and the Church's active prosecution of heresy began shortly thereafter, when the increasing power of the Catharists (Albigensians) was the scandal of Catholic Europe. Canon lawyers declared that if treason to the state demanded death, treason to Christ required no less. After the failure of the Cistercians and Dominicans to win over the Albigensians by preaching, Innocent III in 1208 called for a crusade. After twenty-one years of fighting, the Albigensians were broken, the king and nobles of France enriched, and a violent policy towards heretics justified by its success.

It was Gregory IX who in 1231 originated the papal inquisition by giving the Dominicans the authority to investigate heresy throughout Christendom. The inquisition grew in favor and evolved into the Holy Office, a permanent bureau of investigations.

While the papal inquisition was never as sinister as the notorious Spanish Inquisition of the Renaissance, its practices were appalling enough. Accusers were assured of absolute secrecy for their own protection, so that the accused was never permitted to face them or even to know their names. Often he was not vouchsafed the luxury of knowing the specific charges against him. Dungeons were provided where suspects might languish for months or even years without a hearing. In accordance with Roman law, guilt, rather than innocence, was presumed. The inquisitors placed a high premium on confessions, which, if they could not solicit by persuasion, they elicited by torture, a practice formally approved by Pope Innocent IV in the bull *Ad extirpanda.* The inquisition had a wide range, being extended to relapsed Jews and sorcerers as well as to heretics, and by using the principle of guilt by association flung its nets wide. Even to speak with a suspected heretic was to become suspect oneself. The Synod of Toulouse of 1229 enjoined, among other regulations, that

"Whoever, allowing a heretic to stay on his property either for money or any other cause, if he confesses or is convicted, loses his property forever, and his body is handed over to the civil authority for punishment. . . . (A person) tainted with heresy, (even though he has recanted) must wear two crosses on his coat; the one on the right and the other on the left, and of a different color from his coat. . . . All members of a parish shall vow to the bishop under oath that they will . . . persecute heretics according to their power.

Physical punishments were meted out for crimes of thought, and suspect books, as well as persons, were consigned to the flames.

It would be grossly to misunderstand the problem to imagine that the inquisitors were sadists or monsters. Most of them were normal men simply doing a job, many of them were trained lawyers, and the whole procedure always conformed to a carefully worked-out set of rules. Yet the inquisition is an unfortunate monument to the results of legalism in religion and of authoritarianism in law.

THE march of Christian enthusiasm and organization augured ill for the tranquility of the Jewish community in western Christendom. At the beginning of the Middle Ages there were numerous Jews in western Europe, where, especially in Spain, they established a high culture. Often they settled among the Christians, and it is likely that over the years many yielded to all the pressures of society to conform; more often, they freely and deliberately settled apart in order to maintain their customs and religion. As the father was the center of the Jewish family, so the rabbi and the synagogue were the center of the Jewish community. The independence of the Jews was ordinarily respected by the Christians, who allowed them freedom of worship, self-government, their own law codes, and their own tax collectors.

Jews were often landholders and farmers until the eleventh century, when the feudal system came to demand a Christian oath on the part of every vassal and thus forced many Jews into the cities. In the cities, the Jews were leaders in medicine and in many crafts, particularly those having do with wines and fabrics, but they were barred from most trades by the artisans' gilds, which were religious confraternities limited to Christians. The fact that they were increasingly barred from these trades and from farming induced them to go into commerce, banking, and lending, a sector of the economy they dominated, with the Lombards and Templars, from the eleventh to the fourteenth century.

The worship of the Jewish community in the synagogue centered upon the Scriptures, and the Jews placed a greater emphasis upon learning than the Christians. Most Jewish laymen not only spoke the vernacular language of their environment, but also had some literacy in Hebrew. Jewish scholars, interested in the work of the Christians, mastered Latin as well and sometimes served as tutors in Hebrew to Christian scholars. The great Jewish community in Spain produced some of the best medieval thinkers, the most renowned of whom was Moses ben Maimon or Maimonides (1135–1204), physician, jurist, and philosopher. His *Guide for the Perplexed* is one of the most original philosophical works of his time. Maimonides represents in the Jewish tradition what Aquinas does in the Christian and Averroes in the Moslem: he was the creator of a great synthetic philosophy attempting to bind together the Bible, Jewish tradition, and Greek philosophy.

In the early Middle Ages Christian and Jew lived peaceably together. Nothing like antisemitism existed. There was obvious religious conflict: the Jews believed that the Christians had blasphemously distorted the religion of Israel, and the Christians believed that the Jews were blind in their refusal to recognize in Jesus the true Messiah. This religious conflict was especially bitter because of the close common origins of Christianity and Judaism. But several points are to be kept in mind. The violence of polemic on both sides was limited to religion and had nothing to do with race. When Christian writers condemned the Jews as blind or stupid they applied the same terms with equal zest to the pagan Greeks or other unbelievers. Few overt acts of hostility occurred. Scholarly acquaintance and personal friendship between Christian and Jews were the rule. Gregory the Great, hearing that pillaging of synagogues had occurred in Palermo, ordered the restitution of all stolen property and urged that the Jews "may in no wise be oppressed or suffer any injustice."[4] Louis I personally favored the Jews as administrators and merchants, and there are even two or three recorded instances of Christians converting to Judaism without incurring any punishment beyond harsh language.

Nonetheless, even in the early Middle Ages there were tokens of harder times to come. The Visigothic kings pursued a policy of forced conversion in the seventh century and severely punished Jews who relapsed: this Visigothic tradition was remembered and revived in the Spanish Inquisition of the Renaissance, which was aimed particularly at relapsed Jews. Some Frankish prelates like Amulo of Lyon reacted strongly against Louis the Pious' favor toward the Jews and published heated and vicious anti-Jewish tracts. There are a few isolated instances of popular outrages against the Jews before the end of the eleventh century, though in the twelfth the Christians of Sens still tolerated a synagogue spire higher than that of the cathedral.

It was at the end of the eleventh century, when popular zeal was high and the Crusades under way, that relations between Christian and Jew took a turn for the worse. The change of attitude on the part of the Christians had several roots. First of all the Jews, by isolating themselves in ghettos, holding to their ancient customs, and teaching that they were a race set apart and chosen by God, offended their neighbors. The Jews could not have done otherwise without ceasing to be Jews, but most societies have not been tolerant of those within them who openly deny their values. It is also likely that the business success of the Jews, and most particularly their frequent status as creditors, caused envy and dislike on the part of their competitors.

It was also at this time that the same zeal working for the reform of the Church began to seek the destruction of its supposed enemies—Jew and Moslem as well as heretic. This was the dark side of the golden moon of reform. Popular murders of both heretics and Jews commenced, and reaching appalling proportions amounting to true massacres and pogroms. The mob on its way to the First Crusade stopped along the way and massacred the Jewish communities of several Rhenish towns. There was a similar massacre at York in 1190 and one at Strasbourg in 1349. At Strasbourg the Jews were accused of poisoning the wells and causing the Black Plague:

On Saturday—that was Saint Valentine's Day—they burnt the Jews on a wooden platform in their cemetery. There were about two thousand people of them. Those who wanted to baptize themselves were spared . . . . Many small children were taken out of the fire and baptized against the will of their fathers and mothers. And everything that was owed to the Jews was cancelled, and the Jews had to surrender all pledges and notes that they had taken for debts.[5]

The Cross of Bury St. Edmunds. This cross with its elaborately carved figures has been called a "seminar in the style of the late twelfth century," showing elements of both Romanesque and Gothic. Made for an abbot who was a leader of antisemitic campaigns, the cross is also unusual because its sixty-three inscriptions convey an anti-Jewish message. The inscriptions reflect the mood of a period when events such as the massacre of fifty-seven Jews could occur.

The religious was the outstanding element in the persecution of the Jews. At the back of all the atrocities lay the terrible passage from Saint Matthew (27:xxv): "His blood be on us, and on our children." In the eleventh century the intolerance of the Jewish religion expressed by some of the Fathers and by Bishop Amulo of Lyon bore its fruit in popular frenzy. Commonly believed stories about the Jews became more and more absurd.

Not only did they poison wells, but they kidnapped Christian children and did away with them in ritual murder. "Little Saint Hugh of Lincoln" and "Little Saint William of Norwich" were "child martyrs" popular through the time of Chaucer's *Prioress' Tale* and Marlowe's *Jew of Malta*. Most absurd of all, the Jews were said to steal the eucharist and stab it, and many was the story in which the criminal was caught by the sacred host's flooding the house and street with blood. The Renaissance only heightened distaste for the Jews, as is clear from the character of Shylock, and the rotten tradition finally bore its most hideous fruit in the supposedly enlightened nineteenth and twentieth centuries, when the religious and economic bases of anti-Jewish sentiment were transferred into racial antisemitism.

Most of the Rhenish bishops during the Crusades tried to protect the Jews against the fury of the mobs. As is usually true, the authorities took a while to catch up with the brutality of the people. But by the thirteenth century legalism was rampant in the Church, and a better organized Christian society felt the Jewish presence to be anomalous. Innocent III decreed that Jews should be denied public office, that they should wear dress that distinguished them from Christians, and that converted Jews who lapsed should be severely punished. On the other hand, Saint Bernard condemned the persecutors of the Jews as heretics themselves, and Pope Gregory X in 1272 strongly refuted the charges of ritual murder and insisted that Jews should be preserved from unjust treatment. But voices like those of Saint Bernard and Gregory X were not often raised and less often heard. The record of popes and bishops is spotty.

The Church is most culpable, as is the case with the inquisition, in its unwillingness to speak out against the injustices perpetrated by the state. For it was the state which, as in the case of the heretics, inflicted the most fearful injuries upon the Jews. Supported by popular frenzy and abetted by ecclesiastical connivance, the kings began to find in persecution a convenient means for extorting property and wealth from the Jews. In 1180, by order of Philip II, "the Jews throughout all France were seized in their synagogues and then bespoiled (sic) of their gold and silver and garments, as the Jews themselves had spoiled the Egyptians at their exodus from Egypt. This was a harbinger of their expulsion, which by God's will soon followed."[6] (Actually,

Alleged profanation of the eucharist by Jews (by Paolo Uccello). A woman sells a stolen host to a Jew for vicious purposes.

the final expulsion occurred under Philip IV over a century later.) Edward I drove them from England for similar motives, as did Ferdinand and Isabella from fifteenth-century Spain. In these respects the Jews fared no worse than the Lombards and Templars, who were also persecuted by confiscations and expulsions owing to their wealth, but in other respects they were subjected to far worse indignities: in 1222 a yellow badge two inches by four was imposed upon all the Jews of England above the age of six, a prototype of the yellow star of David used by the Nazis; while in thirteenth-century Germany the approved mark of singularity was a red hat with horns.

THE Crusades are a third unedifying manifestation, after the inquisition and the persecution of the Jews, of popular religious enthusiasm mingled with papal authoritarianism. Some modern historians, with reason, have viewed the Crusades as a manifestation of the western European economic and political expansion that was beginning to get under way in the eleventh century. But the Crusades were primarily religious in purpose. They were one more effort to force the world into the papalist *ordo* and one more expression of popular enthusiasm.

The idea of holy war or conversion by force had first been practiced by the Eastern emperor Heraclius in his seventh-century campaign against the Persians; Charlemagne had forced the Saxons to the Cross; and German missionaries carried the faith to the Slavs with fire and sword. Then, in the later eleventh century, the Christian princes of Spain undertook a holy war against the Moors of the Iberian Peninsula.

This was the earliest and most protracted of the great medieval Crusades. The wealth, power, and cultural richness of Moslem Spain had kept the Christians backed up against the Pyrenees and the Bay of Biscay in Leon and Castile in the west and Aragon in the east. Owing to disunity among the Moslems, the Christian princes, led by Alfonso VI of Leon and Castile and his "Cid Campeador" Rodrigo Diaz, reclaimed vast portions of the peninsula and finally in 1085 regained the ancient Spanish capital of Toledo. The *"Reconquista"* might have been speedily completed had not the Christians themselves been disunified and poorer than the Moslems, had they not been bound by the rules of feudalism to only a few months' campaign a year, and had Moslem Spain not been reunited and revived by the Almoravids from North Africa about 1090. The Christian advance so well begun now continued only in fits and starts, until it was finally consummated in 1492 by Ferdinand and Isabella. Spanish steel, so long kept honed on the reconquest of the peninsula, was then turned to the conquest of whole continents across the Atlantic.

The idea of holy war was thus already well established when the Seljuk Turks irrupted into the Middle East. Before the advent of the Turks relations between Moslems and Christians had become fairly placid. Neither the Moslems, divided between the Mesopotamian 'Abbasids and the Egyptian Fatimids, nor the Byzantines mounted major offensives against the other, and the Moslems ordinarily permitted Christian pilgrims to visit the Holy Land without molestation. Then came the Turks. Originating in central Asia and bursting through Persia and Mesopotamia, they seized Syria and Palestine from the Arabs, who regarded these savage coreligionists as utter barbarians, and swept through Armenia into Asia Minor. There, in 1071 at Manzikert, they inflicted upon the Byzantines their worst defeat since the seventh century. Beset by the Turks and other enemies and weakened internally, the Byzantine Empire could not regain its equilibrium, and finally Emperor Alexius I Comnenus appealed to the pope for help.

Urban II was not slow to respond. The specter of a Turkish conquest of Constantinople was terrifying even to the West; Urban saw in the appeal an opportunity to bring back the East into obedience to Rome; and he believed, correctly, that his leadership of a Crusade would help to unite Europe in the papal ideal of *ordo*. Accordingly at the Council of Clermont in 1095 Urban conjured up a lurid picture of Turkish atrocities, describing how they disemboweled Christian men, raped women, and smeared excrement upon the altars. Appealing for Christian unity in the face of this monstrous enemy and promising forgiveness of sins to anyone who would in penance fight for the liberation of the Holy Land, Urban called for a Crusade [Fr. *croisade,* from *croisé:* "one who has taken up the cross"]. It was the right moment to capture the popular reform enthusiasm then at its height. The crowd shouted back: "God wills it, God wills it," and, after Urban had finished his instructions, they came forward to place upon their breasts the red crosses they would wear while bound for the Holy Land. Those who returned would wear them on their backs.

This "First Crusade" was undertaken by two main groups. The first consisted of a wildly enthusiastic and wholly undisciplined rabble under the leadership of Peter the Hermit, Walter the Penniless, and other popular preachers. Five hordes of "the most stupid and savage refuse of the people, who mingled with their devotion a brutal licence of rapine, prostitution, and drunkenness"[7] ranged across Europe, killing Jews, begging or stealing their keep, yet fixed in their desire to do battle for God against "Mahomet," whom they imagined a devil. More even than the popular heresies, this strange outpouring of crude zeal was a manifestation of the vast and growing energies of what Marxists call the masses. The changes and growing complexities of society rendered many people radically uneasy and insecure. As yet innocent of economic or social goals, their motivation was millennarian—they sought some kind of redemption in this world.

Peter the Hermit preaching the First Crusade.

Having heard of the saving properties of Zion, they took the saying at its most literal and sought salvation at the geographical Jerusalem. It was also a mass popular delusion, for the undisciplined peasants had no chance of reaching the Holy Land. Many died on their way through the Balkans, and more deserted, but a surprising number arrived before the gates of Constantinople and demanded hospitality of Alexius Comnenus.

The horror of the emperor, who had been expecting the pope to send him professionals or mercenaries, may be imagined. He had only one hope: to fulfill the rabble's desire of fighting the Turks before they looted his own city. Accordingly he ordered them shipped over to Asia where the Turks immediately massacred them. Of tens of thousands who crossed from Europe to Asia only a few individuals returned. Such was the fate of a delusion.

The second main group of Crusaders consisted of the nobles of Europe, who cautiously prepared a year before actually setting out. It has often been suggested that their motives were venal, that they wanted land and possessions. This is true of some, particularly of the Normans of southern Italy. But Duke Robert of Normandy and Count Raymond of Toulouse had as much to lose materially by a prolonged absence from their lands in Europe as they had to gain. A second important motive was the scope for deeds of valor the Crusades offered. Fighting was the job of the feudal nobility, and they desired nothing more than to be able to combine warfare with the service of the Prince of Peace. But the primary motivation of the nobles, like that of the peasants, was religious enthusiasm.

Arriving at Constantinople in 1097, "so many potent chiefs and fanatic nations"[8] were only little more gratifying to poor

Alexius Comnenus than the peasant hordes. Alexius' daughter Anna, while finding the Franks exceedingly handsome, was less impressed by their manners: "The Frankish counts are naturally shameless and violent, naturally greedy of money too, and immoderate in everything they wish, and possess a flow of language greater than any other human race; and they did not make their visits to the emperor in any order . . . (and) did not regulate their conversation by an (hourglass). . . ."[9] The emperor, wishing his Frankish allies to promise to restore to him whatever lands they might conquer from the infidel, was obliged to be satisfied with a vague promise that the Crusaders never intended to honor. Thus there was dissension between Crusaders and Byzantines from the very beginning. The expedition would have been doomed had the Moslems not been at the moment even more divided, the Seljuk domains having divided into minor sultanates and principalities.

Alexius had the Frankish nobles transported to Asia, where they fared better than the peasants and won a series of battles which brought them at last to Jerusalem. On July 15, 1099,

> . . . entering the city our pilgrims pursued and killed Saracens up to the Temple of Solomon, in which they had assembled and where they gave battle to us furiously for the whole day so that their blood flowed throughout the whole temple. Finally, having overcome the pagans, our knights seized a great number of men and women, and they killed whom they wished and whom they wished they let live. . . . Soon the crusaders ran throughout the city, seizing gold, silver, horses, mules, and houses full of all kinds of goods. Then rejoicing and weeping from extreme joy our men went to worship at the sepulchre of our Saviour Jesus and thus fulfilled their pledge to Him . . . .[10]

So Christianity came again to the Holy Land.

On the way to the Holy Land, the crusading leaders had not been idle. Raymond of Toulouse had paused to carve himself out a county at Tripoli, Baldwin of Lorraine one at Edessa, and Bohemund of Otranto a principality at Antioch. Baldwin's brother Godfrey of Bouillon had the decency, when the crown of Jerusalem was offered him, to decline it, but his successors were less reticent.

The net result of the First Crusade was to found upon the oriental shores of the Mediterranean four states. Although the

MILES

0 100 200 300 400 500

•York

ENGLAND

Clarendon

Boulogne• FLANDERS

DENMARK

Rhine R.

HOLY PO

Bouillon

LORRAINE

GERMANY

Orléans

Sens

Worms

Strasbourg

Bay of
Biscay

Besançon

ROMAN

Clermont

Compostella

LEON

Lyon

LOMBARDY

PORTUGAL

CASTILE

NAVARRE

PYRENEES

Toulouse

Marseille

Genoa

Venice

Zara

SPAIN

ARAGON

EMPIRE

Toledo

Rome

DOMINIONS

ALMORAVIDS

OF

THE ALMOHADS

Palermo

NORMAN KINGDOM IN THE SOUTH

Otran

Mediter

Tunis

rane

Routes of The Crusades

——————	1096 – 1099
+++++++++	1147 – 1149
▲▼▲▼▲▼	1189 – 1191
⊢—⊢—⊢	1202 – 1204
∘—∘—∘—∘	1228 – 1229
×—×—×—×	1248 – 1254 and 1270

▨ The Crusader States

- - - - - Boundaries

▥ Mongol Empire

▨ Area of The
Latin Empire, 1204

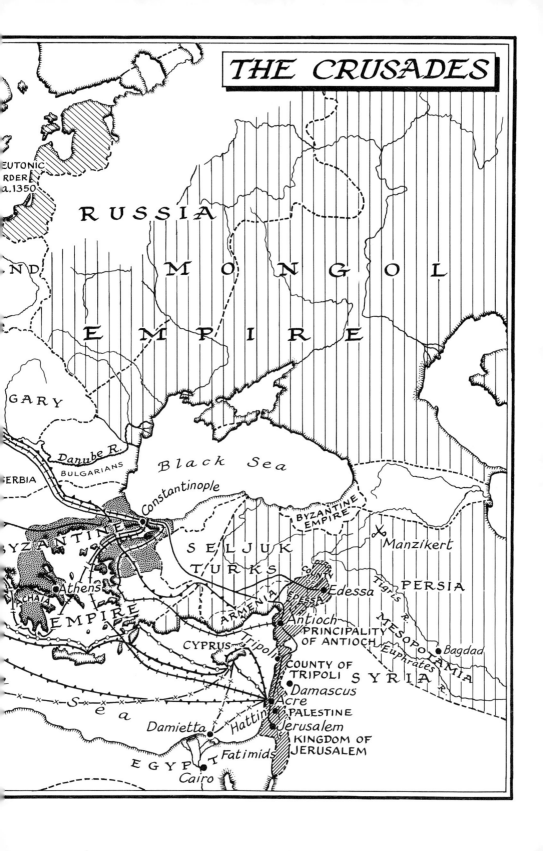

THE CRUSADES

TEUTONIC
ORDER
a.1350

RUSSIA

MONGOL

EMPIRE

LAND

HUNGARY

Danube R.

SERBIA

BULGARIANS

Black Sea

Constantinople

BYZANTINE

BYZANTINE EMPIRE

Manzikert

SELJUK

TURKS

Athens

ARMENIA

CONYA

EDESSA

Tigris R.

PERSIA

Edessa

ACHAIA

EMPIRE

Antioch

PRINCIPALITY
OF ANTIOCH

MESOPOTAMIA

Euphrates R.

Bagdad

CYPRUS

Tripoli

COUNTY OF
TRIPOLI

SYRIA

Damascus

Sea

Acre

PALESTINE

Damietta

Hattin

Jerusalem

KINGDOM OF
JERUSALEM

EGYPT

Fatimids

Cairo

The Crusaders take a town (thirteenth century).

last of them was to survive for one hundred and ninety-two years, none of the crusading states was ever really viable. They were divided among themselves and from the Byzantines, who still claimed the liberated territory as their own; they had to defend a long frontier with few troops; they could attract little permanent settlement from Europe; and they were beset by constant disease.

Their advantages lay partly in the fervor of the crusading military orders like the Templars and Hospitallers. The military orders had much in common with the new monastic orders and orders of canons. They were composed of laymen, who took the vows of poverty, chastity, and obedience and followed a religious Rule. The Hospitallers (Knights of Saint John) were founded about 1099, originally to care for pilgrims, but they soon turned to military activities. The Knights Templar were founded about 1120 as an order purely devoted to the defense of the Holy Land, and similar orders, like the Teutonic Knights in the Baltic region and the Knights of Calatrava in Spain, arose in imitation. The Templars especially came eventually to possess great wealth and influence. The spectacle of religious orders devoted to warfare and wealth illustrates the strange form that religious enthusiasm could take when order was confused with sanctity.

Another advantage of the crusading states was their long coastlines, though even that put them at the mercy of monopolistic and greedy Italian traders who were more interested in a fast ducat than in the defense of the Holy Sepulchre. In fact, their only strong advantage was the disunion of the Moslems; against a reunited Moslem force only the continued zeal of Europe could have preserved them, and Europe was becoming more preoccupied with its own political and economic well being than with the fate of Jerusalem. Never again would the zeal of the First Crusade be matched. The later crusades were universally ill conceived and ill executed.

Tradition has given these later crusades numbers, rather senselessly, for in fact there was a continual going and coming to and from the Holy Land on the part of European knights and princes. Sizable expeditions occurred between the "First Crusade" and the "Second." The "Second Crusade" was a poor affair. Preached by Saint Bernard in 1146, it was adopted by Louis VII of France and Conrad III of Germany, who lost most of their forces in Asia Minor, passed on to Damascus, where they dallied in a half-hearted siege that achieved only a great loss of life from disease among their men, and then returned home.

The Latin states in the Levant were now threatened by the increasing power of Nuredin and then Saladin, rulers who restored Moslem unity by uniting Egypt and Syria. Saladin disastrously defeated the Latin forces at the Horns of Hattin in 1187 and went on to capture Jerusalem. Europe's response was the romantic "Third Crusade" or "Crusade of the Three Kings" (1189–1192). Of the three, Frederick Barbarossa of Germany never arrived in the Holy Land, having drowned while crossing a river in Asia Minor; Philip Augustus of France quickly returned home to spin plots against Richard the Lionhearted; and Richard engaged in chivalric exploits against Saladin, antagonized his allies, and eventually ended up in an Austrian prison while Philip invaded his French possessions. The net result was the concession to the crusaders by Saladin of a ten-mile-wide strip of land along the coast and access to Jerusalem, whose rule, however, the Moslem king retained.

The "Fourth Crusade" began in 1202 under the patronage of Innocent III, who hoped to bring the Eastern Church into obedience to Rome as well as to defeat the Moslems. The Crusaders, mainly petty nobles, could only obtain passage from the Venetians, and had to promise to cut them in on the loot. The

Effigy of Richard the Lionhearted at Fontevrault Abbey.

first act of this holy war was to sack the Christian port of Zara. When Innocent heard of the incident, he tried to call back the Crusade, but it had already gone on toward Constantinople, bearing with it one Alexius, a claimant to the Byzantine throne who contracted to become a Roman Catholic, restore the Eastern Church to communion with the papacy, and pay out a huge sum "for the liberation of the Holy Land." Backed by the crusading army, Alexius IV was enthroned in 1203 and showed his gratitude by paying the crusaders 100,000 marks, of which the Venetians managed to get hold of 86,000. Alexius was murdered the next year, whereupon the crusaders threw themselves wholeheartedly into the rapine of the Christian capital (1204). Stripping churches, raping nuns, destroying statues, books, and paintings, looting houses, and beating people to death, the armies of Christ at last restored the eastern empire to communion with Rome by the expedient of driving out the Byzantine rulers and clergy, ensconcing Baldwin of Flanders as emperor, and dividing the empire into feudal principalities. This grotesque Latin Empire endured until 1261, its main contribution being to sap the strength of the eastern empire and to prepare it for its final extinction by the Turks in 1453.

The Crusades continued to drag on. An attempt to conquer Egypt in 1218 provided only the incongruous spectacle of Saint Francis clad in beggar's robes trying to convert the sultan. In 1228 Frederick II ingratiated himself with the Moslems by lavish entertainment and heretical philosophizing, and by these unusual means achieved a temporary cession of Jerusalem; Saint Louis IX of France made an unsuccessful attempt on Egypt in 1249 and one on Tunis in 1270 that succeeded in cutting down the flower of the French nobility. Jerusalem was finally lost in 1244 and the last fortress of the Latin states, Acre, fell in 1291.

In the meanwhile, two extraordinary events intervened. The first was one of the more peculiar manifestations of that popular zeal and piety that in the thirteenth century was seeking new channels of expression: the mass migration in 1212 of perhaps tens of thousands of children in an effort to reach the Holy Land. A lad near Orléans named Stephen told of receiving a visitation from Christ, who handed him a letter for King Philip Augustus, and the boy began preaching in the countryside and attracting a great following. It is not clear that Stephen himself preached a Crusade, but it is certain that great quantities of children of both sexes and from the age of six upwards began to move southwards from Lorraine and the Rhine, many of them under the leadership of a boy named Nicholas, in an effort to reach Jerusalem. Encouraged by credulous adults, the children were led to believe that God would deliver Jerusalem to their innocence where the nobles had failed to claim it with the sword. A sizable number reached the port of Genoa with Nicholas. Failing to get ship, some went home, and others accompanied Nicholas to Rome, where the pope kindly admonished them to go home. One group, which went to Marseille instead of to Genoa, met with a crueller fate: they found ships, and those who did not end in shipwreck were sold by merchants in the slave markets of North Africa. The significance of this whole episode, like that of the disorderly "Crusade of the Pastoureaux" in 1251, is that it represents the increasing dissatisfaction and sense of power on the part of the people. These strange Crusades were the forerunners of the peasants' rebellions, as well as the heresies, of the next century.

The other extraordinary event was the effort to cement an alliance with the Mongols. These nomadic people had been united into a powerful fighting force by Jenghiz Khan, who by 1223 had conquered an enormous empire stretching from the Pacific to Poland. The strange rumor soon was heard that these savage warriors were Christians. Oddly, there was a portion of truth in this fantastic report. The Nestorian heretics of the early Church had, though forgotten in the West, spread their doctrines eastward, and at the beginning of the thirteenth century there

were several Christian tribes in central Asia, not a few Christian churches in Mongolia itself, and a number of Christian princesses, warriors, and even priests at the court of the Great Khan.

The Catholic Christians of Europe now sent a number of Franciscan missionaries to Mongolia. One of them, William of Rubruck, thus describes his arrival at the Mongol capital: "On Palm Sunday we were near Caracorum. At dawn we blessed branches of willow . . . and about three o'clock we entered the city, the cross raised on high . . . and . . . went to church. The Nestorians came to meet us in procession. On entering the church we found them ready to celebrate Mass . . . ."[11] William also found a large number of Catholics who had been taken prisoner by the Mongols and who expressed their desire to have pastors sent them from Rome.

Not only did Christian missionaries go east, but Mongol embassies met Saint Louis of France in the Sainte-Chapelle and in 1271 negotiated a military alliance with Prince Edward of England. The common hope of Christian and Mongol was that they could effect the destruction of the Moslems by attacking them from both directions, but the Europeans lacked the

A wood carving representing Frederick Barbarossa.

stomach for the enterprise, and the Mongols were left to win their own victories. Hopes for the conversion of the Mongols ran high but were given little substantial support either by the Christian popes or by the Christian kings, and when Jenghiz's grandson Kublai Khan ended the toleration of Christianity in his domains, it quickly lost its importance. A great opportunity for the West had been lost through indifference, and the Mongol Mission, like the Crusades, ended in futility.

THE Crusades did not terminate with the fall of Acre in 1291. Along the Baltic the Teutonic Knights converted the pagan Prussians and Balts by force, and incidentally did battle with Christian Poles and Russians. The Military Orders of the Mediterranean mounted an occasional Crusade, sometimes with the help, but sometimes against the opposition, of the Italians, who often found it more profitable to do business with the infidel. Pierre Dubois at the court of Philip IV of France suggested a great Crusade under French leadership, and in 1396 a vast expedition against the Turks in Hungary failed. The Crusades of the waning Middle Ages merged with the struggles of modern Europe against the Turks, as when a unified Balkan force aided by the West tried unsuccessfully to block the Ottoman advance at Varna in Bulgaria in 1444. Efforts to save Constantinople were ultimately unsuccessful, and that city fell to the Turks in 1453. The old story finally came to an end when in 1917 General Allenby took Jerusalem—not for Christendom, but for the secular interests of the Allies.

What had the Crusades accomplished? It is likely that they hindered, rather than helped, commercial relations with the East. Though the fault lay on both sides, Byzantium and Islam were permanently rendered hostile to the West, with effects that continue to the present: calls for reunion with Rome are still met in the East with reminders of the Crusade of 1202–1204. The Crusades did nothing to enchance cultural contacts between Christianity and Islam. Such as existed were in Spain and Sicily, not in the Levant.

The failure of the Crusades dealt a blow to the prestige of the papacy. Christianity had been perverted by vicious knights and greedy merchants, who inflicted suffering upon hundreds of thousands of Moslems, Jews, and Christians. Whatever justification there may have been for Christendom's reclaiming lands by force that had been wrested from it by force, the Crusades failed even in this non-religious objective. Jerusalem and the East remained in the hands of the Moslems.

Pogroms, inquisition, and Crusades were the effect of passionate but misplaced popular fervor combined with the transformation of the Church from a community to a legalistic society. The law of love had become a love of law.

NOTES

[1] *Les Auteurs chrétiens latins du moyen âge sur les juifs et le judaïsme* (The Hague, 1963).

[2] Cited by Brian Tierney, *The Crisis of Church and State 1050–1300* (Englewood Cliffs, N. J., 1964), pp. 134–135.

[3] Colman Barry, ed. *Readings in Church History* (Westminster, Md., The Newman Press, 1960) 1, 541–542.

[4] Jacob R. Marcus, *The Jew in the Medieval World* (New York, Jewish Publication Society, 1938), p. 113.

[5] Marcus, p. 47.

[6] Marcus, p. 25, from Rigord.

[7] Edward Gibbon, *Decline and Fall*, III, ch. 58, 429–430.

[8] Gibbon, III, ch. 58, 441.

[9] Anna Comnena, *Alexiad*, ed. and trans. E. Dawes, in *The Portable Medieval Reader* edited by James Bruce Ross and Mary M. McLaughlin, Copyright 1949 by the Viking Press, Inc. New York. Reprinted by permission of the Viking Press, Inc.

[10] Anonymous history of the First Crusade, trans. James Bruce Ross in *The Portable Medieval Reader* edited by James Bruce Ross and Mary M. McLaughlin, Copyright 1949 by the Viking Press, Inc. New York. Reprinted by permission of The Viking Press, Inc. p. 443.

[11] William of Rubruck, "Journey," ch. 30, from *The Mongol Mission* translated by a nun of Stanbrook Abbey, edited by Christopher Dawson, Copyright 1955 Sheed & Ward, Inc., New York, 1955, p. 177.

Chapter Nineteen

THE PRACTICE OF POLITICS
IN THE CENTRAL MIDDLE AGES

THE great realms of the West—England, France, Germany, and Italy—continued from 1100 to 1300 to have many characteristics in common. Kings, barons, the Church, and the towns all wished to broaden their influence and enchance their independence at the expense of the others. Insofar as the kings, representing central government, were able to increase their power, disorder was reduced and controlled. Insofar as the opponents of royal power triumphed, tyranny was held at bay. In general, the dangers of disorder and anarchy were greater than those of tyranny, and the extension of royal power appeared beneficial to most observers at the time.

Historians of the last century were fond of finding great metaphysical movements in history, particularly in the direction of "progress," which for many of them meant liberal, laissez-faire nineteenth-century democracy. Consequently they tended to write as if the constitutional issues—the nature of sovereignty or the rights of subjects to representation in the courts or councils—had been clearly understood by medieval kings and barons. They also tended to equate limitations on the king's power as progress in the direction of democracy, and something called the "rise of Parliament" was made the central theme of English history as far back as Magna Carta. In this interpretation, those who supported the rise of Parliament were enlightened; those who, like King John, attempted to check it, were wicked or incompetent. To these historians the history of medieval France appeared unfortunate in comparison with that of England, for in France representative institutions never attained the strength *vis-à-vis* the king that they did in England. There were inconsistencies in this interpretation, for neither the anarchy of later medieval Germany nor that during certain periods of English history, the reign of Stephen (1135–1154) for example, seemed desirable, but these inconsistencies did not inhibit the establishment of the interpretation, often called the "Whig interpretation of history," among the assumptions of generations of scholars.

The Whig interpretation has not disappeared, but for the last forty years its simplicities have been recognized by all historians. The historian faced with the horrors of the twentieth century is less inclined than his grandfathers to subscribe to a simple theory of progress in human affairs. He is instructed enough in the complexities and vagaries of medieval politics to realize that few medieval politicians had much idea of political or constitutional theory. He understands that medieval political history, as Sir Lewis Namier has shown for English eighteenth-century political history, is best understood in terms of the struggle of interest groups for limited political advantage. The contesting parties of the Middle Ages were seldom aware of the long-range constitutional implications of their programs. Each sought to extend its own power, not for the sake of the constitution in generations to come, but for its own immediate advantage.

In all the western European countries one important motor of change was at work. Society was growing more settled and more complex, and commerce, culture, and the other elements of organized, civilized life required order; in turn, establishment of order on a broad basis required the passage of power from smaller units to larger units of government. Then, as government grew, it needed more revenues, and this in turn obliged it to extend its authority further. Reinforcing one another, these tendencies created the national state in England and in France. In Germany and Italy the resistance of princes, bishops, and towns proved sufficient to check the expansion of royal government, but those who resisted the crown in these countries consolidated their own governments in much the way that the kings of France and England were doing.

THE kings, then, sought to extend royal power, not primarily because of theories of kingship deriving from Roman law or elsewhere, but because each individual king needed more soldiers and more money. The kings worked to expand both their private and their public power. The king usually had land which he had not given out to any feudal vassal but ruled directly. This land—the domain—was usually scattered over the country, and it might consist of forest or wasteland, villages or towns. In France, crown land was at the beginning of the twelfth century centered in the Ile de France, the region around Paris; in Germany dynastic quarrels over the crown lands helped weaken the king's position. In England, the king's domain was considerable and was scattered through most areas of the realm.

The domain was worked by freemen and serfs in their villages under the direction of royally appointed stewards. These stewards, unlike feudal barons, were paid employees of the king and owed him complete loyalty. The king was in effect manorial lord in his domains: he collected their revenues directly, in cash or kind, without any feudal intermediary. The kings therefore attempted to maintain and to expand this domain by war, marriage, confiscation, or whatever other means were at hand.

They also had to extend their public power. The royal domain was only a small fraction of the land in any country, the rest being held by feudal lords. The kings attempted to confirm and strengthen the ties binding the feudal lords to them; they made marriage and other alliances with them where possible; they attempted to extend the royal system of law, of administration, and of tax-collecting into the feudal territories. They attempted to limit feudal war among their vassals, to secure their help against common external enemies, and to establish the important principle that no lord could make war on his king. In England and France, time and effort worked to good effect; in Germany the opposite tendency prevailed, and the localities triumphed over the central authority.

In order effectively to advance their power, the kings needed to establish their own independence of the feudal lords, to find other staffs on which to lean. The kings disliked depending on advisers from among the great nobles and clergy to carry out the public administration, and it was often their policy to divert the powers of these public officers to the private household officers—the chamberlain, for example—whose livelihood depended upon royal favor and whose loyalty could therefore be assumed. To these men the kings entrusted the conduct of many of the affairs of state.

Most of all the king needed revenue. Besides the revenues of his domain, he could count upon fines levied by his courts, upon the profits of the mint, and upon other resources, but he also often found it desirable to transform feudal military obligations into monetary payments. Increasing revenues meant greater opportunity to buy land, to pay his administrators, and to create a paid, loyal army, all of which would enhance royal independence.

In the meanwhile, the barons had their own needs and requirements. They too needed to secure order in their own holdings, and they set about consolidating their own domains and building their own administrations in much the way that the kings were doing. When, as in France, the king was eventually able to establish meaningful authority over the principalities, he profited from the work that they had already done. When, in Germany, the king failed to do so, the barons had at least established order and efficient government over smaller territories. Besides expanding their domains and administrations, the barons resisted the encroachments both of the king and of other barons. Northern France in the twelfth century resembles, on a small scale, Europe in the later nineteenth: a constant manipulation of alliances and counter-alliances among the feudal powers.

The barons reacted to the extension of royal power in two ways: they sought to prevent it, or when this failed, to influence it as much as possible. On the one hand they resisted the king's efforts to strengthen his authority over them; on the other hand they tried to divert power in the central government away from the king's private offices and into the public offices which they could more readily control. They sought to maintain and extend the powers of the old Great Council of the realm, the vaguely defined meeting where the king took counsel with his chief tenants. They conjured up vague recollections of the old Germanic right of resistance to an incompetent ruler and often made common cause with the Church. But, even during a great constitutional crisis like Magna Carta in 1215, very few of the participants seem to have been aware of the constitutional implications of their actions.

Before the papal revolution, the kings also turned to the Church, particularly the bishops, as a source of support against the nobility and as a source of revenue, and it is for this reason that the kings so jealously guarded their influence over the bishops. From the thirteenth century, however, Church theorists taught that an unjust monarch might be deposed, and the bishops became more independent. Thus the kings found themselves obliged to rely upon an even broader base of support among the population. The wealth of the citizens and burgers grew at the same time that the king's need for money increased. Upon these newly powerful elements of the community the kings relied increasingly, particularly from the end of the thirteenth century.

Both Church and towns desired nothing so much as the establishment of peace and order so that trade and education might flourish, and they were inclined to support whatever power was most likely to guarantee tranquility. On the other hand, they were both extremely jealous of their own rights and liberties. The towns, often under the control of bishops or barons, were for that reason likely to make common cause with the king, and it was in fact among the towns that in England, France, and Germany alike the kings found their most reliable support. Since many bishops were royally appointed, they also supported the king, but since the papal revolution and the consequent limitations of these appointments, the bishops tended to be more independent and to resist royal intrusions into Church affairs. Hence the support often given the barons by the Church in the conflicts between king and barons in England.

The consequence of these developments was the growth of representative institutions and of the influence of these groups in government. There is no contradiction in the fact that political history from 1100 is the story both of increasing royal power and of increasing representative institutions, for it was primarily the requirements of royal power that called representative institutions into being. Insofar as it is at all possible to speak of popular power in this period, that power was engendered not so much by opposition to, as by cooperation with, the crown.

THE sources for political history 1100–1300 are enormous, including quantities of documents relating to public and private administration and law as well as the works of numerous chroniclers such as Henry of Huntingdon, Rigord, Otto of Freising, and Giovanni Villani, to name only a very few. The greatly increased variety, as well as quantity, of sources affords a very detailed view of the period. Here for the first time the historian begins to be relieved from the limitations placed upon him by lack of sources; and he conversely begins to suffer from the problems that beset the modern historian, who worries less about lack of sources than about selecting what is significant.

FRANCE. The twelfth-century kings of France vigorously attacked the problems that had beset their predecessors. They secured and increased their own domain, they enhanced royal power against the feudality, they added to their revenues, built their administration, and held strong support from both the Church and the towns. They also achieved some success in resisting the formidable threat posed by kings of England who at the same time held the largest and wealthiest fiefs in France. The victory of the kings of France is a monument to the orderly succession of the Capetian line, the requirements of public order pressed by the Church and the towns, the divisions among the nobility, and the extraordinary skill of monarchs like Louis VI, Philip II, Louis IX, and Philip IV.

Louis VI's first contribution was the establishment of firm royal control over the Ile de France, a process that had been begun by his father, Philip I. In 1124 Louis was able to marshal something like a French national resistance against the invading King Henry V of Germany. But the greatest diplomatic coup of this energetic king was the acquisition of Aquitaine. The duke of the largest fief in France, Aquitaine, had since the time of Hugh Capet been virtually independent of the king. Until 1126 he had refused to do homage to Louis at all and had even issued documents as "king of Aquitaine." In 1137 Louis VI was able to arrange the marriage of his son Prince Louis to the heiress to the duchy, Eleanor.

But other dangers still lurked. By 1125, Blois and Champagne, the two countries on either side of the Ile de France, had been united under one dynasty, and this coalition was a constant menace to the crown. In Anjou, the power of Geoffrey Plantagenet (so called because he chose the broomplant—*planta genesta*—as his personal badge) and his heirs was rising. The dukes of Normandy, now also kings of England, threatened the Ile de

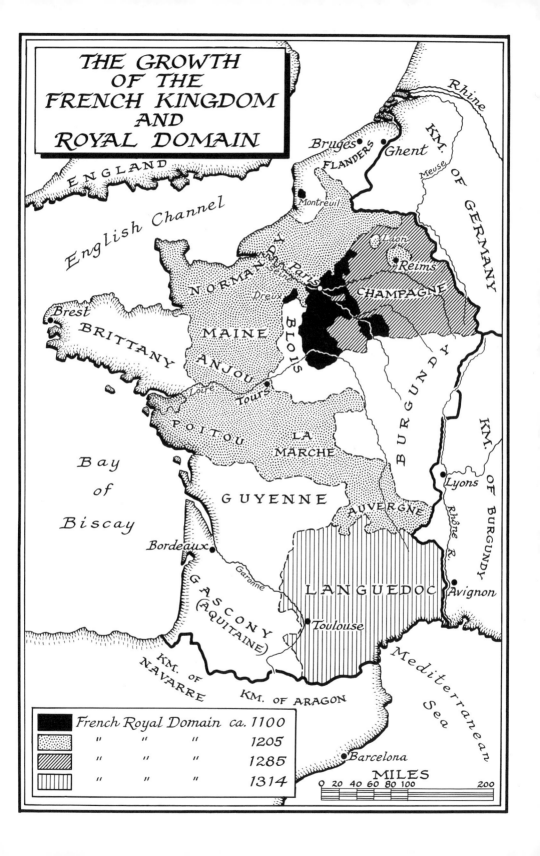

THE GROWTH OF THE FRENCH KINGDOM AND ROYAL DOMAIN

ENGLAND

Bruges
FLANDERS
Ghent
Montreuil

English Channel

KM. OF GERMANY

Rhine

Meuse

Laon
Reims
CHAMPAGNE

NORMANDY
Paris
Seine
Dreux
BLOIS

Brest
BRITTANY
MAINE
ANJOU

Loire
Tours

POITOU
LA MARCHE

BURGUNDY

Lyons

KM. OF BURGUNDY

Bay
of
Biscay

GUYENNE

AUVERGNE

Rhône R.

Bordeaux

Garonne

GASCONY
(AQUITAINE)

LANGUEDOC

Avignon

Toulouse

Mediterranean Sea

KM. OF NAVARRE

KM. OF ARAGON

Barcelona

French Royal Domain ca. 1100
" " " 1205
" " " 1285
" " " 1314

MILES
0 20 40 60 80 100   200

France on the north. One of these dangers was averted when Stephen of Blois was foiled in his effort to secure the English crown and Louis VII temporarily secured Champagne. But the nightmare of the king of France was that England and Normandy would unite with Anjou. The nightmare came true. Geoffrey Plantagenet had married Matilda, the daughter of King Henry I of England, and their son Henry II succeeded in 1154 to the kingdom of England, the duchy of Normandy, and the county of Anjou.

This would have been bad enough for France, but worse followed. The marriage alliance with Aquitaine so carefully arranged by Louis VI ended by bringing sore distress on Louis VII. Mild, pious, and charitable, he could not cope with Eleanor, who was notoriously adulterous, personally vicious, and, in addition to her other sins, unable to provide the king with an heir. Suger, the abbot of Saint-Denis who was the original patron of Gothic architecture as well as the best advisor of both Louis VI and Louis VII, held the marriage together as long as he lived, but after his death Louis procured an anullment (1152). Two months later, Eleanor married Henry Plantagenet, who now ruled an enormous empire.

Eleanor proved no greater boon to Henry than to Louis. She raised constant dissensions and rebellions, first of Henry's sons against him and then, after his death, of the sons against one another. Louis' son, Philip II Augustus (1180–1223), took complete advantage of the situation and mingled in these disputes with unabashed pleasure. Philip, who became king at fourteen, was a vital, though sickly, ruler, who had a shrewd political intelligence and an ability to plan carefully and patiently. He took advantage of Richard the Lionhearted's absence on crusade to encroach upon Normandy, and, when Richard was succeeded by the inept John, he completed the job. John, surnamed Lackland because he lost English territory in France, played into his enemy's hands. He seduced the Lady Isabel of Angoulême away from her fiancé and then refused to come to the French court to answer charges. Philip was accordingly able in 1202 to declare that John, having violated his feudal contract, had forfeited all his lands. This was only theory, but the theory was soon realized, for John, by murdering his young and popular nephew Arthur, drove the Bretons, Angevins, and Normans into

Seal of Philip Augustus.

Philip's camp. By 1205 all northern France had been annexed, and the acquisition of Normandy and Anjou with their fertility and wealth was Philip's greatest contribution to the security of the French crown. The Plantagenets, however, retained control of Aquitaine in the south, and quarrels between the two powers continued. In Germany, England and France both sought to extend their influence; Philip attempted to secure the English crown for his son; in France, disputes over territories in and around Aquitaine were continually recurrent.

Philip constructed an efficient administration to match the extent of his domains. Realizing the need to extend and to generalize taxation in order to support a growing government, he used feudal aids and incidents as much as possible, collected judicial fines, imposed crusading taxes (Philip actually went briefly on crusade, but the tax became a standard source of revenue for kings who never dreamed of setting foot in the Holy Land), and extorted money from the Jews. He took the first step in making Paris a real capital by establishing the *Palais de la Cité* as a permanent center of justice, and he rebuilt the local administration. Until the reign of Philip, this had been in the hands of *prévôts,* tax collectors who were paid by being allowed to pocket much of the money they collected. Philip replaced the *prévôts* with *baillis* in northern France and *sénechaux* in the south. These were civil officers responsible directly to the king for seeing that in every locality royal justice was done and royal taxes collected. Since the *baillis* and *sénéchaux* were moved about from one district to another and were on a strict salary, they were less likely to abuse their position. Only by such institu-

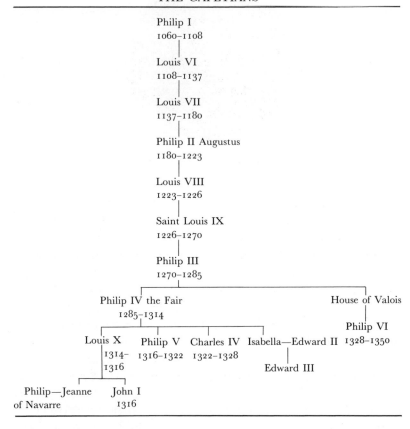

Philip I
1060–1108

Louis VI
1108–1137

Louis VII
1137–1180

Philip II Augustus
1180–1223

Louis VIII
1223–1226

Saint Louis IX
1226–1270

Philip III
1270–1285

Philip IV the Fair
1285–1314

House of Valois

Philip VI
1328–1350

Louis X
1314–1316

Philip V
1316–1322

Charles IV
1322–1328

Isabella—Edward II

Edward III

Philip—Jeanne
of Navarre

John I
1316

tions as these could the king hold together the dominions he
had assembled.

Saint Louis IX (1226–1270), Philip's grandson, inherited
the throne as a child and was long dominated by his mother,
Blanche of Castile. When he grew older, he acquired a charm,
combined with a devotion to justice, that led his subjects to
consider him the ideal Christian king, loving God, justice, and
war. Equally brave in battle, steadfast in captivity, pious in
prayer, and wise in judgment, Louis' axiom was when in doubt
to favor others above oneself and the poor over the rich. His
ascetic sanctity (he had himself whipped and undertook other
mortifications) did not prevent him from being a very astute
politician and adminstrator who systematically dominated the
barons, the communes, and the Church. He put down several

rebellions on the part of the nobles and forbade the construction of private castles. He installed royally appointed mayors in the communes. He established *enquêteurs* (inquisitors) to keep watch over the *baillis* and *sénéchaux,* who were showing too much independence; and he issued royal *ordonnances* without the consent of the barons.

The culmination of these two developments necessary to the creation of a strong monarchy—the consolidation of territory and the consolidation of administration—occurred in the reign of Philip IV the Fair (1285-1314). Philip was as cold and ruthless as he was tall and handsome. A determined politician without the charm or Christian mildness of his grandfather, he determined to rule well and strongly. Philip assimilated Flanders and encroached upon the English position in Aquitaine (or Gascony, as it was increasingly called), sending in royal officials in order to undermine the authority of Edward I, and encouraging French knights to raid the border while Norman ships disrupted Gascon trade. The ultimate issue of these disputes was the Hundred Years' War, which Edward and Philip postponed by the novel expedient of long diplomatic negotiations, during which the beginnings of the modern foreign office and foreign service were made.

In the meanwhile, Philip continued the construction of a strong administration. It has been disputed whether he was himself a great man or whether he

Saint Louis.

was ruled by his advisers. Even contemporaries could not agree. One observer said that "the King of France is pope and emperor"[1]; others, that he was a tool of his own bureaucracy. The latest interpretations insist that Philip was at all times the coordinator of policy, but it is nonetheless true that his ministers began to have the influence that is associated with the cabinet in modern government. These men, Pierre Flote, Guillaume de Nogaret, and Enguerrand de Marigny, were the predecessors of Colbert and Turgot.

Philip pursued his predecessors' policy of controlling the nobility and the towns, and he used provincial assemblies called "estates" to secure popular support of his policies (the Estates General did not yet exist). Philip divided the administration into Parlement (justice), Chambre des Comptes (finance), and great council (advice), all firmly under royal control. The Parlement dealt with appeals and petitions and filled a most important role for a monarchy seeking integration: it heard suits regarding feudal jurisdiction and in this capacity was an instrument of enforcing royal policy in the domains of powerful vassals. Staffed by royal judges, the Parlement usually decided cases in favor of the king.

Philip's increasing need for money to support his growing government led him to increase his exactions from barons, towns, the Lombards, the Jews (whom he expelled after he had robbed them), and, most controversial of all, from the Church and the powerful Knights Templar. Philip's policy towards the Church was the product of financial need. The papacy had been drawing a considerable sum from the French clergy; now the king decided that he too must tap this source of revenue. Unfortunately the pope at this time was Boniface VIII, one of the most immoderate of the medieval popes. Boniface had followed the teachings of the papalist lawyers to their extremes, insisting that the papacy had the right to demand obedience from kings even in specific matters of state. As when Gregory VII met Henry IV in combat, pope and monarch met one another head on. This time it was the papacy that was forced to yield.

Boniface began by declaring Philip's tax of the French clergy improper in the bull *Clericis laicos* (1296); in reply, Philip forbade the export of gold and silver, in effect a block to any further taxation of the French clergy by the pope. Boniface rejoined with a bull, "Inexpressible love," in which he threatened a vast alliance of the king's enemies. As the years passed both sides grew more extreme. Pierre Flote wrote that the French monarchy was superior in honor to the clergy; Boniface threatened to raise an insurrection; Philip burned Boniface's bull and called upon the estates to approve his action. In 1302 Boniface issued the bull *Unam Sanctam,* which marks the height of papalist theory: "We declare, state, and define that it is altogether necessary to salvation for every human creature to be subject to the Roman Pontiff," and the context conveys that this means temporal as well as spiritual subjection. In another context, Boniface is reputed to have exclaimed: "I am king and priest, pope and caesar." It was not that the pope was a megalomaniac: he was in his intemperate fashion expressing what he had been led by the lawyers to believe was tradition. In 1303 he attempted to complete the job by declaring Philip excommunicate.

The response of the monarchy was no less intemperate. Concerting with Boniface's Italian enemies, Philip's man Guillaume de Nogaret in 1303 surprised and kidnapped the pope at Anagni, shortly after which Boniface died. This so-called "Outrage of Anagni" was the preface to the establishment of the papacy at Avignon in southern France in 1305. With imperial power in Italy shattered, the popes could either become the pawns of the Roman noble families, or,

Effigy of Philip IV the Fair.

as Philip IV suggested, withdraw to Avignon where they would be assured of peace and tranquility. They did achieve peace there, but at the price of French domination, which continued until the papacy was returned to Rome in 1378.

Philip IV's reign was on the one hand the culmination of a pragmatic policy of royal extension and on the other the beginning of the transition to modern nationalism. One of the king's lesser advisers, Pierre Dubois, wrote a book on *The Recovery of the Holy Land* in which he spelled out his own formula for Christian society: a French pope, a French Holy Roman Emperor, French kings in eastern Europe, a French emperor in Constantinople, and a king of England docilely serving the wishes of his powerful colleague. For Dubois, the Avignon residence protected the pope from the treacheries of the Romans and procured him "leisure for the government only of souls, and will avoid the intemperance of the Roman air, which is not native to him."[2]

Under Philip IV the Capetian monarchy was on the verge of controlling Europe, but it was quickly brought low after that monarch's death. To the observer who believed in poetic justice, this seemed the result of Philip's crimes, particularly his persecution of the Templars. Desiring to expropriate the vast wealth of that order, Philip, with the acquiescence of his pope, Clement V, in 1311 adjudged the Templars guilty of heresy and perversion and condemned their leaders to death. The master of the order, Jacques de Molay, is said to have pronounced from the stake a solemn curse upon his tormentors. Curse or not, for the first time in the history of the dynasty, Philip's sons were unable to produce a living male heir. The subsequent disputes over the succession, which came to involve the kings of England and Navarre, helped to weaken France and to prepare for the Hundred Years' War. The government, having been burdened by an overambitious foreign policy, was economically weakened. Inflation was encouraged by the debasement of the coinage. To the resentment of the barons, clergy, and burgers who disliked Philip's taxations were added the growing tensions caused by peasant dissatisfaction and unrest. The next century saw not only foreign invasions but internal rebellions. The good luck of the Capetians ended in 1314 with the death of Philip IV, and French dominance of Europe was delayed by more than a century.

ENGLAND. English rulers of the twelfth century built upon the already firm foundations laid by the efficient Anglo-Saxon and Norman administration, and they thus enjoyed advantages denied to their colleagues of France and Germany. The task of the English kings was to extend the royal judicial and administrative system and to link it with local government in a unified system of government. To do this, and to wage war with the Irish, Scots, and French, to say nothing of participating in Crusades, the king needed to expand his revenues and, consequently, to enlist wide support throughout the realm. The result of these policies was to build a powerful monarchy and at the same time to encourage the appearance and development of representative institutions.

One of the most important aspects of the history of England in the twelfth and thirteenth centuries is the achievement of a constitutional balance between the centralizing force in society—the king—and the particularist forces, particularly the barons. William I and Henry I had built up a strong adminstration that already had taken several important steps in the direction of centralized monarchy: the prohibition against anyone's making war against the king; the Oath of Salisbury, a loyalty oath imposed upon all great landholders by William; The Domesday census William ordered made of the whole country; and the use in government by Henry I of men with ability but no feudal power. The long civil war between Stephen of Blois and Henry I's daughter Matilda undermined royal authority, but at least by bad example it convinced most people that royal authority was more attractive than anarchy. According to the settlement reached at the end of the civil war, the son of Matilda and Geoffrey Plantagenet succeeded to the throne at Stephen's death in 1154.

This son was Henry II, twenty-one years old at the time of his accession, a stocky prince who held his weight down by constant exercise. It was energy, physical, mental, and political, that was his most distinguishing characteristic. Fond of hunting, he was unable to sit still in church, passing his time there in conversation or drawing pictures. He was often too impatient to remain sitting while discussing affairs of state, and he not infrequently horrified his servants, courtiers, and administrative staff by deciding early in the morning upon a long journey that

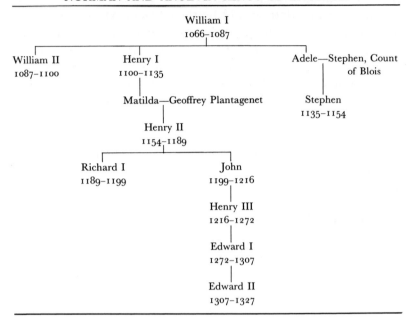

was to begin that day. Then the household knights rushed for their horses, the chancery clerks scrambled for the documents that had to accompany the king everywhere, and in the evening, brought to a halt by the king's command, his followers had to find what lodgings they could for the night. Henry's impatience and violent temper sometimes caused him grief, as in the affair with Becket, but for the most part his driving energy produced a determined diplomacy and political vigor and acumen in dealing with affairs of state. "O Lord," went a saying, "turn the heart of this king that he may know himself to be but man."[3]

Skillfully welding together the most constructive aspects of royal administration, feudalism, and the local courts, Henry began to link the royal courts with the local assemblies, establishing a system of royal justices; he reorganized his administration and, with baronial consent, issued modifications of existing law. In accordance with the medieval idea that law is discovered rather than made, Henry declared that he was going back beyond the civil war to return to the good old customs of his grandfather Henry I. In reality he did much more. He created a unified administrative and legal system that, improved and expanded by Edward I and later monarchs, proved viable and flexible enough to adapt to constant modifications and hence to survive to the present.

Henry II's policy was a logical extension of that of William I and Henry I: to increase governmental efficiency, to establish law and order, and to limit anarchy. Henry possessed the skill and energy requisite to making such a program effective, but his successors were less capable. Richard I spent most of his time abroad at war, and during his reign (1189–1199) the barons reacquired a taste for freedom from royal control.

Richard was succeeded by his brother John. John (1199–1216) inherited the bad temper and sensuousness of his father without his qualities of good judgment. Relying upon personal favorites, prone to fits of rage in which he is said to have become incoherent, subject also to impulses like that which made him carry off Isabel of Angoulême from her fiancé, he was in addition capable of brutality and extreme cruelty. On the death of Richard, John was recognized only in England and Normandy, while Anjou and Brittany acclaimed his nephew Arthur and Aquitaine submitted to the queen-mother Eleanor. With enormous energy John waged successful war against both his mother and his nephew, but his energy was matched by a viciousness that antagonized even those who had at first supported him. Having captured Arthur, as the best report has it, John murdered his nephew with his own hands in a drunken fury. John's unwillingness to abide by the rules of tact, law, morality, or feudal custom not only alienated his French vassals and made it possible for Philip Augustus to strip him of most of his French lands, but alienated the English barons and the English Church as well. Not only did John attempt to enhance the powers of the royal administration and to increase his revenues: any vigorous king would have done this. But he found himself embroiled with the pope over the choice of an archbishop of Canterbury and, once the choice was made, with the new archbishop, Stephen Langton, himself. The barons who held land on both sides of the Channel were enraged at John's blundering French policies, resented his rash temper and violation of feudal sensitivities, and longed for a return to the greater influence they had had under Richard. Discontent culminated in 1215 in a revolt of the barons backed by the archbishop and by the pope.

The chief product of the revolt was the signing of Magna Carta by John in 1215. No medieval document has been the occasion of as much debate. The old Whig interpretation made it the "guarantee of the liberties of the Englishman." If Magna Carta is viewed in the context of its own time, it was nothing quite so spectacular. It was originally called the "Great Charter," not because of its importance, but because of its physical size and to distinguish it from the contemporary "Charter of the Forest." Essentially it was a conservative document in which the Church and the barons demanded a return to what they thought were the old customs of the realm. Basically too it was a feudal document, securing certain rights and privileges for the barons and the Church and ignoring the rest of the people, except by implication. It was intrinsically an expression of the old popular right of resistance as well as of the right to take action against a king who has violated the feudal contract. Yet it went beyond the merely feudal and conservative. From the time of Elizabeth I lawyers used its implications of the rights of the whole people in the term "free man" in order to establish the liberties of the individual. This subsequent history of Magna Carta, in which it came to mean much more than it originally had, is an illustration of the English flexibility with regard to law that made the English system so extraordinarily workable. The English, like other medieval people, subscribed to the theory that law was immutable, but in practice, and almost without being aware of it, they modified and adapted the law to fit the circumstances.

John died in 1216, leaving the throne to an infant son, Henry III. During Henry's minority the barons showed their moderation, or their hopes of dominating the government, in reissuing the Great Charter with revisions favorable to royal power. After 1227, however, Henry III himself assumed the reins of power and, by gradually transferring real power from the public offices, where the barons could control them, into the private offices held by his own loyal supporters, he alienated the barons. By 1258 the conflict was open, culminating in 1265 at the Battle of Evesham, where the royalist forces under the command of Henry's son Prince Edward defeated and killed the

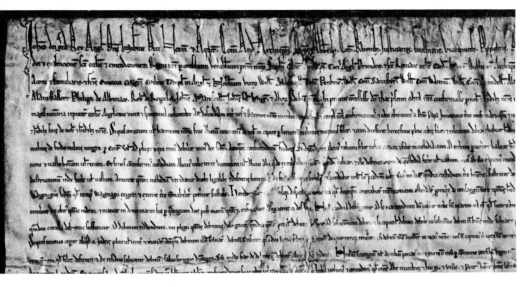

Detail of Magna Carta.

baronial leader Simon de Montfort. From that date the prince, later Edward I, was the effective ruler of the land.

In the meantime, the need of both the king and the barons to court popular support for their cause encouraged increasingly frequent summoning of representative assemblies. The barons had learned to unite and work as a group; and the king had begun to learn the necessity of courting the Church, the burgers, and the wealthy freemen.

Edward I (1272–1307) was one of the most effective monarchs of the Middle Ages. Tall, muscular, and emphatic, he proved himself a courageous and skillful young man in the wars against the barons, and as he grew older gained self-control and moderation as well. Edward came to have a great respect for the law that earned him the title of "the English Justinian." He understood his duty as a king not simply to be the extension of royal power but the securing for everyone his just *libertas,* his proper place in society, and he had a sense of the just claims of all elements of society to a degree highly unusual in his time. He pursued a realistic and energetic foreign policy, fending off Philip IV's encroachments in Gascony, but he was ready to negotiate when reasonable terms were offered. At home, he made

Dominions of the Angevins from 1154

THE THIRTEENTH CENTURY

LIVONIA

Moscow

TEUTONIC
KNIGHTS

EAST
PRUSSIA

POMERANIA

WEST
PRUSSIA

POLAND

R U S S I A

SILESIA

Prague

BOHEMIA

NY

STRIA

nice

H U N G A R Y

Danube R.

SERBIA

BULGARIANS

KM. OF
NAPLES

Melfi

aples

BYZANTINE

KM. OF SICILY

EMPIRE

ARMENIA

CYPRUS

S e a

D O M.   O F   S A L A D I N

those moves to increase the royal administration and revenues that he thought were necessary for the good governance of the realm, but again, when crisis came, he was willing to compromise.

Edward strengthened the royal position by setting the "little council" of personal advisers more clearly apart from the "great council" and making it a kind of cabinet. He determined to strengthen his position through the use of parliament, and he assembled the barons, clergy, gentry, and citizens in a body to hear and approve the royal will. The parliament of Edward I's day was representative in nature, and it was beginning to have some real political power. But for the most part it acted less as a legislative body in the modern sense than as an instrument of royal propaganda. The representatives were sent back to their towns and shires as interpreters of the king's will. The parliament and its statutes were successfully manipulated by Edward I as a means of getting what he wanted done and as a weapon against the independent pretensions of the barons and the pope.

Edward I, like Philip IV, had difficulties with Boniface VIII, and in England this was the occasion of a renewal of effective baronial opposition as well. The conflict culminated in a crisis in 1296–1297. Edward, like Philip, needed more money to run a growing government and a more complicated foreign policy. Trouble in Flanders, Norman piracy, Philip's inroads into Gascony, Edward's own efforts to control Scotland and Wales, all these put unusual demands upon the king's purse. Accordingly Edward imposed new taxes upon both the barons and the clergy, and immediately he found his support dwindling. Boniface VIII's bull *Clericis laicos* against lay taxation of the clergy was meant for Edward as well as for Philip, and the pope's influence was still great. In 1296 both barons and bishops defied the king, and though the settlement of 1297 was a compromise, Edward was forced to withdraw his unusual taxes. The compromise solved nothing and led to renewed struggles between the barons and Edward's heir Edward II, but the crisis had accomplished something else. It prevented Edward I from becoming a Philip IV. It left the baronial opposition, and hence the balance of power, intact.

GERMANY AND ITALY. In Germany and Italy the position of the king was much more defensive than in England or France. The

Boniface VIII.

German and Italian rulers had to try to counteract a disaffection in the Church and an independence among the barons that were both already growing by the beginning of the twelfth century. With frequent shifts of dynasties, continuity of policy and administration was diminished, and the kings had to struggle to keep, let alone to augment, the crown domain. The kings needed desperately to find some reliable ally. They tried in the tradition of the Ottos to enlist the support of the bishops, but many of the bishops were now more loyal to the reformed papacy. They tried to support the lower vassals against the higher, but this only encouraged increasing atomization of power without securing any permanent advantage to the crown. They tried to rely upon the *ministeriales,* like the English serjeants servile in origin and therefore owing everything to the king. But as soon as the *ministeriales* began to grow wealthy and powerful, they identified themselves with the feudal nobility. The kings sought allies in the towns, and in Germany they achieved some success with this policy, but it was an utter failure in Italy, and even in Germany the towns were too sensible of their own interests to support the monarchy any longer than it suited them.

The involvement of the German kings in Italy and their pursuit of imperial schemes were neither so irrational nor so damaging as once was thought, but it is undeniable that they constituted a sizable distraction. The more the kings sought to improve their position in Italy the more problems they encountered. The northern Italian towns preferred independence to any advantage they might get from supporting the emperor, and the papacy was jealous of its independence. Henry VI's marriage to the heiress of Sicily further antagonized the popes, who feared imperial encirclement on north and south, and though Sicily was itself wealthy and efficiently organized, its possession distracted the emperors from dealing with pressing problems in the north. The kings attempted to use frontier lords like Austria and Brandenburg as counterweights against the entrenched barons of central Germany, but again these powers cooperated only when it was to their advantage and strenuously resisted any interference of royal power in their own domains.

The Italian cities and the German princes both lay and ecclesiastical were consolidating their own independence and building viable governments in their own territories. An important question is at what point all efforts of the king to achieve effective rule over his dominions became futile. That point had clearly been reached by the death of Frederick II in 1250, when anarchy ensued, but events had long been leading in that direction. The defeat of the Hohenstaufen by the papacy, the consequent election of the pro-papal Lothar II to the throne in 1124, and then, immediately following Lothar, another shift in

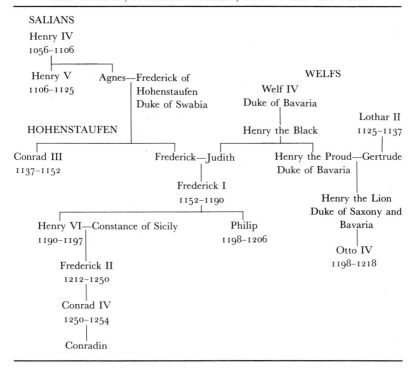

dynasties in favor of the Hohenstaufen, all weakened the imperial office. The Hohenstaufen, whose center of power was in Swabia, never were in a strong position.

The Hohenstaufen power derived from the marriage of Agnes, the daughter of Henry IV, with Frederick of Hohenstaufen, duke of Swabia. The elder son of this marriage, Conrad III, was named Lothar's successor only after having made major concessions to the Church and the barons in order to woo them away from Lothar's heir. Thus competition between dynasties debased the royal power, for every successful candidate had to offer more concessions than his rival. Lothar's heir, Duke Henry the Proud of Bavaria, had by his marriage to Lothar's daughter Gertrude tied the old Welf alliance of Saxony and Bavaria even tighter. Saxony and Bavaria were two of the three most important duchies in the kingdom, and these were now firmly ruled by a family absolutely hostile to the ruling Hohenstaufen. The Welf attack upon imperial power that now ensued was not the result of feudal particularism or opposition to royal power in general as much as it was the expression of implacable hostility to the Hohenstaufen. Conrad III's efforts to deprive Henry the Proud of both duchies failed and only precipitated an open rebellion. Henry the Lion, the heir of Henry the Proud and Gertrude and consequently duke of both Saxony and Bavaria, was an efficient and ruthless ruler who extended his power into the eastern marches, founding colonies and ruling with an iron hand. This formidable ruler was the chief rival of Conrad's son, Frederick I.

Frederick I, called Barbarossa from his red beard, was one of the ablest monarchs of the Middle Ages, and it is a measure of the already desperate state of the empire that he could do little to check the process of deterioration. It has been argued whether Barbarossa was a reactionary looking back to the days of the Ottos or a forward-looking nationalist. Most of all he was a pragmatist who looked about for solutions with a quick and perceptive eye. In his policy towards the nobles he encouraged feudal subtenants against their more powerful masters, and he put much faith in the Brandenburg and Austrian connections to balance the power of Henry the Lion. These were, like the Ottos' assault upon the dukes, short-sighted policies. But he also attempted to bind the nobility closer by establishing *Reichsfürsten,* a new variety of powerful vassals who were to hold their land directly from the king; and he issued an imperial order forbidding feudal wars.

Frederick was initially conciliatory in his approach to the Welfs. He attempted to pacify Henry the Lion by confirming to him both his duchies of Saxony and Bavaria, and a *modus vivendi* was established. But Henry's independent policies continued to rankle, and eventually conflict became open. When Frederick invaded Italy in 1179 he called upon Henry to fulfill his feudal obligations and join the campaign. Henry refused, and Frederick determined to dislodge him. Allying himself with Henry's own discontented vassals, he defeated and exiled the duke (1180). Dividing Henry's duchy of Saxony forever among small vassals, he turned Henry's duchy of Bavaria over to the Wittelsbach family, which ruled until 1918. Thus Frederick disposed of his most powerful enemy. In the meanwhile, he succeeded in streamlining the administration, and exerting some influence over both the bishops and the lesser nobility.

But what Henry II and Philip II could accomplish, Frederick could not. Brandenburg and Austria pursued their own interest, as did the Wittelsbachs in Bavaria. The *Reichsfürsten,* like the *ministeriales,* soon found more in common with the other nobles than with the king. The German towns were becoming more independent; though Frederick held great imperial diets such as that of Besançon in 1157, no representative institutions arose on a national level to express a sense of community of the realm; even the growth of the royal domain was impeded by the peculiar German rule that fiefs to which there was no heir, rather than escheating to the crown, had to be given out to other vassals. Barbarossa's energetic life ended, ironically, in his accidental drowning while on crusade. The final irony is that Frederick, whose policies had failed, soon became a symbol of unity for his people, and the legend grew among those who longed for a return to order that the old king would rise from his tomb and come to rule again.

Frederick's most controversial policy was his determination to secure control of Italy, which many historians have condemned as an absurd effort to recapture imperial grandeur at the expense of royal power. In fact, like Otto the Great, Frederick had good practical reasons for invading Italy. In the first place, Italy was a part of his domains, and he was determined to pacify it. In the second place, the Welfs, as opponents of imperial power, had many supporters in the northern Italian cities as well as in Rome, and Frederick believed it was necessary to secure a strong base of support in Italy as leverage against the Welfs and other feudal opponents in Germany. Finally, much of the king's authority, for good or for ill, had come to depend upon his imperial dignity, and the title of emperor was almost empty if the ruler who claimed it did not have power in Italy, particularly in Rome. The difficulty was that the hostility of both the papacy and most of the towns to any real imperial power in Italy was insurmountable, and support from either of these sources was only temporary. Frederick made numerous expeditions into Italy (1154–55, 1158–62; 1166–68; 1174–76) and each time enjoyed temporary success, but each success only further alienated the Italians. The razing in 1161 of much of the great city of Milan, for example, could compel temporary obedience, but not secure permanent loyalty, to the crown. The Lombard League, backed by the pope, finally inflicted a shattering defeat upon Frederick at Legnano in 1176, the first major battle in which infantry defeated feudal cavalry. This was followed by the Peace of Constance in 1183, which eliminated effective imperial control of northern Italy in favor of the independent cities.

Henry VI, the son of the great emperor, could accomplish even less than his father. Though he pressed theoretical claims to authority over all of Christendom, he was unable in practice to limit feudal particularism. The real situation of this man who dreamed of adding the empire of Constantinople to his domains appeared in 1196, when he offered the German nobles almost anything they wanted if only they would recognize the principle of hereditary succession to the throne. They refused and went ahead to seize what Henry had offered to concede: the heredity of fiefs and the right of bishops to name their own successors. A more effective move was Henry's marriage to Constance, the heiress of the Norman kingdom of Sicily, but the union of north and south, of *impero e regno* ("empire and kingdom") only rendered the papacy more implacable.

The death of Henry VI at an early age plunged Germany into a series of civil wars from which it could not recover, and also left the door open for the triumph of papal power under Innocent III. The blood heir of *impero e regno* was Henry's infant son Frederick, but the Hohenstaufen realized that their position did not permit the luxury of a child candidate and chose Henry's brother Philip as king. A large party among the German princes ignored this choice and named Otto IV, the son of Henry the Lion and therefore the Hohenstaufens' most implacable enemy. England and France immediately plunged in, each recognizing the value of a friendly German ruler: King John took the side of the Welfs, and Philip Augustus that of the Hohenstaufen. Frequent involvement of England and France in German affairs continued for centuries. In this situation Innocent III could hold the balance of power. His chief concern was to prevent a reunification of the empire with Sicily, and this inclined him to the side of the Welfs. But throughout the course of the war, he changed sides to favor whoever was at the moment making more concessions to the Church. Philip died in 1208, after which the young Frederick became the candidate of the Hohenstaufen, and by 1212 that party had so far gained success that the prince could be crowned, though Otto continued his resistance till his death by poison in 1218.

At his coronation Frederick II wore a splendid cape of woven silk decorated with the Sumerian tree of life, two animal combats in the Asian style, and an Arabic prayer to Allah with a date in the fifth century of the Hijra: it was the cape of the cosmopolitan ruler of Sicily, Roger II, and it symbolized both the importance of Sicily to Frederick and his dreams of imperial grandeur. In reality, the result of the civil war between Hohenstaufen and Welf was utter disaster. Both sides had had to make great concessions to the towns and the Church; the Danes and Slavs had attacked the undefended frontiers of Germany; the elective theory of the monarchy had prevailed over the hereditary principle; and English and French interference continued. The road was graded for a continuation of anarchy and a resumption of civil war.

The reign of Frederick II was nonetheless one of the most brilliant in the Middle Ages, owing to his exceptional personality. Called by his contemporaries the "Wonder of the World," he was the author of poetry and technical books, the keeper of an extensive zoo that boasted leopards and a giraffe, and had an extraordinary interest in science. He liked to conduct experiments himself, as when the fancy took him to determine whether rest or exercise were better for the digestion. It was he who, in response to Pope Honorius III's demand for a Crusade to regain Jerusalem, went to the Holy Land, not to fight, but to converse, with his Moslem adversaries.

In Sicily Frederick inherited and enjoyed one of the strongest administrations in Europe. The army was salaried rather than feudal, and the king maintained a widespread system of castles and forts and a huge navy. He collected all customs duties, operated the mint, ran a paid and loyal civil service, kept a chancery that issued documents in Greek and Arabic as well as in Latin, made a census survey, and had a treasury that was the most efficient in the world. It is no wonder that Frederick preferred to live in Palermo rather than in Germany. His reign marked a further extension of royal control: the Constitutions of Melfi in 1220 provided that royal judges were to hear all cases and that the cities would be administered by royal bailiffs.

Frederick hoped to use Sicily as the core of a united kingdom of Italy and in turn to use Italy as a base from which to restore order in Germany. In this he was no more successful than his namesake Frederick I, and for the same reason: the implacable hostility of the papacy and the northern towns, who feared losing their autonomy and their wealth should an imperial authority become effective throughout the peninsula. It is at this time that Florence, Milan, Bologna, Pisa, Genoa, and Venice were beginning to obtain the power and wealth that made them famous in the Renaissance. They did not propose to subordinate these advantages to the imperial welfare. Neither did the heirs of Innocent III in Rome, where papalist theory reinforced political power, plan to submit again to imperial tutelage.

In Germany, ruin was approaching. The civil war had been succeeded by near anarchy as Frederick lingered too long in Italy. Towns, bishops, and even Frederick's son rose in revolt. While the Wonder of the World was nailing down his power in Sicily his control of Germany slipped loose. In the same year as the Constitutions of Melfi, 1220, he was forced to make an "Agreement with the Ecclesiastical Princes" of Germany, giving them free right to dispose of their dioceses as they pleased and promising that he would build no royal castles in, nor impose royal taxes upon, their domains. In 1232 he was obliged to approve a "Statute in Favor of the Princes" that made similar concessions to the lay lords and further gave them full control over courts and markets in their fiefs.

Deterioration was unchecked at the top. But just below, the princes were themselves checking a process that would, if allowed to continue, ultimately be to their disadvantage. They refused to do their feudal duties to the king, but they made certain that they received their due from their own vassals. About 1200, the duke of Bavaria, for example, possessed powers comparable to those of the kings of England and France. The duchy was divided into administrative areas governed by ducal officials. The duke controlled the folk courts. His chancery, curia, and privy council were all firmly in his power. He had all regalian rights—mint, tolls, and taxes—and had established the heredity of the Wittelsbach line. He even had a *Landtag,* an assembly through which he manipulated public opinion. The modern state evolved in Germany, but at the local rather than the national level.

German influence in Europe remained great, and it was extended by trade and conquest into the Slavic lands of the East and into the Baltic, but these advances were taken by nobles, monastic orders like the Cistercians, free settlers, and the military order of the Teutonic Knights, not by the monarchy. The death of Frederick II in 1250 signaled the resumption of civil war with claims to the throne by French and English as well as by German candidates. This period of *Faustrecht,* "rule of the fist" spelled the final end of an effective German monarchy.

By the end of the thirteenth century, the beginnings of the modern state had been established, in France and England on a national scale, and in Italy and Germany at the local level.

NOTES

[1] Cited by Geoffrey Barraclough, *Origins of Modern Germany* (Oxford, 1957), p. 293.

[2] Trans. by Mary M. McLaughlin in *The Portable Medieval Reader* edited by James Bruce Ross and Mary M. McLaughlin, Copyright 1949 by the Viking Press, Inc., New York. Reprinted by permission of the Viking Press, Inc.

Chapter Twenty

MEDIEVAL GOVERNMENT:
THEORY AND PRACTICE

WESTERN legal systems, modern governmental structure, and many current political theories owe much to the agonies and accomplishments of the Middle Ages. Medieval English institutions were particularly influential in forming the present, for they were the most successful and the most refined, and today are the best preserved and best studied. The sources for the constitutional and legal history of England and other medieval states are enormously varied, ranging from constitutional treatises to tax-collection rolls, and even after more than a century of serious scholarship quantities remain unedited and insufficiently studied.

THE innermost aspect of government is law. Upon law depends not only order and safety but individual liberty, both in the modern sense of freedom and in the medieval sense of the fulfillment of one's proper rights and duties. "The distinction between fixed rules and arbitrary options underlies our conception of the liberty of the subject."[1] The idea of liberty is that the sovereign (whether king or popular majority) may not impose its will arbitrarily. The importance of law was even more succinctly expressed by the great constitutional historian Frederick William Maitland: "Law is where life and logic meet." Society without law is inconceivable.

The medieval idea of law derived from Greco-Roman and Judaeo-Christian antecedents. Socrates had declared that the principles of justice were inherent in each man, and Cicero and other Roman jurists argued that there was a "natural law" consisting of eternally valid principles discoverable by reason. Further, in the course of their commerce and conquests, the Romans discovered that all peoples had certain laws in common, such as the prohibition of murder and incest, and the Romans called these regularities "the law of nations." The Middle Ages adopted the products of ancient observation and theory as the rule of "right reason." In addition to the rational law of nature, medieval theory accepted the divine law revealed in the Bible. Together, reason and revelation established absolute principles based upon the conviction that law was eternal and immutable.

To the medieval mind, man's task was first to discover the eternal law—one did not "make" law, one only "discovered" it (*jus dicere non jus facere*)—and second to construct positive (human) law in conformity with the principles of absolute law. If human law conflicted with divine, it was null and void—literally no law at all. Augustine said: "That which is not just seems to be no law at all," and Aquinas agreed: "The force of law depends upon the extent of its justice." *Justitia*, the central principle of medieval law and government, was the proper relation of human law to absolute law. The particular duties of human law in accordance with justice were to foster religion, to further the common welfare, and to aid in the perfection of Christian life in accordance with Saint Paul's dictate that the aim of law is to perfect the Christian personality.

THE practice of law varied. Civil law was opposed to canon law and local law to law of general application. On the continent, Roman law increasingly prevailed; only in England did the old, customary Germanic law retain its vigor, developing into the "common law" of which English-speaking jurists are so justly proud. For the English common law was a remarkable creation. It was "common" in that it made no distinction according to locality or to race, and arose, at least in part, from the extension of royal power and the consent of the people. It was Germanic as opposed to Roman, lay as opposed to ecclesiastical, royal as opposed to private. Judge-made, it was a law of precedent rather than of codes, though it came to encompass writs and statutes as well as judicial decisions.

Its importance can be evaluated in the workings of the English legal system of the twelfth and thirteenth centuries.

Outside the bounds of common law lay the private courts—the immunity courts of feudal lords with their jurisdiction over manorial disputes, minor disputes among tenants, smaller crimes (and, rarely, serious offenses). Outside the bounds also were the church courts, separated from the public tribunals in 1080, and having jurisdiction both *ratione personae* (over the persons of clerics),* and *ratione materiae* (over certain *matters* pertaining to religion, like oaths, blasphemy, and divorce). Within the bounds of the common-law system were the folk courts and the royal courts.

The old, local folk tribunals consisted in England of the "hundred court" and the shire-court. At first all freemen in the locality were obliged to attend these courts, but as this proved an unwieldy system, responsibility was transferred to the tenants of certain properties, an important precedent for representative government. One of the great accomplishments of the English government was the incorporation of local with royal justice. The local courts reached up and the king's courts reached down to join hands in creating the system of common law.

The king's court began as the *curia regis,* an ill-defined group of advisers the king chose on occasion to gather round him. This informal *curia regis* had military and judicial, as well as legislative and administrative, functions. It often acted as a court of appeal. As in the course of the twelfth century government became more complex, the legal functions of this amorphous court were distributed among the court of King's Bench, which traveled about with the king; the court of Common Pleas, which sat at Westminster and heard civil cases; the justices in eyre, who traveled about the realm hearing complaints; and, in the later Middle Ages, the chancery sitting in the capacity of a court of equity. The union of the royal with the local courts was accomplished through the offices of the sheriff, a royal official who presided over the shire-court and was responsible for the collection of taxes and the maintenance of order in the shire; through the itinerant justices and the king's dispensing of justice on his own tours; and, ultimately, through the representatives sent by the shire to report to the king.

*A rule that was often stretched very far, far enough to cover all students, for example; since the penalities assigned by Church courts were light, everyone who could pleaded "benefit of clergy."

The procedure of going to law varied, as it does now, depending on whether the case was civil or criminal. For civil or private wrongs (torts) as opposed to crimes against the public welfare or the "king's peace," the old remedy in English law was self-help: the injured party would attempt to wreak vengeance upon the offender. Such practices encouraged feuds and private wars, and in the course of the twelfth century an alternative was supplied in the form of a growing number of royal *writs*. An injured party would obtain the appropriate writ to oblige his opponent to come to court for a judgment; that is, he would sue him at law. The old rule of self-help survived in the form of wager by battle, in which the plantiff and the defendant, or their deputies, would appear before the court in full armor and do battle, the winner being awarded his case as a judgment of God. For those lower on the social scale than knights, the passage of arms was replaced by endurance contests, such as that in which each party attempted to hold his arms over his head longer than the other. Wager by battle was finally removed from the books only in the nineteenth century.

Criminal procedure began with presentment, similar to what we call indictment: the jury of presentment submitted a list of crimes and suspects to the king's justices, who then called the accused to court. An accused failing to appear had to offer an essoin (excuse) or suffer amercement (a fine). One accused of a serious crime who failed to appear would be considered an outlaw, outside the protection of the law and liable to attack by anyone with impunity. Once the accused appeared in court, he would be faced with one of three procedures. Until about 1150 old Germanic compurgation was often used. In compurgation the accused would take an oath to his own innocence and find a number of (often twelve) compurgators [literally: "those taking an oath with"] to swear that his oath was a true one. The procedure was not wholly absurd since most people feared the spiritual consequences of taking a false oath, but it was obviously open to abuse.

If compurgation failed, or if it were not used, the accused could until 1215 choose to undergo the ordeal. In the ordeal by fire, a red-hot piece of metal was placed in his hand. Then it was removed and the hand bound up. After a lapse of time, the wound was unbound; if it were healing, the man's innocence would be proclaimed, but if it were festering, it was taken as a sign of guilt. The ordeal by hot water was similar, the hand or the whole forearm, depending upon the seriousness of the crime, being plunged into a pot of boiling water. In some crimes the ordeal by cold water was preferred. Here the defendant was bound hand and foot and hurled into a pond or stream. If he floated, it was adjudged that the waters rejected him and that he was therefore guilty; if he sank, he was declared innocent and was fished out by guards who were, hopefully, paying attention. The ordeal depended upon a lively faith in God's immediate intervention in human affairs on the side of the innocent, and, whether as a result of weakening faith or of growing sophistication, the ordeal was increasingly replaced in the twelfth century by trial by jury.

The jury [Fr. *jurer*: "to swear"] was introduced into England by the Normans. Originally the Norman jury was simply a fact-finding body, called the jury of inquest, which the king used for any number of purposes. The first inquest of importance in Anglo-Norman England was that of *Domesday Book*, in which juries of inquest swore to report the census accurately to the king. The jury of presentment, the ancestor of the modern grand jury, came from the same stock. Its duty was to swear to report honestly to the king's officers any crimes that had occurred in its locality. The petty jury, fairly well established from 1215, sat in court and swore to tell the judge the truth about a crime or the men involved in it. They acted more like modern witnesses than a modern petty jury, and the verdict [literally: "true-saying"] of guilty or innocent was left to the judge. It was only in the fourteenth century that the petty juries themselves began giving the verdict.

If all failed and the accused was found guilty, he was subject to a penalty. The nature of judicial penalties underwent change in the course of time. In Anglo-Saxon England, as in most of the Germanic kingdoms, punishment was usually a fine called wergeld, the amount of which was graded according to the seriousness of the injury and the dignity of the person injured. In the progress of time, punishments grew increasingly severe and physical, hanging, whipping, and eventually burning and the pillory being introduced. Prison was introduced in the reign of Henry II but was not a popular medieval institution, the king preferring to execute criminals rather than pay for their keep. This harshness remained generally unmitigated until the nineteenth-century penal reforms.

The interests of royal power and public order worked to increase the scope of royal jurisdiction. Henry II with his assizes and writs, and Edward I with his statutes, enhanced the power of the king and his public courts at the expense of the private courts of the feudal lords and the ecclesiastical courts, broadened the area in which the king might impose his will, and created a strong, coherent system of law built upon Germanic tradition, local responsibility, and royal authority.

The increasing complexity of law called for the training of professional lawyers to replace the clerks or barons who only occasionally turned their attention to law. This professionalization began as early as the reign of Henry II and grew in direct proportion to the expansion of the system of royal justice, assuming definite shape by the time of Edward I. By the reign of Edward III practical law was taught by the example of practical lawyers at the Inns of Court.

FRENCH legal practice differed from the English in much the same way that French politics did. The Capetian kings began with scarcely any control over the systems of justice. The old national assembly of the Carolingians had acted as a kind of high court, and the Germanic local courts had existed in France as in England. But in the collapse of the Carolingian monarchy these local courts were absorbed into the feudal immunity courts. As the king extended his power, there was no wedding of royal with local courts as in England, but an extinction of the feudal courts by the king wherever he found it possible. Hence the legal system, and ultimately the representational system, of France was unbalanced in favor of absolutism. As the power of the monarchy increased, business in the royal courts increased, particulary from the time of Philip Augustus. From the time of Saint Louis, the French kings issued *ordonnances* by royal fiat, as opposed to the English statutes which had to be issued by the king in his Parliament. The French Parlement was never a legislative assembly. At first it was the *curia regis* sitting as a court of appeal; by the reign of Louis IX it consisted largely of professional judges. The French relied earlier than the English upon professional judges, and this, together with the lack of free local courts and the influence of Roman law, which was increasingly influential from the end of the eleventh century, led the French to rely less upon judgment by peers and more upon the authority of magistrates.

THE origins of medieval administration were as informal as those of medieval legal institutions. At the head of the government was a king. The reasons for the prevalence of monarchy are not complicated. Monarchy was the form of government of Israel and of imperial Rome, the two traditions best known to the medieval mind. Further, the distinction between a monarchic and a nonmonarchic form of government is not so great as the tradition of the eighteenth-century revolutions have led us to believe. This is true not only of twentieth-century constitutional monarchies, but of medieval monarchies as well. The kings were in charge of the *respublica,* the commonwealth; they were responsible to Church, feudality, and people, not to speak of God; they were nothing like absolute rulers. The king had several functions. A great medievalist pointed out that the king had a "public" as well as "private body": i.e., an existence as head of state separate from his private existence. It is even possible to say that he had several bodies: he was a private person, a feudal lord, a divinely appointed ruler, and the head of his people, the representative of the *communitas regni.*

Royal government in the early Middle Ages was small beer. Originally the informal *curia regis* (king's court) met sometimes in conjunction with and sometimes apart from the general assembly of freemen like the Mayfield of Carolingian times, but its organization, membership, and function were all wholly undefined and continually varied. The curia had military, administrative, legislative, and judicial functions.

The original purpose of the early assemblies like the Mayfield was military, and this military aspect colored the growth of administration and legislation late into the Middle Ages. Armies continued to have certain legislative characteristics, and civil assemblies certain military functions. Feudal counsel (*consilium*) offered the king in regard to the planning of campaigns was a part and parcel of the advice given him by assemblies and councils. Since the councils had also to *consent* to major wars and campaigns, both the legislative functions of advice and consent had military precedents.

The *curia regis,* as administration, was divided into public and private offices. The king's treasury was originally kept in his bedchamber and in the adjoining wardrobe, the private servant in charge of the chamber (the chamberlain) acting as treasurer. In England by the reign of Henry I a division in the "chamber" (*camera*) had taken place between the wardrobe, where the king's real household expenses were taken care of, and the treasury, which became a public office, the *curia regis ad scaccarium,* or Exchequer. In the thirteenth century one of the great questions of English politics, and the chief source of royal and baronial discord, was how much power was to be wielded by the king's household officers, and how much by the baronial public officers.

For aside from the private household offices, the *curia regis* contained the *consilium,* a word better rendered "counsel" than "council" because of its lack of formal organization. The *consilium* had two functions. When the king called powerful magnates together informally to ask their advice on general problems, historians call it the *magnum consilium;* when a usually smaller group met to consider particular problems of administration, historians call it the *parvum consilium.* These terms are mostly a convenience, because in the Middle Ages the two *consilia* were distinguished from one another neither by definition nor in composition. The same men often appeared in both; neither had any defined membership or responsibility. The distinction is useful, however, because it permits the historian to distinguish between two functions that were gradually, and unnoticed by contemporaries, separating: the consultative function of the *magnum consilium* and the administrative function of the *parvum consilium.* Both represent the *public* aspect of government as opposed to the king's household.

The three great public officers of the *curia* in England after the Norman Conquest were the justiciar, the chancellor, and the treasurer. The justiciar was a viceroy and general administrator. The chancellor, usually a cleric, presided over the chancery, where clerks drew up treaties, charters, and other records. Until the reign of Edward III, when permanent offices in Westminster were established, the chancery often had to follow the king about in carts and to set up its tents wherever he was encamped.

The treasurer presided over the "chamber," as the treasury was originally called. From the twelfth century the chamber was divided into the wardrobe, which remained a private office, and the Exchequer, which became public, under the control of the *consilium*. Henceforward, the "Chancellor of the Exchequer," rather than the treasurer, had chief control over public monies. The Exchequer is, in fact, better described as an occasion than an office or place: it was the occasion when the *consilium* met as administrators of the treasury. This was true at least of the "upper Exchequer," the Exchequer of audit, where was set up the great "chess board" on which the king and his sheriffs played for high stakes. We are fortunate in having a detailed description of the workings of the upper Exchequer in the *Dialogue of the Exchequer* ascribed to Richard Fitznigel:

> DISCIPLE: What is the Exchequer?
> MASTER: The Exchequer is a quadrangular board about ten feet in length and five in breadth placed before those who sit around it in the manner of a table. Running round it there is a raised edge about the height of four fingers, lest anything placed on it should fall off. Above the board is placed a cloth purchased at the Easter term—not an ordinary cloth, but a black one marked with stripes which are the space of a foot or a hand's breadth distant from each other. Within the spaces counters are placed according to their value. . . . But although such a board is called an "Exchequer," nevertheless this name is applied also to the court which sits with the Exchequer. . . .[2]

To this great table of the upper Exchequer the sheriff brought the tally, a stick marked for him by the officers of the lower Exchequer (the Exchequer of receipt) to show how much money he had brought in from his shire. The sheriff had to account for all the public taxes and revenues of the king's domain in the shire entrusted to him. Counters were placed on the table to show how much was due from him, and other counters to show how much he had brought in. The result of the audit was announced in terms of *et quietus est, et debet, et habet de superplusagio.* The rolls of Exchequer, called pipe rolls because of their shape, show among the accounts of Gloucestershire in the reign of Henry I the following:

The king's wardrobe. Stewards hang out clothes and bed linen.
By the king's bed stands a chest similar to that in which the treasury
of the realm was once kept.

The same sheriff accounts for the "farm" of the manor of "Edel-field." He has paid 15 pounds in the Treasury. And he is quit.... The same sheriff accounts for the profits of the forest of Cirencester. He has paid 40 shillings in the Treasury and is quit....[3]

Thus the *curia regis* was advisory body, high court of justice, chancery, and treasury all at once. As time went on, the increasing needs of government brought about further diversification and specialization in the administration. The departments became more distinct and more complex, and their staffs more professionalized.

THE same professionalization that was visible in law and administration also marked the development of military institutions. As royal interests and commitments grew, and as the feudal system became rigid and began losing its military effectiveness, the king turned increasingly to a paid army. Knights were paid to stay in the host longer than their feudal contracts demanded, or they were simply given money fiefs instead of land. Or, even more frequently, the king used scutage and other revenues to pay mercenaries (a soldier is one who is given a salary—Late Lat. *soldus:* "hire"). Scutage, originally a fine levied on knights failing to appear when the host was called, became a normal and acceptable commutation of military service into money that could be used to purchase a professional army. This process, which began as early as the twelfth century, combined in the fourteenth with the increasing effectiveness of bowmen over heavy cavalry to put an end to the military utility of feudalism.

As the local courts linked hands with the royal courts to give England a unified system of law, so royal and local administration also came together, the result being national, and representative, government. The king reached down, as it were, and brought up the existing folk courts, sheriffs, and other organs of local administration into a unified administrative fabric. In France, local power was too much in the hands of the nobility to make this possible, so that the extension of royal administration in France proceeded wholly from the top downwards. It was the *baillis, sénéchaux, and enquêteurs* sent out to the provinces on royal authority that knit the king's dominions together.

Representative institutions existed throughout later medieval Europe: the estates-general and provincial estates of France, the *Landtage* of the German principalities, and the *cortes* of the Iberian peninsula. Practically speaking, these institutions emerged in part from the local folk courts, in part from feudalism, and in part from the king's counsel.

THE history of representative institutions in England is not identical with the history of Parliament. Representation began on the level of local government as a natural, common-sense solution to problems of local government. England, like most medieval countries, was a realm of communities. There was the community of the vill, often identical in boundary with the village; there was the larger community of the hundred, comprising several vills; there was the community of the shire, comprising many hundreds; and, finally, there was the community of the realm. Each of these communities had its own legal and administrative duties, and was responsible for the raising of taxes and the presentment of criminals to the appropriate justices. Every freeman was obliged to attend the regularly scheduled courts of the communities to which he belonged. But it was clear that, with the increasing complexity of governmental problems, with the growth of population, and with the distances that often intervened between a man's home and the court, some kind of representation was necessary.

In English sources, the oldest unit to be represented is the vill, in 1100; the next is the shire and hundred, in 1166; the next is the cathedral chapter, in 1226; the next is the diocesan clergy, in 1254; the next is the "community of the land"—otherwise the barons—in 1258; and the next, the borough in 1265.[4] Only gradually, then, was the idea of representation extended to the community of the realm as a whole.

The origins and nature of the English Parliament were the subject of heated and sometimes acid debate a hundred years ago, and the heat, acidity, and lack of agreement have not abated today. The only firm conclusion that a noted American historian of Parliament can come to is that "we can no longer be so precise about what, originally, Parliament was."[5] Many historians have found the origins of Parliament in the corporate principles of Roman law, but Parliament was not really corporate: it was based upon the shire, which was a "locality, not an order or an estate."[6] What probably happened to produce Parliament was primarily this: the demands of a monarchy that was continually pressing for further centralization and for more revenues caused the king to utilize local institutions for his purposes, thus bringing about a unified system of administration and law. Representatives from these institutions were summoned to the king; it was eventually assumed that they had full power to bind those whom they represented. Then, possibly at this point influenced by Roman corporate theory, these representatives together with the king were considered a corporate entity, the "community of the realm." Even a monarch as inclined to absolutism as Henry VIII was impelled to remark: "We be informed by our judges that we at no time stand so highly in our estate royal as in the time of parliament, wherein we as head and you as members are conjoined and knit together in one body politic." Here the analogy is theological as well as legal: there is more than a hint at a similarity to the mystical Body of Christ.

The date of the origin of Parliament has been equally disputed, partly because it depends upon the definition of the word. A parliament was originally a talk, a meeting, a parley, and the word was used to describe Saint Louis' rendezvous with

Edward I in Parliament. On his left is Llewellyn, prince of Wales, and on his right Alexander, king of Scotland. The smaller figures in the foreground are the secular nobility (to the viewer's right) and the bishops and abbots (to the viewer's left).

his wife on a private stair of the castle in order to escape the jealousy of the queen mother. From the 1240s in England it was used to describe a solemn meeting of the king's advisers, but as yet it denoted neither a body nor even a clearly defined occasion. Some historians have set the date of the origin as early as 1242; others later than 1316. George Cuttino concludes that a true Parliament must have, not only judicial and propaganda functions, but political powers to deal with great decisions of state, and he believes that these powers were present as early as 1316. Another question is whether a Parliament can be so designated before both lords and commons were regularly summoned. From 1258 to 1300 seventy sessions of what might be called "Parliament" were held, but to only nine were representatives of the commons called. Soon thereafter it became not only usual, but necessary, to summon them.

In the latter thirteenth and fourteenth centuries Parliament was transformed from an occasional and ill-defined meeting into a powerful institution. There were three reasons for this. First, power no longer resided wholly with the feudal nobility, and the king needed the support as well as the money of both merchants and gentry. Second, the people wished to have a regular institution to hear grievances and to communicate them to the king. Third, the barons wished to increase their influence upon the administration by means of regular consultations. In 1215 they attempted to impose a permanent regulatory committee upon King John; in the crisis between King Henry III and the barons that occurred in 1258–1265 the idea was revived, and parliaments were called to secure support for the barons' political program. No group had any real idea of what a parliament ought to be, much less of what it was to become; it was a pragmatically conceived product of these converging needs.

Even through the reign of Edward I (1272–1307), Parliament was an act, or an occasion, rather than a body of any definite composition, its function and its membership varying from occasion to occasion. But the struggles between Edward II and the barons made Parliament a permanent institution, and by 1324 it had something like its present shape and function. The theoretical treatise *Modus tenendi parliamentum,* a reliable description of the workings of Parliament in the reign of Edward II, reveals a Parliament engaged in full-scale debate, decision, and legislation.

Parliament was in part a continuation of the old *magnum consilium* gathered to give the king military aid, counsel, and legal judgment. Gradually the composition of the great council was restricted to a smaller gathering of great men, usually described as "barons." By the reign of Edward I it was agreed that barons had a right to attend Parliament, but the only definition of a baron the king could get from his lawyers was tautological: a baron was a man whose fathers had traditionally been called to Parliament. The composition of the *magnum consilium* was of course not wholly arbitrary, for it was by and large the families with the greatest fiefs who were invited. Thus did Edward I summon the earl of Cornwall in 1295:

> The king to his beloved and faithful relative, Edmund, Earl of Cornwall, greeting. Because we wish to have a consultation and meeting with you and with the rest of the principal men of the kingdom, as to provision for remedies against the dangers which in these days are threatening our whole kingdom; we command you, strictly enjoining you in the fidelity and love in which you are bound to us, that on the Lord's day next after the feast of Saint Martin, in the approaching winter, you be present in person at Westminster . . . .[7]

Together with the barons sat "convocation," the bishops and abbots of the realm. This arrangement prevailed until 1340 and then again from the time of the Tudors. The assembly of barons and ecclesiastical magnates came to be known as the House of Lords. This House has persisted in much the same form, though with drastically limited powers, to the present day. Some suggest that the House be reconstituted on the basis of accomplishment and service. The closest approximation to the medieval House of Lords today would be a house composed of leading businessmen, military men, diplomats, administrators, jurists, and scholars.

Others besides barons were summoned to the medieval Parliament. Edward I wrote to the sheriff of Northampton: "We strictly require you to cause two knights from the aforesaid county, two citizens from each city in the same county, and two burgesses from each borough . . . to be elected without delay, and to cause them to come to us at the (same) time and place (as the barons)."

According to Whig historiography, representative government is a Good Thing, particularly as it exists in modern Britain, and the medieval Parliament was growing in the direction of modern democracy by virtue of some mysterious internal metabolism regulated by the providence of the good Whig God. In fact, not only was the House of Commons the product of royal necessity rather than of anything greatly resembling democratic theory, but it in no sense occupied the foreground of medieval government or politics.

The Peers' Lobby, House of Lords.

The ultimate origins of the Commons lie in the idea of the jury, representatives of a locality sworn to bear the record to the court. From 1194 four knights of the shire were sometimes elected to choose two knights from each hundred in order to create a grand jury. In 1213 and 1226 again four discreet knights were elected from each shire to bear the record to the king, that is, to report truly to him on affairs in their shire. Such knights might occasionally present a petition to the king, but their primary function was to give him information and their secondary to act as his messengers to report to the shire whatever he wished conveyed. By the time of Edward I it was established that in addition to the knights (usually two from each shire) there should be elected two citizens from each city (a "city" in the Middle Ages was a town in which a bishop resided) and two from each borough (a town not the residence of a bishop).

Until the fourteenth century the Commons were usually not invited to meet with the great council, but by 1316 their power had greatly increased, in part because of Edward I's failure to cow the realm in 1296–1297 and in part because of his son's difficulties with the barons. After 1327 it was generally agreed that the Commons' consent was necessary to the passage of a statute, and the Commons gradually obtained control over royal requests for taxes, this latter proving their most effective weapon in achieving their later predominance. The Lancastrian kings who usurped the throne from Richard II in 1399 were obliged to court popular support of their questionable rights, and they gave increasing power to Parliament in order to bind both Lords and Commons to their policy.

In accordance with the medieval theory of law, the early Parliaments were thought of as "law-finders" rather than as "law-makers." The only legitimate law being divine law, one could only discover it, not legislate it. But this theory was limited by several considerations. First, even in the early Middle Ages the memory that the Romans had legislated did not disappear. Second, the revival of Roman law in the twelfth century promoted the idea of legislation. Third, the revived theory of Aristotle that the state was a natural human phenomenon reinforced the effect of Roman law and rendered the idea of legislation natural. Fourth and most important, medieval rulers and assemblies were obliged to legislate, whether they wished to or not, and even when they believed they were not doing so, simply by the pressures of change. From the beginning of the fourteenth century at the latest there was an increasingly general recognition of the need, the reality, and the legitimacy of legislative change.

THE king and the representatives of the people: the two greatest questions of medieval political theory were (1) the relation of the individual to the community, and (2) the source, under

God, of ultimate authority. Medieval ideas of government derived from medieval ideas of law. Augustine believed that government was an evil necessary to postlapsarian man (man after the Fall), "natural" or prelapsarian man having required none. Aristotle on the other hand argued that government was natural to "natural man," his definition of "natural" being man as one finds him, the equivalent of Augustine's fallen man. Aquinas followed the Philosopher rather than the Father, holding that man, as a "social animal," naturally forms societies and governments. But Augustine and Aquinas argued that society must be just, it must be in accord with eternal law, "laws that go against the divine law must in no way be observed" (Aquinas) and "The sovereign is not exempt from the law."

But who is the sovereign? Who, on earth, is empowered to declare what eternal law is and to incorporate it into human law? "Law is nothing else than an ordinance of reason for the common good, promulgated by him who has the care of the community," said Aquinas, and "The making of law belongs either to the whole people or to one who has the care of the whole people." There were two types of order proposed in the Middle Ages, the descending and the ascending. In the descending order, God's authority is deputized to emperor, pope, or king, who in turn passes it downwards; in the ascending order, God's authority is given to the whole people, who deputize rulers responsible to them. As Saint Paul said (Romans XIII), "Let every soul be subject unto the higher powers."

The papalist position was "descending." The popes claimed that "plenitude of power" was granted them by God, and a statement of Pope Celestine I was a catch-phrase of the descending theory: "*Docendus est populus, non sequendus*: the people are not to be guides but pupils." The imperialist position was also clearly descending. The kings' position is less clearly definable, because there were various theories of royal power. In papalist theory, the kings received their powers from God through the medium of the pope, and in ecclesiastical theory as a whole, the king was to be chosen in regard to his *idoneity*, that is, his fitness and willingness to rule according to principles of justice defined by the Church. In old Germanic populist theory deriving from ancient tribal procedure, the king was elective, the choice of the nation, in the same way that the chief was the choice of the tribe. This conception continued in the English coronation rites, where the acclamation by the people preceded the enthronement.

The opposite theocratic conception of monarchy was also growing. Its roots were as ancient as the elective principle, for among the ancient Germans "kin-right" existed alongside election, it being assumed that a relative of the chief would succeed him if he were at all agreeable to the tribe, or if he had the power to make himself agreeable. Further, it became customary to regard the kings as descended from a god, an idea beneficial to heredity: most of the Anglo-Saxon kings before the advent of Christianity claimed to be "Woden-born." After the conversion to Christianity, reference back to the Roman tradition of Constantine and the Jewish tradition of David and Solomon with their royal anointing reinforced the notion that the king was more than human and had divinely bestowed powers. "There is such divinity doth hedge a king," says Shakespeare's Claudius to Laertes; and the solemn coronation, the anointing and the liturgical *laudes regiae* ["royal praises" : *Christus vincit, Christus regnat, Christus imperat*] all combined to convey the theocratic nature of the kingship. "After he has been hallowed to King, he has power over his people, and they cannot shake his yoke from off their shoulders."[8] The introduction of Roman law in the twelfth and thirteenth century reinforced the descending theory of royal theocracy, as it made the king the personification of the national "body" or corporation and revived an old phrase: "What has pleased the prince has the force of law."

Yet this was not yet the later absolutist theory of the Divine Right of Kings. There were several limitations upon the idea of theocratic kingship. First, the royal theocratic position was inherently less logical than the imperialist or papalist, since there were many kings, not one, and it is as hard to believe in the divinity of warring kings as in the divinity of warring Olympian gods. Second, in England and certainly in Germany the old elective principle was not wholly forgotten. Third, the idea still prevailed that the king was obliged to rule in accordance with the dictates of eternal law. Fourth, the king was a feudal lord who had, under contract, certain obligations to his vassals. Fifth, and most important, the king's power was limited by practical considerations. Richard II may have tried something like absolutism, but Henry IV's title to the throne was less clear, and that monarch was forced to permit the succession to be regulated in 1404 by an act of Parliament.

From these limitations sprang the idea that under certain conditions it was rightful to revolt against a bad ruler. Among the ancient Germans the tribesmen might rise up against an evil or an incompetent chief; in feudal theory, if the lord broke his contract with his vassal, the vassal was no longer considered bound. The Church held two irreconcilable views. The oldest, and for a long while the strongest, was the idea of passive obedience. If a ruler is evil, we should not resist him, but submit to his tyranny as a chastisement sent by God for our sins. This was Saint Augustine's view. The newer idea was based upon the idea of justice and held that for a king to be king in right he must have idoneity and rule in accordance with justice. Then he is *rex justus*. If he violates the principles of justice, then he may be deposed. This was the idea expressed by Gregory VII in his attitude towards Henry IV: the pope had the right as vicar of Christ to determine when a king had violated justice and might be deposed. Still later, under the influence of Aristotle, Aquinas and others equated the *rex injustus* with the *tyrannus* and suggested that once a king became *tyrannus* he was automatically and literally "no king" at all.

The idea of Gregory VII was still theocratic and "descending." But his position could readily be wedded to an "ascending," populist political theory.

In the twelfth century John of Salisbury, an English poet and philosopher trained in the school of Chartres, published his *Policraticus,* a work in which he took the position that the people had the right to rise up against a tyrant. "To kill a tyrant is not only licit but fair and just . . . . Certainly he who does not pursue the public enemy and take vengeance upon him injures himself and the whole body of the earthly commonwealth . . . . The prince, image of the Deity, ought to be loved, honoured, and cherished; the tyrant, image of the Evil One, ought usually even to be killed."[9] To the objection that the peace of society would be irremediably disrupted if everyone took it upon himself to kill whomever he thought tyrannical, John appealed to papalist theocracy. The people can rise against a tyrant only with the permission of the pope. John's theory, though partly populist, remained partly theocratic.

Later medieval theories became both more and less theocratic. From the twelfth century the rediscovery of Roman law reinforced theocratic royalism, but the revival of Aristotle at about the same time lent weight to the opposite, populist, theory. Aquinas separated the supernatural from the natural *ordo* and placed the state in the latter, so that a natural theory of government like that of Aristotle could be worked out without reference to theocratic principles or the Church.

At the time of the dispute between Philip the Fair and Boniface VIII another important theorist, John of Paris, argued that God spoke through the people and that this was true for the Church as well as for the state. A contemporary of John's, William of Ockham, who was personally anti-papal, applied to the papacy itself the doctrines of resistance reserved by John of Salisbury to the king. The pope, Ockham argued, was appointed by the Christian People to serve them and was responsible to them and only through them to God. Dante (1265–1321) argued in his *De Monarchia* for rule by the emperor, not because of the emperor's divine right, but on the populist ground that the natural need of society was a single ruler.

These tendencies towards populism were most forcefully expressed by a fourteenth-century theorist named Marsilius of Padua, the author of a book entitled *Defensor Pacis*. The people, Marsilius argued, are sovereign, and law depends upon the will of the people, who, however, like any sovereign, should endeavor to conform their will to that of God. Their will is expressed by the *pars valentior* of the populace, a phrase by which Marsilius probably meant, not the "majority," but the "worthy and responsible elements," like the oligarchs who dominated the Italian cities in his day. The ruler was simply the *pars principans,* the "part of the people that rules"; he derives his authority from God through the people. In Marsilius first emerges the modern notion of the ruler as "public servant" rather than lord, an idea that at least until recently was generally accepted in the United States.

Modern theories of justifiable revolution ultimately, though distantly, derive from these medieval ideas of resistance. From Marsilius through Hooker and Locke to the Revolutions of 1688 and 1776, to Jefferson and ultimately to modern peace and civil rights protests, theories of resistance persisted, ever reinforced, if also modified, by new conditions of tyranny.

There was no single direction in the Middle Ages towards either autocracy or populism. The Middle Ages ended having created the conditions for Renaissance and seventeenth-century absolutism. Yet they also created representative institutions and theories of resistance. The only single thrust is towards greater power, complexity, and sophistication in every respect, in both the theory and the practice of government. Unfortunately the most important question raised in the Middle Ages—when, and under what conditions, and by whose authority, may an individual, or must an individual, resist unjust laws or tyrannical rule, and who is to determine what is unjust or tyrannical —has never been answered to the satisfaction of either practical men or philosophers.

NOTES

[1] Helen Cam, *Law-Finders and Law-Makers in Medieval England* (New York, 1963), p. 11.
[2] David Douglas, ed. *English Historical Documents* (London, Eyre and Spottiswoode, 1953), II, 493–494.
[3] Douglas, p. 572.
[4] Helen Cam, "The Theory and Practice of Representation in Medieval England," *History*, xxxviii (1953), 11–26.
[5] George P. Cuttino, "Medieval Parliament Reinterpreted," *Speculum*, xli (1966), 686. Cuttino's article gives a good summary of current views.
[6] Cuttino, p. 682.
[7] For this and the summons to the Commons, see George Burton Adams and H. M. Stephens, *Select Documents of English Constitutional History* (New York, 1902), pp. 83–84.
[8] An English theorist, Aelfric, cited by Percy E. Schramm, *A History of the English Coronation* (Oxford, 1937). p. 141.
[9] Trans. Ewart Lewis, ed. *Medieval Political Ideas* (New York, Alfred A. Knopf, 1954), I, 276–277.

PART FOUR

The
Medieval
Harvest

Chapter Twenty-One

SOCIETY IN THE CENTRAL AND
LATER MIDDLE AGES

THE social and personal environment of the individual is one
of the most important elements of medieval history. The fundamental assumption of medieval society was *ordo:* a divinely
appointed order hierarchically arranged, in which each individual
had his proper place. Society was wholly stratified, the chief
instruments of stratification being the Church, the feudal-
manorial system, and the towns. These three instruments of
stratification created three different, though related, hierarchies.
The division of society into "upper," "middle," and "lower"
classes is more appropriate to the nineteenth than to the thirteenth
century. There was no one elite; there were three.

The first of the three hierarchies was the Church. The
Church as a whole may have ranked as the "first estate" in
political theory, but there was as much social difference between
the archbishop of Mainz and one of his rural parish priests as
between the count of Flanders and one of his serfs.

The second was the old feudal-manorial hierarchy, from
the king and great nobles at the top, through the lesser nobility
and knights, the small freeholders, and the agricultural laborers,
to the serfs. Serfdom was in gradual decline from the twelfth
century, but serfs and paid agricultural laborers together always
made up a large majority of the medieval population.

The third hierarchy was that which evolved with the towns,
beginning in the tenth and eleventh centuries. Here the top
was occupied by the urban "patriciate," consisting of the families
of the great merchants and some of the greatest industrialists.
The urban system became rigid in the course of time. Any

group occupying the top of a hierarchy tends to become exclusive, and the urban patriciate was no exception. By the thirteenth century the patriciate was itself divided into "old families" that had been wealthy long enough to enjoy the comfort, leisure, cultural attainments, and political power that were the aim and goal of wealth, and the *parvenus* who were still striving to transform their economic success into social status. In fourteenth-century London, great care was taken to see that the daughters of wealthy merchants married only the sons of wealthy merchants. Yet the nature of fortunes built upon, and maintained by, business enterprise is that they are more easily dissipated than those based upon land. The American proverb "from shirtsleeves to shirtsleeves in three generations" was often true in the Middle Ages as well. One reason life in the towns was attractive is that upward mobility remained more common there than in the feudal-manorial hierarchy or even that of the Church.

Below the patricians were the lesser merchants, who were hostile to the individuals occupying the patriciate but not to the institution itself, for they hoped one day to occupy it themselves. Below these were the artisans. Only a very few artisans could build up their business to the rank of great industry— although a small number of Flemish and Italian clothmakers managed to do this—and thereby hope for acceptance into the patriciate. Consequently the artisans were generally antagonistic to the merchants, and the pressure they exerted against the patricians was one of the great dynamic forces for social and political change.

Below the artisans were the journeymen, who were treated well by small masters but in large concerns were mere *salariati,* the forerunners of the modern urban proletariat. The hostility of the *salariati* was most commonly directed against their artisan employers, and though they might sometimes join with the artisans against the ruling patriciate, they were also susceptible to the blandishments of the wealthy and sometimes joined forces with them against their employers.

Attempts to construct a single hierarchy consisting of the feudal lords as the "upper class," the bourgeoisie as the "middle class" and the peasants and *salariati* as the "lower class" are absurd. Ranks varied too much both in the countryside and in the towns; the poor artisan can in no sense be equated with either the wealthy merchant or the peasant. Social rankings exist only where comparisons are made, and in the Middle Ages there were few efforts to compare the urban with the feudal-manorial hierarchy. On the occasions when comparisons were made, for example in struggles for control of a public office, then, possibly because of the greater durability of land-based wealth, the nobility outranked the patriciate. When from the sixteenth century society became more unified and contacts between the orders became more common, the idea of one hierarchy with a noble "upper class" and mercantile "middle class" made more sense, and wealthy businessmen began to yearn for patents of nobility.

Society changes when pressure is applied at points of juncture. In the development of the towns, there were three such points. The first was the juncture between the feudal nobility and the towns. Early medieval towns were originally all under the control of one feudal lord or another. Liège belonged to the bishop of Liège, Milan to the archbishop of Milan, and Namur to the count of Namur. This was uncongenial to the town population, which required personal freedom from servitude and collective freedom from burdensome taxes and tolls. In the first urban upheavals whole towns, headed by the wealthy merchants, united against the authority of the feudal lord and demanded to be chartered as communes. The period of economic and political expansion on the part of the towns was therefore a period of unquestioned patrician leadership and domination.

The second juncture was that between the patriciate and the artisans. Once economic prosperity and political independence had been obtained, the smoldering antagonism between these two groups took fire. The flames were fanned by the economic contraction of the later Middle Ages, and the result was a series of popular revolutions against the patriciate. A third juncture, that between the artisans and the industrial laborers, was less subject to pressure at that time, though occasional strikes, mob violence, and eccentric religious manifestations indicated tension. The great battle between employers and employed was postponed until the Industrial Revolution of the nineteenth century.

THERE were several roads a town might take on the way from feudal possession to independent commune. The original power of the lords is illustrated by this grant of a market by King Otto I in 965:

> Let all know that for the love of God we have granted the petition of Adalgus, the reverend archbishop of Hamburg, and have given him permission to establish a market in the place called Bremen. In connection with the market we grant him jurisdiction, tolls, a mint, and all other things connected therewith to which our royal treasury would have a right.[1]

One lord, the king, grants all rights of the market to the archbishop, including the tolls that the merchants found burdensome. By pressure or by purchase the town might gradually obtain certain rights, as did Toulouse, whose count, Alphonse, acknowledged in 1147 that "in no way do I have tallage or tolls in the city of Toulouse. . . ."[2] Or the town might be founded with certain rights, as was the case with the *villes neuves* founded by the kings of France. In 1155 Louis VII established Lorris, granting that

> . . . no inhabitant of the parish of Lorris shall be required to pay a toll or other tax on his provisions. . . . No burgher shall go on an expedition, on foot or on horseback, from which he cannot return the same day to his home if he so desires. . . . No one, neither we nor any other, shall exact from the burghers of Lorris any tallage, tax, or subsidy.[3]

The next step, taken by some of the large towns, was to a commune and complete independence from feudal domination. The transition to the communes took place most easily in much of Italy, where the towns were not as dominated by the feudality as in the North. Moreover, south of the Alps the nobility, rather than living in country castles, chose to dwell within the cities and to associate themselves with their cause—and to complicate the cities' independence once it was attained. Venice, which had been controlled by the Byzantine Empire, found it most easy to obtain independence; the Lombard cities found it more difficult, having to contend with both their bishops and the emperor. The rule of the southern communes came to be lodged in the *consulates,* city governments originally controlled by the feudal lords, but later ruled by consuls elected by the patriciate.

Some of these merchant rulers, like the Medici of Florence, became princes with powers equivalent to those of the feudal rulers in the North.

In the North, the transition to communal independence was difficult. Sometimes charters could be purchased from a needy lord, as London purchased confirmation of its liberties from Richard the Lionhearted; sometimes they could be obtained only by force. The bishops being by far the most conservative and least cooperative of the feudal lords, it was in their cities in northern France, the Low Countries, and the Rhineland where the struggles were most violent. The great uprising at Laon is a grisly example. The townsmen, having passed from protest to revolt and from revolt to bestial violence, hunted through the town for their bishop, who prudently, and apparently characteristically, hid himself in a wine cask. Finding him, the mob pulled him out and mocked at him, and finally one of them,

> . . . lifting his battle-axe brutally dashed out the brains of that sacred, though sinner's head . . . . There brought to his end, his legs were cut off and many another wound inflicted. But Thibaut seeing the ring on the finger of the erstwhile prelate and not being able to draw it off, cut off the dead man's finger and took it. And so stripped to his skin (the bishop) was thrown into a corner in front of his chaplain's house. My God, who shall recount the mocking words that were thrown at him by passersby, as he lay there, and with what clods and stones and dirt his corpse was covered?[4]

The Golden Age of the communes was the twelfth and thirteenth centuries. Thereafter struggles between the patriciate and the artisans were increasingly common. The growing power of the national state also transformed the communes. In Italy a few great cities, their own governments turned into principalities by the Medici and other great merchant princes, absorbed their smaller neighbors. In the North, the kingdoms of France and England and the principalities of Germany absorbed the towns and in time converted the free communal administrations into royal bureaucracies. Only a few "free cities," in fragmented Germany, preserved into the nineteenth century something like their former status.

In the fourteenth and fifteenth centuries social unrest became common enough to affect even the conservative countryside.

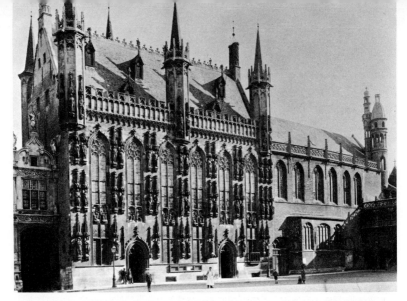

Bruges City Hall (thirteenth century?)—a monument to the wealth and power of the urban patriciate.

The roots of this unrest are both religious and economic. From the early Middle Ages social and religious protest were combined. The sources of heresy were for the most part moral and pietistic, but it is a reasonable, though undemonstrable, assumption that much dissent was socially motivated. Ignorant of their true needs, and taught to believe that salvation came from another world, men were prone to express social discontent in religious terms. This was true of the Patarini of Milan in the eleventh century and was everywhere increasingly true from the twelfth. In thirteenth-century Florence, in France where in 1251 the *Pastoureaux* rose to help Louis IX against the Moslems but then turned to pillaging churches and towns, religion thinly veiled social motives. The Children's Crusade is a similar manifestation. The fifteenth-century Hussites in Bohemia and Wycliffites and Lollards in England as well as those who participated in the flagellation and dancing manias that swept Europe after the plague, were moved at least as much by worldly unhappiness as by the Holy Spirit.

The economic roots of peasant discontent penetrate as deep as the early thirteenth century, when manorial lords, desiring to raise the yield of their land in order to market it for a monetary profit, increased the labor services required of their serfs. The new money economy also created gaps between destitute peasants and those who were able to obtain some wealth, and the depopulation of the fourteenth century obliged manorial lords, in order to keep agricultural production up, to force those tenants who had survived the plague to take on the work of their deceased fellows as well as their own. Free workers were quick to profit from the shortage of labor to demand higher wages, but even they were cheated by the series of "statutes of laborers" that from 1350 prescribed fines or imprisonment for those who refused work in order to press for better pay. Further, the strife that disrupted Christendom in the fourteenth and fifteenth centuries, particularly the Hundred Years' War, not only ravaged peasants' lands but obliged governments to impose increased financial burdens.

In fourteenth- and fifteenth-century Italy and Flanders proletarian revolts were common, and peasants' uprisings or *jacqueries* (from the generic name Jacques applied to French peasants by their contemptuous lords) occurred in England, France, the Low Countries, Spain, Germany, Bohemia, and Hungary. In 1381, as many as sixty thousand peasants and artisans of southern England, under the leadership of Wat Tyler, Jack Straw, and John Ball, marched upon Canterbury and then upon London, where the leading citizens resisted them but where they found thousands of sympathizers among the lower urban class. After burning houses belonging to nobles, lawyers, and clergymen, they murdered the archbishop of Canterbury and would have done more had not Richard II cleverly tricked them into believing that he was sympathetic. Inducing them to meet him outside the city, the king agreed to speak with Wat Tyler, who, however, was murdered by the king's men, whereupon a strong force of London citizenry attacked the rudely armed rebels and dispersed them.

These fourteenth- and fifteenth-century revolts were aimed at real social problems only a little more than their predecessors; their motivation was still largely religious. One of the leaders of the English Peasants' Revolt, John Ball, was a clergyman whose attitude was much like that of Valdes or the other Reformists before him. John Ball advised the doing away with bishops, abbots, priests, and canons, though he was willing to spare the office of archbishop in order to be appointed to it himself. "Are we not all descended from the same parents, Adam and

uant ce vmt le ven
dredp au matm ce
teuple qui eftoit
lothe en la place famte kathe
rine xuant la tour du chafel
x londres comme dit eft fe
commencerent a eulx leuer

The peasants' rebellion of 1381: The mob breaks into Lambeth palace and
murders the archbishop and his men. The archbishop is at the bottom left,
kneeling.

Eve?," he exclaimed, whence the jingle that became so popular
in after years: "When Adam dalf, and Eve span, wo thanne
was a gentilman?"

THESE revolts were protests against social inequality, but their
ideology was still that of Christian theology. The rebels less
often stole objects of value than they destroyed them. Their
ideal was that of Christian poverty, derived from Christ himself,
and afterwards taught by monks and Reformist heretics: it was
the ideal of Saint Francis, and of Savonarola, who had the
"vanities" of Florence burned in the fire. The rebels did not say:
"We want a larger share," but, "Destroy the Mammon of iniquity." *Piers Plowman* complains that the rich ignore the beggars at
their door and that priests are Pharisees who have God ever in
their mouths but who never do his will. "Riches spread upon

Savonarola, *by Fra Bartolommeo.*

riches," says *Piers,* "give rise to all vices." Society was to be saved, not by the better distribution of wealth, but by its destruction.

Yet the Reformists of the later Middle Ages were different in one very important respect from their predecessors. Where the earlier monks and heretics were content to retreat from the world, the rebels now wished to transform it. They were no longer willing to hoard up their own righteousness until the Kingdom of God should come; they were out to rebuild the *societas christiana* upon the true teachings of Christ, and in this they were the direct predecessors of the Protestant Reformers of the sixteenth century. The rebels did not recognize a paradoxical truth: the Church was necessary for the preservation of

Christian tradition, and the Church was necessarily a failure. The Church failed, and the Reformists' efforts also failed, because the radical revolutionary teachings of Jesus were inevitably lost when his teachings were institutionalized; when, in sociological terms, a sect became a church.

MORE important to the individual in the Middle Ages than all of the great religious and political questions were the facts of his everyday life. Far more than the operation of the Exchequer or debates on the number of the sacraments, men were concerned with health, food, sex, shelter, and family relationships. The circumstances of daily living probably mattered to them more than they matter to men in twentieth-century America, for the simple reason that creature comforts were so hard, and miseries so easy, to come by.

In the Middle Ages the pressure of nature bore hard on every man. Against bitter cold, dwellings offered little protection; against storms and floods men had little warning. When unseasonable frost, damp, or drought destroyed an area's crops, there was seldom even adequate means for the shipment of food from a less stricken region. Winter brought pulmonary diseases, and spring and summer contributed plagues, influenza, and dysentery. Dirt was omnipresent, and the disposition of sewage was a constant problem. The peasants simply relieved themselves in the back yard; castles had tower chambers (euphemistically called wardrobes) emptying into a pit or the moat; the houses of the smaller gentry had privies. Big town houses had facilities emptying into cesspits beneath the house, which had to be emptied periodically by servants; smaller houses had outdoor privies, and the city poor had to walk a block or two to public accomodations. These were huge pits over which planks were stretched, and there are some unpleasant reports of careless people slipping and drowning.

On the other hand, the upper classes made a point of personal cleanliness. Bathtubs were common, though they had to be filled with hot water from the kitchen, and, as in modern Japan, one bath was used by the whole family in order of rank. For the less wealthy there were public bath houses in most towns, and in between times people made use of spit baths with washcloths and soap. From the thirteenth century running water was available for the very wealthy and powerful, and Henry III of England (1216–1272) had a whole system for his London palace, including a sewer emptying into the Thames.

Medicine was ineffective. The poor man and his children when stricken died on their pallets in their wretched huts aided only by the ministrations of the village wisewoman with her herbal brews. The man who could afford a physician was in even worse straits, for the learned doctor would feed him pepper to cure a chill or trephine his skull to permit the egress of demons. Some physicans learned from experience, one fourteenth-century doctor advising the use of mouthwash and the boiling of drinking water. Most more often relied upon the textbooks of the ancients. "Experience is untrustworthy, according to Hippocrates," said Peter of Blois. In these circumstances life was short and often wretched, for if disease and famine did not finish a man they might easily reduce him to deformity or at least chronic ill health. When one considers as simple a thing as toothache, and remembers that there were no dentists or false teeth, one is obliged to imagine a population of which a large proportion suffered constant discomfort, though tooth decay was less frequent than today owing to a diet lacking much sugar or refined flour.

DEATH was constantly present. In modern America death has almost ceased to be a fact of life, except for paying the mortician's bill. But in the Middle Ages it was familiar enough to breed contempt. When so much of life was uncomfortable or even miserable, and when most people believed without question that the good man's soul was borne to heaven by angels, death itself was less fearful than now. Medieval men feared God's judgment, or they feared pain, crippling, or deformity, but, because they expected less of life, death seemed not as bad.

IN some ways, medieval food was not inferior to ours. The peasants of course raised food for their own consumption. Bread, whether black, brown, or white, was less refined and more nutritious than most modern breads, so that even poor people got greater quantities of the B vitamins than do most people today. In addition, the peasant obtained protein in milk, cheese, eggs, and beans, though these products became scarcer at the end of the

Middle Ages and the early modern period. He had only a few vegetables and fruits. He enjoyed some fowl and occasionally some small game like squirrel or rabbit, but he was not ordinarily allowed to hunt or fish. One man who could not resist the temptation to poach apologized in court:

Sir, for God's sake do not take it ill of me if I tell thee the truth, how I went the other evening along the bank of this pond and looked at the fish which were playing in the water, so beautiful and so bright, and for the great desire I had for a tench I laid me down on the bank and . . . caught that tench and carried it off . . . .[5]

The upper feudal classes dined more heavily, not only than the medieval peasants, but than we. As Sir Walter Scott long ago observed, the English words for animals on the hoof derive from the Anglo-Saxon: swine, cattle, sheep; but the words for meat on the table—pork, veal, beef, and mutton, derive from French, the language of the Anglo-Norman nobility. In addition to these farmyard animals, the nobility ate quantities of fowl, including duck, pheasant, peacock, and even crane, and game like boar and venison. They also enjoyed meat soups and stews and meat pastries. That these habits were imitated by the wealthy merchants is evident from this sample menu prepared for his young wife's guidance by the Goodman of Paris:

DINNER . . . First course. (Wine of) Grenache and roasts, veal pasties, pimpernel pasties, black-puddings and sausages. Second course. Hares in civey and cutlets, pea soup . . . , salt meat and great joints, a soringue of eels and other fish. Third course. Roast: coneys, partridges, capons, etc., luce, bar, carp, and a quartered pottage. Fourth course. River fish à la dodine, savoury rice, a bourrey with hot sauce and eels reversed. Fifth course. Lark pasties, rissoles, larded milk, sugared flawns. Sixth course. Pears and comfits, medlars and peeled nuts. Hippocras and wafers . . . .[6]

Everyday meals were not as elaborate as this, intended for a dinner party, but even on ordinary occasions the wealthy man in the Middle Ages is estimated to have consumed as much as three pounds of meat a day.

Table manners among the well-to-do were expected to be good. Each person had his own napkin and knife, which he kept in a little box that was set at his place at the table.

The wealthy owned a few cups, dishes, and saucers of silver, but more often thick, unleavened bread was used for plates. There were spoons but no forks, and fingers, as among the Arabs today, preformed many an agile task. A twelfth-century treatise on manners could be read with profit today: there was to be no belching, no touching the nose or ears or using toothpicks at table; elbows were to be kept off the table, and hands and nails were to be carefully washed. Bad manners were boorishness, and no gentleman or lady wished to be known as a boor (a *boor,* cf. Dutch *boer* and German *Bauer,* was literally a farmer or peasant).

The medieval diet, strong in protein and vitamin B, was lacking in vitamins C and D, and as a result there were many cases of scurvy and rickets, diseases which were not known until the nineteenth century to be the result of nutritional deficiency. Wine, beer, and ale were drunk by all, though wine, being more expensive in northern Europe, was there the special drink of the upper classes. Plain water was drunk only by the very poor or the very rash, for supplies were likely to be polluted. Municipal and gild regulations sought to protect the consumer against bad food and dishonest sellers. A butcher who sold tainted meat was run out of town on a rail with a piece of rotten meat tied in front of his nose, and a similar fate awaited the baker who stole his clients' dough or mixed it with impurities.

The medieval diet was, then, in some ways more substantial than ours, though considerably less varied. The difficulty in making any generalizations in regard to standard of living in other respects is even more complicated. Wages were much lower in the Middle Ages than now, but so were prices. A medieval English penny has been estimated as being worth at least forty and perhaps as much as two hundred pence today, and the figure is rising with inflation. But all such indices are essentially meaningless, for the modern wage earner today enjoys television and cars and vacations unimagined by his counterpart seven centuries ago, and it is obviously absurd to construct an index that would tell us how much one would have had to pay for a television in the thirteenth century had there been any. Technology has today made some goods available and cheap. On the other hand, a medieval wage earner would have paid less in real wages for a house, and the furniture he bought

A fraudulent baker is dragged through town on a sled, with a loaf of bread (probably adulterated) around his neck.

would have been better made than today's. His water was sometimes polluted, but the air was clear and his ears exempt from
the assaults of motorcycles and juke boxes. There is no index
that does the job of translating the medieval standard of living
into our terms, especially when we remember that the standard
varied both in their day and in ours. Few people in the
Middle Ages lived as well as the modern middle-class American,
and few lived as badly as the modern lower-class inhabitant of
Calcutta. In most respects life for most Americans and Europeans
is more comfortable now than in thirteenth-century Europe;
that is about all that can be said on the matter.

ATTITUDES toward money were different in the Middle Ages from
what they are today. Christianity glorifies poverty and is mistrustful of riches: Lazarus dying in need is raised to heaven,
and the rich man who fails to help him suffers in hell; a camel
may pass through the eye of a needle more easily than a rich
man may enter the Kingdom of God. Thus through most of
the Middle Ages wealth was not pursued without some shame
and gnawings of conscience. From the thirteenth century,
largely owing to the rise of the bourgeoisie, the glorification of
poverty is muted, except on the part of rebels, and the principle
that poverty, rather than the love of money, is the root of evil
begins to be expressed. This notion is now taken wholly for
granted, although a modern theologian has warned that "need"
quickly becomes "greed" in an affluent society. We are so used to
"wars on poverty" that we find shocking the conviction current

through most of the Middle Ages, that what was needed was a war on riches.

DIFFERENCES in housing and clothing were the clearest distinguishing marks among the classes. The great nobles occupied castles, wooden at first, stone from the later eleventh century. The great hall, a combined living and dining room, was the center of castle life. There was also a chapel and one or more great bedrooms in which large numbers slept. The master and mistress slept in a canopied bed, their men and ladies in smaller beds or pallets on the floor. This proximity, in addition to the fact that most slept naked, gave rise to lewd jokes and stories many of which doubtless had all too good grounds. The windows were small and narrow, and at best the castle was dim, lit only by a few expensive candles or fat-burning lamps that easily flickered and guttered. Until the late Middle Ages the small and narrow windows were unglazed and closed only by shutters, so that one usually had to choose between darkness and cold. The cold, especially in northern Europe, was frightful; the only heat was provided by a fireplace in the great hall or occasional braziers. This fireplace was not, again till the later Middle Ages, connected to a chimney: the smoke merely rose and passed out of a hole in the roof, and on a windy evening it would be inclined to blow all over the hall. The floors were earthen or stone and strewn with rushes and grasses that remained until utterly fouled by offal; then they were either replaced or covered by another layer. The dwelling of the ruling class was dim, dank, smoky, and smelly.

From the fifteenth century, when a man's home no longer needed literally to be his castle, country houses became more comfortable, and in the towns the wealthy merchants were building homes with an eye to comfort. The home of an urban family, originally two rooms over the shop, grew with its family's fortune, and in the fifteenth century increasing attention was paid both to privacy and to elegance. The Goodman of Paris made a list of nineteen helpful household hints for his young wife, including instructions on how to clean house, how to keep sheets and clothes presentable, how to deal with flies, fleas, and other unwelcome fauna, how to cook, and how to comfort her husband when he came home tired from work.

Peasants lived in two-room huts constructed of local materials, one serving as a bedroom and the other as everything else. Through the whole house the barnyard animals wandered at will, though efforts were made to keep them out of the bedroom, where they were inclined to eat the straw mattress. Mud walls and thatched roofs were common; the floor was always of trodden earth, and in the center, on the bare ground, was laid the little cooking fire whenever fuel was available. The windows of course were unglazed. The furniture consisted of stools, a trestle table, and a pot, in addition to a few eating utensils made of wood. The peasants were more fortunate than the urban poor, who lived in one-room alley apartments unblessed by sanitation, ventilation, or light.

A POOR man was instantly distinguishable from a well-to-do man by his bearing, grooming, and clothing. Until the twelfth century the basic dress of all classes was similar: men wore a long loose jacket with a belt around the waist, and hose, tight pants rather like leotards. Over this they might wear a mantle for warmth. Women wore simple robes over their shifts. Men wore underpants; girls and women did not, a custom that produced many a ribald joke about staircases. The difference between the upper and lower classes in clothing was measured by the fineness of cloth, of tailoring, and of color. Poor people wore drab clothes; rich people chose bright colors. Modern male dress is essentially workingman's drab, and a medieval man transported to the New York Stock Exchange might conclude that he had fallen in among oddly well-groomed peasants.

From the twelfth century livelier commerce made changing fashions possible, and the increasing uselessness of the aristocrats encouraged them to adopt clothing useless to serious work. They now delighted in silks and robes richly trimmed with fur. By the fifteenth century, fashions shifted rapidly, and the wealthy began sporting shoes with curled toes, elaborate turbans, or high peaked hats for the ladies, and heavy, fantastically-shaped coats. Thus, like the Chinese mandarins with their long fingernails, they demonstrated to the world that they were a leisure class. Conspicuous consumption began long before the automobile was invented.

In the Middle Ages, sexual practices were on the whole more restrained than they are today, partly perhaps because of Christian morality, but more because of a greater practicality. Although flirting was common among all classes, there were considerable restraints upon going farther. Among all classes children, few of whom had a long education, were married very young, girls on the average between twelve and fourteen, so there was not much time for frivolity before marital responsibilities were undertaken. Among the aristocracy, the virginity of girls was carefully guarded, for a pregnant girl could find no husband, and a virgin daughter could bring much money to a merchant father who married her to the son of an even wealthier man; and promiscuity among the lower classes was restricted by the watchful eye of the manorial lord, who wanted to keep the girls and their offspring on the manor and who wanted no unnecessary quarreling among his tenants. Stability was his desire, and he often forced girls to marry at his convenience. For the same purpose of stability, as well as for the sake of religion, peasants were formally married in the village Church by a priest. A lord who himself fancied a peasant wench was of course always willing to make an exception.

The attitude of the Church towards sex must have had some effect upon behavior. As John Noonan points out, the teaching of the Church has in this regard always been very strict; the only way it could be *more* severe, he says, would be to forbid sexual intercourse altogether. Most of the Fathers and most medieval theologians maintained that sexual intercourse was permissible only within marriage, that it must be done in a normal fashion, and that it must be done for the purpose of procreation. Even then, some of the more extreme writers considered that it was at least venially sinful. Contraception was not only forbidden by the Church, but seldom practised, for it was difficult to replace, let alone increase, population. Nevertheless, both herbal and mechanical contraceptives were well-known from the twelfth century.

But of course sexual morality is always supposed to be declining. In 1110 the monk Guibert of Nogent, mourning the pure old days of his mother's time, exclaimed "Ah! how wretchedly have modesty and honor and the state of maidenhood declined from those times to these . . . ."[7]

FAMILY relationships varied according to time and place in society. Family ties were always important. The tribal groupings of the old Germanic tribes were succeeded by the feudal relationships of man and vassal. But when the feudal system became hereditary, it reaffirmed family solidarity. It is blood relationship that made the aristocracy deliberately exclusive, first of the serjeants, and then of the urban patriciate. The peasant family was always closer knit by necessity, confined as it was to close quarters, and the inbreeding encouraged by the manorial lord meant that a village was likely to be—in the literal sense—one big family.

Family solidarity was greatest among the merchants and artisans of the city, in families that had not only the wealth but the drive to get ahead. The merchant and the artisan took great care and pride in the raising and training of sons and daughters for whom they felt a parental affection heightened by personal anbition: the obedient daughter could be married to a wealthier husband, and the dutiful son could increase the business. In this attitude is the beginning of bourgeois morality.

There was little idea of "childhood" in the Middle Ages. Until about the sixteenth century children were dressed like little adults and allowed to see and hear things that we would be inclined to reserve for more mature eyes and ears. It was the bourgeois family, recognizing the place of a protracted education in advancing their children's careers, that invented the dependent and apprenticed childhood and adolescence with which modern middle-class society is familiar. Neither nobles nor peasants found it useful to educate their children academically.

The sons of medieval merchants were taught to read and write Latin and the vernacular, and to do accounts. They were taught the virtues of obedience, respect for authority, thrift, prudence in investment, and avoidance of unnecessary risk. Gambling—wasting, as it was called—was considered the worst of the vices; eating and drinking were the good, safe, bourgeois amusements. Girls were trained to be obedient to men, to be thrifty and skillful in handling household monies, and to cook and sew. Neither among the merchants nor among the nobles, nor even among the clergy, was there any idea of a liberal education. The practical was at the forefront of the medieval mind even more than that of the modern.

Juggler.

Fool.

IT is difficult to estimate the degree to which religion influenced people's lives. The Church's teachings were seldom questioned, unless they were politically or economically incovenient, and there was common observation of the externals. Many people, perhaps most, attended mass not only on Sundays but on many other occasions. Daily mass was the rule in the castle chapels. The peasants crossed themselves and said their prayers by road-side shrines. There was a general belief that the Divine was near at hand in a very rude and physical fashion: the Blessed Virgin is supposed to have intervened miraculously to save an adulterous monk and his paramour from punishment; a vision of hell recounted by the historian Orderic Vitalis included adulterous women made to ride horses with red-hot nails set in the saddle. The religion of the ordinary man was crude and childish as well as loyal and devout.

FAR from meditating upon the Divine essence, most people spent as much time as they could in joyous recreation. The favorite spectator sport of nobles and peasants alike was watching wan-dering minstrels and jugglers, although public executions were always a welcome diversion. All also enjoyed the blood sports that a fastidious Church still allowed after unkindly forbidding the wholesale slaughter of animals and men so pleasing to the Roman taste. The nobles enjoyed baiting bears or bulls with dogs; the peasants had to be content with cockfights. On cold and wintry days, the nobles enertained themselves with dice, or with the chess and checkers that were learned through commercial contacts with the East, the first mention of chess in a western manuscript being about 1000. Playing cards were introduced in the fifteenth century, as were new rules in chess giving the queen and the bishop more power and making the game more complex. The court jester or fool was a common sight at the noble castle. Often deformed or mentally deranged, the fool could occassionally be clever and even in a minor way influential, for he was allowed liberties of speech and action denied others. The lower classes amused themselves with variations of the nine-men-morris, a game in which the object was to line one's counters up in a row. Reading, impossible for the peasants, was not greatly cultivated by the lay nobility, and a fourteenth-century author commented snidely on "laymen . . . who look in the same way at a book lying upside down as when it is open in its natural way."[8] This was changing by the fourteenth and fifteenth century, especially when the vernacular came to compete with Latin, and the Pastons, English gentry of the fifteenth century, had a good-sized collection of books in French, English, and even a few in Latin.

Outdoor sports were greatly enjoyed by all classes. The nobles hunted, hawked, and held tournaments (general mêlées) and jousts (combats between two knights) to keep their blood spirit up in sluggish times of peace. In the fifteenth century golf (in Scotland) and tennis were introduced. The lower classes enjoyed various field and track sports, racing, throwing the javelin, jousting at barrels or wooden figures, or, from the fourteenth century, archery. The Englishman's skill with the longbow won him considerable advantage on the battlefield as well. Hockey was known quite early, and football seems to have been as old as the Middle Ages themselves. Some fanciful authorities have claimed that football represents the scramble for the head of the sacrificial victim in ancient pagan rites; the more prosaic insist it originated in the good-natured kicking about of pigs'

Bearbaiting: A popular sport of the feudal class.

Peasants playing hockey in a field.

innards at pig-sticking time. Thus was born the modern pigskin, which through the Middle Ages most often took the form of an inflated porcine bladder. Football was so rough that legal measures were taken to restrict it: there are several accounts of murder being done in an overenthusiastic scrimmage.

CERTAIN ways of life and modes of thought were reserved to the feudal aristocracy, the most striking being those of chivalry. In feudalism a man is a lord and a vassal and a knight is simply a *miles,* a warrior, but from the eleventh century he became something more. *Chevalerie,* the French word for knighthood, applies not only to the military and feudal duties of a man but to his general behavior. Knighthood in this sense became an ideology, and the knight became a gentleman. For the first time European aristocrats began to approach the politeness of Japanese society in the same period as portrayed in *The Tale of Genji.* Chivalry became a mystique.

The first sign of the mystique was the initiation rite. Among the old Teutons, every free man was initiated to adulthood at the proper age by being given manly arms. The feudal monopoly of warfare restricted that initiation to the feudal class, and the pattern of training for such initiation became fixed. A feudal father would send his boy off at the age of seven or so to a neighboring or friendly knight for training. The boy, called a valet or page [Fr. *damoiseau*], was trained in arms, riding, hawking, and hunting, and courtesy (the good manners pertaining to a court). At the age of fourteen, he became a squire [Fr. *écuyer:* "shield-bearer"] and was attached to a knight whom he served by bearing his armor and shield, leading his extra horse, helping him dress, arm, or bathe, and carrying messages. In the mean-while his training in arms continued until he was ready to be knighted. In this ceremony he received his arms and his sword from an older knight who then bestowed upon his neck or cheek a blow with the flat of the hand. Later this act, known as dubbing [Fr. *adoubement*], symbolizing the blows a knight must receive and also perhaps reminiscent of confirmation or priestly ordina-tion, was done with the flat of the sword.

Essentially chivalry was a code of mutual respect among warriors emphasizing bravery and personal loyalty, and it became an ethos of its own, not wholly contradictory to Christianity, but wholly distinct. The knights were becoming an *ordo* of their own whose place in Christian society was by no means clear.

From the end of the eleventh century the Church made a concerted effort to Christianize chivalry. At the Council of Clermont Urban II distinguished between robbers and true knights; the Church endeavored to create the idea of the *miles Christi,* the knight of Christ. Intervening in the initiation cere-mony, the Church blessed the sword, which was solemnly placed upon the altar before being given the new knight, and, as he received it, the candidate took an oath to be a good Christian as well as a good warrior. From the thirteenth century, the vigil of arms and purifying bath was added. This was the first, but not the last, time in the Middle Ages that the Church was obliged to try to assimilate a non-Christian ethos: it had equal difficulty in baptizing the mercantile spirit of the towns. There is little evidence that thirteenth-century knights behaved like better Christians than their eleventh-century counterparts.

Yet at least the ideal, if not the practice, of chivalry had been modified, and the traits expected of a *chevalier* were a curious mixture of feudal and Christian virtues. He had to be truthful, honest, brave, and loyal. On no account could he betray his lord. His word was his bond: it was common to let prisoners out on their word, which was very seldom broken. He was courteous. He was stalwart in the face of pain, fatigue, and death. He pursued glory and renown. All of these qualities made up that of *prowess,* that combination of manly vigor with courtesy that was the highest ideal of the knight and upon which his honor depended. To be deemed a *preux chevalier* was the acme of desire, and a man known to lack the qualities of prowess was a disgrace to himself, to his family, and to his lord. To these qualities were added the Christian virtues of piety—the knight often attended daily mass, though he might pass his time there talking about war—of generosity, and of responsibility for the protection of widows, orphans, and the poor. William Marshal (born 1147) was the incarnation of the perfect knight, with his intense loyalty and honesty combined with humility, good manners, generosity, and an insatiable desire for blood combat. The fact that a knight's honor depended upon his courage in battle frequently interfered with tactics, for it was nearly impossible to hold a company of knights in reserve when they were convinced that every minute they remained out of the fray was a blemish upon their shield of honor.

As feudalism grew obsolete and knighthood socially useless, the customs of chivalry grew more colorful and complex, in conformity with the historical rule that institutions tend to become externally more splendid as their utility decreases. Dress and armor grew fantastic. Heraldry became a science with an intricate vocabulary. The exploits of Marshal Boucicaut in the fourteenth century illustrate the fantasies of dying feudalism. During a peace in the Hundred Years' War, Marshal Boucicaut and two companions stationed themselves on the frontier between Boulogne and Calais. Sending heralds three months in advance all over Europe, they announced their intention of jousting with any challenger, who might choose as weapons either blunted or real lances. In the meanwhile the marshal caused magnificent pavilions to be set up near the jousting place, where huge supplies of food and drink were laid in for a party that lasted the whole month. This kind of thing was by no means uncommon, nor were elaborate vows of honor, as when a large group of English knights each placed a patch over one eye till he should have done a deed of glory in honor of his lady fair.

For the ladies were more successful than the Church in transforming chivalry. From the end of the eleventh century an attitude known as "courtly love" emerged in southern France and spread rapidly all over Europe. The result was a revolution in manners which, as C. S. Lewis observed, "has left no corner of our ethics, our imagination, or our daily life untouched. . . . Compared with this revolution the Renaissance is a mere ripple on the surface of literature."[9] The normal attitude of most societies towards women, the prevailing attitude in ancient Greece and Rome, in modern Islam, and in the earlier Middle Ages, was to regard them as brood mares, domestics, and beasts of burden. Courtly love reversed the position of the lady, placing her upon a pedestal as a pure, sensitive being with a nature higher, more refined, and more spiritual, than that of the male. In the Middle Ages, this attitude was confined to the feudal nobility and directed solely at *ladies,* women who themselves were members of the feudal class. The same knight who was capable of the most refined sentiments towards a countess was equally capable, without the slightest sense of inconsistency, of going out an hour later and throwing a peasant girl into a haypile. The attitudes of courtly love were spread by troubadours and minstrels from castle to castle until by the twelfth century they were the common property of the nobility of Germany, England, and the rest of western Europe as well as of France.

Later in the Middle Ages the ideals of courtly love became at once more diluted and more widely diffused. By the end of the fifteenth century courtly love was taken much less seriously by knights, but with increasing literacy and the general refinement of life merchants and industrialists began to adopt the manners of the aristocracy, including the courtly attitude towards ladies. These manners persisted into modern times, reinforced by the Romantic revival of the late eighteenth and early nineteenth centuries, and have only very recently shown signs of disappearing. Even today many of our customs derive from the revolution of courtly love: in America, gentlemen carry parcels for ladies; while in Arabia the men ride the camels and the women walk along behind carrying the groceries. Marks of politeness such as allowing women precedence into doorways or rising when they enter the room are the result of the tradition of courtly love. The enormous preponderance—again until very recently—of love lyrics over other topics among popular songs is a result of courtly love: other cultures preferred war songs or religious songs. Most important, the political and social equality that women in general have begun to win in the twentieth century has its remote origins in the elevation of the lady by the courtly lovers above her previous status of drudge.

Both the nature and origins of courtly love have been disputed by historians and literary critics. The most extreme critics on one side have held that courtly love was never anything more than a very superficial poetic and social convention which no one took seriously; the most extreme on the other side maintain that it was taken so seriously by so many people as to constitute a whole ethic—even a heresy—competing with Christianity. The truth doubtless lies somewhere in between. Courtly love certainly lent itself to exaggeration, but to dismiss it as a game or a fancy is to fail to understand the attractions of romantic, as opposed to purely sensual love.

As worked out by the poets and theoreticians,* courtly love was indeed an ethic with a number of specific rules. The lover, for example, was to tremble at the sight of his beloved; he was to obey her every command without question; he was to fight to the death to defend her honor. These rules were built round a central convention: that courtly love could exist only between a gentleman and a lady and that the lady had to be married to another gentleman of higher status. Courtly love addressed to an unmarried girl, to a lady of lower rank than oneself, or, worst of all, to one's own wife was deemed absurd. At the bottom of this is the idea of romantic love.

No word is more difficult to define than "love": we speak of the love of God and the love of mushroom pizza. Even in our use of the word to describe what passes between a man and a woman we are continually vague, but a description of some of the major differences may help. On one end of the scale there is purely physical love—lust, if you prefer—devoted solely to sexual gratification. Then there is physical love mixed with tenderness and mutual regard and esteem, the kind of love that can grow (or not) with time and is associated with happy marriages or lasting liaisons. On the other end of the scale is Platonic friendship or purely spiritual love; next to that perhaps is the kind of love that persists in a long and happy marriage when the physical has become less important than it once was. But apart from all of these is romantic love. Romantic love views the object of its attention neither as an object of physical satisfaction nor merely as a friend; it is neither purely sensual

---

* The most famous of these was Andrew the Chaplain, who wrote a treatise on "How to Love Like a Gentleman."

nor purely spiritual. The romantic lover sees his beloved as being spiritually above him, a being whom he at once reveres and also desires physically. Courtly love was romantic in this sense. It was strongly sensual, but it emphasized the pleasures of suspense, of yearning, of *Sehnsucht* for the inconceivably beautiful and unattainable. As Yeats observed, "Every touch consumes the myth," and the courtly lovers wished above all to preserve the myth. In getting too easily and too quickly, we lose the pleasures of *attente,* and these pleasures the courtly lovers knew well. Says Mozart's Cherubino:

Sospiro e gemo,	I sigh and moan
Senza voler;	Against my will;
Palpito e tremo,	I tremble and flutter
Senza saper;	Without knowing it;
Non trovo pace	I find peace
Notte nè di,	Neither night nor day;
Ma pur mi piace	Yet it pleases me
Languir così.	To suffer this way.

The origins of courtly love, in most respects a wholly new cultural phenomenon, are disputed. Some historians find them in medieval Latin love poetry, some in Ovid's *Art of Love,* some in Cicero's treatises on friendship, some in Catharist heresy, some in Arabic love poetry, some in devious female propaganda devoted to attracting more attention and service from males. Many of these suggestions are doubtless relevant, but the most important elements in courtly love were three. First, the feudal and chivalric codes. A man already conditioned to feel total loyalty, commitment, and devotion for his lord found it easy enough to transfer these feelings to the lady. Second, the situation of ladies in the feudal castle. A noble lady was left by her husband much of the year while he was at war or at court or simply out hunting. Most girls had been married very young to husbands they had not chosen and had never enjoyed what we would call a romance. They very much needed amusement, but almost every kind of enertainment was barred to them. Love affairs constituted the most dangerous kind of game imaginable, for a man who found that his wife was adulterous could inflict whatever punishment he wished short of actual murder. Courtly love, with its elaborate rituals of flirting, provided the fun, the excitement, and the romance, while bypassing the terrors of adultery. Third, Christianity itself. Christianity reinforced feudal moral restrictions and thus helped to create sexual tension. Moreover, Christianity taught what may be called an ultimate concern for something indescribably good, lovely, beautiful, and unattainable. The courtly lover transferred the language reserved by the Church for God to his lady fair.

To begin with, the lady admired has to be unattainable: she has to be married and of a higher station in life than her admirer. He *adores* and *worships* her, he feels *passion* for her [Latin *passio*: "suffering": cf. the "passion of Christ"]. The lady, rather than God, is the ultimate judge of his conduct; he trembles in her presence like a worshiper before Yahweh; the joy of his love transforms him as thoroughly as the faith of Saint Paul; he abandons all to follow her as the apostles abandoned all to follow Christ. He becomes a *miles amoris* rather than a *miles Christi*. The lady has become his ultimate concern; she has become his God.

Occasionally the conduct of courtly love, like that of chivalry itself, grew fantastic. In Chrétien de Troyes' *The Knight of the Cart,* Lancelot does everything for Guinevere. He crawls over a bridge consisting of the sharpened edge of a sword and, far worse, rides in a cart: a knight was dishonored by riding in any wheeled vehicle. Yet when after many perils he returns to his lady love she turns a cold shoulder, for she has heard that for a split second he hesitated before climbing in. In the thirteenth century, Ulrich von Liechtenstein rode from Venice to Bohemia dressed like the goddess Venus and jousting with all comers, all for the love of a lady whom he had worshiped since he was a page, whose washing water he had reverently drunk, for whom he had chopped off his finger, and who eventually rewarded him for ten years of devotion by pushing him into the moat. But it was precisely the sense of, and love of, the fantastic that the courtly lovers sought, and romantic love became a central part of the romantic view of life put forward by twelfth- and thirteenth-century writers whose world was a world of mystery, of exotic journeys, and of emotional exaltation.

THE effects of the growing diversity and complexity of medieval society had profound effects upon civilization as a whole: serfdom was transformed into paid agricultural labor; feudalism was undermined by the payment of soldiery and the development of archery and firearms; mercantile, artisan, and proletarian classes were forming in the cities; chivalry and courtly love produced new modes of thought; government became more complex. The arts and sciences were advanced, for the accumulation of wealth in cities and the traffic that made them markets for the exchange of ideas encouraged the building of cathedrals, the development of the theatre, and the teaching of philosophy.

NOTES

[1] Quoted by John Mundy and Peter Riesenburg, *The Medieval Town* (New York, 1958), p. 135.
[2] Mundy and Riesenburg, p. 139.
[3] Mundy and Riesenburg, p. 140.
[4] Guibert of Nogent, *Autobiography,* trans. C. C. Swinton Bland (London, E. P. Dutton and Co., 1926) p. 165.
[5] H. S. Bennett, *Life on the English Manor* (Cambridge, Cambridge University Press, 1937), p. 270.
[6] Eileen Power, *The Goodman of Paris* (London, Routledge, 1928), p. 226.
[7] *Autobiography,* trans. C. C. Swinton Bland (London, 1926), pp. 41-42.
[8] Richard de Bury, *The Philobiblion,* in W. O. Hassall, *Medieval England* (New York, 1965), p. 151.
[9] *The Allegory of Love* (Oxford, 1936), p. 4.

Chapter Twenty-Two

REASON, LOVE, AND OBSERVATION

SCHOLASTICISM, having originated in the twelfth-century effort
to synthesize humanism and the Christian tradition, flourished
in the thirteenth. The two most important motors of philosophical
growth were the universities and the gradual incorporation into
the synthesis of the logical and scientific works of Aristotle and
others. Scholasticism took three forms: the scholasticism of reason,
or philosophy; the scholasticism of love, or mystical theology; and
the scholasticism of observation, or what we call science. Of the
three, that of reason dominated the twelfth and thirteenth
centuries and is often thought of as scholasticism *par excellence.*
Certainly no age was more truly an age of reason than that in
which Thomas Aquinas and his colleagues believed that the
human mind might through logic obtain the secrets of the universe and record them in the pages of a *summa.*

The thirteenth century achieved a synthesis in philosophy
in much the way that, through Dante, it achieved one in literature: it worked out the problems that had been posed by
earlier writers. Yet the synthesis was not uniform: there were,
in addition to many lesser variations, three differing trends in
thirteenth-century rational scholasticism: the Aristotelian tradition of using sense observations upon which to base logical
conclusions, the conservative Augustinian tradition of internal
illumination, and, at the end of the century, what might be
called voluntarism, which insisted upon God's freedom of will
as against his intelligibility to human reason.

IN the twelfth century philosophers were still concerned with
the reconciliation of Plato and Christianity; in the thirteenth

they had also to incorporate the Aristotelian materials made available from the latter half of the twelfth century, first from Arabic, and then directly through Greek, sources. The great Aristotelians of the century were William of Auvergne, Alexander of Hales, and Albertus Magnus (Albert the Great). Albert (1193–1280), a truly universal man, was a botanist and geologist as well as a theologian and is the only constructive genius whom posterity has rewarded with the title of "the great," usually reserved to military conquerors. Albert wrote a *summa theologica* and taught at the University of Paris and at Cologne, where he numbered Thomas Aquinas among his pupils.

THOMAS, a great-nephew of the emperor Frederick II, was born into a wealthy and noble Italian family of Aquino in 1225. He had six brothers, all destined by their parents to great careers in politics. Thomas, fat, slow, and pious, was sent at the age of five to the Benedictine abbey of Monte Cassino. He was raised there until the age of fourteen, when he went to the University of Naples to study philosophy. There, impressed by his Dominican teachers, he determined to enter the Order of Preachers himself. His family, who were resigned to his career in the Church, had counted at least upon his becoming abbot of Monte Cassino and looked with little favor upon his plans to become a mendicant. They devoted all their energies to dissuading him from his choice. His brothers are said to have introduced a prostitute into his bed; his mother kidnapped him; his father offered to buy him the archbishopric of Naples. All came to no avail: he was determined to be a friar and a teacher.

Pursuing this ambition, he went to study at Paris, the center of theological learning. There his bulk, seriousness, and slowness earned him the nickname of the "Dumb Ox" until in public disputation the depth of his intelligence became evident. He studied under Albert the Great, taught for a while at Cologne, and then returned in 1252 to Paris, where he spent much of his time until his death in 1274. He retained his humility and shyness, and the blunt directness characteristic of many shy people, refusing to turn questions with witticisms. He also retained his huge bulk, to accomodate which a semicircular concavity had to be excised from his desk. But nothing prevented the fame of his brilliant and thorough mind from growing. So quickly did

Saint Thomas Aquinas, *from a fresco by Fra Angelico.*

it work that he was obliged to dictate, pacing up and down the
room, to several secretaries at once. His fame and piety, as well
as his noble birth, recommended him to the attention of Saint
Louis, and he was a frequent visitor at court. At table he was
wont to stare into space while the other guests laughed and
talked, and on one occasion he interrupted the meal by slamming
his fist onto the table and exclaiming "That is the decisive
point against the Manichaeans!" upon which the tolerant king
called one of his own secretaries to take down the philosopher's
thoughts without delay.

The writings of Thomas Aquinas fill many volumes. The
most important are his great *Summa Theologica* written from

1265 to 1272 as a manual for beginners in theology and his more detailed *Summa contra Gentiles:* "Summa against the Pagans," written in 1259–1264 to aid missionaries in Spain and to combat the secular philosophy imported along with Aristotle from the Arabs. Thomas was an enthusiastic investigator of the new knowledge, but he insisted upon distinguishing that which was acceptable to Christianity from that which was not. His synthesis of the new Aristotelian philosophy with the old Platonic thought at first made his own works suspect to conservative opinion in the Church; but long afterwards his work gained the prominence in Catholic philosophy that it has retained to the present. At the Council of Trent in the sixteenth century the works of Aquinas lay open on the high altar with the Bible as books of reference, and in 1879 the papal encyclical *Aeterni Patris* declared Thomism eternally valid. The limitations of Thomism are today more readily admitted, but the greatness of Thomas himself remains. Even those who find his arguments unconvincing find the grace and skill with which they are presented both intellectually and esthetically impressive.

It was Thomas who perfected the rigorous, logical scholastic method. His reasoning, unlike Anselm's, was *a posteriori* rather than *a priori,* following Aristotle rather than Plato: he begins, like the natural scientist, with sense perceptions. From these sense perceptions pure reason mounts by the rules of logic to encompass all realities including the transcendent. We first study natural theology, in which we proceed with reason unaided by revelation. Then we proceed to revealed theology, in which we add first the tenents of revelation and then the logical deductions from those tenents. In the eighteenth century, Kant objected to this procedure in his *Critique of Pure Reason,* denying that logic could bridge the gap between the observable world of the senses and the transcendent. It is true that Thomas' method differs from that of science in that he buttressed his tower of reason by observation only at the foundations, but this is not a reproach to Thomas, for his purpose is to examine, not the particular attribute of individual beings, but beings in their essence. Thomistic metaphysics neither contradict nor are contradicted by science—they are a wholly different way to truth. Thomas' method has been called that of "essential analysis." Initially his system seems like a universe of fixed, static, Platonic ideas, but in fact he was aware of, and concerned with, both structure and change.

The foundation stone of Thomas' philosophy is the existence of God. Rejecting both Anselm's ontological argument and simple affirmations of faith, Thomas proceeded to five proofs of God's existence consisting of an initial observation of the senses followed by logical elucidation. Simply stated, his first argument proceeds like this: We observe that motion exists. We observe that things are moved, and that everything is moved by another thing. But if we carry this chain of movers to infinity, we have still not explained motion. There must therefore be a first mover. But that first mover must be spiritual. (To recast the argument in modern terms, no material thing moves itself. No one would believe a cogwheel located in Paris capable of moving itself, and if we constructed a chain of cogwheels stretching from Paris to Alpha Centauri capable of moving itself, nor would we admit this of any cogwheel no matter how extended the series.) Hence there is a spiritual first mover, and this all men call God.

Having with this and the four other proofs established the existence of God, Aquinas goes on to investigate what reason tells us must be his attributes. Aquinas was not unaware of the limitations of human reason, maintaining that "the divine substance surpasses every form that our intellect reaches. Thus we are unable to apprehend it by knowing what it is. Yet we are able to have some knowledge of it by knowing what it is not."[1] Reason can tell us what God cannot be, and we assume that what we are left with is something like what he is. God is pure Being, perfect Being lacking nothing. In God is therefore the perfection of every kind of being. Hence he is all that is positive: goodness, simplicity, truth, beauty, love, joy, pure act. Aquinas maintained that although the essence of God cannot be captured in such humanly contrived categories, they are valid in being analogous to God's nature.

God creates the world because he wishes to increase goodness. Since he is perfect, he cannot increase his own goodness, but he can create, out of nothing, creatures who are capable of good.

This created goodness can be conceived of morally or ontologically. A creature is considered morally good if it morally resembles God by having free will and using it freely to do God's will. A creature is ontologically good to the degree that its being resembles God. God is a simple, incorporeal, purely spiritual being. That which is most spiritual is closest to God; that which is least spiritual and most material is farthest away from God. This concept permits the construction of a "great chain of being." God, as absolutely perfect and simple Being and goodness, stands at the top. Below God are the angels, pure though limited spirit, whose existence is not merely a matter of faith but one of logical urgency, for they stand in the gap between God and creatures composed of both form and matter. Below angels are men, below men animals in the order of their intelligence, and below plants inanimate objects. Below everything else is pure matter, which is "tottering on the edge of unreality." For Saint Thomas, in the tradition of Plato, *being* and *reality* are the opposite of what they are for a materialist.

In this system Thomas compares the moral and the ontological, and the comparison carries over to the nature of evil.

Ontologically, evil is negative, a lack of goodness, having no existence. God does not create, or even tolerate, evil, for evil is simply nothing. To ask whether God willed the evil in the universe is like asking whether the cheesemaker made the holes in the Swiss cheese. To the question why God did not make everything as perfect as possible, why he did not, for example, create only angels, Aquinas replies that no one order of things can express God's goodness fully.

Moral evil is a defect of the will and also negative, though not only its practical results, but the evil act of the will itself, are quite real. Moral evil consists of willing what one wants oneself as opposed to what God wants—it is saying, not *thy* will, O lord, but *mine*, be done. The confusion enters when one tries to construct the "Great Chain of Being" to include both the ontological and the moral. Which is the "worse" man, one who falls short of the ideal by having a low intelligence, or one who falls short by willing evil?

This scheme of being, which for Aquinas was a static description of the universe, was in the nineteenth century turned on its side and temporalized as the progressive notion of evolution whereby living things have ascended to higher and higher forms.

The moral plan of the universe is rational. The good man

wills to do God's will, and reason as well as revelation can tell us what that is, for all God's dictates are according to reason: God wills nothing arbitrarily, but everything according to man's needs. Good and evil are objective realities. Hence God forbids theft and adultery, not because it is his whim, but because they disrupt society and make people unhappy. Aristotle had said that the happiness of man consists in realizing his true nature, and Aquinas agreed, adding that man's true nature is union with God.

THE system of Aquinas is one of the most internally consistent ever constructed, but it did not command universal assent even in its own day. Some of his propositions were included in the condemnation of pagan philosophy by the University of Paris in 1277. The condemnation, aimed primarily at the Aristotelianism of Averroes, showed that men were finding it difficult to reconcile the free God of revelation with the God compelled by the rationale of his nature. A double attack was mounted upon the scholasticism of reason by the Augustinian conservatives and a new group—the "voluntarists"—emphasizing the freedom of God's will and the primacy of faith.

The new group included Siger of Brabant, Duns Scotus, and William of Ockham. Siger (born ca. 1235) taught a doctrine of the "two truths": not only must we supplement philosophy with revelation but we must recognize that revelation and reason may often be contradictory. There are some conclusions we accept in philosophy that we cannot accept in faith. But when such contradiction occurs, we must prefer the teachings of faith. Siger's distinction was condemned as heresy in 1277. Duns Scotus (1266-1308), the greatest Scottish philosopher save David Hume, was a Franciscan lecturing at Oxford and then at Paris. So intricate was Duns' thought that the Church bestowed upon him the honorific title "The Subtle Doctor," and the Protestant Reformers, who were unsympathetic to scholastic philosophy, called anyone whose ideas seemed obscure a "duns"—hence our word "dunce." Duns' thought is still difficult to penetrate, and there are today widely divergent views of his significance, some claiming that he represented the most complex development of the scholasticism of reason, others that like Siger he separated philosophy from theology and reason from faith.

The position of William of Ockham (ca. 1300-1349) is

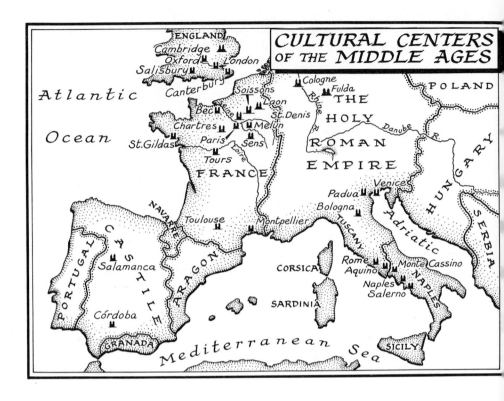

CULTURAL CENTERS OF THE MIDDLE AGES

clearer. Like Duns, he was a Franciscan; he was educated at Oxford and taught at Paris. An enemy of the pope, he was a colleague of Marsilius of Padua in the entourage of the emperor Lewis IV. His most durable contribution to criticism is the celebrated "Ockham's razor": "the simplest explanation consonant with all the facts is usually the best." Even more than Siger, Ockham distinguished between reason and faith. The rational constructs of man have some use in man's own mind, he said, but they are only tools and he must not expect them to correspond with transcendent reality. Only the individual is real; genera and species are human constructs. Rational investigation into the nature of God can show us no more than remote possibilities. We can know the material world through sensory investigation of individual objects; we can know God's world only through faith.

With Siger and Ockham, the split between philosophy and theology, between faith and reason, between religion and science, began. Reason was increasingly applied to empirical observation and bound up with science; religion became the province either of faith or of mystical experience. The scholasticism of reason continued, but from Ockham's time it ceased to command general assent.

THE second kind of scholasticism was the scholasticism of love, or mystical theology. Mystical theology is an effort to systematize mystical practice and is therefore an episode in a long history of Christian mysticism.

Mysticism appears in Islam, Buddhism, Hinduism, and other religions as well as in Christianity, but in Christianity its ultimate origins are in the world-rejecting aspects of that religion, the conviction that this world is so lacking in perfection and reality that the mind must be turned wholly to that other world which is the life of God. The mystical tradition in the Church gained strength with the ascetic practices of the early desert Fathers, and it obtained philosophical justification from Plato through the teaching of Saint Augustine that the way to God is through internal illumination. Augustine argued that though the world is real and can tell us a little something about God and reality, meditation and contemplation of God within the mind provide a better picture of the truth.

Mysticism flourished in the Christian East, as the teachings of Pseudo-Dionysius the Areopagite show, but it had little importance in the West until the twelfth century. Then mysticism emerged as an expression of the religious zeal of the time, and an important reflection of the efforts of reformers to reassert a pure and uncompromised Christianity. Most directly, the revival of mysticism was the product of the shift of the role of monasticism from pillar of society to prophet and judge of society.

The purpose of mysticism is personal experience, of God rather than intellectual understanding. The mystics approved the attempt of reason to find out about God but maintained that it could not go far. Man does not grasp God, God grasps man, and illumination comes as a divine gift, the fruit, not of intellectual labor, but of love. It is difficult to comprehend mysticism since by definition it eludes the intellect: rather than mind speaking to mind, heart speaks to heart, and the language of the heart has always been difficult to translate either into formulae or into rhetoric.

Precisely because of the difficulty of definition, much charlatanry has passed for mysticism, and true mysticism has received much unwarranted criticism from those who are insensitive to it much as a tone-deaf person is insensitive to music. Transcendence is out of fashion in our age of positivism and materialism, but most of us have had at least simple intimations of mysticism. In the mountains or in the forest we have had an experience of union with nature, or of the awesomeness and otherness of a reality behind the facade of material reality, a perception of another world, infinitely cold, clear, and beautiful, and also a little strange and terrifying. But we repress these feelings, ascribing them to hormone reactions or to adolescent romanticism, and thereby limit our experience as a man limits it who refuses to listen to music. Yet even when we do have intimations of the mystical they are only of the simplest kind. The great mystics have undergone long training and discipline; the mysticism of Bernard or John of the Cross is to our simple perceptions as the *Ninth Symphony* is to *Home on the Range*. Mysticism is ineffable and therefore often irritating to those who are not mystics, but it reflects the ineffability of God himself. It is the highest expression of the sacred in the Middle Ages.

The essential quality of mysticism is "sharp, direct, consciousness of the Divine Life"[2] or "the remaking of personality: its entrance into a conscious relation with the Absolute."[3] The key of mysticism is love and life, not knowledge. The apostles, exclaimed Saint Bernard, do not teach us to read Plato, but to live. The Greeks distinguished between *eros* and *agape,* between desire and selfless love. Mysticism is mostly *agape,* selfless love, but it has elements of *eros* as well, yearning for fulfillment in union. Because of the ineffable nature of the mystical experience, the mystic is obliged to communicate almost wholly in metaphors, and one must read mystical language as one reads poetry rather than as one reads an essay. Said Mechtild of Magdeburg:

I cannot dance, O Lord, unless Thou lead me.
If Thou wilt that I leap joyfully
Then must Thou Thyself first dance and sing!
Then will I leap for love
From love to knowledge,

Saint Hildegard of Bingen, a twelfth-century mystic, touched by the fire of the Holy Spirit.

From knowledge to fruition,
From fruition to beyond all human sense.
There I will remain
And circle evermore.[4]

Mysticism is an expression of the sacred view of the universe, the view that everywhere is life, and that there exists beings, not things. Sang Saint Francis in his *Canticle of Brother Sun:*

Praised be thou, my Lord, with all thy creatures,
Especially for Sir Brother Sun.
Through him thou givest us the light of day,
And he is fair and radiant with great splendor,
Of thee, Most High, giving signification.

Praised be thou, my Lord, for Sister Moon and the stars
Formed in the sky, clear, beautiful, and fair.
Praised be thou, my Lord, for Brother Wind,
For air, for weather cloudy and serene and every weather
By which thou to thy creatures givest sustenance.

Praised be thou, my Lord, for Sister Water,
Who is very useful and humble, precious and chaste.

Praised be thou, my Lord, for Brother Fire,
By whom thou dost illuminate the night;
Beauteous is he and jocund, robustious, and strong.

Praised be thou, my Lord, for our Mother Earth,
Who sustains and rules us
And brings forth divers fruits and colored flowers and herbs . . . .[5]

Mysticism is one fulfillment of Christianity. If mysticism is "the personal and intimate encounter of love, and the self-loss of the soul is an utterly transcendent Absolute,"[6] it is a fulfillment of Saint Paul's admonition to empty out the self and to bring Christ in. It is a fulfillment of the Christian teaching that hell consists of separation from God and heaven of union with him. It is a fulfillment of the precept "thou shalt love the Lord thy God with thy whole heart and thy whole soul and thy whole mind," for one does not become a mystic to achieve salvation or to enjoy the peripheral benefits of the mystical life, but wholly because one loves God so much that he can do nothing other. The true mystics are suspicious of visions and ecstasies which they realize can be false or can spring from pride rather than love. "Lift up your heart to God with humble love: and mean God himself, and not what you get out of him,"[7] warns the fourteenth-century *Cloud of Unknowing*, and later describes false mystics:

They experience a spurious warmth, engendered by the fiend, their spiritual enemy, through their pride, and materialism, and spiritual dabbling. And yet, maybe, they imagine it to be the fire of love, lighted and fanned by the grace and goodness of the Holy Ghost. In truth, from this falsehood many evils spring: much hypocrisy and heresy and error.[8]

Finally, mysticism is an expression of the paradoxes of the Gospels. Most strongly do the mystics affirm with Jesus that the first shall be last and the last first, that the poor shall be exalted and the wealthy sent away. If you wish to have everything, says Saint John of the Cross, cling to nothing at all, for a silken thread binds a bird to the ground as surely as an iron band.

Thus far, mysticism has appeared as an experience or an attitude. But to advance beyond the simplest level of mystical experience requires long practice and systematic training, though it is a training, not of the intellect, but of love. Mysticism requires

An initial from a book of Psalms showing the Holy Spirit descending in the form of a dove to illuminate the mystic.

the avoidance of sin, which separates from God: "What does it matter to contemplatives what sort of sin it is, or how great? For when they are engaged in contemplation, they think all sins alike are great in themselves, when the smallest sin separates them from God, and prevents spiritual peace."[9] The mystic separates himself from the temptations of this world by putting a cloud of forgetting between himself and the world. By asceticism and mortification of the body he teaches himself to be indifferent to material demands and by prayer and contemplation he opens his heart to God. The mind cannot penetrate the cloud of unknowing that separates man from God; the mystic pierces the cloud with the dart of love.

In the twelfth century mysticism expanded rapidly in the West. The crisis of western monasticism in the eleventh century had resulted in transforming the monks from servants of society into prophets, judging society and its values from without. The prophetic character of the new monasticism, particularly among the Cistercians, Carthusians, and Francisans, was very conducive to the development of mysticism.

The prevailing atmosphere in western thought at the time being scholastic, the mysticism of the twelfth and thirteenth centuries tended to take on a scholastic hue. Mystics like Saint Bernard of Clairvaux developed a systematic exposition of mysticism in the scholastic manner: Bernard was one of the first to try to describe the mystical life systematically in his treatises *The Steps of Humility* and *On Loving God.*

Unlike Anselm or Aquinas, who began with the principle that God is being, Saint Bernard begins by affirming that God is love. Because God is love, we must love him in order to know him. The example of love that we must follow is Christ himself. God so loved man that he became man and suffered death for him; by this measure must man measure his own love for God: it must be a love that is total and that can stand nothing less than union. But in order to attain union the will must be trained to this love. We withdraw from the world, which is the "Land of Unlikeness to God" and an analogue of hell, to the monastery, which is the "Land of Likeness" and an analogue of heaven. There we practice asceticism to enhance our forgetfulness of this world and to turn our spirit towards God. We practice humility in order to defeat self-esteem and wilfulness. When the mind is prepared by humility and love, it turns to examine the world. But it examines the world, not to categorize or systematize it to fit into the human mind, but rather to be embraced by it. Mere knowledge consists in arranging the world to fit into the mind; but wisdom in opening the mind to the world. We understand the world by seeing God in it. We then examine ourselves in order to learn humility and our neighbor to learn human understanding and love. Next we contemplate God himself, and at last God takes us up, illuminates our reason with grace, and receives our love. This is man's happiness, the restoration of his true nature, which is likeness to God. Bernard's exposition of mysticism had a great influence upon romantic literature, which dwelt upon the individual's lonely quest; and upon courtly love, which used mystical language to apply to a man's devotion to his lady.

The thirteenth-century mystics, like the thirteenth-century scientists, were most of them Franciscans in distinction to the rational scholastics, who were mainly Dominicans. The greatest Franciscan mystic after Francis himself was Saint Bonaventure (1221–1274), who mastered rational theology and politics as well: he taught theology at Paris and as general of the Franciscan Order temporarily saved it from splitting by achieving a moderate compromise between two opposing groups. But his deepest thought was mystical, and, as the author of *The Journey of the Mind to God* and of *The Seven Journeys of Eternity*, he is known to the Church as "the Seraphic Doctor."

As befitted a man who was a theologian as well as a mystic, Bonaventure accepted *a posteriori* reasoning and developed an ingenious, if unconvincing, proof of the temporal finiteness of the universe. If the universe were eternal, he said, then the sun would revolve around the earth an infinity of times; and the moon would revolve an infinity of times; so the sun and moon would revolve an equal number of times; but we know from observation that the moon revolves twelve times for each time the sun revolves once; hence the universe is not eternal. But his logical philosophy was less important than his mystical: we know God, not because we can prove his existence or formulate propositions about him, but because we experience him in our souls.

Rational knowledge of God is impossible, said Bonaventure, because God is different from us in quality as well as in quantity. Knowledge of God can only be equivocal, hazy, and analogous, a proposition that has caused Bonaventure's thought to be described as "negative analogical theology." The understanding of God requires, not logical propositions, but a long and arduous "journey of the spirit." We prepare for this journey by separating ourselves from material concerns. Then we look at the world for reflections or shadows of God (God seen through things). Next we perceive God *in* things, his presence or immanence in the world. Turning within, we see God through ourselves, our will showing his goodness, our intelligence showing his truth. Then we see God *in* ourselves, experiencing his presence within us through grace. Turning to God himself, we see him first

above us, and then in the Trinity. Here "all intellectual operations should be abandoned, and the whole height of our affection should be transferred and transformed into God."[10] Now
before the final union, there may intervene a "dark night of
the soul: when the spirit walks in darkness in a land of aridity,
monotony, and sterility, in the wasteland, as a man walks
alone and afraid in the mountain night, only then to see a
light more marvelous than any earthly dawn." God's being
then is infused into us, and we attain an experience of him as
immediate as any it is possible to have on earth.

There are many variations of the mystical road to God,
all having at their heart the experience of love and union.
In the fourteenth and fifteenth centuries, when the scholasticism
of reason had crumbled, the papacy was discredited by its capture by the French monarchy at Avignon and by the Great
Schism, and social dislocations were growing, there was a movement in the direction of personal, as opposed to institutionalized,
religion, and of prophecy as opposed to the usual channels of
ecclesiastical authority. Heresy and mysticism both benefited from
this situation. The only time mysticism has received as much
attention in Western Christianity as in Buddhism or Hinduism
was during the fourteenth to sixteenth centuries, the age of
Meister Eckhart, John Tauler, Hildegard of Bingen, Catherine
of Siena, the unknown author of the *Cloud of Unknowing,* John
Ruysbroeck, Thomas à Kempis, and John of the Cross. Some of
these later mystics retained the systematized and intellectually
justified mysticism that was the heritage of the scholastics.
Others, like Ruysbroeck, distrusted the intellect and revolted
against the scholastic tradition, pressing instead the claims of the
emotions. But all showed the freedom of the spirit characteristic of mysticism, a characteristic particularly congenial to the
age. The mysticism of Eckhart and Ruysbroeck inspired popular
pious movements like that of the Brethren of the Common Life
in the Low Countries in the fifteenth century. This emphasis
upon individual devotion and freedom of the spirit was a not
inconsiderable precedent for the Reformation.

THE third variety of scholasticism was the scholasticism of observation that eventually turned into modern science.

Early medieval science was wholly dependent upon ancient.

All the scientific knowledge the early Middle Ages possessed was derived from the ancients, and it was taken on authority. The scientific method, which would permit new discoveries, was unknown. Before the twelfth century even the content of ancient science was little understood. When the eye was not fixed upon God, it was turned to the utterly practical; it seldom rested upon the middle ground. For the same period that was so un-productive of science was enormously productive technologically, putting the Greeks and even the Romans to shame. The great innovations of agriculture and transportation of the early Middle Ages were supplemented in the central Middle Ages by numerous mechanical inventions: the clock, the astrolabe, eyeglasses, print-ing, the cannon, varieties of mills and machines constructed upon the new principle of the crank. Roger Bacon in the thirteenth century was sufficiently far-sighted to predict ships propelled by a single man more swiftly than a whole boat filled with oars-men, cars that would move with unbelievable rapidity without benefit of animals, and flying machines borne aloft by a man sitting in the middle and revolving an engine.

From the eleventh century scientific, as opposed to merely technological knowledge, began to revive. The idea that scientific thought did not begin until the Renaissance is wholly false: there was a medieval science, and science in our sense. At first the revival amounted only to the addition of new bodies of material from the translations of Aristotle and other scientific writers, an ex-tension of the content of scientific knowledge without the scien-tific method. But already in the eleventh century signs of the new empiricism were visible: men measured tides, studied volcanoes, and investigated the anatomy of animals. The idea grew that the ancients did not know everything: Roger Bacon announced that "we of the later ages should supply what the ancients lacked," and Adelard of Bath sneered openly at authority and demanded that everything in the material world be investigated.

The breadth of Adelard of Bath's interest can be seen in questions he addressed to a young reader, a kind of twelfth-century encyclopedia of scientific curiosity to be studied before the youth turned his attention to more advanced and specialized subjects. The list asks, among other things: "How different plants grow in the same region. . . . Why, when a plant is grafted, the fruit is that of the grafted part, not of the trunk. . . . Why the seats of imagination, reason, and memory are found in the brain. . . . Why we hear echoes. . . . How or why the globe of the earth is held up in the middle of the air. . . . How the earth moves. . . . Why the waters of the sea are salty. . . . How the ocean does not increase from the influx of rivers." The historian determined to seize upon instances of medieval naïveté may choose to dwell upon another of Adelard's questions—"What food the stars eat, if they are anim(ate)"—but that would be to miss the point that a curiosity for the most part sophisticated was emerging and was determined to develop a method for satisfying itself.[11]

The science of the twelfth through the fourteenth centuries developed three principles now taken for granted but then quite original. The first was a scientific cosmology, a view of the world consistent with the observations of the senses. This implied, not the exclusion of spiritual reality, but an insistence that spiritual beliefs should not contradict the findings of the scientific method in its material preserve. The second principle was the scientific method itself, experimentation. Said Bacon:

> Reasoning draws a conclusion and makes us grant the conclusion, but does not make the conclusion certain . . . unless the mind discovers it by the path of experience . . . (for example), it is generally believed that hot water freezes more quickly than cold water in vessels, and the argument in support of this is advanced that contrary is excited by contrary, just like enemies meeting each other. But it is certain that cold water freezes more quickly for anyone who makes the experiment.[12]

The rational scholastics had destroyed unquestioning trust in authorities; the empirical scholastics now destroyed unquestioning trust in pure reason. The third, and equally important principle established in the Middle Ages was quantification, not only the use of measurements but the use of quantitative concepts in the explanation of the world.

These advances, and particularly that of quantification, were made possible by the progress of mathematics in the eleventh and twelfth centuries. Not only was geometry revived and algebra introduced, but simple arithmetic rendered infinitely easier by the importation of Arabic numerals. (Anyone who doubts this should compare 798 × 47 with DCCXCVIII × XLVII.)

The ten concentric spheres following the medieval cosmology derived from Aristotle. Beyond the tenth sphere, the primum mobile, *is the "Empyrean heaven, the dwelling-place of God and of all the elect."*

In cosmology, there were two schemes, both postulating a geocentric universe. One was a variation of the old Aristotelian system of ten spheres concentric on the earth: the spheres of the moon; Mercury; Venus; the sun; Mars; Jupiter; Saturn; the sphere of the fixed stars; the "crystalline sphere," whose motion explained the precession of the equinoxes; and the tenth heaven, the *primum mobile* which moved everything else. Beyond the tenth sphere was God. The second scheme was the much more precise and delicately adjusted system of deferents and epicycles borrowed from the Arabs. The Arabs meanwhile had made other impressive advances in astronomy. The ninth-century astronomer Thabit calculated the length of the solar year at 365 d. 15 h. 23 m. 25 s., phenomenally close to the modern figure.

Physics made great advances in the later Middle Ages, particularly in the study of motion. It was assumed that from the sphere of the moon upwards bodies behaved differently than on earth and therefore could not be described in terms common to both, but the corollary belief that below the sphere of the moon they did behave with a regularity comprehensible

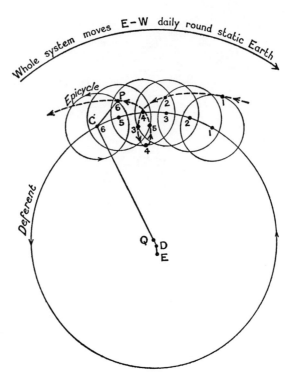

The deferent-epicycle system. In this diagram of Ptolemy's system, the daily motion of the planets is produced by the entire system sharing in the daily rotation of the stellar sphere from East to West. The irregular journey of each planet (P) as seen from the earth (E) is explained by imagining that P moves in a circle (the epicycle) with its center on C which, in turn, moves in a circle (the deferent) with its center on D. D is stationary with respect to E but is not at the center of the earth. In order to explain the non-uniform velocity of C as it travels around the deferent, Ptolemy says that its angular velocity is uniform around a point, the equant (Q), which is inside the deferent but not necessarily at D.

to man made it possible to construct a kinetic physics valid at least for the earth. Thomas Bradwardine (ca. 1295–1349), Nicole Oresme (d. 1382) and Jean Buridan (d. ca. 1358) formulated laws of locomotion (local motion) and of the change of forms (e.g., from hot to cold). Buridan enunciated the impetus theory that motion is not inherent in objects but is the result of an impulse, so that motion can be calculated from the strength of the impulse and the mass of the object impelled.

The Franciscans were among the leaders of empirical as

Plants drawn with skill and scientific accuracy (fifteenth century).

well as mystical scholasticism; science as well as mysticism profited from their general revulsion against the rational scholasticism
dominated by the Dominicans. Two great Franciscan scholars
of Oxford, Robert Grosseteste and Roger Bacon, studied optics
and the behavior of light, investigating perspective and the
properties of prisms, rainbows, and mirrors.

Chemistry was studied chiefly in the form of alchemy, whose
chief purpose was the transmutation of elements. Alchemists
conducted experiments, many of them successful, but as they
concentrated upon changes of color and appearance instead of
changes in mass they contributed few observations of permanent
scientific value. Medieval geology was more impressive. Albert
the Great observed the slowly changing coastline of Flanders
near Bruges, where the sea was constantly creating new sandbars
and strands, and speculated that geological features might be the
product of a slow construction and erosion. Following Avicenna,
Albert also taught that fossils were animals transformed into
stone by means of a mineralizing power. Unfortunately these wise
intuitions, like Augustine's into the nature of time, were not

Techniques of surgery in the Middle Ages—treating fractures.

translated into durable scientific doctrine until centuries later. Albert's descriptions and drawings of plants surpass in accuracy anything previous and in originality anything since the time of Aristotle.

Medicine was very primitive in the West until the eleventh century, and the practices of Western physicians shocked more than one Moslem traveler. But in that century Salerno began to teach medicine, and knowledge improved rapidly. By the thirteenth century concern with, and skill in handling, problems of hygiene and sanitation improved with the knowledge gained from the Arabs and the increased use of experimentation. Galen was no longer an unquestioned authority, and physicans began to issue diagnoses in accordance with experience rather than with the textbook. By the thirteenth century some understanding of contagion had been gained. Lepers were kept isolated, and ships coming into port during a time of plague were quarantined [*quarantina*: lit. "period of forty days"]. The letter of a physician in 1315 to his sons studying at Toulouse shows much sound judgment. They are not to drink or eat too much; they are to boil the well water of Toulouse and the water of the Garonne River before venturing to drink it; they should wash their mouths out with wine after a meal; they are to avoid sleeping in damp places or with cold feet; they must wear a rainhat in bad weather; they are to avoid draughts, to take baths and wash their hair, and to take daily exercise; they should take licorice cough drops for colds.

Techniques of surgery in the Middle Ages—trephining.

THE scholasticism of reason did not continue to command assent after the thirteenth century, but it had settled once and for all the question of how far pure reason might go in investigating the universe. The scholasticism of love deepened and enriched Christianity with a strong mystical tradition. The scholasticism of observation continued to develop until it became modern science. In variety and originality the scholastics of the twelfth and thirteenth centuries rivaled the philosophers of the Greeks or the seventeenth century.

NOTES

[1] *Summa contra Gentiles,* I: 14, ed. Anton Pegis, *Basic Writings of Aquinas* (New York, 1944).
[2] Evelyn Underhill, *Essentials of Mysticism* (New York, 1920), p. 32.
[3] Evelyn Underhill, *Mysticism* (London, 1911), p. 375.
[4] Trans. Lucy Menzies, Mechtild of Magdeburg, *The Revelations* (London, 1953) p. 21.
[5] Ray C. Petry, ed. *Late Medieval Mysticism, The Library of Christian Classics* XIII (Philadelphia, 1957), 124-125. Published in U.S.A. by The Westminster Press. Used by permission.
[6] Underhill, *Essentials,* p. 80.
[7] *The Cloud of Unknowing,* trans. Clifton Wolters (Baltimore, Penguin, 1961), p. 53.
[8] *Cloud,* p. 106.
[9] *Cloud,* p. 99.
[10] *The Mind's Road to God,* VII: 4, trans. George Boas (New York, 1953), p. 44.
[11] Quotations from Adelard, *Questions on Nature,* trans. Mary Martin McLaughlin, in *The Portable Medieval Reader* edited by James Bruce Ross and Mary M. McLaughlin. Copyright 1949 by the Viking Press, Inc. Reprinted by permission of the Viking Press, Inc. Pp. 621-623.
[12] Trans. R. B. Burke, *The Opus Maius of Roger Bacon* (Philadelphia, University of Pennsylvania Press, 1928), II, 583-584.

Chapter Twenty-Three

ART, MUSIC, AND LITERATURE

Modern art in the West is largely private. There is no accepted coherent system of values and goals today, and the language of art is personal, idiosyncratic, and almost secretive. Paintings— even poems—are no longer supposed to have a specific meaning, or, rather, they are supposed to mean whatever you wish them to. C. S. Lewis, having heard seven scholars at total variance on the meaning of a simple twentieth-century poem, observed that Jane Austen—he might have said Henry James—is closer to Shakespeare, Homer, or the Pharaohs than to us. John Donne's poems might occasionally be difficult, Lewis added, but each has a correct interpretation which Donne knew and which the reader can extricate. Donne's art, like the art of the Middle Ages, was public. Medieval art expressed the coherent system of values, mythology, and cosmology of the *ordo christianus*.

The purpose of medieval art, like that of philosophy, science, and mysticism, was to point the way to the transcendent, spiritual reality underlying the material world. Its favorite means of expression was therefore symbolism and allegory. Not all medieval works of art are wholly symbolic, and some are not symbolic at all, but symbol and allegory best served their didactic purpose. Medieval men, lacking the "museum conscience" of today, asked of a painting or a poem moral lessons more often than esthetic. In the thirteenth century William Durand remarked, "Pictures and ornaments in churches are the lessons and the scriptures of the laity." Pictures, statues, architecture, poetry, hymns, sermons, legends, the theater, all taught those who could not read. The liturgy itself was a showing, a semi-dramatic enactment of cosmic reality. These didactic expressions of a coherent society created a highly developed iconography in which almost everything—animals, flowers, objects, scenes from daily life or the Bible—had a transcendent as well as a literal signification. An owl, the bird of darkness and night, often represented Satan; a lamb was Christ the victim; a shepherd was the Good Shepherd, the Lord; fire was martyrdom or religious fervor; a lily was chastity; even a washbasin was Mary the font of purity and grace. This poetic, metaphorical approach to reality is a perfect expression of the teaching of Platonic-Christian idealism that reality is beyond this world, not of it.

Medieval art was Christian, and Christian assumptions lay behind even extrinsically secular works of art. Nothing more clearly indicates that medieval art was for the most part the public expression of the community than the anonymity before the fourteenth century of most painters and sculptors and many poets. They meant by their labors to magnify the Lord rather than themselves, or they saw themselves as mere agents—of God or of society—in a process of transmission and preservation.

Enormously coherent as it was, medieval art varied in content and in form with the locality and the age. There were three great shifts of style, from early medieval to Romanesque, from Romanesque to Gothic,

The Beau Dieu; *sculpture of Christ teaching, from the west front of Amiens Cathedral (thirteenth century).*

and from Gothic to Renaissance neoclassicism. These terms are best applied strictly to the graphic arts; it is not usually helpful to speak of "Romanesque" or "Gothic" literature or music. However, these shifts in the style of the graphic arts were accompanied by related changes in the other arts. The dynamics of change of style are not yet well understood. Sociologists have studied the fashion craze or fad but have yet clearly to elucidate slow, massive, and enduring transmutations of taste. One explanation is in the nature of art itself. The originality and freshness of a style cannot last forever, for its possibilities are exhausted and the searching mind turns to other modes of expression. The old style becomes restricted, imitative, and stale, and often exaggerated and manneristic. Retaining the allegiance of the dull and uncreative, it repels the bold and imaginative. Creative spirits break with tradition and some of their innovations eventually develop into a new style, which in time itself becomes stale.

But changes of style are also the result of growth and change in economics, politics, and social structure. The artist does not live in a vacuum, nor are there many immutable standards of absolute beauty. The artist's idea of what should be done depends to a very great extent upon what people around him, that is to say society, believe should be done. Very often the artist, whether dependent upon money or merely upon praise, becomes the interpreter, rather than the creator, of style. The artistic expression of the very early Middle Ages was conditioned by the fact that the very different sources of western culture had not yet fully mingled: some of the naïveté or even crudity of the seventh century, for example, results from artists' attempts to synthesize classical with Celtic or Teutonic while not knowing quite how to go about it. Increasingly in the following centuries, these traditions having been wed and synthesized, artistic expression gained in self-confidence and felicity.

When early medieval art attempted to imitate the classical, it was unsuccessful, for both its skill and its strength of expression were insufficient to the task. Carolingian art, though it began the process of synthesis, was still largely imitative, but even then Teutonic, Celtic, classical, Byzantine, and even Islamic elements were beginning to blend into a new style, the Romanesque. This new style is difficult to define except in architecture, where it was characterized by massiveness and volume and concern for the enclosure of space. Romanesque painting, not to speak of the other arts (the term "Romanesque" is seldom applied to literature or music), was less distinguishable from what had preceded it. Romanesque style, because it was not a court style like that of the Carolingians, lacked a center or clear boundaries. Rather, it grew up all over Europe with numerous varieties of expression. Perhaps the one characteristic of Romanesque is that it was literally more "Roman-esque" than previous styles. With its massive stone buildings and its monumental sculptures it attempted to create something that, though new and original, was strongly flavored by the Roman past.

This growth of the Romanesque reflects the increasing attention to things Roman throughout society. From the tenth century, the order of the Roman past seemed again not only desirable, but attainable. Knowledge of the Roman past was enhanced by the growth of the classical humanism that flourished in the monasteries once their stability and wealth had been removed from the threat of barbarian attacks. In Charlemagne's time, the poets had vainly boasted of making Aachen a new imperial Rome, but from the later tenth century, the growing order and wealth of society made the dream to some degree possible of fulfillment. The new wealth of bishops and towns permitted them to patronize artists on a grander scale and to purchase materials of sufficient bulk and quality to construct lasting monuments. As in this period the old wooden castles of the feudal warriors yielded to massive stone piles, so the modest ecclesiastical buildings of previous centuries yielded in the eleventh to imposing structures like the abbey of Cluny and the cathedral of Durham.

By the mid-twelfth century yet another style was produced, known in the visual arts as Gothic, and characterized by increasing complexity and technical virtuosity. Though the greatest monuments of Gothic architecture and sculpture are ecclesiastical, the Gothic was everywhere accompanied by a growth of secular approaches and secular subject matter. As towns grew wealthier and kingdoms more peaceful, bishops, kings, and noblemen could afford the luxury of increasing patronage of the arts. But, successful as they had become in the ways of this world. they also increasingly demanded artistic expressions of their

Notre Dame de Paris from the southeast. This cathedral, begun in the twelfth century and completed in the fourteenth, is a well-known example of Gothic. Note the flying buttresses.

secular concern. Moreover, the increasing literacy of the laity, particularly in the towns, coupled with the end of the monastery's monopoly on culture, brought to artistic and literary expression attitudes that heretofore had been largely inarticulate.

In religion, the twelfth and thirteenth centuries were characterized by increased individualism and humanization accompanying the growth of secular values. Heresy, mysticism, pilgrimages, and the new prophetic monasticism were all efforts to achieve personal, as opposed to purely public, religion, and these new qualities were expressed in the arts. Jesus becomes less the pantocrator, the uncreated creator, the impassive sufferer, or the terrible judge; on Gothic crucifixes the man Jesus suffers more as a man; the infant Jesus in his mother's lap even tugs on occasion at his mother's veil.

The cult of Mary was an expression of this search for humanity, for the Virgin exerted herself for those who, like Ebbo the cutthroat, dedicated themselves to her: when Ebbo was caught and hanged, so people believed, she held him up for two days until he could be freed by his friends and not strangle. This humanization produced the naturalism of the

Tympanum at Strasbourg Cathedral: Christ bringing the centurion's daughter back to life. Note the humanity and individuality of the Gothic figures.

Gothic style, a beautiful tension between the transcendent and the material. In the literature of the period, simple piety, self-confidence, and loyalty to *ordo* yields to the self-centered quest of the knight errant, solitary, surrounded by mysterious perils, still pursuing the *peregrinatio* or journey, but a *peregrinatio* less the struggle of the united church militant than the quest of the individual. This new, individual journey occurred on many levels, from Bonaventure's *Journey of the Mind to God,* through Parzival's search for the Grail and Sir Gawain's search for the Green Chapel, to the absurdly romantic quests of Doon de Mayence on behalf of his lady fair.

The final shift in taste that brought about the Renaissance was characterized in part by continued enhancement of secular values as opposed to the religious. As the monastic domination of learning yielded from the twelfth century to the more sophisticated episcopal schools and universities, so now the universities became more independent of ecclesiastical control and new, professional schools arose to train the new, professional classes. The failure of scholasticism and of the papally dominated *ordo christianus,* as well as the moral ill repute of much of the later medieval clergy, meant a decline of the ecclesiastical in art and a corresponding growth of attention to the concern of lawyers, physicians, secular administrators, royal and noble courts, and merchants. The individualism that was growing in the Gothic style, and in the chivalric ideals of fame and distinction both on the battlefield and in love, was consummated in the similar ideals of individual *fama* and *virtus* expressed by Petrarch and later Renaissance men. The Renaissance is best understood, then, not as something radically different from the Middle Ages, but as a change in attitude and style much like that of Romanesque to Gothic. Late Gothic had become artificial, trivial, and exaggerated; it had ceased to be creative. In the fifteenth century men who were conscious that the old styles were moribund sought to replace them with the not wholly compatible aims of realistically imitating nature and of imitating the style, and often the content, of classical literature and art.

THE most important genres of the visual arts during the Middle Ages were architecture (particularly churches, abbeys, and cathedrals), sculpture (especially woodcarvings and reliefs), and painting in the forms of frescoes and book illuminations.

The Romanesque architectural style appeared in a great burst of cathedral building in the early eleventh century; as the monk Radulf Glaber exclaimed, the whole world was putting on a "white mantle of churches." The new cathedrals, massive, huge, and richly decorated, were built with enormous labor. Many eventually took centuries to complete; and the Gothic cathedral of Cologne was not finished until the nineteenth century.

Before the execution of a great cathedral began, the builders always had an architectural plan, though the generations who built it might modify the plan several times. It was drawn by professional architects, not by amateur clergymen, and these architects, at first anonymous, gained both name and reputation in the thirteenth and fourteenth centuries. The architects hired the laborers and craftsmen, and the paintings and carvings were executed by artists who from the twelfth century had professional ateliers. Occasionally some of the labor was undertaken as a pious work by the whole community; more often, money was needed, and a great deal of it. The bishops and abbots expended much of their treasure in building, and what more they needed they received from the town with the help of laymen's fund-raising activities and pious bequests. These means were supplemented by the lucrative, though ethically questionable, sale of indulgences.

Romanesque painting was relatively continuous from the earlier period; Romanesque architecture made a leap in the

An apostle baptizing converts—a scene from the great baptismal font at the Church of Saint Barthélemy in Liège. This is one of the best examples of Romanesque art; the artist was the twelfth-century Renier of Huy.

revival of monumental, free-standing stone sculpture, which had disappeared from the West in the fifth century. Both painting and sculpture were used largely as decorations in the churches and cathedrals. The shift from Romanesque to Gothic in the visual arts is not essentially a matter of dates. Romanesque reached its peak about 1150 but continued into the thirteenth century, while Gothic originated in 1137 and reached its height about 1250. The styles overlapped not only chronologically but technically. Gothic emerged from Romanesque; the styles are often combined; and the distinction between them is often not clear.

There are few styles whose origins can be established as exactly as the Gothic. It was created just north of Paris between 1137 and 1144 when Suger, the adviser of Louis VI and Louis VII, erected a new abbey at Saint Denis. Under the misapprehension that Saint Denis of France was the so-called Dionysius the Areopagite who wrote treatises on the earthy and celestial hierarchies, Suger wished to "build Dionysian theology." He had an idea of the light, color, grace, and upward sweep that he wished to express, and he was immeasurably fortunate in finding an architect creative enough to express these ideas in stone and glass. Together Suger and his unknown architect created a wholly new style whose beauty and sheer originality have few peers in the history of art.

The Gothic style is distinguished by its delicacy, its detail, and above all, its light. By placing the necessary massive supports for the towering walls *outside* the building in the form of flying buttresses, it was possible to create an interior that is light in both senses: the stone work loses its mass and becomes delicate, and the windows become so wide as to constitute a vast wall of color and light. On a bright day at Chartres, or at the Sainte Chapelle in Paris, the light coming through such walls places one wholly within an extraordinary world of soft and diffuse colors.

The Gothic style, instead of placing decorations on or in the cathedral, made the decorations themselves part of the function of the architecture. Not only were the windows works of consummate art, but the pillars, doors, and indeed every part of the cathedral were sculptured. Made possible by new techniques like the use of flying buttresses and by the increasing stabilization of society, which rendered it unnecessary to provide a cathedral with thick walls so that it might double as a fort, these effects were accompanied by increasing naturalism and realism of detail, partly for their own sake, and partly to mirror more accurately the world that was itself a mirror of God.

Every Gothic cathedral was meant to be read as a *speculum naturale,* a mirror of the world. The accurate and detailed carvings present all sorts of plants and beasts both real and imaginary, scenes from the Old and New Testaments, and allegories of virtues and vices. The structure of society is represented in carvings showing the hierarchies of church and state and portraying in their pursuits clergymen, knights, peasants, tradesmen, craftsmen, and men in all other walks of life.

Theology is symbolized in the very structure of the cathedral —the heavy foundation supporting lighter walls in turn holding up the vaulted roof—and both the high vaulting inside and the spire outside reach up towards God. The shape of the cathedral is cruciform, with the altar at the east end facing Jerusalem. Every detail of the creed and many details of popular belief appear in the sculptures and stained glass, from the Trinity through the Creation, the Great Chain of Being, the life of Christ, his passion and resurrection, and the Last Judgment.

The interior of the Abbey Church of Saint Denis, the first Gothic structure.

A Gothic structure of the thirteenth century: Louis IX Sainte Chapelle on the Ile de la Cité in Paris.

Though the Gothic of the fourteenth and fifteenth centuries became artificial, it also moved in mysterious ways into the spare, economic style of Giotto and thence into the Italian Renaissance; and into the beautiful color and exquisite realism of fifteenth-century Flanders, through the northern Renaissance, and thence into Rembrandt and Vermeer.

Music, being unrepresentative, could not be didactic like the visual arts or literature of the Middle Ages, but it was used to evoke religious experience. Early medieval religious music was monophonic and almost purely vocal, though the organ was introduced as early as the tenth century. It was influenced both by Greco-Roman and by Jewish chant and was used in the mass and the monastic Office. Chants developed considerable complexity, the two most important styles being the "Ambrosian" and the "Gregorian," though it is unlikely that either Saint Ambrose or Saint Gregory the Great had much to do with their formation. The eighth century, synthetic in so much else, seems

Roman basilica: Santa Maria Maggiore, Rome, 432 A.D.

CHANGES IN ARCHITECTURAL STYLE

Romanesque: Saint Sernin, Toulouse, 1080–1096.

Gothic: Notre Dame de Paris, 1163–c. 1250.

Neoclassical: Saint Lorenzo, Florence, 1421–1460.

to be the era when the liturgy received its "Gregorian imprint." Music's connection with the liturgy also brought it into the theater, which developed out of the liturgy itself.

By the twelfth century a number of instruments were in use, including the organ, kithara, bagpipe, and viol. Several varieties of musical notation existed, in which Guido of Arezzo (995-1050) was the most famous innovator. Musical theory was studied in the schools as part of the quadrivium, and its relations to mathematics explored.

Secular music, including dances and popular songs, was probably more lively though probably monodic, but little was written down or preserved until the twelfth and the thirteenth centuries.

Though the music of the early Middle Ages was for the most part monophonic, polyphony made an early appearance in the form of the *organum,* in which at first two or more voices followed the same pattern, separated by a fourth interval or a fifth. Later the *organum* grew more complex, and in the eleventh century there are the first signs of harmony. Conceivably the increasing complexity of music may be connected with the increasing complexity of society, for from the twelfth century the towns were the centers of polphony as the monasteries had been of monophony.

The thirteenth century was an age of great innovation, to the extent that a leading historian of music compares it with the sixteenth, eighteenth, and nineteenth. Paris was the center of the new polyphonic style, just as it was the home of the new Gothic style in architecture. The varieties and complexity of polyphony expanded rapidly, and by the fourteenth century the lute, guitar, cymbals, harp, horn, and trumpet were adding their voices to the chorus. The complex polyphony of the later Middle Ages culminated in the fifteenth-century works of Dufay, Okeghem, and Despres, and eventually passed in the Renaissance into the music of di Lasso and Palestrina.

MUCH medieval literature was in Latin, which was the language of scholarly works through the Renaissance, and until the twelfth century of most literary works as well. The outstanding early exceptions were vernacular Irish and English literature, and in the twelfth and thirteenth centuries they too yielded to the

Musicians with rebec (left) and lute.

domination of Latin and French. There was always an oral folk tradition in the vernacular, and French, German, Provençal, Italian, and Spanish literature began to be written in the eleventh century. English vernacular, now called Middle English, appeared again in the thirteenth century, one of the earliest examples being *The Owl and the Nightingale.* Even when in the vernacular, medieval literature was strongly dependent upon classical and early Christian Latin models and tradition.

Most of the themes and conventions of medieval literature arose from the feudal and ecclesiastical milieus. As Dante remarked, there were only three proper subjects for poetry, *salus, virtus,* and *venus:* salvation, bravery, and love; that is, the virtues of the Church, of feudalism, and of the court. The conventions of ecclesiastical literature were derived in part from the classical tradition of rhetoric taught in the schools, witness the rhetorical invocation of the Golden Age, of Nature, or of the Seven Ages of Man. But they were even more derived from the Vulgate Bible and the Fathers. Besides the constant allusions to the

Scriptures and the Fathers, there were the venerable Conventions of martyrdom, miracles, virtues, *peregrinatio,* the world as the mirror of God, the vanity and mutability of earthly things, and the corruption of nature or the social order.

THE feudal virtues are the virtues of the warrior—loyalty, bravery, courage, honor, and generosity—and their corresponding vices. The feudal and ecclesiastical virtues were united in the convention of the *miles Christi* or Christian warrior; and chivalry and courtly love added the conventions of courtesy and the service of the lady.

Warrior conventions and attitudes were expressed in the epic and the romance. Though both manifestations of the same warrior tradition, whose origins lie in the unwritten lays of the Celtic and Teutonic heroic age and in the classical epic, the two are distinguished in style and approach. This warrior literature may be placed in a spectrum—at one extreme is the literature closest to the barbarian lays and at the other that which has been most influenced by Christianity, feudalism, classical models, and chivalry. The spectrum runs from Icelandic literature through *Beowulf,* the *Nibelungenlied,* and the *Song of Roland,* to the romances of Chrétien de Troyes. This spectrum conveys the transformation of the pagan warrior into the feudal knight, then the *miles Christi,* and finally into the *chevalier* rescuing pretty damsels in distress.*

Pre-Christian Teutonic literature was oral, and the epics were all originally oral; the romances, on the other hand, were originally written, though often recited aloud. Almost all the original pre-Christian literature has vanished, the exception being the eddas, sagas, and skaldic poetry of Iceland. A skald was a professional Norse poet, whose verses glorified the king. The *"Poetic Edda"* is a thirteenth-century compilation of ancient pagan lays, mythological or heroic; the *Prose Edda,* by Snorri Sturulson (d. 1241) was in effect a handbook of ancient lore for the use of poets. Snorri, writing in an already converted Iceland, yet preserved the pagan flavor of the old materials: "Then Reginn

---

*The arrangement is not chronological. Icelandic literature was written down in the thirteenth century, while *Beowulf* dates from the eighth. The *Nibelungenlied* is thirteenth century, as is Chrétien, but Roland is twelfth.

came forward saying that Sigurdr had slain his brother, and demanded as a condition of reconciliation that he take Fáfnir's heart and roast it with fire; and Reginn laid him down and drank the blood of Fáfnir, and settled himself to sleep."[1] The sagas, most of them written in the twelfth and thirteenth centuries, were narrative prose of considerable variety, some of which, like the *Volsunga Saga*, derived from ancient paganism and some from Christian, feudal, or even chivalric sources. Most Icelandic literature, whatever its provenance, retained the stark, heroic, and nonmoral qualities of the ancient Norse.

Beowulf, still peopled by dark, stalking things and colored by fearful deeds of blood, received a Christian cast in its written form. The *Nibelungenlied*, written about 1204 but based upon two old legends of the fifth century, the song of Brunhilde and the song of the Burgundians, is a curious piece combining several traditions. The story is the betrayal and conquest of the Burgundians by Attila the Hun, and the savage ferocity, bloodlust, and revenge are the equal of the sagas. But several societies are portrayed at once in the *Nibelungenlied*: the nomadic society of the Huns, the agrarian society of the primitive Teutonic kingdoms, the feudalism represented by Hagen, and even the chivalric society of courtly love, expressed in Siegfried's devotion to Kriemhild.

The Song of Roland is difficult to categorize, and it has been interpreted by critics in a variety of ways. It is no longer considered accurate to describe it as an emasculated version of the old Frankish pagan battle lay or a patchwork of oral traditions. It draws upon the Teutonic oral tradition but on many others as well. Its primary connection is with the growing stock of stories called the "matter of France," as compared with the Arthurian "matter of Britain," and centers upon the exploits of Charlemagne. Classical inspiration is also visible, as is perhaps natural in a period (ca. 1100) when humanistic concern with classical literature was emerging. The classical is felt in the sympathetic treatment of the "pagan" Moslems, almost as if they were Greeks or Trojans, the subtle investigation of motives, the matter-of-fact attitude toward death, and the brooding presence of fate ever impelling Roland towards his doom. Christianity seems correspondingly less evident, appearing only in the perfunctory observance of the sacraments, prayer, and the use of relics, though more particularly in the spirit of crusade against the infidel. The superficiality of Christianity in the poem is illustrated by Archbishop Turpin's readiness to split Moslems in two for the love of Christ. Yet some scholars have found Roland's death remarkably analogous to that of the saints and martyrs of Christian devotional literature.

Most clearly present are the feudal conventions: loyalty, courage, death for one's lord and for one's honor. Chivalry and courtly love do not yet appear: Roland fights for his lord Charlemagne at the side of his feudal companion Oliver and gives little thought to his betrothed, the Princess Alda, who is the only woman in the poem. Oliver expresses the feudal sentiment of the poem best when he exclaims, "The only thing I know is that to yield is worse than to die." *Roland* is not a simple poem and appears less so the more it is read. In its composition of Christian and feudal, Teutonic and classical, it is the fitting expression of an age that was willing to try a variety of ideas, and it is a testament to the artistic skill of the author that he was able to compose such a variety into an esthetically pleasing whole.

The romances of Chrétien de Troyes, Marie de France, and Gottfried of Strasbourg were another variety of warrior literature. Epic and romance are difficult to separate, the differences being in the tragic nature of the epic as opposed to the frequently comic or ironic aspects of the romance; and the entry into the romance of the exaggerated situations and emotions of courtly love. The commonest convention of the romance is the knight errant, riding alone for his lady on a mysterious journey into a darkling wilderness in which lurk myriad grotesque dangers.

Traditionally the romances are divided into the "matter of Rome" (including Rome, Thebes, and Troy), the "matter of France" (Charlemagne and his knights) and the "matter of Britain" (the Celtic Arthur and his knights, and some English heroes like King Horn). Besides these three great "matters" materials come from Islam and even ultimately from the Orient: the character Jehosaphat derives from the Moslem Yosiphat, who in turn is really the Bodhisattva, Gautama Buddha.

A more useful way of categorizing the romances than by "matter" is by the purposes of the writer, whether religious, idealized, or naturalistic and non-Christian. Parzival's quest for the Grail is idealized Christianity (with pagan undertones); but the world of Gawain and the Green Knight and of Tristan and Iseut are both magical and Christian.

IT is impossible wholly to separate clerical from warrior literature, for some at least of the romances and secular lyrics were written by clergymen. But hymns, religious dream-visions, and prose *exempla* and legends (saints' lives designed to be read [*legenda*] at the proper liturgical season) are expressly religious.

Medieval hymns consisted as much of carefully worked rhetorical *conventions* and traditional meters as of spontaneous outpourings of the soul, but it is precisely the enclosing of spirit in form that makes so many of them great works of art. In the thirteenth century in particular appeared several great hymns. Stephen Langton, archbishop of Canterbury at the time of Magna Carta, wrote the *Veni Sancte Spiritus* (translation from Anglican hymnal):

> *Veni sancte spiritus*
> *Et emitte caelitus*
> *lucis tuae radium;*
>
> *Veni, pater pauperum,*
> *veni, dator munerum,*
> *veni, lumen cordium.*
>
> *Consolator optime,*
> *dulcis hospes animae,*
> *dulce refrigerium;*
>
> *In labore requies,*
> *in aestu temperies,*
> *in fletu solacium . . . .*

> Come, thou Holy Spirit, come!
> And from thy celestial home
> Shed a ray of light divine!
> Come, thou father of the poor!
> Come, thou source of all our store!
> Come, within our bosoms shine!
>
> Thou, of comforters the best;
> Thou, the soul's most welcome guest;
> Sweet refreshment here below;

In our labor, rest most sweet;
Grateful coolness in the heat;
Solace in the midst of woe . . .

The most poignant of the great hymns is the anonymous *Stabat Mater* (translation from Anglican hymnal):

Stabat mater dolorosa
iuxta crucem lacrimosa
dum pendebat filius;
cuius animam gementem
consristantem et dolentem
pertransivit gladius . . . .

Quis est homo qui non fleret
matrem Christi si videret
in tanto supplicio?
Quis non posset contristari,
piam matrem contemplari,
dolentem cum filio . . . ?

At the cross her station keeping,
Stood the mournful mother weeping,
Where he hung, the dying Lord:
For her soul of joy bereaved,
Bowed with anguish, deeply grieved,
Felt the sharp and piercing sword . . . .

Who, on Christ's dear mother gazing,
Pierced by anguish so amazing,
Born of woman, would not weep?
Who, on Christ's dear mother thinking,
Such a cup of sorrow drinking,
Would not share her sorrows deep . . . ?

The most powerful is certainly the *Dies Irae* ascribed to Thomas of Celano, which begins:

Dies irae, dies illa,
solvet saeclum in favilla,
teste David cum Sibylla.

Quantus tremor est futurus,
quando iudex est venturus,
cuncta stricte discussurus!

Tuba mirum spargens sonum
per sepulchra regionum,
coget omnes ante thronum.

Mors stupebit et natura
cum resurgit creatura
iudicanti responsura . . . .

which Richard Crashaw interpreted:

Hear'st thou, my soul, what serious things
Both the Psalm and Sibyl sings
Of a sure Judge from whose sharp ray
The world in flames shall fly away?

O that Fire! before whose face
Heaven and earth shall find no place;
O those eyes! whose angry light
Must be the day of that dead night.

O that Trump! whose blast shall run
An even round with th'circling sun,
And urge the murmuring graves to bring
Pale mankind forth to meet his King . . . .

The lyric became increasingly secular in content and was increasingly written in the vernacular, perhaps because girls, who could not read Latin, wanted to be courted in a language they could understand. Most lyrics were concerned with love or nature. They were usually sung or accompanied by music and found brilliant expression with the troubadours, trouvères, and Minnesänger, and with the Goliards. These lyrics are not to be confused with spontaneous, popular ballads, for they were the products of an exquisite art, which, like the Latin hymn, was the better for confining spirit within the forms dictated by rhetorical and poetic tradition.

Sang Walther von der Vogelweide:

Do der sumer komen was,
und die bluomen dur daz gras
wunnelichen sprungen,
aeda die vogele sungen . . .

Summer had come,
And the flowers sprang up
Wondrously through the grass,
And the birds began to sing . . .

An old French lyric of the twelfth century:

En un vergier lez une fontenele,
Dont clere est l'onde et blanche la gravele,
Siet fille a roi, sa main a sa maxele:
En sospirant son douz ami rapele.
Ae cuens Guis amis!
La vostre amors me tout solaz et ris.

In an orchard near a fountain,
whose water was clear, whose borders white,
a princess sat, her hand on her cheek,
and sighing, remembers her sweet love:
Ah, Count Guy, my friend!
How your love gave me comfort and joy.

One of the greatest Provençal troubadours, Bernart de Ventadorn, wrote this *canzon:*

Quan vei la lauzeta mover
De joi ses alas contral rai
Que s'oblid'es laissa chazer
Per la doussor qu'al cor li vai,
Ailas! quals enveja m'en ve
De cui qu'eu veja jauzion!
Meravilhas ai, quar desse
Lo cors de dezirer nom fon.

When I see the lark move its wings in joy in the sun's light and then, forgetting self, falling in the sweetness which goes to its heart, alas, the desire that comes upon me for her whom I should see with joy. I marvel that my heart does not burst with desire.[3]

The Goliardic* songs and lyrics of the Middle Ages have been the subject of much romantic speculation. The vision of the medieval student as the wandering scholar intent upon wine and wenches is as exaggerated as that of a Middle Ages wholly intent upon mystical prayer. Some of the poems are really student poems; more were composed by clergymen for the purposes of satire. Some of the poems are broadly comic, others full of youth and love, others sharply satirical. They are all written in learned Latin, and many of them are exceed-

---

*The term Goliardic, whose origins are unclear, is applied to medieval student literature of an ironic cast.

ingly intricate in rhyme, meter, and allusion. Some are sincerely religious—"Why does the world labor for vainglory?"—but more purely secular, like the "Nun's Lament:"

> *Plangit nonna fletibus*
> *inerrabilibus,*
> *condolens gemitibus,*
> *dicens consocialibus:*
> *heu misella!*
> *nihil est deterius*
> *tali vita;*
> *cum enim sim petulans*
> *et lasciva.*
>
> *Sono tintinnabulum,*
> *repeto psalterium,*
> *gratum linquo somnium*
> *cum dormire cuperem,*
> *heu misella!*
> *pernoctando vigilo*
> *cum non vellem:*
> *iuvenem amplecterer*
> *quam libenter . . . .*

The little nun weeps with indescribable grief, groaning, suffering, saying to her colleagues: a wretched little creature I am! Nothing is worse than this life, for I am wanton and sexy. I ring the bell, I recite the psalms, I get up when I'd rather sleep, O wretched me! I keep vigil all night when I'd much rather be in the arms of a young man . . . .

The song *Praise of Wine* is not only libertine in itself but an open parody on the hymn *Verbum bonum et suave:*

> *Vinum bonum et suave*
> *bibit abbas cum priore;*
> *et conventus de peiore*
> *bibit cum tristitia . . . .*

The abbot and the prior enjoy
The good wine and the sweet;
the rest of the brothers
are obliged to drink the bad . . . .

One of the most intricate, in which there are allusions and subtle wordplays in every stanza, is the Archpoet's; it is in the form of a mock confession, which ends by glorifying the life of drunkeness and lewdness:

> *Aestuans intrinsecus   ira vehementi*
> *in amaritudine   loquor meae menti:*
> *factus de materia   levis elementi*
> *folio sum similis   de quo ludent venti . . . .*

> *Praesul discretissime,   veniam te precor:*
> *morte bona morior,   dulci nece necor,*
> *meum pectus sauciat   puellarum decor,*
> *et quas tactu nequeo,   saltem corde moechor . . . .*

Burning inside with great anger, I bitterly speak thus to my soul: made of the light element (the air), I am like a leaf that the wind plays with . . . . Most excellent bishop, please grant me pardon, for I am dying a good death and making a sweet end. For the beauty of girls wounds me to the quick, and the ones I can't touch I seduce in my heart.

A genre increasingly popular in the later Middle Ages was the secular allegory, the most famous of which is the *Romance of the Rose,* begun in the thirteenth century by Guillaume de Lorris and expanded by Jean de Meun. The secular allegory seized imaginations as thoroughly as the religious allegory had done in the days of Philo and Origen, and the medium continued to be used by Chaucer, Spenser, Swift, and Pope.

THE theater arose in large part from the liturgy. Medieval drama, from which the modern theater derives, has little connection with classical drama, which had been almost extinguished by the sixth century. There is scholarly dispute on the matter, but the majority believe that the theater originated in the addition of tropes—extra words—to the mass. At the gradual of the mass, when the Bible is transferred from the epistle to the Gospel side of the altar, an alleluia was often sung, and sometimes the last syllable was drawn out in a long chant. To help in remembering the music, words were added to the chant, which became known as a sequence. These tropes were then sung by several singers taking parts out in front of the choir screen, perhaps at a side altar. The earliest known dramatic trope is the *Quem queritis* ("Whom are you seeking"), sung at Easter:

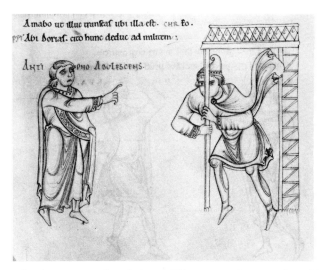

Amabo ut illuc transeas ubi illa est. CHR. Eo.
pp. Abi Sorias. circo hunc deduc ad militem;

ANTI   PHO Adulescens.

Illustration in a manuscript of the twelfth century of a scene from Terence, indicating medieval interest in the secular classics.

ANGELS: Whom are you seeking in the sepulchre, followers of Christ?
THE MARYS: Jesus of Nazareth who was crucified, O dwellers in heaven.
ANGELS: He is not here. He has risen as he foretold. Go, and announce that he is risen from the tomb.

Simple tropes like these were expanded, the dramatic elements were increased, and the action was removed first into the nave, then onto the side porch, then onto the west porch, and finally out into the square. Their connections with the liturgy grew gradually more tenuous, and in the thirteenth century the miracle and morality plays appeared, portraying Biblical scenes or the lives of saints, Saint Nicholas being the most popular subject. In the meanwhile professionalization increased. At first the liturgical actors were priests, then amateur laymen, and in the sixteenth century, members of actors' gilds or other professional troops.

The nature of the transition from the medieval to the secular drama of the sixteenth century is much disputed. It used to be assumed that the comic interludes often staged between the miracle or morality plays were gradually expanded and transformed by Renaissance consciousness of the classical drama, until they became the secular theater of Marlowe and Shakespeare. Modern critics, having found traces of the secular, vernacular drama as far back as the twelfth century, are less inclined to believe that the liturgy was the sole font of the modern stage, though they admit its importance.

THE *fabliau,* or fable, was a popular literary form. It is not known for whom the *fabliaux* were written: peasants, townsmen, or even the aristocracy. In the main their intent is satirical, like the story of the *Priest and the Mulberries,* in which a greedy priest on a journey, reaching up for the highest and juiciest mulberry, is thrown by his horse into a thorn bush. Similar to the *fabliau* is the beast epic, probably (but again not surely) peasant in origin, and a link between the ancient Aesop and the modern Beatrix Potter and Joel Chandler Harris. These stories, chiefly from the Low Countries and Germany, portray animal characters like Reynard the Fox and Ysengrin the Wolf in satires on the greed of churchmen, the cowardice of knights, and the oppression of rulers.

The Divine Comedy of Dante Alighieri (1265–1321) was the masterpiece of medieval literature. It is comparable in matter and in scope to the great epics of the ancient world; it is a great comedy in the sense of a portrait of human life. Written in Italian, it elevated the vernacular to greatness; and, like the Gothic cathedrals, it is a *summa* of medieval thought. In the chaos of the inferno and the order of paradise, in the search for transcendence and the beatific vision, Christian theology is summarized; in the punishments and rewards distributed to the good and the evil, political issues appear; in the vision of the spheres is expressed medieval cosmology; in Dante's devotion to Beatrice is a permutation of courtly love.* The greatness of Dante's conception and the skill of his execution render him, not a mere compiler, but an original and great artist.

THE growth of Renaissance secularism and naturalism at the end of the Middle Ages with Boccaccio and Chaucer is an

*A permutation, because somehow in the course of the thirteenth century the object of devotion shifts from a married woman unattainable by reason of her rank and marriage to a young virgin (Dante's Beatrice and Petrarch's Laura—Shakespeare's Juliet is in some ways similar) unattainable by reason of her purity.

Dante. The Duomo (cathedral) of Florence is at his left; in the background is a representation of his poem.

extension and development of one of the varied characteristics of medieval literature.

Chaucer and Boccaccio themselves were in the medieval tradition. *The Canterbury Tales,* for example, include perfect examples of the beast epic (*The Nun's Priest's Tale*), the *fabliau* (*The Miller's Tale*), the legend (*The Pardoner's Tale*), and the romance (*The Knight's Tale*); and the *Decameron* is in the direct line of medieval bawdy and satire.

Chaucer (*Oil on wood, fifteenth century*).

The Renaissance made a clear break with the Middle Ages even less in literature than in the visual arts, and literary conceptions and conventions that are in large part medieval persist through the ages of Shakespeare and Milton. It is perhaps only in the course of the seventeenth century that the "Elizabethan world picture" (which is in most respects essentially the "medieval world picture") is broken. Then, as Donne complained, "'Tis all in peeces, all cohaerence gone:" the modern world was born.

NOTES

1 *Prose Edda*, trans. A. B. Brodeur, in C. W. Jones, *Medieval Literature in Translation* (New York, 1950), p. 432.
2 Trans. W. T. H. Jackson, *The Literature of the Middle Ages* (New York, Columbia University Press, 1960), p. 246.

Chapter Twenty-Four

THE AUTUMN OF THE MIDDLE AGES: RELIGION AND CULTURE

Fᴿᴼᴹ the fullness of its summer in the thirteenth century, the Middle Ages passed in the fourteenth century into its autumn. The fourteenth and fifteenth centuries are a period of transition, as were the third through the seventh. There are few dichotomies in history, few sudden shifts, and no date when the Middle Ages came to an end. Dates as early as 1300 or as late as 1789 have been suggested, but whatever date is chosen obscures the fact that what happened was a slow change. That change was a little more pronounced than that from Romanesque to Gothic and epic to romance, and somewhat less pronounced than that from Roman to medieval. But like the transition period at the beginning of the Middle Ages, the transition from medieval to modern, which we may arbitrarily define as 1300–1500, was at one and the same time destructive and creative. It was destructive of things typically medieval and can in this sense be described as "the autumn of the Middle Ages." It was creative of things modern and in this sense is often described as "the Renaissance." As the nature and velocity of the change varied radically from region to region of Europe, and as historians no longer subscribe uncritically to the idea of progress or make the value judgment that the modern world is "better" than the medieval world, the period is no longer conceived as one of the coming of light out of darkness. The sophisticated mind rather seeks to understand it in terms both of its creativity of things new and of its dissipation of things old.

Tʜᴇ concept of "Renaissance" or "rebirth," conveying the positive aspects of the period, was first used in the sixteenth century, but as early as the fourteenth, Italian observers were aware that change was taking place. The fourteenth-century Boccaccio said that Dante had revived a creativity in literature that had not existed since the days of Rome, and in the fifteenth century Palmieri asserted that before his time art had been dead for eight hundred years. Petrarch sneered at medieval taste, which he was the first to stigmatize as "Gothic," a term whose pejorative sense is now rejected. This sense of change and belief in change, which came to Italy much earlier than to northern Europe, was itself liberating and conducive to further change and departure from tradition.

But this liberation was very limited. The sober historian, as C. S. Lewis observed, finds few signs of any "vernal enthusiasm" sweeping Europe in the fifteenth century, and Johann Huizinga, the author of *The Waning of the Middle Ages,* went so far as to call the fourteenth and fifteenth centuries a period of "incredible superficiality or feebleness" as compared with the vigorous and creative spirit of the thirteenth century. Huizinga was speaking of northern Europe more than of Italy, but these judgments should at least enjoin hesitation in assigning to the whole age a quality of dawning day and birdsong. In this period of waning, Huizinga suggested, chivalry was caught up in exaggerated clothing, etiquette, and styles; art and literature were enmeshed in petty detail, precious allegory, and affected symbolism; the people were affected by a profound pessimism and after the great plagues were obsessed by a morbidity expressed in grotesque representations of skeletons and "dances of death."

ESSENTIALLY the period is one of transformation of things typically medieval to things typically modern. There was never a complete and perfect synthesis of the Middle Ages, nor any mystical *Zeitgeist* of the time. Over the thousand years separating 1300 from 300 there was constant change and infinite variety. Nonetheless, underneath all this change and variety loose continuities were preserved that after 1300 ever more rapidly dissipated. These continuities, born in the morning twilight of the Middle Ages and now fading in their evening, were: adherence to the ideal, if not to the practice, of Christian unity; adherence to Christian moral principles; confidence in the union of reason and revelation; and adherence to the idea of the unchanging Divine law. From these principles followed the limitation of the power of the state by the Divine law and its subjection to Divine judgment; the consequent limitations of war and of efficiency on the part of the government; and a tendency in the direction of atomization against which men struggled by forming smaller communities: gilds, castle communities, monasteries, or sects. Underlying all were the concepts of *libertas* and *ordo:* that every individual had the *libertas* (the right and the duty) to occupy his proper place in the ideal *ordo* (order) of society.

Now in this period of transition these ideas and attitudes were attenuated, while other ideas and attitudes that had been less typical in the Middle Ages gained power and prominence. The "Renaissance" or the "Autumn," whichever you prefer, was an extension of the Middle Ages, the gradual strengthening and elaboration of certain medieval ideas and institutions to the point at which they could be considered something new: humanism, including both devotion to the classics and to nature; secularism; individualism; and a new view of politics. The period of transition is not the decline of a civilization, for medieval civilization is simply the earliest expression of our own western civilization; much less does the transition represent, as one historian has suggested, the decline of a collective organism obsessed by a death wish. Rather it represents the articulation of a number of changes, some of them simple and striking, others complex and subtle, in economics, society, the Church, the intellectual synthesis, and the idea of sovereignty. In every instance, the changes had their roots deep in the Middle Ages.

THE population boom with its concomitant agricultural, industrial, and commercial expansion came to an end in the fourteenth century. The debate on the extent, date, and nature of its termination is becoming as fierce as that on its beginnings. French historians have always dwelt upon the damaging effects of the Hundred Years' War, English historians upon the Black Death. Some have suggested that contraction was the result of the closing of the "medieval frontier," the end of opportunities for great expansion either on the frontiers of settled Europe or into waste lands within Europe. Still others have argued that the economic contraction of the fourteenth century was but another manifestation of the general deterioration of medieval society otherwise expressed in the turning of war from external crusades to internecine strife, in social struggles, in the breakup of traditional intellectual and political patterns, and even in a general psychological malaise visible in the age's preoccupation with death.

Here as elsewhere, the current tendency is away from exciting generalizations to careful observations. We now know that the fourteenth century was marked not only by the spectacular Black Death of 1347–1350 but by a series of famines and plagues and other natural disasters beginning in the terrible famine of 1315–1317. At the same time there were a number of severe financial and monetary crises, brought about in part by war expenditures exceeding the normal by threefold, in part by the decline of gold and silver mines and a real shortage of money, in part by a rise in prices owing to increased consumer demand, which resulted from the rise of per capita wealth caused by depopulation.

The Black Death, though only one of a number of calamities, was the most important cause of change, destroying as much as 30 to 40 percent of the population in some areas, while leaving others almost untouched. The population reduction brought about by the Death had several diverse effects. It caused a shift in market prices to favor non-agricultural elements. These, particularly the merchants, received a greater per capita share of wealth, which permitted them to invest more and to spend more. For these people the fourteenth and fifteenth centuries— when the Hanseatic League was at its height and English and Dutch commerce was becoming important—were an exciting age of opportunity. A further effect of the Death was to leave agricultural land vacant so that wage earners could occupy them and farm for themselves, adding to the labor shortage and tending to produce higher wages.

The decline of population and the economy continued through the fourteenth and fifteenth centuries, so that the general level of population and economic prosperity was lower in 1500 than in 1300, though some historians posit a fifteenth-century revival. This decline was not everywhere uniform but varied from country to country and even within the same country. While most English towns lost population, London, Bristol, and Southampton maintained their size, and a few towns even grew a little. Bruges and

Burning clothes during the Black Death.

Milan were prosperous. Lombard trade and even agriculture advanced. The decline was not steady, for there were periods of limited recovery after disasters, and it is possible that the gradual revival of population began as early as 1425.

An increasing number of historians, including specialists in Renaissance history like Wallace Ferguson, hold to the theory that the period was one of economic decline, but Ferguson points out that during the decline changes took place facilitating the transition from the medieval to the modern economy. The shift of the population from countryside to town gathered speed; governmental income and activity increased through increased taxation; and business techniques became, possibly as a side effect of decreased prosperity, more effective. The new entrepreneur, for example, was less likely personally to undertake merchant ventures and more likely to remain at home and carry on his business through employees and agents.

In any event, the rapid rise in population and prosperity that had marked the twelfth and thirteenth centuries now came to an end. As we know from sad modern experience, the slowing down of economic advance is in itself a serious disaster, and advance did more than slow in the fourteenth and fifteenth centuries. The period from 1349 to 1470 was a Golden Age only for bacteria.[1] Toward the end of the fifteenth century, another age of expansion began, assisted by the opening of new routes to Asia and the discovery of the New World. The resulting alleged "price revolution" of the sixteenth century reflected a new economy of growth which continued, though with many setbacks, into the phenomenal expansion of Western economy in the eighteenth, nineteenth, and twentieth centuries.

The Black Death: Burial scene at Tournai.

THE discovery of America, the greatest realization conceivable of the myth of the eternal renewal—the opening up of a whole virgin world to European man—has had immeasurable economic, political, and psychological consequences. One has only to guess at the present nature of the world had the Chinese, rather than the Europeans, been the first to effect the discovery.

The origins of the explorations are to be found in the expansion of western Christendom which began in the eighth century with Charlemagne's expeditions against Moslems, Saxons, and Slavs, and which continued in the German *Drang nach Osten,* the Crusades, and the search for routes eastwards to China. The Vivaldi brothers had tried and failed to find a way westward in 1291, but the blocking of the land routes to the East in the fifteenth century forced the Europeans again to search for sea routes and, incidentally, assured the commercial decline of Italy, which had monopolized the old routes, in favor of the Atlantic powers—Portugal, Spain, France, England, and the Netherlands.

The Spanish leadership in the exploration of the New World was a direct outcome of the *Reconquista* from the Moors that had dominated Spanish politics since the eleventh century. The "Catholic Rulers" Ferdinand and Isabella had as their chief purpose the diverting of the energies of the *Reconquista* in constructive directions. The *Reconquista* had ended in the formation of three important kingdoms, Portugal, Castile, and Aragon. Then, in 1469, the marriage of Ferdinand of Aragon and Isabella of Castile founded a union of the two countries which these rulers achieved by three successful policies. They conquered the last Moslem state, the Kingdom of Granada in 1492, expelled the Jews (1492), and expelled the Moslems who refused to embrace Christianity (1502). Their diversion of the forces of a united Spain to the New World and the consequent economic and political advantages helped to make Spain the chief power in Europe for a century.

The voyage of Columbus, though important enough, is itself not as amazing as is sometimes thought. Everyone knew that the world was round and that it was possible to sail westwards to Asia, but everyone also knew that the size of the globe and the frailty of their vessels made the voyage exceedingly hazardous. In spite of the Viking discoveries and legends about a "Western Land," no one seems to have taken the possibility of a continent between Europe and Asia seriously, partly because of the theological implications: if there were people separate from the rest of mankind, then Adam was not the father of all men, and Christ did not die for all, which would be heresy. So firmly were these ideas ingrained that Columbus believed during his explorations of the West Indies that China lay almost directly to the north. As Edmundo O'Gorman has so brilliantly shown, America was not so much discovered as *invented:* the whole conception of a new continent had to be formed by Amerigo Vespucci and others, and it was not everywhere accepted until after 1510. In any event the existence of a whole New World was a novelty that could not but weaken conceptions of the self-contained and unified nature of Christendom.

THE decline of *libertas* and *ordo* encouraged the individualism of the later Middle Ages. No longer certain what the proper order of society was or what their place was in it, men made themselves their own order. The individualism of the Renaissance has been unduly contrasted to the alleged "corporate nature" of medieval society. It is true that medieval theory preached the union of all men in the Mystical Body of Christ, but this did not prevent heresies, rebellions, or personal idiosyncracies. No one could lump Abelard and Saint Bernard together or consider either of them typical of anything. Nor did the theory

A Renaissance individualist: The merchant Giovanni Arnolfini,
by Jan van Eyck (c. 1390–1441).

of a united *societas christiana* prevent bloody wars or political
atomization. Nevertheless, in the autumn of the Middle Ages
there was an increasing tendency to individualism: merchants
and industrialists seeking their own personal fortunes; intellectuals seeking their own personal creeds or modes of expression;
statesmen seeking their own personal power at the expense of
the divine law or the will of the community.

In the world of the intellect, this individualism was one of the
marks of our new age. The earlier Middle Ages had produced
great individualists like Abelard and Frederick II, but traits
like theirs that had been atypical now became normal. The

Renaissance substituted for the medieval virtues of humility and anonymity the virtues of fame and glory, whose roots may lie in romantic chivalry but whose ripe fruits were produced in the fifteenth and sixteenth centuries. The *Autobiography* of the Florentine goldsmith Benvenuto Cellini is the perfect expression of the Renaissance search for personal renown. Cellini's arrogance, conceit, and insensitivity to the personality of anyone but himself make his career the model of those who seek their own glory, rather than God's or that of the community. What Periclean Athens would have considered vicious and idiotic, and scholastic Paris vicious and sinful, was glorified in Renaissance Italy as virtue.

The medieval intellectual consensus showed other signs of transformation. One of the signs of change is the growth of the vernacular. In the general breakdown of the notion of *societas christiana*, localism and nationalism produced in the schools, in the law courts, in administration, and in literature the gradual replacement of the universal Latin language with the vernacular. The vernacular then had in turn a divisive effect upon society. However salutary it is to write a language that the people can read, the declining universality of Latin helped bring about the disunion of Christian society. In China, for example, national unity has been preserved in part owing to the existence of a written language that can be understood by people whose oral communication is unintelligible to one another, and it is conceivable that the preservation of Latin might have worked in that direction in Europe.

The scholastic method continued into the fourteenth and fifteenth centuries, but the separation of faith and reason effected by Siger of Brabant and William of Ockham undercut the scholastic synthesis. Nicholas of Cusa (d. 1464) argued that we can know nothing at all about God, and the skepticism of Ockham extended not only to God but to the phenomenal world. He argued that man's ideas and categories, however internally consistent, have no necessary correspondence to objective reality. One effect of the new skepticism and the separation of faith and reason was to divide those who preferred faith from those who preferred reason, encouraging rationalists to deny the principles of faith and laying the foundation for the "warfare between science and religion." The general movement of the period was away from rational scholasticism and towards experience, in the form of either mysticism or science, a movement in some ways analogous to existential theology today.

Another characteristic of the autumn of the Middle Ages, or the Renaissance, was the growth of humanism. There was a variety of humanism as early as the tenth and eleventh centuries, in the sense of a concern for the classics and a use of classical topics in communication. The mastery and use of classical art, philosophy, and literature by scholars and artists was now at once greatly enhanced and joined with both an increasingly critical attitude and a wide-ranging interest in everything from abstract theology to applied technology. The Fathers and the councils of the Church were studied with as much avidity in the new critical light as was the anatomy of man.

The Renaissance attentiveness to nature, which was, with the classical revival, a strong element in humanism, is represented in Giorgione's (1477–1510) painting of the three philosophers. Giorgione shows, to the right of the picture, Aristotle and Averroes disputing with one another while the Renaissance philosopher gazes off to the left towards mountain, wood, and grotto. This concern with nature in art (and with science in philosophy) was not wholly compatible with imitation of the ancients, for it was new and fresh in its own right. Hence it was one of the forces giving rise to the great battles between the "ancients" and the "moderns" that characterized the seventeenth century. But on the other hand, neither was it wholly new. For a long time it was supposed that Petrarch's ascent of Mount Ventoux in 1336 was the origin of the modern interest in nature and its conflict with older ideas. Petrarch got to the top, admired the view, and then, reading in the volume of Saint Augustine he had conveniently brought with him that all wordly beauty was vanity, made a chastened descent. But Archbishop Anno of Cologne in the eleventh century and other men centuries older than Petrarch had hiked, climbed, and enjoyed mountains wholly without violation of their consciences. The exquisite and accurate reproductions of flowers and trees by the botanist Albert the Great and by the Gothic sculptors indicate the medieval attention to, and love of, nature. Nonetheless, the anatomical sketches of Michelangelo show how much farther this attention to nature progressed in the course of the Renaissance.

The Three Philosophers *by Giorgione (sixteenth century). While Averroes and Aristotle (right) discuss, the Renaissance humanist gazes at a natural scene.*

The Middle Ages had produced their own well-rounded men—Gerbert, Frederick II, Albert the Great—but Renaissance humanism made of the *uomo universale,* the accomplished "Renaissance man," a model and an ideal. This concern produced a greatly improved system of education for the laity. It also produced one of the great original ideas of the period, liberal education: education not for the purpose of a career in Church, state, or commerce, but for the sake of the morally and intellectually good life. This was not only a new, but a noble, ideal, and one all too readily lost sight of.

Concomitant with the growth of interest in nature and in the material world was the growth of intellectual secularism, again a development of ideas that were strong, though not yet dominant, in the central Middle Ages. The secularization of learning and writing was the most important aspect of this development. The merchant class taught its sons and daughters to read and write in order to handle accounts and letters, and even the aristocracy began to explore the delights of learning. Literature and history, written more often now by laymen, turned more often to secular subjects.

THE decline of *libertas* and *ordo* is visible in the decline of the idea of the unified *societas christiana* under the sole sovereignty of God, and, after the twelfth century, under the leadership of the papacy.

The breakdown of the medieval Church in the fourteenth and fifteenth centuries is visible in the decline of the papacy, the attenuation of the ideal of Christian society, and the corresponding rise of private religious opinion in the form of heresy, witchcraft, mysticism, or secularism. The idea of *Christendom* was gradually replaced by that of *Europe,* an entity more visible, more limited, and certainly more secular.

Protestant historians have ascribed this decline of the medieval Church to divine visitation of just punishment upon its corruption. In fact, the Church was then little more debased than before or since. It was not corruption, but the presence of two other conditions, that brought about the decline. First, if these centuries were corrupt, they were also centuries of a growing reform spirit. In the eleventh century, the papacy placed itself at the head of the reform movement and rose to great glory in the following centuries; but in the decades leading up to the sixteenth, it opposed rather than encouraged reform. Instead of welcoming and utilizing reformers as it had done Saint Francis, the Church now rejected them and forced them out, as it did John Hus. It froze out spontaneous religion and spirituality. The second condition leading to decline was the growing consciousness of alternatives among men who saw the papacy debased.

The end of the medieval papacy began in 1294, when a famous hermit of the Abruzzi was, against his will, crowned Pope Celestine V. He soon abdicated, Dante's "coward of the great refusal." Malicious rumor had it that the abdication was prompted by a mysterious voice which in fact emanated from a speaking tube and which belonged to Benedetto Gaetani, who now was chosen Pope Boniface VIII (1294–1303).

According to a contemporary, Boniface entered the papacy like a fox, reigned like a lion, and went out like a dog. Courageous, skilled in canon law, and immeasurably autocratic, he viewed the Church as a political entity and considered it his job to increase its political power. Determined in this pursuit to bring the kings of England and France into line, he also descended deep into Italian family politics and made determined enemies of the powerful Colonna family. He used the "jubilee of 1300" to attract pilgrims to Rome, thereby adding both to his prestige and to his purse. A man who proclaimed himself "king and priest, pope and caesar," he naturally made too many enemies to finish his reign peacefully. At Anagni, while drawing up a bill of excommunication against Philip IV of France, he was surprised by Philip's counselor Guillaume de Nogaret and by Sciarra Colonna, who nearly succeeded in kidnapping him; he died shortly afterwards.

In 1305 the papacy passed to Clement V, a Frenchman who owed his election to the French king and who never dared to go to Rome: for the next generations the popes resided at Avignon in southern France. Petrarch designated Avignon the new "Babylon, the home of all vices and all misery." There, though the popes continued to build theories of papal power, they were able to enforce them against the power of the French kings. The "Babylonian Captivity" did not noticeably lessen the power of the popes, for a pope backed by the French king was stronger than one at the mercy of the Roman nobility, but the arrangement made the papacy more clearly than before a political office.

Efforts were made as early as 1362 to restore the papacy to Rome, and in 1378 an Italian pope, Urban VI, was elected. Urban turned out to be a tyrant to whom even his supporter Saint Catherine of Siena felt impelled to cry: "For the love of Jesus Crucified, Holy Father, soften a little the sudden movement of your temper!" The French cardinals declared Urban's election illegal and chose a pope of their own to reside in Avignon. The result was the Great Schism, which persisted from 1378 to 1415, a period of nearly forty years in which there was one pope at Avignon and another at Rome. In those days no man knew where his obedience should lie, and the division of the Church was exploited, especially by the kings of England and France, for political purposes. The papacy survived in the fifteenth century by yielding itself up to the Italian politicians, but it did so at the cost of its credibility beyond the Alps. The Protestant Reformation followed.

This reformation was delayed until the sixteenth century because the idea of the unified Christian society had not yet broken down to a degree making possible a widespread rejection of the papacy, and because the kings and princes were not yet fully prepared to exploit religious movements to their advantage. Yet movements against the supremacy of the papacy were already, in one form or another, under way.

Churchmen who viewed with despair the collapse of the papacy in the Great Schism could only cast about for theories that would preserve the unity of the Church in the face of papal degradation. There were several at hand. Ancient ecclesiastical theory made the pope only the first among equals in the college of bishops, and canon law up to the time of Hildebrand had upheld the decentralized polity, as opposed to the monarchy, of the Church. Papal domination was achieved by Hildebrand and his successors, but the imperialist polemicists always challenged it. In both ecclesiastical and secular politics the theory of an ascending rather than descending chain of authority was growing. Marsilius of Padua, who preached an ascending, populist theory, suggested in regard to the Church that an ecumenical council, representing the Christian people, should have supreme authority rather than the pope.

Most important were practical considerations. The theory that an unjust or incompetent secular ruler could be deposed had long been accepted; the argument was now applied to the pope as well. Supposing, men asked, a pope should become vicious or insane? Replies that the Holy Spirit would prevent this from happening were not wholly convincing, particularly at the time of the Great Schism. The only practical way to end the schism, it seemed, was to call an ecumenical council, which would sit in judgment upon the popes. The superiority of the council, it seemed to many, was thus clearly implied.

The first conciliar effort to end the schism, at Pisa in 1409, only produced a third pope. The second effort, at Constance in 1414-1415, was both more successful and more significant in matters of theory. Among the theologians and canonists at Constance were Pierre D'Ailly, Jean Gerson, and Francesco Zabarella, the latter two being to some extent influenced by Marsilius.

D'Ailly, under the influence of William of Ockham, wrote a treatise entitled *Useful Proposals* in which he argued that the unity of the Church, rather than originating from, or depending upon, the pope, stood above him, and that as a result a general council could take place with or without his approval. Gerson maintained that a council had the final say in matters of faith and morals and, using populist terms, insisted that the pope was the servant, not the ruler, of the Church. Zabarella argued that the pope could be considered the head of the Church only when he ruled justly and well. All three challenged the Hildebrandine assumption that the Roman Church, that is, the pope and cardinals, were the visible manifestation of the whole Church, and dwelt instead upon the whole Christian people.

Under such influences, the council proceeded to secure the resignation and deposition of the three claimants to the papal throne and the election in 1417, of a new pope, Martin V. At the urging of Gerson, the council passed the decree *Sacrosancta*, affirming the ecumenical council to be the supreme tribunal of Christendom and listing a schedule of necessary reforms. The bishops also expressed their will that a council should be held at least once every ten years. Had these notions prevailed, the papal monarchy would have become limited and constitutional. They did not.

At Basel in 1431 another general council met, its intention originally being to continue limiting papal power. In 1438, however, Eugenius IV succeeded in moving some of the bishops to Ferrara, then to Florence, and finally to Rome, where the council was concluded under papalist auspices. The majority of bishops remained at Basel and elected another pope; the new schism was ended by a compromise of the wearied antagonists in 1449.

The result of all this dissention was the growing power of kings and princes. As the papacy had slain the emperor as head of the Church, so now the princes slew the papacy. As early as 1363 Bernardo Visconti claimed that he was "pope, emperor, and lord" in all his lands, and Rudolf IV of Austria admitted disarmingly, "I want to be pope, archbishop, bishop, archdeacon, and deacon, in my realm." The popes were able to separate the princes from the councils by the end of the fifteenth century and avert the conciliarist threat to papal power; but

Jean Gerson, a leader of the conciliar movement.

in so doing they placed themselves at the mercy of the princes. The sort of mercy the princes would show in the next century is typified in the career of Henry VIII. The destruction of the old *societas christiana* was achieved when the modern notion of the sovereignty of the prince replaced the medieval notion of the sovereignty of God.

THE councils and the princes were not the only sources of protest against papalism, or the only threat to the *societas christiana*. The decline of *libertas* and *ordo* encouraged a growing individualism in religion as well as in the intellectual life. Mysticism was at its strongest in the fourteenth and fifteenth centuries, and semi-mystical cults like the Brethren of the Common Life and the "New Devotion" sprang up in the Low Countries and elsewhere, their most famous protagonists being Gerard Groote and Thomas à Kempis. They, like the prophetic Joan of Arc and Catherine of Siena, represented a more personal, and less public, approach to religion. Again, individualism in religion was encouraged by individualism in culture. The increasing literacy of the laity encouraged individual interpretations of the Bible and of Church history. The educational policies of the Renaissance humanists had much to do with the formation of the idea of the individual, as opposed to the community; with conscience; and eventually with the Protestant Reformation.

The Church was affected not only by the individualism characteristic of the breakdown of *ordo*, but also by the formation of new communities. Popular heresies and movements came to take for their members the place of the old Church. Often these religious movements were unsophisticated manifestations of social discontent. People had not yet learned that it was possible to exert influence for political betterment of their condition in this world, and so transposed social into religious grievances. Thus, while most individualists, like the mystics, retained loyalty to the united Church, there were growing numbers of overt heresies obtaining considerable popular support: the Brethren of the Free Spirit, the Fraticelli, the Guglielmites, the Luciferans, and the Witch Cults. Among the more peculiar were the Flagellants, whose strange practices are still imitated in Corpus Christi processions in Spain and by the isolated but vigorous sect of the Penitentes in New Mexico. In 1349, more than six hundred Flagellants came from the Netherlands to London:

> Sometimes at Saint Paul's and sometimes at other points in the city they made two daily public appearances wearing cloths from the thighs to the ankles, but otherwise stripped bare. Each wore a cap marked with a red cross in front and behind. Each had in his right hand a scourge with three tails. Each tail had a knot and through the middle of it there were sometimes sharp nails fixed. They marched naked in a file one behind the other and whipped themselves with these scourges on their naked and bleeding bodies.[2]

More important were the heresies of John Hus (ca. 1369–1415) and John Wyclif (ca. 1320–1384). Hus, a Bohemian, studied and then taught theology at the University of Prague. In the tradition of the old Reformists and Valdesians, and urged like the conciliarists by the present state of the Church, he began by attacking the corruption of the clergy and was unfortunate enough to support in the schism the papal candidate not approved by the archbishop of Prague. Ecclesiastical reprisals drove Hus eventually to challange the validity of the entire hierarchy and to formulate the theory that the Church was not the visible Church but the invisible community of true believers or elect. Having been granted a safe conduct by Emperor Sigismund, he went to Constance to present his views to the council, and there, in 1415, he was executed at the stake. It is small wonder that Luther later mistrusted the safe conducts promised him by Emperor Charles V. The manner of Hus' death has led the Protestants to claim him as their first martyr:

> When the executioners at once lit (the fire), the master immediately began to sing . . . . And when he began to sing the third time, the wind blew the flame in his face. And thus praying within himself and moving his lips and the head, he expired in the Lord . . . . He seemed to move before he actually died for about the time one can quickly recite "Our Father" two or at most three times.[3]

John Wyclif, from whom Hus drew some of his ideas, was a philosopher at Oxford urging reform and opposing papal exactions in England. Though distrusted by many in power who disliked his teachings and feared their effects upon the restive peasants, he was befriended by John of Gaunt and protected from open persecution. Yet opposition drove Wyclif to greater extremes before his death in 1384, and he was posthumously condemned at the Council of Constance.

Both Hus and Wyclif had followings that outlived them, particularly among the poor and dispossessed. In Bohemia, Hussite sentiment also came from the nationalist nobility, who used religion as a club with which to belabor the emperor. The Hussites, called Taborites from their center at Mount Tabor, itself named after the mountain in Galilee where the risen Christ appeared to his disciples, for years mounted an armed resistance to the emperor, and though they were ultimately defeated, they had destroyed much of the power and wealth of the Bohemian Church.

John Hus being led to execution.

The followers of Wyclif, the Lollards [from Dutch *lollaerd:* "mumbler of prayers"], drew their strength in part from the scholars at Oxford, in part from the lesser gentry, and in a large part from the urban and rural poor. They preached disobedience to unjust popes and bishops, attacked the idea of the indelible priesthood, affirmed the idea of the invisible church, denied transubstantiation, and condemned what they considered the superstitions of pilgrimages and monasticism. They demanded that the Church divest itself of its temporal possessions. The underlying assumption was that all lordship and power on earth depends upon grace and that no one has a right to rule merely because of his position in the earthly hierarchy. The Lollards brought out the first English translation of the entire Bible, and this, in an age of increasing literacy, extended their influence.

The similarity between the doctrines of Hus and Wyclif

and those of the Protestant Reformers is undeniable, and there is reason to suppose a continuity. Popular and reformist dissent had existed in Europe since the eighth century, and there is no reason to suppose that it vanished in the second half of the fourteenth. Though both the Taborites and Lollards were severely reduced and repressed, there is evidence that their sentiments were preserved by many whose grandchildren in the next century received the Reformation with enthusiasm. There is even some vague evidence that Catharism, so gravely reduced in the Albigensian Crusade, persisted. In the sixteenth century one Hans Thon was arrested as a heretic for holding Catharist views, and a map comparing the centers in France of Catharist influence in the thirteenth century with those of Calvinist in the sixteenth will show remarkable congruities. The Reformation was prepared in the fourteenth and fifteenth centuries.

NOTES

[1] Sylvia Thrupp, in the *Economic History Review,* xvii, (1965), 118.
[2] Robert of Avesbury, trans. by W. H. Hassall, *Medieval England* (New York, Harper and Row, Torchbook edition, 1965), p. 156.
[3] Peter of Mladoňovice, trans. by Matthew Spinka, *John Hus and the Council of Constance* (New York, Columbia University Press, 1965), p. 233.

Chapter Twenty-Five

THE AUTUMN OF THE MIDDLE AGES:
SOVEREIGNTY AND THE STATE

THE decline of *libertas* and *ordo* was the decline both of the idea of the Christian society, the great community, and of the structure of the smaller feudal and gild communities.

The feudal system, which had in many respects provided a unified framework for society, was being undermined by the obsolescence of its military functions, and by the fact that the rapidly expanding central governments needed far more money than the old system of feudal dues and incidents could provide. The depression that began early in the fourteenth century made it all the more difficult for the feudality to meet these new demands. From the thirteenth century the uselessness of the feudal cavalry, which had dominated Europe since the eighth century, became increasingly evident. The crossbow and the English longbow, both formidable weapons, had enabled infantry to bring down the great feudal warhorses and their riders. At Bannockburn (1314), Crécy (1346), Agincourt (1415), and Sempach (1386) this point was made. The invention of gunpowder with its power to frighten horses and breach feudal defenses made the importance of infantry even clearer. Knightly armor grew heavier to meet the new threats, but, like the dinosaurs, the feudal cavalry eventually became too heavy to survive.

Perceiving the uselessness of the feudal force, governments turned increasingly in the direction of paid, professional armies. As a result, the rulers grew more interested in a monetary rather than military return from the lands that they gave out. Even on the manorial level, the duties of peasants were increasingly commuted to money payments, and from the fourteenth century indentures became the most common form of contract. As far as the knights were concerned, the governments, which had once grudgingly collected scutage ("shield-money") as a fine from those failing to appear in war, now enthusiastically encouraged their tenants to stay home and to send them the scutage with which they could pay and equip a professional force. It became more common also for rulers, in granting fiefs to their military followers, to substitute for the old land fiefs *fief-rentes* or money fiefs based upon life and provisional tenures rather than upon fixed and hereditary tenures.

All of this so radically transformed feudalism as in effect to transform it into a new set of political, military, and social institutions. Later medieval feudalism was what Professor Mc-Farlane calls "bastard feudalism," a system in which the holding of land is no longer connected with military service. The aristocracy, no longer a military caste, became more interested in profits than in prowess. The castle yielded to the stately home, the illiterate warrior to the cultured gentleman, and might to money. On the other hand, the professional armies made it possible for the prince to wage war and make peace, and in general to conduct his foreign and military policy, with little reference to the will of his subjects. Long vanished was the general levy of the populace of the early Middle Ages, and gone now too was the host of peers. The result was to enhance the power of the prince and his claim to sovereignty, and eventually to encourage autocracy. But at the same time it gave the ruler a flexibility in making and breaking alliances and in fighting wars for very limited objectives. This might seem desirable to us, who live in a world in which the requirements of democratic war ordain that the people must be stirred up to blood lust and to demands for unconditional surrender.

WITH the decline of the idea of the united Christian society, the failure of feudalism, and the decay of other smaller communities like the monasteries and the gilds, the state emerged as the most important entity of the modern world. This was accompanied by a change in the notion of sovereignty. Through most of the Middle Ages the idea was current that only God was sovereign; the new idea was that each prince was sovereign in his own domains. The ultimate authority of God was not rejected, but was only tacitly admitted, and it came to mean very little. Princes no longer considered themselves limited by the power of the emperor, or of the pope, or of any other earthly authority. With the establishment of princely authority came a growth of governmental efficiency and an expansion of the fiscal, military, and religious power of the state. The tendency to anarchy that had dominated the Middle Ages owing to the theories of the limited state and the practical weakness of the state was now replaced by a tendency to autocracy founded upon theories of sovereignty in turn based upon the growing power of the state in practice.

Sovereignty was established in the later Middle Ages on many levels. In Italy, the city state emerged as sovereign out of the wreckage of the imperial power in Italy; in most of Germany and parts of France the nobility were able to establish states, and practical sovereignty, of their own; and in England, France as a whole, and Spain, sovereignty was accomplished at the level of the nation.

A parallel development, only superficially contradictory, was the growth of the power of the people. The breakdown of other communities than the state caused a great deal of social unrest, which was partly expressed by the formation of religious movements but increasingly by political demands. Sometimes the political upheavals were brutish and undirected, like the peasants' rebellions in England and in France: this was often the case when the rebels had no real hope of participating in government. But often, when they had hopes of success, people formed a more moderate program of demands. As the wealth and influence of the mercantile classes or the landed gentry grew, for instance, princes simply could not afford to ignore them. The result was the growth of representative institutions like the English Parliament and of the extraordinary concern of fifteenth-century rulers like the Lancastrians with popular opinion. This advance of popular power was reflected in the political theories of populists like Marsilius of Padua, who argued that the true sovereign was the people and that the prince was merely that "part" of the people ordained to govern.

ITALY was one of the most precocious areas of Europe in the establishment of the idea of princely sovereignty and in the practice of political fragmentation. In the twelfth century the defeat of Frederick Barbarossa by the Lombard League made the northern Italian cities in most respects free of imperial power. The Kingdoms of Sicily and Naples posed no threat to the north, and by the fourteenth century the papacy had lost all chance of extending its temporal domain much farther. Thus the northern Italian cities were permitted to develop their own independence and institutions. City states whose institutions were native and ancient, though sometimes self-consciously modified in imitation of the Greek *polis*, their government was at first republican. Then the urban upper classes replaced the republics with tyrannies. These tyrannies were sometimes of feudal families (like the House of Este at Ferrara or that of the Visconti at Milan), sometimes of military mercenaries (like the Sforza of Milan), and sometimes of the bourgeois patriciate (like the Medici at Florence, whose power culminated in the reign of Lorenzo the Magnificent).

These city states arrogated to themselves sovereign rights. The duchy of Milan, for example, owed its power to a long tradition. Milan had been one of the great centers of the Roman Empire and then the seat of one of the most powerful and distinguished episcopal sees of the West. The importance of its bishop was seconded by a strong nobility that resided in and around the city, not in the countryside. To these advantages was added the growth of a very substantial industry and commerce from the twelfth and thirteenth centuries. By the fourteenth century Milan was one of the most powerful and independent of the city states. The duke of Milan had enormous prestige abroad and enormous powers at home. He recognized no superior authority and, though the citizens of Milan had certain rights, he ruled in an extremely efficient and even authoritarian fashion. Like any king, he developed a centralized bureaucracy complete with privy council, treasury, and chancery, and kept a well-disciplined professional army. His power was so great as to permit him to ignore or to suspend the statutes. His was a viable sovereignty on a small scale.

Though after the sixteenth century the Italian city states faded into insignificance, their form and style, particularly through the influence of political theorists like Machiavelli and historians like Guicciardini, influenced the formation of sovereignty in the rest of Europe. Yet in the brief moment of their flower they created the air that the artists, scholars, and writers of the Renaissance needed to breathe. Further, the ability of the city states to break with both the feudal and the ecclesiastical establishments caused noble birth to become less important than intelligence and skill, and the small size of the states made it possible for such talents to be rewarded with the highest offices of state.

In Germany, sovereignty or near-sovereignty was achieved at the level of the local, feudal domain, when these domains, in the absence of any real competition from the empire, were transformed into principalities.

The idea of the empire in Germany was not yet dead, and it did not wholly vanish until it was abolished by Napoleon in 1806. The emperors continued to make gestures in the direction of imperial power, but Lewis IV was the last to intervene in Italy in the hope of an imperialist restoration. He did so at enormous expense, and at the height of his power could muster no more than 4,000 horses. However, a sense of nationalism was not wholly absent from Germany, as the establishment of the new official name for the empire around 1450 indicates: The Holy Roman Empire of the German Nation. The imperial government was streamlined and professionalized, and the Golden Bull of 1356 established a mechanism for the orderly succession to the throne.

But all this was in vain. It had already been clear in the twelfth century that the imperial power was crumbling, and the *Faustrecht* ("rule of the fist") or anarchy that followed the death of Frederick II's son Conrad IV put an end to any hope of restoration. Seizing the opportunity presented by the civil wars of succession in Germany, the English and French monarchies made of that country the battleground for their competing ambitions. The Golden Bull that stabilized the imperial succession also recognized the practical transformation of Germany into a *Prinzenkreis* ("club of princes"), deeply divided and dominated by certain powerful secular nobles, prince-bishops, and free cities. Switzerland and the Netherlands were moving in the direction of independence. The power and glory of the House of Luxembourg (Charles IV and his successors) derived, not from their imperial

Albert I (1298–1308)
Henry VII (1309–1313)
Lewis IV (1314–1347)
Charles IV (1347–1378)
Wenceslas (1378–1400)
Rupert (1400–1410)
Sigismund (1410–1437)
Albert II (1438–1439)
Frederick III (1440–1493)
Maximilian (1493–1519)

title, but from the strength of their position as rulers of Bohemia, and Prague was their capital. Sigismund, Maximilian, and the great Charles V were not notable because they were emperors, but because of their wide possessions in Bohemia, Hungary, Austria, Burgundy, and eventually Spain and the New World. The imperial symbol of Christian unity was empty.

But it would be a mistake to imagine that because imperial power was waning, the Germany of the medieval autumn was increasingly anarchic. Rather, the failure of the emperor to become a true sovereign permitted other, smaller governments to attain practical sovereignty. In free cities like Frankfurt, in noble domains like the Mark of Brandenburg and the Duchy of Bavaria, and in ecclesiastical principalities like the archbishopric of Cologne, the governors took on the nature of princes. Though in theory they lacked sovereignty, and owed obedience to the emperor, in fact no authority could interfere with them in their own domains. The Markgraf of Brandenburg, for example, kept his own army, held his own diets, maintained his own administration, established his own law courts, coined his own money, and regulated his own Church, exactly as if he had been king of England or France. The princes united in pacts to keep the general peace and successfully repressed disorder by building up the jurisdiction of the courts and destroying anarchic institutions like the blood-feud.

The establishment of the German principalities prevented further atomization and anarchy. But the disadvantages of not having viable sovereignty established at a broader level are obvious. The clash of interests among the principalities provoked wars;

their jealousy of their own independence encouraged the forma-
tion of independent and mutually hostile Churches during the
Reformation; and the ultimate results were the savage Thirty
Years' War and the prevention of German unity until 1870.

NATIONALISM was the expression of sovereignty at something
between the universal and local levels. It was the natural product
of the breakdown of the united Christian society on the one hand
and feudal fragmentation on the other. It has been, of course,
the most enduring variety of sovereignty produced by the autumn
of the Middle Ages.

The word *natio* had been used in the earlier Middle Ages,
but in the simple sense of place of birth or even "family" (*natio*
in its root sense simply means "birth"). The universities had
nationes, but there the term meant students from a particular
district, which might be as large as England or as small as Rome
or Tuscany. On the other hand, the earlier Middle Ages certainly
knew the *state:* the Church was itself a state, and so were the
monarchies of Theoderic and Otto the Great. But neither early
medieval "nation" nor early medieval "state" fit the modern idea
of a nation.

The characteristics of the true nation are five: political unity;
a certain degree of civilization; a certain religious, linguistic and
cultural unity; common cultural traditions; and, most important,
a consciousness of these unities, a belief in nationhood. This last
is the essential point, and the history of a nation is really the
history of the consciousness of a people that they are a nation.

When the kings had the power to develop the political
unity of the state over a wide area of some cultural homogeneity,
and when the universal community of Christian society and local,
limited communities had lost their dominion over the minds of
men, the people turned to the state to express their sense of
community, and it was then that the nation was born. There are
some signs of popular national consciousness as early as the
twelfth century, as indicated by the "Sweet France" of the *Song
of Roland.* This consciousness emerged more clearly at the end
of the thirteenth century with the growing power of the French
and English monarchies, was heightened by the passions gen-
erated by the Hundred Years' War and by the charismatic career
of Joan of Arc, was encouraged by the dissensions of the Great

Schism, and was accepted as a principle at the Council of Constance when the bishops were divided according to nations.

In both England and France, then, there was a strong movement of nationalism in the fourteenth and fifteenth centuries, which was expressed in the thrust towards both royal absolutism and popular representation, ideas apparently contradictory but reconcilable within the framework of nationalism.

In England, the growing power of the kings managed to subdue the nobility without destroying it, and the ancient opposition of feudality and Church to royal power was subsumed, with that of the towns and gentry, in Parliament, which represented all the estates of the realm. The failure of either king or Parliament to destroy the other meant that each would continue to check the other's drive for power. The result was a balance of power that characterized the English constitution of the eighteenth century and made possible the development of a strong and loyal nationalism. The elements of nationalism, central power, and popular identification with the state were developed in England in a strong and balanced fashion.

The strong monarchy of Edward I was prevented from attaining the tyrannical proportions of that of Philip IV by the crisis of 1297, when nobles and Church together successfully defied the king's efforts to expand taxation. Under Edward's incompetent successor Edward II (1307–1327) the barons rose again in an attempt to drive out the king's favorites and bring public offices under their own control. Edward's temporary victory, enshrined in the royalist Statute of York in 1322, served only to further envenom his enemies, and he was finally forced to abdicate and then was murdered.

The victory over Edward II was no real victory for the barons, whose program was reactionary and unrealistic. The development of nationalist politics, and indeed, the practical demands of government, required the growth of the central authority in royal hands, and against this pragmatic necessity the baronial program was as ineffective as that of the opponents of "big government" in the modern United States.

Under Edward III, whose attention was fixed on France, there was no overt baronial unrest, but the custom of annual parliaments was quietly established. The pragmatic and compelling need of Edward III for money to carry on his French wars obliged him to rely more heavily upon public support and hence upon Parliament than had his predecessors.

The conflict broke out again under Richard II. Sensitive, proud, and determined to rule, he was at first popular and able to force the baronial opposition (the "Lords Appellant") to retreat. At last his absolutist tendencies carried him too far, and after significant sections of the population were alienated, it became possible for Duke John of Gaunt and his son Henry Bolingbroke to administer Richard a fate similar to Edward II's. Shakespeare has captured the pathos of the fallen king; and a contemporary of Richard's, Adam of Usk, did so more succinctly:

And now those in whom Richard, late king, did put his trust for help were fallen. And when he heard thereof, he grieved more sorely and mourned even to death, which came to him most miserably . . . as he lay in chains in the castle of Pontefract, tormented by Sir (Thomas) Swineford with starving fare . . . .[1]

For all his unfortunate end, which served as a precedent for the Convention of 1688 that declared James II deposed, Richard II had moved England closer to absolutism. The process was reversed under his successors, the Lancastrians. The claim of Bolingbroke, who took the title Henry IV, was weak, and this initial flaw, in addition to other domestic difficulties and the exigencies of the French war, obliged the Lancastrians to yield power to Parliament. The Whig historians praised the enlightenment of the House of Lancaster and its willingness to "experiment" with Parliamentary government: in fact the Lancastrians would have liked nothing better than to maintain the royal authority they asserted; they simply found themselves incapable of doing so.

The opposition to the Lancastrians was mounted by the House of York in a series of civil wars that romantics called the Wars of the Roses, but that were really a continuation of the old baronial wars with the difference that the Yorkists desired, not so much to limit, as to possess, the monarchy. Those who seek a date dividing medieval from modern in English history are coming to realize that the accession of Edward IV of York in 1461 was at least as important as that of Henry VII Tudor in 1485. The

Richard II and his wife, Anne of Bohemia.

Yorkists found themselves in a stronger position both domestically and abroad than the Lancastrians (the war in France was over), and asserted strong royal control and introduced centralizing innovations that would be adopted and expanded by the Tudors. The years from the death of Edward IV in 1483 to the victory of the Tudors at Bosworth in 1485 saw the last spasm of the baronial wars. Henceforward opposition to the monarchy would be mounted, as it was in the Civil War of the seventeeth century, by Parliament and by wide sections of the populace.

The French monarchy began the fourteenth century with enormous prestige and power, but the reign of Philip IV was followed by a sudden and complete reversal of fortune. The failure of Philip's children to produce heirs created a dispute over the crown that eventually brought in the king of England; and the disastrous Capetian policy of granting *appanages* (great fiefs) to the younger brothers of kings bore fruit in the rebellions of the dukes of Burgundy. The "Hundred Years' War," plagues, famines, and peasant rebellions reduced the kingdom of France to a shambles and permitted the king of England to assume the French crown in 1422.

The "Hundred Years' War" is a misnomer, for there was not one war, but several, and they lasted more than a hundred years. The entry of England into French politics following the Norman conquest began a conflict that continued intermittently thereafter, the king of England's position as the greatest vassal of the king of France being highly conducive to strife.

The immediate precedents of the War were set as far back as 1259 at the Treaty of Paris. There, in return for territorial concessions and freedom to pursue his ambitions in Sicily, Henry III foolishly promised Louis IX that Aquitaine (or Gascony as it was now called) should be treated as a French fief and not as the personal possession of the English king. Philip IV used this agreement to send in French officers, to divert pleas from Westminster to Paris, and otherwise to assert French sovereignty. Gascon and Norman ships fought and pirated one another on the high seas, and a general war was averted only when Edward I and Philip IV agreed to arbitrate. In the meanwhile Edward was building a coalition of pro-English forces in Germany and Flanders, a foreshadowing of the policy used against Napoleon five hundred years later, while France on its side was finding a natural ally in Scotland.

In 1329 Edward III did homage to King Philip VI of France, promising to bear him faith and loyalty. But that homage soon proved empty. Border provocations in Gascony, French aid to Scotland, and the chivalric desire for war and booty prompted Edward to lay claim to the French throne. It has been disputed whether Edward was serious; his claim was certainly poor. If the claim of Philip V that the royal title could not pass through a woman were accepted, Edward's claim was null, since it came from his mother Isabella. If, on the other hand, title *could* pass through a woman, then the heir was Charles the Bad King of

THE FRENCH AND ENGLISH MONARCHIES AT THE TIME OF THE HUNDRED YEARS' WAR:
THE HOUSES OF VALOIS, BURGUNDY, LANCASTER, AND YORK

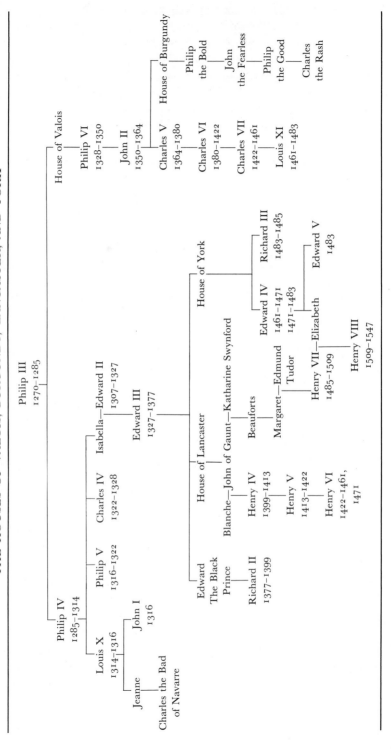

*Edward II of England doing homage to Philip IV the Fair for the
Plantagenet possessions in Aquitaine. The dress of the king of France is
decorated with fleurs de lys; that of the king of England with the English lion.*

Navarre, the grandson of Louis X. It may be assumed that
Edward's claim was meant as a bargaining principle.

After the usual provocations, Philip VI declared Edward's
fief confiscated in 1337, and the War was on. The first phase
(1337–1360) was characterized by spectacular English victories.
At Sluys in 1340 the French navy was destroyed. At Crécy in
1346 the English archers under Edward III wiped out the much
larger French army, and in 1356 Edward's son, Edward the Black
Prince, administered an almost identical defeat at Poitiers. In
the meanwhile, Charles of Navarre also laid claim to the throne
and allied himself with a revolt of students and artisans at Paris
(1355), and in 1358 the great peasants' risings, or Jacqueries,
occurred. The king of France, John II, had himself been made
prisoner at Poitiers, and the French were obliged to yield.

The Peace of Bretigny (1360) gave the English a huge ransom for the person of King John, and important territorial ad-
ditions, among them the strategically and economically important

port of Calais. The "peace" was marked by border skirmishes, the brutal ravaging of the countryside by the "free companies," and a war between the English and French candidates for the throne of Castile. King Charles V, who came to the throne in 1364, had as a boy seen from his tower window the red glow of the fires lit by the English, and he was determined to drive them out. Avoiding big battles, and using both diplomacy and harrassment, this able ruler was able to reduce English power considerably, but his achievements were undone by his death in 1380. The heir to the throne, Charles VI, was a minor, and a civil war broke out between the "Armagnacs," supporters of the duke of Orléans, who wished to pursue the war against the English, and the students and burgers, who supported the duke of Burgundy and neutrality. By 1399 the dynastic situation of both countries was shaky and a peace was signed that endured sixteen years.

In 1415 Henry V, feeling the Lancastrian throne well settled, and having determined to revive the old claims to the French throne, landed at Harfleur and marched through Normandy with a success equal to that of Edward III. On Saint Crispin's day he inflicted upon the French chivalry at Agincourt a defeat even more disastrous than that of Crécy. The will to resist had been further sapped when at Paris the Burgundians massacred the Armagnacs, using as their excuse a big lie worthy of Hitler: that the Armagnacs favored surrender to the English! By this time King Charles VI was completely insane and had to be forcibly restrained by burly attendants; the French could not resist, and in 1420 the Treaty of Troyes provided for the marriage of Henry V with Catherine of France and for the accession of Henry to the French throne upon the death of Charles VI. Two years later Charles died but so, ironically, did Henry. Under the terms of the treaty, the kingdoms of England and France passed to the infant Henry VI, son of Henry V and Catherine, while the Dauphin Charles, the son of Charles VI, retreated to brood in Bourges.

France was now suddenly lifted from the lowest depths to the greatest heights by one of the most extraordinary figures of history, Joan of Arc, the peasant girl of Domremy who believed that she heard the saints telling her that God intended her to save France. Joan has appeared a great saint to many modern writers; a few have taken the charges of witchcraft lodged against her seriously and suggested that she may have belonged to a witch-cult. She is certainly a symbol of the rising national consciousness brought about by the war, for it is most unusual in the medieval context for an unlettered inhabitant of a remote eastern province on the borders of the empire, or indeed for anyone, to evince such loyalty to an entity called France. This patriotism is perhaps the most extraordinary aspect of an extraordinary career. Her religious enthusiasm is best understood in the context of the movements of lay prophecy that were common in her day: in many respects she resembled Margery Kempe, the unlettered English mystic and prophetess.

When Joan arrived at the Dauphin's court at Chinon, the story goes, the Dauphin tried to test her prophetic abilities by disguising himself as one of his courtiers but that Joan, introduced at court in her country clothes, went immediately to him and saluted him as her king. Whether out of belief or out of desperation, the Dauphin put her in charge of a force to lift the siege of Orléans, the last great fortress resisting the English. The almost incredible truth that Charles placed this teen-age girl at the head of his army is accompanied by the equally unbelievable fact that she was able to command the respect and to fire the courage of his soldiers, and succeeded in defeating the English and raising the siege. The triumphant Maid of Orléans now led Charles VII to be crowned at the traditional coronation site of France, the cathedral of Reims.

Her triumph was short-lived. The next year she was captured by the Burgundians who turned her over to the English. After a trial under the presidency of Bishop Cauchon and under the influence of the English, she was condemned and burned at Rouen as a heretic and a witch. The king whom she had created found it inconvenient to attempt to save her. Thus in the space of three years her fantastic career was brought to a close. But she had imparted a confidence and vigor to the French armies that enabled them to conquer Normandy and finally, in 1453, capture Bordeaux, for more than three centuries the capital of English influence on the continent.

The defeat of the English and Burgundians gave the French new enthusiasm, and France, like many other nations which gain or recover their unity, went on to expand its influence. The suc-

Burgundian Dominions

MILES
0   100   200   300   400   500

THE END OF THE MIDDLE AGES

TEUTONIC ORDER

LITHUANIA

POLAND

Dnieper

HUNGARY

MOLDAVIA

YEDISAN

WALLACHIA

SERBIA

Danube

BULGARIA

Black Sea

TURKISH EMPIRE

Constantinople

ANATOLIA

Aegean Sea

Mytilene

TO VENICE

TO VENICE

TO VENICE

TO VENICE

CYPRUS
(To VENICE)

Sea

CRETE (To VENICE)

Joan of Arc at the stake in Rouen.

cessors of Charles VII pursued expansionist policies in Spain, Italy, and Germany. On the other hand the English, freed from their continental obsession, were able to turn their energies overseas to the New World. The experience of the war encouraged national feelings in both England and France; its termination permitted their effective expression.

The Hundred Years' War was the last great medieval war. As May McKisack observed:

> Men sensitive to beauty must have shared something of Froissart's delight in the pageantry of war, in "the fresh, shining armor, the banners waving in the wind, the companies in good order, riding a soft pace," in the sight of a famous knight like Sir John Chandos, "with his banner before him and his company about him, with his coat of arms on him, great and large. . . ."[2]

IN France, the growing power of the kings was opposed by the great nobility, particularly the dukes of Burgundy, and the eventual autocracy of the Bourbons was made possible when the kings defeated the nobles in pitched battle during the Hundred Years' War. Though the war, and the career of Joan of Arc, created a sense of nationalism in France, there was never much popular participation in the French government, except perhaps in the reign of Charles VII; the provincial estates were always instruments of royal policy and propaganda rather than truly advisory bodies. Ordonnances of 1439 and 1445 established a permanent standing army and taxes that continued without further consultation with the people until the French Revolution. From the reign of Louis XI, the movement of French politics in the direction of the *Ancien Régime* was clearly visible. The lack of balance in the French constitution visible already in the fifteenth century is the ultimate root of the Revolution of 1789.

In the midst of the Hundred Years' War new sovereignties analogous to the German principalities were nearly established in France. The most important of these was Burgundy. Duke Philip the Bold (1364–1404), who received the *appanage* of Burgundy as the younger brother of Charles V, was an able and ambitious ruler, and gradually acquired lands until at the height of Burgundian power his successors ruled Burgundy, Lorraine, Luxembourg, Flanders, Holland, and Picardy, a state that nearly surrounded France and, by cooperating with the English, nearly brought down the French monarchy. The alliance with England, the glories and grandeur of the Burgundian court at Dijon, and the extent of the Burgundian domains led some of the dukes, as well as some modern historians, to dream of the reestablishment of a "middle kingdom" between Germany and France. This idea ignores the almost totally French nature of the Burgundian state. It was too French ever to have become a separate kingdom.

It did, on the other hand, approach sovereignty on the princely level. The duke created a court and institutions in direct and systematic imitation of French royal institutions. He centralized his control over his vast domains as much as possible, and he set up at Dijon not only a brilliant court but a whole centralized administration, including a treasury, a parlement, and an assembly of estates. The duke coined his own money and had his own system of taxation. But Burgundian sovereignty was never developed to the utmost. The Burgundian dukes were never willing or able to break with the king entirely, and royal taxes were often collected, while appeals from Burgundian courts often went to the parlement at Paris. Burgundian sovereignty was finally eclipsed at the death of the ambitious and unlucky Duke Charles the Rash (1467–1477), whose lands were divided between Louis XI and the Emperor Maximilian. Essentially, it was the extraordinary victory of the French kings over the nobles, including the English, that brought down Burgundy, which could not continue to exist as the only one of the French principalities preserving its independence of the crown.

In 1453 two great cities fell: Bordeaux and Constantinople. The fall of Bordeaux marked the end of the Hundred Years' War and heralded the advent of the modern French and English kingdoms. That of Constantinople marked the end of the Byzantine Empire, an event that had enormous consequences for both East and West.

The opponents of the Eastern Christians had since the eleventh century been the Seljuk Turks, but in the early fourteenth century a new Turkish power arose in Anatolia, the Ottomans. Efficient and ruthless, they gradually reduced the territories and power of the Byzantine and other Balkan powers, and by 1450 they had established an empire that included most of the southern Balkans and Asia Minor. The Byzantine emperor was deprived of all his domains except the capital and was obliged to rely upon the walls of Constantinople, and upon the Venetians and Hungarians, to hold off the Turks. The Venetians were more concerned with their own affairs than with saving the empire, and the Hungarians were weakened by internal dissensions in the 1440s. No real force stood in the way of Mehmet the Conqueror (1451–1481) in his design to annex a city already surrounded by his armies.

The Sultan Mehmet was a determined and crafty man who had promised the Italians at the siege of Mytilene that if they surrendered they might keep their heads—and then ordered their bodies sawed in two. An admirer of Alexander the Great, he declared that "I shall go from East to West as formerly the Westerners penetrated the East."[3] In 1453, circumventing the impregnable sea walls of Constantinople by bringing his galleys overland on rollers to the Golden Horn, Mehmet entered the bravely, but hopelessly, defended city. So, as the western empire had ended with Romulus Augustulus, who bore the names of the founders of the city and of the empire, the eastern empire perished with Constantine XI, who bore the name of the founder of the second Rome. Even the name of the city was changed to Istanbul [the Turkish understanding of the Greek *eis tên polin*: "into the city"].

The destruction of Byzantium and the consequent isolation of Russia and the other Orthodox peoples from the rest of Chris-

Mehmet II, the conqueror of Constantinople (by Gentile Bellini).

tendom has had effects visible today. The conception of "western civilization," which was growing out of the idea of Christendom at this time, was formed to exclude the Orthodox Christians in the East; and the severing of the routes of commerce and culture between East and West by the Turks encouraged both their mutual differences and the expansion of the West in the direction of the New World.

By 1500, or at least by the Reformation, the transition period that had begun in 1300 was over, and the medieval had been transformed into the modern world. But medieval contributions did not end with the Renaissance. The Protestants of the Reformation were not only in the tradition of later medieval religious dissent, they chose Saint Augustine to be their chief guide in theology. Medieval confidence in reason, though shaken by Siger and Ockham, did not disappear until the days of Kant, Hume, and Freud. Theocentricity continued through the nineteenth and into the twentieth century. Feudal institutions remained, though an empty shell, until the French Revolution, and chivalric manners in love and war until the Second World War. Religious unity, though vitiated by the Reformation, remained strong in the Catholic Church and shows signs of ecumenical revival today. Parliament, law-courts, universities, and the concepts of the limited state, of the social contract, of national sovereignty, all these and much more with which we are familiar were formed in the Middle Ages.

There is a cultural core in western civilization that is ill defined but very real. It consists of the tradition of art, literature, philosophy, myth, and religion that began for us with the ancient Jews and Greeks and grew with accretions through the succeeding centuries. It contains Homer and Sophocles, Vergil and Horace, Plato and Saint Paul and Augustine, the Parthenon and the Sainte-Chapelle, the Song of Solomon and the Song of Roland, Dante and Milton and Goethe, Palestrina, Bach, and Mozart, and all the others. Familiarity with this growing and continuous culture created in western civilization a sense of community, a mutual understanding and familiarity that has bound century to century and generation to generation. This continuity is the essence of civilization. There are certain philosophical, literary, religious, or political ideas that would have been recognized in fifth-century B.C. Athens, first-century Rome, eighth-century Aachen, thirteenth-century Paris, fifteenth-century Milan, and nineteenth-century Cambridge. The historian, reflecting upon the importance for civilization of maintaining a living sense of this continuity and of these traditions, is concerned with their dilution in the twentieth century, for they are increasingly relegated to the domain of the scholar while the "practical man" goes about his business suffering (though he does not know how much he suffers) from a cultural amnesia that blots three thousand years from his mind. The historian recognizes in the study of medieval history, as in that of the other humane subjects, a partial remedy for that growing sickness.

NOTES

[1] Trans. E. M. Thompson (Oxford, 1904) p. 198.

[2] May McKisack, *The Fourteenth Century* (Oxford, Clarendon Press, 1959), p. 249.

[3] Daniel Waley, *Later Medieval Europe* (New York, 1964), p. 209.

Bibliography

These short select bibliographies list the latest, most widely available, or best books on the material covered in each chapter. Original sources are omitted, having been mentioned in the text. Periodical articles and books in languages other than English are included only when they are of unusual interest. Books available in paperback are marked with an asterisk. Books useful for several chapters are listed under the first. For fuller bibliographies and for the latest periodical materials the reader should go to these journals in particular: the *American Historical Review, English Historical Review, Historische Zeitschrift, Revue historique, Revue d'histoire ecclésiastique,* and *Speculum.* A good, short bibliography is that of R. H. C. Davis, *Medieval European History,* pamphlet No. 67 of "Helps for Students of History" published by the Historical Association (London, 1963). In what follows, the first names of authors are as a rule given even when not habitually used, in order to facilitate finding the books.

INTRODUCTION

Evans, Joan, ed. *The Flowering of the Middle Ages.* London, 1966.
McEvedy, Colin. *The Penguin Atlas of Medieval History.* Baltimore, 1961.
Rice, David Talbot, ed. *The Dawn of Western Civilization.* London, 1965.

CHAPTER ONE

* Burckhardt, Jakob. *The Age of Constantine the Great.* New York, 1949.
  Cambridge Ancient History.
  Gibbon, Edward. *The Decline and Fall of the Roman Empire,* chapters 1–13. 2 vols. New York, 1932.
* Hadas, Moses. *A History of Rome.* New York, 1956.
  Hammond, Mason. *The Antonine Monarchy.* Rome, 1959.
  Jones, Arnold H. M. *The Decline of the Ancient World.* New York, 1966.
  ———. *The Later Roman Empire 284–602.* 2 vols. Norman (Okla.), 1964.
* Lot, Ferdinand. *The End of the Ancient World and the Beginnings of the Middle Ages.* New York, 1961.
  Momigliano, Arnaldo. "Christianity and the Decline of the Roman Empire," in *The Conflict between Paganism and Christianity.* Oxford, 1963.

Parker, Henry M. D. *A History of the Roman World from A. D. 138 to 337,* 2d ed. London, 1958.
* Rostovtzeff, Michael. *Rome,* trans. J. D. Duff. New York, 1960.
——. *The Social and Economic History of the Roman Empire,* 2d ed. 2 vols. Oxford, 1957.
White, Lynn, Jr., ed. *The Transformation of the Roman World.* Berkeley and Los Angeles, 1966.

CHAPTER TWO

* Bultmann, Rudolf. *Primitive Christianity in Its Contemporary Setting.* New York, 1956.
Burrows, Millar. *The Dead Sea Scrolls.* New York, 1955.
——. *More Light on the Dead Sea Scrolls: New Scrolls and New Interpretations.* New York, 1958.
Daniélou, Jean, and Henri C. Marrou. *The First Six Hundred Years.* Vol. 1 of *The Christian Centuries.* New York, 1964.
* Grant, Frederick C. *An Introduction to New Testament Thought.* New York, 1950.
* Hatch, Edwin. *The Influence of Greek Ideas on Christianity.* New York, 1957.
Moore, George Foot. *Judaism in the Age of the Tanaim.* 3 vols. Cambridge (Mass.), 1927–30.
* Nock, Arthur Darby. *St. Paul.* New York, 1963.
Robinson, James. *A New Quest of the Historical Jesus.* London, 1959.
Schweitzer, Albert. *The Quest of the Historical Jesus,* 3d ed. New York, 1961.

CHAPTER THREE

Alföldi, András. *The Conversion of Constantine and Pagan Rome.* Oxford, 1948. *Cambridge Medieval History,* vol. 1.
* Chambers, Mortimer, ed. *The Fall of Rome.* New York, 1963.
* Cochrane, C. N. *Christianity and Classical Culture.* New York, 1957.
Décarreaux, Jean. *Monks and Civilization.* London, 1964.
Dörries, Herman. *Constantine and Religious Liberty,* trans. Roland H. Bainton. New Haven, 1960.
* Jonas, Hans. *The Gnostic Religion.* Boston, 1958.
* Jones, A. H. M. *Constantine and the Conversion of Europe.* New York, 1962.

CHAPTER FOUR

* D'Arcy, Martin C., et al. *Saint Augustine, His Age, Life, and Thought.* New York, 1957.
Fransen, Peter. "Three Ways of Dogmatic Thought," in *Cross Currents,* XIII, 1963.
Ladner, Gerhart. *The Idea of Reform.* Cambridge (Mass.), 1959.
Przywara, Erich. *An Augustine Synthesis.* New York, 1958.
* Van der Meer, Frederik. *Augustine the Bishop.* New York, 1961.

CHAPTER FIVE

* Bark, William Carrol. *Origins of the Medieval World.* Stanford, 1958.
* Blair, Peter Hunter. *An introduction to Anglo-Saxon England.* Cambridge (Eng.), 1956. *Cambridge Medieval History,* vols. 1 and 2. (Eng.), 1956.
  Deanesly, Margaret. *A History of Early Medieval Europe from 476 to 911,* 2d ed. New York, 1960.
* Duckett, Eleanor Shipley. *The Gateway to the Middle Ages.* 3 vols. New York, 1961.
* Havighurst, Alfred F., ed. *The Pirenne Thesis.* Boston, 1958.
  Laistner, Max L. W. *Thought and Letters in Western Europe A.D. 500–900,* 2d ed. London, 1957.
  Musset, Lucien. *Les Invasions: les vagues germaniques.* Paris, 1965.
* Pirenne, Henri. *Mohammed and Charlemagne.* New York, 1957.
* Wallace-Hadrill, John M. *The Barbarian West.* New York, 1962.
  ——. *The Long-Haired Kings and Other Studies in Frankish History.* New York, 1962.

CHAPTER SIX

* Andrae, Tor. *Mohammed, the Man and His Faith.* London, 1936.
  Barker, John. *Justinian and the Later Roman Empire.* Madison, 1966.
* Baynes, Norman H., and H. St.L. B. Moss, eds. *Byzantium.* Oxford, 1948. *Cambridge Medieval History,* vols. 2 and 4.
  Dvornik, Francis. *The Making of Central and Eastern Europe.* London, 1949.
* Geanokoplos, Deano J. *Byzantine East and Latin West.* New York, 1966.
* Guillaume, Alfred. *Islam,* 2d ed. Harmondsworth, 1956.
  Hitti, Philip K. *History of the Arabs from the Earliest Times to the Present,* 7th ed. London, 1960.
* Hussey, Joan M. *The Byzantine World.* New York, 1961.
* Lewis, Bernard. *The Arabs in History,* 4th ed. London, 1958.
  Ostrogorsky, George. *A History of the Byzantine State.* Oxford, 1956.
  Riasanovsky, Nicholas. *A History of Russia.* New York, 1963.
  Southern, Richard W. *Western Views of Islam in the Middle Ages.* Cambridge (Mass.), 1962.
* Vasiliev, Alexander A. *History of the Byzantine Empire 324–1453,* 3d ed. Madison, 1961.
* von Grunebaum, Gustave. *Medieval Islam: A Study in Cultural Orientation,* 2d ed. Chicago, 1961.
  Watt, W. Montgomery. *A History of Islamic Spain.* Edinburgh, 1965.

CHAPTER SEVEN

Cambridge Medieval History, vol. 2.
* Leclercq, Jean. *The Love of Learning and the Desire for God.* New York, 1961.
  Levison, Wilhelm. *England and the Continent in the Eighth Century.* Oxford, 1946.
  Mann, Horace K. *The Lives of the Popes in the Early Middle Ages,* 2d ed. 14 vols. London, 1925–32.
  Ullmann, Walter. *The Growth of Papal Government in the Middle Ages,* 2d ed. London, 1962.

CHAPTER EIGHT

* Bloch, Marc. *Feudal Society.* 2 vols. London, 1961.
* Brøndsted, Johannes. *The Vikings.* Baltimore, 1960.
  Cambridge Medieval History, vols. 2 and 3.
* Duckett, Eleanor Shipley. *Alfred the Great.* Chicago, 1957.
  ——. *Carolingian Portraits.* Ann Arbor, 1962.
  Kern, Fritz. *Kingship and Law in the Middle Ages.* Oxford, 1939.
  Morrison, Karl Frederick. *The Two Kingdoms: Ecclesiology in Carolingian Political Thought.* Princeton, 1964.
* Munz, Peter. *The Origin of the Carolingian Empire.* Dunedin (N.Z.), 1960.
  Oleson, Tryggvi J. *Early Voyages and Northern Approaches 1000–1632.* London, 1964.
  Sawyer, P. H. *The Age of the Vikings.* New York, 1962.
* Sullivan, Richard, ed. *The Coronation of Charlemagne.* Boston, 1959.
* Winston, Richard. *Charlemagne, from the Hammer to the Cross.* New York, 1956.

CHAPTER NINE

Cambridge Medieval History, vols. 2 and 3.
Coulbourn, Rushton, ed. *Feudalism in History.* Princeton, 1956.
* Ganshof, François L. *Feudalism,* 2d ed. New York, 1961.
  Hollister, C. Warren. *The Military Organization of Norman England.* Oxford, 1965.
  Painter, Sidney. *William Marshal.* Baltimore, 1933.
  Pollock, Frederick and F. W. Maitland. *The History of English Law before the Time of Edward I,* 2d ed.(reprint). 2 vols. Cambridge (Eng.), 1952.
  Poole, Austin Lane. *Obligations of Society in the XII and XIII Centuries.* Oxford, 1946.
  Stenton, Frank M. *The First Century of English Feudalism, 1066–1166,* 2d ed. Oxford, 1961.
* Stephenson, Carl. *Medieval Feudalism.* Ithaca, 1956.
* Strayer, Joseph R. *Feudalism.* New York, 1965.
* Thrupp, Sylvia, ed. *Early Medieval Society.* New York, 1967.

CHAPTER TEN

Beech, George T. *A Rural Society in Medieval France: The Gatine of Poitou in the Eleventh and Twelfth Centuries.* Baltimore, 1964.
* Bennett, Henry S. *Life on the English Manor.* Cambridge (Eng.), 1960.
  Beresford, Maurice W., and J. K. S. St.Joseph. *Medieval England, an Aerial Survey.* Cambridge (Eng.), 1958.
  Bloch, Marc. *Land and Work in Mediaeval Europe,* trans. J.E. Anderson. Berkeley and Los Angeles, 1967.
  Cambridge Economic History, vol. 1, 2d ed. Cambridge, 1966.
  Cambridge Medieval History. vol. 3.
  Duby, Georges. *L'Economie rurale et la vie des campagnes dans l'Occident médiéval.* 2 vols. Paris, 1962.
  Finberg, Herbert P. R. *Tavistock Abbey, A Study in the Social and Economic History of Devon.* Cambridge (Eng.), 1951.

Herlihy, David. "The Agrarian Revolution in Southern France and
   Italy 801–1150," *Speculum,* xxxiii (1958).
Homans, George Caspar. *English Villagers of the Thirteenth Century.*
   Cambridge (Mass.), 1941.
Morgan, Marjorie M. *The English Lands of the Abbey of Bec.* Oxford, 1946.
Neilson, Nellie. *Medieval Agrarian Economy.* New York, 1936.
Orwin, Charles S., and Christabel S. Orwin. *The Open Fields,* 2d ed.
   New York, 1954.
Raftis, J. Ambrose. *The Estates of Ramsey Abbey.* Toronto, 1957.
——. *Tenure and Mobility: Studies in the Social History of the Mediaeval
   English Village.* Toronto, 1964.
* White, Lynn, jr. *Medieval Technology and Social Change.* New York, 1966.

CHAPTER ELEVEN

Amann, Emile, and Auguste Dumas. *L'Eglise au pouvoir des laïques.*
   Paris, 1948.
Cantor, Norman F. "The Crisis of Western Monasticism 1050–1130,"
   American Historical Review, lxvi (1950).
Evans, Joan. *Monastic Life at Cluny 910–1157.* London, 1931.
Johnson, Edgar N. *The Secular Activities of the German Episcopate.*
   Lincoln (Neb.), 1932.
Lea, Henry Charles. *A History of Sacerdotal Celibacy in the Middle Ages,*
   3d ed. London, 1907.
Russell, Jeffrey B. *Dissent and Reform in the Early Middle Ages.* Berkeley
   and Los Angeles, 1965.

CHAPTER TWELVE

Bolgar, R. R. *The Classical Heritage and Its Beneficiaries.* New York, 1964.
* Curtius, Ernst. *European Literature and the Latin Middle Ages.* New
   York, 1963.
Duckett, Eleanor Shipley. *Alcuin, Friend of Charlemagne.* New York, 1951.
Hanning, Robert W. *The Vision of History in Early Britain.* New York,
   1966.
* Hinks, Roger. *Carolingian Art.* Ann Arbor, 1962.
Ladner, Gerhart. "Greatness in Mediaeval History," *Catholic Historical
   Review,* l (1964).
Poole, Reginald Lane. *Chronicles and Annals: A Brief Outline of Their
   Origin and Growth.* Oxford, 1926.
Prescott, H. F. M. *Son of Dust*(a novel). New York, 1956.
Stenton, Frank M., ed. *The Bayeux Tapestry.* London, 1957.
Thompson, James Westfall. *The Literacy of the Laity in the Middle Ages.*
   New York, 1960.

CHAPTER THIRTEEN

Barraclough, Geoffrey. *Mediaeval Germany.* 2 vols. Oxford, 1938.
* ——. *The Origins of Modern Germany,* 2d ed. New York, 1966.
Brooke, Christopher. *Europe in the Central Middle Ages 987–1125.* New
   York, 1964.

* Duckett, Eleanor Shipley. *Alfred the Great.* Chicago, 1956.
* Fawtier, Robert. *The Capetian Kings of France.* New York, 1966.
* Petit-Dutaillis. *The Feudal Monarchy in France and England.* New York, 1964.
* Poole, Austin Lane. *From Domesday Book to Magna Carta.* Oxford, 1951.
 Stenton, Frank M. *Anglo-Saxon England,* 2d ed. Oxford, 1950.

CHAPTER FOURTEEN

* Adelson, Howard. *Medieval Commerce.* Princeton, 1962.
 Baldwin, John W. *The Medieval Theories of the Just Price.* Philadelphia,
  1959.
 Bridbury, A. R. *Economic Growth. England in the Later Middle Ages.*
  London, 1962.
 Cambridge Economic History, vols. 2 and 3.
 Ferguson, Wallace K. "Recent Trends in the Economic Historiography
  of the Renaissance," *Studies in the Renaissance,* VII (1960).
 Heaton, Herbert. *Economic History of Europe,* 2d ed. New York, 1948.
 Herlihy, David. *Pisa in the Early Renaissance.* New Haven, 1958.
 Lopez, Robert S., and H. A. Miskimin. "The Economic Depression of
  the Renaissance," *Economic History Review,* XIV (1961–62).
* Mundy, John H., and Peter Riesenberg. *The Medieval Town.* New
  York, 1958.
* Pirenne, Henri. *Economic and Social History of Medieval Europe.* New
  York, 1956.
* ——. *Medieval Cities.* New York, 1956.
 Russell, Josiah C. *British Medieval Population.* Albuquerque, 1948.
 ——. "Ancient and Medieval Population," *Transactions of the American
  Philosophical Society,* XLVIII, part 2 (Philadelphia, 1958).
* Thrupp, Sylvia. *The Merchant Class of Medieval London.* Ann Arbor, 1962.

CHAPTER FIFTEEN

 Brooke, Christopher. *Europe in the Central Middle Ages 987–1125.* New
  York, 1964.
 Brooke, Zachary N. *The English Church and the Papacy,* 2d ed. Cambridge
  (Eng.), 1952.
 Cambridge Medieval History, vol. 5.
 Cantor, Norman F. *Church, Kingship, and Lay Investiture in England
  1089–1135.* Princeton, 1958.
 Carlyle, Robert W., and A. J. Carlyle. *A History of Mediaeval Political
  Theory in the West,* 4th impression. Edinburgh and London, 1962.
 Morrison, Karl F. "Canossa: a Revision," *Traditio,* XVIII (1962).
 Parker, Thomas M. *Christianity and the State in the Light of History.*
  London, 1955.
 Tellenbach, Gerd. *Church, State and Christian Society at the Time of the
  Investiture Contest.* Oxford, 1940.
 Ullmann, Walter. *The Growth of Papal Government in the Middle Ages,* 2d
  ed. London, 1962.
* Williams, Schafer, ed. *The Gregorian Epoch: Reformation, Revolution, Reaction.*
  Boston, 1964.

CHAPTER SIXTEEN

Bouyer, Louis. *The Cistercian Heritage.* London, 1958.
Brooke, Rosalind B. *Early Franciscan Government.* Cambridge (Eng.), 1959.
Cambridge Medieval History, vols. 5 and 6.
Colvin, Howard M. *The White Canons in England.* Oxford, 1951.
Dickinson, John C. *Monastic Life in Medieval England.* New York, 1962.
——. *The Origins of the Austin Canons and Their Introduction into England.* London, 1950.
* Jarrett, Bede. *The Life of Saint Dominic.* Garden City (N.Y.), 1964.
Knowles, David. *The Monastic Order in England,* 2d ed. Cambridge (Eng.), 1963.
——. *The Religious Orders in England.* 3 vols. Cambridge (Eng.), 1957–62.
Lea, Henry Charles. *History of the Inquisition of the Middle Ages.* 3 vols. New York, 1887.
Leff, Gordon. *Heresy in the Later Middle Ages.* To appear.
Lortz, Joseph, ed. *Bernhard von Clairvaux: Mönch und Mystiker.* Wiesbaden, 1955.
Sabatier, Paul. *Life of Saint Francis of Assisi.* New York, 1923.

CHAPTER SEVENTEEN

Cambridge Medieval History, vol. 6.
Clagett, Marshall, et al. *Twelfth-Century Europe and the Foundations of Modern Society.* Madison, 1966.
* Copleston, Frederick C. *A History of Philosophy,* 2d ed., vol. 2. New York, 1961.
Daly, Lowrie J. *The Medieval University.* New York, 1961.
* Gilson, Etienne. *Heloise and Abelard.* Ann Arbor, 1960.
* Haskins, Charles Homer. *The Renaissance of the Twelfth Century.* New York, 1957.
* ——. *The Rise of Universities.* Ithaca, 1957.
Kibre, Pearl. *Nations in the Mediaeval European Universities.* Cambridge (Mass.), 1948.
* Knowles, David. *The Evolution of Medieval Thought.* Baltimore, 1962.
* Leff, Gordon. *Medieval Thought—Saint Augustine to Ockham.* Baltimore, 1958.
* Pieper, Josef. *Scholasticism.* New York, 1960.
Rashdall, Hastings. *The Universities of Europe in the Middle Ages,* 2d ed., revised by Frederick M. Powicke and A. B. Enden. 3 vols. Oxford, 1936.
* Southern, Richard W. *The Making of the Middle Ages.* New Haven, 1962.
——. *Saint Anselm and His Biographer.* Cambridge (Eng.), 1963.
* von Grunebaum, Gustave. *Medieval Islam,* 2d ed. Chicago, 1961.
* Wieruszowski, Helene. *The Medieval University.* New York, 1966.

CHAPTER EIGHTEEN

* Atiya, Aziz S. *Crusade, Commerce and Culture.* New York, 1966.
——. *The Crusade: Historiography and Bibliography.* Bloomington, 1962.
——. *The Crusade in the Later Middle Ages.* London, 1938.

* Brundage, James A. *The Crusades: Motives and Achievements.* Boston, 1964.
Cambridge Medieval History, vols. 5, 6, 7.
Lawrence, Clifford H. *The English Church and the Papacy in the Middle Ages.* New York, 1965.
Mortimer, Robert C. *Western Canon Law.* Berkeley, 1953.
* Runciman, Steven. *A History of the Crusades.* 3 vols. New York, 1964–67.
* ——. *The Mediaeval Manichee.* New York, 1961.
Setton, Kenneth M., ed. *A History of the Crusades.* 5 vols. projected. Philadelphia, 1955– .
* Tierney, Brian. *The Crisis of Church and State 1050–1300.* Englewood Cliffs (N.J.), 1964.
Ullmann, Walter. *The Growth of Papal Government in the Middle Ages,* 2d ed. London, 1962.

CHAPTER NINETEEN

* Barraclough, Geoffrey. *The Origins of Modern Germany,* 2d ed. New York, 1966.
Boase, Thomas S. R. *Boniface VIII.* London, 1933.
Brooke, Christopher N. L. *From Alfred to Henry III 871–1272.* Edinburgh, 1961.
* Cam, Helen M. *England before Elizabeth,* 2d ed. New York, 1960.
Cambridge Medieval History, vols. 5 and 6.
Cuttino, George P. *English Diplomatic Administration 1259–1339.* London, 1940.
* Fawtier, Robert. *The Capetian Kings of France.* New York, 1966.
Holt, James C. *The Making of Magna Carta.* Cambridge (Eng.), 1965.
Jolliffe, John E. A. *Angevin Kingship.* London, 1955.
Kantorowicz, Ernst. *Frederick the Second 1194–1250.* New York, 1967.
* Painter, Sidney. *The Reign of King John.* Baltimore, 1966.
Powicke, Frederick M. *King Henry III and the Lord Edward.* Oxford, 1947.
——. *Stephen Langton.* Oxford, 1928.
* Runciman, Steven. *The Sicilian Vespers: A History of the Mediterranean World in the Later Thirteenth Century.* Baltimore, 1960.
* Sayles, George O. *The Medieval Foundations of England.* Cranbury (N.J.), 1961.
Strayer, Joseph R. "Philip the Fair—A Constitutional King," *American Historical Review,* LXII (1956).

CHAPTER TWENTY

Cam, Helen. *Law-Finders and Law-Makers in Medieval England.* New York, 1963.
Cambridge Medieval History, vols. 5 and 6.
Carlyle, Robert W., and A. J. Carlyle. *A History of Mediaeval Political Theory in the West.* 6 vols. Edinburgh and London, 1903–1906.
Chrimes, Stanley B. *An Introduction to the Administrative History of Mediaeval England.* Oxford, 1952.
Hollister, C. Warren. *Anglo-Saxon Military Institutions.* Oxford, 1962.
——. *The Military Organization of Norman England.* Oxford, 1965.
Kantorowicz, Ernst. *The King's Two Bodies.* Princeton, 1957.

———. *Laudes Regiae.* Berkeley, 1946.

Keeney, Barnaby C. *Judgment by Peers.* Cambridge (Mass.), 1949.

Kern, Fritz. *Kingship and Law in the Middle Ages.* Oxford, 1956.

Lewis, Ewart, ed. *Medieval Political Ideas.* 2 vols. New York, 1954.

Lyon, Bryce. *A Constitutional and Legal History of Medieval England.* New York, 1960.

Post, Gaines. *Studies in Medieval Legal Thought.* Princeton, 1964.

Richardson, Henry G., and G. O. Sayles. *The Governance of Mediaeval England from the Conquest to Magna Carta.* Edinburgh, 1963.

* Ullman, Walter. *A History of Political Thought in the Middle Ages,* Baltimore, 1965.

———. *Medieval Papalism.* London, 1949.

———. *Principles of Government and Politics in the Middle Ages.* New York, 1961.

Vinogradoff, Paul. *Roman Law in Medieval Europe.* New York, 1909.

CHAPTER TWENTY-ONE

* Boissonade, Prosper. *Life and Work in Medieval Europe.* New York, 1964.

Brucker, Gene. *Florentine Politics and Society 1343–1378.* Princeton, 1962.

Clifford, Esther R. *A Knight of Great Renown: the Life and Times of Othon de Grandson.* Chicago, 1961.

Cunnington, Cecil W., and P. Cunnington. *Handbook of English Mediaeval Costume.* London, 1952.

Evans, Joan. *Life in Medieval France,* 2d ed. London, 1957.

* Huizinga, Johan. *The Waning of the Middle Ages.* New York, 1954.

* Labarge, Margaret Wade. *A Baronial Household of the Thirteenth Century.* New York, 1965.

Lewis, C. S. *The Allegory of Love.* New York, 1958.

* Noonan, John T., Jr. *Contraception.* Cambridge (Mass.), 1965.

* Oldenbourg, Zoë. *The Cornerstone* (a novel). New York, 1965.

———. *The World Is Not Enough* (a novel). New York, 1948.

* Painter, Sidney. *French Chivalry.* Ithaca, 1957.

Poole, Austin Lane. *Medieval England,* 2d ed. 2 vols. Oxford, 1958.

* Power, Eileen. *Medieval People.* Garden City (N.Y.), 1956.

CHAPTER TWENTY-TWO

Clagett, Marshall. *The Science of Mechanics in the Middle Ages.* Madison, 1959.

* Copleston, Frederick C. *Aquinas.* Harmondsworth, 1955.

* —. *A History of Philosophy,* vols. 2 and 3. Garden City (N.Y.), 1962–63.

* Crombie, Alistair C. *Medieval and Early Modern Science,* 2d ed. 2 vols. New York, 1959.

Gilson, Etienne. *The Mystical Theology of Saint Bernard.* New York, 1940.

Harris, Charles R. S. *Duns Scotus.* 2 vols. Oxford, 1927.

* Husik, Isaac. *A History of Medieval Jewish Philosophy.* New York, 1958.

* Knowles, David. *The English Mystical Tradition.* New York, 1965.

* Lovejoy, Arthur O. *The Great Chain of Being.* New York, 1960.

Petry, Ray C., ed. *Late Medieval Mysticism, The Library of Christian Classics* XIII. Philadelphia, 1957.
* Underhill, Evelyn. *The Essentials of Mysticism,* 2d ed. New York, 1960.
* ——. *Mysticism,* 12th ed. New York, 1961.

CHAPTER TWENTY-THREE

Hardison, O. B., Jr. *Christian Rite and Christian Drama in the Middle Ages.* Baltimore, 1965.
Jackson, William T. H. *The Literature of the Middle Ages.* New York, 1960.
Janson, Horst W. *History of Art.* New York, 1962.
Jantzen, Hans. *High Gothic.* New York, 1962.
Lewis, C. S. *The Discarded Image: An Introduction to Medieval and Renaissance Literature.* Cambridge (Eng.), 1964.
* Mâle, Emile. *The Gothic Image.* New York, 1958. First published as *Religious Art in France of the Thirteenth Century.* New York, 1913.
Morey, Charles R. *Medieval Art.* New York, 1942.
* Panofsky, Erwin. *Gothic Art and Scholasticism.* New York, 1957.
Reese, Gustave. *Music in the Middle Ages.* New York, 1940.
* Southern, Richard W. *The Making of the Middle Ages,* esp. the chapter "From Epic to Romance." New Haven, 1962.
von Simson, Otto. *The Gothic Cathedral.* New York, 1956.
* Waddell, Helen. *The Wandering Scholars.* Garden City (N.Y.), 1955.
* Weston, Jessie L. *From Ritual to Romance.* Garden City (N.Y.), 1957.

CHAPTERS TWENTY-FOUR AND TWENTY-FIVE

* Burckhardt, Jakob. *The Civilization of the Renaissance in Italy,* 8th ed. 2 vols. New York, 1958.
Cambridge Medieval History, vols. 7, 8.
Cuttino, George P. "Historical Revision: The Causes of the Hundred Years' War," *Speculum,* XXXI (1956).
* Dannenfeldt, Karl H. *The Renaissance: Medieval or Modern?.* Boston, 1959.
Ferguson, Wallace K. *The Renaissance in Historical Thought.* Boston, 1948.
Hale, John R., et al., eds. *Europe in the Late Middle Ages.* Evanston, 1965.
Hay, Denys. *Europe in the Fourteenth and Fifteenth Centuries.* New York, 1966.
* ——. *The Renaissance Debate.* New York, 1965.
Heers, Jacques. *L'Occident aux XIV et XV siècles. Aspects économiques et sociaux.* Paris, 1963.
* Huizinga, Johan. *The Waning of the Middle Ages.* Garden City (N.Y.), 1954.
Jacob, Ernest F. *Essays in the Conciliar Epoch,* 3d ed. Notre Dame (Ind.), 1963.
Lyon, Bryce. *From Fief to Indenture. The Transition from Feudal to Non-feudal Contract in Western Europe.* Cambridge (Mass.), 1957.
* Mollat, Guillaume. *The Popes at Avignon,* 9th ed. New York, 1965.
O'Gorman, Edmundo. *The Invention of America.* Bloomington, 1961.
* Perroy, Edouard. *The Hundred Years War.* New York, 1965.
Runciman, Steven. *The Fall of Constantinople 1453.* Cambridge (Eng.), 1965.
Tierney, Brian. *Foundations of the Conciliar Theory.* Cambridge (Eng.), 1955.
Ullman, Walter. *The Origins of the Great Schism.* London, 1948.
Waley, Daniel. *Later Medieval Europe.* New York, 1964.

Chronological Lists

I. SIGNIFICANT POPES MENTIONED IN BOOK

Clement I (90–99)
Julius I (337–352)
Innocent I (402–417)
Leo I the Great (440–461)
Gelasius I (492–496)
John I (523–526)
Gregory I the Great (590–604)
Honorius I (625–638)
Martin I (649–655)
Gregory II (715–731)
Gregory III (731–741)
Zachary (741–752)
Stephen III (752–757)
Hadrian I (772–795)
Leo III (795–816)
Nicholas I (858–867)
Hadrian II (867–872)
John VIII (872–882)
Formosus (891–896)
Sergius III (904–911)
John XII (955–963)

Sylvester II (999–1003)
Benedict IX (1032–1048)
Gregory VI (1045–1046)
Leo IX (1048–1054)
Stephen IX (1057–1058)
Nicholas II (1059–1061)
Alexander II (1061–1073)
Gregory VII (1073–1085)
Urban II (1088–1099)
Paschal II (1099–1118)
Calixtus II (1119–1124)
Innocent II (1130–1143)
Alexander III (1159–1181)
Innocent III (1198–1216)
Gregory IX (1227–1241)
Celestine V (1294)
Boniface VIII (1294–1303)
Clement V (1305–1314)
Urban VI (1378–1389)
Alexander V (1409–1410)
Pius II (1458–1464)

II. SIGNIFICANT ROMAN AND BYZANTINE EMPERORS MENTIONED IN BOOK

Augustus (27 B.C.–14 A.D.)
Tiberius (14–37)
Nero (54–68)
Domitian (81–96)
Trajan (98–117)
Hadrian (117–138)
Marcus Aurelius (161–180)
Commodus (180–192)
Septimius Severus (193–211)
Caracalla (211–217)
Heliogabalus (218–222)
Aurelian (270–275)
Diocletian (284–305)
Maximian (286–305)

Constantine I the Great (311–337)
Licinius (311–324)
Constantius II (337–361)
Constans I (337–350)
Julian the Apostate (361–363)
Valens (364–378)
Theodosius I the Great (379–395)
Theodosius II (408–450)
Julius Nepos (473–475)
Romulus Augustulus (475–476)
Zeno (474–491)
Anastasius I (491–518)
Justinian I the Great (527–565)
Maurice (582–602)

Phocas I (602–610)
Leo III the Isaurian (717–741)
Constantine V Copronymous (741–775)
Irene (797–802)
Basil II (963–1025)
Alexius I Comnenus (1081–1118)
Constantine XI (1448–1453)

John II (1118–1143)
Manuel I (1143–1180)
Alexius IV (1203–1204)
Alexius V (1204)
Latin Emperors from 1204 to 1261
Michael VIII (1261–1282)

FOR THE DATES OF THE ENGLISH, GERMAN, AND FRENCH RULERS,
SEE THE CHRONOLOGICAL TABLES IN THE TEXT.

Illustration Credits

TITLE PAGE   Alinari—Art Reference Bureau (from Cappelone degli Spagnoli in Santa Maria Novella, Florence).

CHAPTER ONE   Page 17: Alinari—Art Reference Bureau. Page 23: Alinari —Art Reference Bureau. Page 32: Courtesy of the Yugoslav State Tourist Office, New York.

CHAPTER TWO   Page 38: Copyright Fototeca Unione—Art Reference Bureau (Tomb beneath St. Peter's, Rome). Page 41: Anderson—Art Reference Bureau (Lateran Museum). Page 44: The Hebrew University of Jerusalem (on exhibition at the Shrine of the Book, Jerusalem). Page 52: With the kind permission of Professor Micheal Gough from his book, *The Early Christians* (London: Thames & Hudson; U. S. A.: Frederick A. Praeger); the drawing was made by Mrs. Mary Gough. Page 54: Art Reference Bureau (Pontifical Commission of Sacred Archives, Rights Reserved).

CHAPTER THREE   Page 60: Alinari—Art Reference Bureau (Basilica on the Forum, Palazzodei Conservatori, Rome). Page 62: Cliché des Musées Nationaux, Louvre.

CHAPTER FOUR   Page 81: Art Reference Bureau (Lateran Museum, Vatican Archive, Rome).

CHAPTER FIVE   Page 92: Codex Vigilanus, San Lorenzo de El Escorial (José de Prado Herranz, Photographer). Page 97: Art Reference Bureau (Stiftsbibliothek, St. Gallen). Page 98: The Library, Trinity College, Dublin (The Green Studio, Ltd., Photographers). Page 100: Alinari—Art Reference Bureau. Page 107: Consulate General of Iceland.

CHAPTER SIX   Page 118: Alinari—Art Reference Bureau. Page 121: Marburg—Art Reference Bureau (Church of Hosios Lukos, Delphi). Page 124: Art Reference Bureau (Bibliothèque Nationale, Paris). Page 133: Edinburgh University Library. Page 137: Anderson—Art Reference Bureau.

CHAPTER SEVEN   Page 143: Art Reference Bureau (Copyright Fototeca Unione, Rome). Page 162: Alinari—Art Reference Bureau (Piazza S. Giovanni in Lateran Tricolinio, Rome).

CHAPTER EIGHT   Page 171: Marburg—Art Reference Bureau (Aachen Cathedral). Page 175: Art Reference Bureau (Bibliothèque Nationale, Paris). Page 178: Photographie Giraudon (Bibliothèque Nationale, Paris). Page 183: Copyright Universitetets Oldsaksamling, Oslo. Page 184: Ole J. Kragh, Copenhagen (Gyldendalske Boghandel). Page 186: Copyright Universitetets Oldsaksamling, Oslo.

CHAPTER NINE   Page 197: Bibliothèque Nationale, Paris. Page 201: Copyright British Museum. Page 202: *top,* Copyright *Country Life,* London;

bottom, Copyright *Country Life,* London. Page 203: *top,* Alinari—Art Reference Bureau; *bottom,* Copyright A. C. L.—Art Reference Bureau.

CHAPTER TEN   Page 213: drawing based on a panel in the Dome of Modena Cathedral. Page 215: *top,* Courtesy of the Master and Fellows of Trinity College, Cambridge; *middle,* from Paul Lacroix, *Manners, Customs, and Dress during the Middle Ages,* no date; *bottom,* Marburg—Art Reference Bureau. Page 218: Copyright Universitetets Oldsaksamling, Oslo. Page 223: Landesmuseum für Vor-Und Frühgeschichte.

CHAPTER ELEVEN   Page 241: from Annales Benedictinae.

CHAPTER TWELVE   Page 247: By kind permission of the Abbess, Abbaye Sainte Croix, Congrègations des Dames de la Charité de St. Benoit. Page 250: Bibliothèque Nationale, Paris. Page 255: Copyright British Museum. Page 259: By courtesy of the Master and Fellows of Corpus Christi College, Cambridge. Page 261: Art Reference Bureau (Bibliothèque Nationale, Paris). Page 265: Marburg—Art Reference Bureau. Page 266: Art Reference Bureau (Municipal Library, Epernay). Page 267: Copyright British Museum. Page 269: Art Reference Bureau (Treasury, Monza Cathedral).

CHAPTER THIRTEEN   Page 276: Marburg—Art Reference Bureau. Page 280: Kunsthistorisches Museum, Vienna. Page 285: Art Reference Bureau (Staatsbibliothek, Munich).

CHAPTER FOURTEEN   Page 308: Paul Lacroix, *Manners, Customs, and Dress during the Middle Ages,* no date, (from the Library of Rouen). Page 309: Copyright British Museum. Page 310: Copyright British Museum. Page 316: Copyright British Museum. Page 318: Marburg—Art Reference Bureau (Schwarzhaüpterhaüs). Page 319: Marburg—Art Reference Bureau (Altstadt von Süden). Page 321: Agraci—Art Reference Bureau (Bibliothèque de l'Arsenal). Page 322: Art Reference Bureau (Archives Photographique, Paris). Page 323: Copyright Reserved, Her Majesty the Queen, from Windsor Castle. Page 324: State Archives of Prato (Carlo Siliani, Photographer). Page 325: Copyright British Museum.

CHAPTER FIFTEEN   Page 333: The Vatican Library. Page 347: Marburg—Art Reference Bureau (Fontrevault Abbey). Page 349: Copyright British Museum. Page 351: The Bodleian Library, Oxford.

CHAPTER SIXTEEN   Page 358: Copyright *Country Life,* London. Page 360: J. C. Dickinson, *Monastic Life in Medieval England,* p. 145, reprinted by permission of A. & C. Black, Ltd., London. Page 363: Alinari—Art Reference Bureau. Page 365: Alinari—Art Reference Bureau. Page 366: Alinari—Art Reference Bureau (Museo di San Marco, Florence). Page 369: Anderson—Art Reference Bureau (Opera del Duomo, Siena). Page 371: Reproduced by permission of the Syndics of the Fitzwilliam Museum, Cambridge.

CHAPTER SEVENTEEN   Page 383: Bulloz—Art Reference Bureau. Page 392: Copyright Bibliothèque Royale, Brussels.

CHAPTER EIGHTEEN   Page 405: The Metropolitan Museum of Art, The Cloisters Collection, Purchase, 1963. Page 407: Alinari—Art Reference Bureau

(Palazzo Ducale, Urbino). Page 410: Bibliothèque de l'Arsenal. Page 414: Bibliothèque Nationale, Paris. Page 416: Photographie Giraudon. Page 418: Marburg—Art Reference Bureau (St. Zeno).

CHAPTER NINETEEN   Page 429: Archives Nationales, Paris. Page 431: Marburg—Art Reference Bureau (Mainneville). Page 433: Marburg—Art Reference Bureau (Abbey of St. Denis). Page 439: Sam J. Harrop, Lincoln, England, from Art Reference Bureau (by permission of Lincoln Cathedral). Page 443: Alinari—Art Reference Bureau (Vatican Basilica—Grotto).

CHAPTER TWENTY   Page 461: Copyright Bibliothèque Royale, Brussels. Page 464: Copyright Society of Antiquaries, Burlington House. Page 467: Copyright A12257, A. F. Kersting, London.

CHAPTER TWENTY-ONE   Page 482: Copyright A. C. L.—Art Reference Bureau. Page 484: Copyright British Museum. Page 485: Alinari—Art Reference Bureau (Museum of San Marco, Florence). Page 490: By courtesy of the Corporation of London (R. B. Fleming & Co., Ltd., Photographers). Page 495: *left,* Copyright British Museum; *right,* Copyright British Museum. Page 497: *left,* Copyright British Museum; *right,* Copyright British Museum.

CHAPTER TWENTY-TWO   Page 507: Brogi—Art Reference Bureau (Museum of San Marco, Florence). Page 515: Manuscript of the *Scivias.* Page 523: By permission of the Syndics of the University Library, Cambridge, England. Page 524: A. C. Crombie, *Medieval and Early Modern Science,* Volume I, p. 84, reprinted by permission of Harvard University Press. Page 525: Biblioteca Marciana, Venice. Page 526: Copyright British Museum. Page 527: Copyright British Museum.

CHAPTER TWENTY-THREE   Page 529: Marburg—Art Reference Bureau. Page 532: Marburg—Art Reference Bureau. Page 533: Marburg—Art Reference Bureau. Page 535: Copyright A. C. L.—Art Reference Bureau. Page 537: *left,* Marburg—Art Reference Bureau; *right,* Marburg—Art Reference Bureau. Page 538: *top,* Marburg—Art Reference Bureau; *bottom,* Marburg—Art Reference Bureau. Page 539: *top,* Marburg—Art Reference Bureau; *bottom,* Alinari—Art Reference Bureau. Page 541: San Lorenzo de El Escorial (José de Prado Herranz, Photographer). Page 551: The Bodleian Library, Oxford. Page 553: Alinari—Art Reference Bureau (Domenico di Francesco detto Michelino in Florence Cathedral). Page 554: By permission of the Harvard College Library.

CHAPTER TWENTY-FOUR   Page 559: The Bodleian Library, Oxford. Page 560: Copyright Bibliothèque Royale, Brussels. Page 562: Marburg—Art Reference Bureau (Staatliche Museum, Berlin). Page 565: Kunsthistorisches Museum, Vienna. Page 570: J. Lenfant, *Histoire des Concile de Constance,* Volume II. Page 573: New York Public Library.

CHAPTER TWENTY-FIVE   Page 584: Marburg—Art Reference Bureau (Westminster Abbey). Page 587: Art Reference Bureau (Bibliothèque Nationale, Paris). Page 592: Photographie Giraudon (Bibliothèque Nationale, Paris). Page 595: Reproduced by courtesy of the Trustees, The National Gallery, London.

Index

Law (*continued*)
422, 468, 472; Moslem, 116;
Byzantine, 116, 120; Frankish,
145, 191; feudal, 199, 200, 204;
manorial, 222, 223–224; canon,
329, 348, 385, 397–398; French,
432, 457–458; English, 453–457
Lea, Henry Charles, 11
"Legend of Saint Sylvester," 160
Legends, 545, 553
Legnano, battle of (1176), 448
Leo I the Great (pope), 69, 72
Leo III (pope), 170–172, 239
Leo IX (pope), 126, 329, 331, 335,
341
Leo III the Isaurian (emperor), 118,
119–121, 133, 159, 160
Leon and Castile, 286, 335, 408
Lewis IV (Germany), 512, 579, 580
Lewis, C. S., 499, 528, 556
Libelli de Lite, 327
Liber judiciorum, 144
Liber sanctorum, 230
Libertas, 5, 328, 439, 557, 561, 566,
570, 575
Licinius (emperor), 59, 60
Liège, 233–234, 305, 313, 344
Lille, 319
Literacy, 248–249, 302, 374, 494,
573
Literature, 107, 113, 249, 250, 540–
542; Roman, 30, 31; Christian,
47; Celtic, 96, 540–541; early
medieval, 112, 113, 253, 260–262;
Carolingian, 168; vernacular, 296;
Islamic, 502; courtly, 503; English,
540–541, 543; Scandinavian, 542–
543; German, 543; French, 543–
544; "Matter of Britain," 543,
544; "Matter of France," 543,
544; "Matter of Rome," 544
Little Flowers of Saint Francis, 355
Liturgy, 93, 125, 156, 157, 159,
237–238, 367
Liudprand of Cremona, 116, 252,
275, 285–286
Logoi spermatikoi, 35
Loire, 187, 291
Lollards, 372, 373, 482, 573, 574
Lombard, Maurice, 304
Lombard League, 448, 578

Lombards, 91, 93, 96, 106, 117, 125,
140, 141, 148, 156, 158, 159, 160,
161, 162, 163, 169, 170, 174, 281,
293
Lombards (merchants), 402, 407,
432, 559
Lombardy, 106, 344, 384, 480
London, 305, 306, 317, 558; com-
promise of (1107), 345, 347; free
city of, 481
"Lords Appellant," 583
Lorenzo the Magnificent, 578
Lorraine (Lotharingia), 177, 233,
239, 275, 277, 280, 281, 328, 329,
593
Lorris, 307, 480
Lorris, Guillaume de, 550
Lothar I (Germany), 174–177, 281
Lothar II (Germany), 331, 345, 444,
445
Lothar II (Italy), 177
Louis I the Pious (France), 151, 167,
168, 173–177, 239, 274, 403, 404
Louis VI (France), 290, 307, 359,
426–428, 430, 535–536
Louis VII (France), 388, 415, 428,
430, 480, 535–536
Louis VIII (France), 430
Louis IX (France) (St. Louis),
199, 416, 418, 426, 430–431, 457,
482, 507, 585
Louis X (France), 430, 586, 587
Louis XI (France), 586, 593
Louis II the German, 174, 176
Louis III the Child (Germany),
176, 177, 275
Lübeck, 317
Luciferans, 371, 571
Lucius III (pope), 370
Lupus of Ferrières, 168, 248, 249,
252
Luther, Martin, 373, 572
Luxembourg, 593; House of, 579
Lyon, 305, 319, 369, 370
Lyric poetry, 547–550

Mabillon, Jean, 9
Macedonian Dynasty, 122
Machiavelli, Niccolò, 578
McKisack, May, 592
Magdeburg, 284

Magic, 243, 251, 401
Magna Carta, 210, 421, 424, 438
Magyars, 93, 99, 117, 179, 182, 187, 230
Maieul (abbot of Cluny), 182
Maimonides, Moses, 377, 403
Mainz, 307
Maitland, Frederick William, 10, 452
Manasses of Reims, 230
Manegold of Lautenbach, 379
Mani, 67
Manichaeism, 52, 67, 80, 371; and St. Augustine, 78–79
Manor, 188, 193, 212, 214–215, 477
Mansus, 198, 199
Manzikert, battle of (1071), 122, 409
Marcomanni, 25
Marie de France, 544
Marigny, Enguerrand de, 432
Marlowe, Christopher, 552
Marozia, Princess, 236
Marseille, 317, 321
Marshal, William, 208–210, 499
Marsilius of Padua, 472, 512, 568, 577
Martial (Latin poet), 29
Martin I (pope), 158
Martin V (pope), 569
Martyrologies, 263
Masters of Cavalry, 59
Masters of Infantry, 59
Mathematics, 136, 523
Matilda (of England), 208, 292, 428, 435, 436
Matilda (of Tuscany), 339, 343, 344
Maurists, 9
Mawalī, 135
Maxentius, 58
Maximian (emperor), 31, 32, 33
Maximilian (Germany), 580, 593
Mayfield, 190, 458
Mecca, 119, 127, 130, 132
Mechanical inventions, 521
Mechtild of Magdeburg, 514–515
Medici, 481, 578
Medicine, 136, 487, 526
Medieval Academy of America, 11
Medina, 119, 130
Megingaud of Eichstätt, 232
Mehmet the Conqueror, 594

Meissen, 284
Melun, 381
Merchant Adventurers, 320
Merchet, 225
Merovech, 104
Merovingian Dynasty, 104, 106, 111, 144–146, 148–149, 174, 178, 179, 343
Messalina, 29
Metalogicon, 386
Methodius, St., 127
Metz, 141, 146
Meun, Jean de, 550
Michael Psellos, 116
Michelangelo, 564
Migne, 10
Milan, 72, 77, 79, 281–282, 305, 307, 332, 342, 448, 450, 482, 559, 578
Millennarianism, 370
Milvian Bridge, battle of (312), 58, 60
Ministeriales, 279, 444
Minnesänger, 547
Minnesota "runestone," 185
Missi dominici, 192
Missionary work, 50, 91, 153–156, 163, 230, 238; Irish, 96–98; at the end of 8th century, 141; Charles Martel and, 148; methods of, 152–153; in 7th and 8th centuries, 152–155; Willibrord and, 154; Boniface and, 154–155
Mithraism, 37, 39, 52
Modus tenendi parliamentum, 465
Mohammed, 119, 127–132, 138
Mohammed and Charlemagne, 110
Molesme, 357
Monasticism, 92, 142, 148, 153, 156, 163, 231, 254, 301, 328, 332, 355–366, 396, 576; early, 64–66; Irish, 96–98; growth of, in 6th and 7th centuries, 149–152; St. Benedict and, 150–152; St. Boniface and, 154–155, 229, 230, 239; reforms and influence of, 239–243; Peter Damian and, 240–242, 356, 361; Cistercian, 356–361; St. Bernard and, 358–360; St. Francis and, 362–364; St. Dominic and, 364–366. *See also* under individual orders

Rather of Verona and of Liège, 231, 334

Ravenna, 100, 123, 160, 162, 384; exarchate of, 159–161

Raymond of Toulouse, 410, 411

Realism, 380, 381

Recared (Visigothic king), 144, 157

Receswinth (Visigothic king), 144

Reconquista, 138, 560

Reeve, 222

Reformation, 38, 77, 187, 355, 372, 373, 485, 511, 520, 568, 571, 574, 581, 595, 596

Reformists, 483, 485, 486, 572

Reform movement, 229–244

Regino of Prüm, 275

Reichsfürsten, 446, 447

Reims, 233, 305, 589

Religion: Christian, 37–55; popular attitudes toward Christian, 495; Roman, 30, 37, 59–62

Renaissance, 8, 89, 123, 170, 236, 268–269, 317, 386, 389, 521, 551, 552, 559, 563; Carolingian, 168, 246–250; 12th century, 245, 374; slave trade during, 316; concept of, 374, 555–557; Jews in, 404, 406; "courtly love" and, 499–500; beginnings of, 533–534; Latin and, 540; and break with Middle Ages, 554–557; humanism in, 564–566, 571, 595

Reval, 318

Rhetoric, 249, 388

Rhine, 317

Rhône, 317

Richard I the Lionhearted (England), 209–210, 415, 428, 436, 437, 481

Richard II (England), 468, 470, 483, 583, 586

Richard III (England), 586

Richer, 275

Riga, 318

Rigord, 425

Ring, the (fortress system), 169

Robert I (France), 182

Robert II the Pious (France), 290, 400

Robert Guiscard, 293

Robertians: *see* Capetians

Robert of Courçon, 390

Robert of Jumièges, 294, 295

Robert of Molesme, 357

Robert of Normandy, 295, 410

Robert the Strong, 182

Rockingham, council of, 346

Roger II (Sicily), 293, 449

Roland, Count, 169; *see also Song of Roland*

Rollo, 293

Rolls Series (or *Rerum Britannicarum Medii Aevi Scriptores*), 10

Romance, 544–545, 553

Romance of the Rose, 550

Romanitas, 110, 111

Romantics, 10

Rome: life in, 16–18, 28–29; fall of (410), 19 ff., 63, 80, 87, 101; religion in, 30; synod of (1076), 342; *see also* Papacy

Romulus Augustulus, 64, 73, 101

Roncesvalles, Pass of, 169

Roscelin, 381

Roswitha of Gandersheim, 262

Rouen, 339, 589

Rudolf IV of Austria, 569

Rudolf of Burgundy, 182

Rudolf of Rheinfelden, 343

Rule, Essene, 44

Rupert, 580

Russia, 99, 283, 419, 595; incorporated into Eastern Orthodox Church, 127

Ruysbroeck, John, 520

Sachsenspiegel, 385

Sacred, idea of the, 5–6, 253, 363

Ste-Chapelle, 418, 536

St. Denis, abbey of, 149, 161–162, 382, 535; fair of, 319

Ste-Geneviève, School of, 381

St. Gildas, monastery of, 382

St. Philibert, monks of, 187

St. Victor, School of, 380

Saladin, 415

Salian dynasty, 276, 278, 283, 345, 445

Salic law, 145

Salisbury Oath, 296, 435

Sanitation, 486

San Vitale, 123

Saône, 188

Sardinia, 179

Steps of Humility, 518
Steward, 222
Stigand, 114, 294, 295
Stilicho, 63, 111
Stirrups, 147, 197
Stoicism, 30, 34, 35, 46, 76
Stourbridge, fair of, 319
Strabo, 94, 250, 252
Stralsund, Treaty of, 318
Strasbourg, 404; meeting and oaths of, 177
Strauss, David Friedrich, 40, 41
Straw, Jack, 483
Studion, abbey of, 121
Sturulson, Snorri, 542
Style, shifts in, 529–530, 535–536, 537, 555; *see also* Art
Suetonius, 39
Suevi, 93, 99, 101
Sufis, 377
Suger of St. Denis, 359, 428, 535–536
Summa contra Gentiles, 508
Summa theologiae, 507
Sunna, 127
Superstition, 228, 243
Sutri, 329, 340
Swabia, 281, 445
Sweden, 101, 182, 317, 318
Sweyn Forkbeard, 185
Switzerland, 182, 188, 579
Syagrius, 104
Sylvester I (pope), 161
Sylvester II (pope), 231, 251, 252, 286, 376, 565
Sylvester III (pope), 331
Symeon Logothetes, 116
Symmachus, 57, 62, 77
Syria, 25, 27, 65, 76, 119, 132, 134, 408, 415

Taborites, 572, 574
Tacitus, 28, 29, 39, 57
Tagaste, 78, 79
Talas River, battle of (751), 133
Tale of Genji, 497
Tallage, 224
Tammuz, 41
Tarik, 132
Tauler, John, 520

Taunton, 306
Technology, 7, 107, 219–221, 270, 521
Teilhard de Chardin, 258
Templars, 322, 402, 407, 414, 432, 434
Terence, 112, 248
Tertry, battle of (687), 146
Tertullian, 54, 66, 77
Teutonic Knights, 414, 419, 451
Teutons, 63, 64, 67, 93, 94, 96, 101–110, 111, 117, 123, 125, 140, 141, 142, 147, 153, 186–187, 246, 267, 277; and Christianity, 90–92; classified, 99
Thabit, 523
Theater, 7, 550–552
Theobald of Canterbury, 347, 348
Theoderic I the Great, 101, 106, 111, 112, 142–143, 581
Theodore and Hadrian, 248
Theodosius I the Great (emperor), 62, 63, 71, 72, 77, 338
Theodosius III (emperor), 119
Theodulf, 246, 250, 265
Theology, 5–6, 46, 80–88, 112, 123–124, 230, 249, 250, 254, 301, 375, 380–381, 384, 508–513, 519–520, 536; Moslem, 130–132, 138
Theophanes, 116
Theophano, 286
Theophylact, House of, 236
Thessalonikê, 72
Thietmar of Merseburg, 275
Thomas à Kempis, 520, 571
Thomas Aquinas: *see* Aquinas
Thomas Becket, St., 347–350, 368, 436
Thomas of Celano, 355, 363, 546
Thon, Hans, 574
Thuringia, 99, 152
Thuringians, 104
Tiberius (emperor), 22
Tibet, 270
Tongres, 104
Toulouse, 372; synod of (1229), 401
Tours, 105, 250, 291, 307, 321
Tours (Poitiers), battle of (733), 132, 147
Tower of London, 296
Town halls, 307